CW00349237

1001 EASY WAYS FOR EARTH-WISE LIVING

1001 EASY WAYS FOR EARTH-WISE LIVING

Natural and eco-friendly ideas that can make a real difference to your life

Reader's Digest

1001 EASY WAYS FOR EARTH-WISE LIVING

CONTRIBUTORS Pamela Allardice, Sarah Baker, Georgina Bitcon, Scott Forbes, Frank Gardner, Rebecca Gilling, Alison Haynes, Paul Klymenko, Lynn Lewis, Bryn Lynar, Sharon Natoli, Peter Needham, Rosemary Ann Ogilvie, Jennifer Stackhouse

PROJECT EDITOR Tracy Tucker

PROJECT DESIGNER Lena Lowe

TEXT EDITORS Sue Grose-Hodge, Sarah Baker, Helen Cooney, Scott Forbes, Carol Natsis

SENIOR EDITOR Samantha Kent

DESIGN CONCEPT Sue Rawkins

SENIOR DESIGNER Kylie Mulquin

DESIGN ASSISTANCE Adrian Crestani, Annette Fitzgerald, Claire Potter

FRONT COVER DESIGN i2i Design

PUBLISHING COORDINATOR Françoise Toman

PICTURE RESEARCHERS Annette Crueger, Joanna Collard, Kylie Mulquin

COMMISSIONED PHOTOGRAPHY Ad-Libitum

PROOFREADER Susan McCreery

INDEXER Diane Harriman

PRODUCTION MANAGER GENERAL BOOKS Janelle Garside

READER'S DIGEST GENERAL BOOKS

EDITORIAL DIRECTOR Elaine Russell

MANAGING EDITOR Rosemary McDonald

ART DIRECTOR Carole Orbell

1001 Easy Ways for Earth-wise Living is published by
Reader's Digest (Australia) Pty Limited
80 Bay Street, Ultimo, NSW 2007
www.readersdigest.com.au, www.readersdigest.co.nz

First published 2006

National Library of Australia Cataloguing-in-Publication data:
1001 easy ways for earth-wise living: natural and eco-friendly ideas that can make a real difference to your life.

Includes index.
ISBN 1 921077 36 0.

1. Organic living. 2. Green products. I. Reader's Digest (Australia).
640.41

Prepress by Sinnott Bros, Sydney
Printed and bound by Leo Paper Products, China

We are interested in receiving your comments on the contents of this book.
Write to: The Editor, General Books Editorial,
Reader's Digest (Australia) Pty Limited,
GPO Box 4353, Sydney, NSW 2001
or email us at bookeditors.au@readersdigest.com

To order additional copies of *1001 Easy Ways for Earth-wise Living*
call 1300 303 210 (Australia) or 0800 540 032 (New Zealand)
or email us at customerservice@au.readersdigest.com

CONTENTS

Earth-wise Gardening 218

Out and About 278

GETTING STARTED

Here are hundreds of easy ways to protect your family's health, save you money and safeguard the environment. If you adopt just a handful of the simple, earth-wise living tips in this book, you'll not only save money, you'll also be contributing to a healthier environment that will benefit everybody.

ABOVE *A clean bedroom that is free of clutter is essential for people who suffer from dust allergies.*

OPPOSITE *Eating fresh, whole foods, drying your washing in the sun, growing your own herbs and getting plenty of exercise will all contribute to a healthy, earth-wise lifestyle.*

WHAT IS EARTH-WISE LIVING?

We all want to lead happy, balanced lives. We want to feel fit and well, have more leisure time, save money on household bills and have a positive effect on the environment. By adopting an earth-wise approach to living, you can achieve all this.

Being earth-wise means living more in harmony with the natural world. In fact, this is a good, commonsense rule of thumb to apply to many aspects of modern life.

For instance, is the meal you put on the dinner table every night made from fresh, whole food, free of additives such as artificial colours, flavours and preservatives? By avoiding processed food, you are ensuring that your family enjoys a healthy diet, full of protein, vitamins and minerals, essential for long-term health and wellbeing.

And if you buy certified organically grown food, you can be sure that it has been grown naturally, without any harmful chemical fertilisers and pesticides.

Perhaps you already recycle your bottles, cans and paper, use cloth shopping bags instead of plastic ones and wash your clothes in cold water. You'd like to do more, but aren't sure where to start.

Whether you live in a suburban house on a large block or in a tiny apartment in the middle of the city, there are tips and suggestions in this book to suit you.

For example, if you're concerned about the rising cost of fuel, you could try walking or cycling at least part of the way to work each day. Doing so will improve your health and fitness as well as save you money on fuel and transport costs and reduce air pollution.

At home, if you have no room for a sprawling vegetable garden, think about growing organic herbs and a few salad vegetables on your balcony or windowsill. You'll always have fresh herbs for cooking and the ingredients for a garden salad, they'll cost you next to nothing and you can be happy in the knowledge that they are safe to eat.

ABOVE *Ginger tea is a safe, natural remedy for nausea.*

BELOW *Clean mirrors with just a spray of plain soda water, then polish dry.*

WHAT ARE THE BENEFITS?

Invariably the earth-wise approach will simplify your life while saving you money on shopping and household bills. For every earth-wise tip you adopt, you are making a difference to the environment – whether it is saving energy and water, cutting down on air pollution or adding less to landfills. Protecting the environment benefits everybody.

For instance, did you know that the air in the average household can be up to three times more polluted than the air outside? A major contributor to this household pollution is the arsenal of chemical cleaners used in the average home.

But you don't need all those expensive products when a handful of versatile natural products will do the job just as well, perhaps better. If you are concerned about using chemicals in your home but aren't sure what to avoid, consider putting together an earth-wise cleaning kit.

You may have a packet of bicarbonate of soda in your pantry and use it only for cooking, but you may be unaware that you can use it for lots of other jobs around the home. Try bicarb next time you clean the oven, polish the kitchen sink, unblock household drains, deodorise furnishings and carpet, remove stains from linen and even brush your teeth! Bicarb, one of the key items in the earth-wise cleaning kit, is cheap, easy to use and a natural substance that doesn't pollute the air or waterways.

WHAT CAN YOU DO?

Start making changes slowly. Next time you buy toilet paper, consider buying a brand made from recycled, unbleached paper. Next time you need to replace a light bulb, try out a low-energy compact fluorescent lamp. Some last for 12 years! This not only saves you money on energy bills but also saves on the burning of fossil fuels, a major contributor to air pollution, to produce that energy.

Another thing you can do is cut down on what you buy or use in the first place. If you buy a takeaway coffee every day at work, take along your own cup rather than add to the millions of disposable cups discarded each year.

Laptop computers require fewer materials to make, and although they may seem expensive, they use up to 90 per cent less energy than desktop computers.

Refuse plastic bags when you shop. Use cloth bags instead – most supermarkets sell cloth or synthetic bags that can be used over and over again. In one year alone, Australians cut their consumption of plastic bags by a staggering 1 billion, and some country towns have declared themselves 'plastic bag-free'. So next time your newsagency starts to pop your favourite magazine into a plastic bag, ask them not to.

There are also more expensive purchases you could consider avoiding or recycling. For example, many people in Australia discard their mobile phones every 18–24 months when they buy a later model. This results in millions of mobile phones going to landfill and releasing nickel and other metals into the soil and groundwater. But the phones can be recycled and the batteries can be melted down and made into other products. There are numerous phone recycling programs operating in Australia and New Zealand.

So before you throw something out – whether it's a glass jar or an item of furniture that's seen better days – consider whether it can be reused or recycled, or given away. Even some toxic items, such as ink cartridges, can now be recycled. If you're not sure, check with your local council. Most councils have a recycling program (in fact, Australia leads the world in newspaper recycling). To check what recycling schemes are available in your area, you could look up this website: www.recyclingnearyou.com.au.

As you become more confident with your earth-wise approach, try branching out. When you select a standard grocery item from the supermarket shelf, check the label first – are there lots of additives indicating that the item has been highly processed?

For example, if you like eating a brand name toasted muesli for breakfast, you may not realise that the toasting process adds sugar and fat. Alternatively, you could save money by making your own toasted muesli – that way, you know exactly what's in it and you can tailor it to suit your dietary needs, too. And if you buy the ingredients in bulk, you'll cut down on the amount of packaging you accumulate – that's less clutter to deal with and also less waste.

Organic, seasonal produce tastes delicious and contains no harmful chemicals. When you buy truss tomatoes, they'll last longer if you leave them on the vine until you're ready to use them.

Hot water accounts for about 30 per cent of household energy use. Try washing your clothes with cold water and see how much money you save.

Some local councils offer discounts if you install a rainwater tank on your property. Use the rainwater to water your garden.

There are also some major environmental concerns that affect our daily lives. If you live in an area that's subject to water restrictions, saving water will be a major household issue for you. Some areas have prohibitive rates for high water-users, too. There are many simple things you can do to cut down on your water usage and save money at the same time.

For instance, fill a 1-litre plastic bottle with water and place it in your toilet cistern – every time you flush the toilet, you'll save 1 litre of water.

Next time you buy a washing machine, think about buying a front-loader. They use up to 60 per cent less water than top-loading machines. If you fix a dripping tap as soon as you notice it, you could be saving up to 90 litres of water a week. And there are lots of other things you can do around your home to save water – install a water-saving shower rose, buy a rainwater tank or use 'grey' water on your garden.

OUR GUIDE TO MAKING CHANGES

Earth-wise Living can be used as both a comprehensive reference book and a source of inspiring ideas, with tips covering every aspect of daily life, from health and beauty to servicing your car. Statistics that will inspire you to make small but beneficial changes are highlighted throughout the text, and informative coverage on some important environmental issues is given in bite-sized chunks so that you'll be equipped with the knowledge to make your own choices.

In 'The Natural Home' we tell you how to have an energy-efficient home and also save money on energy and water bills. And if you are building or renovating, you can check our advice on how to have an earth-wise, healthy home.

'Around the Home', the next chapter, tells you how to clean and care for your home and its contents without using harsh chemical cleaners. We also show you how to deal with household pests the natural way and how to care for your family pets with some simple, home-made remedies.

In 'The Healthy Body' we give you a comprehensive guide to nutrition as well as a handy introduction to getting fit, whether you prefer to do aerobic exercise, strength training or non-impact exercise.

This chapter ends with helpful hints on how to get a good night's sleep.

Clear skin and shiny hair are both signs of inner health and vitality. 'Feeling Well' will help you to work out your own beauty routine, using our home-made treatments. We also introduce you to massage and other natural therapies as well as natural remedies for a wide range of minor and serious ailments.

In 'Earth-wise Gardening' you'll learn how to work with nature to have a low-maintenance, water-wise and organic garden that will provide you with fresh produce, flowers and colourful foliage all year.

Finally, in 'Out and About', we give you a comprehensive guide to shopping the earth-wise way. We also tell you how you can save money and safeguard the environment by choosing the right form of transport for your needs – whether it's a car, a bike or your own two feet! And we show you how to 'tread lightly' on the earth when you're travelling.

So why not start making some easy, stress-free changes now, and save yourself money and time as well as lead a healthier, safer life?

ORGANIC AND BIODYNAMIC SYMBOLS

If you buy a product labelled with one of these logos, it means that it has been certified as having been grown and processed organically or biodynamically – without most conventional chemical pesticides and fertilisers made with synthetic ingredients.

PLASTICS IDENTIFICATION CODE FOR RECYCLING

All plastics can be recycled but it's only economically viable for some local councils to collect codes 1 to 3 from households.

Code	Virgin use	Recycled use
1 PET	Soft-drink and mineral-water bottles, filling for sleeping bags and pillows, textile fibres	Soft-drink and detergent bottles, clear film for packaging, carpet fibres, fleecy jackets
 2 HDPE	Crinkly shopping bags, freezer bags, milk and cream bottles, bottles for shampoo and cleaners, milk crates	Compost bins, detergent bottles, crates, agricultural pipes, pallets, kerbside recycling crates, garden edging
 3 V	Unplasticised vinyl for clear cordial and juice bottles etc; plasticised vinyl for garden hoses, shoe soles, tubing	Detergent bottles, plumbing fittings for unplasticised vinyl; hose inner core, industrial flooring for plasticised vinyl
4 LDPE	Black plastic sheeting, ice-cream container lids, garbage bins and bags	Film for builders, industry, plant nursery bags
 5 PP	Potato-chip bags, ice-cream containers, drinking straws, hinged lunch boxes	Compost bins, kerbside recycling crates, worm factories, building panels
 6 PS	Polystyrene for yoghurt containers, plastic cutlery, imitation crystal glassware; expanded polystyrene for hot-drink cups, takeaway food containers, meat trays, produce boxes	Polystyrene clothes pegs, coathangers, office accessories, spools, rulers, video/CD boxes; for expanded polystyrene picture frame mouldings, under slab pods
 7 OTHER	All other plastics, including acrylic and nylon	Wheels and castors, outdoor furniture, marine structures

The Natural Home

You'll create a healthier, more comfortable home environment if you select natural materials and efficient appliances, and adopt energy- and water-saving habits. You'll also help the environment and save dramatically on living costs.

THE NATURAL HOME...

EFFICIENT LIVING

■ Learn simple ways to save energy and money – immediately. See page 18. ■ Gas or electric, portable or central – what's the best kind of heating for your home? See page 24. ■ Invest in energy-efficient lighting and reap the rewards, page 32. ■ By simply installing an efficient showerhead you can slash your water usage, and your water bills. See page 34.

ROOM BY ROOM

■ Cook up a storm without it costing a fortune. See page 40. ■ Follow our guide to clothes washing and watch your water bills shrink, page 46. ■ Working at home can be an earth-wise choice. Make it work for you and the environment, page 52.

BUILDING AND RENOVATING

■ Building a house from scratch offers an ideal opportunity to create an earth-wise home. See page 54. ■ Selecting the right building materials can make all the difference to your costs and comfort, page 58. ■ Simple renovations can dramatically improve the energy efficiency of your home – and increase its value. See page 62. ■ Choosing natural floor and wall coverings and paints and varnishes will help minimise your exposure to potentially harmful chemicals, page 64.

EFFICIENT LIVING

Careful use of natural resources will save you money and create a healthier, more comfortable home.

The energy-efficient home

Using less energy around the home is much easier to achieve than you might think. Tapping into the sun's warmth and light, making simple design changes, choosing and using your appliances wisely, and changing a few old habits can make all the difference – to your energy bills, your comfort and the environment.

TOP TWELVE ENERGY SAVERS

1 Make the most of the sun's warmth by installing large windows on the northern side of your house. To stay cool in summer, install awnings, eaves or blinds that block the high summer sun.

2 Make sure that your home is well insulated. A properly insulated home can be up to 10°C warmer in winter and as much as 7°C cooler in summer.

3 Whenever the weather permits, use a clothes line instead of a dryer to dry your washing. You'll save money and help cut greenhouse gases by about 3 kilograms for every load of washing.

4 One of the simplest ways to save energy is to switch off appliances at the wall when you won't be using them for a few hours. Keeping appliances on stand-by can account for 10 per cent of a household electricity bill.

5 If you have central heating and an adjustable thermostat, try turning your heating down a fraction. You may not notice a big difference heat-wise, but you could make big savings: a reduction of 1°C can cut bills by 10 per cent.

6 Plug gaps around windows and doors and any other external openings using draught excluders and weather strips. Draughtproofing can cut household heat loss by up to 25 per cent in winter.

ENERGY RATINGS EXPLAINED

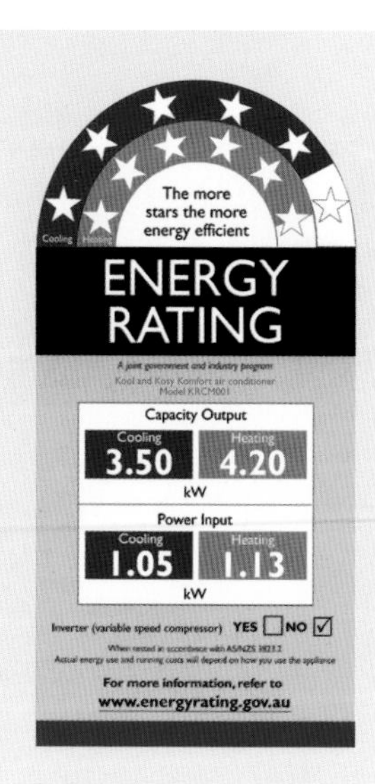

Energy Rating labels are now mandatory in Australia and New Zealand on refrigerators, freezers, washing machines, clothes dryers, dishwashers, single-phase airconditioners and gas heaters.

WHAT IT MEANS The rating consists of two elements: a star rating and a consumption indicator. The more stars an appliance has been awarded on the scale of 1–6, the more efficient it is.

HOW TO CHOOSE The consumption indicator shows how much energy the appliance uses (usually kilowatts per hour or year); so, if two items have the same star rating, choose the one with the lower rate of consumption.

THINK LONG TERM Some appliances with higher star ratings are more expensive, but will save you money in the long run. One extra star in an Energy Rating can result in savings of 10 per cent per year.

READY RECKONER To calculate the running cost, and how quickly you would recover any extra expense, find the price of a kilowatt hour on your electricity bill, then multiply it by the consumption figure.

Simply insulating a ceiling can SAVE AS MUCH AS 40 per cent on heating and cooling costs.

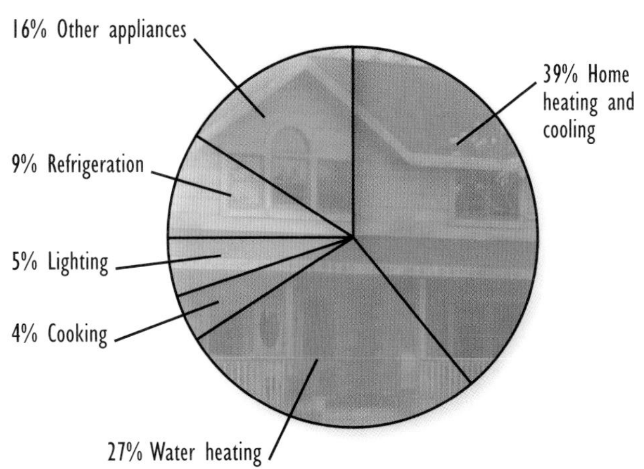

HOUSEHOLD ENERGY USE

Heating and cooling account for the largest chunk of energy used in the home; heating water is the other big user. These figures are for Australian homes, but New Zealand statistics are comparable.

Source: Australian Greenhouse Office

7 Reduce heat loss by up to one-third in winter by covering windows with heavy, lined, close-fitting curtains and a closed pelmet.

8 Replace standard incandescent light bulbs with compact fluorescent lamps (CFLs). Though a little more expensive than conventional bulbs, CFLs are much more efficient, creating an equivalent light at a significantly lower wattage – a 25-watt CFL is as bright as a 100-watt regular bulb. As a result, CFLs can last 10 times as long and use 80 per cent less energy.

9 Select appliances that are both energy-efficient and the right size for your needs – a 284-litre fridge will use 20 per cent more energy than a 210-litre fridge, even if they both have the same Energy Rating.

10 If you have a choice between natural gas and conventional electricity, go with gas. Not only is natural gas normally cheaper, it produces one-third of the greenhouse gas emissions of electricity from coal-fired power stations.

11 Make sure that your hot-water tank and pipes are properly insulated. In an average home, heating water accounts for more than one-quarter of the household energy bill; and as much as half of total water-heating costs can be due to heat loss.

12 Next time you change your hot-water system, consider buying an energy-efficient gas, solar or electric-heat-pump unit. These systems cost more to purchase, but are much cheaper to run. They will save you money in the long term, and help reduce greenhouse gases.

TOP TIP

Working out how energy-efficient your home is can simply be a matter of taking a close look at your habits, bills, appliances and fittings. Many energy authorities and suppliers provide information and tools that will assist, and some even offer onsite assessments. Alternatively, seek advice from building designers who specialise in sustainability. See *Resources*, p. 316.

hot links

Advice on saving energy and money: www.energysmart.com.au; www.ccsa.asn.au/CC1/reduce%20use.htm; www.energywise.co.nz/inmyhome/inmyhome.asp

Select energy-efficient appliances: http://search.energyrating.gov.au

Find out how much greenhouse gas your household emits: www.greenpower.com.au/go/calculator.cgi

One extra star in an Energy Rating can result in savings of **10 per cent** per year.

The energy we use

Most households in Australia use electricity that comes from coal, a non-renewable resource. It's cheap and convenient to use but the environmental costs are high. The good news is that greener energy is now readily available. It's no less reliable and, when combined with energy-efficient practices, is not expensive.

WHERE DOES IT COME FROM?

- In Australia, 90 per cent of electricity is produced by burning coal. Energy is wasted during conversion and the process generates huge quantities of carbon dioxide and other greenhouse gases, which contribute to global warming.
- Hydro-electricity provides most of Tasmania's energy and 60–70 per cent of household electricity in New Zealand. It is a renewable form of energy, but construction of dams and power stations can produce large amounts of greenhouse gases and damage the environment. Smaller, low-impact schemes are becoming more common.
- Natural gas, the most readily available alternative to conventional electricity, is also non-renewable, but much 'cleaner', producing about one-third of the greenhouse gas emissions of grid electricity.
- Liquified petroleum gas (LPG) is available to many consumers where piped natural gas is not. Transport and storage increases its adverse environmental impact and its price – it can cost two to three times as much as natural gas.
- Wood provides some energy for many homes. Although it produces some pollutants, wood can be renewable and generates relatively low greenhouse gas emissions.
- Renewable energy sources, such as solar, wind, biomass and geothermal energy, produce only a tiny portion of the energy we need. But governments are seeking to increase their use.

DIY ENERGY

If you want to be self-sufficient, consider setting up a renewable energy system at home.

- An effective way to do this is to install solar panels (photovoltaic cells) on your roof. They convert

GOING GREEN THE EASY WAY

Most energy retailers can provide you with power derived from renewable energy sources for little more than the cost of regular, non-renewable sources – so going green involves just a few simple steps.

- Find out if your local energy retailer has a renewable energy option. If it doesn't, contact a green energy scheme, such as Green Power in Australia, which can direct you to accredited suppliers.
- Select how much green energy you wish to purchase. Most suppliers offer different plans, with renewable energy making up a proportion – say 50 per cent – or all of your supply. In some cases, you can select the kind of renewable energy you wish to use.
- Confirm the precise cost of the program. Some schemes cost a little more than standard energy supplies, but a number of companies now offer green power at the same price as conventional electricity.
- Apply to have your service switched over. The retailer will normally organise the changeover so that there are no interruptions to your supply.
- Monitor your energy use to make sure you are keeping consumption and greenhouse gases to a minimum. Most energy suppliers now provide information on usage patterns and greenhouse gas output on their bills.

Switching an average home to green energy cuts greenhouse emissions by as much as taking three cars off the road each year.

sunlight into electricity, storing it in batteries for subsequent use.
- In remote areas, consider using a small wind generator if you have an appropriately windy site, and/or a micro-hydro generator if you have access to a river or creek.
- Find out if you can link these systems to the grid, for back-up and so that any surplus energy you create can be traded for energy credits.
- Check whether rebates are available for installing such systems.
- Discuss your needs with specialist suppliers before buying.

Change to energy-efficient products to cut household greenhouse gas emissions in half.

hot links

Lists of accredited green energy suppliers: www.greenpower.gov.au/pages/Home-Who-Sells.php
Advice on alternative technologies and renewable energy: www.ata.org.au
Information on New Zealand's renewable energy: energywise.co.nz/renewableenergy/renewableenergy.asp
Wind energy: www.meridianenergy.co.nz/WindProjects

Comparing energy supplies

Energy source	Production	Advantages	Disadvantages
Coal-fired electricity	Burning coal heats water that drives turbines to make electricity.	Readily available.	Non-renewable. Inefficient. High water use and greenhouse gases.
Hydro-electricity	Running water drives turbines that generate electricity.	Renewable. Readily available.	Set-up generates greenhouse gases and damages environment.
Natural gas	Gas piped to consumer and burnt on site.	Efficient. Lower greenhouse gas output than coal-fired electricity.	Not available everywhere. Non-renewable. Limited applications.
LPG	Gas supplied in cylinders and tanks and burnt on site.	Widely available. Low greenhouse gas emissions.	Expensive. Transportation to site uses additional energy.
Solar	Solar energy converted to power using photovoltaic cells.	Abundant, free, renewable. No greenhouse gas emissions.	Not yet available in all areas. Expensive to set up.
Wind	Wind drives turbines that produce electricity.	Free, clean. No greenhouse gas emissions.	Expensive to set up. Turbines obtrusive and may endanger birds.
Wave/Tidal	Waves or tides power turbines that produce electricity.	Source readily available, renewable and close to cities.	Difficult and expensive to harness wave power efficiently.
Biomass	Plant matter is burned to power electricity generators.	Potentially renewable. Recycles agricultural waste.	Cultivation and burning of fuel can yield low levels of pollutants.
Landfill	Methane from rotting rubbish is burned to power generators.	Recycles waste. Helps prevent methane build-up in atmosphere.	Expensive. Requires large quantities of waste.
Geothermal	Heat, steam or hot water from the earth's interior drives generators.	Inexpensive once set up. Efficient.	Limited to areas of geothermal activity or appropriate geology.

In most areas, GOVERNMENT REBATES are available to householders who install renewable energy systems.

Insulation basics

One of the most efficient ways to save energy and money at home is to insulate your house properly. Good insulation will keep heat inside in winter and outside in summer. As a result, you won't need to use nearly as many energy-hungry heating and cooling devices and, best of all, you may be able to cut your heating and cooling bills in half.

GETTING STARTED

Before you purchase insulation materials, take a look at your environment, the orientation of your house, potential causes of heat loss, and what is possible given the state of your home.

- Think about your local climate and what you want to achieve. Is it more important to limit heat loss in winter or heat build-up in summer?
- Consider how easy it will be to install insulation. The easiest time is during construction or renovations. However, ceilings and floors can be insulated at almost any time, so long as there is access to a crawl space.
- Factor in long-term savings. Overhauling your home insulation may seem expensive and time-consuming, but it can pay for itself in less than 5 years in the form of reduced heating costs.
- If you have existing insulation that is inefficient, consider adding another, thicker layer to improve its performance.
- Make sure you insulate all areas of the home – floors as well as ceilings and walls – completely. A 5 per cent gap can reduce potential benefits by up to 50 per cent.
- To maximise the effects of insulation, check that all air outlets, such as chimneys and vents, are shut off when not in use.

SELECTING MATERIALS

There are two main types of insulation materials, which can be used either separately or together.

- Reflective insulation is usually made from aluminium foil laminated onto paper or plastic. It works by reflecting and resisting heat. It is highly effective at preventing summer heat gain via the roof.

Pay less

Effective insulation can result in dramatic reductions in your energy bills:

- Insulating the roof and ceiling will save you between 20 and 40 per cent of heating and cooling costs.
- Insulating the walls can cut the same costs by another 10 per cent or more.
- Insulate the floor and you could reduce the same costs by 5–10 per cent.

Common insulation materials

Type	Form	Notes
Cellulose fibre	Shredded paper or fibre pellets; boards	Safe and biodegradable. Treated with borax to make fire-resistant and deter pests; settling can reduce efficiency.
Fibreglass	Loose fill, blankets, batts	Widely available, easy to install; fire-resistant. Fibres may irritate skin, emit fumes; non-biodegradable.
Polyester	Batts and rolls	Effective and versatile; non-toxic. Must not be compressed or moistened; non-biodegradable.
Reflective foil	Rolls and batts (some with foil backing)	Effective; blocks moisture. Needs to remain dust-free and have air space of at least 25 mm; non-biodegradable.
Rock-wool	Batts and loose granules	Effective, good soundproofing. Must not be compressed or moistened; may irritate skin; non-biodegradable.
Wool	Loose fill or batts and rolls	Safe, renewable source; recyclable, biodegradable. Needs to be treated against rotting and to deter vermin.

■ ■ ■ **A well-insulated home** is as much as 10°C WARMER in winter and up to 7°C cooler in summer.

Without adequate insulation, your hard-earned cash is literally disappearing into thin air.

- Bulk insulation works by trapping small pockets of air, which in turn inhibit heat flow. It can be made from a variety of materials including glass fibre, wool and cellulose fibre, and comes in several forms such as batts, loose fill and boards.
- Products combining the two types of insulation are available. For example, you can buy foil-backed blankets or foil-backed batts.

ADDING INSULATION

Loose fill is used mainly for flat ceilings and confined spaces. Batts and rolls can be used for ceilings, pitched roofs, walls and floors. Look for biodegradable materials with no health risks.

- Avoid loose-fill bulk insulation if your roof space is draughty; alternatively, apply a sealant to its top surface to hold it in place.
- Keep bulk insulation dry at all times. If condensation is a problem, fit a 'vapour barrier' – usually reflective foil – on the warm side of the insulation material. Installing roof vents will also help. Exhaust fans should be properly ducted to prevent moisture build-up in the roof.
- Avoid installing insulation within approximately 90 mm of heating flues or exhaust fans, or on top of or within roughly 25 mm of recessed light fittings.
- When working with fibreglass and rock-wool fibres, wear protective clothing and a mask as the fibres can irritate the skin, nose and eyes.
- If fitting insulation over wiring, check with a licensed electrician that it's safe to cover it first.

DRAUGHTPROOFING

As well as adding insulation, you should seal all gaps and holes. Draughtproofing can cut heat loss by up to 25 per cent in winter.

- If you can see light around a door or window, or hear whistling, then air may be getting in and out. To find less obvious leaks, wet your hand and hold it in front of doors, windows and other openings. You'll feel any draught on your damp hand.
- Draughtproof doors and windows with foam strips or permanent mouldings. Use a permanent draught excluder or 'door sausage' to seal a gap at the bottom of a door.
- Seal narrow gaps with foam seals or mouldings. If that isn't possible, use a liquid caulking compound. Latex- and silicone-based sealants are the least toxic. Exterior caulking products may emit toxic fumes.
- Window panes cause up to 20 per cent of heat loss in winter, so make sure you also cover windows with curtains and a pelmet.

WHAT IS THE R VALUE?

Insulation materials usually carry an R value. This measures its resistance to heat flow – in other words, its effectiveness. The higher the rating, the better. Most materials come in ratings ranging from 1.0 to 3.5.

- Look for ceiling insulation with an R value of at least 2.5 and wall insulation with a rating of 1.0 to 1.5.
- The ideal R value for your home depends on the local climate, and there are suggested standards for different locations – contact your local authority or energy department for details.

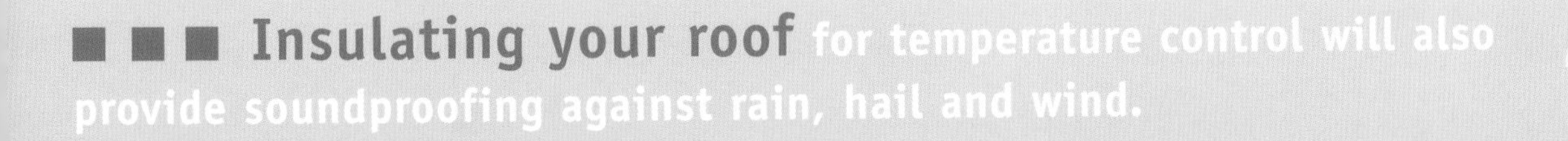

Insulating your roof for temperature control will also provide soundproofing against rain, hail and wind.

Warming solutions

Your home can be warm without costing the earth. It's especially worth thinking about the effectiveness of your heating as it's usually one of the biggest energy consumers in the house (often *the* biggest), and can be a major drain on your funds. The good news is that there are plenty of commonsense savings that you can make.

FIRST STEPS

A few simple changes to your existing set-up can cut your heating bills significantly.

- On sunny days in winter, open up the house to the north and west to let the sun's warmth in.
- Make sure your house is well insulated. Seal gaps around doors and windows. Cover windows with thick curtains and pelmets.
- Move heaters away from windows to avoid unnecessary heat loss.
- Before turning the heating up, think about putting on another layer of clothing instead.
- Remember to turn your heating off before you go out of the house and to turn it off or down low before you go to bed.
- Close doors between heated and unheated areas to keep the warmth in the area you are heating.
- In gas fires, dust can block air intakes, causing faulty combustion and emission of toxic fumes, including carbon monoxide. If you notice a gas flame burning orange or yellow rather than blue, it's time to get your heater serviced.
- Check that your heating appliances are operating efficiently. If in doubt, have them serviced, as they may be using surplus energy.

THE RIGHT SYSTEM

When choosing a heating system, you need to look at the amount of space you have to heat and at how much, how often and for how long that space needs to be heated. Look, too, at the system's ongoing costs and its potential environmental impact.

- If you live in a small apartment and only need to heat your home during the coldest days of winter, then a space heater will probably suffice. Choose a portable one so that you can move it from room to room as required.
- If you have a number of rooms and need to heat them on a regular basis, consider buying an efficient, fixed space heater for the living

WHAT'S IN A NAME?

There are two main types of heating, radiant and convective, and two main ways this heat is delivered, space and central heating.

- Radiant heat: heats directly using a flame or hot electrical element.
- Convective heat: warms and circulates the air.
- Space heating: uses an appliance to heat a single room or part of a house.
- Central heating: directs heat from a central heat source to rooms via pipes.

~ STAR SAVER ~

Install ceiling fans to push warm air that accumulates near the ceiling back to ground level – where you need it! The cost of installation will be offset by long-term savings of as much as 10 per cent of your heating costs.

Try to limit the area you need to heat. If you can halve the area you have to heat, you'll halve your heating costs.

area and portable space heaters for rooms such as bedrooms, which are used only part of the time.

- Central heating may only be worth the additional expense if you need to heat living areas *and* other rooms for three or more months of the year.
- Overall, gas heaters are more economical to run and generate lower levels of greenhouse gases. Where gas is not available, a reverse-cycle airconditioner is the next best option.

Comparing space heaters

Type	Pros	Cons
Bar heater	Inexpensive, portable; direct heat warms body quickly.	Expensive to run; red-hot element poses fire risk.
Fan heater	Inexpensive, portable; heats small rooms quickly.	Expensive to run; ineffective in large rooms.
Convection heater	Inexpensive, portable; heats small rooms quickly.	Expensive to run; ineffective in rooms with high ceilings.
Oil-filled column heater	Good for moderate to large rooms with high ceilings; can be portable.	Expensive to run; takes time to heat up and cool down.
Reverse-cycle heat pump	Economical; the most efficient and earth-wise electric option.	Expensive to buy and install.
Wall heater	Off-peak storage heaters can be economical.	Otherwise expensive to run.
Flued gas heater	Economical, powerful heat; low greenhouse gas emissions.	Expensive to buy and install; imitation flames pose fire risk.
Unflued gas heater	Portable, economical and efficient; low greenhouse gas emissions.	Moderately expensive to buy; increases indoor air pollution.
Open wood fire	Potentially environmentally friendly; atmospheric and attractive.	Highly inefficient, polluting; fire risk from flames, sparks.
Slow-combustion wood fire	Potentially environmentally friendly; efficient.	Moderately expensive to install; fire risk from sparks.

- When buying an electric space heater, make sure the heater's output is appropriate for the area you want to warm. Don't buy a large heater for a small room as it will cost more and make the room too warm. Conversely, it's no good trying to heat a large space with a small heater – your costs will soar and you won't even feel warm.
- To work out the ideal kilowattage, calculate the volume of the area to be heated (height × length × width in metres) then divide the total by 20. Buy a more powerful machine if your room is badly insulated.
- Look for electric heaters that shut off when they overheat.
- With portable space heaters, look for systems that will switch themselves off automatically if they are accidentally knocked over.
- When buying a reverse-cycle airconditioner, opt for one that has a high efficiency rating and a thermostat. Adjustable louvres and a programmable timer are also desirable features. Note that these units may not work at full efficiency in very cold conditions (under 5°C).

■ ■ ■ **By increasing the efficiency** of your heating, you can cut overall household energy use by up to 20 per cent.

GAS ISSUES

Burning gas produces carbon monoxide, carbon dioxide, nitric oxide and nitrogen dioxide, as well as small amounts of formaldehyde and sulphur dioxide. It also creates water vapour, which can in turn increase levels of condensation and mould.

- For cleaner air, choose a flued heater, which channels toxic fumes outdoors via a pipe or chimney.
- Unflued heaters are generally less expensive and less energy efficient than flued heaters (to compare gas heaters, check their Energy Rating labels). If you do choose an unflued heater, make sure the room you use it in is well ventilated. If there are no air vents, or they are blocked, open a window or door regularly to let pollutants out.
- Don't leave an unflued gas heater on overnight or use one in a bedroom or bathroom.
- To monitor oxygen levels in a heated room, choose a heater with an oxygen depletion indicator. It will let you know when the oxygen level is low. Overheating indicators are also a sensible safety precaution.
- LPG is an option in areas where natural gas is not available. But although portable LPG heaters produce similarly low levels of greenhouse emissions to natural gas heaters, they are more expensive to run, sometimes costing as much as portable electric heaters.
- Choose a gas heater with electronic ignition rather than a pilot light that burns constantly. If you have a heater with a pilot light, turn the pilot light off in summer when you are not using the heater.

WOOD FIRES

Burning wood can be a positive choice from an environmental point of view as it has minimal greenhouse impact if the wood is obtained from a sustainable source and not transported far. Overall, however, it is an inefficient form of heating because so much of the heat is lost.

- Make sure your wood comes from a sustainable source such as a timber plantation.
- Make sure you use clean, high-quality wood that has been dried, or 'seasoned', for at least a year. This will help minimise air pollution.
- Do not collect firewood from parks as it provides vital habitat and nesting material for animals.
- Do not use wood that has been coated with varnish, paint or other

WARNING!

▼ Some states have set a maximum permitted power output for unflued gas heaters, and in Victoria these heaters are banned altogether. Check with your local energy authority.

Comparing central heating systems

Source	Set-up cost	Operating cost	Greenhouse emissions
Ducted: electric reverse-cycle	Moderate	Low to moderate	High
Ducted: gas	Moderate	Low	Low
Ducted: LPG	Moderate	High	Low
Electric thin film	High	Moderate to high	High
Hydronic: electric	High	Moderate to high	High
Hydronic: gas	High	Low	Low
Hydronic: LPG	High	High	Low
Hydronic: wood/solar	High	Low	Low
In-slab floor	High	Moderate to high	High with electricity, low with gas, even lower with wood or solar plus gas

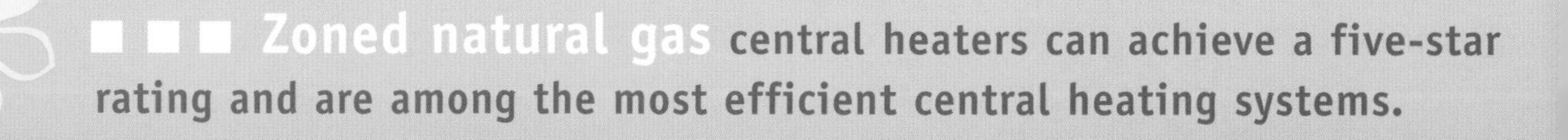

About 90 per cent of the heat from an open fire goes straight up the chimney.

chemicals as it could emit toxic fumes. Driftwood may contain chemicals as well as salt that can erode or rust a fireplace.

- Don't let logs smoulder for long periods, such as overnight, as this increases the output of pollutants.
- Have your chimney checked and cleaned once a year to make sure it is working efficiently.
- Add wood ash to your compost – it's an excellent source of potassium, which promotes healthy plant growth.
- Improve the efficiency of an open fire by installing a fireplace insert. This is a metal frame that allows air to circulate around the fire in the fireplace, pick up heat and flow back into the room. It can raise the efficiency of an open fire to 35 per cent.
- Fit a fan to your wood heater. It will help circulate warm air and can raise efficiency by up to 8 per cent.
- If burning wood will be your main heat source, install a slow-combustion heater (pictured below). These are cheap to run, emit minimal pollutants, and operate at up to 70 per cent efficiency, compared with 10 per cent for an open fire.

CENTRAL HEATING

Central heating sounds cosy, but can be expensive if not used frugally. If you do opt for central heating, consider your options carefully and look for systems and features that will reduce costs and cut greenhouse emissions.

- If your lifestyle is such that you're out of the house most of the day and only want to warm a room or two in the evenings and on weekends, you are likely to find the total cost of a central heating system is much higher than using one or more efficient space heaters.
- If you opt for central heating, make sure you buy a zoned system – one that lets you turn heat off and on in each room or at least different parts of the house. This can easily halve your heating costs.
- Consider the pros and cons of the main types of central heating: ducted air, hydronic (hot-water), thin film and in-slab heating. Most can be fuelled by electricity (including solar), gas or LPG.
- Choose a system with a high efficiency rating.
- Make sure that the system is the right size and has the right amount of power for your home.
- Look for well-insulated ducts with an R rating of at least 1.5, and check regularly for air leaks – you don't want to pay for heating the roof space!
- Make sure the system has a programmable thermostat that will allow you to control the temperature at different times of day.

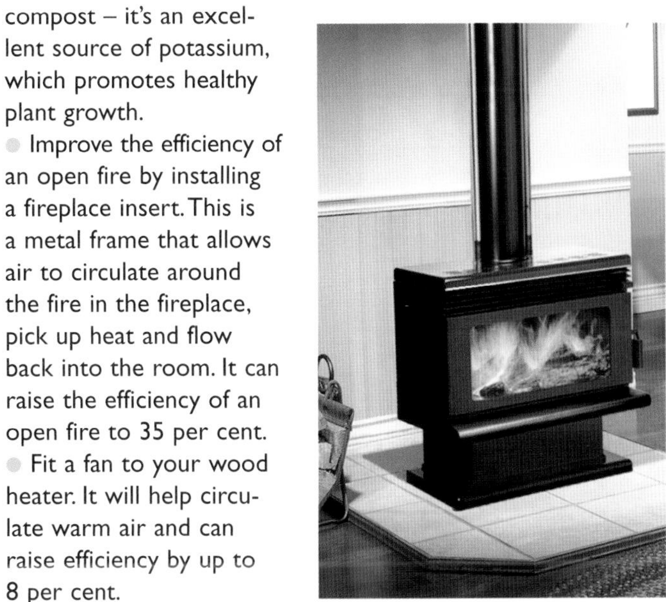

Central heating supply

- **Ducted** Warm air is heated by a central furnace and then circulated to rooms through long, flexible tubes or ducts, usually located under the floor or in the roof space.
- **Electric thin film** Heat is generated by electric elements set in thin films usually fixed behind the ceilings, walls or floor.
- **Hydronic** Water is heated by a furnace and then circulated through pipes to metal radiators, usually mounted on walls.
- **In-slab floor** Heat is produced by electric coils or hot-water pipes set in a concrete-slab floor.

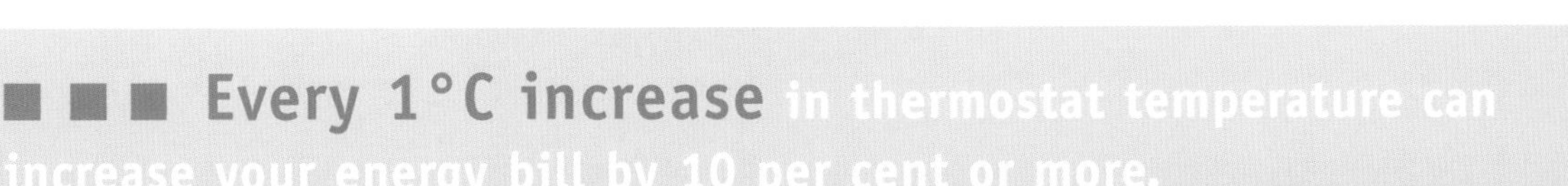

Heating water

In an average household, heating water accounts for the second largest proportion of energy use. That means the potential for savings is great. Reducing your water usage and making adjustments to your system can help cut costs, but installing a new energy-efficient heater may provide the greatest long-term gains.

HOT-WATER SAVERS

- Think before turning on the hot water. Will cold water suffice – for example, for rinsing dishes and washing clothes? This simple step can save up to 25 per cent of your water-heating bill.
- Keep your thermostat setting fairly low – about 60°C (but over 55°C to kill off bacteria). Having the water too hot is a waste of energy and means that you use more cold water to make it cooler. Lowering the temperature also reduces the risk of scalds.
- Fix a dripping hot tap. It could be wasting up to 10 bathtubs full of hot water a month.
- Try to avoid using hot water in short spurts throughout the day. Instead, do several jobs that need hot water at once. This way, less water is left in the pipes to go cold.
- Take shorter showers and save up to 23 litres of water a minute.
- Install tap aerators and flow restrictors. These limit the flow without reducing pressure.
- Install an AAA water-efficient showerhead and you could cut hot-water usage by up to half.
- Make sure your hot-water pipes and tank are well insulated, especially if they are outside. Up to half of your hot water bill is spent on reheating water that has gone cold.

ELECTRIC HEATERS

Traditional electric water heaters are inexpensive to buy and relatively easy to install. But running costs are high (up to six times those of a good solar system).

- Think twice before choosing a conventional electric heater. It can emit four times as much greenhouse gas as a natural gas, electric heat pump or electric-boosted solar heater, and twelve times as much as a gas-boosted solar heater.
- If electricity is your best option, consider an electric heat pump. It extracts heat from the atmosphere and pumps it into the water tank.

✓ BUY WISELY

- Make sure you weigh up the initial cost of a water heater against ongoing running costs and its environmental impact.
- Compare instantaneous systems, which heat on demand, with storage systems, which maintain a full tank at a set temperature. Gas instantaneous systems are more efficient and economical than gas or electric storage systems.
- Calculate what size of tank you require. If your tank is too small, you'll run out of hot water; too big and you'll waste money and energy keeping unused water hot.

Hot-water power

Type of system	Initial cost	Running cost	Greenhouse emissions
Electric heat pump	High	Low	Low
Electric storage	Low	High (low if off-peak)	High
Natural gas, instantaneous	Low	Low	Low
Natural gas, storage	Low	Low	Low
Solar with electric booster	High	Low	Medium
Solar with natural gas booster	High	Low	Low

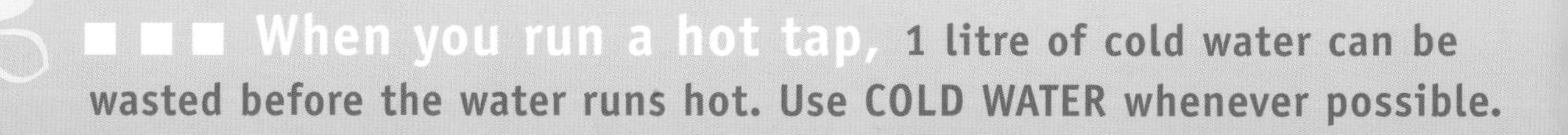

■ ■ ■ **When you run a hot tap,** 1 litre of cold water can be wasted before the water runs hot. Use COLD WATER whenever possible.

~ *STAR SAVER* ~

Overall, a gas-boosted solar water heater is the cheapest to run and the most energy-efficient. Running costs are up to 80 per cent lower than an equivalent electric storage system, which means it should pay for itself in 5–10 years.

Though expensive to install, it is eco-friendly and economical, using 70 per cent less electricity than a conventional electric water heater.

- To make further savings, connect your heat pump to a timer and set it to use off-peak energy supplies.
- Find out if your local authority offers rebates or incentives for installing heat-pump systems.

GAS HEATERS

Gas water heaters, whether instantaneous or storage-based, are generally more economical and eco-friendly than electric heaters – though you are still using a non-renewable resource.

- Look for efficiency rating labels and give preference to systems awarded five or six stars. Such systems may qualify you for rebates.
- If you opt for an instantaneous system, avoid units with pilot lights as these waste valuable energy and emit as much as an extra 300 kilograms of greenhouse gases a year.

SOLAR HEATERS

Solar systems are a viable option in almost every part of Australia and New Zealand, and can meet up to 80 per cent of household water-heating needs – a booster system, powered by gas, electricity or solid fuel, makes up the shortfall. The main component is a set of panels fixed to the roof.

- Find out if you will qualify for a government loan, rebate or credit for installing a solar hot water system. This can make installation a lot more affordable.
- Investigate converting your existing gas or electric storage heater to solar power. This is possible with most modern systems.
- When installing a solar system, choose a sunny, north-facing spot, no more than 20 degrees east or west of north – ideally one that receives direct sunlight between 8 am and 4 pm.
- Place the system at an angle of between 15 and 50 degrees. If your roof doesn't allow for this, you can use a mounting frame, but this will increase the cost of the system.
- Make sure your roof is strong enough to support the system – some are quite heavy.
- Place the storage tank as close as possible to the solar collectors in order to minimise heat loss from connecting pipes.
- Set the thermostat on the booster to a maximum of 60°C. The lower the setting, the lower the amount of energy needed to supplement the solar heating.
- Make the most efficient use you can of your solar water heating. For example, do jobs that require large amounts of hot water early in the day, so that the water that refills the tank will be heated by the sun over the rest of the day rather than by a booster source at night.

hot links

For information on solar energy: www.anzses.org; www.eeca.govt.nz/renewable-energy/solar
Accredited suppliers and installers of solar water heaters: www.seav.sustainability.vic.gov.au/renewable_energy/policies_and_initiatives/shw; www.solarindustries.org.nz

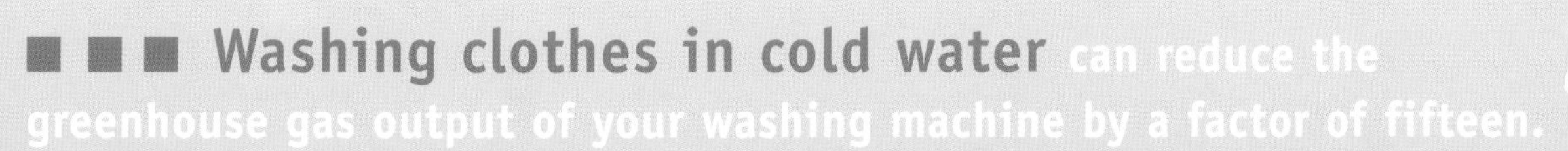

■ ■ ■ **Washing clothes in cold water** can reduce the greenhouse gas output of your washing machine by a factor of fifteen.

Staying cool

Before you flick the switch for instant cool – and huge power bills – think about your options. Is your house well insulated? Is there ample shading and ventilation? When the answer's yes, cooling devices will run more efficiently and your bills will be a lot lower.

SIMPLE STRATEGIES

Take a good look around your house to see if you can make any modifications that will help keep hot air out and let cooling breezes come in.

- On hot days, make sure windows, blinds and curtains are closed to keep heat out and the interior shaded and cool.
- When it's already hot inside, try opening windows on opposite sides of the house to create cooling cross-ventilation.
- At night, when the temperature drops, open the doors and windows to let cold air inside. Turning on extractor fans in bathrooms and kitchens for a short time can help draw the warm air outside.
- Hang damp sheets outside your windows. The evaporating water will have a cooling effect.
- If you live in a house with two or more storeys, consider using the lower floors during the day, as they should be cooler.
- Install temporary shutters or awnings over north- and west-facing windows. They will block the sun's heat, but can be removed in winter to let the sun in when you need it most. Alternatively, modify the eaves of your house so that they keep summer sun out but let winter sun in. The ideal width of eaves will vary depending on your latitude.
- Check that your house, and especially the roof, is well insulated. Reflective insulation placed under the roof can dramatically reduce heat build-up in summer.
- Remove paving from outside north-facing windows as it will contribute to heat build-up. Replace with a cooling plant cover such as grass or low-lying plants or shrubs.

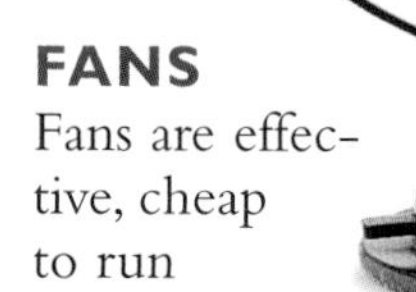

FANS

Fans are effective, cheap to run and energy-efficient. They work not by lowering the temperature, but by circulating air over your body, which evaporates moisture, making you feel cool.

- Portable fans are effective for personal cooling. Look for models that have variable speed settings and oscillate (turn from side to side).
- For room cooling, consider installing ceiling fans. Place the fan above the light fitting (to avoid a flickering effect) and at least 2.1 m above the floor.
- Choose four-bladed fans with tilted or scoop-edged blades for the best air circulation. Despite a higher initial outlay, more expensive fans

PROS & CONS

USING AN AIRCONDITIONER

Airconditioners are highly effective at lowering air temperatures and also help reduce humidity. In recent years, cheaper, more efficient models have become available, including compact reverse-cycle units that also provide heating. But airconditioners are still the most expensive cooling systems to buy and run – the operating cost per hour of a medium-sized unit is 30 times that of a ceiling fan – and the least energy-efficient. Excess use of airconditioners during hot spells is thought to be one of the main causes of electricity-grid overloads and blackouts, and their high energy consumption is a major contributor to household greenhouse gas emissions.

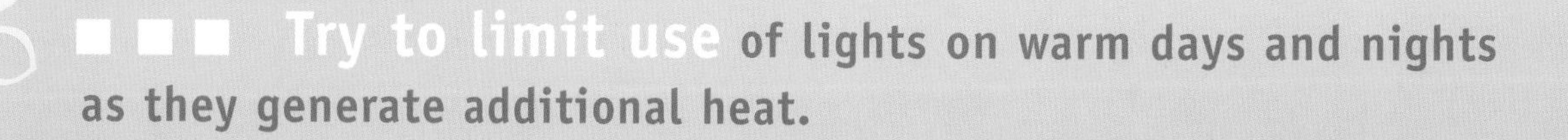

~ STAR SAVER ~

Using fans with your airconditioner can cut costs. Raise the thermostat on your cooling system and turn on your fan – the moving air makes higher temperatures feel more comfortable. Fans cost just a few cents an hour to run, but every degree you can turn up your airconditioner saves up to 10 per cent of cooling costs.

with stronger motors are quieter and last longer. A reverse function will allow you to use the fan to push heat downwards in winter.

- If you need to cool every room, consider a whole-house fan. It consists of a large fan set in the roof, which sucks air out of the room below, while drawing fresh air in through open windows and doors.

EVAPORATIVE COOLERS

These systems work by drawing air through a water-moistened filter to cool it. The cool air is then blown through the house. Available as portable, fixed-unit or ducted systems, they are fairly inexpensive and use relatively little energy, but can be noisy, obtrusive and use a lot of water.

- Before buying, consider your local climate. Evaporative coolers work more efficiently in areas where the average relative humidity is low.
- For a room of under 25 sq.m, you can use a portable model. Fixed units will cool a room of up to 50 sq.m, but can cost five times as much.
- On portable units, look for directional shutters, variable speed settings and a water-level gauge – all will help you monitor and increase the efficiency of the system.
- When cooling, keep windows and doors open to let damp air out.
- Install the unit on the side of the house facing prevailing warm winds. That way, you can block the warm air and open the windows on the other side to let moisture out.
- If the weather is particularly humid, turn the water supply off and use just the fan.
- During cold weather, cover your roof unit and close vents to stop heat escaping.

AIRCONDITIONERS

- Split systems, which have separate indoor and outdoor elements linked by piping, are generally cheaper, quieter and use less energy than fixed units, which consist of a box mounted on a window or outside wall. Ducted systems use the most energy and are the most expensive to buy and run.
- As a rule of thumb, you'll need a system with 100–140 watts (0.1–0.14 kW) per sq.m of living room and 80–100 watts (0.08–0.1 kW) per sq.m of bedroom, depending on your climate and house design. Discuss with your supplier.
- Select units with a high Energy Rating. They may cost a little more but will soon pay for themselves. Each extra star means a saving of about 10 per cent in running costs.

TOP TIP

If you live in a hot climate, think about adding a pergola on the north side of the house. Cover it with deciduous vines or a shadecloth and in summer it will block up to 80 per cent of the sun's heat. Remove the shadecloth in winter; the vines will shed their leaves and let the sun shine through.

- If you opt for a ducted system, choose one with zoning – the ability to switch cooling on or off in different parts of the house. This will minimise energy use and costs.
- Select a model with a programmable timer and thermostat, economy settings and adjustable speeds and louvres.
- Install the unit out of direct sunlight and don't block its outlet with furniture or curtains.
- For maximum efficiency, shut doors and windows in the room where the unit is operating.
- Don't set the thermostat too low (26–27°C should be cool enough), and remember to turn it off when you go out.
- Clean the filters regularly and keep coils and fans free of dust.

■ ■ ■ **When using cooling systems,** minimise the area being cooled. Close doors to areas not being used.

Switched-on lighting

Lighting might account for as little as 5 per cent of household energy costs, but it's part of your expenditure and energy output that can easily be cut – by more than half, if you're careful. Start by opening up your house to nature's free and highly efficient light source, the sun. Then look at adopting low-energy, long-life technologies.

NATURAL LIGHTING

Maximising your use of natural light will save on lighting bills, warm your home and help eliminate germs and dust mites.

- Paint interior walls in pale shades and use mirrors to reflect natural light, particularly in dark rooms.
- On bright, sunny days (that aren't too hot) open blinds and curtains to admit as much light as possible.
- If your house is especially dark, think about installing large windows on the north side of the house, or even French doors. Make windows taller rather than wider, to admit more light.
- Situate work areas, such as desks and kitchen sinks and benches, close to sources of natural light.
- Consider installing skylights in dark corners such as hallways or small rooms with no windows. To minimise heat flow, make sure they are covered at night and shaded at midday in summer.
- A cheap and effective alternative to a skylight is a sky tube or solar tube (pictured above). It concentrates and reflects natural light through a diffuser into the room below. The light generated is the equivalent of a 100-watt bulb. A sky tube loses less heat than a skylight and can be fitted with an exhaust fan as well as a light for night-time.

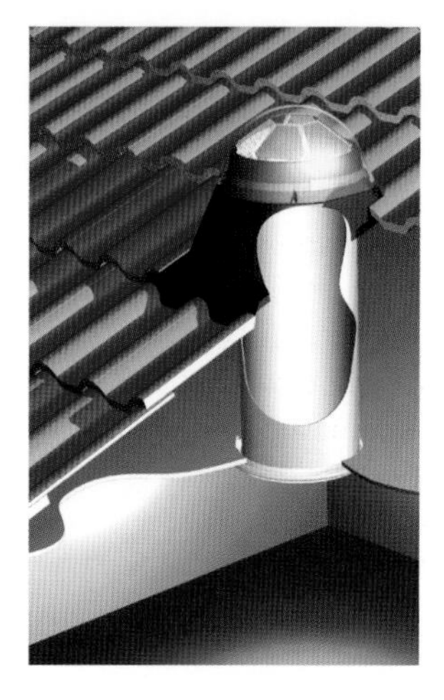

Watt's the difference?

Incandescent bulb wattage	CFL equivalent wattage
40	9–11
60	13–15
75	18–20
100	23–25
150	30–35

WHICH KIND OF LIGHTING?

Aesthetics are important when it comes to lighting, but choosing the right light for each location is just as crucial. An appropriate, efficient light will not only increase comfort, it will also save energy and reduce long-term costs. Fortunately, a host of efficient lighting options is available.

- Conventional incandescent light bulbs are inefficient because most of the energy used to run them is turned into heat rather than light. Though they are cheap to buy, they have to be replaced regularly. Limit your use of incandescent bulbs to areas where you need light instantly and only for a short time, such as a bathroom or pantry.
- Consider using halogen bulbs, which throw a bright light similar to natural light, to illuminate a work area or to spotlight a painting. They are expensive to buy, but usually last twice as long as regular bulbs.
- Think twice before installing halogen downlighting. These lights throw hard-edged spotlights rather than ambient light, so it takes up to six of them to light the same area as a single incandescent bulb.
- Remember that low-voltage halogen lights need transformers, so you'll need to fit downlight transformers in your roof cavity.
- If your home has a concrete slab ceiling, your only halogen option will be the 240-volt variety. These don't require a transformer, but the bulbs are more expensive than the low-voltage varieties.

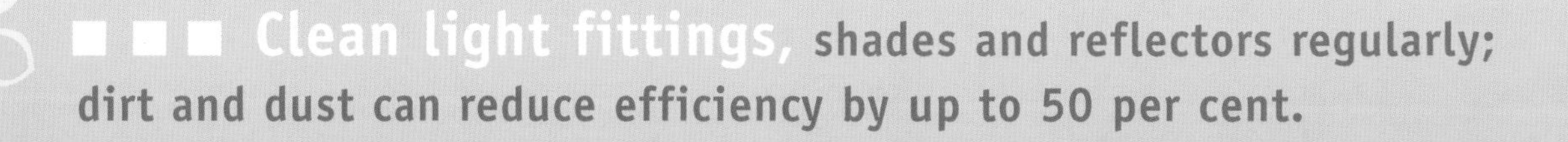

SAVE WITH FLUOROS

Fluorescent lights consume about one quarter of the energy of equivalent incandescent bulbs and last up to fifteen times longer. They are available in two forms: traditional tube lights, which are cheaper but require special fittings, and compact fluorescent lamps (CFLs), which fit standard light sockets. They come in a range of tones and wattages, making them suitable for most uses.

- Use fluorescent lights where you need light for long periods – for example in kitchens or living areas.
- Next time you need to replace a conventional light bulb, try a CFL, then gradually replace all incandescent bulbs in high-use areas.
- Generally, it's wise to select a slightly higher wattage for CFLs than is usually recommended by the manufacturer because they tend to dim a little over time. Use the table opposite as a guide.
- Look for CFLs that come in two pieces, a fitting and a bulb. That allows you to replace just the bulb rather than the whole unit.

SMART LIGHTING

- Select the lowest acceptable wattage for all lights. More watts mean you use more power.
- Remember to turn lights off whenever you leave a room. That includes fluorescent lights, though very frequent turning on and off of these lights should be avoided because it shortens their life span.
- Use low-wattage lights for general room lighting, saving more powerful lights for places where you need to do close work.
- Remember that a low-wattage light placed closer to where it is needed is more efficient than using a stronger light placed further away.
- Avoid lights with multiple bulbs as they are inefficient – about six 25-watt bulbs are needed to match the output of one 100-watt bulb.
- Don't install light fittings that obscure the light. Some can block up to 50 per cent of the light.
- Use timers or light or heat sensors to control outside lights.
- Install contact switches in cupboards so that lights go on when you open the cupboard and off when you close it.
- Use dimmer switches to reduce energy use. They can be attached to all incandescent light fittings, though you'll need a special transformer for low-voltage halogen lamps. They do not work with fluorescent bulbs. If you constantly use dimmer light, put in a lower-wattage bulb.

~ STAR SAVER ~

Gradually replace your 100-watt regular light bulbs with 23- to 25-watt compact fluorescent bulbs. They will last up to 10 times as long, pay for themselves in about a year and a half, then pay for themselves at least twice again during the rest of their lifetime.

TOP TIP

Solar-powered garden lights can be the ideal solution for gentle night lighting of garden paths and driveways, which can be difficult to connect to household electricity. They cost nothing to run, as they soak up the sun's power during the day through a panel and store it in a battery that powers the lights at night.

Types of artificial lighting

Lighting type	Purchase cost	Life span in hours	Running costs	Energy use
Fluorescent	Medium	6000–15,000	Low	Low
Halogen	Medium	2000–4000	Medium	Medium
Incandescent	Low	1000–2500	High	High

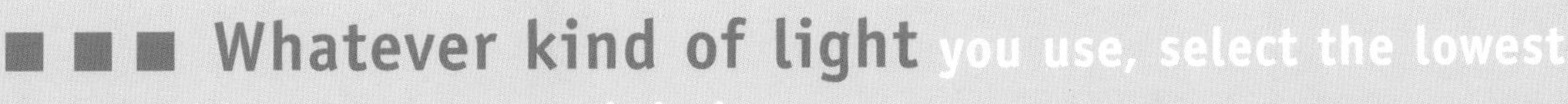

Water-wise living

By adopting water-wise habits and making some minor adjustments to your plumbing, it's possible to halve your water consumption. You'll be helping reduce pressure on limited water supplies, protecting the environment by reducing your sewerage outputs and saving money at the same time.

EASY WAYS TO SAVE WATER

- Take shorter showers. Every minute less spent in the shower can save up to 23 litres of water, depending on the efficiency of your showerhead.
- If you have a leaking tap, fix it at once – it could be wasting up to 2000 litres of water a month. Don't keep tightening the tap as this will wear the washer and make the leak worse.
- Whenever you turn a tap on and are waiting for cold water to run hot, catch the cold water in a jug or bucket and then use it – for watering indoor plants, filling the kettle, or any other purpose. You could save up to 4 litres of water each time.

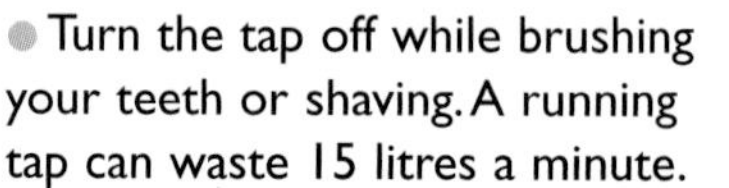

- Turn the tap off while brushing your teeth or shaving. A running tap can waste 15 litres a minute.
- If you have one, use the half-flush option on your toilet whenever appropriate. You can save about 8 litres per flush.
- Don't run your washing machine until you have a full load. Reducing the number of washes you do can save huge amounts of water – some top-loading washing machines can use as much as 240 litres per wash.
- Use your dishwasher only when it is full. You can save up to 50 litres for every wash you don't do.
- If you are washing dishes by hand, rinse them in a sink full of cold water rather than under a running tap – which could use 15 litres a minute.

AVERAGE HOUSEHOLD WATER USE IN AUSTRALIA

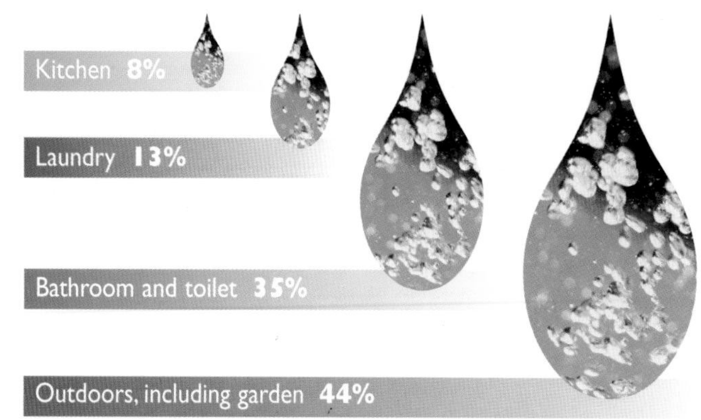

Source: Australian Bureau of Statistics

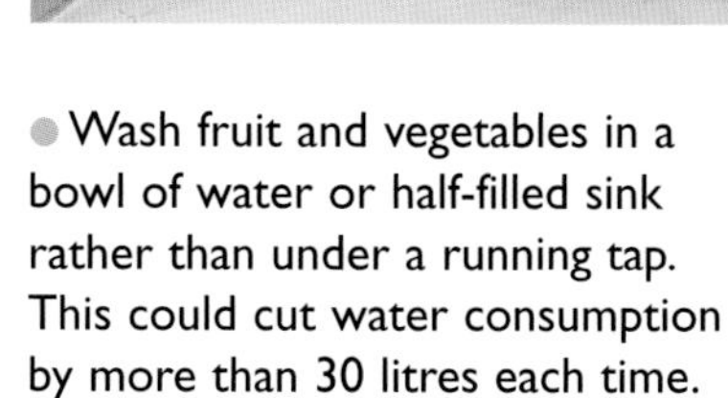

- Wash fruit and vegetables in a bowl of water or half-filled sink rather than under a running tap. This could cut water consumption by more than 30 litres each time.
- When washing the car, use a bucket and sponge rather than a hose. Use just 6 buckets and you'll save more than 150 litres per wash.
- To clean driveways, paths and paved areas, sweep with a broom instead of hosing.
- Gradually reduce how frequently you water the garden – this will encourage plants to put down strong, deep roots.
- Don't water the garden during the heat of the day; instead water in the cool of the evening or in the early morning.
- Even when water restrictions aren't in force, use minimal water on the lawn. Increase drought-resistance of grass by not cutting it too short (about 3 cm is ideal); by aerating it occasionally with a garden fork to improve water penetration; and by not over-fertilising because the more fertiliser you use, the more water you need to keep the grass lush.

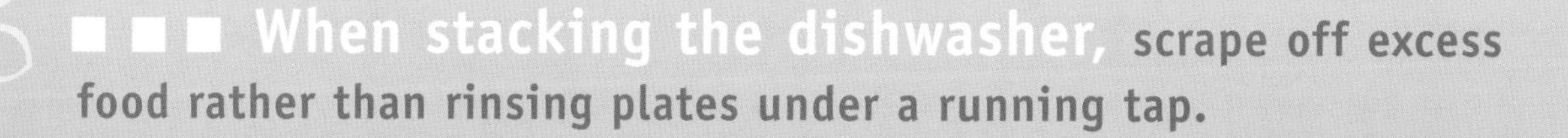

■ ■ ■ **When stacking the dishwasher,** scrape off excess food rather than rinsing plates under a running tap.

Top Tip

Small leaks can waste huge amounts of water – that you are paying for – so it's a good idea to run this check for a leaking pipe every now and then. Turn off all taps and machines that use water. Write down the reading on your water meter. Check it again half an hour later. If it has gone up, you have a leak. Call a plumber if you can't find the leak yourself.

~ *FLYING START* ~

Switch to an AAA-rated water-saving showerhead. It's the cheapest and most effective change you can make inside your home to save water – it can save up to 50,000 litres a year. Some water authorities will provide, install and even offer rebates for using these devices.

WATER-SAVING HARDWARE

A range of accessories and fittings is available to help you save water. Check with your local authority whether all plumbing work has to be carried out by a licensed plumber. In some jurisdictions, doing it yourself can nullify related insurance cover.

- Replace separate taps with a single-lever mixer tap. This will help you adjust the water temperature more rapidly, thereby saving water.
- Ask a plumber to fit aerators and flow regulators to taps (or fit taps that incorporate these devices). They reduce the flow of water without diminishing pressure – in other words, without you really noticing a difference.
- Update your cistern to a high-efficiency dual flush system. This can reduce flush volume from 11 litres to 3 litres.
- If your cistern doesn't have a half-flush option, consider reducing the flush volume by installing a commercially available flush regulator or by inserting a plastic bottle full of water in the cistern, well away from the flush mechanism.
- To avoid wasting cold water left in hot-water pipes, install a recirculating system, which sends unused water back to the heater, or a heat-tracing system, which uses minimal power to keep the water in the pipes warm.

EFFICIENCY RATINGS

When buying appliances that use water, look for models bearing Water Rating 'star' labels or Water Conservation Rating 'AAAAA' labels (the former will gradually replace the latter).

- These efficiency ratings cover showerheads, dishwashers, washing machines, taps, toilet equipment and flow regulators.
- Water Rating labels indicate efficiency using a rating of between one and six stars and a consumption figure. The more stars, the more efficient the product.
- Water Conservation Rating labels grade products from A to AAAAA. The higher the number of As, the higher the level of water efficiency.
- Appliances with high ratings may cost more but will offer significant long-term savings.
- All of the rated products meet Australian Standards performance levels, so they are of high quality.
- Water-efficient products not only save water and money, but also energy – and thereby limit greenhouse gas emissions.

hot links

Information on the Water Conservation Rating and Labelling (AAAAA) Scheme: www.wsaa.asn.au
Information on the Water Efficiency Labelling and Standards (WELS) Scheme: www.waterrating.gov.au
Advice on water conservation: www.savewater.com.au; www.waitakere.govt.nz/CnlSer/wtr/wtrsavetips.asp

Collecting water

Installing a rainwater tank will save you money on water bills and provide a back-up supply for times of drought. You'll also be doing your bit to help preserve valuable drinking water. Water from a rainwater tank can be used not just for the garden and washing the car, but also for flushing toilets and washing clothes.

CHOOSING A TANK

Rainwater tanks work by funnelling water that falls on a roof through the gutters and downpipes to a tank. When buying, explore your options carefully.

- Contact your local water authority and council to find out if there are any restrictions on the size or type of tank you can install.
- Ask about rebates available to home owners who install tanks.
- Survey your property to find the best place for a tank. Remember they don't have to take up a huge amount of space. Consider side passages and areas under the house or adjacent to outbuildings.

DESIGNED TO FIT

Water tanks now come in all shapes and sizes. Take a look at the following options.

- Gutter systems hang from gutters and use gravity to supply outdoor taps. They hold up to 1500 litres.
- Slimline tanks are rectangular polyethylene modules that slot together. They can be placed against walls and in narrow spaces where normal tanks would not fit.
- Water fences and water walls are plastic containers that double as a fence or screen in a garden.
- Bladder tanks, made of flexible plastic, fit under floors or decks, and can be linked for extra capacity.

What kind of tank?

Material	Advantages	Disadvantages
Concrete	Large capacity; can be installed underground or under buildings; long-lasting; keeps light out	Expensive; excavation required to install underground; can crack
Fibreglass	Economical; light; resistant to high temperatures and corrosion	Fragile, prone to cracking; may let light in; some types not suitable for drinking water
Plastic (polyethylene)	Economical; light; UV-resistant; huge range of shapes, colours, sizes and capacities	Longevity depends on level of UV treatment; can be an eyesore
Steel	Economical; reasonably light; range of sizes and shapes	Limited life span; prone to rust; can be an eyesore

PLUMBING AND ACCESSORIES

Tanks can be placed and plumbed according to different needs, and a range of devices is available to help you monitor and maintain supply.

- Ask your supplier to check that your roofing and guttering materials are safe – roofs made with asbestos, covered with lead flashings, painted with lead paint, or covered with tar or bitumen are not.
- Make sure your tank is installed by a qualified plumber and conforms to local legislation.
- Think about having your tank linked to the plumbing so that it provides water for the toilet and/or washing clothes. Some authorities provide an extra rebate for this.
- If you link the tank to the toilet or laundry, make sure you connect it to a mains top-up system, which maintains a minimum amount of water during dry spells, and a back-flow prevention device, to prevent mains and tank supplies mixing.
- Look at placing the tank above ground level (or using a gutter system) so that gravity provides all the pressure you need. But bear in mind that there are restrictions on tank height in many areas.

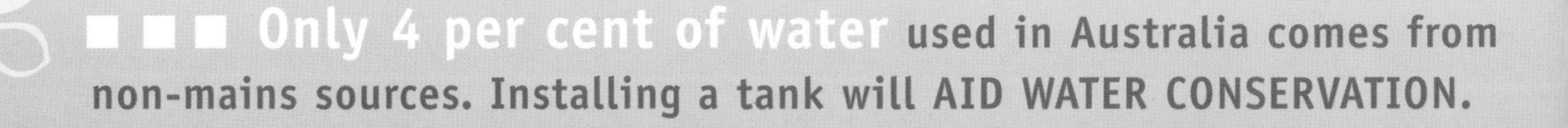

■ ■ ■ **Only 4 per cent of water** used in Australia comes from non-mains sources. Installing a tank will AID WATER CONSERVATION.

- To increase water pressure in non-gravity-fed tanks, fit an electric pump. These are inexpensive and easy to use, but can be noisy.
- Fit a first-flush diverter. It diverts initial runoff, which usually carries most of the accumulated dirt and debris, into a separate collector.
- Buy a dipstick or level indicator to monitor water levels in the tank.
- Add screens to keep debris, vermin and insects out. Screens should be fitted to all inlets and outlets.
- Consider purchasing gutter shields or covers to keep leaves out and improve water quality.

MAINTENANCE

- Use your tank water regularly. This will make your investment worthwhile and ensure that the water doesn't stagnate.
- Drain and clean the tank at least once every 2 years.
- If you don't have gutter shields or covers, regularly cut back trees and bushes that overhang the roof.
- Check that the covers on top of your tank and any other openings fit snugly. Any light that enters the tank will encourage algae to grow.
- Make sure rainwater does not flow into your mains supply.
- Do not drink the water from the tank unless it has been purified.

WHAT SIZE RAINWATER TANK?

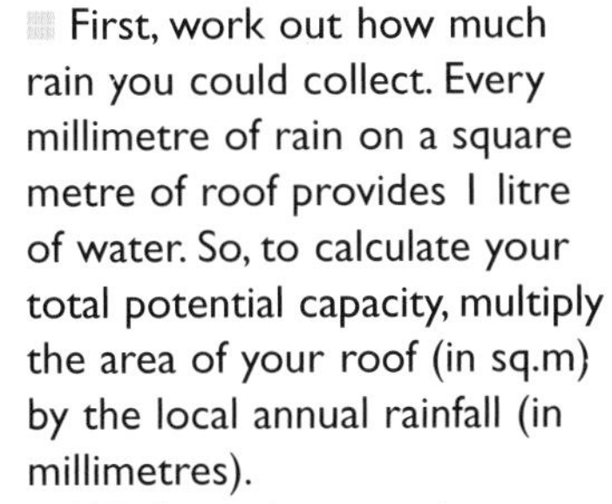

Take some time to work out where you want to use rainwater and how much you need. Also, look into local rainfall patterns. If most of the rain in your area falls in one season, then it is likely that your tank won't cover your garden watering needs in the dry months. In a domestic situation, a tank with a 2000–5000 litre capacity should suffice.

- First, work out how much rain you could collect. Every millimetre of rain on a square metre of roof provides 1 litre of water. So, to calculate your total potential capacity, multiply the area of your roof (in sq.m) by the local annual rainfall (in millimetres).
- Work out how much water you want to collect by using the water usage figures below.
- Evaluate how much you will need of the total water you could collect from your roof – you probably won't be able to, or want to, catch it all.
- Now you are ready to choose your tank. Make sure you choose one that suits your budget and remember to factor in costs for delivery, installation and any accessories you will require.

AVERAGE WATER USAGE

Toilet

Non-efficient full flush	11 litres
Non-efficient half flush	5.5 litres
Efficient full flush	6 litres
Efficient half flush	3 litres

Shower

Non-efficient showerhead	Up to 23 litres a minute
Efficient showerhead	9 litres a minute

Bath

Low bath	50 litres
Full bath	150 litres

Dishwashing

By hand	18 litres
Non-efficient machine	36 litres
Efficient machine	16 litres

Clothes washing

Non-efficient top-loader	Up to 240 litres
Efficient top-loader	110 litres
Efficient front-loader	100 litres

General use

Washing, brushing teeth, etc	18 litres per person per day

Garden

Sprinkler	1000 litres an hour

Washing car

Hose	17 litres a minute

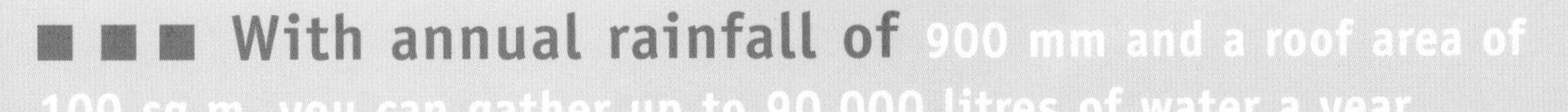

■ ■ ■ **With annual rainfall of 900 mm and a roof area of 100 sq.m, you can gather up to 90,000 litres of water a year.**

Recycling water

Every household generates a large amount of wastewater that simply flows down the drain. Not all of this water needs to go to waste. By planning a safe system in consultation with your local council and plumber, you can capture and divert your grey water to irrigate the garden, flush the toilets and wash your clothes.

GROUND RULES

Recycling water is not especially difficult, but it is not as straightforward as collecting rainwater, and must be planned and carried out carefully to ensure health, environmental and legal requirements are met.

- Check local council and water authority regulations carefully. Some councils and water authorities do not allow reuse of wastewater; others encourage it by offering rebates for money spent on water-saving and water-recycling devices.
- Do not use black water as it contains high levels of bacteria.
- Unless you treat the water, use grey water only from the shower, bath, basin and washing machine. Do not use water from the kitchen as it contains grease and food scraps that encourage the growth of bacteria and attract pests.
- Restrict the use of untreated grey water to the garden. Use only treated grey water to flush toilets and wash clothes (although final rinse water from a washing machine can probably be reused in a subsequent wash without treatment).
- Even grey water from the bathroom and laundry can contain pathogens that spread disease. Use the water immediately, handle it with care and make sure you wash your hands afterwards.
- Keep children and pets away from grey water.
- Never put grey water on fruit and vegetables that may be eaten raw.
- Ensure that grey water doesn't flow from your property onto neighbouring property. You could be liable for any damage or illness that occurs as a result of this.
- Seek advice from a specialist plumber or consultant who is familiar with recycling systems and local regulations and requirements.
- Make sure all members of the household and visitors understand what is being done and how to help.

BUY WISELY

A wide range of water recycling systems is available, including reed-bed and sand filters, aerated wastewater treatment systems and ultraviolet disinfection systems. Before buying, ask yourself and your supplier these questions.

- Is the system approved by the local council and water authority?
- What kind of guarantees come with the system?
- Does the cost include delivery and installation?
- How much space and energy will it use, and how much will it cost to run?
- Will the recycled water be suitable for indoor use? If so, how do I connect the recycling system to my toilet cistern and/or my washing machine?
- Does it have many parts that can break down, such as pumps?
- Is it noisy?
- Does it use chemicals?
- How will I know if it's not working?
- Does it require periodical emptying or desludging?
- How does it deal with small amounts of household chemicals, such as bleach?

WATER WORDS

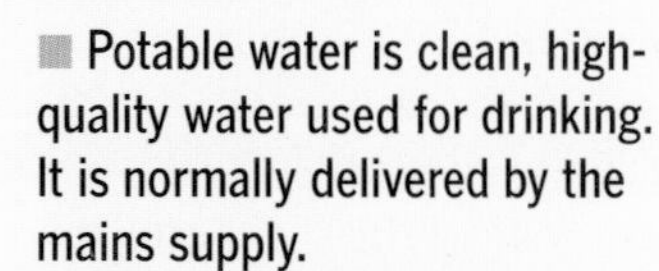

Household water is described in different ways according to its quality and potential use.

- Potable water is clean, high-quality water used for drinking. It is normally delivered by the mains supply.
- Black water is wastewater from toilets and bidets. It contains high levels of bacteria and pollutants.
- Grey water is wastewater from other sources such as the bath, shower and sinks.

■ ■ ■ **An inefficient washing machine, used six times a week, can drain away 1400 litres of recyclable water every 7 days.**

Reduce the drain on drinking water supplies by reusing grey water.

RECYCLING OPTIONS

Grey water can be recycled in various ways, ranging from manual collection to high-tech treatment systems. You can:

- Collect it in a bowl, bucket or hand pump, and pour it into a tank linked to a garden irrigation system. Do not pour it straight onto the garden as it can be a health hazard (see also *Water for the garden,* p. 246).
- Attach a hose to the outlet on your washing machine and connect it to your irrigation system.
- Ask a plumber to divert the wastewater pipe from a basin, bath or shower to an irrigation system. The pipe must have a valve to direct excess water into the sewer. Or have your plumber install a water diverter, which lets you redirect wastewater to an irrigation system whenever appropriate. Some of these devices incorporate a filter.
- Buy a commercially available recycling system. Make sure any models you consider will provide an appropriate level of treatment and are approved by your local council.

SYSTEM MAINTENANCE

- Do not store wastewater for more than 24 hours as bacteria may breed in it.
- Make sure all your unused wastewater is directed into the sewage system. Do not allow excess grey water to drain into stormwater outlets.
- Take care to keep your grey water separate from the mains water. If necessary, install a backflow prevention device.
- Use colour-coded pipes or prominent labels to distinguish recycled water outlets.
- Drain and clean your grey water tank and pipes regularly.
- Have your grey water recycling system serviced professionally and regularly, as recommended by the supplier.
- If you go away for an extended period, take the recycling system apart, clean it carefully and then store it empty and dry.

WARNING!

▼ To avoid human exposure to grey water, it is better to use a subsurface irrigation system to water the garden, or a surface system covered by mulch.

IMPROVING WATER QUALITY

Your recycled water will be safer and more useful if you carefully control the first use of the water, minimising the number of pollutants and chemicals you add.

- Use biodegradable, preferably plant-based cleaning products with no added phosphates. Check that all the ingredients in the product are 100 per cent biodegradable, not just the surfactant.
- Use the minimum recommended amounts of detergents and cleaners.
- If you use a phosphate-free, plant-based laundry powder, you can dilute wash water by combining it with rinse water or by watering the garden with wash water then applying the rinse water immediately afterwards.
- To avoid salt build-up in soil, check that your water isn't saline to begin with (sometimes the case with bore water).
- Use a filter in your washing machine and clean it regularly to minimise levels of lint, hair and pollutants in grey water.
- Never pour paints, pesticides, solvents or medicines down the sink or toilet. Check with your local council for advice on disposing of these materials.
- Don't divert water that has been used to wash nappies or has been used by a sick person.

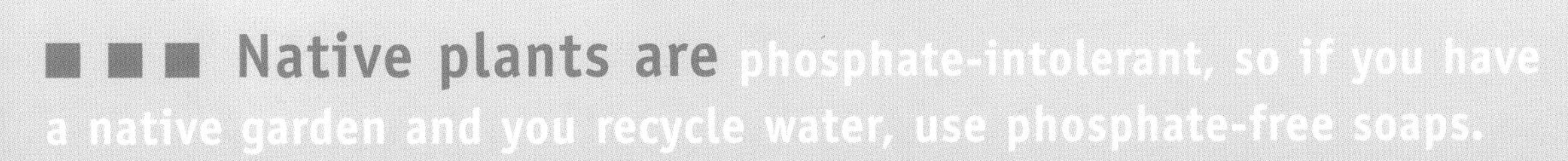

ROOM BY ROOM

Different strategies are required to make each part of the house energy-efficient, comfortable and healthy.

The efficient kitchen

Our kitchens are big energy and water users and they are the main source of household waste, so it's well worth taking the time to evaluate your kitchen routines and to make some changes. Using resources wisely, running energy-efficient appliances, and recycling as much as possible will pay dividends for you, your home and the environment.

TEN COOL SAVERS

1 Fridges and freezers are energy-hungry appliances, so, when it's time to buy, choose high-efficiency models. In turn, this will help you make significant financial savings over the long term.

2 Don't be tempted to keep an old fridge running as a back-up unless you really need it. Old fridges are likely to be more energy-hungry than newer, more energy-efficient models.

3 Locate your fridge in a cool spot, away from heat-producing appliances, and make sure there is an air space of at least 8 cm around the coils at the back. A lack of space or ventilation can reduce efficiency by up to 15 per cent.

4 Don't set the thermostat too cold. The optimum temperature for a fridge is about 3 to 4°C; for a freezer it's -18 to -15°C. Every 1°C reduction can increase energy use by 5 per cent.

5 Open the door as little as possible. For every minute it is open, it takes the fridge 3 minutes to cool down again.

6 Keep the fridge at least two-thirds full. Food retains cold better than air does, so an empty fridge actually requires more energy to stay cold.

7 Regularly check that the seals are working properly. To do this, close the door over a piece of paper; if you can pull the paper out easily, the seal isn't strong enough. Tighten the hinges or replace the seals. (You can use this method to check oven seals too.)

8 Defrost the freezer every 3 months or so if it's not a frost-free model. Never let more than 5 mm of frost accumulate.

9 Clean the coils at the back annually to keep it working efficiently.

10 If you go away for a long period, empty the fridge, turn it off and leave the door open.

BUY WISELY

- Look for a fridge or freezer with a high Energy Rating. The highest rated models may cost a little more but can use half the energy of the lowest rated appliances.
- Ask suppliers whether they can offer appliances that use environmentally friendly Greenfreeze technology (see *Greenfreeze*, p. 41).
- Don't buy a bigger fridge or freezer than you need. A 284-litre fridge and a 210-litre fridge might have the same Energy Rating, but the 284-litre fridge will use 20 per cent more energy than the 210-litre fridge.
- If you're tossing up between two small fridges or one large one, go for the large one as it will generally be more cost-effective.
- If you want a large, separate freezer, a chest freezer is likely to be more economical than an upright freezer because most models of this type have thicker insulation, which retains cold air more efficiently.

Avoid buying fridges with unnecessary extras, such as ice-makers. They COST MORE to buy and use more energy.

STOVE SENSE

There are no energy ratings for cooking appliances, so you have to use other criteria to make an earth-wise choice.

- If possible, choose natural gas rather than electricity for cooking, especially for a stovetop. Gas stovetops cost half as much to run as electric ones and yield about half the amount of greenhouse gases.
- Don't buy anything larger than you need. In general, the larger the stove, the more energy it will use.
- Choose a stovetop with a range of ring sizes. This will help you control energy use.
- If you buy an electric stovetop, bear in mind that coil hotplates tend to be cheaper and more efficient than solid or ceramic hotplates.
- If you opt for electricity, consider induction hotplates. These are up to 30 per cent more efficient than standard hotplates. Each induction hotplate has a switch and an electromagnetic inductor coil. When a pan is placed on the hotplate, a magnetic field is created, causing the pan, but not the stovetop, to heat up. Little energy is wasted, and temperature control is precise.

~ STAR SAVER ~

Choose an oven with a fan. Fan-forced ovens are up to 25 per cent more efficient and produce up to 35 per cent less greenhouse gas than ovens without a fan.

COST-EFFECTIVE COOKING

- Use a microwave for small dishes and reheating. Microwaves use less energy and yield much lower greenhouse emissions than stovetops.
- Invest in a pressure cooker. It will cook the food in a third of the time required by a conventional stovetop, using one-third as much energy.
- To reduce the cooking time of frozen foods, thaw them thoroughly in the fridge before cooking.
- Match the size of your pan to the hotplate, and keep the flame as low as possible. If the flame extends beyond the edge of the saucepan base, you are wasting energy.
- Cooking one small dish in an oven is inefficient. If you are going to switch on the oven, make it worthwhile by cooking several dishes at once.
- Avoid opening the oven door as much as possible when cooking. The oven loses about 15°C of heat every time you do so.

TOP TIP

If you can cook something using a small appliance such as a toaster, slow cooker or electric frypan, do so. A toaster, for example, will generate one-quarter of the greenhouse gas emissions produced by an electric grill to do the same job.

Greenfreeze

- Until the late 1980s, the main coolants used in fridges were chlorofluorocarbons, or CFCs. These damaged the ozone layer and were banned.
- CFCs were then replaced with hydrofluorocarbons (HFCs) and hydrochlorofluorocarbons (HCFCs). Unfortunately these were also found to damage the ozone layer and, in the case of HFCs, increase global warming.
- Working with scientists, Greenpeace developed an ozone-friendly cooling technology. Known as Greenfreeze, it uses natural hydrocarbons.
- More than 100 million Greenfreeze appliances have been sold worldwide. However, few models have reached Australasian markets; ask your supplier for information.

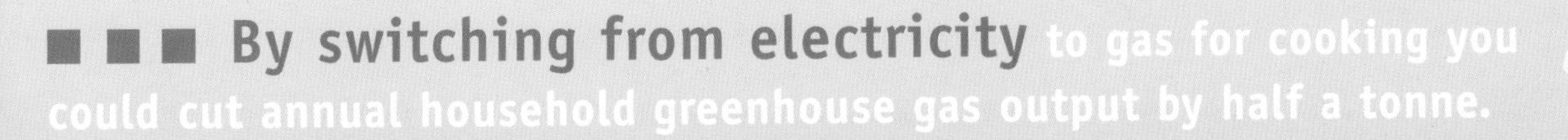

~ FUTURE GLIMPSE ~

Students at the University of New South Wales have attracted worldwide attention by designing a dishwasher that needs neither detergent nor water. Called the Rockpool, it uses high pressure to turn frozen carbon dioxide (dry ice) into a fluid that dissolves dirt and grease. Commercial production would currently be prohibitively expensive, but the technology may soon find its way into other products.

SIMPLE WATER SAVERS

We use about 8 per cent of our annual domestic water supply in the kitchen. The following tips will help you cut consumption.

- If you have an old-model dishwasher, consider washing small amounts of dishes by hand.
- When washing dishes by hand, rinse them in a second sink or basin filled with cold water rather than under a running tap.
- Wash fruit and vegetables in a basin or bowl of water rather than under a running tap. Reuse the water afterwards by pouring it on your lawn or plants.
- Defrost food in the fridge rather than under running water.
- Keep a jug of iced water on the bench, so that when you feel like a drink you won't waste water waiting for the tap to run cold.

CHOOSING AND USING A DISHWASHER

A major consumer of water and energy in the kitchen is an automatic dishwasher. Dishwashers can, however, be quite efficient if you select the right model and use it wisely.

- When purchasing a dishwasher, choose one with a high Energy Rating as well as a high Water Rating – in both cases, the higher the number of stars, the better.
- Make sure the dishwasher has a wide range of settings, including an economy setting. This will give you more options for saving energy. Run the dishwasher on the economy setting whenever possible.
- Look for models that have a half-load option. Some have two drawers that can be used separately or together. Using a half-load can save over 9 litres of water per wash.
- Consider buying machines that can be run on cold water. When

PROS & CONS

DISHWASHER OR SINK?

Washing dishes in the sink certainly saves energy and, if you are careful not to waste water while rinsing, it can be the best option in terms of water use, too. But if you have a modern, high-efficiency dishwasher and use it correctly – running a full load on an economy setting – you may use just 16 litres of water each time. That's 2 litres less than the average hand wash uses. In comparison, an older (1980s), low-efficiency dishwasher is likely to use about 36 litres of water.

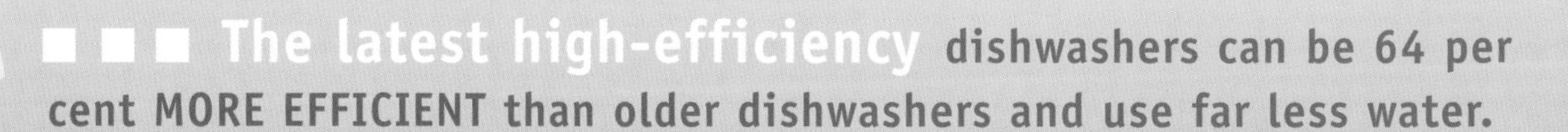

The latest high-efficiency dishwashers can be 64 per cent MORE EFFICIENT than older dishwashers and use far less water.

COMPOST CHECKLIST

Most biodegradable materials can be put into the compost heap, but careful screening of scraps will make for better results. The greater the variety of ingredients, the better the compost. For best results, chop up coarse materials.

What to put in

✔ Fruit and vegetable peelings and cores – great for getting compost started
✔ Cooked table scraps
✔ Coffee grounds – supply proteins and oils
✔ Tea-leaves and unbleached tea bags – add welcome nitrogen
✔ Old bread
✔ Eggshells
✔ Shredded newspaper – in small amounts
✔ Wood shavings, sawdust or fire ash
✔ Household dust and hair
✔ Garden waste – leaves, non-woody prunings, grass

What to leave out

✘ Fats and oils
✘ Meat and bones – take too long to break down and can attract pests
✘ Citrus peel – fine in small quantities, but contains a preservative that can inhibit decomposition
✘ Corn cobs – take too long to decompose
✘ Salt
✘ Anything that has been treated with chemicals
✘ Weed seeds
✘ Diseased plant material
✘ Dog or cat faeces

hot water is required, the machine heats it, generally using less energy than a conventional water heater. Otherwise, always choose a cycle with a cold rinse, if that is available.

- If your dishwasher uses hot water and you have an off-peak hot water option, run the dishwasher at night when it will cost less.
- When purchasing a dishwasher, choose one that permits 'no-heat' or air-drying. If your dishwasher does have a heat-drying function, turn it off and let the dishes air dry. This can reduce energy use by more than 10 per cent.
- Use the dishwasher only when it is fully loaded.
- Rather than rinsing plates before you put them in the machine, which can double your water use, simply scrape excess food into your garbage bin. Most modern machines will be able to filter the rest.
- To ensure efficient dishwasher operation, follow closely the manufacturer's instructions for loading dishes and selecting programs.
- For optimal operation, clean the filter regularly.
- To avoid the chemical pollutants in many dishwashing powders and tablets, look for environmentally friendly, preferably plant-based, alternatives. These are available from specialist suppliers.

WASTE NOT

- Try to reduce the amount of food packaging you bring home. Buy fruit and vegetables loose or take your own bags to collect your shopping.
- Reuse packaging as much as you can. Bottles, jars and plastic containers can be washed and reused time and time again.
- Recycle as much of your rubbish as you can, but make sure you follow your local council guidelines (see *Recycling*, p. 104).
- Do not put food scraps down the toilet or sink. Instead recycle them using a garden compost heap or, if space is tight, a worm farm (see *Feeding your garden*, p. 242).
- Put a strainer in your sink plughole to catch food scraps, then add them to the compost.
- Avoid using sink waste-disposal units as these use extra water and flush food scraps into waste pipes.

■ ■ ■ **About half of the rubbish** we discard is food scraps and garden cuttings, which can easily be RECYCLED in a compost heap.

The water-wise bathroom

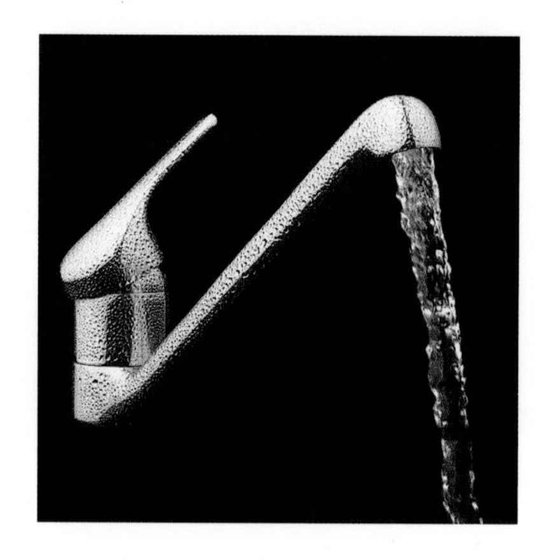

The bathroom is the room where we use the largest amount of water, but it's also the room where we can make the greatest contribution to conserving this valuable resource. Installing a water-saving showerhead will lower your household water consumption more than any other change, but don't stop there – there are many other ways to save on water bills.

SEND LESS DOWN THE DRAIN

- Fit an AAA-rated showerhead. This can reduce water output by at least 9 litres a minute. Alternatively, have a plumber install a flow restrictor to reduce the amount of water your shower emits.
- Take shorter showers. Every minute less can save as much as 23 litres of water. If you find this difficult, buy a timer and set it to 3 or 4 minutes to remind you to get out.
- When waiting for a shower to run hot, catch the cold water in a bucket. Later, you can use the water on your indoor plants or in the garden. Keep a container handy at the basin, too.
- Having a bath generally uses more water than taking a shower, so savour one as an occasional treat. Don't overfill the bath: add just enough water to cover yourself when lying down.
- Check the water temperature as the bath fills, to avoid running it too hot and then having to add lots of cold water to cool it down.
- Check the plug in the bath to make sure it isn't letting out any water. Add a metal strainer to the plug hole to prevent hair and other solids clogging outlet pipes.
- Consider installing a grey water system to recycle water from the bath, shower and basin. The water can be used on the garden, for flushing the toilet, even for washing clothes (see *Recycling water*, p. 38).

AT THE BASIN

- Install aerating taps. These reduce water flow by up to 50 per cent, saving up to 5000 litres a year. Another option is to fit screw-on aerators to existing taps.
- Consider a single-lever mixing tap: it will help you obtain the right water temperature more quickly.
- When you turn the taps on, don't turn them on full blast – up to 90 per cent of the water may be wasted. Get into the habit of releasing just as much as you need.
- Don't leave the tap running when you are brushing your teeth. A running tap can waste as much as 17 litres of water a minute.
- When shaving, fill a cup with water and rinse your razor there instead of under a running tap or in a full sink of water.

PROS & CONS

BATH OR SHOWER?

A bath is generally assumed to use far more water than a shower, but it depends on the efficiency of your shower and how frugal you are in the bath. A low bath will use about 50 litres of water, whereas a full one may consume 150 litres. An inefficient showerhead can use up to 23 litres a minute; so, within just over 2 minutes, you'll have used as much as a low bath and if you hang around for 7 minutes, you'll have used more than a full bath. In contrast, an efficient showerhead uses just 9 litres a minute, so a 3- or 4-minute shower will consume significantly less than a low bath.

FIXTURES AND ACCESSORIES

- Choose ceramics for fixtures, and natural materials such as wood, stone, or bamboo for soap dishes, laundry baskets, etc. Where possible, avoid plastic items, such as PVC shower curtains, as they are derived from non-renewable petroleum.
- When your towels wear out, consider replacing them with towels made from environmentally friendly, non-chlorine-bleached materials such as hemp or organic

■ ■ ■ **Take shorter showers:** every minute less spent in the shower can save up to 23 litres of water.

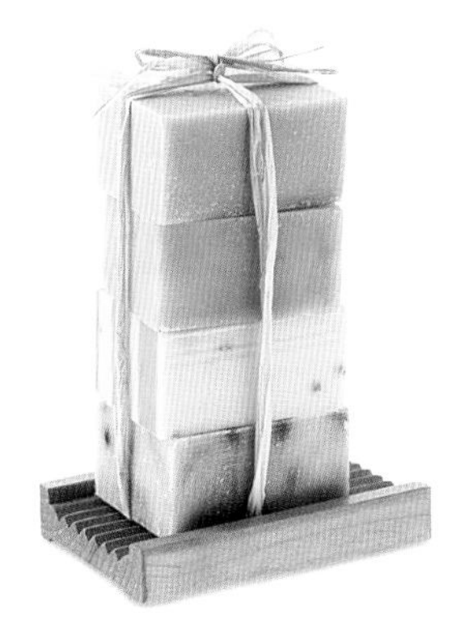

~ *STAR SAVER* ~

Even a tiny leak in a toilet cistern can waste 36 litres of water a day, and a more noticeable leak might dispense a staggering 96,000 litres a year. To check whether your toilet is losing water, add a drop or two of food colouring to the cistern and leave it for a few hours. If it leaks through to the toilet, have the cistern fixed at once.

cotton, which are available from specialist shops. Alternatively, if you buy ordinary cotton towels, make sure that they are of a high quality, so that they will last. Avoid synthetic face sponges made from non-renewable petrochemicals.

- Avoid disposables, such as disposable razors, as they increase waste.
- Choose pure soap or vegetable-based soaps and bath gels, without synthetic additives, especially if you are planning to use your grey water.
- Minimise use of your extractor fan. On warm days, open a window instead. Provided you have a bathroom window that opens to the outside, avoid or disconnect fans that stay on while the light is on.
- If you don't have a window that you can open, consider installing a vented skylight.

TOILET TRAINING

- When buying a new toilet, choose a model with a high Water Rating or Water Conservation Rating.
- Fit an efficient dual-flush toilet and use the half-flush option. It can save about 8 litres of water per flush.
- Alternatively, install a toilet-flush regulator (or cistern system convertor), available from hardware shops. This allows you to control the amount of water that is flushed: the water is released for only as long as you hold the button. It can save as much as 5000 litres of water a year.
- Even if you don't have a dual-flush toilet, you can still reduce the amount of water used per flush by installing your own regulator. Fill a large plastic bottle with water and put it in the cistern, making sure it doesn't interfere with the flush mechanism. Its size will dictate how much you save: a 3-litre container will save 3 litres of water per flush.
- Always buy toilet paper made from recycled paper, and avoid papers that have been chlorine-bleached or have had perfumes or colours added to them.
- Use biodegradable toilet cleaners that have low toxicity, such as plant-based organic products (available from specialist suppliers) or borax and vinegar. Many antibacterial disinfectants destroy the bacteria required to break down sewage.
- Do not put sanitary towels, tampons or condoms down the toilet as they are likely to cause blockages in the outlet pipes.

THE WATER-FREE LOO

A composting toilet requires no water and relatively little maintenance. The waste drops into a large tank in the subfloor, where it slides slowly down a sloping base. By the time it reaches the lowest part of the tank, where a door allows access, it has turned into A-grade organic manure.

WHY DO IT? If water is in short supply or normal sewerage services are not available – or you just want to do your utmost for the environment.

CHOOSING A SYSTEM Buy a commercially available model. It will have been tried and tested and come with a range of accessories. Make sure, however, that it meets local authority regulations.

ESSENTIAL FEATURES Air ducts or a fan to aerate the waste. An extractor fan to dissipate fumes.

OPTIONAL EXTRAS A hatch that allows you to add organic matter. A heater to maintain an optimum temperature in cool areas. Revolving tanks to stagger delivery of compost. A solar panel to run the fan.

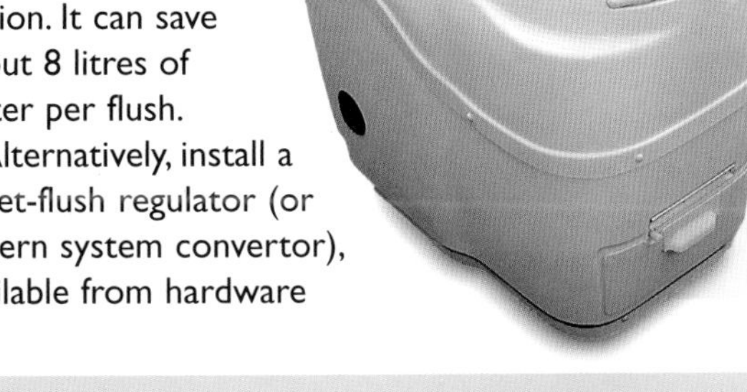

Fixing even a tiny leak in a toilet cistern might save 36 litres of water every day.

The earth-wise laundry

The earth-wise laundry works on simple principles: use less energy in washing and heating water, and use cold water whenever possible. Also, opt for environmentally preferred soaps and powders that are no more expensive, just as good for your fabrics and better for the garden if you want to reuse the water.

WASHING SENSE

- Wait until you have a full load before running your machine. If you have to do a smaller wash, remember to reset the water level.
- Stick to a short cycle, which is usually sufficient for all but heavily soiled items.
- Don't use any more detergent than you need. It won't make the clothes any cleaner, they'll be more difficult to rinse properly and you will waste soap and energy – for every 100 grams of detergent that is produced, about 1.3 kilograms of greenhouse gases are emitted.
- Use eco-friendly detergents and soaps that are petrochemical- and phosphate-free or low in phosphate. (See also *Choose carefully*, p 74.) Choose concentrated forms – they don't have the bulking agents of other products, are cheaper and need less packaging.
- If your washing machine has a suds or rinse-water save feature, use it. If not, collect final rinse water from a top-loader by holding the outlet pipe over a bucket, and pour it back into the machine before starting the next wash.
- Clean the washing machine filter regularly to keep your machine working efficiently.
- Look at installing a diverter to redirect wastewater from your machine to a garden irrigation system (see *Recycling water*, p. 38).

~ *STAR SAVER* ~

Eighty per cent of the energy required for a hot wash is used to heat the water, so use a cold wash whenever you can. You'll also cut greenhouse emissions as a hot wash generates 15 times as much greenhouse gas as a cold wash.

IDEAL WASHING MACHINE FEATURES

- ✔ Variable temperature control – to allow use of cold water
- ✔ Load-size sensor or other reduced-load function – minimises water usage
- ✔ Range of wash cycles to suit different fabrics – gentler on clothes
- ✔ High spin speed (front-loaders mainly) – saves on drying time, and energy if you use a dryer
- ✔ Suds- or rinse-water saver – recycles rinse water for use in subsequent washes
- ✔ Anti-crease features, for example, permanent press cycles or end-of-cycle tumble functions (front-loaders), or rinse or spin 'hold' functions (top-loaders) – reduce the need for ironing

CHOOSING A WASHING MACHINE

- Buy the most efficient model that you can find. Washing machines carry star ratings for both energy and water efficiency. The higher the number of stars (or, in some cases, As for water efficiency), the more efficient the machine. Front-loading machines are generally more efficient than top-loaders.
- Choose a capacity appropriate to your needs. For example, if you have a big family or regularly do large loads, you should select a

■ ■ ■ **Washing your clothes in cold water uses approximately 90 per cent less energy than if you use hot water.**

larger machine. Multiple washes in a smaller-capacity washing machine will use more energy and more water.

- Check how much water the machine uses per wash – the less the better. Look for models that allow you to vary water levels to match the size of the wash. Alternatively, opt for machines that sense the load size or allow you to set the load size.
- Make sure that the machine has a cold wash cycle; you will still need separate hot and cold water tap fittings for connection. Avoid machines that take cold water only, heating it when hot water is required, as this process is usually less efficient than using your piped hot water – especially if your water is heated by gas or solar power (the latter heats your water for free).

DRY WISELY

- Whenever the weather permits, hang your washing outside to dry. Ultraviolet light from the sun will help eliminate bacteria and dust mites. Even on damp days, choose to use a clothes horse placed under shelter or indoors rather than a dryer.
- Shake and smooth out clothes prior to hanging them, to reduce the need for ironing.
- A mechanical clothes dryer is energy-hungry and generates significant amounts of greenhouse gases, so use it as little as possible. When you do, switch it to a medium setting rather than high.
- Don't overload the machine or overdry the clothes. Both use unnecessary energy; overloading will also crease your clothes and overdrying will increase wear.
- Do separate loads of heavy and light items, as mixing them will increase the drying time.
- Run your machine at night. If you have off-peak electricity, you will save money; even if you don't, you'll help reduce demand for energy at peak times.
- Use your washing machine spin cycle to dry clothes as much as possible before putting them in the dryer. This can cut greenhouse emissions by up to 2 kilograms per load.
- Make sure the room your dryer is in is well ventilated. Humidity can reduce the machine's efficiency.
- Clean the lint filter in your machine after every load. If it is clogged it will use more energy and can be a fire hazard.

CHOOSING A DRYER

- Choose a model with a high Energy Rating. But bear in mind that dryers are generally inefficient; few attain three stars or more.
- Look for models with these features: sensors that automatically switch off the machine when the clothes are dry; reverse tumble; a wide range of fabric and temperature settings, including a cool-down option; an external rack for drying additional items using exhaust air; and an accessible lint filter.
- Consider investing in a gas-fired or heat-pump dryer. These are more expensive than electric dryers, but much more efficient, so they will save you money in the long run.

PROS & CONS

FRONT-LOADERS OR TOP-LOADERS?

Top-loading washing machines are very popular and generally cheaper than front-loaders; they also wash more quickly. However, buying a front-loading machine should save you money in the long run and will be better for the environment. Front-loaders normally use less water – an efficient model can use more than 100 litres less per wash than an inefficient top-loader. In addition, front-loaders consume about 40 per cent less energy than top-loaders and about half as much detergent. They also wash more gently, so your clothes will last longer!

■ ■ ■ **A front-loader** can use 40 per cent less energy, a third less water and half as much detergent as a top-loader.

The natural bedroom

We spend about one-third of our lives in the bedroom, so it pays to make it as healthy a place as possible. Investing in quality beds and bedding may cost extra, but will increase comfort, contribute to good health and protect resources. It will also save you money in the long run, as quality products last longer.

WHICH BED?

Many of the beds and most of the mattresses we buy incorporate synthetic materials. These materials are derived from non-renewable petrochemicals, can contain volatile organic compounds (VOCs) that emit harmful fumes (see *Clearing the air*, p. 98) and are seldom recyclable.

- When selecting your next bed, opt for a base made of natural materials, preferably wood from a sustainable source, and sealed with non-toxic, biodegradable stains or varnishes. Avoid bases made of wood composites, such as particleboard, as these are often made with adhesives containing VOCs.
- When choosing your next mattress, consider one that is made of natural, biodegradable materials, such as cotton, wool or natural latex (which is harvested sustainably from rubber trees). Research what's available on the Internet and visit natural bedding outlets before making your choice.
- If you are prepared to spend for the long term, consider a pure latex mattress – many are guaranteed for 10 years and can last up to 25 years. Latex is light and offers good support. It is also less likely to harbour dust mites than other materials, is naturally antibacterial and is resistant to moisture build-up. Check with the manufacturer that no chemicals have been added.
- Cotton and wool mattresses are generally reasonably inexpensive, comfortable, durable and allow good air circulation; wool is also an effective heat regulator. They do, however, require regular airing in the sun to avoid compaction (and to ensure that moisture retention and dust mites are kept to a minimum), and are often heavy and difficult to manoeuvre. Check with the manufacturers that no chemicals have been added.
- Good-quality inner spring mattresses are widely available for reasonable prices. They can offer good back support and last for 10 years or more. Bear in mind, however, that most such mattresses are made using synthetic materials, particularly polyurethane foams, which may emit chemical fumes.
- If you opt for a mattress made of synthetic materials, contact the maker and ask about potentially harmful chemicals, such as flame retardants (see *Healthy living areas*, p. 50), that might have been used in production. Some companies adhere voluntarily to European safety standards that regulate chemical emissions, but no standards or labelling schemes identify low-VOC products in Australasia.
- If you buy beds and bedding that you suspect may contain VOCs, let them stand in a well-ventilated space for a couple of weeks before

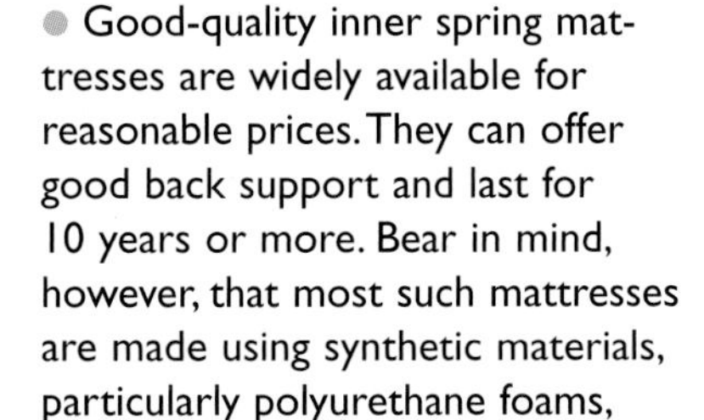

Buying a second-hand wooden bed base makes economic *and* environmental sense. Second-hand bases are usually cheaper than new ones, and older bases are often made of high-quality timbers that are no longer available. If chemicals were used during production, any emissions will have fallen to a harmless level. Just make sure the bed isn't coated with lead-based paint.

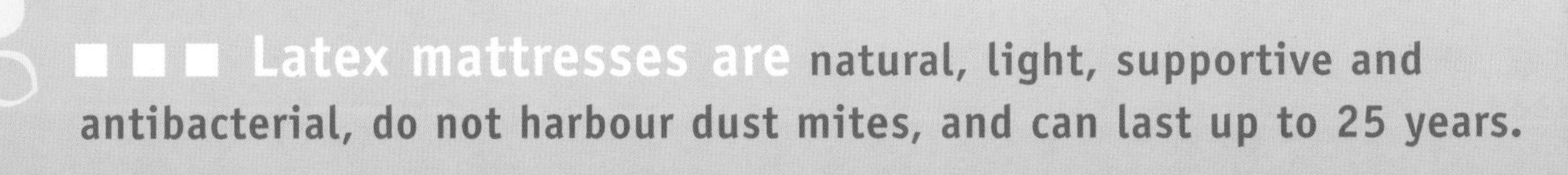

use, and continue to air them regularly. Fumes will diminish over time.

- If you purchase a bed base or bedroom furniture made of a wood composite, consider sealing it with eco-friendly paint or varnish to minimise off-gassing of fumes.

GREENER BEDDING

- Choose sheets made of natural fibres derived from environmentally friendly sources.
- Consider wool blankets instead of a doona. Heavy doonas often make us too hot, resulting in disturbed sleep patterns. Wool is particularly good at trapping heat, and using three or four blankets allows you to adjust the covering to suit the temperature.
- If you buy a doona, opt for natural fillings and coverings, such as wool, cotton or down, rather than synthetics.
- Select pillows containing natural materials such as down, wool, cotton or latex.
- Place a protector made of natural fibres, such as wool or cotton, around or on top of your mattress. This will help absorb sweat, protect you from dust mites in the mattress, and can make an old mattress more comfortable.

Avoid dark cotton sheets – the darker the colour, the more chemicals are used to fix the dye.

SLEEP RIGHT

- Keep furniture to a minimum so that you can dust and vacuum easily and regularly.
- Choose furniture made with wood from a sustainable source. Check that varnishes and stains are low in toxicity and biodegradable.
- Refresh the air in the bedroom by opening windows every day.
- Pull back the covers every morning to air the sheets for a few hours. This will help evaporate perspiration and get rid of dust mites.
- When you change the sheets, let the mattress air for a while. Vacuuming the mattress and spraying it with a solution of eucalyptus oil will minimise dust mites.
- Hang your bedding in the sun for 3 hours to eliminate dust mites, mould and mildew.
- If dust or dust mites continue to be a problem, remove carpets, heavy curtains, padded headboards and cushions. Consider storing clothes in another room.
- Minimise the number of electrical appliances in your bedroom to reduce your exposure to electromagnetic fields (see *Harmful rays*, p. 101), and keep your bed away from power sources – even those on the other side of a wall.

COTTON Inexpensive, comfortable, lets air circulate, wears well. Conventional production uses large amounts of water as well as fertilisers, pesticides and bleaches. Requires large doses of chemicals to absorb dyes.

DUCK and GOOSE DOWN Natural, soft, light. Effective heat and moisture regulator. Usually a by-product of breeding ducks for food. Moderately expensive.

HEMP Strong, breathes well, naturally hypoallergenic and antibacterial. Production requires relatively little water and few or no pesticides. Absorbs dyes easily without chemical additives. Not yet widely available; moderately expensive.

ORGANIC COTTON Same qualities as conventional cotton, but produced without chemicals and dyes. End product is therefore safer, but more expensive.

POLYESTER Inexpensive, easy to maintain, but doesn't breathe well. Derived from non-renewable petroleum; production yields toxic waste. Can contain VOCs.

WOOL Renewable, plentiful. Effective heat and moisture regulator, naturally flame retardant. May contain pesticide residues, and dyed and treated wool may contain chemicals. Moderately expensive.

Healthy living areas

Living areas aren't always the healthiest of places. We tend to sit in them for long periods, often with a heater on or watching television, possibly breathing in fumes from fittings and furniture. Ventilating the room and choosing natural materials and efficient appliances will protect health, enhance comfort and save money.

NATURAL COMFORT

- Try to not bring furnishings and fittings into your home that are made with synthetic products. As well as being derived from non-renewable petroleum, these often contain volatile organic compounds (VOCs), which emit harmful fumes (see *Clearing the air*, p. 98).
- If you have been living with your furniture a long time, chances are emissions from treated fabrics and chemical finishes have depleted. But next time something needs replacing, buy items made from natural materials that have not been treated with chemicals. Quiz your supplier and manufacturer, if need be.
- Consider doing without carpets – especially if any family members suffer from allergies or asthma – as carpets harbour dust mites and dirt. New synthetic carpets, and some natural fibre carpets that have been treated with fire retardants, are also likely to contain VOCs.
- If you do choose carpet, opt for natural fibres; wool carpets are a good choice and are naturally fire-resistant, so normally don't require chemical retardants.
- Let as much sun into living areas as possible to provide warmth and invigorating sunlight. Sunlight will also help eliminate dust mites.
- Make sure your living area is well ventilated – open windows regularly.
- Keep plants, such as spathiphyllums and kentia palms, in living areas to help clear the air of chemical fumes (see *Natural air filters*, p. 101).
- In winter, heat the room efficiently and cleanly so that you are comfortable but avoid overheating or increasing air pollution.

BROMINATED FLAME RETARDANTS

WHAT ARE THEY? Brominated flame retardants (BFRs) are chemicals used to reduce the flammability of carpets, curtains, televisions, computers and other furnishings and appliances.

WHAT'S THE PROBLEM? Tests have shown that the chemicals accumulate in household dust and are absorbed by our bodies; high levels have been found in blood and breast milk.

WHY DOES IT MATTER? Certain BFRs, known as PBDEs (polybrominated diphenyl ethers), have been shown to disrupt thyroid hormone function in animals, and may cause foetal damage.

WHAT'S BEING DONE? The PBDEs known as penta and octa have been banned in Europe and

parts of the United States, and are being phased out of industrial use in Australia. Environmental groups are campaigning for other PBDEs to be phased out, too.

WHAT CAN I DO? Ask retailers or manufacturers whether textiles or appliances have been treated with these retardants. If you can't find a BFR-free product, make sure you frequently ventilate the area where the item is used.

WINDOW COVERINGS

What you hang over your windows can make a big difference to your comfort – and to your energy bills.

- If you live in a warm climate, blinds are a good choice. They will block sunlight and limit heat build-up, and allow you to open the windows and let air circulate while keeping out the hot, bright sun.
- In colder climates, fit heavy, lined curtains. These can cut heat loss by up to one-third in winter. Make sure the curtains fit closely to the window, and extend beyond the bottom and sides of the frame.

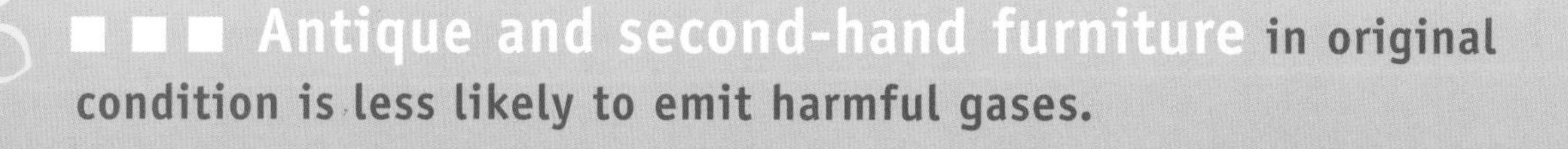

Antique and second-hand furniture in original condition is less likely to emit harmful gases.

The power used by equipment in standby mode can account for more than 10 per cent of household energy use.

- Add a close-fitting box pelmet to the top of the window frame to prevent draughts coming in over the top of the curtain.
- Avoid synthetic materials or any materials treated with stain repellents and fire retardants as they may emit fumes.

BUYING FURNITURE

- Buy for comfort and longevity as well as for looks. Think twice about buying something that is the height of fashion. You are more likely to discard it after a few years and it is less likely to be recycled.
- Invest in good-quality furniture. It may cost more initially, but is likely to last longer.
- Choose natural materials that come from sustainable sources and are biodegradable. Many of these materials, such as wood, are easier to repair than plastics or synthetics.
- Avoid furniture made from synthetic foam or composite wood products as these often contain VOCs, including formaldehyde, a probable carcinogen. Second-hand items are better in this respect as any chemical emissions will have dwindled to insignificant levels.
- Opt for wood that's been treated with natural or low-toxicity oils, varnishes and stains.
- Reject stain-repellent or fire-retardant treatments as these chemicals can emit toxic fumes.
- Look for labels that identify eco-friendly goods, such as Environmental Choice labels and the Forest Stewardship Council trademark.

HOME ENTERTAINMENT

Careful selection and use of home-entertainment appliances can help the environment and your bank balance.

- Limit the number of appliances you have in living areas. Get rid of items you seldom use.
- Consider purchasing combination units such as video-DVD, TV-DVD or CD-DVD players. These can help limit energy use and electromagnetic fields.
- Choose products made by companies that have agreed to eliminate toxic chemicals from production. Check manufacturers' web sites and environmental labelling programs for information.
- When buying equipment, look for energy-efficient models, preferably bearing the Energy Star logo.
- Switch appliances off when not in use, rather than leaving them on standby. You'll save energy – and money, too.

ENERGY STARS

The Energy Star logo is awarded to energy-efficient home electronics and office equipment.

- Energy Star products switch to sleep mode when not in use, and/or use less energy in sleep mode.
- Energy Star home electronics, for example, use about 75 per cent less energy than standard products when in sleep mode.

THE TRUTH ABOUT...

STANDBY MODE

When an appliance is turned on but not playing, or appears to be off but can be switched on by a remote control, it is in standby mode. Equipment such as televisions, DVD players, stereos and computers are in standby mode for 60 per cent of their life span, and standby can account for more than 10 per cent of household energy use. By switching off your appliances at the wall or using Energy Star products, you can make substantial savings.

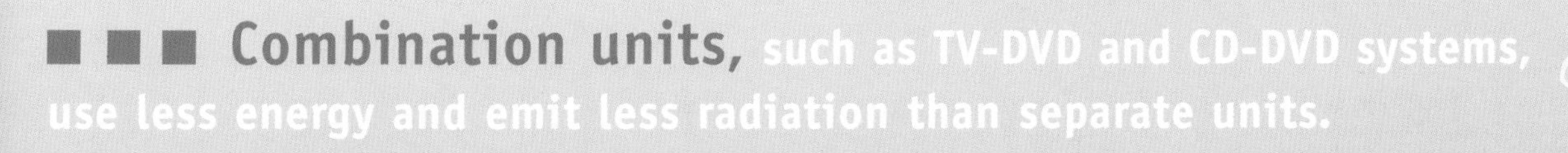

Combination units, such as TV-DVD and CD-DVD systems, use less energy and emit less radiation than separate units.

The home office

Most of us now have a computer at home and many of us have a home office. Even a small set-up can be a drain on energy and a cause of waste and pollution. Take a good look at your workspace and practices to make sure you are doing all you can to look after yourself, your resources and the environment.

PLANNING YOUR OFFICE

- Minimise clutter so that you can easily dust, clean and access files, equipment and cables.
- Make sure your office is well ventilated as office equipment is a significant source of heat and unhealthy fumes.
- Avoid office furniture made from wood composites, which can contain high levels of volatile organic compounds (VOCs). Choose solid wood instead.
- Consider buying second-hand furniture to recycle materials, save money and reduce chemical fumes.
- Maximise your use of natural light. Your screen may need to be kept in shade to limit reflections, but try to place a separate desk or table near a window so that you can read in natural light.
- For artificial lighting, use energy-efficient compact fluorescent bulbs.

EARTH-WISE PAPER USE

✔ Print only when necessary.
✔ Check for errors on screen before printing.
✔ Use print previews to check documents before printing.
✔ Print on both sides of paper.
✔ Use email instead of regular mail and back-up onto a disk rather than paper.
✔ Reuse whenever you can: use the other side of printed pages for notes, use adhesive labels to cover old addresses.
✔ Put all office waste paper (except for thermal fax paper) in council recycling.

✘ Don't design documents to include pages with little type, such as separate title pages.
✘ Don't use unnecessarily wide margins or large typefaces.
✘ Don't throw envelopes away if they can be recycled.
✘ Don't use a cover sheet when faxing.
✘ Don't use adhesive labels on new envelopes.
✘ Don't buy envelopes with plastic windows as these cannot be recycled; alternatives, made of a material called 'glassine', are available.

BUYING EQUIPMENT

- Select energy-efficient products, preferably bearing an Energy Star (see *Energy stars*, p. 51) or Environmental Choice label.
- Favour manufacturers with sound environmental policies. Reports on the green credentials of computer companies can be found on the Internet.
- Choose a computer that you will be able to upgrade easily.
- Consider a laptop. It can use up to 90 per cent less energy than a desktop machine, and can be easily hooked up to a monitor, keyboard and conventional mouse.

SELECTING PERIPHERALS

- To save energy, have peripherals, such as CD drives, installed inside the computer rather than purchasing separate units, or buy units that are powered by the computer.
- Consider multifunction machines, such as a combination printer, fax and scanner, which can save energy.
- When costing printers, make sure you factor in the lifespan and price of cartridge refills.
- Instead of buying a fax machine, investigate whether you can use fax software and your modem; or, if you have a scanner, scan documents and send them as email.

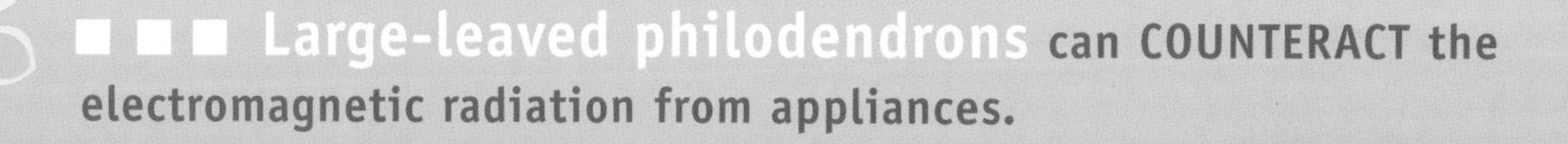

- If you need a fax machine, choose one that uses plain paper, so that you can use both sides of each page, and look for models that scan both sides of a page, to save energy.
- Think twice about buying a photocopier as it will use a lot of energy. If you only need copies now and again, use your scanner or fax machine, or a local print shop.

EFFICIENT COMPUTING

- Make sure you are using your equipment's energy-saving features.
- Select the shortest acceptable period of inactivity before your computer switches to sleep mode.
- Switch off appliances at the wall when you are not using them. Make sure any that have to stay on permanently are Energy Star products.
- Avoid screen savers. They are unnecessary on modern LCD screens and do not reduce energy use. Use sleep mode or switch off.
- If your computer doesn't have energy-saving features, turn off the monitor when you're not using it, since the monitor uses up to 80 per cent of the power used.

USING CONSUMABLES

- Opt for folders, binders and dividers made from recyclable materials. Avoid plastics.
- Buy refillable pencils and pens.
- Choose paper and packaging made from recycled paper.
- Avoid chlorine-bleached paper: look for 'chlorine-free' or 'oxygen-bleached' labels.
- Select the 'draft' or 'rough' print option to conserve toner.
- Use suppliers who obtain materials from eco-friendly sources and operate recycling programs.

E-WASTE

Huge quantities of office equipment are dumped every year – so-called 'e-waste' – adding dangerous toxins to landfills. Reuse or recycle.

- Try to reuse peripherals and other components.
- Donate your old computer to a non-profit organisation or a friend.
- Ask if the manufacturer of your computer will recycle a redundant machine. Some companies even recycle competitors' computers.
- Alternatively, look for an accredited computer recycler.
- Recycle or refill printer cartridges. In Australia, you can take used cartridges to post offices and retailers that participate in the Cartridges 4 Planet Ark scheme. Many suppliers refill used cartridges. Make sure using refills won't damage the printer or void your warranty.

Every year in Australia, 2 million computers are purchased and more than 3 million become redundant. As many as 5 million old computers may lie in storage.

hot links

Check out the Silicon Valley Toxics Coalition campaign for responsible technology: www.svtc.org/icrt/index.html
Electronic waste: www.envict.org.au/inform.php?menu=6&item=532; www.mfe.govt.nz/issues/waste/special/e-waste
Energy Star: www.energystar.gov.au; www.energystar.govt.nz/index.aspx
Find out about printer cartridge recycling near you: www.planetark.com/cartridges
Learn how to select environmentally friendly office paper: www.wilderness.org.au/campaigns/forests/consumer/friendly_office_paper

Home work

Working from home is an earth-wise option! If you do it even part-time, you not only free up time for yourself but also make a contribution to the environment by helping to:

- **Reduce traffic.** You'll possibly take a car off the road or at least help reduce the number of commuters travelling at rush hour.
- **Save fuel.** Especially if you normally drive to work, savings in petrol can be significant.
- **Cut pollution.** Any reduction in car use, or in any other kind of mechanised transport, helps reduce air pollution, including emissions that contribute to global warming.

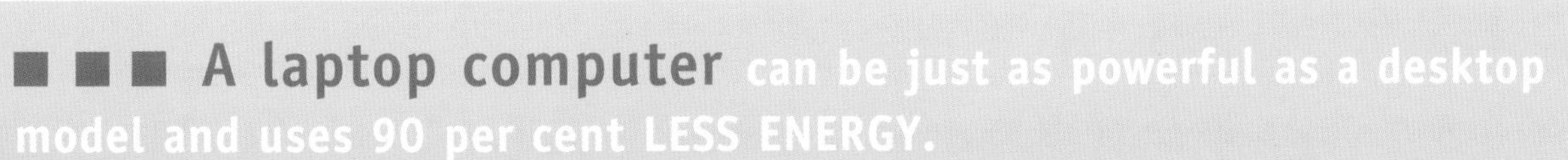

BUILDING AND RENOVATING

When building a new home or renovating an old one, careful design and selection of materials will bring long-term benefits.

Building a new home

Making good use of a site's natural features will help you construct a home that is comfortable, efficient and economical to run. The key to earth-wise building design is aspect. Orientate your house to capitalise on warming sunlight and cooling breezes, and you'll be way out in front in terms of energy efficiency.

STARTING SMART

Before you start designing, it's critical that you think through what you want and obtain advice from the right people.

- Read up on environmentally friendly design; there is a host of books and web sites on the subject.
- Contact local authorities to find out about building regulations. Ask, too, about rebates and grants for building eco-friendly homes.
- Make a detailed wish list of features for your new house. Work out how many bedrooms you need. Think about storage space. Don't make the house any bigger than is necessary – every 10 sq.m costs about as much as a new car.
- Look for architects and/or builders experienced in designing eco-friendly homes. Make appointments with a number of them to discuss your ideas.
- Once you have plans, get at least three quotes from contractors you think you can work with.
- Visit homes that prospective contractors have built or designed. Evaluate the success of the design and how the workmanship has weathered. If possible, talk to the owners and find out what they like and dislike about their houses.
- Check the architect or builder's record for costings, reusing materials, cleaning up and waste disposal.
- Make sure every detail is thought through and discussed before building starts – it's much more difficult to change things afterwards.

CHOOSING A SITE

- When looking for a site, consider its proximity to your workplace and to local services. Being near these places can reduce your dependency on mechanised transport. On the other hand, if you can work from home, you might want to be in a quieter, less polluted rural area.
- Examine the topography, or lie of the land. Is the site on a slope? If so, develop a design that avoids large-scale excavation – it's usually expensive, and can damage natural habitats, increase erosion and pollute stormwater outlets.
- Study the local climate and the site's orientation. Does it get plenty of sun? The more the better, as you can use sunlight to warm your home. Where do the prevailing winds come from? Can they be blocked or used to your advantage?
- Look at neighbouring buildings. How close are they? Are they going to block sunlight? Will your house block their light?
- At a rural site, check the availability of services such as water, gas, electricity, phone and refuse collection. How will this affect costs and your choice of energy sources?

~ *STAR SAVER* ~

Don't dismiss the idea of a kit home. You may well find that making some earth-wise adjustments to a conventional kit house is a much cheaper option than building a custom-designed home. Some modestly priced, eco-friendly kit homes are also available.

Some banks offer reduced interest rates on loans for eco-friendly homes. Ask around and you could SAVE THOUSANDS!

WHAT IS PASSIVE DESIGN?

Passive design makes the most of the natural features of a site. It uses sunlight to provide natural – and free – heating, breezes for cooling, and vegetation for shade.

- To maximise natural heating, orientate the house towards north or just east of north, and build across a wide east–west axis. Place the most frequently used rooms on the north and install large windows here to let in plenty of sun. Less frequently used rooms can be on the south side, and have smaller windows.
- Use eaves or awnings to provide the appropriate amount of shade. For hot climates, you want shade year-round, so wide eaves are the best. For cooler climates, design narrow eaves or incorporate moveable awnings to keep the mid-summer sun out but let winter sun in. The optimum width of the eaves will depend on your latitude.
- In temperate areas, limit window size on the east and west sides, and make sure there is plenty of shade, especially on the west side – try using storage areas as a buffer here.
- Design the house to make appropriate use of prevailing winds. In hot climates, design so that cooling breezes blow through the rooms. In cool climates, site the house so that it is sheltered from prevailing cold winds, or plant trees and shrubs to block the winds.
- Use vegetation for shade. Deciduous trees provide shade in summer but admit sunlight in winter; evergreens shade year-round. Cultivate grasses and other low-lying plants in front of north-facing windows to limit reflected heat and glare.
- Choose appropriate building materials. Dense materials such as brick and concrete have a high 'thermal mass', meaning they will absorb heat by day and redistribute it at night; that makes them better for cooler areas. Lighter materials have a lower thermal mass, meaning they retain little heat, and are therefore better for hot areas.

hot links

Learn about passive design and view earth-wise houses in Australia and New Zealand: www.solarhouseday.com
Get advice from the Royal Australian Institute of Architects: www.archicentre.com.au
Find a builder experienced in eco-friendly design: www.greensmart.com.au
Find a building designer near you: www.bdaa.com.au
Contact New Zealand architects and designers committed to eco-friendly principles: www.ecoprojects.co.nz/about.asp

Passive design and climate

Climate	Site	Design	Materials	Insulation	Sun and shade
Cool	Maximum exposure to sun; shelter from prevailing cold winds	Compact with minimal external walls; living areas on north	Heavier materials, dark colours	Mainly bulk insulation	Large north-facing windows; narrow eaves or moveable awnings
Hot	Plenty of shade and cooling breezes	Long and narrow to maximise cross-ventilation	Lightweight, light-coloured	Mainly reflective insulation	Shade whole building year-round; wide eaves

*Table provides a basic guide only. Further adjustments will be required depending on exactly how hot or cool, and how humid or arid, your climate is.

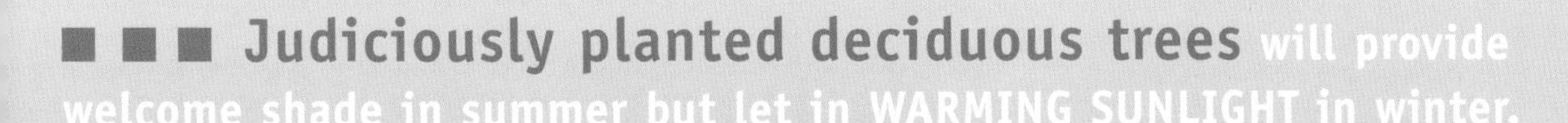

Built-in efficiency

Building a home from scratch gives you the opportunity to arrange rooms for maximum energy-efficiency and comfort. It also allows you to include money- and energy-saving features that are expensive and difficult to add to existing homes.

BEST-LAID PLANS

- Position so called 'wet areas' – the toilet, bathroom, laundry and kitchen – close to each other to minimise the length of water pipes required to reach each area. The longer the pipes, the more hot water goes cold sitting in them, the farther new hot water has to travel and the more water is wasted.

TOP TIP

The WERS (Window Energy Rating Scheme) can help you choose the right windows for your climate. The scheme rates windows for their effectiveness in heating, cooling and preventing fading of carpets and other fabrics, on a scale of 1–5 stars for each. The higher the number of stars, the more effective the window.

- Group rooms that you will need to heat or cool at the same time, such as living areas or bedrooms.
- In cool climates, avoid making open-plan areas too large or they will be difficult to heat. Having doors between rooms means that they can be heated separately. Also, keep your ceilings lower than 2.7 m; any higher and it's difficult and expensive to warm the room.
- Work with your architect to use space efficiently; for example, minimise hallways in your design as they tend to be a waste of space.
- In cold areas, include external rooms, such as porches and laundries. These will act as air locks, keeping cold air out of the main part of the house. In hot areas, create shaded outdoor living spaces.

INSTALL NOW, SAVE LATER

- Insulate your house appropriately. Insulation is tremendously effective in controlling heat loss and gain. It's easy to install when building – much more difficult to add later (see *Insulation basics*, p. 22).
- If you are considering central heating, think about incorporating underfloor heating that uses hot-water pipes powered by solar heating and a gas back-up. It's economical and eco-friendly. (Electric underfloor heating, in contrast, results in high greenhouse emissions.)
- For water-heating, opt for a solar or electric heat-pump system. These are by far the most efficient systems and if you can absorb the moderately high purchase price in your building costs, you will reap the benefits later.
- Consider installing grid-linked solar panels to generate electricity. Rebates are available to reduce the initial cost, and, combined with energy-efficiency measures, the panels can insulate you against rises in electricity tariffs. Surplus energy can be fed back into the grid, potentially eliminating power bills. The system will also add value to your home.
- Look at incorporating a rainwater tank to cater for watering the garden. A range of designs is available (see *Collecting water*, p. 36).
- Talk to a plumber about installing a grey water diverter. This can divert waste water from your bath, shower, or washing machine to a garden irrigation system. You might also be able to use your grey water for flushing toilets or washing clothes (see *Recycling water*, p. 38).
- Make sure the plumbing fittings you choose are water-efficient and choose toilets with dual-flush cisterns. These items are compulsory in new homes in some areas.

■ ■ ■ Install your own energy-generating system and then you can SELL SURPLUS ENERGY to your mains supplier.

~ *STAR SAVER* ~

Ask your electrical contractor to install separate switches for every light bulb rather than a single switch for several bulbs, which wastes energy and money. And plan from the start to use energy-efficient fluorescent light bulbs.

WINDOW DESIGN

Windows are a major source of heat loss and gain, and therefore a key element in any design.

- Choose the appropriate size of windows for the orientation and climate. Large windows on the north side of the home will maximise natural heating. But large windows on the south side may cause heat loss.
- Wooden frames are attractive, provide good insulation and are eco-friendly if the timber comes from a renewable source. But bear in mind that they can be expensive to buy, especially if custom-made, and require periodical maintenance to ensure the wood does not rot. They are also hard to seal because the wood swells and contracts with changes in temperature.
- PVC frames are durable, require little maintenance and provide good insulation, but they are made from non-renewable resources and their production is a source of pollution.
- Aluminium frames are lightweight and durable. But because aluminium is a good conductor of heat, they can become hot to touch and also require some kind of insulation (a 'thermal break') or treatment to make them energy-efficient. In addition, the production of aluminium uses large amounts of energy.
- Make windows taller rather than wider. This will let more light in.
- Select appropriate glass for your climate. Some types are absorbent, meaning that they allow heat into the house; others are reflective, meaning that they keep heat out.
- Consider double-glazing for cold areas. It's expensive to install, but can cut heat loss by as much as 50 per cent. It can also help block outside noise.
- In warm areas, consider fitting insect screens over windows so that you can leave windows open and let cooling breezes in.
- Louvres, either in the form of louvred glass panels or louvred shutters, are a useful feature for warm climates, allowing you to admit and direct cooling breezes.

RATING SCHEMES

Various rating schemes and software programs can be used to assess the efficiency of your design and exactly how further modifications will affect it. Ask your architect or local authority for information.

- **NatHERS** Developed by the CSIRO and funded by the Australian and New Zealand Minerals and Energy Council, the Nationwide House Energy Rating Scheme is now widely used. Some local authorities demand a minimum 3.5-star NatHERS rating before granting building approval.
- **NABERS** The National Australian Built Environment Rating System (www.nabers.com.au) measures the environmental impact of an existing building's regular operation.
- **BASIX** A web-based assessment tool operated by the NSW Government (www.basix.nsw.gov.au), the Building Sustainability Index measures the efficiency of a new home design, in particular with regard to water use, greenhouse gas emissions and thermal comfort. All new homes and additions to existing homes in NSW must now comply.
- **FIRST RATE** Developed by Victoria's Sustainable Energy Authority (www.seav.vic.gov.au), this scheme is being used to grade all new houses in Victoria.
- **BERS** Used widely in Queensland, the Building Energy Rating Scheme (www.solarlogic.com.au) is regarded as the most effective assessment tool for tropical climates. A similar package, QRate, is available for coastal subtropical areas.
- **GREEN HOME SCHEME** This national, independent scheme run by BRANZ (Building Research Association of New Zealand, www.branz.co.nz), rates the environmental impact of new homes.
- **TUSC** Developed by Waitakere City Council, TUSC (Tools for Urban Sustainability: Code of Practice, www.tusc.org.nz) allows users to assess designs against various sustainability indices.

Building materials

It's important to select the right building materials for your design needs and climate, but also to choose materials that are eco-friendly. To do that, you'll need to consider the environmental impact of a material's production, supply and use, and its potential for recycling. Seek further advice from an architect or builder.

EIGHT TIPS FOR CHOOSING MATERIALS

1 Choose for durability. You'll save money in the long run and there is a greater likelihood of the materials being recycled later.

2 Select materials whose extraction, production, transportation and/or delivery uses low amounts of energy. This energy is sometimes referred to as the 'embodied energy' of a material, and is measured in megajoules per kilogram.

3 Consider in particular the environmental impact of a material's production. Trees, for example, absorb far more greenhouse gases than the production of timber creates; conversely, producing plastics, metals and bricks uses large amounts of energy and is polluting.

4 Whenever possible, opt for materials made from renewable resources. Wood is renewable if it comes from a sustainable source such as a plantation; bricks, plastics and metals are usually made from non-renewable materials, but recycled forms are now available.

5 Choose local materials over imported ones. Long-distance transportation adds considerably to the cost of materials and produces large amounts of greenhouse gases.

6 Avoid materials that have been treated with chemicals. Many of these treatments are toxic and continue to emit, or off-gas, potentially harmful gases for years; some treatments, such as pentachlorophenol, a wood preservative, have been banned overseas. Look for organic treatments such as natural oils.

7 Purchase recycled materials or materials that have a high recycled content, such as recycled aluminium or recycled concrete. These are becoming much more widely available.

8 Reuse materials wherever possible. Resist the temptation to demolish a home and start from scratch if the existing building could be overhauled. If you do demolish, evaluate which materials can be reused and what might be of interest to a second-hand building centre.

How much energy does it take?

Material	Embodied energy*	Material	Embodied energy*
Aluminium	170.0	Particle board	8.0
Copper	100.0	Cement	5.6
Plastics	90.0	Fibre cement	4.8
PVC	80.0	Plasterboard	4.4
Acrylic paint	61.5	Gypsum plaster	2.9
Galvanised steel	38.0	Bricks	2.5
Hardboard	24.2	Hardwood, kiln-dried	2.0
Glass	12.7	Concrete blocks	1.5
MDF	11.3	Rammed earth	0.7
Plywood	10.4	Hardwood, air-dried	0.5

* Measured in megajoules per kilogram. Generally, the lower the figure, the more environmentally friendly the material. But note that values may be affected by many factors, such as distance between place of manufacture and purchase.

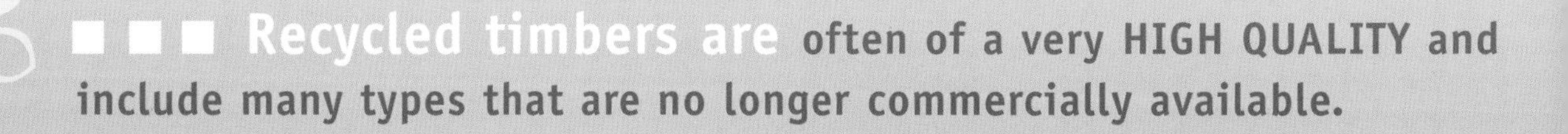

■ ■ ■ **Recycled timbers are** often of a very HIGH QUALITY and include many types that are no longer commercially available.

OUTBACK INSPIRATION

At the Gloria Lee Environmental Centre at Arrillhjere, 30 km west of Alice Springs, a house belonging to and designed by Arrernte woman Olive Peltharre Veverbrants is a model for energy-efficient outback living. The house (right) has minimal operating costs and needs no airconditioning, despite the high summer temperatures. It includes these features.

- Walls built with 14,000 mudbricks sourced and made on-site, which retain heat in winter.
- Orientation to utilise prevailing breezes for cooling.
- Wide eaves to shade the house in summer and absorb heat in winter.
- Colorbond roof painted off-white to reflect heat.
- Roof-canopy ventilation to let rising heat out.
- Ceiling fans on timers.
- Solar panels (with wood-fired backup) for running appliances and heating water.
- Two large rainwater tanks linked to a rooftop header tank that feeds the house by gravity.
- Grey water diverter linked to garden irrigation system.
- Worm farm for recycling organic waste.

WASTE NOT

- Calculate requirements carefully. Don't order more than you need.
- Base your design on standard sizes so that special measures don't have to be ordered.
- Take your time to measure everything accurately to avoid waste. Measure twice and cut once!
- Keep different types of materials separate so that any excess can easily be returned or recycled.
- Keep the time between delivery and use of materials as short as possible. That way, there's less time for materials to be damaged.
- Handle materials carefully to avoid damaging and, consequently, wasting them.
- Choose suppliers who will take back excess materials.
- Return surplus materials to suppliers for recycling, and recycle other leftovers in other ways.

hot links

Learn how to choose sustainable timber and other materials: www.rainforestinfo.org.au/good_wood/contents.htm
Consult a database of eco-friendly building materials and suppliers: www.ecospecifier.org/content/view/full/45
Review lists of forest-friendly timbers and suppliers: www.timbershop.org.au
Learn about ecoSelect timbers and stockists: www.ecoselect.com.au
Consult Greenpeace's guide to forest-friendly timbers and retailers: www.greenpeace.org.nz/campaigns/forests/goodwoodguide.asp

BUY RECYCLED

A wide range of recycled building materials is now available, offering opportunities to reuse and save. Look for the following:

- Timber: flooring, lining boards, skirting boards. Recycled timber is often of a high quality and/or a type that is no longer widely available.
- Bricks: older bricks can be aesthetically pleasing and add character to a home.
- Stone: attractive stone blocks, including marble, slate and sandstone, are often available for reuse.
- Doors: including internal and external doors, French doors, screen doors and security doors.
- Windows: from antique leadlight and stained glass to sliding aluminium models.
- Fireplaces: grates, surrounds and mantlepieces of marble, carved wood and cast iron.
- Light fittings: from Art Deco lamps to chandeliers. Just make sure they conform to modern safety standards.
- Porcelain: baths, basins, cisterns, laundry tubs – all can be given a new lease of life by re-enamelling.

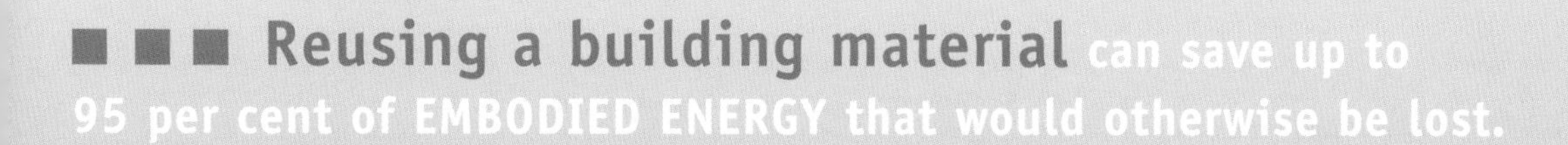

The production of timber generates 1500 times less greenhouse gases than the manufacture of aluminium.

GOOD WOOD

The fact that there are a number of readily available plantation timbers for building means that using timber extracted from rainforests and old-growth forests can and should be avoided. Always check where wood comes from and select wisely.

- Avoid timbers like meranti and merbau, which come from South-East Asian rainforests.
- Give preference to plantation timbers that are grown for building, harvested, then replanted. The most widely available plantation timbers suited to building needs are radiata pine, hoop pine and cypress pine.
- Look for Forest Stewardship Council and Australian Forestry Standard labels, which certify that timber is from a sustainable source.
- Select durable, termite-resistant timbers, such as cypress pine for flooring, to minimise the need for chemical treatments. Some timbers are treated to prevent borer or fungus; seek out non-toxic, oil-based preservatives and borax and boron-compound treatments rather than more toxic ones.
- Buy recycled wood whenever possible. Sources include specialist recyclers, demolition companies and suppliers of second-hand building materials. Watch out for lead-based paints and old nails.
- Try bamboo for flooring. It's sustainable, durable and cost-effective.

TOXIC TREATMENTS

If possible, avoid wood products treated with the following:

- Copper chrome arsenate (CCA). Wood treated with CCA cannot be mulched or burned as it yields toxins, including arsenic. CCA is being phased out of residential use and for play areas and public seating in North America, the EU and Australia.
- Ammoniacal Copper Quaternary (ACQ). Though in theory more eco-friendly than CCA, ACQ is still difficult to dispose of safely.
- Creosote. Highly toxic, it can irritate the eyes and skin and cannot be disposed of safely. It is no longer sold for domestic use in Australia or New Zealand, but is occasionally used for telegraph and power poles and some industrial applications.
- Pentachlorophenol (PCP or 'penta'). An organochlorine wood preservative (related to DDT and Agent Orange), PCP has been linked to fatigue, nausea, allergies and cancer. It is banned in many countries, including New Zealand, but is still being used in Australia.
- Light organic solvent preservative (LOSP). It often contains PCP and other toxins. Its production releases large quantities of hydrocarbon solvent gas and it can leach into soil.
- Chemical insecticides. Some ingredients in insecticides, such as lindane, dieldrin and benzene hexachloride, are suspected carcinogens.

Building materials

Material	Uses
Aluminium	Mouldings, window frames
Brick (clay)	Walls, paths, driveways
Concrete	Floors, walls, supports
Fibre cement sheeting	Cladding
Glass	Windows, doors, skylights; br
Mudbrick	Walls, floors
Plasterboard	Lining walls
Plastics	Window frames, water pipes, gutters, floor and wall coveri
Steel	Frames, supports
Stone and composite stone	Walls, floors, supports
Straw bale	Walls
Timber	Floors, walls, supports and roof frames

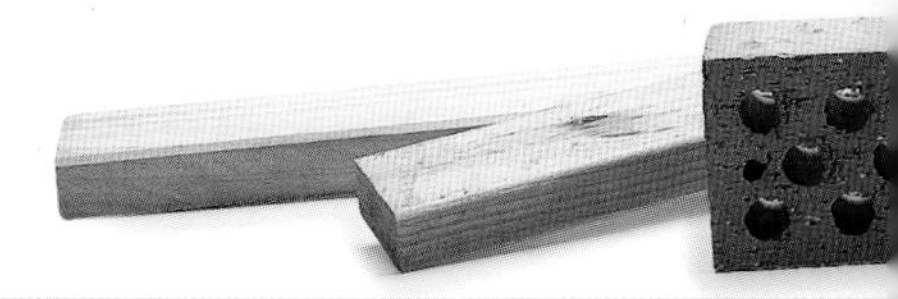

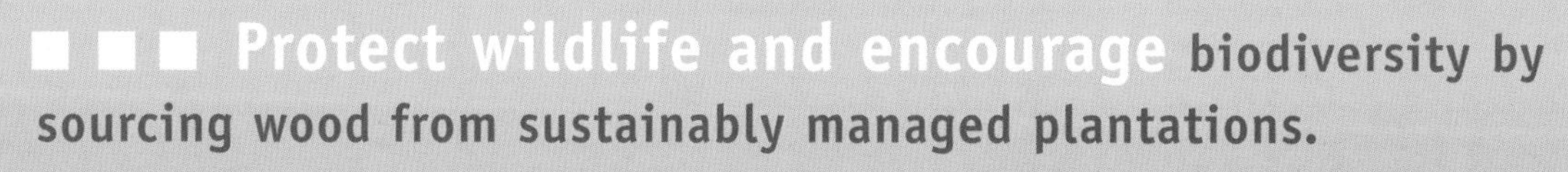

dvantages	Disadvantages	Earth-wise tips
rong, lightweight, can be recycled	Production is very energy-intensive and polluting.	Avoid, or use recycled aluminium.
ersatile, good thermal mass	Production is energy-intensive and uses non-renewable resources.	Look for recycled bricks.
igh thermal mass, strong, durable, conomical, resists termites nd earthquakes	Production involves quarrying and creates greenhouse emissions; poor insulator, needs reinforcing.	Use autoclaved aerated concrete (AAC), which is lightweight, energy-efficient and non-toxic, or concrete made with recycled aggregate.
ow embodied energy, light, expensive, good thermal properties, an be rendered	Not as strong as some other options; associated with cheap housing and asbestos (no longer used).	Try lime wash as a surface treatment: it's suitable and environmentally benign.
table, long-lasting, efficient, recyclable	Production is energy-intensive, uses non-renewable minerals.	Seek out recycled windows; buy energy-efficient new glass.
ource material can be found on site, ng-lasting, biodegradable, high thermal ass; pest- and fire-resistant	Making bricks is labour-intensive; requires soil with high clay content; poor insulator.	Bricks can be purchased ready-made.
otentially recyclable, breathes, rgely natural	Some plasterboards contain toxic chemicals and glass fibres.	Look for recycled plasterboard and non-synthetic boards with natural fixatives.
ight, durable, resistant to damp, ater and pests	Made from non-renewable resources; production is energy-intensive and polluting; may off-gas.	Look for renewable alternatives; avoid PVC – opt for PVC-free polypropylene or polybutylene instead.
rong, economical, durable, recyclable	Production is energy-intensive and highly polluting; coatings are often polluting.	Buy recycled steel or opt for renewable timber.
bundant, durable, high thermal mass, conomical if available on site; no oxic emissions	Non-renewable; extraction and transportation can be energy-intensive.	Use salvaged stone or products made with waste stone from local sources.
heap, renewable, good insulator	Is bulkier than other materials; requires specialised construction.	Avoid chemical pest treatments and use eco-friendly render.
trong, easy to work with, versatile, otentially renewable, biodegradable	Some timber is non-renewable; often treated with toxic chemicals.	Use recycled wood or timber from sustainable sources, with no chemical treatments.

■ ■ ■ **Calculate your needs** carefully to avoid wasting materials. MEASURE TWICE AND CUT ONCE!

Earth-wise renovating

Making an older home energy-efficient, a process known as retrofitting, can involve anything from minor renovations to a major structural makeover – but it will usually be worth the effort. If you are buying a new house, what you buy will influence how costly and difficult any earth-wise renovations will be.

WHAT TO LOOK FOR

When you are looking for a home, look closely at how energy-efficient it is and how easy it will be to make improvements.

- Is the building's orientation appropriate for the climate? In a temperate area, you want plenty of winter sun. In a hot area, you need shade and cooling breezes.
- How easy will it be to admit more sunlight or cooling breezes?
- Does the house get too much sun? A west-facing living area with large windows can be a heat trap.
- Are the kitchen, bathroom and laundry – the so-called 'wet areas' – close together? If they are, you will be starting with a house design that works well for hot-water usage.
- Is the house well insulated? How easy will it be to alter the insulation or add more?
- Is the house draughty? Are there gaps that could be sealed?
- What kind of heating and cooling systems does the house have and how efficient are they? How easy would they be to replace?
- Does the building contain any hazardous materials? Check for lead paint and pipes, asbestos panels and roofing, and fibreglass insulation.
- Is there enough space for your needs in the garden? Is there a clothes line, or room for one, in an appropriate place?

~ *FLYING START* ~

It's often easier and more economical to buy a smaller, cheaper house and add the eco-friendly features you want than to find them in an existing house at the top of your price range. Cost this approach before you start house hunting.

WHERE TO START

When planning renovations, start by thinking about the following.

- Consider whether you can change the allocation of space within the house in order to group rooms with similar uses. Can you bring wet areas closer together? Can you move living areas to the north side of the house?
- Look at your options for improving insulation. Depending on the extent of the renovations you are planning, your options may be limited. Plan for maximum effect with minimum upheaval – the roof is a good place to begin. Carefully select the right type of insulation for your climate and house (see *Insulation basics*, p. 22).
- Think about adding new windows to let more light and heat in. Could you open up the north-eastern side of the house to let in the morning sun or add a north-facing clerestory window, or skylight, at the back of the house to introduce light and heat into dark rooms?
- Consider adding a small room, such as a porch or laundry, between external doors and the outside. This will create an air lock, preventing heat loss in winter and heat gain in summer.
- Look at whether you can add doors between living areas and sleeping areas so that those zones can be heated and cooled separately. Seal off the bottom of a staircase to prevent heat rising to unused upper floors.
- Check doors, windows and other external openings for draughts and close any gaps using draught excluders or weather strips.

■ ■ ■ **Adding larger windows to the north side of your home will increase NATURAL LIGHT and passive heating.**

- If draughtproofing windows does not fix them, install energy-efficient frames and glazing. Think about installing double-glazing if you live in a cold climate, and fit heavy curtains and pelmets to minimise heat loss.
- Examine how you can make your heating more efficient. Can you have gas piped to rooms that need it? If you live in a cold area, could you easily install a natural gas, zoned central heating system? This works best if you have sufficient space under the floor for a furnace and ducts (underfloor ducts are more efficient than ceiling ducts); if you don't, a reverse-cycle system may work better.
- Consider installing grid-linked solar panels to generate electricity from the sun. You'll reduce your power bills – possibly to zero – and cut your greenhouse gas emissions significantly. Just make sure your house has a sturdy, north-facing roof to support the panels.
- Redesign your garden to use plants to improve your home's energy-efficiency. On the north side of the house, use a pergola to block the summer sun, or plant low-growing grasses and shrubs to reduce reflected heat and glare. Plant deciduous trees on the east and west sides to exclude the sun in summer but admit it in winter.

WATER, HOT AND COLD

- Install water-efficient shower-heads and taps, and make sure you have dual-flush toilet cisterns.
- When you replace appliances, such as dishwashers and washing machines, select models for maximum water- and energy-efficiency.
- Look at the efficiency of your hot-water service. Solar water heaters can be installed fairly easily.
- Think about installing a rainwater tank to supply water for the garden. A large underground tank probably won't be an option, but a wide variety of tanks is now available, many of which can be installed unobtrusively.
- Consider further adaptations to your water supply, including using grey water for toilets and washing machines (see *Collecting water*, p. 36, and *Recycling water*, p. 38).

WHEN THE JOB'S DONE

When you've finished renovating, consider what you can salvage. With a little extra thought, many materials can have a new lease of life elsewhere.

- Contact your local authority, waste depot or recycling contractors to find out what can be reused.
- Remember that a wide range of materials can be recycled, including aluminium, bricks, glass, concrete, gypsum plasterboard, paper, many plastics, steel and timber.
- While renovations are in progress, use sorting boxes to separate recyclable materials such as wood, metal and electrical wires.
- Save bricks and stones and timber offcuts for future projects.
- Donate leftover paint to charities and community groups.
- Keep extra roof tiles and ceramic or slate floor tiles to replace any that get damaged. Or use them in other ways, such as for lawn edges.
- Find other uses for surplus timber, including old flooring, window frames and beams.

ASBESTOS ALERT

Asbestos was widely used as a building material until the 1980s. It was a component in roofing and guttering, but was most common in 'fibro' sheeting. Although no longer used, it is now a major hazard for renovators who remove it or disturb it while building. If breathed in, asbestos dust can cause fatal respiratory diseases.

- Asbestos is most dangerous when broken up, as this allows fibres to become airborne. So always avoid cutting, sanding or drilling into boards that may contain asbestos.
- Where the material is in good condition, often the best option is to leave it in place and seal it with paint.
- If asbestos has to be removed, have it done by a specialist contractor – who will wear the appropriate protective clothing. This is mandatory in most Australian states and strongly recommended elsewhere.

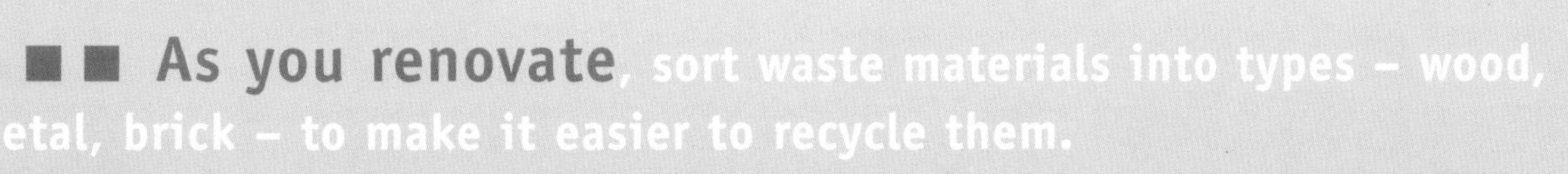

As you renovate, sort waste materials into types – wood, metal, brick – to make it easier to recycle them.

Finishing off

Your choice of floor and wall coverings will be influenced by your lifestyle and the local climate, but it is wise to give equal consideration to the effect these products can have on indoor air quality. By choosing carefully, you can minimise your exposure to harmful chemicals – and be kinder to the environment.

FLOORING AND FLOOR COVERINGS

The production of some types of flooring, such as synthetic carpets, has a high environmental cost, so consider other more natural choices first.

- Think about your needs in different rooms. Ask yourself if you really need wall-to-wall carpet. Hard-wearing surfaces are ideal for areas of heavy traffic such as halls and kitchens, whereas softer coverings might be preferable in bedrooms and some living areas.
- Although attractive and comfortable, new carpet is likely to emit toxic chemicals due to treatments during production. If you do want carpet, choose one that is made with natural fibres and ideally without any chemical treatments.
- If carpet underlay is required, select recycled rubber or natural latex instead of synthetics, which require large amounts of energy to produce and emit harmful gases.
- Ask your carpet layer to fix the carpet in place using mechanical fixings – tacks or staples – rather than synthetic adhesives. If adhesive is essential, use a non-toxic adhesive or a water-based adhesive, which has low levels of toxic volatile organic compounds (VOCs).
- Whatever type of carpet you lay, ventilate the area well when fitting and do not use the room for at least 3 days. Avoid laying new carpet in rooms where babies or pregnant women will sleep.
- Consider timber floors. They are soft underfoot, easy to clean and don't harbour dust mites. Choose boards made from timber that has

PROS & CONS

CARPETS

Conventional carpets create a feeling of warmth and luxury, especially in cold climates. They provide thermal and acoustic insulation and are hard-wearing and attractive. But environmental problems arise at almost every stage of their production and use. Their manufacture involves dozens of polluting chemicals. Once in place, carpets off-gas chemicals, including harmful VOCs, for long periods – even some natural-fibre carpets are treated with toxic stain repellents and fire retardants that can continue to evaporate for years. Carpets also harbour dust mites that cause allergies and trigger asthma attacks, and the dust tends to absorb other toxins from the atmosphere.

WARNING!

▼ Make sure the positive effects of natural flooring aren't diminished or eliminated as a result of the use of harmful chemical adhesives and stains. Try to use natural finishes only.

TOP TIP

To remove old wallpaper, use a mixture of vinegar and water (about 300 ml vinegar to a standard bucket of water). It will loosen the old glue, making it easier to peel off the paper with a scraper. Alternatively, use a steam stripper.

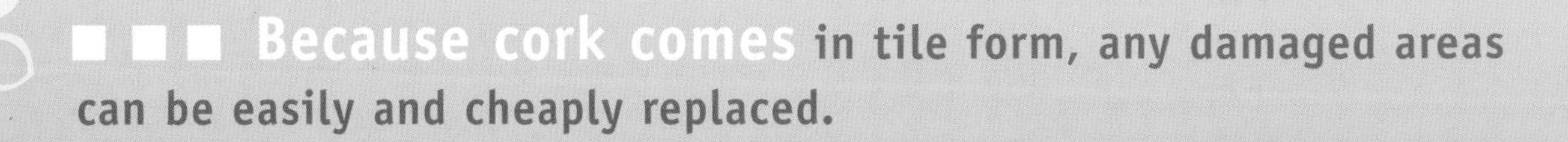

been harvested sustainably, or, better still, source some good-quality second-hand boards. Often the timber in these is far superior to what is currently available. Make sure any new wood is not treated with chemical treatments or sealants.

- Consider stone or slate flooring, especially if found locally or from a second-hand supplier. Though non-renewable, these materials are abundant, durable and absorb heat.
- For high-traffic areas, especially in a warm climate, think about using ceramic or terracotta tiles. They are derived from non-renewable but abundant sources, require relatively little energy to manufacture, do not off-gas and are recyclable.
- Rather than covering a concrete floor, try applying a finish to it. Polished concrete is hard-wearing, waterproof and attractive, especially if a natural tint is added when the concrete is poured, and chemical sealants are not necessary.
- Terrazzo tiles are another good warm-climate alternative. They consist of second-grade marble chips set into concrete, which is then polished. They're attractive and a lot cheaper than marble!
- Try to avoid PVC (or vinyl) flooring. Its production releases large amounts of toxic chemicals, it causes as many problems for allergy sufferers as carpet, and on disposal it leaches chemicals into landfills.

WALL COVERINGS

- Keep things simple. Do without wall linings and coverings unless they improve efficiency – by, for example, acting as an insulator. Choose easy-to-apply finishes such as renders, washes and paints.
- Ask yourself whether you need wallpaper. It might be pretty and help disguise an uneven wall, but some wallpapers contain harmful inks and dyes, fungicides and VOCs.
- If you have your heart set on wallpaper, investigate earth-wise options such as recycled papers, and use water-based wallpaper paste instead of chemical-based glues. To prevent fungal growth, add borax to the paste.
- Consider cork tiles for areas where you require good sound and heat insulation. Cork is renewable and recyclable. Seal it with beeswax or natural oil.
- For wet areas such as bathrooms and kitchens, ceramic tiles are a good choice as they are easy to clean and discourage mould and bacteria. Reinforced glass is an alternative for kitchens.

EARTH-WISE FLOORING

A wide range of natural, renewable flooring materials is available. Make sure the materials have not been treated with chemicals and avoid synthetic adhesives.

BAMBOO (*top*) Floorboards made from this prolific plant are moisture-resistant and durable, don't warp and are free of knots and other flaws found in wood. Check no formaldehyde glues or synthetic sealants have been applied.

COIR Derived from the outer husk of the coconut, coir is woven into a coarse material that is particularly hard wearing. It's ideal for areas of heavy traffic such as halls and living areas.

CORK (*centre*) The bark of the cork tree, cork is harvested just once every 9 years, then regenerates. Cultivation requires no irrigation, fertilisers or pesticides. Cork is soft and warm, an excellent insulator and does not collect dust.

JUTE Made from fibres of the stalks of the *Cochorus* or jute plant, jute provides a soft, absorbent material that is ideal for bedrooms but less appropriate for kitchens, bathrooms or living areas.

LINO (*bottom*) Made from flax fibre and oil, ground cork, wood, flour and natural resins, then fixed to a natural backing such as jute, lino emits no toxic gases and is antistatic, easy to clean and biodegradable.

SEAGRASS Woven from the fibres of various species of seagrasses, this material is tough, hard-wearing and naturally antistatic and stain-resistant. Not suited to damp rooms.

SISAL Made from the fibres of the agave plant, sisal is durable, naturally antibacterial and antistatic.

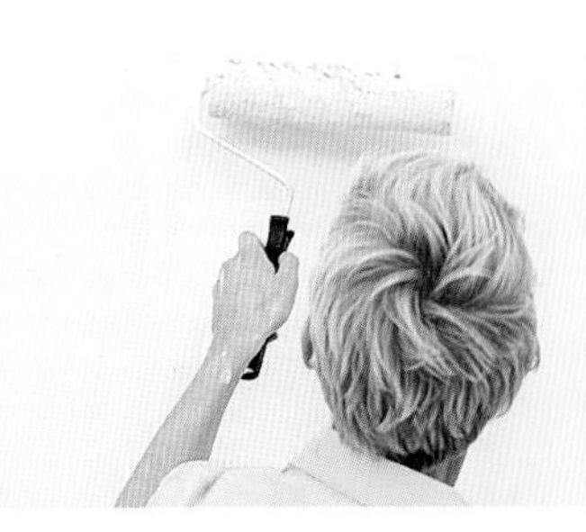

Levels of VOCs in a newly painted house can be up to 1000 times higher than outdoor levels.

THE TOP COAT

Conventional paints are among the most polluting substances we use in our homes. But a wide range of less harmful products is now readily available.

- Try to use paints that are VOC-free or low-VOC rather than conventional paints, especially indoors. If you are committed to an all-natural approach, choose lime washes or organic paints made from all-natural ingredients.
- Think carefully before you choose conventional paint. Its production involves the use of hundreds of chemicals and the finished products often contain toxins such as heavy metals and VOCs, some of which may be carcinogenic. After application, these paints continue to emit harmful fumes for at least 6 months – and often much longer. Non-biodegradable, they leach chemicals into waste heaps.
- Keep in mind that although water-based (acrylic) paints are generally safer than oil-based paints, they can still contain numerous harmful chemical additives.
- If you can achieve a smooth surface with minimal preparation, paint over old paint rather than remove it. Wear a dust mask when sanding to avoid inhaling dust from old paints or varnishes.
- To remove old paint, use a water-based, solvent-free paint stripper, a hot-air gun or a scraper and plenty of elbow grease. Avoid conventional chemical paint strippers as they contain hazardous substances such as methylene chloride and dichloromethane, both thought to be carcinogenic.
- Be wary of old paints containing lead, used as a drying agent in paint prior to 1950 and now known to be highly toxic. If you are unsure of what you are dealing with, get a paint fragment tested by your local Occupational Health and Safety department or Environment Protection Authority, or buy a testing kit from a hardware store. If the paint is in good condition, it is often best to leave it in place; otherwise have a specialist remove it.
- To wash down a wall for painting, use a solution of washing soda and water. Add ½ cup washing soda to 500 ml water for a regular solution. For a mild solution, add just 1 tablespoon washing soda to every 500 ml water; for a stronger solution, add 1 cup washing soda to every 500 ml water.
- Use a special painter's mask when painting. These are available from hardware stores and are different from dust masks, which should not be used as they will trap fumes near your mouth and nose.
- Whatever type of paint you are using, make sure the room you are working in is well ventilated. If possible, air the room for a week before using it after painting.

SAFER PAINTS

The main alternatives to conventional paints are listed below, with the safest options first.

MILK PAINT A mixture of casein, a protein found in milk, and earth pigments, milk paint has a smooth matt finish suitable for interior walls and furnishings.

LIME WASH Made from lime and natural pigments, lime wash gives walls – exterior and interior – a soft, weathered look.

NATURAL/ORGANIC PAINTS These are usually made from vegetable and mineral extracts bound with natural oils or resins. Some natural paints still contain conventional pigments such as titanium oxide and natural solvents that can be low-level irritants.

VOC-FREE PAINTS These have the same make-up as conventional paints, but exclude the harmful VOCs. They tend to be expensive.

LOW-VOC PAINTS These are made from petrochemicals but with reduced levels of VOCs. They may still contain harmful chemical additives.

If you suspect your old paintwork contains lead, you can test it with a kit from a hardware shop.

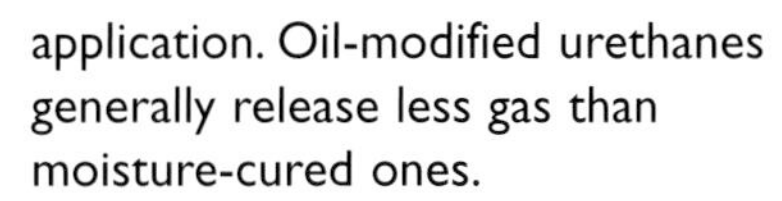

USING NATURAL PAINTS

- Use natural paints soon after purchase, as they contain few preservatives and so don't last long.
- Allow for extended drying times. Natural paints don't contain chemical drying agents.
- Natural paints tend to be thinner than regular paints. When painting a ceiling, cut a slit in a sponge and thread it onto your brush to prevent paint running down your arm.
- Wear a mask when mixing powders as some can be caustic.
- Remember: natural paint leftovers can be added to your compost!

SEALING WOOD

- Avoid polyurethane wood sealants. Many contain di-isocyanate, a respiratory irritant, and all contain a range of other VOCs. The most toxic are the 2-part coatings that have to be mixed before application. Oil-modified urethanes generally release less gas than moisture-cured ones.
- Try natural oils, which penetrate the wood but allow it to breathe. Products based on tung oil, from the tung tree, are a good choice, but make sure they don't contain synthetic resins.
- Use beeswax to create a durable, attractive surface. The wax can be applied on top of natural oil.
- Consider natural stains. Lime finishes come in a range of colours that give an aged look to wood while highlighting its grain. Other washes and stains give timber a light colouring while allowing the grain to show through.
- Remember that some natural sealants such as oils and beeswax may need to be applied more often than synthetics to keep the wood in good condition.

CLEANING UP

- To clean brushes after using water-based paints, wipe off excess with newspaper, then wash the brushes in a bucket of water. Pour the water on waste ground, away from food plants or drains, or, as a last resort, down the sink.
- To clean brushes used with solvent-based (oil-based) paints, use a non-toxic thinner or natural turpentine-based product; or boil the brushes in vinegar then wash them in water. Try to avoid excessive use of mineral turpentines as many contain benzene, a carcinogen.
- Never pour unused paints or solvents down the sink or into drains. Old tins of natural or water-based paint can go in the bin, but old tins of solvent-based paint cannot. Ask your council if it organises pick-ups of unwanted chemicals or if you can drop the tins off at a waste depot.

TOP TIP

Try shellac for painting wooden shelves and to seal treated wood or wood-composite products that may emit toxic fumes. Derived from a resin exuded by the Asian lac insect, shellac is 100 per cent natural, easy to apply, smells good and dries to a matt finish in 2–3 hours. It can be used on plain wood surfaces or painted ones.

MAKE YOUR OWN MILK PAINT

Milk has been used for centuries as the base for an easy-to-make house paint. Though milk paint is now available commercially, you can make your own using casein (a milk protein) and natural pigment, available from hardware stores.

250 g casein powder
465 ml water
50 g pigment

- Mix the casein powder with 340 ml water. Whisk to a thick batter and leave to stand for 30 minutes.
- Add the rest of the water and whisk again to a creamy consistency. Let it stand for 15 minutes.
- Mix the pigment with a little water to make a thin paste, then add it to the casein mixture. Stir thoroughly to distribute the colour. It's then ready to use, but apply it quickly.

Around the Home

Clean and manage your house the natural way. With an earth-wise cleaning kit and a battery of commonsense strategies, you can tackle dirt and stains, keep pests at bay and care for your pets without using harmful chemicals.

AROUND THE HOME...

EARTH-WISE CLEANING

■ What's in commercial cleaning agents? Are they harmful? See page 74. ■ Make your own cleaners and disinfectants, page 76. ■ Don't use harsh bleaches to remove stains from household linen – sometimes it's as easy as hanging it in the sun, page 88. ■ Tackle any stain with our natural stain-remover kit, page 90. ■ Use natural substances such as lemon juice to clean glass, metals and ceramics. See our recipes on page 94. ■ Keep your valuables in excellent condition with our simple care and cleaning tips, page 96. ■ The air inside your home may be up to three times more polluted than outdoors. Find out what you can do about it on page 98.

WASTE WATCH

■ 'Reduce, reuse, recycle' should be your guiding principle for managing household waste. Be inspired by our ideas on page 102. ■ Whether it's a printer cartridge or a tin of old paint, if you can't recycle an item in your home, dispose of it responsibly, page 104.

HOUSEHOLD PESTS

■ Keep your kitchen pest-free with natural deterrents. See page 108. ■ Make your own non-toxic traps to keep rodents, flies and other household invaders under control, page 112. ■ Get rid of termites and keep them away, page 114.

CARING FOR YOUR PET

■ Which is better for your pet – commercial pet food or home-made food? See page 118. ■ For many minor ailments, you can treat your pet at home with simple, natural remedies, page 122. ■ Dogs and cats are prone to parasitic pests, such as fleas and intestinal worms. See page 126.

EARTH-WISE CLEANING

By rethinking your approach to cleaning, you can save money and reduce your impact on the environment.

Keeping a clean home

A clean home is both a pleasure to live in and essential for healthy living. Maintaining a regular cleaning routine keeps dirt under control and moulds and allergy-producing substances in check. Cleaning little but often is the key – if you catch dust and spills before they turn to grime, you won't need harsh chemical cleaners.

TEN STEPS TO BETTER CLEANING

1 Stop the dirt before it comes inside. Place good-quality dirt-absorbing mats at all entrances to the home. Your carpets will stay cleaner and last longer.

2 Initiate a shoe-free policy in the household to avoid the problem of tracking in oil and dirt from outside. Provide a shoe rack at the door and a chair nearby, to encourage people to oblige.

3 Try to tidy up as you go. If you haven't the time, clear up small messes as they occur and you won't have a big job to deal with at the end of the day.

4 Instead of reaching for the strongest chemical cleaner first, look for environmentally responsible cleaning alternatives. Mostly, they will work just as well.

5 Act fast on spills and stains. You'll not only find your cleaning is more effective, you'll also need fewer chemicals to do the job.

6 Give cleaners time to work and you'll find you need less of them. Leave mould and oven cleaners to work overnight, for example.

7 See how little you can get away with. Use less when applying household cleaners, whether they're commercial brands or more natural alternatives. You may find a wipe with a damp cloth is all you need.

8 Use elbow grease. Brushes, scourers and cloths are the first line of defence against dirt and reduce the need for harsh, fast-acting chemicals.

9 Use recycled materials to clean kitchen and bathroom surfaces. Old cotton T-shirts and towels are perfect. They're economical and longer-lasting than disposable wipes and paper towels.

10 Work out a minimum cleaning routine to keep your home functioning efficiently. That way, even if you're extra busy, at least you know you've covered the basics each week.

CLEANING TOOL KIT

You need surprisingly few tools to clean your home. Either recycle from everyday staples or buy quality equipment that will last.

RECYCLE

- T-shirts and cotton towels: cut to usable sizes for a constant supply of absorbent cleaning cloths.
- Single cotton or wool socks: pull on your hand and use as a duster.
- Toothbrushes: use to clean around taps and hard-to-access areas.
- Shaving brushes and paintbrushes: use for dusting delicate items.
- Spray bottles: keep on hand for homemade cleaning solutions.

■ ■ ■ **Using cleaning aids such as scrubbing brushes and steel wool reduces the need for fast-acting chemicals.**

BUY NEW

- Long-handled soft broom: more expensive brooms with good-quality bristles will pick up the dirt better and last longer.
- Dustpan and brush: buy several and store near high-activity areas ready for quick clean-ups.
- Long-handled sponge mop and bucket: choose good-quality mops with sturdy replaceable heads.
- For the kitchen: washing-up brush, vegetable scrubbing brush and fine steel wool scourer.
- For the bathroom: toilet brush and bucket.

MICROFIBRE KNOW-HOW

- Start with an all-purpose cloth or mitt. There are a variety of grades for different applications, from cleaning glass to washing cars.
- Buy wisely – the most expensive microfibre cloth is not necessarily the best, but the very cheapest do tend to be inferior.
- Don't use fabric softeners when laundering microfibre cloths. They smooth the fibres, rendering them useless. Also avoid tumble-drying.
- Clean your windows with a microfibre cloth just after it's come out of the washing machine. It will be at just the right dampness after the spin cycle.
- Damp microfibre cloths will remove bacteria. Wipe the surface dry after use as an extra precaution.

WEEKLY ROUTINE

- ✔ Vacuum and dust rooms
- ✔ Clean stove and grill pan
- ✔ Wipe over kitchen cupboards and fridge
- ✔ Wash and disinfect bins
- ✔ Clean toilet and wipe down bathroom basin
- ✔ Shake out doormats
- ✔ Sweep entrances and outside living areas

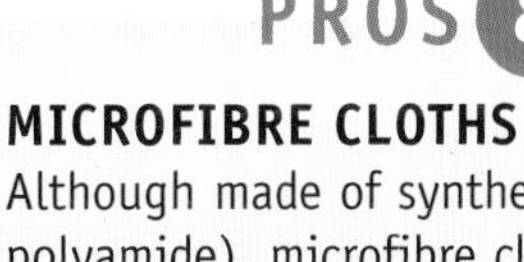

MICROFIBRE CLOTHS

Although made of synthetic fibres (polyester and polyamide), microfibre cloths do have a place in the earth-wise tool kit. Because of the way the fibres are arranged, microfibre cloths pick up dirt without the addition of chemical cleansers. They're much more absorbent than natural textiles, pick up and hold dirt and grease without scratching, are easy to use on almost any surface and can be washed and used repeatedly. Buy good-quality cloths that will last and make worthwhile the energy used in their production.

The frequent use of household cleaning chemicals can cause asthma attacks and breathing difficulties.

VACUUM CLEANERS

A weekly vacuum will pick up dust before it turns to grime and keep dust mites and carpet beetles at bay. Consider these points when buying your next cleaner.

- Higher wattage vacuum cleaners don't necessarily have a more powerful suction. Do your homework before buying, ask for a demonstration and make sure the machine you choose suits the surfaces you want to clean.
- Do you want a bag or non-bag system? Disposable paper bags make less mess than canisters or fabric bags, but are less cost-effective.
- Ask about the filter system, especially if anyone in your family is asthmatic or suffers from allergies. The best filters, known as HEPA (high efficiency particulate air) filters, capture tiny particles of dust and allergens that would otherwise be blown back into the air through the vacuum's exhaust system.
- Consider models with a gauge that alerts you to when the bag or canister needs replacing. Full bags waste energy – both yours and the motor's.
- Look for models with a variable power button, which allows you to use less suction on delicate items.
- A powerhead attachment will use more energy, but will increase carpet cleaning efficiency.
- If you clean mostly carpet, look for a cleaner that offers pile adjustment. This saves wear and tear on your carpet and the vacuum motor.

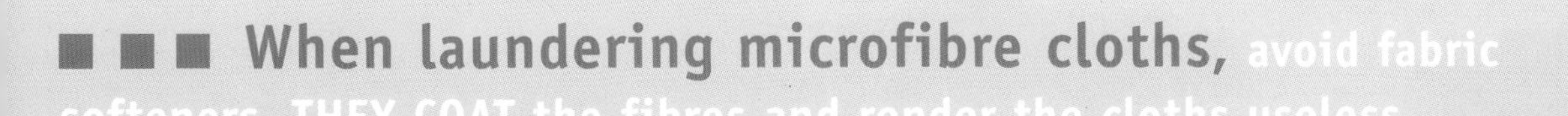

Choose carefully

Knowing which chemicals to avoid in commercial cleaning products is difficult. It's a complex subject and not everyone agrees on which substances are harmful. Many labels are short on ingredients and, even when they are included, are hard to understand. Before selecting a chemical cleaner try to find out what the ingredients are likely to be.

CLEANING AGENTS: WHAT'S IN THEM?

If you want to know what's in a cleaner or detergent you use regularly, and it's not on the label, you will need to contact the manufacturer.

- Use the caller information number on the product label (usually a free-call number) to enquire about ingredients or ask for a Material Safety Data Sheet (MSDS), which will identify any dangerous ingredients. Most companies will oblige – if not, it may be wise to select an alternative product.
- A number of personal care and cleaning products contain a class of surfactants (dirt removers) called alkylphenol ethoxylates. Two of these (nonylphenol and octylphenol) are hormone disruptors, which mimic the hormone oestrogen, and can affect the reproductive systems of fish, birds and mammals. In addition, they biodegrade slowly.
- The antibacterial agent triclosan is found in some dishwashing liquids, antimicrobial soaps and dishcloths. It has been found to react with chlorine in water to form chloroform, is closely related to dioxin and is not readily biodegradable.
- Volatile organic compounds (VOCs), including toluene and trichlorethylene, are found in some spot removers and floor waxes and polishes. Some VOCs are linked to cancer, and others, such as formaldehyde (formalin), an ingredient in some laundry detergents, can cause health problems such as nausea, wheezing and skin rashes.
- Quaternary ammonium compounds, such as benzalkonium chloride, cetrimonium bromide, quaternium-15 and quaternium 1-29, are used in many cleaning products as germicides, preservatives and surfactants. They can cause irritation to the eyes as well as a variety of allergic symptoms.

AIR FRESHENERS

- Don't use a smell – particularly a manufactured one – to cover up another smell. A number of air fresheners contain VOCs, which are hazardous to human health.
- Some air fresheners contain paradichlorobenzene, a chlorine derivative that has recently been linked to both liver and nerve damage.
- Be careful when buying essential oils. Some have been diluted with synthetic scents, which can be harmful to inhale, particularly for people with allergies. To be sure of what you are buying, look for labels that state, '100 per cent pure essential oil' or something similar.

Use in moderation

- **Ammonia** is generally not considered harmful to the environment. However, it can be harmful to people with respiratory problems. Use in a well-ventilated area and never mix with chlorine bleaches.
- **Hydrogen peroxide** is an oxidising bleach that breaks down quickly into water and oxygen. Use in preference to bleaches that contain chlorine.
- **Methylated spirits** should be 95 per cent alcohol (ethanol, usually derived from plants) and 5 per cent methanol (a petroleum by-product that is poisonous). Do not inhale or ingest and do not tip down the drain.

Ecologically friendly washing powders are better value for money because they cut out unnecessary bulking agents.

SAFETY FIRST

If you choose to use chemical cleansers, take care to minimise health risks.

- Open windows so fresh air can dissipate fumes and pollutants.
- Wear rubber gloves and long-sleeved clothing. For heavy-duty jobs, wear a mask and goggles.
- Do not mix cleaners. You risk creating a more toxic substance.
- Use rub-on cleaners rather than sprays to avoid inhaling.
- Rinse cleaned surfaces well to remove chemical residues.
- Avoid using chemical cleansers in cooking and eating areas.

OVEN CLEANERS

- Avoid oven cleaners with sodium hydroxide (caustic soda). It's highly corrosive and can cause severe irritation, deep burns and blindness.
- Products labelled 'non-corrosive' may contain ethanolamine, a solvent that can cause headaches and asthmatic reactions as well as affect the central nervous system.
- Diethyl glycol alkyl ethers (ethylene glycol ethers or EGEs) are found in some oven cleaners and have been linked with birth defects.

WARNING!

▼ Don't mix chemical cleaners with very hot water as this may promote the escape of volatile chemicals into the atmosphere.

HOUSEHOLD BLEACHES

- Watch out for chlorine, which is present in many household bleaches and mould removers. It can react with other dangerous organic matter in sewage to form toxic, very persistent chemicals called organochlorines.
- Avoid products that contain chlorine in forms such as sodium hypochlorite, a lung and eye irritant that releases toxic fumes when mixed with ammonia or acid-based cleaners (including vinegar).

LAUNDRY PRODUCTS

- Look for 'no phosphate' on the label. This means no added phosphate and a background level of less than 0.5 per cent. Products marked 'P' have less than 7.8 grams of phosphate per wash and are the next best choice.
- Some laundry detergents and general cleaners contain artificial musks as a perfume. These are persistent chemicals, both in the environment and in the human body, and some may be neurotoxic.

TOILET CLEANERS

- Think carefully before using a commercial toilet cleaner. Many contain corrosive acids as well as dyes and deodorisers that are irritating to the eyes and skin and may be carcinogenic.
- Don't buy 'in-tank' cleaners that contain paradichlorobenzene, a chemical solvent that accumulates in the body and has been linked to liver and nerve damage.

THE TRUTH ABOUT...

PHOSPHATE

Algal blooms are choking up our waterways and the culprit is phosphate. We use it in detergents, and farmers use it in fertilisers. Although phosphates exist in nature, when concentrations are too high algae thrives, producing blooms that cut out oxygen and other nutrients to river life.

hot links

Toxic chemicals around the house and alternatives: www.tec.org.au/member/tec/projects/tcye/Household.html

Labelling specifications and links to the Global Ecolabelling Network: www.aela.org.au; www.enviro-choice.org.nz

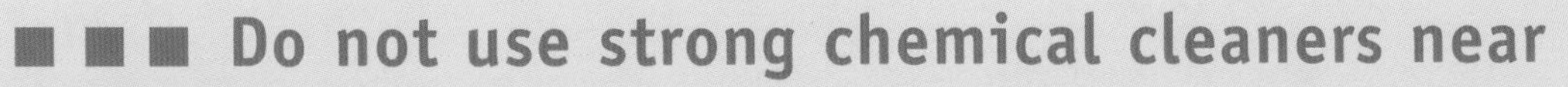

■ ■ ■ Do not use strong chemical cleaners near children. They can be adversely affected, even by small quantities.

Greener cleaners

Cleaning without chemicals is not only possible, most of the time it's equally effective. Natural cleaning products are also much safer for us and for the environment. Making your own cleaners is inexpensive and, best of all, you know exactly what's gone into them.

WHY USE NATURAL CLEANING AGENTS?

- Natural cleaning products are often cheaper. Less is spent on advertising and the savings are passed on to you, the consumer.
- Homemade cleaning products are often composed of just one substance – the cleaning agent – whereas many commercial products contain additives that bulk up the product and add cosmetic appeal.
- Allergy sufferers, people with sensitive skins and those with asthma or other breathing difficulties are far less likely to react badly to natural cleansers.

WARNING!

▼ Although washing soda is not harmful to the environment, it is a strong chemical – so always wear gloves when using it.

- Chemicals that break down quickly are better for waterways. If you don't have the time to make your own cleaners, buy cleaners that are low in toxicity and biodegrade quickly.
- Low chemical use in the kitchen, laundry and bathroom means you should be able to re-use the rinsing or 'grey' water on your plants when rainwater is scarce.

Pure soap is one of the safest and cheapest washing products around.

THE EARTH-WISE CLEANING KIT

BICARBONATE OF SODA

- Use bicarb (baking soda) when you need a mild abrasive. It's composed of sodium bicarbonate, a slightly alkaline substance, which has very low toxicity, and cleans by forming a mild detergent when it reacts with grease and oil.

BORAX

- A naturally occurring alkaline mineral salt, borax will dissolve grease, remove stains, deodorise, disinfect, bleach, inhibit mould, soften water and fabric – and kill ants and cockroaches. It doesn't persist for long in the environment, but it is toxic if ingested, so use with care, especially around pets and small children.

GLYCERINE

- A by-product of the soap-making process, glycerine is a useful cleaning ingredient because it helps mix oil with water and dissolves many forms of dirt. Most glycerine comes from vegetable oil or animal fats (tallow), but about 10 per cent is produced from petroleum.

LEMON JUICE

- Squeeze a lemon for a milder and much better smelling substitute for bleach. It's also good for inhibiting mould growth, deodorising and removing stains.

SALT

- Salt is excellent for scouring pans and kitchen utensils as the grains act as a mild abrasive as well as a disinfectant.

SOAP FLAKES

- Buy pure soap flakes or make your own by grating a bar of laundry or pure soap. It's 100 per cent biodegradable, low in toxicity and, unlike detergent, doesn't contribute to algal problems in waterways. Keep flakes in an airtight container.

■ ■ ■ **To clean a smelly bin,** add a few drops of eucalyptus oil to hot water, swill around the bin, pour out, then wipe.

ECO LABELS

As manufacturers target the growing eco market, you'll be able to find safer products more easily.

- Look out for Environmental Choice logos in Australia and Ecolabelling Trust logos in New Zealand, to guide you to cleaning products that are safe to use.
- Log onto the Internet and check out accredited products. Some may be available at local stores, or you may be able to order direct.

TEA-TREE AND EUCALYPTUS OILS

- Use these cleaners and natural disinfectants to finish off after washing down surfaces.

WASHING SODA

- Washing soda (sodium carbonate) is moderately alkaline and is a good cleaning staple for the kitchen. It's particularly good for cutting grease, but also removes stains and softens water.

WHITE VINEGAR

- A good substitute for toilet cleaners. Also use to remove bathroom scum, hard water deposits and tarnishes on metal.

MAKE YOUR OWN

SCOURING PASTE

The simplest cleaner of all. Use for sinks, oven doors, stovetops and inside mugs.

4 tbsp bicarb
1 tbsp water

- Mix ingredients into a stiff paste and apply with a damp sponge. Buff residue with a dry cloth.

BICARB CLEANER

A general cleaner that is safe for use anywhere in the home.

1 tsp bicarb
1 tsp pure soap flakes
squeeze of lemon or dash of white vinegar
1 cup warm water

- Mix ingredients and shake until soap is dissolved. Spray and wipe with a kitchen sponge.

VINEGAR CLEANER

All-purpose and long-lasting, this cleaner removes grease and dirt. Ideal for use on stainless steel sinks, tiled and wooden surfaces and plastic finishes, such as fridge shelves and telephones.

2 cups white vinegar
1 cup water
25 drops eucalyptus oil

- Combine all ingredients in a spray bottle. Shake well before use, spray onto a soft damp cloth and rub. There's no need to rinse.

LAVENDER DISINFECTANT

Keeps bathroom surfaces safe and smelling sweet. It also makes a marvellous spray when ironing bed linen.

25 drops lavender essential oil
2 tbsp methylated spirits or vodka
500 ml distilled water

- Add the oil to the alcohol in a clean dry bottle and leave to dissolve for 24 hours.
- Add water and decant into a spray bottle. Shake mixture thoroughly before use.

SOAP AND BORAX CLEANER

This cleaner is so useful you may want to make it up in large quantities. It's great for benchtops.

2 tsp borax
1 heaped tsp pure soap flakes
3 cups water

- Mix ingredients well. Spray and wipe with a damp sponge. Store in an airtight container.

LEMON CREAM CLEANSER

This slightly abrasive cleaner is good for baths, basins, benches and stovetops.

squirt of phosphate-free liquid detergent
½ cup bicarb
1 tsp vegetable glycerine
lemon essential oil

- Stir enough detergent into bicarb to make a soft paste. Add glycerine and several drops of the oil. Apply with a damp sponge, then rinse.

Warm soapy water cleans most stovetops. Use bicarb on a soft cloth to REMOVE STUBBORN STAINS.

A clean kitchen

The kitchen is the room with the most potential for accumulating grease and spills. If you get into the habit of a daily cleaning routine, it's easy to keep it clean without using harsh commercial products. If you add a little time into the equation, it's possible to get rid of even hard-to-remove dirt using gentle cleaners.

ROUTINE CLEANING

- Wipe over kitchen counters and sinks daily with a cloth sprinkled with bicarbonate of soda (bicarb), then dampen with eucalyptus oil and wipe again.
- Use a solution of salt – about a teaspoon to a cup of water – to clean the sink. It's very effective and almost cost-free.

- Keep the drains clear. Catch food debris with a sink strainer and put tea leaves and coffee grounds into the compost bin.
- Don't put the fat and oil from saucepans down the drain. Scrape into an old milk carton, freeze, then throw into the garbage bin. This way the oil won't leak into your bin.
- Clean fridges once every few weeks. Check use-by dates on cartons and jars and get rid of perishable foods that are past their prime. Don't use commercial cleaning products on fridge shelves – they may contain harsh solvents that undermine the plastic. Instead, wipe them down with a paste of bicarb and water.
- Check the seals on bottles and containers in the pantry every six months or so and wipe up any spills as they can attract kitchen pests.
- To clean and deodorise a microwave oven, add the juice and skin of a lemon to a bowl of water and place inside the microwave. Run on high for 2–5 minutes. Remove and wipe the oven interior clean. Always cover food in the microwave to cut down on spills and splatters.
- Wipe out your oven while it is still warm with a damp cloth dipped in bicarb. If it needs more of a clean, apply a paste of bicarb and white vinegar to all surfaces, leave for an hour, then wipe away the residue and rinse with a damp cloth.
- Rub matt-finish stainless steel rangehoods and exhaust fans with a clean dry cloth from time to time. If you do this regularly, thick grease won't have time to build up, and a polish is all you need.
- Wipe over shiny stainless steel rangehoods and exhaust fans with a damp cloth sprinkled with a little bicarb. Buff with a clean dry cloth.

WARNING!

▼ If you have a catalytic self-cleaning oven, do not use any of the cleaning methods described here unless your user's manual says it's safe to do so.

DEALING WITH BAKED-ON DIRT

- Sprinkle saucepans with washing soda. Gently add boiling water and leave for 30 minutes before washing as normal. Alternatively, pour a thin layer of cooking oil over burnt pans and heat gently. Allow to cool, drain off the oil and wash as normal.
- Clean an oven dish by dipping it in very hot water and quickly turning it upside down on a flat surface. Leave for 15 minutes. The trapped steam will loosen the residue making it much easier to clean off.
- Soak oven shelves overnight in a solution of 1 cup washing soda per litre of hot water. You may need to use the laundry tub, or turn shelves occasionally for even cleaning. Wear rubber gloves for this task.

- Heat the oven to 200°C, then turn it off. Place a small bowl of cloudy ammonia in the centre, and a bowl of boiling water on the bottom. Close the oven door and leave overnight. Wipe out in the morning with warm, soapy water.
- Place wet cloths over the stovetop and leave for at least half an hour. The dirt should wipe off much more easily without the need for caustic products. If that doesn't work, leave the cloths on overnight.

TRICKY SPOTS

- Cut pieces of thick paper or newspaper to fit on the tops of high cupboards, where grease from cooking settles and gathers dust. Change the paper twice annually and you won't need to clean.
- Scrub the mildew from the folds of fridge door seals with an old toothbrush dipped in white vinegar.

Top Tip

Wet dishcloths and kitchen sponges harbour bacteria. Soak cloths each night in a solution of boiling water with a good dash of vinegar and a few drops of eucalyptus oil. Rinse well in the morning.

~ STAR SAVER ~

Bicarbonate of soda, which has very low toxicity and is economical, is an excellent choice as an all-purpose cleaner in the kitchen. It's gentle enough to use in fridges and on chrome and aluminium without scratching. To clean pots and pans, rub over with a paste of bicarb on a damp cloth and rinse.

- Pull out the fridge, microwave and dishwasher once or twice a year to clean behind them. These appliances provide warm dark places where cockroaches like to hide and breed.
- Wipe around the knobs of your stovetop with the end of a teaspoon wrapped in a scrap of damp cloth.
- If the S-bend under your sink is blocked, pour in 1 cup bicarb followed by 1 cup vinegar. When the fizzing stops, follow with a kettle of boiling water, then use a plunger to push the blockage through.
- Tie the hood from an old sweatshirt to the end of a broom and use it to clear cobwebs on ceilings.

DIY detergent

Use a teaspoon or two in hot water for washing dishes.

1½ cups soap flakes
¾ cup water
1½ cups washing soda
1½ cups white vinegar
lemon essential oil

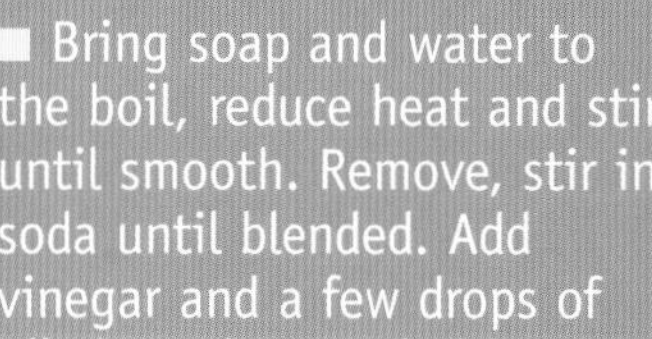

- Bring soap and water to the boil, reduce heat and stir until smooth. Remove, stir in soda until blended. Add vinegar and a few drops of oil. Store in a sealed bottle.

Use splatter guards on grill pans and DON'T OVERFILL SAUCEPANS – that way you won't have the spills to clean up.

A clean bathroom

Some chemicals are absorbed through the skin, so avoid using bleaches and tough abrasives in the bathroom. If you or a family member has allergies to chemicals, try cleaning the room with a gentle shampoo. Other mild detergents, like dishwashing liquid will also work well on tiles and porcelain, especially in conjunction with a fine scouring pad.

SHOWERS AND BATHS

- A paste of bicarbonate of soda (bicarb) and water can be used all around the bathroom, from the sink to the shower. Use it with a cloth or a non-scratching scourer.
- Never use an abrasive cleaner on baths because it may scratch the surface. A little dishwashing liquid on a cloth is a good alternative.
- Clean soap scum from a glass shower screen by mixing 2 parts salt with 1 part vinegar. Rub onto the screen with a cloth (or even fine steel wool), then rinse and dry.
- If you have a bad back, buy an extra toilet brush and use it to scrub the bath.
- To disinfect the shower recess, and to clean mould from grout, mix ¼ cup borax with 2 cups very hot water and ¼ teaspoon tea-tree oil. Shake in a spray bottle until the borax dissolves. Spray on surfaces, leave overnight and rinse.
- After cleaning the shower, wipe over the tiles and screen with a few drops of almond oil to prevent the build-up of soap scum.
- To prevent the bathroom mirror fogging up while showering, wipe it over with glycerine or a thin film of shaving cream. Buff with a dry cloth.
- Re-use plastic orange nets in the bathroom as scourers, or to hold children's bath toys.

HAND BASINS

- Old nylon stockings work well for cleaning bathroom porcelain that scratches easily. Use them with a mild abrasive, such as bicarb or salt.
- Running low on bicarb? Cream of tartar is a good substitute for cleaning porcelain.
- Rub lemon juice around plugholes to remove grease and lime scale. Another way to remove lime scale is by rubbing hard with a plastic scourer and neat dishwashing liquid.
- For the orange-brown stains that result from dripping taps, rub vigorously with a mixture of 1 teaspoon salt to ½ cup white vinegar. This also works for hard-water deposits.

GETTING RID OF MOULD

Unfortunately, mould and bathrooms often go hand in hand. Good ventilation is essential to prevent it. Open windows and install an exhaust fan if necessary. After showering, air and dry damp towels outside to keep moisture down.

- Stop mould from forming by treating susceptible surfaces with a mixture of 2 teaspoons borax and 1 cup white vinegar. Spray or apply with a cloth and leave for 30 minutes before wiping off.
- Apply a paste of bicarb and water to clean the grout between shower or floor tiles. Scrub with an old toothbrush and then rinse.
- To reduce mould on a shower curtain, get into the habit of drying the curtain with a towel after each shower.
- To clean mould off a shower curtain, scrub with bicarb. Or use a paste made from vinegar or lemon juice and borax. Rub the curtain vigorously and rinse well.

Add a few drops of pine oil or tea-tree oil to the toilet bowl for EXTRA DISINFECTANT POWER.

- Use old toothbrushes or denture brushes sprinkled with bicarb to clean fiddly crevices around taps and plugs. Another good cleaning agent is toothpaste. Try it on taps as well as teeth – it will give your chrome added sparkle.
- To remove oily deposits or lime scale from around taps, try wrapping them in a cloth soaked in white vinegar and leave for about half an hour before rinsing.

TOP TIP

Dilute ½ cup vinegar in 2 litres water to clean mirrors, window glass and tiles. It's better than plain water because it doesn't leave a water mark.

TOILETS

- Don't put anything except for human waste and biodegradable toilet paper down a toilet. Anything else can either block the drain or pollute the environment.
- Put the toilet lid down before flushing the cistern if your toilet is in the bathroom. Otherwise you risk getting fine mist particles of toilet water all over the room, including your toothbrush.
- Don't use a proprietary toilet cleaner. Many use strong acids and some use toxic chemicals such as paradichlorobenzene.
- Clean inside toilet bowl by sprinkling dampened surface with borax and spray with vinegar (1 cup borax to ¼ cup vinegar). Let it sit for an hour or two to give the solution time to work, then scrub with a long-handled brush and flush.
- To remove a stubborn toilet bowl ring, apply a paste of neat borax and lemon juice. Leave overnight, scrub well and flush.
- Use any general cleaner such as a colourless, scent-free dishwashing liquid or soap solution to clean the outside of the toilet bowl and the toilet seat.

- Burn off the smell of toilet odours with an aromatherapy oil burner, a candle or simply light a match. These odours are not harmful, so an open window is generally enough to clear the air.
- Clean out the toilet cistern every now and then if you use grey water as it can get a bit smelly. To empty the cistern, turn off the control valve on the inlet pipe. Then flush the toilet; once the cistern has emptied, it won't refill.

NATURAL DISINFECTANTS

- **BORAX** Kills bacteria and deodorises. Mix with hot water and vinegar or lemon juice to get rid of stubborn stains in toilet bowls. Can also be used instead of bleach to combat recurring mould.
- **LEMON JUICE** An effective and pleasant-smelling alternative to bleach. Useful as a mould-inhibitor as well as a disinfectant. For stubborn mildew stains on shower curtains, rub with lemon juice and dry in the sun.
- **SALT** Dissolve in water to use as a mild disinfectant in kitchens and bathrooms. Salt is also good for cleaning surfaces that require a gentle abrasive. Mixes well with vinegar and water as a surface cleaner.
- **SOAP** Washes away bacteria and is an important part of basic sanitation. Pure soap flakes are available in supermarkets, or you could make your own by grating a bar of pure soap.
- **TEA-TREE AND EUCALYPTUS OILS** Strong but pleasant-smelling and economical to use as you need just a few drops. Add to hot water when wiping down surfaces.

Floors

Regular vacuuming is a good idea for all floors, but is essential if you have carpets, to remove the dirt and grit that can wear away carpet fibres. Don't let dirt build up on hard floors either. You'll need only use a broom and a quick sponge-mop with warm soapy water to remove the dirt.

CARPETS

- Don't forget to vacuum under couches, behind furniture and along skirting boards. It will keep carpet beetles and moths in check and help to remove dust mites and pet fur, which often accumulate in hard-to-reach spots. This is especially important if family members suffer from allergies.
- Scoop or scrape away all solid spills with a blunt knife or spoon. Blot liquids with a clean cloth, pressing firmly to soak up all the spill. Proceed cautiously if you are at all concerned about colour-fastness.
- Try using soda water to get rid of the rancid smells that can be left behind on carpets from some foods, animal messes and vomit. Or rub a little bicarbonate of soda on the spot with a damp cloth.
- Pour soda water or mineral water on to liquid spills on carpets. The bubbles make the spillage rise to the surface where you can blot it with a clean cloth.
- Sprinkle bicarbonate of soda on natural and synthetic floor coverings to remove grease, dirt and odours. Leave for 15 to 30 minutes and then vacuum up powder. For heavy grease stains, you may need to use cornflour.

TOP TIP

Act quickly and you can remove all traces of a red wine stain, even on a pale carpet. Mop any excess liquid with an absorbent cloth. Then saturate the spill with white wine and leave it to seep in for 10 minutes. Rinse with a clean cloth and lukewarm water.

- Remove candle wax from carpets by scraping off as much as possible with a blunt knife and then covering with a tissue, blotting paper or brown wrapping paper. Hold a hot iron just above it and press the paper down to blot the carpet. Use several sheets if necessary.
- Never use an alkaline product (some laundry detergents are alkaline) on a wool carpet as it can damage the fibres and cause fading of fabric dyes.

LINOLEUM AND VINYL

- Avoid using ammonia products and abrasive cleaners on linoleum and vinyl as they'll dull the surface. Instead, mop with water and a little detergent and rinse.
- It's best to avoid cleaning linoleum with strong alkaline products, but if you do, rinse the floor well to avoid cracking, shrinking and/or discolouration.
- Remove scuff marks with a pencil eraser, or try rubbing with neat dishwashing liquid. Finish by wiping clean with a damp cloth.
- Blot or scoop spillages as soon as possible to reduce the chance of a permanent mark. If you're not quick enough, try removing stains with a fine nylon pad and neat detergent, a pencil eraser or an all-purpose cleaner.

■ ■ ■ Use a pencil eraser or eucalyptus oil to remove SCUFF MARKS on hard floors, such as timber and linoleum.

PROS & CONS

STEAM-CLEANING

Steam mops are a non-chemical method of cleaning hard floors. They don't use much electricity, and some produce vapour with a low enough water content that you can safely steam-clean curtains, carpets, mattresses and upholstery. However, if you are considering a steam-cleaner, bear in mind they are only a practical option if you clean regularly. They can't pick up dust, and mop heads can get very dirty. Removable mop-head covers can be thrown in with regular washing.

~ FUTURE GLIMPSE ~

Several manufacturers already sell a 'robot' or automatic vacuum cleaner. It looks like a giant, flat pod, and moves around the room by itself, detecting and avoiding walls and other obstacles. It is cordless, and when not in use sits in a charging bay. Because it works on batteries, it is a low energy consumer.

TILED FLOORS

- Sweep or vacuum over sealed ceramic, terrazzo or marble tiles and sponge-mop with a bucket of warm water and 2 cups vinegar.
- Use a little bicarbonate of soda to remove marks on glazed tiles. For marks on unglazed tiles, rub gently with fine steel wool, again using bicarb if more abrasion is needed.
- Use a borax solution (dissolve ½ cup borax in a bucket of hot water) to thoroughly clean and disinfect tiled surfaces.

FLOORBOARDS

- For unsealed timber, sweep then polish with a cloth impregnated with linseed oil.
- For sealed timber, sweep then sponge-mop with just water or water and a little detergent.
- Wash an oil-finished timber or polyurethane floor with 1 part methylated spirits to 10 parts hot water. Then buff with a dry cloth.
- Sprinkle sticky patches on an oil-finished floor with flour and wipe over with a damp cloth.

MAKE YOUR OWN

STRONG CLEANER FOR HARD FLOORS

This cleaner contains washing soda, which can be damaging on the skin, so wear protective gloves when using it. Do not use on timber floors.

1 tbsp liquid soap
¼ cup white vinegar
¼ cup washing soda
3 litres hot water

- Mix all the ingredients in a bucket.
- Rinse with clean water after use.

CARPET STAIN FOAM

Use as a foam for carpets and upholstery.

2 cups pure soap flakes
½ cup methylated spirits
25 ml eucalyptus oil

- Shake ingredients together in a large jar until combined. Add a little hot water if the mixture is too hard to mix – but leave it quite thick. Store in a sealed jar.
- To use: mix 2–3 tbsp of mixture into 1 litre of very hot water and whisk until suds form.
- Rub just the foam over the carpet stain and leave for 10 minutes. Wipe away with a damp sponge dipped in white vinegar (this neutralises the alkalinity left by the foam).
- Blot thoroughly with a clean pad.
- For extra tough stains, add ¼ cup washing soda to the hot water with the foam mix and whisk until soda crystals have completely dissolved.

Rub half a lemon sprinkled generously with salt into RUST STAINS on linoleum or vinyl and then rinse with water.

Keeping outdoors spick-and-span

A courtyard, balcony or deck is an extra room you can use for relaxing or entertaining, but in the fresh air. Because outdoor living areas are open to the elements, cleaning them is a little different from indoor cleaning. By following a few basic rules and procedures you can make your outdoor room a pleasant place all year round without resorting to harsh cleaning chemicals.

BARBECUE DRILL

A dirty barbecue not only cooks less efficiently but also attracts vermin, so make sure you clean it properly each time you cook.

- When you have finished using the barbecue, clean off as much food residue as you can.
- Turn the barbecue to *High* (or choose the *Clean Burn* setting if you have one) to burn off fat and any remaining residue.
- While the plate is still very hot, sprinkle it with salt, leave to cool, and then brush clean.
- Using a wire brush, scrub the grates and hotplate with a paste of bicarbonate of soda and water. Wipe clean, then dry with a cloth.
- Once the barbecue is clean, apply a coat of canola oil to the grates and hotplate to help prevent rust.

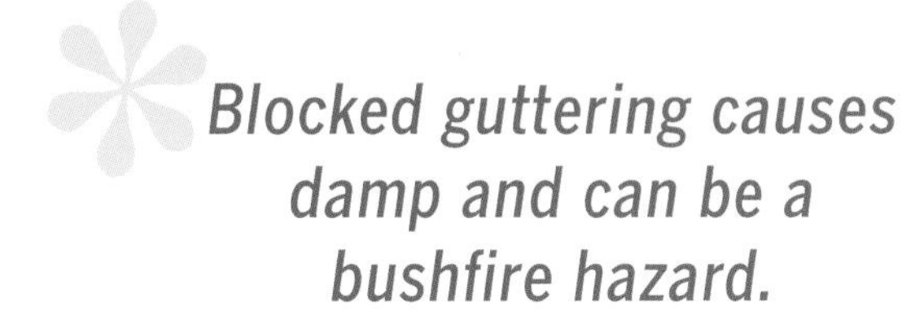

Blocked guttering causes damp and can be a bushfire hazard.

GARDEN TOOLS

Clean garden tools each time you use them. They will last longer and be easier to use.

- Regularly wipe wooden handles with a mixture of 1 part vinegar, 1 part boiled linseed oil and 1 part natural turpentine.
- Wipe the metal parts of tools with a damp rag that has been dipped in linseed oil.
- To prevent dirt build-up on the underside of your lawnmower, apply a little vegetable oil on the cleaned metal.

TOP TIP

To give your barbecue a thorough clean, try this 'steam-cleaning' method. First, heat the barbecue until it is very hot, then dip a long-handled wire brush in water and quickly scrub it across the grates and plate. As the water touches the hot surface, it will evaporate and clean.

OUTDOOR FURNITURE

A little care and some regular maintenance will add years to the life of your outdoor furniture.

- You can scrub most types of outdoor furniture. Use a nylon-bristled brush that has been dipped in a bucket of warm water, to which a squirt of phosphate-free dishwashing liquid has been added. To rinse, wipe down with several clean, wet rags.
- Scrub wooden furniture and allow to dry. Sand lightly to restore the colour, then oil with a solution of 2 cups raw linseed oil and ½ cup natural turpentine.
- Wipe aluminium furniture with warm water and a dash of vinegar, and then dry. Don't use ammonia or bicarbonate of soda, which can discolour aluminium.
- Regularly tighten the screws on wooden outdoor furniture.
- Act quickly to touch up any chips or scratches on metal and wrought iron furniture so it won't rust.
- To prevent the growth of mould, be sure to keep cane and wicker furniture dry.

If there are trees near your house, consider installing guttering mesh to avoid having to clean the gutters frequently.

Quick fixes for stains

Treat outdoor spills and stains immediately. Try one of these cleaning solutions.

- For oil or grease spilled on concrete or pavers, sprinkle with a clay-type cat litter, leave it to absorb the spill, then sweep it up.
- Combine equal amounts of fuller's earth and bicarbonate of soda with enough water to make a wet paste, then spread over greasy stains and allow to dry. Sweep up the residue.
- Wash stains on concrete, brick or pavers with a solution of 1 tbsp borax to 1 litre hot water. (High concentrations of borax will kill plants, so take care.)

CANVAS FURNITURE

- Regularly brush off the dirt and, if water restrictions permit, hose down canvas furniture and awnings with clean, cold water.
- To prevent mould, make sure that any canvas article is dry before you fold or store it.
- Treat bird poo and mildew stains on canvas with a paste of salt and lemon juice. Leave it in the sun until the stain disappears, then rinse off.
- Scrub canvas director's chairs with water and mild soap. Treat any stubborn stains with a paste of bicarbonate of soda. Leave the paste on the canvas for 5 minutes, then rinse off.
- To remove mould from a canvas umbrella, scrub it inside and out with soapy water. Sprinkle any stains with bicarbonate of soda, leave for an hour or so, and then rinse off.

PLAY EQUIPMENT

- Keep animal droppings and rubbish out of the sandpit by covering it when it is not in use.
- If a wading pool seems dirty, clean it with a solution of ¼ cup bicarbonate of soda in 4 litres water.
- Regularly scrub play equipment – such as swings and slides – with warm soapy water and a soft-bristled brush to remove grime, sticky handprints and bird poo.

GOLDEN OUTDOOR RULES

- ✔ Use a broom, not a hose, to clean hard surfaces. Keep a stiff heavy-duty broom solely for outdoor use.
- ✔ A regular sweep will prevent a build-up of mould-causing leaves, twigs and other organic debris.
- ✔ Keep courtyard drainage grates free of leaves and pet hair.
- ✔ Clear guttering and downpipes regularly.
- ✔ Store canvas chairs and umbrellas out of the weather, otherwise they will rot.
- ✔ Make sure the water in your water feature is clean and free of mosquito larvae.
- ✔ To prevent rusting, put garden tools back where they belong after each use.
- ✔ Store your hose on a reel to keep it neat and prevent it from forming kinks or knots. It will work more efficiently and last longer.

PAVED AREAS

Moss can be unsightly and even dangerous on paved areas. Try one of these cleaning solutions.

- Add about a handful of salt to a 5:1 solution of water and vinegar. Paint the solution onto the moss, then sweep the moss away when it is dry.
- Spray a solution of 1 part vinegar to 1 part methylated spirits.
- Pour a kettle of boiling water over the moss.
- For bad moss infestations, clean paved areas with a high-pressure washer (but first check the water restrictions in your area).

■ ■ ■ **Clean swimming pool tiles** with a little bicarbonate of soda on a soft cloth.

Wash and wear

Looking after your clothes properly will give them a longer life. Whether you wash by hand or machine, select appropriate washing methods and cycles and use non-toxic products. You can avoid the expense of dry-cleaning, and the chemicals associated with it, by washing most items carefully at home.

ASSESSING THE WASH

- Consider whether you need to wash an item of clothing after wearing it only once. Freshen it by hanging it outside to air for a day.
- Many clothes that are labelled 'dry-clean only' can in fact be hand-washed with care.
- Silks and woollens, including furnishings, can often be washed safely by hand in lukewarm or cold water.
- To give you more wearings between cleans, spot-clean clothes that should only be dry-cleaned.
- Use pure soap flakes for washing as they're kind to your hands as well as to fabrics.
- Machine washing, even on a gentle cycle, may be rough on clothes, so hand wash special items.

MACHINE WASHING

- By sorting your washing (whites/coloureds, lightly/heavily soiled, fabric types) you can choose the optimum cycle for your load and get better results.
- Reduce wear and tear by emptying pockets, tying tapes, turning denim and corduroy inside out, and doing up buttons and zips.
- Be sure to treat grime and stains before you wash. Either soak the soiled garments overnight or use a pre-wash stain remover.
- Most laundry loads can be done in cold water, which saves energy and saves you money.
- Put small or delicate items in an old pillowcase, or special washing bag, before laundering.
- Wipe out the drum of the washing machine (and around the door seal of a front-loader) after the final load. If the machine tends to smell musty, run a full cycle with 2 cups of vinegar, but no soap.

ALL-PURPOSE LAUNDRY 'POWDER'

½ cup washing soda
1 cup finely grated pure soap
½ cup salt
½ cup borax
½ cup bicarbonate of soda

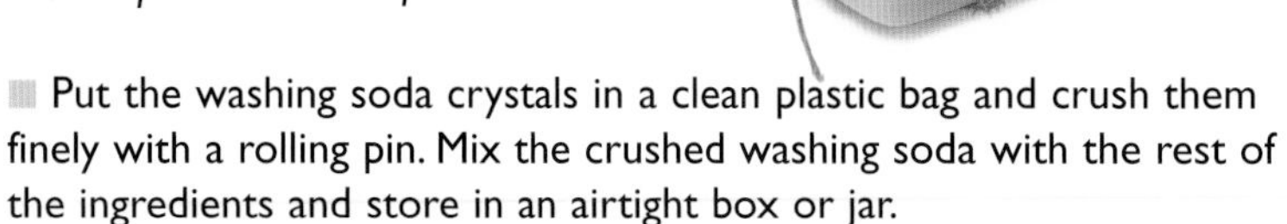

- Put the washing soda crystals in a clean plastic bag and crush them finely with a rolling pin. Mix the crushed washing soda with the rest of the ingredients and store in an airtight box or jar.
- Use 1 tbsp for a small load, 1½ for a medium load and 2 for a large load. Dissolve in a jug of hot water before adding to a top-loading machine. For a front-loader, dissolve the 'powder' in a small amount of hot water and add to the dispenser.
- If using it for hand washing, be sure to wear rubber gloves.

TOP TIP

To remove scorch marks after ironing at too high a temperature, soak the affected area in pure lemon juice for 30 minutes. Rinse in warm water, then dry in the sun. Both the lemon juice and the sunlight have a bleaching action.

■ ■ ■ **Rub underarm sweat stains** with a paste of vegetable glycerine and cream of tartar. Leave for 24 hours before washing.

THE TRUTH ABOUT...

DRY-CLEANING

Dry-cleaning involves the use of 'perc' (perchloroethylene), a potentially toxic chemical that belongs to the organochlorine family. Environmentally persistent, it can cause headaches, dizziness, nausea and, with prolonged exposure, liver and kidney damage as well as cancer. Safer alternatives include liquid carbon dioxide and wet-cleaning methods, but they are relatively new and may be hard to find. Check which method your local drycleaner uses. In the meantime, consider if a particular item of clothing needs to be dry-cleaned, and air dry-cleaned clothes in a well-ventilated place for a day or two, to make sure any chemicals have dissipated.

Fabric softeners

Commercial fabric softeners make your clothes feel soft and smell fresh, but contain potentially harmful chemicals and synthetic fragrances. Try these natural fabric softeners instead.

- Add 1 cup white vinegar to your washing machine during the rinse cycle. If your washing machine is a front-loader, add 2 tbsp white vinegar to the fabric conditioner dispenser.
- For a fresh fragrance, add a few drops of lavender, lemon, rose or eucalyptus essential oil to the vinegar.
- Bicarbonate of soda is also an excellent fabric softener. Add 1/4 cup to the wash with a few drops of essential oil.

Take advantage of sunlight's natural freshening, bleaching and antibacterial properties by drying your household washing outside whenever you can.

PRE-WASH STAIN REMOVAL

Treating dirt and stains before you wash makes the whole cleaning process much more effective. (See also *Tackling stains the natural way*, p. 90.)

- Add 1/4 cup borax to 500 ml water. Pour the mixture into a spray bottle. Use it on stains before washing but shake the bottle first.
- For stubborn stains, mix together 3 tablespoons mild, colour-free dishwashing liquid, 3 tablespoons vegetable glycerine and 375 ml water in a spray bottle. Spray. Leave for 15–30 minutes before washing.
- Rub collars with a paste made from 1 tablespoon vinegar and 1 teaspoon bicarbonate of soda.
- Soak soiled nappies overnight in a bucket of hot water with 1/2–1 cup borax. Wash as usual, adding 1 cup vinegar to the rinse.

DRYING AND IRONING

- Whenever possible, use the elements to dry your clothes. The sun and wind are free, and a clothes line is cheap, long-lasting and kinder to fabrics than a clothes dryer.
- If you have to use the drier, use the 'cool down' cycle. Sometimes called a 'permanent press' cycle because it dries with cool rather than warm air, it creases clothing less and so cuts down on the need for ironing.
- When it's raining, use a fold-away drying rack indoors or install an airer that can be elevated near the ceiling in a utility room or laundry.
- Most of your clothes won't need ironing if you smooth and neatly fold everything as you take it down from the washing line.
- To avoid ironing some woollen clothes, such as tailored suits, hang them in the bathroom when you're having a shower. The creases will drop out in the steam.

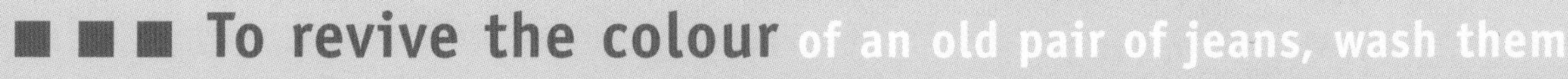

■ ■ ■ **To revive the colour** of an old pair of jeans, wash them with a brand-new pair.

Household laundry

There's more to laundry than just keeping your clothes clean. Tea towels, bath towels, table linen and bedding also need regular attention. In the case of quilts, doonas and pillows, this doesn't necessarily involve frequent washing – regular shaking, turning and airing are also important for keeping them fresh.

BLANKET CARE

- ✔ Soak a very dirty non-woollen blanket for 20 minutes, then wash it on a gentle cycle in warm water.
- ✔ Gently wash a woollen blanket on a machine wool cycle or (preferably) by hand, using warm water, never hot.
- ✔ Gently squeeze out the washed blanket, then roll it in towels to remove excess water. Dry flat or draped over several lines on your clothes line.
- ✗ To avoid matting the fibres of the wool (felting), don't rub or wring out the blanket.
- ✗ Don't tumble-dry a woollen blanket as it could become damaged.

BATH, KITCHEN AND TABLE LINEN

Wash bathroom and kitchen towels and linen regularly and, if possible, dry them in the sun to keep them fresh and hygienic.

- Before you use them, soak new towels in a sink of water with a handful of bicarbonate of soda, then wash as usual, adding 1 cup vinegar to the final rinse. This softens the fabric and removes any chemicals used in manufacturing.
- Machine wash all bath towels frequently. Damp towelling fabric is a breeding ground for bacteria.
- To fluff up and keep the pile soft, shake a washed towel before pegging it out, and again when it's dry.
- Soften scratchy bath and kitchen towels by soaking them overnight in a bucket of warm water with ½ cup Epsom salts. Do not rinse.
- Soak dirty tea towels overnight in a solution of 2 tablespoons cream of tartar per litre of boiling water, then wash them as usual.
- To remove grease from and disinfect kitchen linen, add 2 tablespoons borax to the washing water.

- Keep linen tablecloths white by soaking them overnight in a laundry tub of water with 1 cup cream of tartar, then wash as usual.
- To remove candle wax from a tablecloth, harden the wax with an ice cube, then scrape it off. Dab the residue with eucalyptus oil and launder as usual. Alternatively, try placing the cloth in the freezer and then proceed with the eucalyptus oil and washing.

BED LINEN AND BEDDING

Sheets, pillowcases and doona covers should be washed weekly. Bulkier bedding items – such as pillows, blankets and doonas – may not need frequent washing, but they can also be laundered when necessary.

- Machine wash sheets, pillowcases, doona covers and mattress protectors and dry them on the clothes line if possible.
- Polyester, foam and feather pillows are all washable, but make sure they are absolutely dry before using them. Regularly air them between washes.
- Depending on their size, pillows can be washed in a washing machine on a warm, gentle cycle with reduced spin.

■ ■ ■ **If you shake and fold** bed linen as you take it down from the line, it will NOT NEED IRONING.

Besides containing potentially harmful chemicals, commercial fabric conditioner reduces the absorbency of towels and tea towels, even though they feel softer.

- You can also wash pillows by hand in soapy water or with wool wash. Rinse several times and dry flat outside in the shade, turning over and shaking frequently.
- Air doonas outside once a week.
- Most doonas – whether filled with feathers, polyester, cotton, wool or a combination – can be washed. Check the care label for precise instructions.
- To wash a doona, knead it in warm, soapy water (or use wool wash) in the bath. Rinse well in several changes of water.
- It's better not to wring, spin-dry or line-dry a doona. To keep the filling evenly distributed, squeeze out as much water as you can and dry the doona flat on the grass (on an old sheet), turning and shaking it frequently.
- If necessary, fluff up pillows and doonas in the tumble-dryer for about 10 minutes. For doonas, add 2 or 3 clean tennis balls to the drum to help break up the feathers.

SAFE STAIN REMOVAL

Try one of these gentler alternatives to harsh chlorine bleach.

- Lemon juice can remove stubborn stains, including rust. And don't forget that the sun can whiten and brighten whites.
- Hydrogen peroxide breaks down into oxygen and water and is a much milder chemical bleach than chlorine. It can be used safely on most fabrics. Use it in moderation.
- To remove lipstick from napkins and collars, dab with eucalyptus oil until the lipstick disappears, then wash as usual.
- Remove brown stains from stored table linen by rubbing them with a paste of bicarbonate of soda and lemon juice before washing.
- Sponge a tomato sauce stain with cold water, then rub in a little vegetable glycerine. Leave for half an hour, then wash the garment as usual.

BRIGHTER WHITES

Instead of buying off-the-shelf laundry products with chlorine bleaches and fluorescers, try some of these tips to brighten up your whites.

- Add 1 cup each methylated spirits and cloudy ammonia to the washing water to help dissolve and lift off settled dirt.
- Add ½ cup borax to the machine wash. Borax is active only at temperatures above 60°C, so it must be used in hot water.
- Use old-fashioned washing blue in the final rinse to whiten your whites. Made from the pigment indigo, washing blue creates an optical illusion that makes white fabric look whiter.
- Washing white bed linen with blue towels has a similar bluing effect.

EUCALYPTUS WOOL WASH

This recipe has been used to wash wool for generations. It's ideal for blankets, quilts and pillows. The eucalyptus oil helps to keep the wool soft and also repels moths.

2 cups soap flakes
½ cup methylated spirits
25 ml eucalyptus oil

- Add all the ingredients together in a wide-mouthed jar and shake until combined.
- Use 2 tbsp wool wash per litre of warm water, then rinse.

Add vinegar to the final rinse to keep face washers fresh and sanitised.

Tackling stains the natural way

Stains are inevitable but there's no need to resort to harsh chemicals to deal with them. There are two simple tricks to successful stain removal: the first is to keep a natural stain removal kit on hand and the second is to act quickly. Sometimes you may not need anything more than nature's greatest solvent – water.

TEN RULES FOR STAIN REMOVAL

1 Take immediate action. The faster you act, the better your chances of completely removing the stain.

2 Mop up the excess. Try to blot up as much of a spill as possible with a clean rag or paper towel. Lift off solids with a knife blade.

3 Don't let the stain dry out. If you can't deal with it straight away, sponge the stain with cold water, spray it with soda water or cover it with a damp towel.

4 Re-lubricate a dry stain. If a stain does dry (or you find an old one), rub it with vegetable glycerine before removing it.

5 Don't use hot water. It 'sets' many stains, making them much more difficult to remove. Always use cold or tepid water when you first tackle a stain.

6 Start with the gentlest approach. Quite often all you need for removing a stain is soda water or a soapy solution.

7 Always move from the outside in. To avoid leaving a ring, start from the outer edge of a stain and work towards the centre.

8 Don't scrub at a stain. Instead, place an absorbent pad beneath the stain and dab it with the remover solution, forcing it through the fibres. Make sure you change the pad frequently.

9 Work from the back of the fabric to the front. If possible, place the absorbent pad on the stain itself on the right side of the fabric and apply stain remover from the wrong side of the fabric.

10 More is not necessarily better. If a cleaner is not working, don't increase the strength of the solution. Rinse it away, and try something else.

NATURAL STAIN REMOVER KIT

From the supermarket:

- ✔ Bicarbonate of soda (baking soda)
- ✔ Borax
- ✔ Cloudy ammonia
- ✔ Cream of tartar
- ✔ Eucalyptus oil
- ✔ Lemon juice
- ✔ Methylated spirits
- ✔ Phosphate-free, colourless dishwashing liquid
- ✔ Pure soap or soap flakes
- ✔ Salt
- ✔ Soda water
- ✔ Washing soda (sodium carbonate)
- ✔ White vinegar

From the health food shop:

- ✔ Vegetable glycerine

From the chemist:

- ✔ Epsom salts
- ✔ Hydrogen peroxide

QUICK FIXES

When you're away from home and disaster strikes, one of the following tricks might get you out of trouble.

- If possible, sponge with cold water immediately.
- Pour on a little soda or mineral water, then mop up the excess.
- Cover a fruit or wine stain with salt to absorb some of the liquid.
- Sprinkle a grease stain with flour or cornflour.
- Place a slice of wet bread over a beetroot stain.
- Tip white wine onto a red wine stain, then blot.

■ ■ ■ **To remove** plant sap from fabric, rub the stain with EUCALYPTUS OIL until the stain disappears, then launder as usual.

Stain removal at a glance

Stain	Treat with	What to do
Ballpoint pen	Eucalyptus oil, methylated spirits	Sponge with a cloth dipped in eucalyptus oil or methylated spirits.
Beer, beetroot	Borax, water	Dab with, or soak in, a solution of 2 tbsp borax per 500 ml water.
Berries	White vinegar, lemon juice	Rub with vinegar or juice. Leave for an hour or two, then launder.
Blood (new)	Cold water, salt	Soak in cold water. Add a handful of salt for stubborn stains.
Blood (old)	Vegetable glycerine, cold water	Rub with glycerine to soften, then proceed as for new blood.
Chocolate, coffee	Borax, water	Dab with, or soak in, a solution of 2 tbsp borax per 500 ml water.
Cosmetics	Cloudy ammonia, water	Dab with a solution of 1 part cloudy ammonia per 3 parts water.
Egg, fruit juice	Borax, cold water (not hot)	Dab with, or soak in, a solution of 2 tbsp borax per 500 ml water.
Grass	Water, sugar, eucalyptus oil	Dampen stain with water and sprinkle with sugar. Roll up, leave for 1 hour, then launder. Rub stubborn stains with eucalyptus oil.
Grease, oil	Cornflour, washing soda, eucalyptus oil	Sprinkle spot with cornflour. Place stain between several layers of paper towel and iron gently. Repeat if necessary. Soak stubborn stains in water with 1 tbsp washing soda and 1 tsp eucalyptus oil.
Mildew, mould	Cream of tartar, lemon juice, hydrogen peroxide	Cover spots with a paste of cream of tartar and lemon juice. Leave until dry, then brush off and launder. Or dab spot with a 3 per cent solution of hydrogen peroxide.
Milk	Water, soap, vinegar	Rinse immediately in soapy water, then soak in water with a dash of vinegar for 10 minutes. Rinse.
Nail polish	Methylated spirits	Dab quickly with a damp cloth, then sponge with spirits.
Rust	Salt, lemon juice	Mix salt and lemon juice to make a paste. Rub into stain, leave 10–20 minutes, then rinse out.
Scorch mark	Vegetable glycerine, borax	Cover the mark with a mix of vegetable glycerine and borax. Leave to dry, then brush.
Shoe polish	Eucalyptus oil, methylated spirits	Place stain on absorbent pad and dab with oil or spirits, moving pad frequently so that the stain is over a clean spot.
Soft drink, tea	Borax, warm water	Dab with, or soak in, a solution of 2 tbsp borax per 500 ml water.
Turmeric (curry)	Hydrogen peroxide (3 per cent)	Dab stain with neat hydrogen peroxide.
Vomit	Borax, water, eucalyptus oil	Scrape up solids. Dab or soak in a solution of 2 tbsp borax per 500 ml water, with a few drops of eucalyptus oil.
Wine, red	Soda water, borax, water	Apply soda water immediately. If stain persists, soak in a solution of 2 tbsp borax per 500 ml water.
Wine, white	Soda water	Apply soda water immediately, then launder as usual.

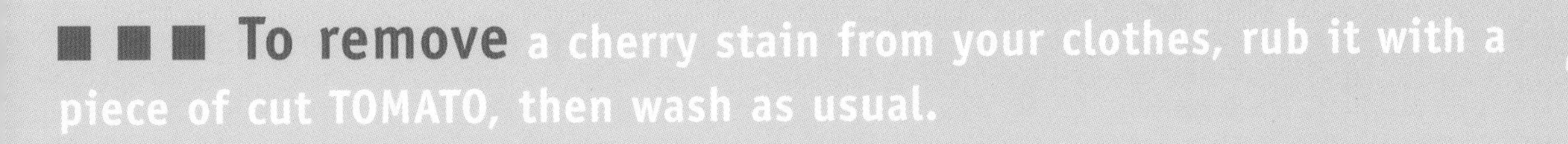

■ ■ ■ **To remove** a cherry stain from your clothes, rub it with a piece of cut TOMATO, then wash as usual.

Caring for furniture

With some basic precautions and a little care, good furniture can last for many years. Regular maintenance with gentle cleaners and conditioners such as beeswax, vinegar and pure soap can bring new life to well-used furniture and preserve its natural sheen.

EIGHT TIPS FOR WOOD

1 Wooden furniture (and upholstered pieces too) will last longer if they are kept out of direct sunlight. Ultraviolet rays bleach and damage both wood and fabric.

2 Avoid placing good furniture in very damp or very dry places, or near hot fires, heating vents or radiators. With high moisture levels wood expands, but as the atmosphere becomes less humid, wood may develop cracks. Cracking may also occur in very dry or hot conditions.

3 Protect wooden surfaces from heat and spills with coasters, tablemats and heat pads. To remove cigarette burns, try rubbing with some toothpaste.

4 Start any cleaning routine with dusting, using a slightly damp cloth. If you apply polish to dusty wood, you will simply grind in the dirt and you may damage the surface.

5 Clean wood, if necessary, with a mild soap and water. For unfinished wood or finishes other than polyurethane, use the suds only on a barely damp sponge or cloth. This avoids overwetting.

6 To clean and condition unfinished and lightly finished surfaces, try a simple polish made from equal amounts of olive (or linseed) oil and white vinegar mixed with a few drops of essential oil. Apply it with a soft cloth.

7 To clean raw pine, always use cold water and soap, as hot water can turn it yellow. To remove grease spots, rub with fine-grade sandpaper and wipe with a damp cloth.

8 A French-polish finish is susceptible to damage by heat and all solvents, including water. Wipe the surface carefully with a barely damp cloth. If it needs waxing, use only pure, softened beeswax, working in the direction of the grain.

THE TRUTH ABOUT...

FURNITURE POLISH

Commercial polishes and waxes may contain ingredients such as phenol, nitrobenzene or petroleum distillates. These substances are highly flammable and are also harmful when inhaled or ingested or if they come in contact with the skin. Normally remaining in the environment for only a few days, they may persist for longer when released in larger amounts or over an extended period. Some polishes also contain fine abrasive materials, which can wear away a finish over time.

BE WAX WISE

Wax protects and nourishes unfinished or lightly finished wood as well as fills in fine scratches and gives wood a soft sheen.

- ✔ Always dust and clean before waxing, otherwise you'll seal in the dirt.
- ✔ Choose a solid wax based on beeswax (or make your own).
- ✔ Allow wax to dry before giving the surface a good buff with a soft cloth.
- ✘ Avoid cream waxes, which contain solvents that can soften and remove lower layers of wax.

■ ■ ■ **To banish musty smells,** sprinkle upholstery with bicarbonate of soda, then vacuum up after an hour or two.

~ STAR SAVER ~

To extend the life of a sagging cane seat, upturn the chair and cover the seat bottom with a towel wrung out in a solution of 1 cup salt dissolved in 1 cup boiling water. Leave for about 30 minutes. As it dries, the cane will shrink and tighten. Don't sit on it for 24 hours.

QUICK FIXES

It's surprisingly easy to fix or disguise minor blemishes in wooden furniture using materials you have to hand. And it costs next to nothing.

- To remove white water stains, apply a little toothpaste, fine wood ash or smooth peanut butter with a damp cloth. Rub in the direction of the grain, or try rubbing the mark with half a walnut or pecan nut. Finish with polish.
- Hide a scratch by dabbing it with iodine (for mahogany and dark wood), instant coffee dissolved in vegetable oil, or a wax crayon in a similar colour to the wood.
- Saturate a dried paint spot with linseed oil until it softens, then gently lift it off with a knife blade.
- Cover a shallow dent with several layers of damp paper towel, then carefully iron the towels until dry. This causes the wood fibres to swell and fill the dent. Try this method on a wooden floor too.

NATURAL FIBRES

- To keep wicker, cane and bamboo furniture looking good, regularly dust it or, better still, vacuum it with the brush attachment.
- A damp, soapy cloth will remove most surface dirt. Add washing soda for extra cleaning power.

- Untreated cane and wicker enjoy an annual moisturising treatment. In the shade, spray the furniture lightly with a garden hose, scrubbing with a soft brush if necessary. Leave outdoors to dry thoroughly.
- Try scrubbing bamboo with a solution of warm soapy water mixed with a little borax. Rinse in salt water and dry well.
- Rub cleaned and dried furniture with a little linseed or citrus oil. This is especially important for moisturising natural, unfinished fibres which are prone to drying out.

FABRIC AND LEATHER

- To keep upholstery dust-free, vacuum it regularly. Dusty furniture eventually becomes dirty.
- Clean fabric without over-wetting it. Using an electric beater, combine 1 part mild detergent with 4 parts warm water. Brush the foam only onto dirty areas or stains. Blot dry with a clean, white cloth.
- To remove tea, coffee and red wine stains, sponge fabric with a solution of 4 tablespoons borax dissolved in 600 ml water. Blot with a paper towel pad.
- Clean very dirty or stained leather with a solution of 1 tablespoon vinegar to ½ bucket warm water and dry thoroughly with a soft towel. Or work saddle soap (from saddleries and hardware stores) into a rich lather, then buff with a soft cloth.
- Polish and nourish leather by rubbing with a mixture of 1 part vinegar to 2 parts linseed oil. Buff to a gentle shine with a soft cloth.

HOME-MADE FURNITURE POLISH

125 g beeswax, grated
500 ml raw linseed oil (for dark wood) or olive oil (for pale wood)
1 tsp lavender or rosemary essential oil

- Melt the wax in a heat-proof bowl over a saucepan of simmering water.
- Carefully add the oil and stir over heat for 3 minutes.
- Remove from the heat and stir in essential oil.
- Transfer to a clean jar and allow to set.
- Using a soft cloth, rub sparingly into the wood, leave for 30 minutes, and then polish off.

■ ■ ■ **Remove grease spots** on leather furniture by rubbing them with EUCALYPTUS OIL, then finish with polish.

Caring for glass, metals and ceramics

Commercial metal and glass cleaners are often chemical cocktails, containing a range of potentially harmful ingredients that can be inhaled or come in contact with the skin. It's not worth taking the risk. Common natural substances such as lemon juice and salt come into their own in the care of glass, metals and ceramics.

SPARKLING GLASS

- One of the simplest and least toxic ways to clean mirror and window glass is to spray it with plain soda water, then polish dry.
- Vinegar and water will clean most windows. Add a little detergent, if you're still getting streaks.
- Wipe a glass tabletop with lemon juice, then polish it with a soft, lint-free cloth.
- Remove scratch marks with toothpaste. Work to and fro with a clean cloth.
- When washing glassware, add a little lemon juice or vinegar to the rinse water to add extra sparkle.
- Hand wash glasses in hot water with pure soap. To avoid streaking, rinse and dry straight away. Hold stem-ware by the bowl and not by the more fragile stem.

For fragrant home-made cleaners, add a few drops of essential oil, which is less allergenic than synthetic perfume.

MAKING YOUR METAL SHINE

ALUMINIUM

Aluminium is a hard-wearing metal, but is vulnerable to alkaline cleansers, such as chlorine bleach, washing soda and bicarbonate of soda, which all cause staining and pitting.

- Don't leave food to stand or soak in an aluminium saucepan, as this will pit the surface irreparably. (Refer to page 284 for health concerns about aluminium.)
- To avoid staining, never wash aluminium saucepans and cake tins in the dishwasher.
- To loosen burnt-on food in an aluminium pan, try boiling an onion in it.

BRASS AND COPPER

Many brass and copper items are sold with a protective lacquer coating. Simply wash these with soapy water. The following methods are for uncoated items.

- A paste of salt and lemon juice is a good basic cleaner for both brass and copper. First, rub it in, then rinse well.
- For stubborn marks on brass, try rubbing the stain with white tooth-paste and a couple of drops of olive oil, then rinse with warm water before polishing dry.
- Don't scour copper cookware. To remove poisonous green stains, clean with a solution of 1 part salt and 2 parts white vinegar. Rinse, dry and polish.

THE TRUTH ABOUT...

GLASS AND METAL CLEANERS

Most commercial window cleaners contain ammonia, alcohol and detergents. Some have butyl cellosolve, a chemical that is readily absorbed through the skin and can cause health problems. Metal polishes may contain abrasives such as pumice, as well as volatile and harmful substances such as solvents, kerosene and white spirits. It is considerably less toxic, cheaper and just as effective to make your own cleaners.

■ ■ ■ Clean stained, streaky or dirty glass by rubbing with a paste of 1 part vinegar to 1 part salt.

TOP TIP

To clean a narrow-necked glass vase or decanter, add a mixture of rock salt and vinegar, crushed egg shells and vinegar, or tea leaves and vinegar. Swirl around and stand for several hours if necessary. Rinse well.

MAKE YOUR OWN METAL POLISHES

ALL-PURPOSE POLISH

Try this inexpensive polish to clean brass, copper, bronze, pewter and stainless steel.

salt
plain flour
white vinegar

- Combine equal parts of salt and flour, then add enough vinegar to make a stiff paste.
- Apply sparingly to metal items, then allow to dry for 1–2 hours.
- Rinse off and polish thoroughly with a soft cloth.
- Take care not to use too much polish, as this may wear away the details of raised designs.

BRASS CLEANER

This low-toxicity cleaner is suitable for deeply tarnished or intricately etched brass items. Citric acid is available at supermarkets.

25 g citric acid
3 litres hot water

- Dissolve the citric acid in hot water in a large pot or the kitchen sink.
- Place the pieces of brass in the solution and leave to soak for 5 minutes.
- Scrub gently with an old toothbrush, then rinse and dry.

BRONZE

- Don't wash bronze, but do dust it regularly. Polish from time to time with a cloth dipped in linseed oil, then buff with a soft cloth.

CAST IRON

- To remove rust from cast iron, rub with fine sandpaper or steel wool, make sure that it is dry, and then wipe with vegetable oil.
- Always wash seasoned, cast-iron cookware by hand. Dry immediately and wipe over with vegetable oil to prevent rusting.

CHROME

- Clean chrome with a damp sponge sprinkled with bicarbonate of soda. Cider vinegar is also effective.

PEWTER

- Remove dirt and grime from pewter by washing in a solution of warm water and dishwashing liquid.
- For stubborn dirt on pewter, mix finely powdered whiting (from a hardware store) with a little vegetable oil and rub over with a soft cloth. Polish with a clean cloth.

STAINLESS STEEL

- Soak dingy stainless steel cutlery for 10 minutes in a sinkful of boiling water with 3 tablespoons bicarbonate of soda. It will sparkle.

CERAMICS

- Remove baked-on food from glazed earthenware by soaking it in hot, soapy water, then scraping gently with a plastic scourer.
- Wash unglazed earthenware in hot water only. Detergent will leach into the clay pores and then into your food the next time you cook.
- Soak unglazed pots with stubborn stains or baked-on food in water with 1–4 tablespoons bicarbonate of soda added. Do not scour.
- Remove tannin stains from a teapot by filling it with 1 part bicarbonate of soda to 2 parts hot water. Leave to stand overnight. Rinse thoroughly and dry.
- To remove tea stains from china, rub with crushed salt on a soft cloth.

Saucepan cleaner

Try this simple recipe to clean and brighten your aluminium saucepans. Apple or citrus peel can be substituted for vinegar.

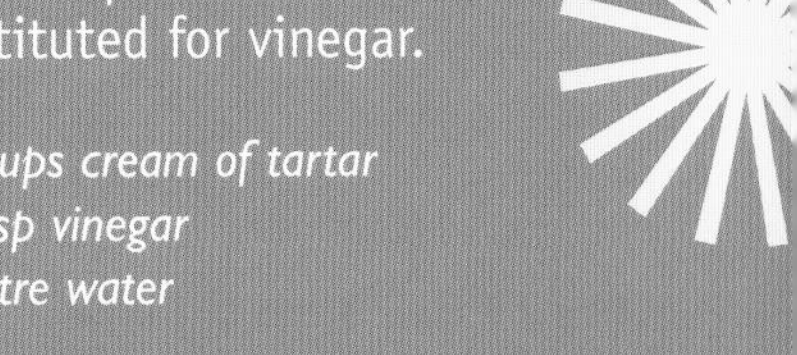

2 cups cream of tartar
2 tsp vinegar
1 litre water

Add cream of tartar and vinegar to water and boil for 10 minutes.

■ ■ ■ **Buttermilk will clean copper.** Wipe it on, leave for 10 minutes and then wipe it off.

Caring for valuables

Whether for sentimental or financial reasons, it makes sense to look after your valuables, and you can do so by taking a little care and without resorting to chemical cleaners. Detergents, hair spray, perfume, sunlight and water can all spell disaster for some delicate items. When in doubt, ask an expert.

POLISHING SILVER

- White toothpaste and a little olive oil makes a good polish for items that can't be immersed, but don't rub too hard or you'll wear away the silver coating.
- Try making your own earth-wise silver polish by combining equal parts of whiting (powdered chalk, available from hardware stores), cloudy ammonia, methylated spirits and water.
- Use an old shaving or stencil brush to work the polish into the crevices on finely patterned or filigree silver. Cover the bristles with a soft cloth to polish off.
- Don't wash bone or ivory handles in hot water. It accelerates the natural yellowing process.
- To whiten bone or ivory handles or remove stains from them, make a paste with a little lemon juice and salt, rub into the handles, rinse in tepid water and dry.

SHINING JEWELS

You may prefer to take special pieces to a jeweller for cleaning. When cleaning at home, make sure you do so in a bowl, not under the tap – don't risk seeing a family heirloom disappear down the plughole.

- Keep precious pieces in top condition by storing separately to avoid tangles or the scratching that may occur when gemstones of different hardness touch one other.
- Unless you're sure what a piece of jewellery is made of and what it should be cleaned with, avoid using water, detergent, bicarbonate of soda, ammonia and commercial cloths and dips. Amber, bone, coral, ivory, lapis lazuli, malachite, opal, shells or turquoise should never be washed, although wiping with a damp cloth will not harm them.
- A gentle brushing with white toothpaste and an old soft toothbrush will remove film and grime from a diamond. Rinse in warm water and dry with a lint-free soft cloth.
- Make a cleaning solution for gold and silver jewellery set with hard stones, such as diamonds, sapphires and rubies (but not pearls), by mixing equal parts of water and cloudy ammonia in a jar. Soak jewellery for 30 minutes, scrubbing crevices with an old soft toothbrush. Rinse and dry with a soft cloth.

CHINA AND CRYSTAL

- Always wash fragile, antique or gilded china and crystal in warm, soapy water.
- Delicate items should be wiped with a dishcloth or soft sponge only (not a brush) to prevent scratching.

Easy silver cleaning

Like many 'old-fashioned' remedies, this silver-cleaning method has a sound scientific basis: it relies on a process called galvanic coupling, which takes place between the two metals.

a couple of sheets of aluminium foil
1 tbsp salt
1 tbsp bicarbonate of soda

- Line the bottom of a non-metal bucket or large bowl with a couple of sheets of aluminium foil. Add the salt and bicarbonate of soda to the bucket or bowl. Fill with boiling water.
- Immerse washable silver articles (sterling or plated) in the solution and allow to soak for an hour or two (the foil will get darker).
- Remove the silverware, rinse and dry thoroughly to restore its shine.

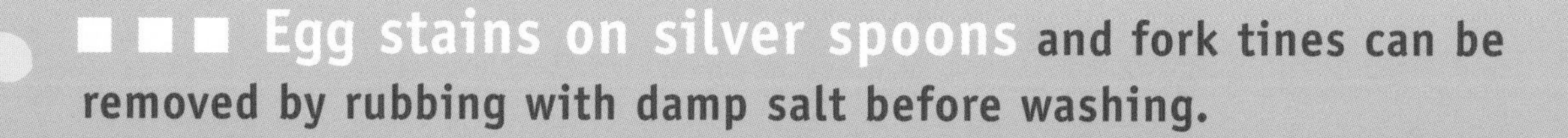

KEEPING PEARLS LUSTROUS

Cultured pearls owe their unique lustre to the nacre coating that forms around a bead inserted into a clam or oyster.

- ✔ After wearing, wipe the pearls with a chamois to remove any traces of perspiration. Perspiration is acidic and can damage the surface of pearls.
- ✔ To avoid damaging the nacre coating, apply perfume and hair spray before you put on your pearl necklace, and always remove a pearl ring before using hand or body lotion.
- ✔ Wash very dirty pearls in mild soapy water with a soft cloth. Spread on a moist cloth to air-dry gradually.
- ✔ Pearls prefer a little moisture, so dampen them with salty water from time to time and allow to air-dry.
- ✘ To preserve their patina, never clean pearls with solutions containing ammonia or detergents, and avoid abrasive cleaners.
- ✘ Don't wrap pearls in cotton or wool, as these materials may cause the pearls to dry out and crack.

To keep silver cutlery in tip-top condition, hand wash in warm, soapy water, then rinse and dry immediately to avoid tarnishing.

WARNING!

▼ Dampness may damage artworks hung in bathrooms or kitchens, and bright sunlight is likely to fade them.

- Wash, or at least rinse, delicate china as soon as possible after use to prevent damage to the glaze.
- Rinse crystal in clean, hot water with ¼ cup white vinegar added and air-dry upside down on a rack.
- To clean a red wine stain from a crystal decanter, put 2 teaspoons each bicarbonate of soda and cream of tartar into the decanter with 1 cup tepid water and shake well. Empty, then add more warm water with a little cloudy ammonia. Shake, empty and rinse well.
- To remove the hairline cracks that sometimes appear in the glaze on fine china, soak the item overnight in warm milk, then hand wash.

BOOKS AND PICTURES

- Dust books at least once a year, using a heavy make-up brush on the closed pages.
- Open books regularly to reduce dampness and prevent dust from setting too deep.
- To rid a book of a musty smell, try storing it in a paper bag filled with crumpled newspaper.
- Gently clean leather book covers with a damp cloth. Use vegetable oil only if absolutely necessary, as it tends to darken the cover and encourage mould.
- Keep paintings and prints away from humidity, sudden changes of temperature and too much light.
- Clean unpainted wooden picture frames with a soft cloth dipped in linseed oil.
- Clean painted frames with a cloth moistened with a mild soap solution.
- Use acid-free paper next to much-loved photographs, and store negatives and old prints out of sunlight, at an even temperature.
- Lie heavy books flat to prevent pages tearing away from the spine.
- Use book ends to prevent books from slumping against each other and becoming distorted.
- To prevent pictures fading, replace ordinary glass with ultra-violet treated glass. Though more expensive, it ensures longer life.

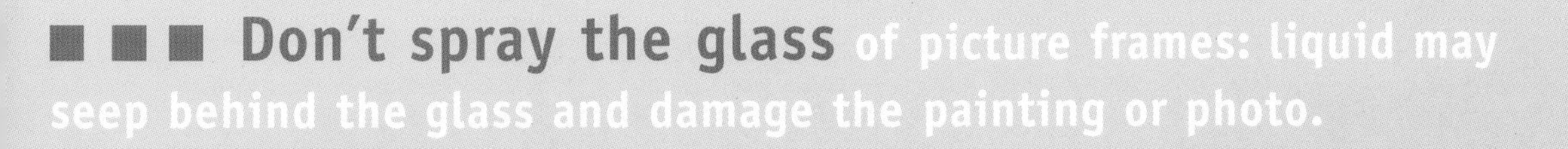

■ ■ ■ **Don't spray the glass** of picture frames: liquid may seep behind the glass and damage the painting or photo.

Clearing the air

Most of us think of our home as a refuge from environmental problems, so it may come as a surprise to learn that the air inside our home is often two to three times more polluted than outdoors. The causes of indoor air pollution are many and varied, but sensible household management can minimise the effects.

KEEPING FUMES OUT

Burning fuels and any other materials indoors can release potentially dangerous gases, including nitrogen dioxide, which can irritate the eyes and throat, and carbon monoxide, which in low doses can cause headaches and fatigue, and in high doses can be fatal.

- Do not smoke cigarettes, cigars or pipes indoors. Not only are they bad for your health but they also release hundreds of toxins into the air, including benzene, which is a potential carcinogen.
- Choose heaters and stoves that are flued. If you have unflued heaters of any kind, ensure adequate ventilation. Children exposed to unflued gas appliances are more likely to get chest colds.
- Make sure heaters and stovetops are kept in good condition. If a gas flame burns yellow, it may be emitting dangerous gases, including carbon monoxide. Have the appliance serviced at once.
- Check chimneys and flues regularly for blockages and leaks.
- Make sure doors on wood-fired stoves close tightly.
- If your garage is joined to your home, make sure there is an air lock or air-tight door between house and garage. Motor vehicle exhaust fumes contain carbon monoxide and benzene.

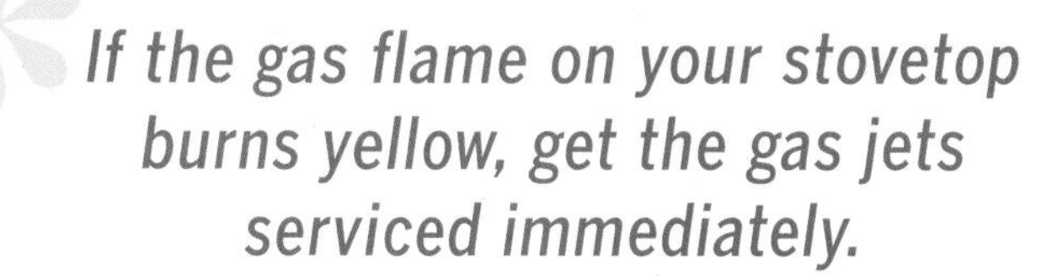

If the gas flame on your stovetop burns yellow, get the gas jets serviced immediately.

WHAT WE CAN'T SEE

Many household products, from paints and varnishes to furniture and carpets, emit chemical gases. Simple precautions will minimise your exposure.

- Try not to buy furniture made of wood composites, such as particleboard, fibreboard or plywood, as these are often made with volatile organic compounds (VOCs). Alternatively, seal with non-toxic varnish to prevent fumes escaping, or store in a well-ventilated spot for a week before installing indoors.

THE TRUTH ABOUT...

VOLATILE ORGANIC COMPOUNDS

Used in the production of many household items, volatile organic compounds, or VOCs, continue to evaporate, or 'off-gas', at room temperature for years. Many are toxic and their emissions can cause a range of ailments, from eye irritation to fatigue and dizziness; some, such as benzene and formaldehyde, are potentially carcinogenic. A number of countries have developed labelling programs that indicate emission levels from consumer products, but no such program exists in Australia or New Zealand. Identifying safer products is therefore extremely difficult, and the best strategy is to buy untreated natural materials whenever possible.

■ ■ ■ If you need a carpet, select NATURAL FIBRES and ask the fitter to use mechanical methods rather than adhesives.

Causes of indoor chemical pollution

Category	Sources	Dangers	Solutions
Asbestos	Fibro panels, asbestos roofing and guttering	Airborne dust causes serious respiratory diseases including lung cancer.	Seal asbestos materials or have them removed by a specialist.
Brominated flame retardants	Carpets, soft furnishings, televisions, computers	PBDEs (polybrominated diphenyl ethers) can interfere with thyroid hormones and cause foetal damage.	Seek out products made without brominated flame retardants.
Cleaning products	Detergents, floor cleaners, oven cleaners, chlorine, bleaches, etc.	Petrochemicals and other toxins can damage immune system and brain.	Use simple but effective substances such as bicarbonate of soda and vinegar; buy plant-based products.
Combustion gases	Use of unflued heaters, fireplaces and, to a much lesser extent, gas cookers	Toxic fumes irritate airways, exacerbate asthma and sinus problems.	Use flued or electric appliances, or ensure adequate ventilation when using unflued devices.
Lead	Dust from old lead paint, contaminated water from lead-soldered pipes	Low-level poisoning causes learning difficulties; more severe poisoning can damage kidneys and brain.	Seal suspect paint or have it removed by a specialist; filter suspect water.
Pesticides	Pest extermination treatments, pest sprays and strips	Some can affect the nervous system, some are carcinogens, others are endocrine disruptors.	Use non-chemical barriers (screens, nets) and/or plant-based insecticides (such as pyrethrum).
Solvents	Paints, glues, cleaning products, pesticides, marker pens, etc.	Linked to allergies, asthma, birth defects, brain damage, cancer.	Seek out solvent-free alternatives; use solvent-based products in well-ventilated areas, preferably outside.
Tobacco	Smoking of cigarettes, cigars, pipes	Mixture of 2000 substances, including 40 carcinogens. Irritates nose, eyes and throat, exacerbates respiratory problems, causes lung cancer.	Give up smoking; ban smoking inside the home.
VOCs (off-gassing)	Paints, vinyl, carpets, particle-board furniture, stain repellents	Can irritate airways and cause allergies, cancer, damage to nervous system.	Avoid synthetics; use natural materials and plant-based products.

- Select natural materials rather than synthetics. Many synthetic foams and fabrics emit VOCs.
- Use low-toxicity cleaning agents or try products that work without chemicals, such as microfibre cloths.
- Purchase toiletries, cosmetics and perfumes that are free of chemicals and synthetic fragrances.
- Avoid aerosol sprays, including insect repellents and hair sprays, as they emit a fine mist that is easily inhaled. Use roll-on, pump spray or pump products.
- Try not to use perfumes and sprays in rooms where you spend long periods, such as the bedroom.
- If you need to disguise an unpleasant odour, choose a natural alternative to a chemical-based air freshener. Tea-tree oil and eucalyptus oil are effective.
- Choose materials carefully when building, renovating or decorating. Use natural materials and plant-based paints, varnishes and sealants.
- When buying paint, paint stripper, adhesive, fuel or other chemical products, buy only as much as you need, to avoid storing them in the house. If you have to keep such products, put them in a well-ventilated spot, preferably outside.

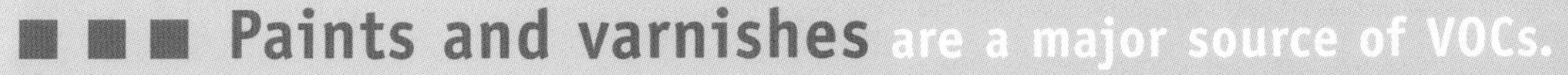

Natural air fresheners

Problem	Solution
Kitchen bins	Clean and deodorise with a solution of 1 tsp lemon juice to 1 litre water.
Outdoor bins	To wash, add a handful of washing soda to 1 litre hot water. Sprinkle with bicarbonate of soda to catch residual odours.
Smelly fridges	Place a small open bowl of bicarbonate of soda on one of the refrigerator shelves and change it regularly.
Smelly toilets	Light a scented candle for a few seconds and it will burn off the offending air-bound molecules. A match will also work.

Tests have shown that house plants can reduce levels of VOCs by between 50 and 70 per cent.

- Make sure you carefully follow the manufacturer's safety and usage instructions when using chemical products, including cleaning agents, paints, varnishes, sealants and adhesives.
- Before removing old paint from a wall or piece of furniture, check it for lead. Used widely up to 1970, lead is known to cause neurological damage, especially in children. If necessary, have a sample tested by your local Occupational Health and Safety department or Environment Protection Authority, or buy a testing kit from a hardware shop. If the paint is in good condition, it is often best to leave it in place; if not, have a specialist remove it.
- Keep any old asbestos boards, tiles or panels in good condition or have them removed by a professional. Airborne asbestos particles can cause a range of lung diseases, including cancer.

BREATHE EASIER

Nature contributes to the mix of pollutants we live with from day to day, in the form of moulds, mildew and fungi, pollen, dust mites, bacteria from pet and pest droppings and saliva and skin particles from pets. All will proliferate in damp conditions and can become airborne. In turn they can trigger asthma, allergies and some serious diseases.

- If dampness is a problem, check your damp course, if you have one, or add a new one. If your house lies on a concrete slab, have the underslab waterproofing checked by a specialist. Sometimes holes appear, allowing moisture into the house. A surface treatment is usually the most effective solution to this problem.
- Keep the subfloor and attic well ventilated to prevent condensation. Think about adding new pressed-metal vents to the subfloor. For the attic, look at using 'whirlybird' ventilators, which use the power of the wind to extract stale air.
- Eliminate any standing water or permanently wet surfaces under or close to the house.
- If your ventilation is not satisfactory, use extractor fans to remove moist air from bathrooms and kitchens. These can also help remove chemical fumes emitted by heaters, stovetops and synthetic furnishings and materials.
- Clean and dry water-damaged carpets and building materials immediately or consider removing them altogether. Damp materials provide an ideal breeding ground for mould and bacteria.
- Make sure humidifiers and airconditioners are always kept clean. Micro-organisms that breed in these places can give rise to significant respiratory

■ ■ ■ Bicarbonate of soda absorbs the molecules we notice as unpleasant smells. Use it as an air freshener.

diseases. Clean evaporation trays in these appliances and in refrigerators regularly.

- Keep pets clean and free of insect infestations (see *Pest-free pets*, p. 126).
- Clean, dust and ventilate your house regularly to minimise pollen, dust mites, and animal skin flakes, droppings and hair. Dust mites do not tolerate hot water or vinegar, so wiping surfaces with a hot vinegar solution is a good way to get rid of them.
- Air beds, bedding and mattresses regularly. Wash bedding in hot water or hang it in the sun for 3 hours to eliminate dust mites, mould and mildew.
- If you or anyone else in your household suffers from allergies or asthma, consider removing carpets and other furnishings that might attract dust mites. Healthier flooring alternatives include hardwood, cork, linoleum or tiled floors.
- Sleep with a window open, if it's convenient and safe. You spend long periods in the bedroom breathing out carbon dioxide and water vapour, so it's a good idea to let fresh air in as often as possible.

hot links

Discover more about indoor air pollution: www.tec.org.au/member/tec/projects/ToxicChemicals/iap1.html; www.epa.gov/iaq/ia-intro.html

Learn about the dangers of household chemicals: www.oztoxics.org/ntn/cis.html; www.rainforestinfo.org.au/good_wood/indr_air.htm

Get information on lead poisoning: www.lead.org.au/fs-index.html

HARMFUL RAYS

Power sources and electrical appliances all create electromagnetic fields (EMFs). Recent research has suggested that these fields could be associated with an increased risk of certain cancers and Alzheimer's disease. To reduce any potential risk:

- Minimise the number of appliances you have on at any one time.
- Don't sit next to appliances for long periods.
- Remove unnecessary appliances from bedrooms or unplug them before you go to sleep, especially any that incorporate a transformer.
- Don't sleep with your head close to a power source or an appliance (keep your alarm clock about a metre from your head, for instance).
- Don't put your bed against a wall if a meter box is on the other side.
- When buying a computer, select a model with an LCD screen. These emit much less radiation than old-fashioned CRT (cathode ray tube) screens, and use much less energy.

Eliminating sources of pollution and ensuring good ventilation are the best ways to improve indoor air quality, but plants can also be used to filter out toxins. Placing three or more in an average-sized room has been shown to reduce levels of VOCs by 50–70 per cent. While the micro-organisms in the potting mix do most of the cleaning, different plants soak up different pollutants, so use a variety. Proven performers include:

DEVIL'S IVY (*Epipremnum pinnatum* 'Aureum') Also known as pothos, this hardy indoor creeper enjoys warm temperatures (15–30°C) and high humidity. In bright light, it should be watered regularly, though overwatering can cause root rot. Poorly maintained plants are susceptible to mealy bug, mites and thrips.

DRACAENA Especially *Dracaena deremensis* 'Janet Craig' and *Dracaena marginata*. Dracaenas grow well indoors, requiring moderate warmth (over 12°C), regular watering and medium to bright light, though the 'Janet Craig' can tolerate low light.

KENTIA PALM (*Howea forsteriana*) A relatively slow-growing, the kentia can tolerate low light and dry conditions – water it when the soil starts to dry out. An occasional spell outdoors in a well-watered, shaded area will help keep it healthy.

PEACE LILY (*pictured*) Especially *Spathiphyllum* 'Petite' and 'Sensation'. These plants grow well in medium light and will cope with airconditioning, but won't tolerate direct sun. Stand them on a tray of moistened pebbles and mist the leaves occasionally to deter two-spotted mites.

QUEENSLAND UMBRELLA TREE (*Schefflera actinophylla* 'Amate') This bushy plant with large leathery leaves should be kept warm (over 13°C) and allowed to dry out a little between waterings. Spray the leaves with warm water and watch for scale insects, two-spotted mites and aphids.

Other plants that have been shown to reduce pollution are bamboo palm, Boston fern, chrysanthemums, gerbera daisy, philodendrons, rubber and spider plants.

WASTE WATCH

Reduce, reuse and recycle: adopt this three-pronged approach and you'll be surprised how much you can save.

Reduce and reuse

Choosing products with little or no packaging is an easy way to reduce what comes into your home and what ends up in landfill. Reusing instead of throwing away makes economic sense – not only that, devising ingenious ways to reuse household items is fun. And whatever you put out for recycling will find its way back to you in other products.

MINIMISING WASTE

- Try to use paper rather than plastic bags when packing fruit and vegetables for weighing.
- Make sure you take reusable bags with you when shopping and refuse plastic carry bags.
- Look for products that have minimum or recyclable packaging, or that come in refillable and/or returnable containers. Some health shops and food cooperatives even encourage customers to bring their own containers.
- Choose reusable products, such as rechargeable batteries, rather than the disposable alternatives.

REUSING MATERIALS

Many items that are normally consigned straight to the garbage can be modified to serve all sorts of useful purposes.

PAPER PRODUCTS

- Roll used giftwrap around empty cardboard tubes to keep it crease-free, ready for the next time you need to wrap a present, or use it to line shelves or drawers.
- Make gift tags by cutting motifs from giftwrap or pictures from old greetings cards and glueing them to cards.
- Open out paper carry bags and decorate with a stamp or potato print to make wrapping paper.
- Clip or staple your scrap paper into notepads to keep by the phone or in the kitchen.
- Make sure you use both sides of the paper in your printer or fax machine before recycling.
- Shred newspaper as mulch for the garden or use it several sheets thick on garden beds as a weed mat.
- Use old newspapers as a lining for your pet's basket or kennel. They can be easily and cheaply replaced.

TURNING OLD INTO NEW

For lots of clever ideas on reusing household items, check the Internet. Here are a few ideas to get you started.

- Running out of skirt hangers? Attach two clothes pegs (hinged) at either end of a coathanger.
- Use polystyrene trays as drip catchers for oily bottles.
- Reuse empty squeeze detergent bottles for storing home-made cleaning products, or to water indoor plants.
- Remove the lids from tin cans and convert the cans into hangers for epiphytes (air plants) or bulbs.

- Make a hole in the lid of an empty coffee tin, pop a ball of string inside and thread the end out through the hole for tangle-free use.
- Small, empty vegetable oil cans can be turned into attractive pots for holding cooking utensils.
- Store items such as photos and receipts in old shoeboxes.
- Cut off the legs of old pantihose and use for securing plants to stakes – they won't cut into the plant stem.
- If you've gathered lots of old pantihose, use them to stuff cushions and toys.
- Use an empty film canister to hold a travel sewing kit.

~ *FLYING START* ~

A worm farm reduces garbage by turning organic waste and paper into nutrient-rich castings for plants. Generally available from a garden centre or your council, a worm farm will fit in a small space in a garage or shed, on a shady balcony or under overhanging eaves. It's a great way to reduce your rubbish immediately.

- Sheets of newspaper are useful for cleaning greasy pans and barbecues, as well as for wrapping food scraps that can't go in the compost.
- Use newspaper instead of plastic bags to line your kitchen garbage bin.

CARTONS, JARS AND CANS

- Use an egg carton or cut-down milk carton with drainage holes cut in the bottom for seed propagation. Once the seedlings are big enough, plant the carton or each detached 'egg cup' directly in the ground. The carton will protect the seedling, then biodegrade and disappear.
- Wash plastic milk and juice containers thoroughly and use them to freeze soups and sauces, or fill with water and freeze to make cooler bricks.
- Use old juice and dairy cartons as peel-away moulds for home-made soap and candles.
- Save glass jars and bottles for preserving, jam making and pickling.
- Refill pretty or unusual-shaped glass bottles with home-made herb oil or vinegar for gifts.
- Keep airtight glass jars for storing herbs, rice, lentils and pulses. These foods benefit from being stored this way and the glass allows you to see at a glance what's inside.

- Use glass jars for holding salad dressings and leftover sauce. It's easier to clean these liquids out of glass than out of plastic.
- Cut the top half off a plastic soft drink bottle to make a handy funnel for the garage or the kitchen.
- Wash out old herb and spice jars and use them for holding small items such as elastic bands, safety pins, paper clips, a little sewing kit, or nails and screws.
- Use small tins to make attractive candle holders for the garden or a city balcony.

CLOTHES AND FABRICS

Clothes, bedding, towels and curtains that have seen better days can still be put to good use or given a new lease of life.

- Save old shirts to wear for gardening or painting.
- Socks that are past darning come in handy as polishing cloths, padding for the ends of ladders and cobweb dusters (fitted over brooms).
- Turn odd socks into hand puppets to amuse young children: just sew on buttons and fabric scraps.
- Cut the legs of well-worn trousers to make gardening shorts.
- Remove the wires from an old electric blanket and use the blanket as an underlay on your bed.
- Sheets that are beyond saving and faded curtains make good drop cloths for decorating.
- Sew discarded curtains into bags for storing good coats, suits and dresses.
- Use fabric scraps for quilting – baby blankets, pot holders or bags.

Canny party lights

clean tins
paper and pencil
adhesive tape
hammer and nail
vice
wire, 0.9 mm (optional)

- Hammer down any sharp edges, then fill the tin with water. Place in the freezer until frozen solid. (The ice will stop the tin collapsing when you hammer into it.)
- Cut a piece of paper to fit around the tin and draw a design of holes on it. Tape the paper around the frozen tin.
- Place the tin in the vice to hold it, then hammer the nail through the design to transfer the pattern to the tin.
- If you're going to want to hang the tin up, make two extra holes in the top for attaching a wire handle.
- Allow the ice to melt, and dry the tin. Place a candle or tea-light inside.

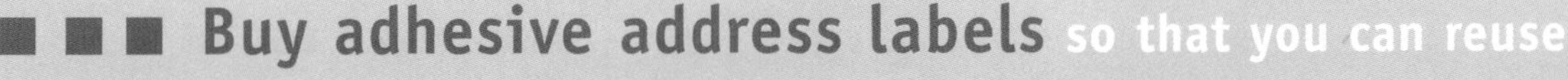

■ ■ ■ **Buy adhesive address labels** so that you can reuse envelopes that are still in good condition.

Recycling

The best kind of recycling is giving things you don't want to someone who really needs them. Next best is making sure waste that can be recycled is separated from regular rubbish ready for kerbside pickup. In Australia and New Zealand about 40 per cent of packaging waste is recycled.

PASS IT ON

Before you toss away old items consider whether you can give them away instead.

- Doctors' and hospital waiting rooms often need magazines and children's toys or books.
- Many charities will take furniture that is in good condition; some will take electrical appliances.
- Many charities use old greetings cards to make new ones, which they then resell.
- Old school textbooks can be donated, via various charities, to children in the developing world.
- Corks from wine bottles are collected by charities, such as Guides Australia, for recycling.
- Beekeepers and people who sell jam at markets or school fetes are always on the lookout for jars.
- Vets and pet shops will often accept newspaper for shredding.
- Charities will accept odd balls of wool that can be knitted into squares to make blankets.
- Old spectacles can be donated to people in need overseas. Ask your optometrist for information.
- Charities collect clothes, bedding and other textiles to sell for funds, distribute to people in need or turn into rags that they sell to industry.
- At least one company shreds old shoes to make athletic mats.

~ STAR SAVER ~

Recycling, or 'reverse garbage', cooperatives operate in a number of Australian states, collecting surplus materials of all kinds from businesses, and reselling them very cheaply. Someone's trash is always someone else's treasure.

SAFE DISPOSAL

Some things cannot be recycled but do require thoughtful disposal to avoid contaminating the environment or harming others.

- Ask your pharmacist how to dispose of out-of-date medicines and other drugs. Do not throw them in the garbage or flush them down the toilet.
- Check with your local council or the Poisons Information Centre before you throw out the miscellaneous old tins and bottles in your garage or garden shed. Many of them will contain hazardous chemicals.
- If you have decided to get rid of all the toxic cleaning products in your laundry and kitchen, don't simply throw them in the garbage. Contact your local council for information on disposal.

SORTING WITH CARE

If unrecyclable items are mixed with recyclable ones, the batch becomes useless, so it's important to sort your recycling carefully. Just a piece of a ceramic cup, for example, can make a tonne of glass unusable.

- Plastic (PET) bottles come in seven different types, numbered 1–7 (see *Getting started*, p. 13). Each council takes a different combination of types, so always check with your council first.
- Take the caps off all bottles.
- Separate rubber bands and plastic wrap from paper.
- Remove the plastic cap and nozzle from steel aerosol cans, but do not attempt to crush them.
- Some councils require you to remove the plastic window from window envelopes before recycling.
- Do not put recyclables in plastic bags.

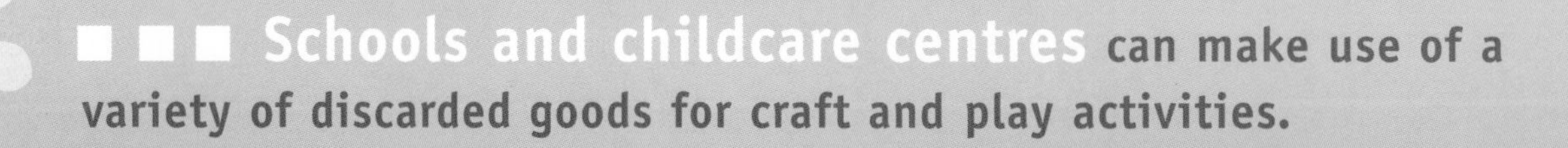

■ ■ ■ **Schools and childcare centres can make use of a variety of discarded goods for craft and play activities.**

HAZARDOUS WASTE

Some items are recyclable but contain heavy metals or toxic chemicals that must be handled with care and disposed of carefully. Find out what can be recycled and how to do it from your council or on the Internet.

- Ask if your council takes car and household batteries for recycling. Many batteries contain heavy metals such as lead, zinc and cadmium. Some retailers recycle batteries.
- Drain used motor oil into a clean container and take it to your local garage or council depot for recycling.
- Find out if paint cans can be included with domestic waste or if they have to be taken to the depot separately.
- Ask at mobile phone shops if they will accept your old mobile phone for recycling.
- Recycle printer and toner cartridges. Some suppliers take back used cartridges, and Planet Ark operates a free collection service in Australia.
- Relatively new computers can be given to charities; older models can be recycled for parts. Consult the Internet.
- White goods and electrical appliances, working or not, are accepted by most councils. Refrigerators need to be disposed of carefully to make sure refrigerant does not leak into the environment.
- Most councils offer information about where you can take a car to be recycled safely.
- Rubber tyres can be recycled into new products. Contact your local council or tyre dealer.
- To recycle scrap metal, check with your council or in the Yellow Pages.

RECYCLING CHECKLIST

Most local governments operate a kerbside recycling service. Many also offer additional disposal services and can supply information about companies that can take the waste that they are unable to deal with. Always check with your own council what they will take. Rinse out bottles, jars, cans and milk cartons before leaving them out.

Can be recycled

- ✔ Glass jars and bottles: remove lids
- ✔ Paper: newspapers, magazines, telephone directories (sometimes there's a special collection), envelopes, computer paper, paper packaging, cardboard, pizza boxes (not accepted by all councils)
- ✔ Steel cans
- ✔ Steel aerosol cans
- ✔ Steel jam jar lids
- ✔ Metal bottle tops
- ✔ Aluminium cans
- ✔ Aluminium foil (not accepted by all councils)
- ✔ Milk and fruit juice cartons (not accepted by all councils)
- ✔ PET plastics: check which types your council accepts; remove lids
- ✔ Green waste: but use in compost or worm farm first

Cannot be recycled

- ✗ Plastic bags (some large supermarkets provide bins to collect these for recycling)
- ✗ Oven-proof, window or mirror glass
- ✗ Food wrappers
- ✗ Facial tissues
- ✗ Polystyrene food or beverage containers
- ✗ Wax-coated cardboard
- ✗ Cellophane and foil giftwrap
- ✗ Plastic-covered paper
- ✗ Drinking glasses
- ✗ Light bulbs
- ✗ Ceramics

hot links

Guide to recycling in your local area:
www.recyclingnearyou.com.au
www.reducerubbish.govt.nz/regional-pages/index.html
How to recycle used vehicle oil:
www.oilrecycling.gov.au
Safe disposal of out-of-date and unwanted medicines: www.returnmed.com.au
Recycling symbols:
www.resource.nsw.gov.au/signs/main.htm
www.ronz.org.nz/nz_recycling_symbols/index.html

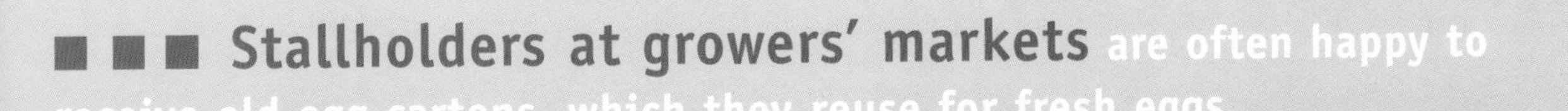

As good as new

There's often no need to buy replacements for worn but otherwise useful items. You can breathe new life into old furniture or fabrics at little or no expense, and exercise your creative skills as well. With a few simple techniques, you can save a favourite piece from the scrap heap or revive junk shop bargains.

WOODEN TREASURES

- To brighten a dulled lacquer or varnish finish, mix a little traditional white, non-gel toothpaste with water and rub it on with a cloth.
- You can remove old French polish (shellac) with methylated spirits and elbow grease.
- When dismantling furniture, always use a spare piece of wood to cushion any hammering. If you hammer the furniture directly you may split or bruise the wood.
- If you have a drawer that sticks, check for worn parts and sand swollen sides. If that doesn't work, rub all sliding parts with candle wax.
- Dismantle loose drawers and reglue them. Undo screws and tap the joints apart. Dab hot vinegar on the separated joints to loosen and remove old glue.
- To fix blistered veneer, cut with a razor knife, slide wood glue underneath with a palette knife and press the veneer back into place. Cover with greaseproof paper and put a heavy weight on top.
- To make an effective paint stripper, mix a thick paste of washing soda and water. Neutralise the stripped surface with vinegar, then wipe with a damp rag.

WARNING!

▼ Many conventional paint strippers contain methylene chloride and dichloromethane, both likely carcinogens. Use a non-toxic stripper or a hot air gun instead.

Fixing a tear

Sewing up a tear in leather, vinyl or certain heavy fabrics may do more harm than good. Try gluing on a patch instead.

- Use a razor blade to cut a neat circle or square around the rip.
- Glue a backing of similar material behind the hole.
- Trace the hole on paper to use as a pattern.
- Cut the patch from an inside or underside area of the upholstery.
- Carefully glue the patch onto the backing.

METAL MAKEOVERS

- Reuse aluminium foil to rub away pinprick rust spots on chrome furniture and taps. Just crumple into a manageable wad and rub.
- Rub pitted chrome furniture frames with steel wool and methylated spirits to remove rust spots. Polish with a little olive oil.
- Polish painted iron or aluminium furniture with beeswax or carnauba wax to provide extra protection, especially if the furniture is likely to be used outside.
- If old nylon webbing is riveted to an aluminium frame and cannot be removed, consider screwing 12 mm thick Western red cedar slats to the frame over the top instead of replacing the webbing.
- Use scrapers, wire brushes and sandpaper to remove rust from cast iron before priming and repainting.
- To loosen water-based paint, soak the item in boiling water. For oil-based paint, soak overnight in a bucket of water with 250 grams fireplace ash, if you have it.

■ ■ ■ **Avoid paint strippers** altogether by using a hot-air gun to loosen paint before scraping off.

RE-COVER A DIRECTOR'S CHAIR

Brighten up an old director's chair with a new cover and a touch of paint or wood stain. Thick canvas or deckchair fabric is best, as it withstands damp. Clean, stain or paint the chair before replacing the covers.

- Carefully remove the old fabric from the chair with a craft knife, gently easing out the nails and taking care not to damage the wood. If the nails won't come out easily, hammer them in and cut the fabric free.
- Open out the old seat fabric and use it as a pattern to cut out the new seat, allowing an extra 2 cm at the back and front edges for hems.
- Machine the hems and press under a 5-cm allowance at the left and right edges.
- Lay a folded end of fabric on the outside of one rail. Collapse the chair and fix the cover in place with six tacks. Repeat the process on the other side.
- Remove the back support, chiselling out the nails if necessary, and then sliding it off.
- Measure the old back support, adding 5 cm at each side and 2 cm for hems at top and bottom.
- Cut out the new back support to match the size measured and then machine the hems.
- From behind, secure one side of the support on the inside of the back post with four tacks.
- Wind the fabric around the post, pull across the front of the chair and fold around the other back post, securing with tacks.

REVIVING FABRICS

- Try lengthening curtains by inserting coordinated bands of a similar weight fabric or by adding a border at the bottom.
- Turn faded curtains into a set of cushion covers, dyeing them to match your decor.
- A dye bath will rejuvenate towels and bedlinen.
- Extend the life of worn sheets by cutting them in half and resewing them with the threadbare part on the outer edges. Strengthen the edges with binding if necessary.
- Make a felted throw by putting pure wool jumpers from op shops in the washing machine and washing them on a hot cycle until the fabric shrinks and felts. Cut equal-sized squares from this felted fabric (the wool fibres are now so matted that the edges will not unravel) and stitch them together to create a cosy wool throw or bedspread.

Pieces of torn, worn or stained clothing and curtains are great for making a scrap quilt.

DYEING

Using dyes, you can change the colour of most items made of fabric. Remember, loose weaves dye better than close weaves and natural textiles dye more satisfactorily than synthetics.

- Before dyeing, always wash items in the hottest water they can stand. This removes manufacturers' finishes, grease and dirt.
- Hot dyes result in faster colours, but be sure that your fabric can withstand hot water.
- Add a pinch of bicarbonate of soda to a hot dye mixture to help it spread evenly.
- Use cold-water dyes on fine-textured fabric such as silk or muslin.
- Make natural dyes from household and garden items, such as onion skins, turmeric, tea and coffee, berries and flowers. For best effect, most require mordants – chemical fixatives – but these can be toxic and should be handled with care. Explore the Internet or your local library for detailed recipes and instructions.

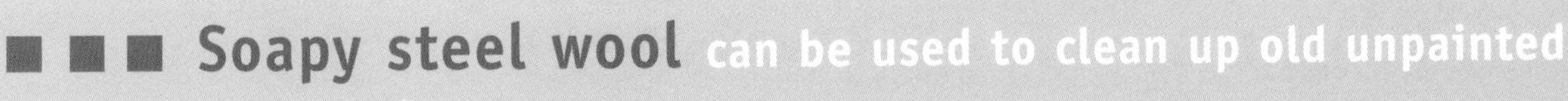

■ ■ ■ **Soapy steel wool** can be used to clean up old unpainted aluminium chair frames.

HOUSEHOLD PESTS

A clean, pest-free home is essential to your family's wellbeing. A little natural know-how can help.

Banish kitchen pests

Ants, cockroaches and pantry moths (weevils) gather in the kitchen because it's warm and has a plentiful food supply, but this is the last place you'd want to use pesticides containing toxic chemicals. Natural alternatives are just as effective and better value too. Always try the least toxic treatments first.

KEEP A CLEAN SHIP

Commonsense is the first line of attack in keeping pests at bay. They can't have a party if there's nothing to eat.

- Keep kitchen benches spotless and train the family to clean up after themselves.
- Transfer everything in the pantry into pest-proof storage containers. Weevils often come home with you from the shops, and leaving unopened packets around not only provides food for the weevils already in your kitchen, but possibly introduces more to your cupboards.
- Keep an eye on use-by dates and use your groceries in date order. Avoid buying too much and doubling up on items you rarely use.
- Wipe up shelf spills and regularly clean cupboards, washing them out with detergent. Add a few drops of pest-repelling oil of cloves to the washing water.
- Even if you find just one weevil egg or grub in a product, throw the whole thing out. (Flours and grains can be composted.)
- To deter weevils, scatter bay leaves or cloves on cupboard shelves and tape them inside container lids.

BASIC KNOW-HOW

- ✔ Block gaps in walls, around pipes and between skirting boards and floors to prevent pests getting in and then breeding.
- ✔ Keep your kitchen garbage bin firmly covered. Empty it frequently.
- ✔ Use sticky traps, baits and fly swats. They harm only the insects that get caught in them and not humans, pets or native animals.
- ✘ Don't leave dirty dishes lying around. Make sure you do the washing-up before you go to bed each night.
- ✘ Don't let loose papers accumulate; keep them in a sealed box.
- ✘ Don't turn out natural predators such as huntsman spiders and daddy-long-legs. They trap and eat flies and other insects.

ANTS

Ants are a nuisance only when they decide to move in, so try to encourage them to leave before taking more drastic measures.

- Avoid leaving uncovered food on kitchen benches.
- Wipe up spills immediately.
- Wipe out the oven and grill pan after you've used them.
- If you can, keep outside garbage bins away from the house.
- Try placing pots of ant-repellent herbs such as mint, pennyroyal, rue or tansy – or dried bunches of these herbs – near trouble spots.
- Consider creating a barrier at the ants' entry points. For example, sprinkle a narrow, unbroken trail of

■ ■ ■ **Spray a trail of ants** with a solution of 2 cups water per 5 ml dishwashing liquid, from a trigger bottle.

Top Tip

Try this effective ant deterrent. Mix equal parts jam and borax, place in jar lids and put in the ants' path. If small children or pets are around, place the bait in empty 300 ml or cut-down milk cartons, tape the tops closed and pierce a few holes around the bottom so the ants can get to the bait.

cayenne pepper, black pepper or salt across their path. Or draw a line with chalk.

- Frequently wipe the windowsill with oil of cloves or eucalyptus oil. Ants dislike these strong odours.
- Dust cracks in cupboards with diatomaceous earth. The tiny sharp particles of this fossilised silica are lethal to crawling insects, but don't affect humans or pets. Use food-grade, not pool-grade, which may irritate your lungs.

COCKROACHES

Don't put out the welcome mat, and try to disturb them regularly so that they don't get too comfortable! Fewer places for them to live means fewer cockroaches.

- To deter newcomers, install good-quality screens on all your doors and windows.
- Make sure you promptly fix leaking taps and pipes – cockroaches love damp, dark, warm places. They will even congregate in the cavity of your dishwasher door!
- Thoroughly clear away all food each night, including any pet food and birdseed.
- Regularly move around loose stored items, such as plastic bags, towels, toiletries and under-sink products because cockroaches love to nest among them.
- Place sticky traps near cockroach breeding areas. Try mixing a low-toxicity bait, such as borax, with sugar or jam in a small lid.
- Rather than using surface sprays, environmentally friendly pest controllers use a heat gun to flush out cockroaches from under cupboards and behind fridges. This burns their wings, causing them to die later.
- To discourage cockroaches, save the ends off cucumbers and place them in cupboards. Other repellents are vanilla beans, dried pyrethrum daisies and pyrethrum dust (from garden centres) – although the latter should be used with caution and strictly according to package instructions.
- Smear the inside of a glass jar with oil, then half fill it with beer. They'll get in, but they won't be able to get out!

Insecticides – what to avoid

Chemicals	How they affect us
Organophosphates: *malathion, parathion, chlorpyrifos, diazinon*	Readily absorbed through skin. Poisoning symptoms include headaches, dizziness and diarrhoea. Tend not to persist in the environment more than a few months.
Carbamates: *aldicarb, carbaryl, bendiocarb, propoxur*	Moderately to highly toxic if swallowed. Some can be absorbed through the skin. Break down quickly in the environment.

Once widely used in pest control, organochlorine insecticides such as aldrin and dieldrin were banned in Australia in 1995 (DDT was banned in 1987). They accumulate in the fatty tissue of animals and cause serious health problems. Today's insecticides are toxic but less persistent in the environment.

USE IN MODERATION

If you need chemical help, here are the least toxic and least persistent options.

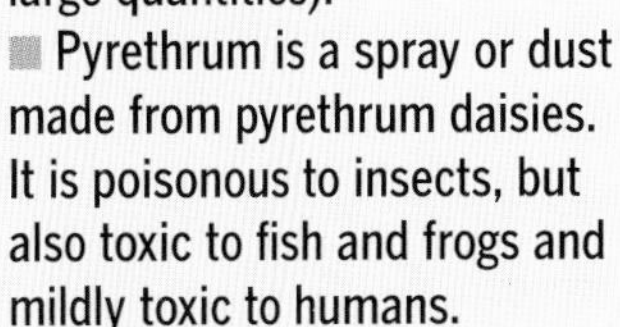

- Borax, a strong alkali, is poisonous to plants and insects (and to humans too, if taken in large quantities).
- Pyrethrum is a spray or dust made from pyrethrum daisies. It is poisonous to insects, but also toxic to fish and frogs and mildly toxic to humans.
- Pyrethroids are a synthetic form of pyrethrum. They are highly toxic to insects and aquatic life, and mildly toxic to mammals. Pyrethroids take longer to break down than natural pyrethrum and should be used only when necessary.

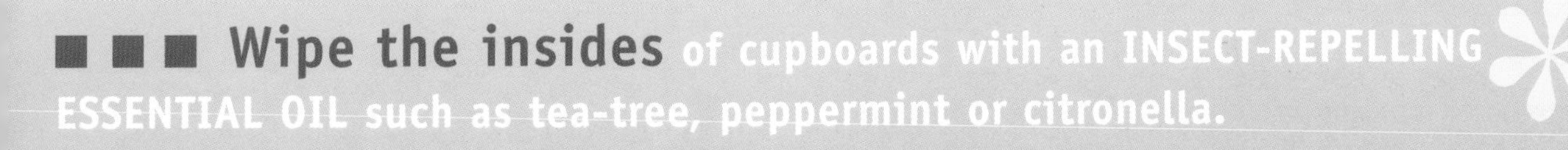

Too close for comfort

Fleas and dust mites like the warmth and comfort of our homes. Moths and carpet beetles eat the textiles we wear and use. Making a house less comfortable for pests is one way of dealing with them without resorting to chemicals, while using natural products that will repel fleas, moths and carpet beetles is another.

FLEAS

- If you have pets, make it a priority to check and treat them for fleas.
- Vacuum thoroughly and regularly to remove fleas and their eggs and larvae from carpets and floors. Burn the vacuum bag, or seal it in a plastic bag and place it in the hot sun or in the freezer for 48 hours. This will kill any fleas, larvae or eggs.
- For a persistent infestation, clean thoroughly and then spray pyrethrum in cracks and crevices, and anywhere you've seen fleas.

THE GOOD EARTH

Diatomaceous earth (DE) is the fossilised remains of tiny prehistoric algae called 'diatoms'. It feels like talcum powder, but its razor-sharp microscopic particles of silica kill insects on contact or when they ingest it.

- It's safe and free of chemicals and has no effect on mammals.
- Use only food- or garden-grade DE. The DE used for swimming pool filters is a finer powder, and a potentially dangerous lung irritant.
- Check garden centres or web sites for natural, untreated DE. Do not buy it from pool shops.

CLOTHES MOTHS AND CARPET BEETLES

The larvae of moths devour your stored clothes after hatching from eggs that have been deposited by adult moths. And it's the larvae of carpet beetles that damage your carpets.

- Clothes moths prefer dirty or stained clothing, so make sure stored clothes are perfectly clean before you put them away.
- Kill moth eggs and larvae by washing clothes (but not woollens) on the hottest suitable washing-machine cycle. Hang them in the sun for a couple of hours.
- Store moth-prone woollens and linen in chests made from camphorwood, which repels moths.
- Instead of commercial moth balls, use camphorwood or red cedar balls. Alternatively, sprinkle Epsom salts, dried herbs or whole cloves among your clothes.
- Fill muslin sachets with spice mixes and dried herbs, such as lavender, and tuck them in with your woollens.
- Vacuum your wardrobe regularly and finish by wiping it out with eucalyptus or lavender essential oil.
- Adult carpet beetles may enter the house on plant material. Check cut flowers for any activity as you arrange them in vases.
- Check your piano felts for signs of carpet beetle infestation. Vacuum carefully, then place a few bay leaves inside the piano. They will act as a natural repellent.

KEEP FLEAS AWAY

FLEA POWDER

500 g bicarbonate of soda
20 drops pennyroyal essential oil

- Mix bicarbonate of soda and oil together thoroughly.
- Sprinkle over carpets and furniture using a sifter or fine-mesh strainer with a teaspoon.
- Leave for at least 1 hour, and then vacuum.

FLEA SPRAY

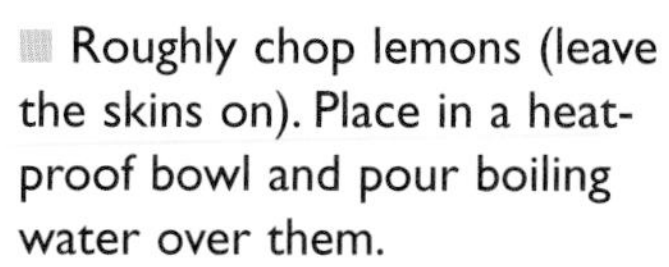

2 lemons
500 ml boiling water

- Roughly chop lemons (leave the skins on). Place in a heat-proof bowl and pour boiling water over them.
- Steep the mixture overnight, then strain into a spray bottle.
- Spray a mist over vacuumed carpets and clean pet bedding.

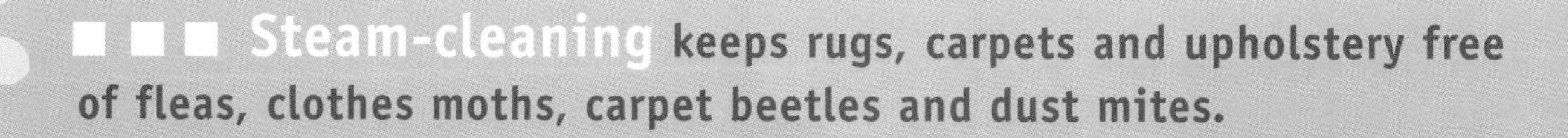

■ ■ ■ **Steam-cleaning keeps rugs, carpets and upholstery free of fleas, clothes moths, carpet beetles and dust mites.**

MAKE A MOTH-REPELLENT POMANDER

The pomander's effect lasts for years. You can buy orris root powder from chemists and craft stores.

• *Tie the pomander with a ribbon and hang it in a wardrobe.*

1 Use tape to divide a thin-skinned orange into quarters. Starting at the stalk end, push in whole cloves.

2 Roll the orange in a mix of 2 tsp each orris root powder, ground cloves and cinnamon, until coated.

3 Replace the tape with a decorative ribbon, then hang the orange in an airy place until it is dry.

~ FLYING START ~

Regularly vacuuming floors and carpets is the best defence against fleas, moths, carpet beetles and dust mites, especially under beds and along skirting boards where dust, dead insects and human skin particles accumulate, providing food for larvae.

DUST MITES

Dust mites thrive in warm, humid conditions and are found in clothing, bedding, carpets and soft furnishings.

- If anyone in your household has a dust-mite allergy, consider getting rid of the carpets and curtains.
- To help reduce dust mite numbers, wash all bedding regularly in hot water with soap powder and a good dash of eucalyptus oil. If you can, dry it in the sun.
- Dust mites don't like dry living conditions. Let the sun and air into the house as often as possible and consider using a dehumidifier in damp bedrooms. Regularly air blankets, doonas, soft furnishings and rugs in the sun.
- Consider buying allergen-resistant bedding – special microporous covers are available for mattresses, pillows and doonas. Their fine holes prevent dust mite infestation but still allow the air to circulate.
- Frequently vacuum floors, bed bases and mattresses using a powerful vacuum cleaner with a high-energy particulate air (HEPA) filter, which removes dust and allergens very efficiently. Regularly steam cleaning carpet and upholstery will also help.
- Limit the number of dust traps by keeping as much as possible behind cupboard doors. Open bookcases, cluttered under-bed surfaces and the tops of wardrobes are particular dust hazards.
- Put children's soft toys into the freezer for 24 hours to kill dust mites. Wash them at any temperature to remove dust mite faeces.

hot links

Information about pesticides and their alternatives:
www.beyondpesticides.org
Natural insect pest control: http://eartheasy.com/live_natpest_control.htm
Safer solutions for common pests:
www.tec.org.au/ipm/online/common.html

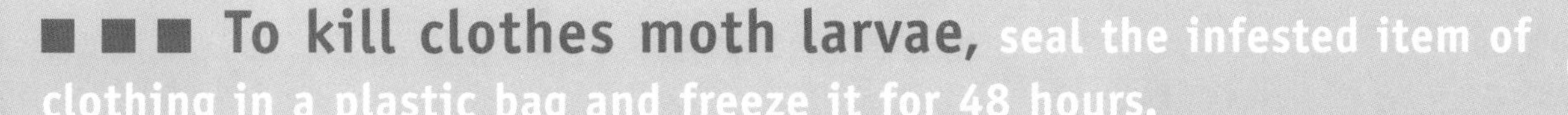

■ ■ ■ **To kill clothes moth larvae,** seal the infested item of clothing in a plastic bag and freeze it for 48 hours.

Invaders from outside

Mosquitoes, rodents, spiders and flies may be a nuisance outdoors, where they usually breed. But they'll also invade a home if they can find a way in. Keeping them out of the house is the key to keeping them under control.

MOSQUITOES

Besides disturbing your sleep, mozzies spread disease to both people and pets. Keep them at bay by installing screens on windows and doors, sleeping under a net and using natural deterrents.

- Outdoors, burn citronella candles to help repel mozzies.
- Indoors, burn lavender or peppermint essential oil in a vaporiser.
- Consider planting tansy or basil around the edges of your outdoor eating area.
- Use a natural repellent on your skin. Choose from apple cider vinegar or diluted essential oils, such as pennyroyal, tea-tree, lemon balm or lavender.

Discourage mozzies by placing a tiny saucer of oil of cloves by your bed.

BUZZ OFF!

To repel mosquitoes, try this mixture of oils.

I part lavender oil
I part eucalyptus oil
I part pennyroyal oil
3 parts unscented moisturiser or almond oil

Mix well. Apply to the skin liberally and frequently. If you have sensitive skin, apply small amounts on exposed areas.

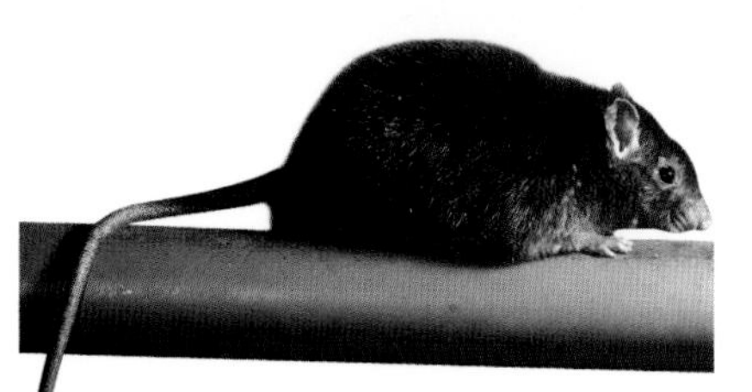

RATS AND MICE

If you see one rodent, there are sure to be others. Ignore it, and there will soon be many more!

- Store food – particularly rodent favourites such as chocolate, flour and cereals – in sealed containers.
- Seal cracks that rats and mice can squeeze through with mortar or metal sheeting. Steel wool is a good temporary measure.
- Dab peppermint oil around entry points. Rats and mice hate it.
- Keep outdoor areas near the house clean, and clear potential rat hideouts, such as dense clumps of weeds or open compost bins.

TRAPPING TIPS

To catch rats and mice, use traps instead of rat poison, which can harm other small creatures.

- To decide where to put traps, sprinkle flour in likely places and check for footprints.
- For bait, try pumpkin, brazil nuts, peanut butter with rolled oats or sunflower seeds.
- If you think you have more than one rodent, use several traps at once. As a rule of thumb, use twice as many traps as you think you have rodents, in groups of two or three.

MOSQUITO MANAGEMENT

Mosquitoes breed in still water; even the smallest amount will do.

- ✔ Remove any stagnant water left in pots, buckets and plant saucers.
- ✔ Make sure that water runs freely in your roof guttering, downpipes and open drainage pipes.
- ✔ Fit fine mesh screens over inlets to water tanks.
- ✔ Empty and renew your pet's water bowl every day.
- ✔ If you have a pond, keep fish or frogs to eat mosquito larvae.
- ✔ If your garden has a water feature, turn it on regularly to get the water moving and stop mozzies breeding.

Soothe an itchy mosquito bite with a mixture of equal parts vinegar and bicarbonate of soda.

MAKE YOUR OWN FLY-PAPERS

This traditional and natural method of catching flies doesn't give off toxic fumes or bad odours. You'll need brown and white sugar, golden syrup and strips of masking tape.

• Hang fly-papers up with string near windows and doors. The flies are attracted to the sweet coating, and then get trapped on the sticky surface.

1 Cut six 60 cm lengths of masking tape and fold each in half crosswise, with the sticky sides together, to make 30 cm strips. Pierce a hole at the top of each strip with a skewer and set aside.

2 Combine 200 ml golden syrup with 2 tbsp each brown and white sugar. Soak the strips in the sticky mixture overnight. Remove them, scrape off the excess syrup and thread kitchen twine through the holes.

- Check the traps regularly, leaving them for three days before collecting. Set them again in a week's time.
- In cold weather, rodents like warmth. Cut a small entrance to a box and put a baited trap and a lamp inside. Check it daily. Don't move the trap until you've caught your rat.

FLIES

If flies are a constant nuisance, check that you are not attracting them or making it easy for them to get inside your home.

- Are there screens on your doors and windows?
- Have you wiped spills from the kitchen bench?
- Has uncovered food been left on the kitchen bench?
- Has the dog left its bone on the doormat?
- Is there something 'on the nose' in the kitchen bin?
- Is the cat-litter tray dirty?

NO-SPRAY TACTICS

- One annoying fly? Use a fly swat.
- Trap flies with sticky fly-papers (from hardware shops). Or make your own, as shown above.
- To repel flies, try burning basil, lavender, peppermint or eucalyptus essential oil in a vaporiser.

SPIDERS

Most spiders are best left alone. Inside, keep them under control by clearing their webs frequently.

- Keep any poisonous spider populations at bay by clearing likely hiding places in the garden, such as rubbish heaps and empty cans. Be sure to wear gloves as you do so.
- Before you put them on, shake out garden shoes, gumboots and garden gloves.
- Tolerate daddy-long-leg spiders. They are highly venomous to other spiders but not to humans, as their pincers can't puncture human skin. If there are too many, clear most of the cobwebs, but let some stay put.
- If you need to remove a huntsman spider (opposite, top right), cover it with a large glass, slip a sheet of paper beneath, then take it outside and release it.

WARNING!

▼ Don't undertake large-scale spraying under the house because it only encourages spiders to move to safer locations, which may include inside your home.

■ ■ ■ **Wipe mirrors and glass** with a little vinegar to STOP FLIES from landing on them and leaving spots.

Undercover enemies

The word 'termite' can strike fear into the heart of any home owner. Who wants to see their most valuable asset literally being eaten away? But it is possible to take positive steps to protect your property from invasion, and if you do need to call in professional help, you can still aim to be as informed and earth-wise as possible in your choice of treatment.

TEN WAYS TO BEAT TERMITES

Termites, also known as white ants, are part of the natural decay system of bushland. However, they move into houses when their natural habitat is disturbed by building in the surrounding area.

1 Have your house inspected annually by a licensed pest controller, preferably one who is also environmentally aware.

2 Make sure there is easy access to all concealed areas.

3 Look for mud-covered trails from termite nests (sometimes concealed under trees) to food sources such as verandah posts, sleeper retaining walls or the wood inside your house.

4 Regularly check for signs of termite activity, such as springy floors, hollow-sounding wood and discoloured paint.

WARNING!

▼ Some chemicals used for termite control are extremely dangerous. Always refuse treatments that contain organophosphates or arsenic.

5 Listen carefully for sounds of activity near timber structures. Termites feed inside wood, and when they are well entrenched it may be possible to hear them, particularly late at night when there is less ambient noise.

6 Termites find damp soil appealing, so don't let damp spots develop near the house. Fix a dripping airconditioner, an outlet from the hot-water system or a leaky outside tap by catching water in a container and regularly emptying it onto the garden. Check that downpipes direct water away from the edge of the house.

7 Make sure the house sub-floor area is adequately ventilated and that any air vents are free from obstruction. Increased moisture levels and fungal growth attract termites. If necessary, install some extra ventilation.

8 Don't allow wood of any sort (even firewood) to be stored near or under your home, or close to any timber structures.

9 Don't build soil up against the house or around timber structures, such as fences. Raised soil can block ventilation holes or damp courses, allowing termites to find a safe passage to floors, beams and other internal timberwork.

10 If you suspect you have active termites, don't disturb them or they may flee, making their nest difficult to find. Call an expert.

TOP TIP

Termites may colonise wood-based mulches in your garden. Be sure to consider this when choosing mulch. If you live in a high-risk area, try a pebble mulch instead.

■ ■ ■ **Let your neighbours know** when you are treating termites. Ideally, they should treat their houses at the same time.

Choosing a termite treatment

Treatment	Description	Pros	Cons
Physical barrier	Graded stone or a termite-resistant waterproof membrane	Non-toxic	Needs to be applied during building; not suitable for existing buildings
Chemical barrier	Applied to soil around house. Kills and repels termites; isolates colony	Fast-acting	Does not eradicate colony; chemicals of varying toxicity are put into the soil
Chemical dusting	Insecticide applied directly to termite workings	If used correctly, can eradicate the source	Even new generation insect-growth regulators (IGRs) are mildly toxic
Chemical baits	Insecticide baits placed in strategic positions	Reduced toxicity in the new-generation baits; uses smaller amounts of toxin	Labour intensive; can be very slow-acting

The least toxic termite treatment involves bait only, with an insect growth regulator, and no chemical barriers.

NEW BUILDING

If you're embarking on new construction or an extension, there are several preventive measures you can take.

- Ask your builder about termite regulations for buildings in your area.
- Before building, get advice from an environmentally aware pest controller on preventive measures.
- Install non-toxic physical barriers, such as graded stone or a termite-resistant membrane.
- Lift wooden posts from ground contact with metal stirrups.
- Fit brick piers and other sub-floor constructions with ant caps and termite barriers.
- If necessary, lay ag-pipes to ensure good drainage around the site. These pipes have holes that drain water away and prevent pooling.
- Make sure your builder factors in adequate sub-floor ventilation.
- Wherever possible, build in access to concealed areas.
- Organise the removal of tree stumps and roots from the site. Consolidate the soil before pouring the foundations to minimise cracks in the concrete slab; termites don't eat concrete but can enter timber walls through surface cracks.
- After construction is complete, clear all leftover timber from the building site. Don't use it as landfill.
- Avoid CCA-treated timber. These timber products have been banned in some states and regions, so check with your local authority. Ask your builder to use timber that has been treated with a non-arsenic preservative. Alternatively, choose termite- and rot-resistant hardwood for construction.

Need help?

Sometimes you will need help from an expert. Don't feel defeated – you can still make earth-wise choices.

- Ask friends and neighbours for their recommendations and draw up a short list.
- Ask about experience, accreditation, methods and chemicals, and about the least toxic alternatives available.
- Run a web search on the chemicals proposed by the various experts.
- Be wary of free quotes. A diligent pest controller spends time investigating and reporting, and you should expect to pay for this. It could save you money in the long run.
- A reputable controller should provide you with references from previous customers. Phone them and ask whether they were satisfied with the service.

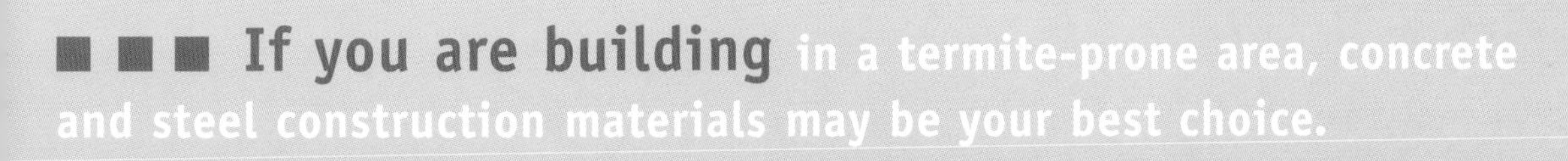

■ ■ ■ **If you are building** in a termite-prone area, concrete and steel construction materials may be your best choice.

CARING FOR YOUR PET

The animals we keep as pets depend on us to make sure they live healthy and happy lives.

Pets, naturally

Companion animals bring joy to the lives of millions of people – and they're good for our health too. Responsible pet ownership means looking after your animals and making sure they don't harm native fauna or the environment.

WHICH PET?

Pet ownership requires planning and commitment. Before making a decision on whether to bring a pet into your home, here are some questions to ask yourself.

- Is everyone in the family willing to help care for an animal?
- Does anyone in the family suffer from allergies?
- What sort of pet will be best for your lifestyle and the size and type of home you live in? Will it suit the surrounding environment?
- Do you want a young animal or an adult one? Puppies and kittens need a lot more attention.
- How big will your dog grow? How much exercise will it need? Learn as much as possible about the characteristics and requirements of the different breeds you are considering. There are many informative web sites.
- What sort of pet will be suitable for young children?
- Will you be able to afford expenses such as pet food, vet care and insurance over the long term?

KEEPING OUR WILDLIFE SAFE

Pets that are allowed to wander indiscriminately pose a threat to native wildlife and to themselves. By taking a few simple precautions, it's easy to minimise the impact your pet makes on the environment.

- Don't let your dog wander unchecked. Make sure it can't get out during the day and keep it on a leash in 'lead only' areas outdoors.
- Consider keeping your cat or dog inside at night. This is one of the most effective ways to stop it hunting.
- Have your pet de-sexed. This will make it less likely to roam and encounter wildlife. And fewer unwanted pregnancies will mean there are fewer feral animals on the loose.
- Put a bell on your cat to warn native animals and birds of its approach.
- Don't feed stray animals – they may turn feral. Contact the RSPCA or ask your local council to pick them up.

Choose non-toxic paints and wood preservatives when making a CAGE OR KENNEL for your outdoor pet to live in.

PROS & CONS

OWNING A PET

Pets can make excellent companions, and there's no doubt that the regular routine of having to exercise a dog is good for our health – pet owners suffer less from high blood pressure and heart attacks and tend to recover more quickly from illness and surgery. Children who are brought up with pets are likely to learn respect for animals. But owning a pet is a long-term responsibility. And, unfortunately, even the most good-natured cats and dogs have the instincts of wild animals and pose a threat to native mammals, birds, reptiles and amphibians.

~ *FLYING START* ~

Adopting a pet from a shelter or rescue organisation is a worthwhile experience, and it goes some way to alleviating the burden of unwanted animals. You'll have to pay a fee, but it will be less than a pet shop would charge. In most cases, the animal will be immunised, spayed or neutered and microchipped.

HEALTHY HABITS

Animal faeces carry parasites which can infect people and pollute the environment. There are a number of precautions you can take to prevent infection.

- When out walking your dog, keep an eye on your pet and try to stop it from defecating on footpaths, in children's sandpits and near drains. Dog faeces are a major source of water pollution in urban areas.
- Pick up dog faeces with a biodegradable plastic bag or a pooper-scooper. Many councils provide labelled bins and plastic bags for faeces collection.
- Clean your cat's litter tray regularly in scalding water or use a low-toxicity cleanser to kill germs. Biodegradable, environmentally friendly litters such as recycled paper pellets are available from supermarkets. Or you can line your cat's tray with torn-up newspapers.
- Wash your hands thoroughly after direct contact with dogs and cats, especially before meals, to prevent catching diseases. Don't allow dogs to lick the faces of family members.
- Toxoplasmosis can be caught through contact with cat faeces. It's a systemic disease that cats acquire from eating infected raw meat. Pregnant women are particularly at risk, so take extra care.

NATIVE KNOW-HOW

Rescuing a sick or injured animal and nurturing it back to health can be very satisfying. If your cat or dog injures a native animal, there are practical ways to help improve its chances of survival.

- Cover the animal with a towel and place it in an escape-proof box. Place the box in a warm, quiet room and do not disturb it. Don't try to feed, handle or display the animal, as stress of any kind can result in death.
- Take the injured animal to a veterinarian or contact a wildlife rescue organisation. They will give you expert advice on what to do.
- If you see an injured animal on the road, stop and assess its condition. If it is safe to do so, move the animal off the road. Even if the animal is dead, check for a pouch – there may be live young inside.
- If the animal recovers, remember that in most cases you will need a licence to keep a native animal. Check the requirements with your local wildlife authority.

hot links

Good general sites: www.rspca.org.au; www.rspcanz.org.nz
Finding the right pet: www.petnet.com.au/petlovers.html
Microchipping: www.catprotection.org.au/html/be_a_responsible_cat_owner.html
Responsible pet ownership to protect native fauna: www.deh.gov.au/biodiversity/threatened/publications/pets.html

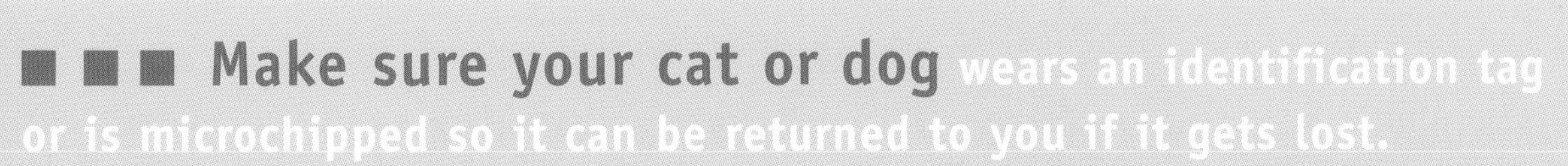

A balanced diet

Pets need a balanced, healthy diet and adequate exercise just as much as we do. The quality and choice of pet foods has improved and there are now many natural products on the market, allowing you to feed your animals a diet as free from artificial chemicals and preservatives as possible. What you feed your pet will need to suit your budget and the way you live.

CHOOSING A DIET

It's a tough choice choosing the right diet for your pet. Commercially prepared food is convenient but it may be expensive; home-made food is cheaper but requires some planning.

- Try to offer your pet variety, both for the sake of its health and to keep it interested. If you want to change your pet's diet, it's best to introduce new foods gradually.
- Observe your pet's appearance, behaviour and general health. These are your best guides to whether you are feeding your pet a balanced and healthy diet. Seek veterinary help if you are unsure whether your pet is getting the nutrients it needs.

FOOD IN THE RAW

Many experts and vets advocate feeding dogs and cats a raw food diet. There are a number of sound reasons for following this advice.

- A mixed diet of raw meat, bones and vegetables most closely approximates your pet's genetically programmed ideal diet.
- Eating raw food is good for your pet's oral health. It encourages stronger teeth and gums and your pet will be less likely to have bad breath.
- Raw bones are a good source of calcium. They also supply small amounts of cartilage, bone marrow and minerals that are vital for strong, healthy bones.
- A good bone provides your pet with dietary roughage.
- Cooked bones are not good for cats. They can shatter, blunt the teeth and even choke the animal. Also, cooking bones greatly reduces the availability of calcium, a vital mineral for cats.

COMMERCIAL PET FOOD

Pets may thrive on commercially prepared food. The Pet Food Industry Association of Australia (PFIAA) has developed detailed guidelines for the labelling, marketing and nutritional claims of pet foods. Many owners put their trust in this, feeling confident that their pet is getting products of a high standard with the right balance of nutrients.

- Choose good-quality commercial dry foods from pet shops and veterinarians. They may cost more, but are superior to the economy brands sold in supermarkets.
- Good-quality varieties usually contain high-quality fibre. Cheaper commercial tinned foods contain fermentable fibre, which may cause flatulence, larger faeces and more odour. Preparing home-made food gives you more control over the fibre content of your pet's diet.
- Look for commercial brands that contain anti-oxidants and accurately measured vitamin and mineral supplements. This information is often prominently displayed on the product's packaging.

✓ BUY WISELY

- Look for cheaper cuts of meat or bones at the butcher. Trim off any very fatty meat and, if you can afford it, buy organic.
- Consider less fashionable cuts of meat, such as offal. Liver is particularly good. However, avoid sheep's liver for dogs because it can cause hydatids if it comes from infected sheep.

■ ■ ■ **Pick dandelions,** pansies, puha, curly kale and parsley for your rabbits and guinea pigs to snack on.

ORGANIC PET FOOD

Buying foods that have been certified 'organic' is your guarantee that they have been produced using no chemicals, pesticides, hormones or antibiotics, and that they are not genetically modified. Buying organic meat ensures that it comes from healthy animals. Canned and dried organic foods are also available, but because they are imported are often more expensive. Foods labelled as 'natural' are cheaper than organic ones, but manufacturers may give little information about the way they have been produced. Read the labels carefully to be sure.

HOME-MADE FOOD

It can be hard to gauge whether a home-made diet is cheaper than a commercially prepared one. A combination of both is probably the key to achieving a healthy, happy pet.

- Learn about your animal's nutritional needs. You will need to take into account its breed, age, size and lifestyle.
- Consider home-made food for a pet with medical problems, special nutritional requirements due to age, or one that has allergies to certain colourings or preservatives.
- Supplement your pet's diet with scraps and leftovers, but make sure the food you are adding is not too fatty, salty or full of preservatives.

VEGETABLE VARIETY

Anti-oxidants are present in some vegetables, but are absent in many commercial pet foods. They defuse toxic molecules called free radicals, which may be a factor in some cancers, heart and lung disease, and cataracts.

- Add a small quantity of raw vegetables to your cat's diet. Cats fed a meat-only diet are more likely to suffer from renal failure in old age.
- Slice vegetables thinly, or lightly cook to aid your pet's digestion. This mimics the way vegetables are eaten by dogs and cats in the wild – partly digested from the stomach of their prey. Large, raw chunks will pass straight through the gut with little benefit to the animal.
- Serve vegetables in small portions to avoid flatulence.
- If you choose to feed your dog a vegetarian diet, consult your vet to ensure it is getting all the nutrients it needs.

SNACKS AND SUPPLEMENTS

Pets like variety in what they eat. Give them a treat by adding a few natural supplements to their diet. Many of the following suggestions are kitchen scraps or can be found growing wild.

BIRDS

- Bake some leftover wholemeal bread to harden it. Wait until it cools and then clip it to the side of the cage for your birds to nibble on.
- Pick up a pine cone for your parrot or parakeet. They love pecking the seed-stuffed cones and it will keep their beaks trim.

TOP TIP

See if your cat or dog will eat a little broccoli, brussels sprouts or cauliflower. These vegetables contain compounds that stimulate the body's natural defences to help it neutralise carcinogens – the cancer-causing compounds. Lightly cook the vegetables first before adding them to your pet's meal.

THE CAT'S WHISKERS

This quick and easy meal will add valuable fibre to your cat's diet.

2 cups brown rice
1 kg lean beef, minced
1 tsp salt
2 tsp wheat germ

- Cook rice and set aside.
- Cook remaining ingredients in a non-stick pan with a little water for 15 minutes.
- Mix meat mixture with cooked rice.
- Divide the mixture into daily serve-size portions and freeze until required.

● Chop up some fruit for variety. It's good for birds, but avoid pits or seeds from apples, cherries, peaches and avocados.

OFF-LIMIT FOODS

✗ Don't give chocolate to cats and dogs. Though they may be keen to eat it, chocolate is toxic to them. Coffee, alcohol and wild mushrooms are also bad for pets.

✗ Don't give pet birds dairy products or salty foods such as chips, which can cause seizures.

✗ Don't add onions or anything onion-flavoured to your pet's home-cooked meals. Onions can cause haemolytic anaemia, a condition in which red blood cells are destroyed.

✗ Don't feed cats raw egg white. A chemical in it neutralises the vitamin biotin, which is essential for good health.

Try giving your dog or cat cooked pumpkin – it's an excellent source of fibre and vitamins.

● Regularly offer your birds handfuls of thistles or seeding grasses you have collected, along with the soil-covered roots. Don't give them lawn clippings because the grass may have been sprayed with insecticides or treated with fertilisers, both of which are highly toxic to birds.

● Attach fresh hay to the cage for birds to pick through.

● Wash all vegetables, fruit and grasses in case they have been sprayed with chemicals, or buy organic produce.

CATS AND DOGS

● Grate or slice small slivers of carrots and apples into your cat's food. Fruit and vegetables are good for your pet's waistline and great for keeping teeth clean and breath fresh. Dogs will eat them readily.

● Provide wheatgrass for your cat to chew on if it doesn't have access to a garden. Grass stimulates a cat's immune system, helps sweeten the breath and helps it regurgitate fur balls.

● Grow catmint (also known as catnip) or parsley in pots and place on a windowsill. They're both good sources of fibre for your cat.

FISH

● Add regular supplies of fresh aquatic plants to your fish tank or pond. Plants are a good additional food source for fish, as well as offering a place to shelter and helping to oxygenate the water.

● Blanch a lettuce leaf or a slice of zucchini in boiling water and attach it to the glass of the fish tank with a suction clip. You can also try a slice of orange or lemon. Wash the fruit thoroughly first, in case there are some chemicals residues on the skin .

● Give your aquarium fish a snack of mosquito larvae – they enjoy them, and live food is a welcome supplement to a constant diet of artificial or prepared food. And if mosquitoes are multiplying in your garden pond, this is an excellent way of reducing their numbers.

hot links

Cat diet information: www.cathelp-online.com/health
Fact sheets about pets: www.petinfo4u.com
Information about dogs: www.canismajor.com/dog; www.doglinks.co.nz/health/healthcare.htm
Expert pet information: http://peteducation.com
Bird care: www.birdhealth.com.au/bird/birds.html

If you feed your pet mostly tinned food, try to give it A FRESH FOOD SNACK once or twice a week.

Exercise and play

Exercise is essential for pets, particularly animals that spend much of their time indoors. It's good for their physical health and keeps them alert and interested in the outside world. It can be as simple as a good, brisk walk of 15 to 30 minutes twice a day for a dog or 15 minutes playing with a cat.

WHY EXERCISE?

- You'll save on vet bills. Pets that are overweight and under-exercised are much more likely to suffer from a range of ailments.
- Your house and garden will look better. Bored and lonely animals often take out their frustration by causing damage to their immediate surroundings.
- You'll stay on better terms with your neighbours. A confined dog is an unhappy dog, and behavioural problems such as excessive barking, aggression and possessiveness can be the result.
- If you walk your dog daily, you'll find yourself becoming healthier along with your pet.

BUDGET PLAYTHINGS

You don't need to buy expensive novelties for pets. With a little imagination you can make toys from everyday household items that will keep them just as happy.

- Recycle a cardboard box. Cut holes in the top and sides large enough for your cat or puppy to wriggle through. Throw in a couple of its favourite toys and watch it pop in and out of the box.
- Open a brown paper bag. Cats and kittens love to hide inside and pounce on people as they pass by.
- Secure one end of a long piece of string to a slim bamboo pole or piece of thin dowel with some tape and tie the other end to a ball of paper or a catnip toy mouse. Cats never seem to tire of chasing this simple and fun toy around.
- Give your teething puppy an old soccer ball to chew on. Let enough air out of the ball so that it can get a good grip on the leather.

ORGANISED ACTIVITIES

If your dog is very lively and has energy to spare, consider organised, competitive activities. You may find this a worthwhile extra expense.

- Obedience trials test retrieving over hurdles, obeying hand signals and scent discrimination.
- Agility trials are timed events which direct your dog through a course made up of a variety of planks, tunnels, jumps and other obstacles.
- Lure coursing is a sport for dogs that use their eyes, rather than their noses, for hunting. It involves chasing an object and is a fast and physically demanding sport in which speed, agility and stamina are tested.
- Herding trials to train sheepdogs and cattle dogs may be available in your area. Check with breed societies and pet clubs.

TOP TIP

Encourage your dog to swim. It will give it a great workout and it doesn't cost a cent.

WARNING!

▼ Don't exercise your dog in the heat of the day. Heatstroke is a real risk. Dogs rely on panting to release excess heat, but this cooling system isn't very efficient, particularly in very hot weather.

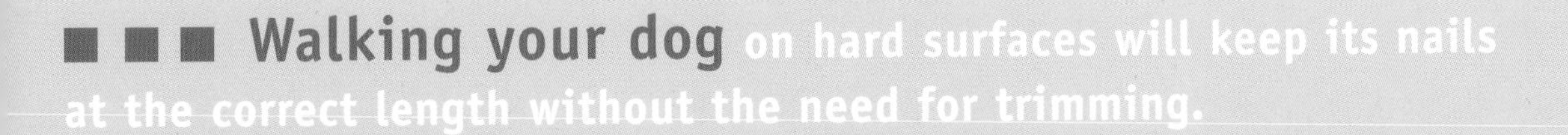

■ ■ ■ **Walking your dog** on hard surfaces will keep its nails at the correct length without the need for trimming.

Natural remedies

If you know what's wrong with your pet, basic medical care and simple, effective treatments can be carried out at home for minor ailments. Many remedies can be made from inexpensive cooking ingredients, bathroom staples and garden produce. But always remember, if any symptoms persist, seek veterinary help.

COMMON AILMENTS

ACNE

- If you find slightly crusty bumps under your pet's chin and around its mouth, wash the area with mild soap, rinse well with warm water and dry thoroughly – acne thrives in damp places. Plastic food dishes can harbour bacteria that cause this problem, so use china, glass or metal.

ARTHRITIS

- Massage the hips, back, neck and legs gently but firmly for a few minutes every day to improve blood flow and to keep muscles and joints as loose as possible. Concentrate on the areas surrounding the joints. Carefully move the legs through their full range of motion.
- Wrap a hot-water bottle in a towel (to prevent burning) and apply to the sore, aching areas.
- Swimming is great exercise for arthritic dogs that love the water.
- Add parsley, grated ginger, linseed oil or sunflower oil to the diet.

CONSTIPATION

- Mix 1/4 teaspoon to 1 teaspoon psyllium fibre powder (depending on the size of your pet) into moist food to prevent constipation.
- Offer more water, and add a small amount of cooked pumpkin and green vegetables to the diet. If your pet is a reluctant drinker, add a little salty gravy to its food to help it work up a thirst.

DANDRUFF

- Add linoleic acid to your dog's food. The best sources are safflower and sunflower oils. Add about 1/2 teaspoon (for a small dog) to 1 tablespoon (for a large dog).

DIARRHOEA

- Don't offer your pet any solid food for a couple of days.
- Provide plenty of water and an electrolyte solution to avoid dehydration. Give your pet ice cubes to lick or chew on if it won't drink water.
- Soothe your pet's upset stomach during the first day of fasting by giving a few teaspoons of slippery elm powder mixed to a paste with

ROSEMARY RELIEF

Use this aromatic rosemary infusion to treat arthritis.

1 cup boiling water
1 tsp fresh rosemary leaves

- Pour boiling water over the rosemary. Stir and cover for 15 minutes.
- Strain and store in the fridge.
- Mix a little into your pet's food.

PROS & CONS

ALTERNATIVE MEDICINE

Should you treat your pet with human treatments such as essential oils, acupuncture, homeopathy or herbal remedies? The efficacy of natural therapy treatments is open to debate but in the case of essential oils, the answer is a definite no. Animals' olfactory organs are much more sensitive than those of humans and the inhalation of strong, concentrated scents can be dangerous to them. You can discuss treatment options with a vet trained in holistic medicine if you're interested in alternative medicine.

Use a plastic eye-dropper or small syringe to give your cat clear, warm CHICKEN BROTH when it is unwell.

De-sex your male cat – it'll be less likely to fight, so you'll save on vet bills.

apple juice. This will encourage the growth of gut-friendly bacteria in the intestines.

- Try changing your pet's diet from red meat to a white meat such as chicken. Some animals have specific allergies, usually to proteins or preservatives.
- Once the diarrhoea has stopped, offer bland food such as boiled rice with a little poached, skinless white chicken meat for 1 to 4 days. Gradually reintroduce your pet's usual food.
- Diarrhoea can also be caused by intestinal worms, so treat your pet for an infestation, especially if this is the likely cause.
- Consult your vet if the diarrhoea continues for more than 2 days, or if it is bloody, or seems painful.
- Overeating and scavenging can cause diarrhoea. Don't overfeed and secure your garbage bin from raids.

TOP TIP

Apply the gel from a cut aloe vera leaf directly onto scalds, sunburn or hotspots caused by excessive scratching. The gel takes the sting out of scalds and sunburn and soothes an itch with its moisturising properties. Always break off the more mature leaves from the aloe vera plant.

DRY PAWS

- If you live in a cold area, check dogs' paw pads in winter. They can become dry, particularly if they spend a lot of time out in the snow. Rub a daily smear of calendula ointment over the affected areas.

GRAZES

- Wash the affected area gently, using gauze pads soaked in warm, salty water or a dilute antiseptic of tea-tree oil. Rinse with warm water and pat dry with gauze pads. Don't use cotton balls as fibres can stick to the wound.
- Apply arnica ointment, a herbal and homeopathic remedy that has anti-inflammatory and pain-killing properties. It can also be used to treat bruises, sprains and swellings. However, do not use it on deep, open wounds.
- Secure a gauze bandage over the graze if necessary. This may stop your pet scratching it.

PAIN

- If your pet needs time to recuperate, give it a safe quiet place to lie down. Line a cardboard box with newspaper and an old blanket, and place it in a room where it won't be disturbed.

- For outdoor pets, line a car tyre with an old blanket in your garage or carport. Use a hot-water bottle (covered to prevent burns) to make your pet feel more comfortable.

SCALDS

- Swab scalds immediately with cold water. Hold a pack of ice cubes in a cloth against the wound for at least 10 minutes, or longer for severe burns. Apply some aloe vera gel or comfrey leaves and bandage.

SKIN IRRITATIONS

- Check with your vet what may have caused the irritation. It could be fleas, contact with grass or plants such as wandering jew or buffalo grass, mange mites, tick larvae, an allergy to food or inhaled particles such as pollen or house dust mites.

Remove all milk products from your pet's diet when it is suffering from diarrhoea. Milk can cause or aggravate the condition.

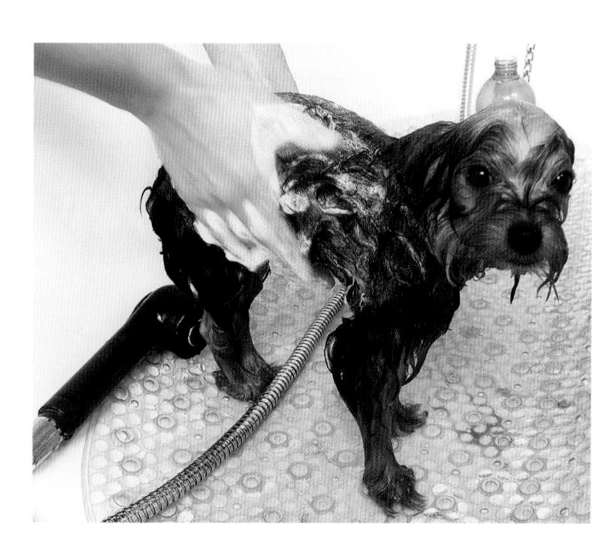

PROS & CONS

SHOULD I SHAMPOO MY PET?
Dogs and cats have naturally waterproof coats that usually don't need washing unless the animal has rolled in something smelly or in a substance that irritates the skin. Cats are diligent self-groomers so they rarely need a wash, whereas dogs, especially outdoor dogs, may need washing two or three times a year. Shampooing too often reduces the coat's ability to repel water by depleting the natural oils in the fur. Choose a shampoo made specifically for pets, or make your own – the pH level of your pet's skin differs from that of humans. Regular brushing will assist in removing dead hair and accumulated dirt.

- Wash your pet's feet with cold water after it has been playing on freshly cut or dew-dampened grass.
- If your pet suffers from a grass allergy, make cotton booties from an old T-shirt. Secure the material with a sticky bandage so it won't be chewed off easily.
- Give your pet a bath in cool water if it is scratching excessively. Warm water makes the irritation worse. Add a handful of colloidal oatmeal (available from pet shops, chemists and health food shops) to the water. The oatmeal moisturises the skin and soothes skin irritations.
- Apply an oatmeal conditioner after washing, as this can also help reduce skin irritation.

Dress your grass-allergic dog in an old cotton T-shirt to give it some protection when it is playing outside in the garden.

SUNBURN

- Consider whether your pet is susceptible to sunburn. Dogs that are light- or white-skinned, such as Dalmatians, and those that have short hair, are prime candidates. White- and short-haired cats are particularly susceptible too.
- Try to ensure your pet doesn't spend the hottest hours of the day (usually between 11 am and 2 pm) in direct sunlight. Watch out for cats and dogs that love to laze in the sun, as they can suffer from burnt ear tips and sunburnt noses. Repeated sunburn may lead to skin cancers.
- Relieve the discomfort and sting of sunburn by spraying the affected area with cool water mixed with witch hazel – it has a numbing effect. You can also apply some cooling and soothing aloe vera gel directly on the skin.

WARNING!

▼ A deep, open wound that has dirt embedded in it, or that will not stop bleeding, needs immediate veterinary attention.

TOOTH AND GUM PROBLEMS

- Give dogs and cats raw meaty bones and crunchy vegetables regularly to chew on. The scraping action helps prevent tartar build-up, which can lead to gum disease.
- Gently massage your pet's gums and teeth if it will let you. This helps to clean teeth and gums if done regularly. Finger toothbrushes and dog and cat toothpaste are available from both pet shops and vets.
- Relieve your puppy's teething pain by giving it an old linen tea towel or

■ ■ ■ Sit your allergy-affected pet in the bathroom when you shower. STEAM SOOTHES a sore, irritated nose.

ALL-PURPOSE DOG AND CAT SHAMPOO

2 cups water
2 tsp liquid castile soap (this has a high olive oil content)
2 tbsp aloe vera gel
1 tbsp vegetable glycerine or vegetable oil

- Combine all the ingredients in a jar. Shake to blend.
- Wet the coat thoroughly, pour on shampoo and work into a lather.
- Rinse thoroughly and towel dry.

a cotton face washer to chew on. Wet the washer and twist it before putting it in the freezer for an hour. The cold will help relieve the pain of sore, swollen and irritated gums.

URINARY TRACT INFECTIONS

- Stir a small amount of cranberry juice or 250–1000 mg vitamin C powder into your pet's food. This can help to acidify the urine and stop the infection-causing bacteria multiplying in the bladder. Citrus juice has a similar effect and may also ease painful urination.
- Consult your vet if there is blood in the urine. This is usually a sign of infection and your pet may need to commence a course of antibiotics immediately. Leaving it too long may worsen the situation and cause unnecessary suffering for your pet.

GROOMING

- Combing or brushing your cat or dog regularly is an essential part of preventive health care. It keeps the fur clean and tangle-free and is an opportunity to check for signs of potential health problems.
- Brush long-haired cats and dogs at least once a week to avoid matting. Brushing can become more time-consuming and difficult the longer you leave it, so it's wise to do it regularly.
- To untangle your pet's fur, first sprinkle a little cornflour on the mats, and then brush them out gently. While there's no need to buy a commercial de-tangler, fur that is heavily matted may need the help of a professional groomer.
- Use a flea comb regularly in warmer weather.
- To make your dog's coat smell pleasant and look shiny, apply tea-tree oil to the grooming brush.
- Check your pet's ears weekly. The ear canals should be clean, with no signs of inflammation, unpleasant odour or redness.
- Clean out the ears gently once a month with an equal mixture of rubbing alcohol and hydrogen peroxide (available from chemists). Soak a piece of gauze in the solution and wrap it around your fingers, gently using it to swab away any accumulated debris.
- Alternatively, use 1 part lemon juice to 3 parts water, or witch hazel extract for a gentle and effective ear-cleaning solution. Don't probe deeply into the ears or you could damage your pet's hearing.
- Gently and carefully clean around the eyes with a cotton wool ball dipped in lukewarm water or warm black tea. You can also use olive oil in place of water, though some cats will not tolerate it well.

CAT MASSAGE

Cats, particularly older ones, enjoy slow and gentle massage. It can be calming for the anxious feline and can have therapeutic benefits for arthritic cats. Some owners also notice behavioural changes – a previously indifferent cat may become more affectionate.

- Rest your cat gently on your lap. Pay particular attention to the position your cat prefers. The key is to make your pet feel as comfortable as possible before starting the massage.
- Start slowly, using a light, even pressure. Older cats often have frail bones and stiff joints. Explore your cat's body contours. Use different parts of your hands during the massage – palms, fingertips, finger pads, thumbs.
- Gently stroke different areas of your cat's body, including the neck, behind the ears, the top of the head and under the chin. Move on to the leg and hip joints, carefully and gently rotating them as you go.

Pest-free pets

Keeping your pet free from parasites and diseases is vital for its health and happiness, and that of your family, particularly small children, who often have close contact with them. Earth-wise control methods for parasites include chemical-free treatments you can carry out at home and basic household hygiene procedures. Vaccinations are generally recommended to control viral diseases. Discuss this with your vet.

PESKY PARASITES

Preventive measures go a long way in combating the parasites that pets inevitably come into contact with, both from other animals and the environment.

FLEAS

- Groom your pet regularly with a flea comb. A flea collar may help, but fleas are becoming more resistant to the chemicals they contain.
- Use an insect growth regulator. This non-toxic and relatively new form of flea control works by transmitting hormones into the flea eggs and larvae, helping to reduce fleas as long as all pets in the household are treated with the same product. They are available from your veterinarian and come in a variety of forms, including aerosols that are sprayed directly onto your pet and your furnishings, and as tablets that you give your pet with its food.
- Add some brewer's yeast (available in health food shops) to your pet's food. It contains substances that produce a skin odour known to deter fleas. Use 2 tablespoons yeast per 4 kilograms of the animal's body weight and add to moist food.
- Wash your pet's bedding every week (and any fabric toys or rugs) in the hottest water the fabric can stand and leave to dry in the sun. Launder loose covers on furniture regularly as well, along with any rugs and curtains.
- Vacuum carpets, curtains and upholstered furniture once a week. Sprinkle a layer of table salt over your upholstery and carpets and leave overnight before vacuuming.

STOP THE ITCH!

FLEA SPRAY

For use on your dog or cat. It can also be sprayed on your pet's bedding. It smells good, too.

1 cup water
4–6 drops tea-tree oil
4–6 drops lavender oil

- Mix ingredients together and pour into a spray bottle.
- Keep sprayer by the door and spritz your dog or cat each time it goes outside, taking care to avoid the eyes.

TICK AND FLEA SHAMPOO

Oatmeal shampoo can be purchased from health food shops and pet suppliers.

1/4 cup oatmeal shampoo
1/4 cup water
4 drops tea-tree oil

- Mix together in a bottle and shake well.
- Shampoo your dog once a week, or as necessary.

■ ■ ■ **If your dog won't swallow its medicine, try disguising it by dipping the pill in some PEANUT BUTTER.**

Pest and virus check – the symptoms

Pest/virus	What is it?	What are the symptoms?
Fleas	Small insect with piercing mouthparts. Feeds on animal blood. Spread by contact with infested animals.	Skin irritations, skin biting, excessive scratching, allergic reactions. In extreme cases, death from secondary infection.
Heartworm	Parasitic roundworms (nematodes) that live in the arteries of the lungs and in the heart.	Difficulty breathing when exercising, persistent cough, vomiting, reluctance to move, reduced appetite, weight loss.
Intestinal worms	Segmented parasitic worms. Spread by eating infected meat and offal.	Dull coat, swollen belly, pale gums, licking around the anus, dragging the bottom, vomiting, spaghetti-like eggs in stools.
Ticks	Small arachnid with piercing mouthparts. Injects host with poison, affecting muscles and respiratory system.	Unsteady gait, fever, weakness, muscle aches, loss of appetite.
Viruses	Distemper, hepatitis, parvovirus, feline enteritis, feline immunodeficiency virus (AIDS), feline leukemia virus.	Decreased appetite, vomiting, swollen belly, soft or liquid stools, or blood in stools, whining in discomfort.

HEARTWORM

- This disease is spread to dogs and cats by mosquitoes, so it's important to eliminate areas of standing water that can serve as breeding grounds.
- Keep your pets indoors as much as possible during times when mosquitoes are most active – dawn and dusk during spring and summer.

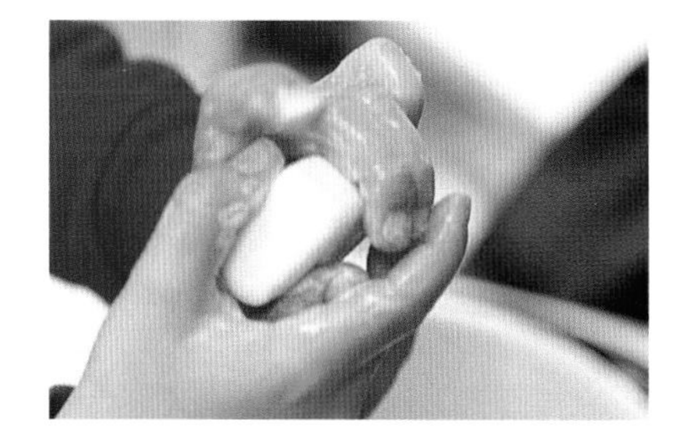

INTESTINAL WORMS

- Make sure children wash their hands after playing in a sandpit or with a pet. They can pick up round-worm larvae from both sources.
- Fleas are a source of tapeworm infection. If your pet has a flea problem, tackle it first – it will help to prevent tapeworm infestation.
- Don't let your pet eat rodents. Rats and mice transmit tapeworm.
- If your pet shows any symptoms, ask your vet to provide a safe, effective de-worming medicine.

TICKS

- Ticks occur in urban areas as well as in the countryside. Make sure you check your pet regularly.
- Seek immediate veterinary help if you sense your pet is in danger. It may have difficulty breathing and be unsteady on its legs.
- Check for tiny lumps by rubbing gently back and forth through your pet's fur, feeling the whole body. It should take 10 to 30 minutes, depending on the animal's size.
- Use a tick hook or tweezers to remove a tick. Fingers are the least efficient tool as you are likely to squeeze its body and cause more poison to be injected. Don't worry if the head is left in the skin: it will die and eventually fall out.

VIRUSES

- Most vaccine manufacturers recommend giving dogs and cats a temporary vaccination at 6 to 8 weeks of age, followed by adult or full vaccination at 12 to 14 weeks.
- Annual boosters are the subject of some controversy, so you should seek advice from your vet or from a holistic practitioner about their necessity for your pet.

hot links

Advice about vaccinations:
www.wholisticanimal.com/petvaccinations.html
Useful information on ticks:
www.ozpets.com.au/health/articles/HC10004.shtml
Online veterinary services:
www.vetservice.co.nz/content/pet_index.php

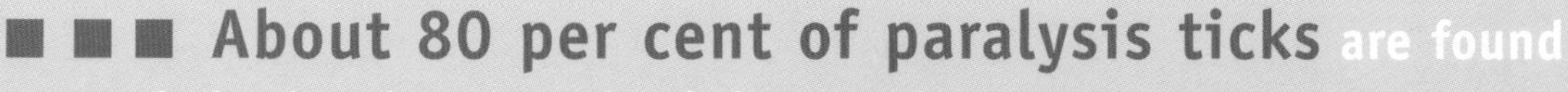

The Healthy Body

A healthy, balanced diet and a sensible exercise routine are the foundation of a healthy body and long-term good health. With our guide to making the most of seasonal produce, you'll be able to enjoy fresh, healthy food all year round.

THE HEALTHY BODY...

EATING WELL

For great tips on buying fresh fruit and vegetables, see page 134. More than 3000 food additives are used in food processing. See what you should avoid, page 138. Use our key to deciphering food labels, page 141. There are lots of traditional ways to preserve food and enjoy the best of seasonal produce all year round, page 144. Turn leftovers into delicious staples for the freezer, page 151.

NUTRITION BASICS

Make healthy eating a lifetime habit by following our guide to eating well, page 152. What is the food pyramid? How does it help you eat a balanced diet? See page 155. See our guide to putting a 'rainbow on your plate' with fruit and vegetables every day, page 158. Try our natural energy boosters, page 160.

EXERCISE FOR LIFE

There are lots of ways to introduce exercise into your daily routine without paying for expensive gym membership. See page 162. Start your aerobic fitness program at your own front door – put on a pair of comfortable shoes and just start walking, page 164. Try our DIY weights workout on page 166. Discover the benefits of stretching and other non-impact forms of exercise, from yoga to tai chi, page 168. Check out our tips on achieving a good night's sleep, page 170.

EATING WELL

Fresh, flavoursome food is one of life's great joys. Make informed choices about the food you buy.

Fresh is best

Many kinds of vegetables, fruit and perishable goods start to lose nutrition and flavour from the moment they're harvested. By making 'fresh, local, seasonal' your mantra, and eating them as soon as possible, you'll enjoy top taste and great health, while saving money and creating minimal impact on the environment.

TEN WAYS TO GET FRESH

1 The best way to get the freshest produce is to grow your own. If you can't, the next best thing is to buy fresh, local produce. The longer produce is stored, and the further it has to travel, the less nutritional value it provides. About 10 per cent is lost – particularly vitamin C – in the journey from farm to table.

2 Purchase food in season. Learn what's available month to month and you'll avoid buying produce that's been in cold storage for long periods. Also take advantage of produce gluts, when retailers often sell items more cheaply.

3 Buy food in small quantities and use it quickly, even if you have to shop more than once a week. It's worthwhile, because you eat produce that's as fresh and nutritious as possible.

4 Handle fragile vegetables and herbs with care, as they bruise easily and rapidly deteriorate.

5 Brush up on correct storage procedures – they help maintain freshness. Your grocer and butcher can advise you on the best methods and will often provide leaflets on storage ideas and preparation tips.

6 Prepare vegetables just before eating or cooking. Once cut, they start to lose vitamins. Soaking cut vegetables in water also leaches nutrients. Seal cut, unused portions tightly in a plastic bag in the fridge.

7 Ripen fruit at room temperature away from direct sunlight, which can destroy nutrients such as vitamins A and C. Refrigeration inactivates the ripening process.

8 Eat meat and fish within 2 days of purchase. Refrigerate or freeze fish as soon as possible – the high fatty acid content deteriorates quickly. Always store meat and fish in the lowest part of the fridge or in the chiller compartment to stop juices dripping onto other refrigerator contents, such as vegetables.

9 When shopping, think about your week's menu and plan to eat the most perishable items first. Leafy greens and herbs have a high water content and tend to go limp and lose their crunch very quickly, while ripe berries and stone fruit bruise easily. Root vegetables, pumpkin, broccoli, apples and oranges, for example, are hardier and last longer if stored correctly.

10 Drink fresh fruit and vegetable juices within 3–4 hours of squeezing. The longer you leave juice exposed to the air, the more it becomes oxidised and begins to lose important nutritional value. Consider adding some of the pulp back in – it's high in fibre.

Check retail and e-tail bookshops for books with 'quick and easy' recipes or 'meals in minutes'.

PROS & CONS

FOOD IRRADIATION

Irradiation is used to reduce food spoilage and extend shelf life. It involves exposing food to a radioactive source, which destroys micro-organisms such as moulds and yeasts, as well as bacteria that can cause food poisoning. The food doesn't come into contact with the energy source and therefore can't be contaminated by radioactivity. There is evidence, however, that in some foods the process reduces the amount of nutrients that help protect us against cancer and other diseases. Irradiation may also cause changes in the taste, texture and appearance of the treated food. The only foods irradiated in Australia and New Zealand are tropical fruit, herbs, spices and herbal infusions.

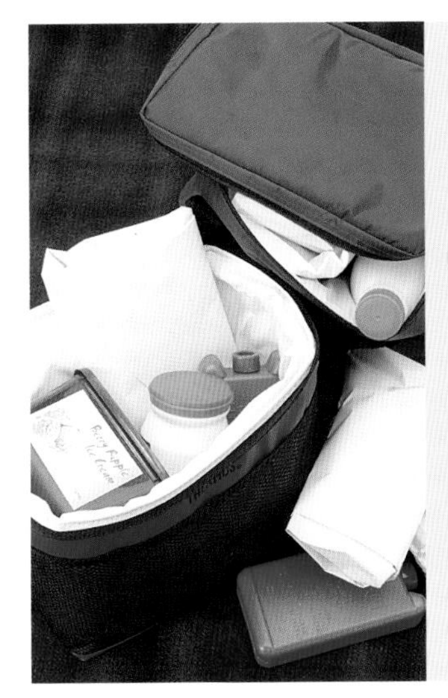

TOP TIP

Carry chiller bags in the boot of the car to ensure perishable food such as meat, fish, dairy produce and herbs don't deteriorate on the way home. Add in some ice bricks too – they will help keep a low, even temperature inside the bag.

IF NOT FRESH...

While fresh is best, sometimes it's not readily available. Consider these issues if you live in an area where access to fresh food is limited.

Food processing creates greenhouse gases through manufacture, packaging and transport.

- Frozen vegetables are probably the healthiest alternatives to fresh. Vegetables are snap-frozen as soon as they are picked and have a similar vitamin content to that of fresh produce.
- Canned produce may contain added sugar or salt. Much canned fruit is packed in heavy syrups, and canned vegetables may be high in sodium. Choose fruit canned in its own juice with no added sugar, and vegetables with no added salt.
- Canning involves exposing fruit and vegetables to extremely high temperatures, which may destroy some vitamins. If you buy food in cans, try to ensure you don't end up stockpiling and then eating old produce. Cans lose an additional 5–10 per cent of vitamins for every year the food is stored.
- Refining removes a lot of the fibre from grains and cereals. Fibre is essential for helping prevent digestive tract cancers, including colon cancer. Refined grains and cereals are also lower in essential nutrients, including iron, vitamin E, the B vitamins, chromium and magnesium.
- Buy dried legumes and whole grains in small quantities and store in the refrigerator to keep them fresh for as long as possible. They're subject to moth attack and faster deterioration in humid areas.
- Dried fruit is a great pantry stand-by. It is a concentrated source of iron and potassium and can be rehydrated to create delicious desserts. Try soaking dried apricots, pears, apples, prunes and a cinnamon stick in water or apple juice overnight. Serve warm with a dollop of ricotta.
- Foods preserved by salting and pickling carry an increased risk of cancer if you eat large amounts of them. Try rinsing off some of the excess salt before you eat them.
- Eating processed fatty meats such as salami, bacon, cured ham and hot dogs may increase the risk of certain types of cancer.
- Consider buying whole spices – the flavours are more authentic, they're cheaper and stay fresher for longer than packet ground spices. Simply grind them up in a mortar and pestle or a coffee grinder kept solely for this purpose.
- Store nuts and seeds in the freezer to keep them fresh for longer. Being rich in oil, they can become rancid very quickly.

■ ■ ■ **The fossil fuel** energy used to produce meat protein is highest for beef and lamb and lowest for FREE-RANGE POULTRY.

Buying fresh

It's worth knowing what to look for when you're shopping for produce. It can make all the difference between buying fruit and vegetables that are nutritious and stay fresh for days, and the disappointment of discovering you've picked food that's past its use-by date. Check out these hints from a seasoned buyer.

FRUIT AND VEGETABLES

Look for firm, brightly coloured and blemish-free produce. Avoid wrinkled, cracked or broken skins or dry, brittle stems and, when buying fruit, choose pieces that feel heavy for their size.

- Avocados: Skin colour isn't an indication of ripeness. Only 'Hass' changes colour from dark green to purplish-black. It's ripe if it feels soft when pressed near the stem end.
- Melons: A clean, sunken scar indicates that the stem was pulled from a ripe melon. The more intense the smell, the riper the fruit.
- Pawpaw or papaya: Pawpaws ripen from the bottom up towards the stem. Look for colour at least halfway up the fruit.
- Peaches and nectarines: Look for the characteristic red blush with a creamy or gold undertone and a good aroma. Avoid green or hard fruit: once fruit is picked, it lacks flavour and usually shrivels and toughens rather than ripens.
- Pears: Tree-ripened fruit can have a mushy texture. It's one fruit that should be picked early and allowed to ripen in storage.
- Pineapples: Some varieties stay green longer than others, so skin colour is not a reliable guide to ripeness. Go for a fragrant aroma.
- Potatoes: Avoid those with peeling skin, green spots, or with shoots from the eyes.
- Soft fruit: Avoid packages with juice leaks; it can be a sign that produce is damaged or going mouldy.
- Sweet corn: Choose corn with the husk on – a bright-green husk is best; a dry and yellowed husk indicates age.
- Watermelon: If the melon is ripe, the rind should have a cream or yellowish undercolour and the seeds will rattle when you shake it.

MEAT, FISH AND SHELLFISH

Smell is a good indicator of freshness. Meat should be pink or red. Whole fish should be shiny, with reddish gills and clear, bulging eyes.

- Avoid packages of meat with lots of liquid – the meat may be dry as a result of losing moisture.
- Choose beef that is red, not brown, with fat that is white, not yellow. Some meat display cases use

Health nut

Fresh nuts and seeds taste great and have many health benefits. As they age, their oils oxidise and become rancid, creating a bitter flavour. The best and cheapest way to buy nuts and seeds is in the shell. Choose nuts that feel heavy for their size: if they feel light, they may be withered inside. If you're buying packaged shelled nuts, buy them from a health food shop with a high turnover. Avoid purchasing them in bulk from bins because their sensitivity to light, heat and oxygen will cause shelled nuts to oxidise quickly.

SUSTAINABLE FISH LIST

Avoid	Buy instead
✗ Blue warehou	✓ Barramundi
✗ Deep sea perch/ orange roughy	✓ Blue-eyed cod
✗ Eastern gemfish/hake	✓ Bream
✗ Redfish	✓ Coral trout
✗ Shark/flake	✓ Flathead
✗ Silver trevally	✓ Leatherjacket
✗ Southern bluefin tuna	✓ Mullet
✗ Swordfish	✓ Snapper
	✓ Whiting

■ ■ ■ **Look for 'heritage'** tomatoes at markets and organic stores. They're FULL OF FLAVOUR – just like tomatoes used to taste.

fluorescent lights to make the meat look redder. Check the colour away from artificial light.

- Look for lamb and pork with a pink to pale red colour, little fat and a smooth, firm texture. Visible bone ends in pork should be red: the whiter the tips of the bone, the older the animal.
- Chicken should have unblemished skin and flesh. Test the breastbone on whole birds: the more flexible it is, the younger the bird and the more tender the flesh.
- Avoid buying endangered fish species and those that are caught by harmful methods, such as long lines, which snare other animals.
- Select fish fillets that look firm and springy. Avoid discoloured or limp flesh. Moistness is not a reliable indicator of age, as fish are often sprayed with water to make them look fresh.
- When selecting live mussels, oysters and clams, their shells should be tightly closed, or close up when tapped.
- Check the flesh of shucked mussels, oysters and clams. It should be shiny and plump, and there should be little liquid in the shell. Scallops should be dry, plump, creamy in colour and sweet-smelling.

- When buying raw prawns, try to select ones that look firm. Limp prawns are old prawns.
- If buying live crabs, check that they are indeed alive – they should be moving their legs.

When you're buying fruit, weigh it in your hands. The heavier the fruit, the greater the juice content.

Best time to buy

Season	Fruit and vegetables
Summer	Apricots, blueberries, mangoes, melons, strawberries Sweet corn, zucchini
Midsummer	Cherries
Summer to autumn	Pawpaw (papaya) Beans (green), tomatoes
Summer and autumn	Figs, raspberries Capsicum, celery, eggplant
Late summer to early autumn	Grapes
Late summer, autumn and late winter	Apples, passionfruit
Early autumn	Blackberries
Autumn	Kiwifruit, quinces Beetroot, mushrooms, silver beet
Autumn and winter	Limes, mandarins, pears Broccoli, leeks, onions, sweet potatoes
Winter	Oranges (navel), oranges (Valencia), rhubarb (red) Artichokes (Jerusalem), avocados brussels sprouts, cabbage, celeriac, English spinach, parsnips, pumpkin, turnips
Late winter	Oranges (Seville)
Winter and early spring	Cauliflower
Winter and spring	Lemons Fennel
Late winter to spring	Artichokes (globe), swedes
Spring	Asparagus
Spring and early summer	Beans (broad), peas

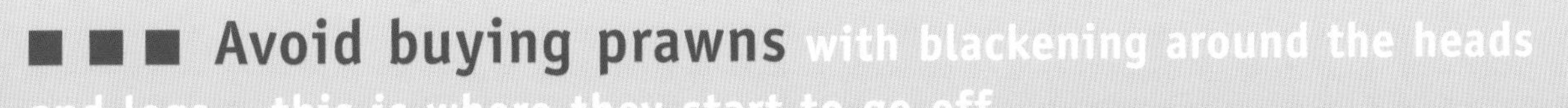

■ ■ ■ **Avoid buying prawns** with blackening around the heads and legs – this is where they start to go off.

What's in the food we eat?

More than 7200 registered pesticides, herbicides and fungicides are used in agricultural production in Australia and New Zealand. While these chemicals are considered safe by regulating authorities, some have been associated with health problems. Unless you eat only what you yourself grow, or purchase certified organic produce, it's likely that the food you buy has been produced using chemicals.

REDUCING CHEMICALS

Pesticides, herbicides, hormones and antibiotics are often used in farming to boost production. Here are some practical ways to help minimise your exposure.

- Grow your own vegetables and fruit – it's the most reliable way of knowing that no harmful substances have been used in their production.
- Purchase produce from farmers' markets or the farm gate. Ask vendors about chemicals used, if any. While some farmers are not certified organic, they may classify themselves as 'almost organic', using natural fertilisers and minimal amounts of chemicals responsibly.
- Quiz greengrocers about their produce. However, if they buy through central cooperatives or markets, they may not know whether chemicals were used.
- Wash all fruit and vegetables thoroughly. Don't use detergent.
- Remove the outer leaves of vegetables and peel non-organic vegetables and fruit to significantly reduce pesticide intake.
- Hormones and antibiotics can be stored in animal fat. Choose lean meat and trim any visible fat from meat before cooking.

- Cook meat, chicken and fish thoroughly and eat cooked vegetables as well as raw. Cooking helps break down chemical residues.
- Eat legumes and soy products to reduce exposure to the hormones and pesticides used on livestock.

PROS & CONS

GM FOODS

Genetically modified (GM) products are created when microbiologists insert the genetic material from one species into the DNA of another, with the aim of producing improved characteristics, such as resistance to insect pests and pesticides, or better flavour or nutrient content. The risks associated with the consumption of GM foods over the long term aren't yet known, as GM crops have only been available for a limited time. Because it's difficult to protect non-GM crops from pollination by GM varieties, there are growing fears that GM crops may change agricultural biodiversity and create dangerous 'super' pests, weeds and viruses.

GM crop	Product
Canola	Canola oil
Corn/maize	Corn oil, cornstarch/cornflour, corn syrup, maltodextrin (for desserts and sweets)
Cottonseed	Blended vegetable oils, snack foods
Potatoes	Potato chips
Soy	Soy oil, soy flour, soy protein, soy lecithin, soy sauce, soy milk, tofu, miso
Sugar beet	Sweetener (sucrose) for drinks, desserts and sweets

■ ■ ■ **Eating a range of foods is better for us nutritionally and reduces the likelihood of exposure to a single pesticide.**

FISH ALERT

Some fish contain small amounts of methylmercury, a toxic substance derived from mercury, which occurs naturally in the underwater environment.

- To minimise the risk, especially if you're pregnant or breastfeeding, moderate your intake of large fish at the top of the food chain. These include shark, swordfish, ray, barramundi, gemfish, ling, orange roughy and southern bluefin tuna.

EARTH-WISE CHECKLIST

Although surveys of commonly eaten foods have found no harmful levels of residues of agricultural chemicals in Australian and New Zealand foods, some items contain more concentrated levels of chemicals or are sprayed more heavily for pests and diseases than other foods. Put these on your organic shopping list:

- Potatoes and onions
- All cruciferous vegetables such as cabbage, cauliflower, broccoli, bok choy and brussels sprouts
- Apples, mangoes and strawberries
- Chocolate, coffee and tea
- Dried fruit
- Nuts and seeds

GM FOOD TIPS

No GM crops are grown commercially in New Zealand, and no GM fruit, vegetables or meat are sold. In Australia, there are a number of GM crops allowed to be grown commercially. These include cotton, soybeans, sugar beet, potatoes and canola.

- About 60 per cent of processed food – both imported and local – now contains genetically modified (GM) ingredients, additives or processing. By law, this must be shown on food labels – check the fine print on packaging.
- Be aware that labels may not tell the whole story. For example, tiny quantities of GM material used in flavourings won't be listed.
- If you don't want to consume GM foods, choose products that state they are 'GM-free', avoid products listed in the table (see opposite), which may be derived from imported or local GM crops, or buy certified organic produce.

hot links

Greenpeace GE-Free Food Guide: www.truefood.org.au/guide2.html; www.gefreefood.org.nz
Chemicals in food: www.nzfsa.govt.nz/consumers/food-safety-topics/chemicals-in-food/index.htm
Food additives: www.answers.com/topic/list-of-food-additives

THE GOOD EGG

Any shopper knows that there's a dazzling array of choice when it comes to buying eggs. Here's what the labels really mean.

- **ANTIBIOTIC-, HORMONE- and PRESERVATIVE-FREE** Food authorities state that hens have not been fed artificial preservatives and hormones since the 1950s. Eggs can't be sold to the public if hens have been given antibiotics.
- **BARN-LAID** Up to 5000 hens may be kept in a large barn divided into pens, usually under artificial lighting. They have room to spread their wings, bathe in dust, perch and scratch for food. The practice of beak trimming is limited.
- **FREE-RANGE** There is no legal definition of free-range but in theory it means that the hens are allowed to roam outside from daylight to dusk and have unrestricted access to food and water.
- **OMEGA-3-ENRICHED** Hens consume a diet enriched with omega-3 fatty acids and vitamin E (from ground flaxseed or fish oil), producing eggs with a higher content of omega-3 essential fatty acids.
- **ORGANIC** Accreditation from a nationally certified body ensures the hens are fed with organic grain and the eggs are not contaminated with chemical fertilisers and pesticides.
- **VEGETARIAN** Hens are fed a diet that contains no meat or meat by-products. They are usually caged so that their diet can be controlled.
- **VITAMIN-ENRICHED** Extra vitamins have been added to the hens' diet. Because eggs are naturally rich in vitamins and minerals, this is largely unnecessary.

In a survey, 92 per cent of Australians wanted all GM ingredients labelled, including products made from GM-fed animals.

Food additives

More than 3000 additives can be used in food processing to improve the safety, appearance, flavour and shelf life of foods. Additives must be approved by Food Standards Australia New Zealand before they can be used, but some cause adverse reactions in certain people. Check labels carefully before you buy.

Take your glasses with you when you go shopping – information about food additives and additive numbers on labels is usually in small print.

FOCUS ON FOOD ADDITIVES

All food additives must be included in the ingredient list found on product packages.

- Responses to food additives vary between individuals: one person may tolerate a substance that makes someone else quite ill. Check *Additives to avoid*, p. 139, if you suffer from food allergies or intolerances, asthma or PKU (phenylketonuria: a congenital metabolic disorder) and try to avoid the additives listed.
- Check food labels carefully if you're vegetarian or vegan. Many of the common food additives, such as emulsifiers, gelatine, glycerol, maltodextrins and natural flavours are derived from animals.
- Avoid buying products with a long list of additives. These foods are likely to be highly processed and may have low nutritional value.
- Be aware that fast foods and supermarket-bought convenience foods often contain synthetic flavours that mimic natural ones. To avoid these, base your diet on fresh foods such as fruits, vegetables, legumes, nuts and lean meats.
- If you're trying to avoid caffeine in soft drinks, labelling laws now make it easier to do so. If guarana, a plant from South America that has high levels of natural caffeine, has been added, it too must be labelled as containing caffeine.
- Watch out for monosodium glutamate (MSG), a flavour enhancer often included in salad dressings, soups and potato chips. Its use allows the manufacturer to reduce the amount of other ingredients in their products. For example, you may get less chicken in chicken soup if MSG is present.
- If you want to eliminate any risk of the potential effects of chemicals on your health, try to buy certified organic produce only.

ADDED NATURALLY

Some food additives come from natural sources and act as disease-preventing phyto-nutrients. The additives below do this. They are derived from carotenoids – the substances that give plants their colour – and are used to colour food.

- ✔ Anthocyanins 163: grape skins or blackcurrants
- ✔ Beta-carotene 160a: plant pigment
- ✔ Lutein 161b: marigolds and green leaves
- ✔ Lycopene 160d: various plant sources
- ✔ Paprika oleoresin 160c: paprika (*Capsicum annuum*)
- ✔ Rubixanthin 161d: rose hips
- ✔ Violoxanthin 161e: yellow pansies

■ ■ ■ **When buying imported produce** be aware that farmers in developing countries may use chemicals banned here.

Additives to avoid

Additive	Purpose	Possible side effects
Aspartame 951	A chemical sweetener widely used in diet soft drinks.	Not safe for people suffering phenylketonuria (PKU). May cause migraine headaches.
Benzoates 210, 211, 212, 213, 216, 218	Sodium benzoate is used as a preservative in margarine, pickles, preserves, jams, soft drinks and fruit juices. Benzoic acid is a common ingredient in flavourings such as chocolate added to beverages, sweets, baked goods and chewing gum.	May cause adverse effects in sensitive people, especially hyperactive children.
Butylated hydroxyanisole (BHA) 320	Petroleum-derived anti-oxidant used to prevent oils, fats, and fat-containing foods from becoming rancid. Sometimes added to food packaging materials.	May cause adverse effects in sensitive people. Try to limit exposure for children. Suspected carcinogen.
Butylated hydroxytoluene (BHT) 321	Petroleum-derived anti-oxidant used to prevent oils, fats, and fat-containing foods from becoming rancid. Sometimes added to food packaging materials.	May cause adverse effects in sensitive people. Try to limit exposure for children. Suspected carcinogen.
Colourings 102, 107, 110, 122, 123, 124, 127, 129, 132, 133, 142, 151, 155, 160b	These add colour, provide uniform colour or restore original colour to a wide range of foods, although colourings are not permitted in meat, fish, poultry, fruits and vegetables.	Colourings may cause hyperactivity in sensitive children. Others cause a range of allergic reactions such as skin rashes and other more serious conditions such as breathing problems.
Disodium 5'-ribonucleotides 635	Flavour enhancer known as the 'new MSG', it can be added to foods stating 'no MSG'.	May cause adverse effects in sensitive people.
Monosodium glutamate (MSG) 621	Flavour enhancer used in many foods, including bottled Chinese sauces.	Unsuitable for pregnant women, infants and children, for asthmatics and salicylate-sensitive people. May cause reactions such as nausea and headaches in sensitive individuals.
Nitrites 249, 250, 251, 252	Preservatives and curing agents commonly used in preserved and luncheon meats.	May cause adverse effects in sensitive people, especially hyperactive children.
Sulphites 220, 221, 222, 223, 224, 225, 228	Preservatives used to prevent dried fruit from desiccation and stiffening; also used to preserve frozen potatoes, and wine.	May cause allergic reaction in sensitive people.
Tertiary butylhydroquinone 319	Petroleum-derived anti-oxidant used in fast foods and baking sprays, and to spray food packaging to prevent colour change and rancidity.	May cause adverse effects in sensitive people, especially hyperactive children.

■ ■ ■ **Check the label** for caffeine. It occurs naturally in tea, coffee and chocolate but is added to ENERGY DRINKS.

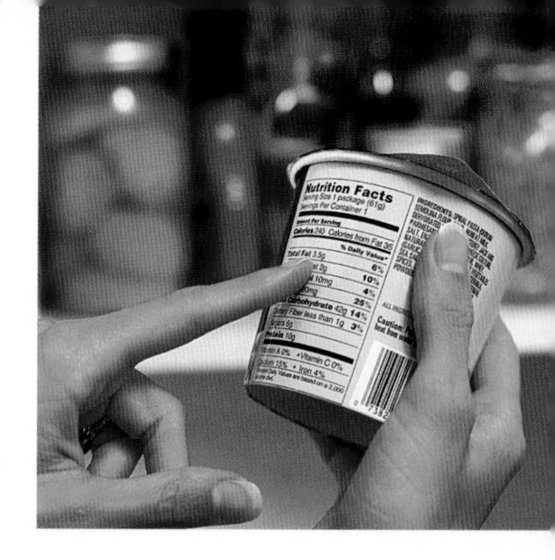

Know your labels

The information on food labels is essential reading if you have a food allergy or intolerance, if you want to cut down on kilojoules, fat, sugar or salt, have special dietary needs or prefer to avoid GM foods or additives. Many food additives are listed simply as code numbers to replace long names appearing on labels.

READ THE SMALL PRINT

- Check the listing of ingredients. They're ranked in descending order, calculated by weight. For example, if an orange juice drink lists its ingredients as glucose, sucrose, oranges, colouring, flavouring and preservative, you'll know that sugars (glucose and sucrose) are the main ingredient in this product.
- Compare products by looking for the percentage of the key or characterising ingredient. For example, in strawberry yoghurt, strawberry is the characterising ingredient and the percentage of strawberries must be shown.
- Use the nutrition information for 100 grams to make comparisons. The label shows the contents in two formats: per serve and per 100 grams. The amount per serve is a measure chosen by the manufacturer and can vary between different brands and products. Remember: the suggested serving size may be so small that it doesn't reflect realistic portions, possibly to disguise the number of kilojoules it contains.
- Check for warnings such as the presence of potential allergens including peanuts and other nuts, seafood, fish, milk, eggs, soy and gluten-containing cereals if you or a family member are susceptible. Food manufacturers are obliged to disclose this information even if it's just a trace amount. For example, the label might read 'This product may contain traces of nuts'.
- Look for advisory statements about substances that pose potential health risks. Information about substances such as quinine, aspartame (contains phenylalanine) and guarana (contains caffeine) must now be included on labels.
- If you want to buy local products, check the wording on the label carefully. 'Product of Australia' means the product must be made in Australia, with all major ingredients coming from Australia. However, 'Made in Australia' means it may be manufactured from both local and imported ingredients, as long as 50 per cent of the production cost is incurred in Australia.
- If you want to be sure that you're buying foods without genetically modified (GM) ingredients, look for 'GM-free' on the label. Exemptions from GM labelling include foods which may contain ingredients produced from animals that were fed GM feed and highly refined foods made from GM crops.

'No added sugars' means that no extra sugar has been added to a product, over and above any natural sugars already present, such as those in fruit (fructose).

TOP TIP

If you want the real thing, be extra careful when buying flavoured foods. Choose an 'apricot-flavoured' product over one that has 'apricot flavour' or 'flavouring'. The difference is that an apricot-flavoured yoghurt, for example, must contain apricots but a yoghurt with apricot flavour need not contain any apricots.

- Look for the Heart Foundation Tick – it's on foods that are tested to ensure they meet strict standards for sodium (salt), saturated fat, kilojoules, trans fat, calcium and fibre. Not all companies apply for the Tick, so its absence from the label doesn't necessarily mean the food is unhealthy.
- Foods labelled 'Organically grown' may contain additives. Sulphur dioxide (a preservative) may be added to organic wines, for example, but minimum quantities are used. All wine additives are shown on Australian labels; in New Zealand, only sulphur dioxide must appear.

FATS FACT-FILE

Even the most straightforward labels sometimes need a little translation. Look out for these descriptions if you're trying to reduce your fat intake and consider their true meanings.

- **Fat-free** This is not completely accurate, as products labelled in this way are permitted to contain up to 0.15 per cent fat.
- **Low-fat** This means the product contains less than 1.5 per cent fat for liquids, and less than 3 per cent fat for solid foods.
- **Reduced-fat** There must be a minimum 25 per cent reduction of the normal amount for the product.
- **Light or 'lite'** This doesn't necessarily mean light in fat or kilojoules. Light olive oil, for example, is light in colour. 'Lite' potato chips have the same fat content as the traditional variety, but are often just cut more thinly.
- **All-natural** Ingredients such as fat and oil may still be present. They're completely natural, but may not be especially healthy.
- **Cholesterol-free or no cholesterol** This doesn't mean the product is low in fat. It may still contain fat – even in high amounts – and this will add to your kilojoule count. What it does mean is that the fat is mono-unsaturated, so it won't lead to heart disease.

The international additive numbering system

Numbers	Additives	What they do
100–181	Colourings	Restore original colour lost in processing; add colour; give the food a uniform colour.
200–297	Preservatives and food acids	Preservatives prevent or slow food spoilage arising from bacteria and fungi. Food acids ensure a constant acid level.
300–385	Anti-oxidants, mineral salts and food acids	Anti-oxidants prevent rancidity and discolouration. Mineral salts improve texture. Food acids ensure a constant acid level.
400–492	Emulsifiers, stabilisers, and thickeners	Emulsifiers keep oil and water mixtures from separating. Stabilisers ensure even distribution. Thickeners thicken, bind and stabilise.
500–586	Anti-caking agents, firming agents	Anti-caking agents prevent particles sticking together. Firming agents retain the natural texture of produce.
600–641	Flavour enhancers	Improve flavour and aroma.
900–1202	Sweetening and bleaching agents; propellants	Enhance sweetness and whiten. Give food a shiny appearance, prevent excess frothing when boiling. Propellants are used in aerosols to release contents.
1400–1450	Thickeners	Thicken, bind and stabilise.
1505–1521	Sequestrants and solvents	Sequestrants help prevent food spoilage. Solvents hold substances in a solution or suspension.

Eating organic

How can you ensure that the foods you buy are the purest available, free of chemicals, drugs or genetically modified substances? It's simple: choose certified organic produce. Eaten fresh, organic food is as nature intended – flavoursome, full of nutrients and produced in harmony with the environment.

WHY BUY ORGANIC?

- Organic standards prohibit the use of the synthetic fertilisers, pesticides and herbicides that are widely used in conventional farming – safer for both the farmers and the consumer. They also forbid genetic modification as well as the routine dosing of animals with antibiotics and growth hormones.
- Organic agriculture allows fewer dangerous wastes into the environment than conventional farming. Run-off from synthetic pesticides and fertilisers contaminates waterways and pollutes drinking water. Many birds, animals and insects die because they have eaten plants that have been sprayed with chemicals, or because they have consumed chemicals themselves – either directly or through the food chain.
- Conventional farming uses more petroleum than any other industry, primarily through the production of synthetic fertilisers and pesticides.
- Organic guidelines ensure a more humane treatment of animals than conventional farming. For example, organic farmers don't use artificial lighting to increase productivity.
- Organic farmers regard soil as the foundation of the food chain and constantly work to improve its structure. Thus they reduce the risk of topsoil being washed or blown away, in turn reducing erosion.
- Organic practices encourage biodiversity, while conventional farming focuses on monoculture, which increases the susceptibility of crops to disease and pest infestations.
- Organic food tastes better! Just ask anyone who grows their own.

WARNING!

▼ Meat that is labelled 'hormone-free' or 'chemical-free' isn't necessarily organic. The label means that no growth hormones were fed to the animals.

TIPS FOR GOING ORGANIC

If you don't want to go 100 per cent organic, minimise your exposure to agricultural chemicals by buying organic versions of the produce you use most.

- Look for a label displaying the name and logo of an accredited organisation certifying that the product is organic or biodynamic (see the symbols on page 13).

~ STAR SAVER ~

You can save money on organic produce by buying direct – from the farm gate, from farmers' markets and from local 'co-ops'. Online, home-delivery sources can be economical too as they frequently bypass one or two links in the supply chain.

PROS & CONS

ORGANIC FOOD

Most organic food costs more than conventionally farmed foods for two reasons: organic farms tend to be smaller than conventional farms, and organic farming is much more labour and management intensive. However, by buying food that is certified organic, you can be sure that the farmer hasn't used any methods or chemicals that could ultimately harm you or the environment. In this way you might regard the cost as a worthwhile investment in both your health and the health of the environment, which benefits everybody.

■ ■ ■ **Organic farmers combat insect pests using farming practices such as crop rotation and crop diversity.**

- The organic fruit and vegetables you buy may not be uniform in size and shape. They're grown for their nutritional content and taste, not their looks.
- Don't be put off by the different colour of some organic dried fruit. For example, organic apricots are darker in colour and more flavourful because they don't contain the preservative sulphur dioxide.

- Some organic foods have a shorter shelf life than conventionally grown produce, because they don't contain preservatives. Don't store them for too long before eating.
- To save on packaging, buy organic grains, cereals and pulses loose. Select a natural foods shop with a high turnover.
- Check produce carefully before buying. An organic label doesn't mean it's always as fresh or nutritious as it should be.
- Don't be put off if your organic fruit or vegetables come with the odd insect. It proves that what you're buying hasn't been treated with chemicals.

Organic certification

Organisation	Qualification
Bio-Dynamic Research Institute (BDRI)	Certifies biodynamic operations to the Demeter standard; an international trademark registered in Australia since 1967.
National Association for Sustainable Agriculture Australia (NASAA)	Certifies the organic industry and organic produce as organic or biodynamic.
Australian Certified Organic (ACO)	The largest certification organisation in Australia. Certifies the organic industry and organic and biodynamic produce.
Organic Growers of Australia (OGA)	Certifies farmers and processors producing a range of foods.
Tasmanian Organic Producers (TOP)	Certifies organic and biodynamic food that has been either grown or made in Tasmania.
Organic Food Chain (OFC)	A grower-owned and -operated organisation.
Safe Food Queensland (SFQ)	Run by the Queensland government, SFQ is the most recent certification organisation in Australia.
International Federation of Organic Agriculture Movements (IFOAM)	The major international organic organisation.
Australian Quarantine and Inspection Service (AQIS)	Provides inspection and certification for a range of exports.
Bio-Grow New Zealand	New Zealand's leading organic certification body, internationally recognised and one of only 20 certification agencies worldwide to hold IFOAM accreditation.
AgriQuality New Zealand	Provides a range of independent, internationally recognised certification, including NZFSA Organic Certification.
Bio Dynamic Farming and Gardening Association in NZ Inc.	Certifies biodynamic operations to the Demeter standard in New Zealand.

hot links

Explore the world of organics and find organic products and services:
www.organicchoice.com.au
www.theorganicsdirectory.com.au
www.organicpathways.co.nz
www.soil-health.org.nz

■ ■ ■ **Try organic beer, made from hops, wheat and malt – heavily sprayed crops when farmed conventionally – and spring water.**

Storing and preserving

Bottle and preserve fruits and vegetables when they are in season – they're at their most choice and plentiful and it's usually when they're cheapest to buy. Storing fresh foods correctly will help maintain freshness, but remember the longer fresh produce is stored the less nutrional value it provides.

GARDEN TO PANTRY

Choose unblemished garden produce to give it the best chance of storing well. Keep it in a dry, dark, cool place, away from strong-smelling substances.

- Choose fruit that ripens late in the season as it keeps best. Some varieties of apples, such as Cox's and Bramley's, keep better than others. Pick pears before they ripen.
- Store apples and pears on shelves or in boxes in a dark, slightly moist environment. Ensure the fruit doesn't touch each other, or wrap each one in greaseproof paper, or newspaper if necessary. This stops rotting fungi and bacteria from spreading.
- Don't wash vegetables before storing them, as this speeds up the deterioration process.
- To store onions and garlic string them together when they are completely dry and hang them from the ceiling. Alternatively, hang them in bags, or in nylon pantihose.
- If you grow pumpkins for storage, leave the fruit on the vine until the plant dies, then leave the fruit to dry in the full sun for a few days. Collect the pumpkins and hang them individually in net produce bags, ensuring they don't touch one another. They should keep for a few months.

- Pack root vegetables, such as potatoes and carrots, in barely moist sand or sawdust in large containers so the roots don't touch, otherwise they will rot.
- String chillies together by threading a large needle with double thread, and poking the needle through the chilli, just below the green cap. Hang the chillies in a sunny place to dry.
- Preserve herbs by drying bunches in a warm, airy space. Hang them upside-down to drain the essential oils into the leaves. Once they are dry, strip the leaves from the stems and store in airtight containers in a cool place away from the sun.
- Check produce regularly and remove any rotting fruit or vegetables. This prevents mould from spreading.

Food for the pantry

Type of food	Life span
Bottled fruit	6–12 months
Chutneys	6 months; refrigerate after opening
Fruit butters	No more than 2 weeks, but can be frozen
Jams, jellies and marmalades	6 months; refrigerate after opening
Pickles	1–2 months; refrigerate after opening
Vinegars	3–6 months

Warning!

If food stored in jars shows any of these signs, throw it out.

- The contents shoot out when the lid is opened. When opening a jar, point the lid away from your face.
- The jar or lid has mould on it, or food has leaked out during storage.
- The liquid contents appear to be bubbling or look discoloured.
- The food looks slimy, cloudy, shrivelled or spongy.
- The contents smell 'off'.

■ ■ ■ **Bring a taste of summer to winter vegetables by adding a spoonful of HOME-MADE summer relish or chutney.**

~ **STAR SAVER** ~

Make your own herbal or fruit vinegars. It's easy to do and costs a fraction of the price of the varieties sold in gourmet delicatessens. Store them in attractive wine bottles topped with a pourer-stopper. They make great gifts, too.

PRESERVING METHODS

Preserving food is a great way to make the most of cheap and plentiful seasonal produce.

BOTTLING AND CANNING

- This is a time-consuming but effective method of preserving tomatoes and other fruits. Heat is used to kill bacteria, yeasts and fungi, and to halt enzyme activity.
- Sealing the jars or cans prevents the reintroduction of spoiling micro-organisms.

DRYING

- This inactivates the bacteria, yeast, enzymes and fungi in food, which all need moisture to thrive. A home drying machine is easy to use for all sorts of fruits and vegetables and involves less preparation time.

FREEZING

- This method retards the growth and activity of micro-organisms, allowing food to retain its quality for periods of up to a year. All you need is a freezer.

SUN-DRIED TOMATOES

If you live in an unpolluted area that has hot, sunny summers, you can easily make your own sun-dried tomatoes. If not, dry them in the oven.

IN THE SUN

The key to success is drying the fruit over a block of 3 or 4 uninterrupted sunny days.

- Make drying frames from four 1-m lengths of untreated wood. Stretch nylon mesh or cheesecloth across the top, and tack it to the underside of the frame. Reinforce the frame by tacking criss-crossed string underneath.
- Core Roma tomatoes and cut them in half.
- Place the fruit in a single layer on the frame, and leave it out in the sun all day. Remove the tomatoes as they dry, and bring the whole lot inside at night.
- Repeat this procedure for 3 or 4 days, as required. (If you use cherry tomatoes they'll be ready in a day.)
- To destroy any insect eggs, spread the dried tomatoes on a baking tray and place it in an oven preheated to 100°C for 10–15 minutes.

IN THE OVEN

You can dry tomatoes in the oven as long as you use the lowest heat setting. This will prevent them from burning.

- Spread halved and cored Roma tomatoes, cut side up, on wire racks over oven trays.
- Sprinkle the tomatoes with salt, and leave them in the oven at the lowest temperature for 6–8 hours. Turn them regularly, until dried.

STORING

- To store your dried tomatoes, pack them into sterilised jars, cover with olive oil and seal.
- Alternatively, use some airtight containers without oil and store them in the fridge.
- If you plan to keep the dried tomatoes for a long time, just freeze them.

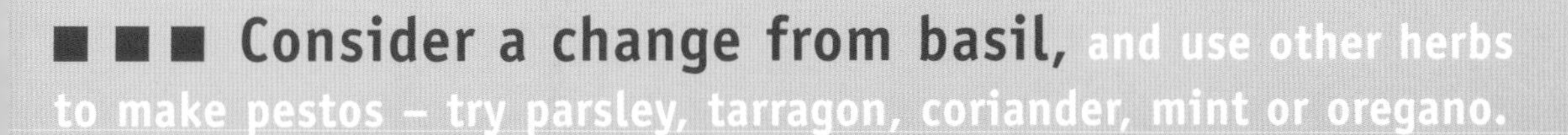

■ ■ ■ **Consider a change from basil,** and use other herbs to make pestos – try parsley, tarragon, coriander, mint or oregano.

Recipes for the pantry

Another way to make the most of your garden harvest or a glut of seasonal produce is to make it into delicious condiments such as vinegars, chutneys and relishes. They'll contain no preservatives, be full of flavour and will cost much less than shop-bought items. They also make wonderful gifts.

HERB VINEGARS

Tarragon, basil, dill and rosemary are the classic herbs for vinegars, but oregano, thyme, parsley, mint and nasturtium leaves are all delicious too. If you like a particular herb, try it.

1 cup herbs
2 cups white wine or apple cider vinegar with minimum 5% acidity
unbleached coffee filter paper or cheesecloth

- Gather your favourite herbs in the morning after the dew has evaporated, but before the mid-morning sun hits the leaves.
- Wash off any grit or small insects and blot dry with clean towels.
- Next, remove the leaves from each of the stems.

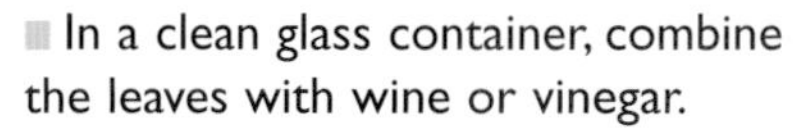

- In a clean glass container, combine the leaves with wine or vinegar.
- Cover the container, and leave it in a cool, dark place. Stir or shake the mixture every couple of days.
- Taste the vinegar after 1 week. If the flavour is intense enough, strain through a coffee filter or some clean cheesecloth into a sterilised wine bottle. Cork and cap, label and store in a cool, dark place.

FRUIT VINEGARS

This is a great way to use soft or damaged fruit. Almost any fruit works well, but raspberry, strawberry, blueberry and cherry vinegars are sensational.

1 cup fruit, washed, dried and mashed or roughly chopped
2 cups vinegar with minimum 5% acidity, red for dark fruit, white for light fruit
approx. 1/8 to 1/2 cup sugar or 1/2 tbsp to 1/3 cup honey

- Place the fruit and vinegar in a clean glass container. Cover, and put it in a cool, dark place to macerate for a week.
- Taste to check the flavour. If you want a really intense flavour, strain out the old fruit and replace it with a new batch.

- Leave for another week or two. Repeat as often as necessary to achieve the flavour you want.
- When you're satisfied with the flavour, strain the vinegar into a small saucepan.
- Add sugar or honey to taste.
- Bring the mixture to the boil, stirring to dissolve the sugar. Then reduce the heat and allow the vinegar to simmer for 3 minutes, skimming if necessary.
- Leave to cool, then bottle. Cork and cap, label and store in a cool, dark place.

TASTY GREEN TOMATO CHUTNEY

500 g Granny Smith apples, peeled, cored and chopped
2 kg mixed green and red tomatoes, peeled and roughly chopped
500 g onions, chopped
4 large cloves garlic, crushed
1 tbsp sea salt
3 tbsp pickling spice, a blend of whole or coarsely cut spices (from supermarkets), tied in sterilised cheesecloth
2 1/2 cups apple cider vinegar
500 g sugar

Preserving food at home is a rewarding way to capture the taste of home-grown or locally produced fruits and vegetables.

In a large preserving pan or stockpot, combine the apples, tomatoes, onions, garlic, salt, spice bag, and half the vinegar.
Bring to the boil, lower the heat and simmer, stirring frequently, for 1 hour, until the chutney is thick.
Dissolve the sugar in the remaining vinegar and add it to the chutney. Simmer, stirring occasionally, for another 1½ hours, until the chutney is very thick.
Remove the spice bag, and spoon the chutney into warm, sterilised jars. Seal, label and store in a cool, dark place. To allow the flavours to develop, leave the chutney for a month before using it.

CARAMELISED RED ONION RELISH

2 large red onions, peeled and sliced very thinly
¼ cup firmly packed, dark brown sugar
1 cup dry red wine
3 tbsp balsamic vinegar
dash sea salt
freshly milled black pepper
wide-mouthed 500 ml jar

In a heavy non-stick frying pan, combine the onions and sugar and cook, stirring frequently, over a medium-high heat, uncovered, for about 25 minutes until the onions turn golden and start to caramelise.
Add the wine and vinegar and bring to the boil over a high heat. Reduce the heat to low and cook for about 15 minutes, stirring often, until most of the liquid has evaporated.
Season to taste with salt and pepper, and ladle into the jar. Cool, seal and label. Store in the fridge and use within 3 weeks. Or store it for a longer time in the freezer.

MARMALADE

This recipe makes enough marmalade to fill three 450-gram jars.

skins of 3 navel oranges
1 lemon
3 cups filtered water
1 kg sugar

Chop the orange skins very finely.
Chop the lemon into small pieces.
Put the orange skins and the lemon in a large glass bowl with the filtered water. Leave for 24 hours.
Transfer the mixture into a large preserving pan or stockpot. Bring to the boil, reduce the heat and simmer until the rind is very tender (about 30 minutes).
Remove from the heat, cover and stand for another 24 hours.
Put a saucer into the freezer. You'll use this later to test whether the marmalade has set.
Measure the mixture, and add 1 cup sugar for each cup of pulp.
Bring to the boil, stirring to dissolve the sugar. Boil until the mixture gels.
To check whether it has set, put 1 teaspoon of marmalade onto the cold saucer, leave for a minute and push the jam with your finger. If it's ready, it will wrinkle.
Pour into warm, sterilised jars, seal and label.

PRESERVED LEMONS

Make several batches of this recipe when lemons are at their peak and they'll last you a year. This recipe will fill a 750-ml jar.

5 lemons
80 g sea salt
4 whole cloves
4 cardamom pods, bruised
1 tsp coriander seeds
2 bay leaves
1½ cups olive or canola oil

Wash and dry the lemons, then cut them into quarters lengthways.
Put the lemons in a colander that has been placed over a bowl and sprinkle them evenly with salt.
Leave to stand for 24 hours. The skins should soften as the juices run out of the lemons.
Pack into a sterilised jar with the spices and bay leaves. Completely cover the lemons with oil.
Seal the jars, and leave in the fridge for 1 month before using.
Serve the preserved lemons thinly sliced or finely chopped with a Greek salad, Moroccan tajines, sprinkled over fish or in dips.

BRANDIED CHERRIES

1 kg large, sweet cherries
2 cups sugar
750 ml bottle brandy

Thoroughly wash and dry the cherries. Stems and pits may be removed, or left in.
Pack the cherries into a large sterilised jar.
Mix together the sugar and brandy, and pour over the cherries. Seal, and leave in a cool, dark place for a month, turning the jar every day to dissolve the sugar.

Follow the instructions in recipes carefully. Altering the amounts may affect the QUALITY AND SAFETY of preserved foods.

Freezing foods

Always freeze fresh foods when they are at their peak. For best flavour and nutrition, vegetables – especially peas, sweet corn and broad beans, which convert sugar to starch within hours of being picked – should be frozen as soon as they're harvested. Leftovers can be handy if you freeze them soon after cooking.

GARDEN TO FREEZER

- Pick basil regularly through summer to prevent it going to seed. Make it into pesto, and package it in small portions – around a quarter of a cup – before freezing. Frozen pesto doesn't go brown, which tends to happen when it is stored in the fridge.
- Grate zucchini coarsely (in a food processor or manually) and put it into a large strainer to drain, pressing out as much liquid as possible. Package in 1- or 2-cup portions and freeze. Use in fritters, pancakes, bread, pies and on pasta.
- Cut capsicums into quarters, remove the seeds and white membranes, arrange them on a grill tray with the skin side facing up. Grill on *High* until the skins are black. Cover the capsicum with an old tea towel, and when the pieces are cool enough to handle, lift off the skins. Freeze in portion sizes for instant roast capsicum.
- Pick spinach leaves and remove the stalks. Blanch the leaves for a few seconds in boiling water or, alternatively, fry them in a little olive oil. Drain, squeeze out any extra moisture, and freeze in serving-sized portions. Frozen spinach is a great stand-by for cooked dishes.
- Don't waste the zest of organic or home-grown citrus fruits. Before squeezing, pare the zest with a citrus zester and store it in an airtight container in the freezer, adding to it continually. Use it as needed.
- Freeze herbs in ice-cube trays. First, wash and chop the herbs, then place a small portion in each ice-cube compartment. Cover with boiling filtered water and place the tray in the freezer. When solid, transfer the cubes to a freezer bag. Toss into sauces, casseroles or soups.
- Squeeze the juice of lemons and limes, then freeze them in ice-cube trays to use later.

BLANCHING VEGETABLES

To retain their colour, taste and texture, most vegetables need blanching before freezing.

- Use a large stockpot that has a double steamer insert and bring about 15 cm of water to the boil.
- Place the vegetables in a thin layer in each basket, put the lid on and begin timing. The smaller and more tender the item, the less time it needs in the steamer.
- To halt the cooking process, plunge the vegetables into a sink of iced water. Freeze water in milk or juice cartons the night before to ensure the water is really icy.

DEFROSTING TIPS

✔ Use defrosted fish within 1–2 days.

✔ Thaw minced meats in the refrigerator.

✔ Precooked foods that are low in moisture content, such as baked goods, can be thawed at room temperature.

✘ Never defrost perishable foods on the kitchen counter, outdoors or even in your home's coolest room. Thawing at room temperature can stimulate the breeding of micro-organisms, which may lead to food poisoning.

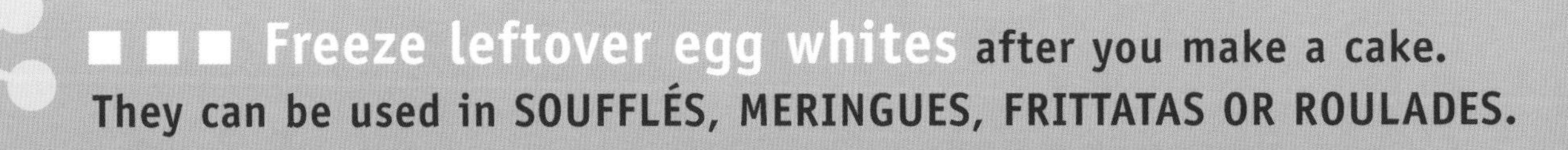

ROASTED TOMATO SAUCE

This sauce freezes beautifully, so make plenty when summer tomatoes are at their peak.

1 kg medium, ripe red tomatoes
olive oil
5–10 cloves garlic, sliced
1 ½ tbsp balsamic vinegar

Slice each tomato across the middle and place the halves on lightly oiled baking sheets.
Drizzle each tomato half with a little olive oil.
Put some garlic slices on top of each tomato.
Place the sheets in a 190°C oven and roast for about an hour – note that larger tomatoes may take longer – until the edges are slightly blackened and the liquid in the pan has evaporated.
Scrape them into a food processor and process to a rough purée. Press it through a sieve to remove seeds and skin.
Add the balsamic vinegar. Taste and season with freshly cracked black pepper.
Serve tossed through pasta, with some shaved parmesan.

Not for freezing

So many foods freeze successfully that it's easier to mention those that don't.

- Raw eggs in their shells
- Hard-boiled eggs
- Boiled white potatoes
- Raw potatoes
- Commercial cottage cheese
- Salads or desserts made with gelatine
- Salad vegetables, such as lettuce, tomatoes, radishes and cucumbers
- Cakes with cream fillings
- Cakes with icings made from egg whites
- Custard pies, cream pies or pies with meringue

GUIDELINES FOR FREEZING

- To prevent bacterial growth, you need to freeze leftovers as soon as possible – in fact, immediately if they contain meat. To speed up the cooling process, store leftovers in small, shallow containers.
- To prevent freezer burn (resulting in dehydrated food), use airtight containers. Remove as much air as possible from the container before sealing solid foods.

- Allow for expansion when freezing liquids or semi-liquid foods. A good guide is to leave a space of about 3 cm below the rim of the container you're using.
- Avoid overloading your freezer with new foods. If you plan to do a major cooking and freezing session, reduce the temperature to the lowest point at least 24 hours in advance. Once all the foods are frozen, return the thermostat to its usual setting.
- Don't forget to label your containers with the contents and the date on which they were frozen. In general, vegetables will keep for 10 months if home-frozen, but for 8 months if purchased. Check the guidelines in your freezer manual and don't keep anything for longer than 12 months.

WARNING!

▼ Do not freeze raw fish you have purchased unless you are certain it really is fresh and hasn't been frozen before.

- The higher the oil content of the fish, the less well it will freeze. Lean fish such as flathead or snapper, for example, can be frozen for up to 6 months, while oily fish such as salmon and trout should be eaten within 3 months.
- Raw shellfish can be stored in the freezer for up to 6 months. If you are freezing cooked shellfish, cook it as soon as possible after purchase and store it in the freezer for up to 3 months.
- If you have leftover stock or coconut milk, freeze it instead of throwing it out.
- Freeze leftover wine and add it to stews and marinades.

■ ■ ■ **The loss of texture** that freezing causes is more noticeable in fruit, which is eaten raw, than in cooked vegetables.

The efficient cook

With forward planning you can cook and freeze seasonal produce when it's at its peak – and cheap and plentiful. And by using leftovers economically and cooking healthy 'fast-food' recipes that use less gas and electricity, you'll reduce your time in the kitchen as well as save money.

MAKE A LITTLE EXTRA

When preparing dinner, make extra portions to use in meals the following day. It's a good way of saving time as well as money on your energy bills. Or freeze extra portions to use later – they're a great stand-by for busy days.

- When grilling or roasting chicken breasts or lamb fillets, cook a few more at the same time and use them in sandwiches the next day.
- Boil extra potatoes and pasta to use in a potato or pasta salad. Once it is cooked, toss the pasta in a little oil to prevent it from drying out, and cover it almost immediately.
- When making pizza dough, make two or three times the quantity and freeze the surplus. Yeast dough keeps for up to 2 months in the freezer.
- When boiling eggs, cook a couple more to use in spinach salad, sandwiches and potato salad.
- Instead of frying onions for particular meals, consider doing a large batch at a time and freezing it. Frying a number of onions takes only a little more power than one or two.
- Next time you cook butter beans or soy beans, cook the whole packet and freeze what you don't use. Whiz to a purée in a blender, and package in 1-cup portions to add later to blended soups or mashed potato, or for use in bean cakes.
- When making crepes, prepare a large batch and freeze what you don't eat in a stack, separated by greaseproof paper circles. You can save the paper and reuse it with the next batch.
- When making shortcrust pastry, double the quantity and freeze half, either as a dough ball or pressed into a pie tin, ready for blind baking.
- Make the most of seasonal produce and cook a double batch of healthy fruit or vegetable muffins. They freeze well, and are ideal for a quick breakfast or nutritious snack.
- Cook large batches of samosas, spinach and feta triangles or other small pastry-encased goodies, and freeze the leftovers for another day.
- If you frequently use a particular type of nut – such as walnuts – in your cooking, buy a couple of kilograms of very fresh nuts, chop them roughly by hand or in a food processor, and freeze them.

Don't boil the goodness out of food. Cook vegetables until they are only just tender. Steaming is a good way to preserve the nutrients.

PROS & CONS

IS MICROWAVE COOKING SAFE?

Microwave ovens save on energy by using a fraction of the cooking time of conventional ovens. But does microwaving have an effect on your food and your health? It seems likely that microwaving actually retains more vitamins, minerals and nutrients in food than boiling. The process is not harmful because the radiation stops once the oven has been turned off. However, there is a health risk if the food is not heated evenly all the way through – a drawback of microwaves – as this won't kill all the bacteria.

Use leftover steamed vegetables in a frittata. Just add beaten eggs and some cheese and cook it as for an omelette.

TASTY LEFTOVERS

Don't throw away leftovers. With a little planning and imagination, they can become freezer staples.

BEANS

- Mash and freeze. Add to soups, mashed potatoes and fish cakes.
- Make a delicious dip by mashing beans with a little thick but low-fat yoghurt and a dash of chilli.
- Serve in a taco with chopped onions, tomatoes, avocados, shredded lettuce and grated cheese.

POTATOES

- Make potato cakes or fish cakes.
- For a treat, add some chopped cooked onion, chopped parsley and plenty of cracked black pepper to leftover mashed potato and fry in a little olive oil in a non-stick pan until golden brown and crispy.
- Brush potato skins with a little oil and bake in a hot oven until crisp and golden. Serve with a spicy salsa, chutney or dip.

RICE

- Leftover rice makes an instant piecrust. Combine 2 cups with a beaten egg and press over the base of a lightly oiled pie or quiche tin. Bake in a preheated 180°C oven for 10 minutes. Add a filling and bake for the specified time.
- Use leftover rice in a rice salad, or make fried rice or rice pudding.
- Leftover risotto loses its characterising moisture and therefore doesn't reheat well. However, it can be turned into delicious risotto

cakes. Mix in an egg for easier handling and shape the rice into round patties. Coat in flour, shake off the excess and shallow-fry in hot oil.

STOCK

- Use leftovers to make stock. Freeze it in ice-cube trays and use it when you need it. It's much tastier than the bought variety. Simmer some vegetable trimmings – such as broccoli and cauliflower stalks, cabbage cores and parsley stems – and leftover chicken, beef or fish bones for a couple of hours.

TOP TIP

Wraps – pita bread, tortillas, lavash bread, roti or tissue-thin mountain bread – are great for using small amounts of leftovers for lunch the following day. Simply season with anything from a little pepper or balsamic vinegar to sweet chilli sauce or tahini, wrap and serve.

COOK AND LEAVE

Save on gas or electricity, and give yourself time to do other things in the kitchen by switching off the cooker once you have brought these carbohydrate foods to the boil and letting them cook in the residual heat.

- **COUSCOUS** Delicious and quick to prepare. Just combine equal quantities of couscous and hot water or hot stock in a small bowl, stir well to combine, cover and leave for 10–15 minutes. Fluff with a fork and serve.
- **RICE** Bring a large saucepan of water to the boil, add the rice, stir it quickly to separate the grains, and bring to the boil again. Remove the saucepan from the heat, cover and let it stand. Start checking white rice after 5 minutes to see if it is cooked, brown rice after 15 minutes. Though some types may take up to 30 or 40 minutes, long-grain varieties cook in less time than short-grain ones.
- **SOBA NOODLES and RICE VERMICELLI** Place the noodles in a bowl, pour over plenty of boiling water, stir to separate the noodles, then leave for about 10 minutes. After that, they'll be perfectly cooked and ready to serve.

Turn leftover bread – or home-made bread failures – into breadcrumbs and freeze. They're much nicer than shop-bought crumbs.

NUTRITION BASICS

Eating a broad variety of good natural foods can help you live a long, healthy and active life.

Healthy habits

There's no single blueprint for eating a healthy diet, just two simple principles. Give your body a variety of different foods, including unprocessed foods, every day and eat – and drink – in moderation. While miracle ingredients and diet fads come and go, these keys to good health will never change.

Making changes to the way you eat is easier if you do it gradually, getting comfortable with each step before moving onto the next. Every step will help to make healthy eating a natural, painless part of your lifestyle.

Experts tell us that it takes 21 days to form a new habit – that's only 3 weeks to a healthier diet.

1 Start the day well by eating a fibre-rich breakfast of porridge or natural muesli topped with fruit. Eating breakfast keeps you mentally and physically alert.

2 Keep coffee and caffeine-containing soft drinks to a minimum – they give only a short burst of caffeine-fuelled energy. Try one or two cups daily of black or green tea. Tea contains anti-oxidants which are associated with lower rates of cancer and heart disease. A cup of black or green tea has about half the caffeine of a cup of coffee.

3 Slowly reduce the amount of sugar you take in tea or coffee. It's better to retrain your palate than to use artificial sweeteners, so that you lower your desire for sweet foods and drinks overall.

4 When baking cakes or biscuits, substitute half wholemeal flour for white flour, gradually increasing it as your taste changes. Eat wholegrain bread more often than white – it has more B vitamins and twice as much fibre. Experiment with different types made from a variety of grains.

5 Buy brown rice and wholemeal or spelt pasta rather than white to boost fibre and B vitamin intake. Introduce it gradually as part of a mixed dish if the family resists.

6 Gradually increase the variety of fruit and vegetables you eat to seven servings a day. For example, including a piece of fruit with your breakfast and one as a snack, having a salad with lunch and two cups of cooked vegetables for dinner would give you your daily requirement.

7 Replace sugar- and fat-filled snacks such as biscuits, pastries and chocolate with fruit. It doesn't have to be dull – try dried fruit or a tropical fruit salad for variety.

8 Try to do without deep-fried takeaway foods to reduce your saturated fat intake. Also, try to use just a scrape of butter, polyunsaturated or mono-unsaturated margarine. Or experiment with a nut butter or mashed avocado on bread. Try cold-pressed macadamia or canola oil for cooking.

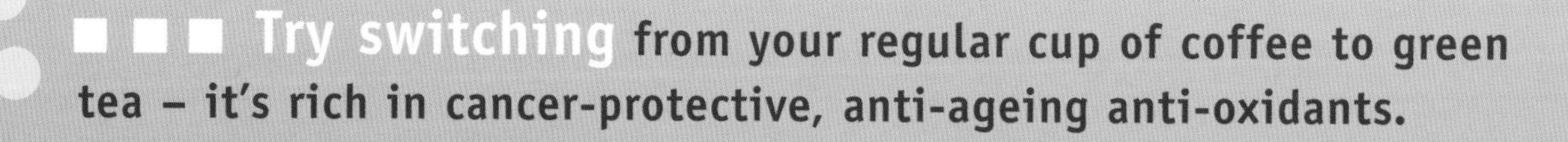

HEALTHY BURGERS

If you love burgers, here's a healthy version. This recipe makes two burgers. Save time – double the burger mixture and freeze it for later use.

75 g top quality minced beef
2 garlic cloves, crushed
½ small carrot, grated
½ small fresh beetroot, grated
¼ cup cooked kidney beans, mashed
1 tbsp parsley, roughly chopped
1 egg
2 tbsp wholemeal breadcrumbs
1 tbsp olive oil
¼ onion, sliced in rings
2 avocado slices
2 tomato slices
few lettuce leaves, torn

Mix the beef, garlic, carrot, beetroot, kidney beans, parsley, egg and breadcrumbs together in a large bowl. Form the mixture into two small patties.

Heat the oil and cook the onion rings in a frying pan over a low heat for 10 minutes or so, until they are caramelised – brown but not burnt.

Meanwhile, fry the meat patties in a non-stick pan on both sides until brown.

Hollow out two crisp wholemeal buns. Place the burgers and the onion rings on the buns and pile with the avocado, tomato and lettuce.

THE TRUTH ABOUT...

FAST FOOD

Takeaway food scores high on convenience, but low in the health stakes. While some fast-food chains have made an effort to introduce more fresh vegetables and fruit onto their menus, others have actually increased their serving sizes – and their profits. Even the healthier options, such as accompanying side salads, can sometimes be compromised by creamy salad dressings and fluffy bread rolls with high levels of sugar and low levels of fibre. If you enjoy hamburgers and hot dogs, try to limit them to a once-a-week treat – and pass on the extras like cheese, fried onions and bacon.

9 Drink enough water. Moderately active adults need about 2 litres per day. Check your hydration by looking at the colour of your urine. It should be pale yellow or clear.

10 Use less salt, or cut it out altogether. Excess salt over time can result in a rise in blood pressure. It's easy to avoid too much salt if you eat mainly fresh food because most of the salt in our diet comes from processed food. Instead of reaching for the salt shaker, use herbs, spices and other natural flavourings such as fresh lemon or lime juice.

11 Eat dairy products in moderation. Low-fat or no-fat milks, yoghurts and ice-creams help keep saturated fat intake down.

12 Learn to love soy. It's an excellent source of plant protein and appears to reduce the risk of heart disease by helping lower cholesterol levels. It's also been shown to protect against breast cancer in women and prostate cancer in men. Aim for at least one serving a day of soy milk or soy yoghurt, tofu or tempeh.

13 Choose lean cuts of red meat and minimise your intake of processed meats such as salami, bacon and sausages. Lean meat is a good source of iron, zinc, vitamin B_{12} and high-quality protein whereas high intakes of processed meats have been associated with a greater risk of bowel cancer.

14 Eat more fish to increase your intake of beneficial omega-3 essential fatty acids. Aim for two to four meals a week and choose oily fish such as salmon, mackerel, sardines and mullet.

15 Prepare vegetarian meals occasionally. Include legumes, such as kidney beans, soy beans, chick peas or lentils. These have a low glycaemic index (GI) so you'll feel fuller for longer. Their high fibre content also helps prevent constipation.

A balanced diet

Eating the right mix of earth-wise foods is not only essential to good health and vitality, it also gives us added resilience to combat the stresses of modern living. Check below to see if you're getting enough of the body's basic building blocks of protein, carbohydrates, fats and oils.

PROTEIN

Animal foods – necessary for the growth and repair of hair, skin, muscles and bones – contain the full spectrum of essential amino acids needed to make protein. If you're vegetarian or vegan, it's essential to eat a broad selection of plant foods to obtain enough amino acids to make protein.

MEAT AND HEALTH

Eating lean meat can make an important nutritional contribution to your diet. But be careful – fatty and processed meats add too much saturated fat and salt to daily intakes. The type and amount of meat eaten is an important consideration for maintaining good health. In general, eating less animal protein and more fresh unprocessed food is better for our bodies.

- Eat lean red meat about three to four times a week. Include fish and legume-based meals at least several times a week, and skinless chicken for variety. Consumption of excessive amounts of high-fat animal protein is linked to heart disease, high blood pressure, some cancers and kidney disease.
- When you want to include meat on the menu, stick to a palm-sized piece of lean meat and increase the serving size of vegetables or salad.
- Fatty meats, many processed meats and chicken skin are high in saturated fat, which is not good for heart health. Avoid duck and goose, which have more fat, and choose skinless chicken or turkey.
- If chewing meat becomes difficult as you get older, try lean mince and softer stewed meats, and add other easy-to-chew sources of protein to your diet, such as eggs, legumes and soy products.
- Try game, such as kangaroo and venison. This lean and healthy option is good nutritionally because it is relatively low in saturated fat Game is available from some supermarkets and butchers.
- Large-scale grazing of livestock degrades the environment in many ways, including the acceleration of soil erosion and the production of methane, a greenhouse gas. If you are cutting down on meat, choose free-range and organic products. They use less intensive, more environmentally sustainable practices.

TIPS FOR VEGETARIANS

- Devise a menu that combines whole grains, nuts, seeds and legumes, such as dried beans, lentils and split peas – together they supply all the essential amino acids. Try dhal with rice, hummus with flat bread or kidney beans with tortillas.
- Eat more soy products, such as tofu, tempeh and miso. They're the best alternative to meat for providing complete protein. Soy protein is rich in phyto-oestrogens or isoflavones, which may help to lower cholesterol, inhibit the growth of cancer cells and ease the symptoms of menopause.

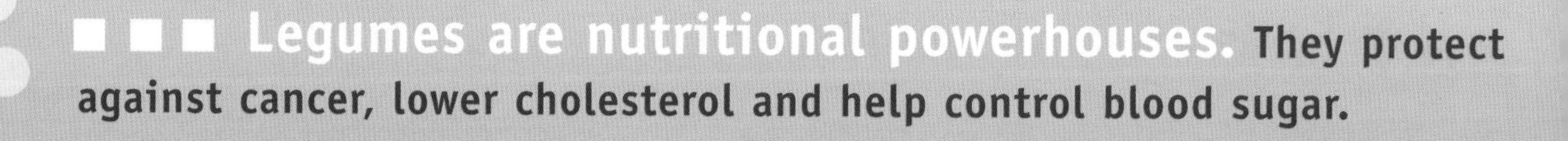

■ ■ ■ Legumes are nutritional powerhouses. They protect against cancer, lower cholesterol and help control blood sugar.

THE RIGHT BALANCE

The triangle shown here has changed the emphasis of the food pyramid of a decade ago. It is now recognised that whole grains and plant-based oils and fats play an important part in a healthy diet.

EAT PLENTY OF PLANT FOODS
Wholemeal bread and wholegrain cereals
Brown rice, wholemeal pasta and noodles
Nuts and legumes
Fruit and vegetables

EAT MODERATE AMOUNTS OF ANIMAL FOODS
Milk, yoghurt, cheese
Meat, fish, poultry and eggs

EAT LESS
Refined grains
Animal fats
Margarine
Fried foods
Sweets

TOP TIP

Start the day with a high-fibre wholegrain breakfast cereal. The carbohydrates are digested slowly and provide a longer lasting source of energy to keep you feeling satisfied throughout the morning.

Don't let any single food – however good for you – dominate your diet, as inevitably it will produce imbalances in the body.

- Try spelt pasta – it's an excellent protein source for vegetarians and its protein content is 10–25 per cent greater than common varieties of commercial wheat pasta.
- Eat wheat germ, lentils, pumpkin seeds and unsalted nuts for their high protein content.
- Eat plenty of legumes, such as beans and split peas. Not only are they high in protein, but also high in fibre and very low in saturated fat.
- If you're not a vegan, add dairy foods or eggs to your daily diet. They provide a good-quality protein source, particularly for young children and some older people who may find it difficult to eat the volume of grains and beans needed to meet daily protein requirements.

CARBOHYDRATES

Carbohydrates are found in food as either starches or sugars. Starches, also referred to as complex carbohydrates, are found in breads, breakfast cereals, rice, pasta, and starchy vegetables such as potatoes and corn. This type of carbohydrate supplies the body with the energy needed to carry out normal daily functions.

- Try to limit your intake of refined carbohydrate foods, such as sugar, sweets and biscuits. (Carbohydrate can either be refined or unrefined, referring to how much processing the food has gone through.) They'll give you a quick energy boost, but it will quickly fade.
- Choose carbohydrate-rich foods in the form of whole grains, brown rice and legumes, such as chickpeas and kidney beans. They'll give you more energy in the long term than refined varieties, such as white bread, and they contain more essential nutrients.
- Experiment with the variety of whole grains that are now available – millet, rye, buckwheat, and the rediscovered 'ancient' grains such as spelt, kamut, quinoa and amaranth. An additional bonus is that by purchasing these you will be supporting crop biodiversity.
- Aim for a serving of dried beans, peas or lentils for lunch or dinner each day or, at the very least, a couple of times a week. Sneak them

■ ■ ■ **A mainly vegetarian,** unprocessed diet promotes healthy digestion and also protects against heart disease and cancer.

into family meals: add kidney beans to spaghetti bolognaise or mash a cup of butter beans and stir into mashed potatoes or pumpkin.

- Add canned borlotti beans to vegetable or minestrone soup – it boosts the fibre content and increases zinc and iron as well.
- Snack on fresh raw sesame, sunflower or pumpkin seeds, or sprinkle them on home-baked muffins. They're also a great garnish for salads, pasta, steamed vegetables or casseroles.

GET THE GI FACTS

The glycaemic index is a guide devised by nutritionists to identify the rate at which foods break down from carbohydrates to sugar in the blood. Carbohydrates that raise blood sugar more slowly, and by a smaller amount, are healthier for you in the long term than those that raise it more quickly. Look for the GI symbol on some food packaging. It tells you that a product has been glycaemic index tested. Foods containing carbohydrate are measured on a scale of 1 to 100.

- Choose to eat foods with a low glycaemic index (less than 55). They give you a longer lasting source of energy (where your blood sugar levels rise and fall gradually).
- Slow-burning energy foods including legumes, low-fat dairy products, wholegrain breads and breakfast cereals are better for diabetics and people trying to lose weight. Because low GI foods are digested more slowly, they help you to feel fuller for longer, keeping your hunger under control.
- Eat foods rated high on the index (more than 70), such as potatoes, sugary foods and white bread, before you exercise and you'll experience a fast burst of energy.
- Don't get carried away with GI. The GI value of some healthy foods can be higher than a less nutritious food. Fifty grams of fresh ripe pineapple, for example, has a higher GI than the same amount of chocolate because the fruit contains more glucose. So, while the GI is a valuable tool, always choose foods on the basis of their nutritional value.

FATS AND OILS

Our bodies need the right balance of essential fatty acids to build strong, flexible cell membranes. For good health, choose unsaturated fats (generally from vegetable sources and fish) rather than the saturated fats (mainly from animal-based foods, fast food and baked goods), which increase the risk of heart disease.

- Avoid eating too many saturated fats from foods such as fatty meats, cakes, biscuits, pastries, pies, butter and lard. These fats are solid, or semi-solid, at room temperature and increase the risk of heart disease and Type 2 diabetes.
- Choose mono-unsaturated fats, such as olive and canola oils, and poly-unsaturated fats such as sunflower and safflower oils, which are liquid at room temperature. Fats and oils rich in omega-3 fatty acids are the best. These include walnut, linseed and mustard seed oils.
- Eat more oily coldwater fish such as salmon, trout and mackerel. They contain beneficial omega-3 fatty acids that are essential for a healthy nervous system, help lower 'bad' LDL cholesterol and also contribute

PROS & CONS

FISH FARMS

Aquaculture allows us to eat fresh fish, such as salmon, year-round. This is good for our omega-3 intake and it helps to conserve dwindling ocean populations. Some of the world's oceans and waterways, however, are being fished solely for the purpose of supplying food to the farmed-fish industry, depleting local stocks. Fish farming can also pollute surrounding water with faeces and uneaten food. When you can, opt for fresh deep-sea fish from local waters.

Read the labels on processed foods. Compare the saturated fat content of similar products to help you make healthier choices.

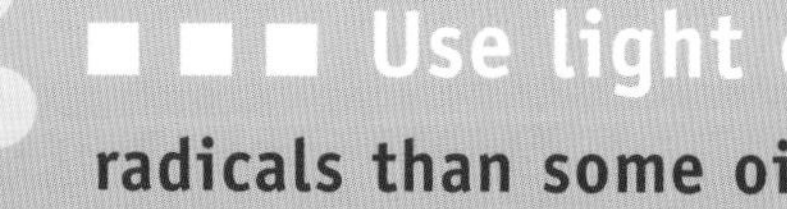

Use light olive oil for stir-frying. It produces fewer free radicals than some oils when it's heated and contains anti-oxidants.

FRIENDS AND FOES

Brush up on the latest health and nutrition terminology.

- ANTI-OXIDANTS diffuse free radicals and protect cells from damage. Many of the phyto-chemicals present in plant foods act as anti-oxidants.
- 'BAD' CHOLESTEROL (LDL) sticks to the walls of your arteries, restricting blood flow. Eating too much saturated fat increases your blood level of LDL.
- FREE RADICALS are molecules that roam your system causing cell damage. Found naturally in your body, they are also produced by external influences, such as sunlight and pollution.
- 'GOOD' CHOLESTEROL (HDL) mops up the 'bad' cholesterol. HDL can be increased by regular exercise and weight reduction.

SPREAD IT ON

- **AVOCADO** Mash avocado as a spread on sandwiches. It tastes delicious, is rich in beneficial essential fatty acids and loaded with vitamins, minerals and fibre.
- **DIPS** Check the refrigerated section in your supermarket for tasty and healthy dips you can use as a spread, such as hummus.
- **LOW-FAT CHEESES** Instead of butter, use cottage cheese or fresh ricotta. Both make a great base for other fillings.
- **NUT BUTTERS** Purchase a brand that doesn't contain partially hydrogenated oils. Alternatively, try making them at home. For peanut butter, simply combine 500 grams roasted peanuts with ¼ cup peanut oil and ½ tsp salt in a food processor. Process mixture until it reaches the desired texture: smooth or chunky.
- **OILS** Use a little extra-virgin olive oil or cold-pressed walnut oil on bread.

to keeping arteries flexible. A fish meal can be quick and easy too – stir smoked salmon through cooked pasta and sprinkle with chopped dill and black pepper.

- Minimise consumption of full-cream dairy products, which contain saturated fat. Consider skim or low-fat milk and yoghurt, cottage cheese and ricotta.
- Try to minimise animal fat. Remove the skin from poultry, where most of the fat is stored.
- Take 1 tablespoon of cold-pressed flaxseed oil daily as a supplement or use the oil to dress a salad or steamed vegetables. Flaxseed contains almost twice the amount of omega-3 found in fish oils, but is of a different type.
- Avoid cooking or buying deep-fried foods. At home, grill or stir-fry using oil with a high smoking point, such as safflower, corn, soybean, olive or macadamia.
- Read the packaging to avoid hidden fat, especially in processed food, biscuits and tinned soups. Make sure to avoid dripping, lard, copha, palm oil, shortening, milk solids, cream, coconut oil and cocoa butter.

- Be aware that 'oven-baked' and 'toasted' processed foods can be high in fat. And avoid anything that contains 'hydrogenated' or 'trans fats', which are saturated fats. Margarine and spreads produced in Australia and New Zealand contain low levels of trans fats.
- If you like eating chips but would like to avoid the fat, switch to a baked variety. Or try rice crackers or air-popped popcorn.

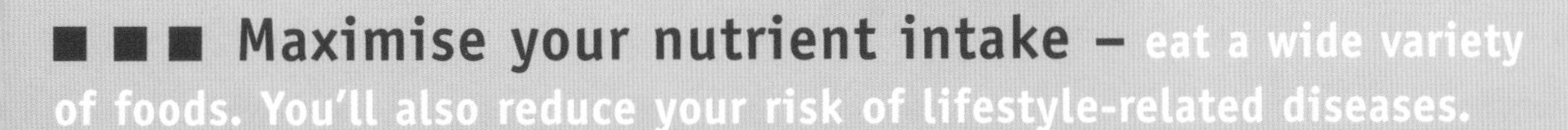

Maximise your nutrient intake – eat a wide variety of foods. You'll also reduce your risk of lifestyle-related diseases.

Fruit and vegetables

Even if you do nothing else to change your diet, eating more fresh fruit and vegetables will make a huge difference to your health and vitality, conferring greater protection against many chronic and degenerative diseases and helping to combat the effects of too many environmental toxins.

A diet rich in fruit, vegetables, whole grains and legumes can reduce the risk of breast cancer.

WHY EAT YOUR GREENS?

What we were told when we were children is true – eating our greens is good for us. Here's why.

- The fibre contained in leafy green vegetables acts like a scrubbing brush in the gut, helping to reduce the absorption of microbial toxins into the body.
- Eating more fruit and vegetables satisfies your hunger and means you'll be less likely to reach for high-fat, high-sugar and low-fibre foods.
- Eating a diet high in unprocessed and natural foods is one of the best things you can do for your health, along with taking enough exercise and getting sufficient rest.
- Green leafy vegetables are high in folate and iron and assist in healthy cell development.
- The phyto-chemicals in vegetables and other plant foods may help to ward off the toxic effects of ozone, the main component of smog, smoke and environmental pollution.

DIY DETOX

Add these superfoods to your shopping list to reduce the effects of environmental toxins and maximise health and wellbeing.

- Berries: rich in anti-oxidants, they strengthen the immune system, protect eyesight and may assist with improved memory. Choose from blueberries, raspberries, strawberries, mulberries, blackberries, cranberries and loganberries.
- Broccoli: contains sulforaphane, a phyto-chemical that protects our bodies from free radicals and pollutants before they attack healthy cells. Cauliflower, brussels sprouts and cabbage also contain sulforaphane.
- Citrus fruits: brimming with phyto-chemicals and vitamin C, they have strong anti-oxidant properties important for the immune system.

TOP TIP

Eating 1 cup raw baby spinach or 1/2 cup cooked spinach or silver beet daily may cut your risk of lung cancer by as much as a half, even if you were once a heavy smoker.

Vegetables for health

Food	Benefits
Red, yellow and orange vegetables	Protect against heart disease, diabetes and arthritis. Also help protect vision.
Green leafy vegetables, cruciferous vegetables: broccoli, cauliflower, brussels sprouts, cabbage	Neutralise free radicals. Stimulate anti-cancer enzymes. Helpful in preventing asthma.
Allium vegetables: onions, garlic, leeks, chives	Fight against infections, boost cardiovascular health and lower 'bad' LDL cholesterol. Have anti-inflammatory properties.
Asian mushrooms: shiitake, enoki, oyster, wood ear, maitake	Protect against viruses and tumours. Boost immune system function.
Sea vegetables: agar-agar, dulse, nori, kombu, wakame, arame	Promote strong bones, help prevent colon cancer, lower LDL cholesterol, improve insulin sensitivity.

Try to eat seven serves of fruit and vegetables every day. Experiment with different varieties and new cooking methods.

CHOLESTEROL BUSTERS

The anti-oxidants in fruit and vegetables help prevent cholesterol moving out of the blood and into the lining of the blood vessels. The deeper the skin colour, the greater the anti-oxidant punch.

- Avocado and grapefruit: rich in glutathione, an anti-oxidant which helps oxidise fats and neutralise harmful free radicals.
- Blueberries: contain more anti-oxidants called anthocyanins than any other food. Cranberries, raspberries and strawberries are also rich in these. They also save cells from premature ageing.
- Cabbage: contains potent anti-oxidants. Choose both red and green varieties and eat raw, sliced thinly in salads. It's delicious (raw or lightly cooked) with garlic, a touch of brown sugar and a little orange juice.
- Carrots: the beta carotene, responsible for the colour of carrots, is a powerful anti-oxidant.
- Grapes: the quercetin in red grapes (also found in onions) keeps 'bad' LDL cholesterol from turning toxic and attacking the arteries.
- Onions: choose red and brown varieties. Use raw in salads to maximise the allyl sulphides, chemicals that lower the risk of stomach and colon cancer. Include an onion, raw or cooked, in your daily diet. You'll lower your blood pressure too.
- Soy beans: high in the B vitamins, calcium and iron, soy contains anti-oxidants that reduce 'bad' LDL cholesterol and raise your 'good' HDL cholesterol.
- Tomatoes: the richest source of lycopene, which controls the build-up of cholesterol in arteries. It's better absorbed from cooked tomatoes, so try them sautéed with mushrooms on toast for breakfast. Apricots are also a good source.

PROS & CONS

TO JUICE OR NOT TO JUICE?

Delicious, fresh, natural juices are great for delivering a quick energy boost, especially on hot summer days. However, for maximum nutritional impact you need to eat the whole fruit or vegetable, as most of the fibre that is so important for preventing constipation and cancers of the digestive tract is discarded in the juicing process. To retain the fibre, blend fruits in a blender, then combine the thick fruit puree with a little low-fat milk or soy milk and a dash of honey, and you have a delicious and sustaining smoothie.

COLOUR YOUR PLATE

The beautiful colours of fruits and vegetables, created by plant nutrients called carotenoids, confer different health benefits and disease protection. Aim to have at least one serving of fruit and vegetables, raw or cooked, from each colour every day.

FRUIT • Apples • Grapes • Honeydew melon • Kiwifruit • Limes • Pears

VEGETABLES • Artichokes • Asparagus • Avocado • Beans • Bok choy • Broccoli • Broccolini • Brussels sprouts • Cabbage • Capsicum • Celery • Choko • Cucumber • Endive • English spinach • Lettuce • Okra • Parsley • Peas • Rocket • Watercress • Zucchini

FRUIT • Apricots • Bananas • Grapefruit • Lemons • Mangoes • Nectarines • Oranges • Passionfruit • Pawpaw • Peaches • Pears • Persimmons • Pineapple • Rockmelon • Tangerines

VEGETABLES • Beetroot • Capsicum • Carrot • Pumpkin • Squash • Swedes • Sweet corn • Sweet potatoes

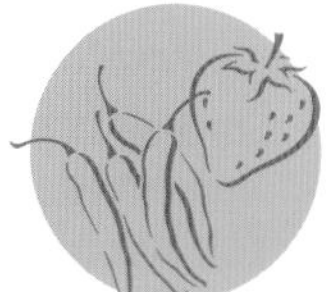

FRUIT • Apples • Blood oranges • Cherries • Cranberries • Grapefruit (pink) • Grapes • Pomegranates • Raspberries • Rhubarb • Strawberries • Watermelon

VEGETABLES • Beetroot • Cabbage • Capsicum • Chillies • Onions • Potatoes • Radicchio • Radishes • Tomatoes

FRUIT • Blackberries • Blackcurrants • Black cherries • Blueberries • Figs • Grapes • Plums • Raisins

VEGETABLES • Eggplant • Potatoes

FRUIT • Dates • Lychees • Raisins • Sultanas

VEGETABLES • Cauliflower • Jerusalem artichokes • Mushrooms • Onions • Parsnips • Potatoes • Spring onions • Turnips

■ ■ ■ **Eat apples to your heart's content.** They contain pectin, a soluble fibre that helps to lower your cholesterol.

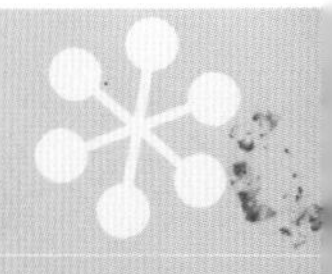

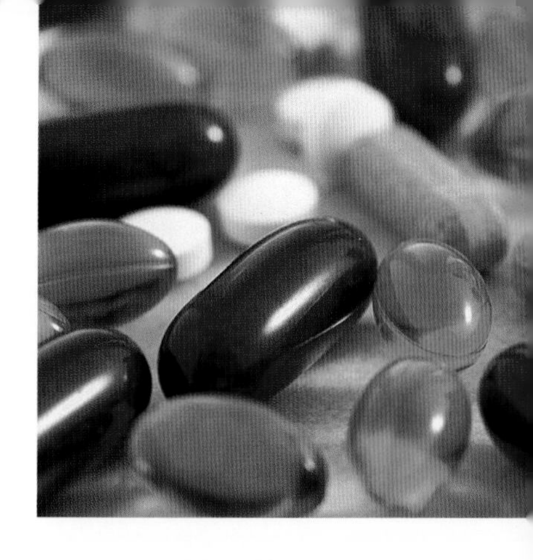

Energy boosters

We obtain energy from our food and our energy levels are greatly influenced by diet. Given the right foods and enough water, we can be very resilient to the stresses of modern living. Sometimes, however, illness or stress puts us at higher risk of vitamin deficiency or dehydration, and we need extra help.

THE ESSENTIAL INGREDIENT

Water is essential for good health and vitality. It makes up 60 per cent of the body, and is needed for carrying important nutrients and chemicals to cells and tissues, and in regulating temperature.

- Check your daily water intake, particularly as you get older. As we age, we tend to lose our perception of thirst and drink too little water, so cells can become dehydrated.
- Make a point of sipping water throughout the day. Aim to drink about 8 glasses, or 2 litres. If you find this difficult, break the quantity down so you drink ½ glass every 30 minutes, or ¼ glass every 15 minutes.
- Drinking water is an effective antidote to feelings of fatigue or confusion. These may be signs that you are dehydrated.

SUPPLEMENTS

While supplements should never replace healthy eating, there are times when you may need an additional energy boost.

- During pregnancy, after an illness or following a stressful episode.
- If you're feeling your years (no matter what your age). Consider taking a daily multivitamin supplement if you're over fifty.
- To provide maximum protection against cancer, osteoporosis and heart disease in adults.
- To help alleviate marginal nutritional deficiencies, which make their presence felt only through vague symptoms such as lethargy and tiredness.
- To allow you to get enough nutrients if you're on a restricted diet. Vegans and vegetarians, for example, may not be getting enough iron, vitamin B_{12} and calcium from their food.
- If you suspect you may have a food intolerance and as a result have cut whole food groups out of your diet.

GET VALUE FOR MONEY

- Buy supplements from a natural therapy clinic, a chemist that specialises in health supplements or a health food shop. That way you'll have experts on hand to advise you on the right formulation.

GET JUICED!

Fight your next low-energy slump by trying one of these easy-to-make supercharged juices and smoothies.

- WAKE-UP CALL: Blend 1 cup rice or soy milk, 1 banana, 4 dried apricots, 1 tbsp LSA, 1 tsp honey and a sprinkle of nutmeg until smooth. It's packed with energy-giving B vitamins.
- FATIGUE BUSTER: Juice orange or grapefruit, beetroot, apple, carrot and a slice of ginger for a juice full of phyto-chemicals.
- BERRY BUZZ: Juice strawberries and blueberries, then add cranberry juice and a squeeze of lime – enjoy a burst of vitamin C!

STAY VITAL

- ✔ Eat a small amount of raw food daily
- ✔ Drink about 2 litres of water every day
- ✔ Eat whole grains, legumes, nuts and seeds
- ✘ Don't skip meals
- ✘ Don't smoke
- ✘ Forget quick energy fixes

■ ■ ■ **Eat foods rich in potassium,** like oranges, bananas and apricots, to replenish your energy if you've been very active.

If you suffer from hypoglycaemia, keep a bowl full of apples in the office or at home – they're excellent at stabilising blood sugar levels.

- Compare the number of equivalent dosage tablets in the container across several brands to get the best value.
- Check the nutrient dose on the packaging. It's usually prefixed by the abbreviation 'Equiv'. For example, 1 gram of the supplement calcium carbonate might give you the equivalent of 400 mg of calcium whereas 1 gram of oyster shell supplement may only supply 350 mg.
- A high-potency multivitamin and mineral formulation gives you the maximum benefit. While these high-potency brands can be quite expensive, you are paying for therapeutic doses and the proper balance of complementary – and quality – nutrients.
- The most economical way to take vitamin C is in the powdered form.
- Try to purchase natural forms of vitamin E (d-alpha-tocopherol), as they may be more effective – although more expensive – than the synthetic form (dl-alpha-tocopherol). For best results, look for a brand of natural vitamin E that contains mixed tocopherols.
- When buying liquid herbal extracts, ask a qualified herbalist or pharmacist to make up a formula rather than purchasing an off-the-shelf proprietary brand. In most cases it will be cheaper.
- Consider purchasing your nutritional supplements online. It's possible to save up to 50 per cent of the recommended retail price.

TOP TIP

Eating fresh fruit will increase your liquid intake so you won't need to drink so many glasses of water. Try watermelon, which is 98 per cent water.

THE HIGHS AND LOWS

There are several foods and drinks that give an instant lift when we're feeling low in energy. The effect of these pick-me-ups is short-lived and they may not be the best choice for optimal health over the long term. Try to minimise your intake of them.

■ **COFFEE and TEA** The caffeine in these beverages (though much lower in tea) causes the release of several chemicals, including adrenaline, which prompts the release of blood sugar, making us feel energised and motivated. However, these effects don't last long, so within an hour or two you start to feel tired and unmotivated once more.
Healthy alternatives: herbal or fruit infusions.

■ **REFINED GRAINS** While easily digested and relatively quick to cook, these foods can release energy rapidly, causing rapid spikes – and equally rapid dips – in blood sugar. They are also lower in fibre than the whole grains they are derived from.
Healthy alternatives: brown rice, whole grains, oats and quinoa.

■ **SOFT DRINKS** These are one of the most problematic of all quick-hit substances because the sugar and kilojoules come without any nutrients. The sugar provides a quick hit – and so does the caffeine in some cola drinks.
Healthy alternatives: natural fruit juice, smoothies made with low-fat milk, rice milk or soy milk.

■ **SUGARY FOODS** Depending on the variety you eat, sugary foods can produce a rapid rise in blood sugar, causing levels to spike rapidly, then drop off, leaving you feeling tired and hungry. They're often very high in kilojoules without many nutrients.
Healthy alternatives: dried apricots, sultanas, fresh fruit.

EXERCISE FOR LIFE

Regular exercise makes you feel well and has long-term benefits for your health. You'll sleep better too.

Getting fit

Daily exercise is essential for good health. It keeps your body in good condition, reduces the risk of heart disease and helps control your weight. You don't have to take out an expensive gym membership – just start from your own front door. It's never too late to begin.

EXERCISE AND THE ENVIRONMENT

There are two earth-wise issues you should consider when you exercise. Are you working out in a clean, safe environment? And is the venue you're using environmentally friendly?

- Avoid walking or running near main roads, or during peak hour, as smog from traffic and other sources is unhealthy to breathe. Your overall wellbeing won't improve if you're unwittingly exposing yourself to pollutants. If you suffer from asthma, you need to be particularly vigilant.
- When walking, running or cycling at night, wear reflective clothing so you can be seen clearly.
- Be aware that playing sport outdoors at night requires floodlights that can be energy intensive, triggering emissions of gases that are linked to global warming.
- If you play golf or use a sportsground, check whether recycled water and environmentally friendly products are used on the grass.
- Check pollution reports on the news before swimming at city beaches. The water is more likely to be polluted 2 to 3 days after heavy rain, when run-off from stormwater drains is discharged into the sea. Also, some beaches are near offshore sewage treatment plants. Call your local council for information.
- If you love to surf but find that you're fighting infections all summer long, listen to your body and stay out of the water. It may be polluted, even if it hasn't officially been declared hazardous.

GETTING THE RIGHT MINDSET

- Start exercising slowly and build up gradually. Don't, for example, attempt a 5-km sprint if you're new to running. Your body won't be ready for it, and disappointment is guaranteed if your expectations are too high.
- Go at your own pace and don't worry if you seem to be progressing more slowly than you would like. Your body will tell you when it's time to notch things up a gear.
- Find something you like doing. Choose a moderate (not strenuous) activity that gets your heart pumping a bit harder while you're having some fun. If you find that going to the gym isn't your thing, choose something you think you'll enjoy.
- If you have a swimming pool, consider setting up an aquarobics group with friends and neighbours. Share the cost of hiring a personal trainer to run the classes.
- Stick with your chosen activity, even if you find it hard at first. The key to long-term fitness is simply exercising on a regular basis.
- To avoid the boredom that can accompany routine – and to give you more time outdoors in the sunshine getting your vitamin D, which increases calcium absorption and helps prevent breast cancer – play a favourite sport, such as tennis or golf, on a regular basis.
- If you need encouragement, ask a friend to exercise with you. Making an arrangement to meet someone for an exercise session will make it more difficult to avoid working out when you don't feel like it.
- If it helps to set goals, set them. However, bear in mind that they need to be achievable, not impossible – don't expect instant results. Make sure you celebrate your successes.

~ *STAR SAVER* ~

Check out the big online bookshops for fitness videos or DVDs: there are hundreds available, from high-impact aerobics and kickboxing, through body shaping and weights workouts, to walking, dance, Pilates and yoga routines. You can purchase several fitness videos/DVDs for less than the price of an annual gym membership, and they'll serve you well for years.

A SENSIBLE WORKOUT

Don't begin your exercise with a pre-workout stretch. It's now thought that this may do more harm than good, because it's impossible to properly stretch cold muscles.

- To avoid dehydration, drink plenty of filtered water before, during and after your workout.
- Start any workout slowly to reduce the risk of injuring cold muscles and ending up with expensive medical bills. Gradually increase the intensity of the workout over 5 to 10 minutes. The higher your body temperature, the better your muscles will perform and the more efficiently they will use oxygen and nutrients.
- At the end of a session, allow enough time to warm down and bring your heart rate back to normal. Ideally, allocate sufficient time to your workout to do some deep stretching while your muscles are still warm.
- Cool down properly from your warm-down before taking a shower. Wait 5 to 10 minutes, then have a lukewarm shower, otherwise your elevated body temperature, combined with the heat of the water, may lead to dizziness, dehydration or faintness.

INCIDENTAL EXERCISE

We expend far less effort than we once did in everyday life, thanks to cars, labour-saving equipment and domestic outsourcing. Here are some tips on how to work a little more exercise into your daily routine.

- Instead of paying someone else to do it, wash the car, clean the windows, mow the lawn, rake the leaves, scrub the bathroom or do the vacuuming yourself. It's all good aerobic exercise, and you'll save money.
- Walk up escalators and, if you can, use the stairs instead of taking lifts. Make your legs work harder by not using the handrail.
- Play with your children or grandchildren instead of supervising their games from the sidelines. Walk them to school if it's a local one. The daily exercise will be good for you and give the children a healthy habit for life.
- When you sit down, try to do so very slowly, using your muscles to control your movements rather than flopping down into a chair.
- As you stand up, let your abdominal muscles do the work. Don't use your arms and don't rock your body to gain momentum.
- If you need to post a letter or buy a carton of milk, walk to the local postbox or shop, don't automatically use the car.
- When lifting bags of groceries into the car, use muscle power rather than momentum.

Ten-minute workouts

Here's how to devote the equivalent of half an hour a day to exercising if you can't find an unbroken 30 minutes.

- Divide your workout into 15 10-minute sessions per week, comprising 10 aerobic sessions, 3 strength training sessions and 2 stretching or yoga sessions – or use different combinations, according to whatever suits you best.
- Divide the 10 minutes into 2 minutes of warming up, 6 minutes of working out and 2 minutes of warming down.
- Make sure you really exert yourself when you're working out. It's the only way short spurts of exercise can be effective. Try to put in an effort that rates 4 on a scale of one to five.

■ ■ ■ **Regular weight-bearing exercise** builds up STRONGER BONES and counteracts the development of osteoporosis.

Aerobic exercise

Any sort of activity that makes you breathe more deeply and pumps up your heart rate is aerobic exercise. It's something anyone can do, regardless of age or athletic ability. Everyday chores can be aerobic, but walking, running, swimming and cycling can be more enjoyable ways of increasing aerobic activity.

THE BENEFITS

- You'll lose weight. People who include short bursts of exercise in their daily routines lose weight and are more likely to keep it off than people who maintain traditional 45-minute, three-times-a-week exercise programs.
- There is less risk of serious illness. As well as enjoying increased energy and vitality, you'll derive permanent benefits, including a reduced risk of cardiovascular disease, high blood pressure, diabetes and cancer.
- When you're really pushing your boundaries, you'll experience runner's high, the temporary natural 'high' runners and elite athletes speak of. Vigorous aerobic exercise releases 'feel-good' brain chemicals called endorphins, which are the body's natural opiates.
- You'll slow the ageing process. Some effects of ageing will slow down because aerobic exercise helps counter the inevitable decline in maximum oxygen consumption that occurs with the passing years. The proof is evident even in people in their seventies and eighties.
- Exercising in the open air gives you the chance to appreciate the natural world. Tree-lined streets and local parks are pleasant environments in which to walk or run, and weekend bushwalking is an ideal way to relax and re-connect with the landscape.
- You'll beat the blues. Regular moderate aerobic exercise is helpful in treating and preventing mild depression and it doesn't have the side effects that can go with taking prescription drugs.
- You'll save money and help the environment. Walking, running or cycling instead of driving or catching public transport will save you money and cut down on fuel emissions at the same time.

BUY WISELY

■ If you want to exercise at home, don't buy a stationary bicycle or another indoor exercise machine, such as a treadmill, without trying it out first. These machines are expensive and even though they can produce great results, using them day in, day out can become boring. That's why so many are listed for sale in the weekend classifieds! Hire the item for at least 3 months and, if you do decide to buy after hiring, check out the classifieds. You'll save a lot of money by buying secondhand.

WALKING FOR HEALTH

Walking for exercise means you can start from your front door. It's free and you won't be contributing to global warming by using petrol-driven transport. And the convenience factor is a big plus, making it far more likely that you'll stick to it over the long term.

- Just put on a comfortable pair of shoes, go outside and walk around the block. Do the same tomorrow, and the next day and the next, for the next month – even if you don't feel like it. The important thing is to cement the exercise habit.
- Once you're feeling fit, aim for a brisk 30-minute walk at least 3 or 4 times a week.
- If you want to check that your daily routine is enough to keep you fit, use a pedometer, a device that measures the number of steps you take. Aim for 10,000 steps a day. Just getting off the bus a stop before

■ ■ ■ **By cycling to work every day, you'll be doing your little bit to combat global warming while getting fit at the same time.**

your destination could be all you need to do.

- Rev it up a bit if you're getting less from your workout as you become fitter, or if your routine becomes boring. Vary your routes and add some hills. Start with a mild grade and build up to the steeper ones.
- Do some interval training to increase your fitness. Start with 30-second intervals and increase your pace to about 75 per cent of your top speed, then drop back to your normal pace for 30 seconds. Gradually increase the length of your speed intervals to 3 minutes.
- Take smaller steps when you want to power up your walking. The natural inclination is to take longer strides but it's actually more effective to shorten them and focus on walking faster.

- **CYCLING** This is a good exercise for developing the heart and lungs. However, unless you have access to safe cycling paths, being on the road involves a higher risk of serious injury.
- **GARDENING** Working in the garden can be a gentle or vigorous form of exercise, and has earth-wise benefits.
- **HOBBIES** Rollerblading, skateboarding, dancing and ice-skating are all fun activities that provide a good workout for the heart, lungs and muscles.
- **SWIMMING** This works all the major muscle groups with little risk of injury. If possible, swim in fresh water or the sea to avoid the chlorine in public pools.
- **WALKING and RUNNING** These are the two most convenient, inexpensive and efficient ways of keeping fit. All you need is a pair of good athletic shoes.

Count your steps: 100–110 per minute is a leisurely stroll; 120–130 is a moderate workout; 140–150 is serious training.

THE RIGHT SHOE

Never skimp on the quality of your athletic shoes. If your feet aren't properly supported, you'll be out of action in no time.

- Select shoes that are especially designed for your chosen activity – it will make a big difference to your comfort and performance. Cross trainers are recommended for aerobic exercises or for multiple activities.
- To avoid paying full retail price, check out sales and factory outlets. During the rest of the year, keep your eyes peeled for both e-tail and retail two-for-the-price-of-one offers.
- Consider buying less well known brands of athletic shoes as they can offer equal quality for a much lower price. And be aware that in the past certain prestige brands have been linked to unethical labour practices in developing countries.
- Take your old trainers to the shoe shop. In some sports outlets, the assistants can offer advice on what to buy, based on the pattern of wear in your old shoes. For instance, if you tend to lean towards the instep, they'll recommend a shoe with additional support in that part of the shoe.
- Get advice from a podiatrist, who will recognise any problems you may have and can give you objective advice on what sort of shoe to buy.

If you don't enjoy exercising on your own, try a team sport like basketball, or join an aerobics class.

Strength training

Training with weights is suitable for all ages and particularly good for people over the age of 55, who have the most to gain from increasing their muscle strength. Strength training has many advantages, from improving the ability to carry out everyday chores to alleviating depression and anxiety.

THE BENEFITS

- You won't need to go on a diet. Toned muscles increase kilojoule burn, so even when you're resting, your body is using about 7 per cent more energy and reducing the possibility of weight gain.
- Strength training helps to prevent osteoporosis by increasing bone density and reversing bone loss, just as weight-bearing exercise such as walking or jogging does.
- It is also great for lower-back health. Toned abdominal muscles support the lower back, reducing the risk of spinal injury.
- You'll notice the improvement in your capacity for aerobic exercise. Strengthening the muscles you use for walking, for example, will allow you to up the ante and improve your pace or take on more challenging terrain.
- Excess body fat will be reduced. However, don't be disappointed if the scales don't reflect this loss. Your weight may not change because the muscle you're building is heavier than the fat you're shedding.
- Your internal health will improve. Strength training helps to lower cholesterol and triglyceride levels (the forms in which most fat exists in the body), lessening the risk of heart attack. This type of training also helps the body to process blood sugar more efficiently, lessening the risk of diabetes and benefiting people with insulin resistance.
- With greater strength and increased flexibility, you'll find you suffer from fewer muscle and joint aches and pains.

WHAT YOU NEED

- ✔ The green light from your doctor if you're over forty
- ✔ Loose, comfortable clothing
- ✔ Set of adjustable dumbbells (or make your own)
- ✔ Enough space if you're working out at home
- ✔ Three uninterrupted sessions of 5–10 minutes per week

Regular weight training will increase bone density by up to 2 per cent every year, regardless of age or sex.

WEIGHTS WORKOUT

You don't have to join a gym to increase your muscle fitness and strength, though it can help to give you an idea of what's involved and learn the techniques correctly. If you prefer to work out at home, here are some suggestions.

- Buy or rent a weights-workout or strength-training fitness DVD or video to learn how to do the moves. This will also help you to prevent injury.
- Don't spend money on weights until you're sure you like this form of strength training. In the meantime, make your own. Start out with two 450-gram cans of beans or tomatoes as hand weights.
- Begin your training program by working out for 5–10 minutes with very light weights (not more than 500 grams) and performing one set of 8 repetitions for each exercise.
- Gradually build yourself up to 20–30 minutes by increasing the number of repetitions in a set to 16, and then increasing the number of sets to three or four.

■ ■ ■ Strength training will improve your self-esteem and body image as well as make your body stronger.

- Once you're ready for heavier weights, use 1-litre plastic milk or juice containers (with handles) filled with water or sand. As you progress, you'll need different amounts of weights for different body areas, so create several sets of 'hand weights'. In this way, you'll save money and recycle at the same time.
- If you want muscle definition, not bulk, use lighter weights and increase the number of repetitions.

TOP TIP

To ensure you don't lose muscle fitness when you're travelling, buy a resistance band from a sporting-goods shop. It weighs only a few grams and will take up almost no space in your luggage.

If you want to create bigger muscles, use heavier weights and do fewer repetitions.
- Try using resistance bands to build muscle. They're inexpensive, portable and come in various sizes.

BICEPS CURLS

- Sit on a chair with your legs apart, your right elbow resting on your right thigh, and your left palm resting on your left thigh in order to support your upper body.
- Hold a hand weight in your right hand, positioned near your collarbone. Slowly lower your right arm towards the ground until it is almost completely extended, but avoid locking your elbow. Slowly raise your arm towards your shoulder again.
- Repeat using your left arm.
- Repeat 4, 8, 12 or 16 times to make a full set. Do 3 or 4 sets for both arms.

TRICEPS CURLS

- Stand with your feet hip-width apart. Hold a single weight in both hands above your head (pictured above right).
- Slowly bend your elbows and lower the weight behind your head down to your shoulders, then slowly raise your arms in the air again.
- Repeat 4, 8, 12 or 16 times to make a full set. Do 3 or 4 sets.

UPRIGHT ROWS

- Stand with your feet hip-width apart. Hold a weight in each hand, arms hanging down against the front of your body, thumbs touching.
- Now, slowly bring the weights up your body to almost touch the outer tips of your shoulders: your arms will be out to the sides like chicken wings. Slowly return to the starting position.
- Repeat 4, 8, 12 or 16 times to make a full set. Do 3 or 4 sets.

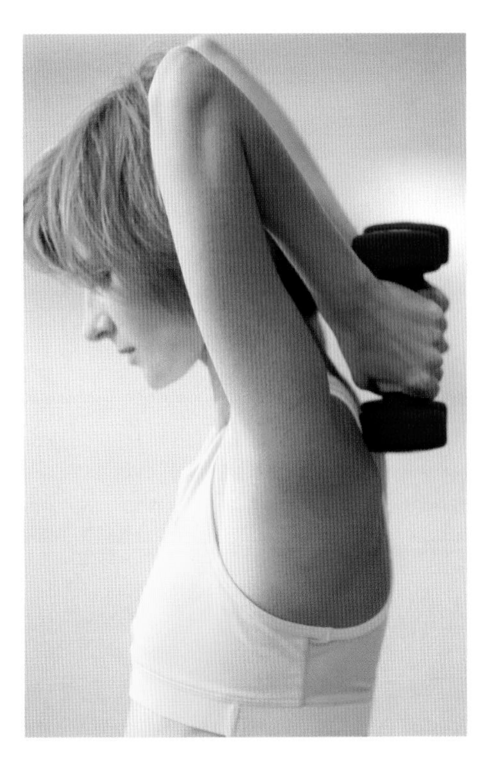

SHOULDER RAISES

- Stand with your feet hip-width apart. Hold a weight in each hand, with your arms hanging down against the front of your body, elbows not locked, thumbs touching each other.
- Slowly raise your right arm straight up in front of your body to shoulder height so that your arm is at right angles to your torso. Slowly lower your arm back to the starting position.
- Repeat the same movement with your left arm.
- Repeat 4, 8, 12 or 16 times to make a full set. Do 3 or 4 sets for both arms.

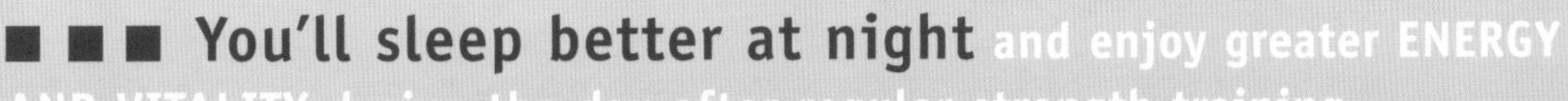

■ ■ ■ **You'll sleep better at night** and enjoy greater ENERGY AND VITALITY during the day after regular strength training.

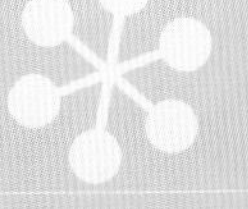

Non-impact exercise

Since the mid-1990s, there's been a shift from high-impact exercise to gentler disciplines that provide an equally effective workout without punishing the body. A feature of yoga, Pilates and tai chi, stretching is simple, doesn't take up much time and can mostly be done at home.

KEEPING YOUR SPINE FLEXIBLE

The spine is the body's lifeline, so whether you work hard in a manual job or sit at a computer all day, it pays to keep it flexible.

- Try spinal rolls and twists, which are excellent for spinal flexibility. Or attend a yoga class to learn poses such as the 'bridge' and the 'cobra'.

WARNING!

▼ If you're pregnant, or have suffered a spinal or neck injury, it's advisable to seek professional advice before stretching.

- Lie down on the floor, with a folded towel supporting the back of your neck. Stretch your arms at shoulder level, palms upwards. Relax in this position for 10–15 minutes. It will release muscular tension, relieve joint pressure and allow your spine's shock absorbers to plump up with fluid.
- Sit on a chair with your feet shoulder-width apart. Slowly lean forwards and down, placing your hands beside the outsides of your feet. Let your head hang down loosely between your knees, but don't put any strain on your neck muscles. Hold the position for 30 seconds and then very slowly return to a normal sitting position.

SPINAL ROLLS

Try to do these spinal roll exercises two or three times a day. If your back is very tight and lacks flexibility, at first you may feel as though you are rolling on square wheels! But do persevere because as your body warms up, you'll feel your spine gradually loosen as the vertebrae in your neck and spine are massaged by the action, and the rolls will become smoother.

THE BENEFITS OF STRETCHING

Stretching relaxes the body and tunes the mind. It's essential for everyone to maintain easy movement, but it's particularly important for people who sit at a desk most of the day. Here are the benefits.

- Increases the body's range of motion.
- Develops body awareness, making you alert to any subtle changes in performance, which helps to prevent injury.
- Helps avoid or alleviate back, shoulder and neck problems.
- Reduces effort and muscle tension in everyday actions.
- Builds endurance and strength.
- Increases physical and mental confidence.
- Promotes circulation.
- Helps control breathing, which leads to greater relaxation.
- Makes aerobic exercise easier, because flexible muscles are less likely to be strained.

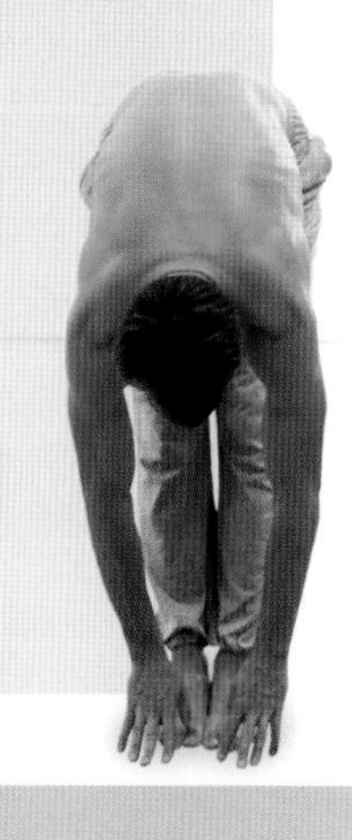

TOP TIP

If you are sedentary for much of the day, try sitting on an exercise ball. It will make you sit up straight and you can use it for stretching exercises.

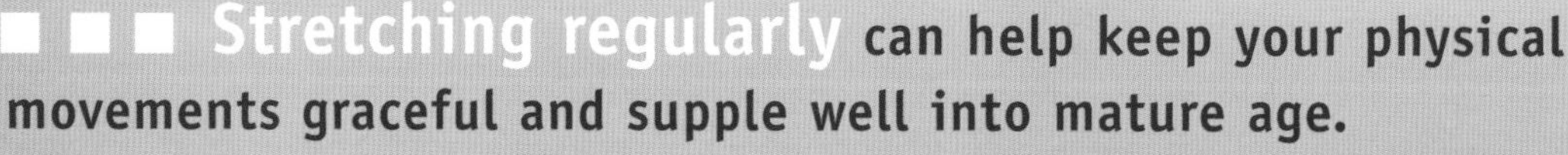

■ ■ ■ **Stretching regularly** can help keep your physical movements graceful and supple well into mature age.

Stretching is a simple, painless way of keeping the muscles supple and building flexibility and endurance.

- Sit on the floor. The surface should be well-padded.
- Draw your knees up to your chest and then bend your head towards them. Link your hands behind your knees.
- Keeping your spine rounded, rock slightly forwards, then roll backwards onto the floor, but avoid going so far back that your neck is in contact with the ground.
- Without stopping, roll up again into the sitting position.
- Perform 4–6 continuous rolls to start with.
- Rest.
- Repeat the whole procedure about three or four times.
- Build up to 12 rolls per set.

OFFICE EXERCISE

If you sit at a desk or computer for long periods, this is a good exercise for avoiding stiffness. If possible, do it every few hours.

- Stand up, with your feet together, and raise both arms straight above your head, stretching your whole body upwards.
- Lower your arms.
- Repeat the first step.
- Now, position your feet so that they are hip-distance apart and fold your arms on top of your head, clasping your elbows with opposite hands as you do so.
- Slowly bend forwards and, with your arms still clasped, stretch forwards and down from your tailbone. Try to touch the floor with your forearms if you can, but don't push yourself.
- Remain in this position for several seconds. You'll feel your spine stretching as you do so. Then slowly unroll yourself.

hot links

Pilates Institute of Australasia: www.pilates.com.au
Tai chi Australia: www.taichiaustralia.com.au
Australian Society of Teachers of the Alexander Technique: www.alexandertechnique.org.au
Australian Feldenkrais Guild: www.feldenkrais.org.au

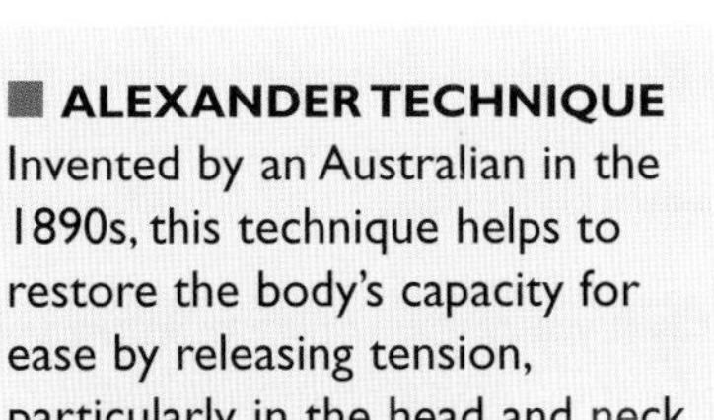

ALEXANDER TECHNIQUE Invented by an Australian in the 1890s, this technique helps to restore the body's capacity for ease by releasing tension, particularly in the head and neck. It aims to allow the body to reach its full potential.

BIKRAM YOGA Developed in India, yoga merges physical and mental exercises. Bikram is a newer form of the practice that benefits blood circulation, improves cardiovascular conditioning and improves detoxification by increasing perspiration. Classes are conducted in rooms heated to 37°C to increase muscle and tissue elasticity and reduce the risk of injury. However, exercising in such extreme heat carries health risks.

FELDENKRAIS METHOD Developed in the 1940s, Feldenkrais is a practical discipline to help develop awareness of body movement. The aim is to recognise any tensions and correct them by focusing on small, precise movements. Feldenkrais is usually taught one to one, or in small classes.

HATHA YOGA Hatha is the most popular type of yoga among Westerners. Techniques using asana (poses) and pranayama (breath) gently control the mind and senses without strain.

IYENGAR YOGA Similar to Hatha, Iyengar uses props such as belts to help bring the body into the correct positions. There's also a focus on holding the poses for a length of time.

PILATES Invented in the early 20th century by Joseph Pilates, Pilates combines East and West, gymnastic and yogic principles, mind and body. Exercises are designed to oxygenate, then stretch, strengthen and finally re-stretch a particular muscle group.

TAI CHI Mind, body and spirit are integrated in this Chinese discipline. Many older people practise its graceful forms as a way of staying healthy and vital. Benefits those with arthritis as the exercises strengthen and improve flexibility and range of motion without pain.

A good night's sleep

It's important for your health to have a sound sleep every night. While many people take it for granted, for some, especially those in mid-life, a good night's sleep can become increasingly difficult to achieve. There are many earth-wise ways of learning to sleep well without resorting to prescription medicines.

Have a bath before bed. The warm water will raise your body temperature, making you naturally sleepy.

FOURTEEN STEPS TO BEDTIME BLISS

1 Try to go to bed and get up at the same time – or within an hour of your usual time.

2 Avoid indulging in daytime naps as they may interfere with your night-time sleep.

3 Caffeine is a stimulant that is found in coffee and chocolate. Avoid both for several hours before bedtime. Experiment to see what suits you and your body: some people find caffeine consumed any time after 10 am is enough to prevent them from sleeping.

4 Alcohol and tobacco can also disrupt sleep, so avoid them for 3 hours before bedtime. Again, you may need to abstain for longer.

5 Try to eat at least 3 hours before bedtime so the process of digesting food doesn't keep you awake. If this routine isn't convenient, consider eating your main meal at lunch, and a lighter meal in the evening.

6 If you are a light sleeper, go to bed only when you are really tired. You may find that spending less time in bed produces a deeper, more restful sleep.

7 Regular exercise should guarantee a good night's sleep, but try to complete your workout at least 2 hours before going to bed.

8 Establish a calming bedtime ritual, such as meditation or a soak in a warm bath. Add a few drops of relaxing lavender essential oil.

9 Ensure your bedroom is comfortable, dark and free of clutter.

10 If your bedroom is noisy, buy a 'white noise' machine to block out external noise, or play New Age music very softly.

11 Watch your fluid intake at night. If you do go to the toilet after bedtime, don't turn the lights on. They can signal 'daylight' to the pineal gland, halting melatonin production and making it impossible to go back to sleep.

12 If you are on any medication, check to see whether there are side effects that include insomnia. If there are, ask your doctor about different drugs or consider natural alternatives.

13 Use your bedroom only for sleeping. Set aside another time and place for planning, thinking and worrying so you are less likely to toss and turn at night.

14 Sex does not always act like a sleeping draught. You may find it so stimulating that you stay awake for hours.

Pack earplugs and eyeshades to block out unwanted noise and light when you're travelling, especially on a plane trip.

To work effectively, supplements and herbal remedies should be taken just before going to bed. Take the herbs as a tincture, made up by a herbalist or pharmacist, or make them into a tea.

■ **JAMAICAN DOGWOOD** (*Piscidia erythrina*) This herb also eases migraine, period cramps and neuralgia.
■ **LIME FLOWER** (*Tilia* x *europaea*) A sedative herb, it also eases nervous tension, migraine and palpitations.
■ **MELATONIN** Available in New Zealand from health food shops, but only by prescription in Australia. A naturally occurring hormone from the pineal gland, melatonin helps set the brain's internal clock. However,

it hasn't been studied in humans and must not be taken by women who are pregnant or breastfeeding or by people with certain diseases. Seek medical advice before using it.
■ **PASSIONFLOWER** (*Passiflora incarnata*) This is a sedative herb that is also beneficial for nervous tension and neuralgia.
■ **SKULLCAP** (*Scutellaria lateriflora*) A sedative herb that combines well with valerian, skullcap is helpful in easing nervous tension and anxiety.
■ **VALERIAN** (*Valeriana officinalis*) (*left*) This herb has tranquillising properties that reduce anxiety and stress, helping people who find it hard to switch off mentally. Take it in the form of capsules or tea.

RESTLESS LEGS SYNDROME

This neuromuscular disorder is a common cause of insomnia. People who suffer from it experience an overwhelming desire to move their legs.

- Try taking 35–60 mg folic acid daily. People with a family history of the condition often respond to high doses of this supplement.
- If there is no family history of restless leg syndrome, ask your doctor to check your iron levels. But never take iron supplements unless a deficiency is confirmed, as excess iron can harm your health.
- Magnesium and vitamin E may be effective against this syndrome as well as muscle cramps. Take 250 mg magnesium at night, and 400–800 IU natural vitamin E during the day.
- If you're over 50, try taking 80 mg liquid extract of the herb *Ginkgo biloba* three times daily.

STOP SNORING!

Snoring may be caused by having a blocked nose, an allergy, lying on your back, drinking too much alcohol or being overweight.

- Use an air filter in your bedroom and keep pets out. Remove any rugs too as they can harbour dust mites.
- Avoid alcohol and other sedatives because of their relaxing effect on the throat muscles.
- Ease congestion by applying mentholated vapour balm to your chest.
- To stop sleeping on your back, wear a T-shirt with a golf ball sewn into a pocket on the back.
- Health food shops stock homeopathic tablets that may help, and don't have any side effects.
- If you suspect you have sleep apnoea – where the throat muscles collapse during sleep and block the airway – seek medical advice.

RELAXATION TECHNIQUE

- Lie on your back, and shut your eyes.
- Breathe in and clench your toes down towards the soles of your feet. Hold for a count of 10, release and exhale.
- Repeat the same 'breathe in-clench-hold-release-exhale' sequence for every major muscle group in your body, working up from your feet, to your buttocks, shoulders and, finally, to your chest and neck.
- Lastly, smile as widely as you can, hold, release and relax. Stretch – and go to sleep.

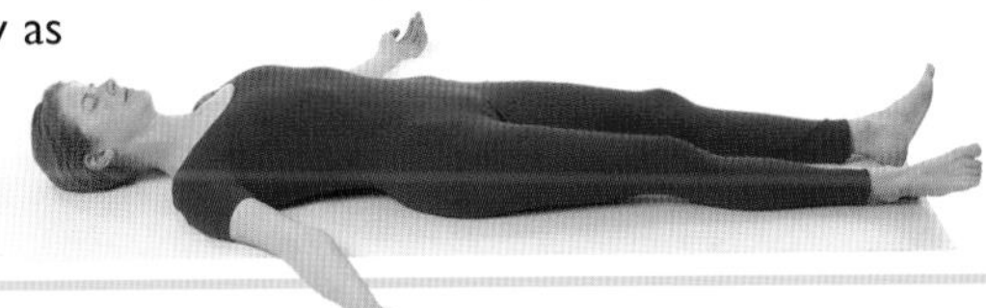

■ ■ ■ **Avoid prescription sleeping drugs.** They produce side effects and eventually you'll need a higher dose to get the same effect.

Feeling Well

A lifestyle that includes exercise and a balanced diet is the best way to ensure good health. But if you do suffer from minor ailments or even a serious health condition, there are lots of natural remedies that may help.

FEELING WELL...

LOOKING GOOD

- Try our home beauty treatments on page 176.
- Work out the best skincare program for your skin type, page 178.
- Give yourself a home spa treatment with natural ingredients, page 180.
- Try our natural home-made hair tints, page 185.
- Pamper your body with body scrubs, massage oils and fragrant powders. See page 186.

HOLISTIC HEALTH

■ Modern life is full of stressful situations. Try one of our stress busters, page 190. ■ Learn about the power of positive thinking, meditation and other relaxation techniques, page 194. ■ What are natural therapies, and do they really work? See page 196. ■ Discover the power of hands-on healing, page 198.

NATURAL REMEDIES

■ Fight off winter ailments with some simple strategies, page 202. ■ Treat minor ailments naturally at home, page 204.

■ Next time you have a headache, try our natural remedies, page 206. ■ If you have a serious health condition, making some simple lifestyle choices may help. See page 212. ■ Check out our guide to the top 30 earth-wise medicines, page 216.

LOOKING GOOD

A glowing complexion, shiny hair and a confident smile are all measures of health and vitality.

A healthy complexion

If you eat well, sleep well, take regular exercise and maintain an earth-wise skincare program, you don't need to spend a fortune on cosmetics and commercial treatments. Regular care using natural ingredients – as well as staying out of the sun – really does make a difference.

TEN-STEP FACIAL

1 Keep out of the sun as much as possible. This is the single best preventive strategy to avoid premature ageing and the risk of developing skin cancer. Outdoors, wear a wide-brimmed hat and loose, light, long-sleeved clothing rather than shorts and brief tops.

2 Use sunscreen. Keep it in a handy place – your handbag, car, gardening kit, picnic basket or golf bag – and apply it about 30 minutes before you go out, as it takes this long to become effective.

3 Eat a diet high in natural fibre because digestive problems can result in skin blemishes. Good health starts from the inside out, so include lots of fruit, raw vegetables and whole grains in your diet.

4 Try to minimise or completely avoid exposure to your skin's natural enemies. For example, stress, too many late nights, coffee, alcohol and cigarettes can all play a part in making you look less than your best.

5 Avoid using soap. Its alkalinity tends to strip the natural acid mantle of the skin. Choose a gentle cleansing oil or cream instead.

6 Moisturise your face every day. As well as minimising the appearance of fine lines and countering flakiness and dryness, a rich moisturiser will plump up your skin, creating a smoother, more even appearance.

7 Drink 8 glasses of water a day. Your skin should contain about 15 per cent water. However, in air-conditioned offices where the humidity level is 8–10 per cent, this moisture evaporates faster than it can be replaced.

8 Give your skin time to rest and breathe occasionally by cleansing it thoroughly and leaving it free of moisturisers and make-up. Your skin will benefit from the deep cleansing. For best results, do this after a facial or a facial steam.

9 Apply fruit acids in the form of a face mask. If used regularly, the acids and enzymes in the fruit help to slough off dead skin cells, fade age spots and make your skin appear brighter. Save money by making your own face masks rather than buying expensive commercial products.

10 Regular aerobic exercise gives you instantly glowing skin and it's also a great natural foundation for good health. Choose an activity that you enjoy and make it part of your daily routine.

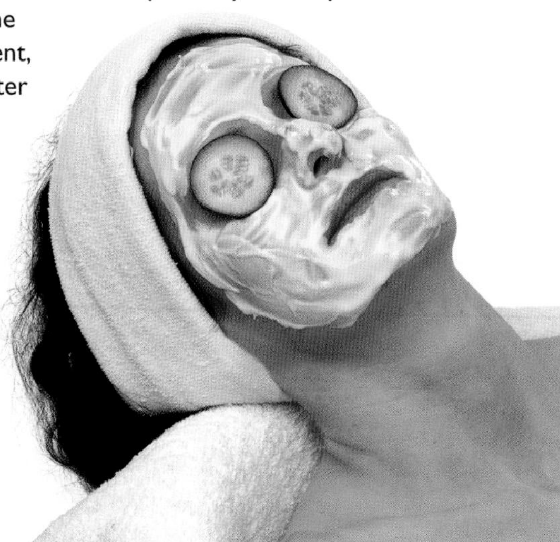

HOME BEAUTY TREATMENTS

FRUITY FACIAL

This mask provides the mild peeling properties of fruit acids plus generous quantities of vitamin A to heal and revitalise your skin. It also contains enzymes that remove dead cells.

1 ripe peach, peeled
1 tsp brandy
a little cornflour

- Mash ingredients together into a workable paste.
- Smooth over your face, avoiding your lips and eyes.
- Rinse off after 20 minutes.

SCRUB UP!

Try this facial scrub for an almost instant improvement in skin texture and appearance.

1 tbsp natural yoghurt
1 tsp brewer's yeast
1 tsp finely ground bran
1 tsp sugar

- Thoroughly mix all the ingredients together.
- Massage the scrub into your skin before the sugar dissolves. Rinse off with lukewarm water.

BASIC MOISTURISER

This moisturiser was invented by a Greek doctor, Galen, in the second century AD.

5 tbsp distilled water
5 tbsp rosewater
1 tsp borax
5 tbsp grated white beeswax
18 tbsp olive oil

- Combine the water and rosewater, stir in the borax and set aside.
- Place the beeswax in the top of a double boiler and melt it over a gentle heat. When it is liquid, pour in the oil and stir. Pour in the borax solution and continue to stir as it becomes opaque.
- Remove from the heat and stir until the mixture has thickened and cooled. Store in a glass jar away from heat and light.

NATURAL FACELIFT

Facial massage not only feels wonderful, it also improves circulation and muscle tone, relieves tension and makes the skin more supple. Save money by doing it yourself at home.

- Dip your fingertips into a little olive or almond oil, then close your eyes. Sweep your fingertips up from your chin and over your cheeks. Make large circles at your temples. Then, moving out from an imaginary midline, smooth your fingers across your forehead.
- Using quick, light movements, pinch gently along your jawline. Lift your ears up, and back and forward, in gentle circles.
- Massage the scalp with slow, firm movements, then finish by pressing the hollows on the back of your neck where the spine and skull join.
- Once you've mastered the routine, consider teaching a friend, so you can massage each other.

TREAT SURFACE VEINS

- You can improve broken surface veins on your cheeks and nose by eating plenty of foods that contain vitamin C and the bioflavonoids – for example, citrus fruits, parsley, capsicum and potatoes.

THE TRUTH ABOUT...

SUNSCREENS

We're constantly warned of the importance of sun protection – experts recommend that we stay indoors between 11 am and 2 pm and wear sunscreen, sunglasses and protective clothing. Yet many sunscreens contain some doubtful chemicals, such as diethanolamine (DEA) and triethanolamine (TEA), both possible carcinogens, and the parabens, which may mimic oestrogen in the body. For those who apply sunscreen regularly, a safer choice may be zinc oxide, the ultraviolet-blocker, which now comes in a light, invisible form.

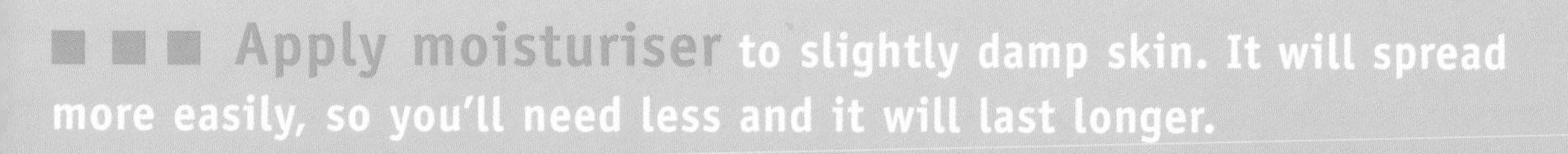

Apply moisturiser to slightly damp skin. It will spread more easily, so you'll need less and it will last longer.

Understanding your skin

All sorts of factors can affect your skin – diet, sleep and exercise as well as hormonal imbalances and environmental hazards, such as air pollution. Though you can't control all these influences, you can at least eat well, exercise regularly and make sure that your skincare regimen is safe.

WHAT TYPE OF SKIN DO YOU HAVE?

Most people have oily skin, dry skin or a combination of both. Take this quick test to find out what type of skin you have.

- First, cut three strips from a sheet of plain, thin tissue.
- In the morning, before you wash your face, press one strip on your nose and chin, one on your forehead and one on a cheek.
- If any one of the strips becomes translucent and sticks to your skin, this indicates oily skin.
- If all the tissue strips are unmarked, you have dry skin.
- If the strips over your forehead, nose and chin (the 'T-zone') are translucent and the other one is unmarked, you have what is known as 'combination' skin.
- If you have combination skin, follow the tips for oily or dry skin below, as appropriate – you'll need to mix and match the treatments to find out what works best for you. Try different products on the different areas of your face. You may find that light, oil-free products are best overall.

DRY SKIN CARE

Dry skin can be caused by underactive sebaceous glands, drying weather conditions, air-conditioning and a poor diet.

- Ensure that you get enough essential fatty acids in your diet by using olive or flaxseed oil in your salad dressings.
- Try to cut down, or even cut out, your intake of fast foods.
- Eat plenty of fresh fruit and vegetables, and avoid eating processed foods as much as you can.
- Take vitamins A and D in the form of fish liver oil, fresh carrot juice and EPA (eicosapentaenoic acid) and DHA (docosahexaenoic acid) in supplement form.
- Look after your skin by using the following natural ingredients in masks, washes, poultices or steam treatments: avocado (revitalises), carrot (moisturises; a good source of the 'skin vitamins' A and E), grapes (encourage cell renewal and brighten the complexion) and peach (soothing and anti-inflammatory).
- Use a rich cream on your face night and day. Look for ingredients that are particularly nourishing and soothing, such as vitamin E and evening primrose oil.
- After a hot bath or shower, apply moisturiser all over your body.
- Avoid any skin products that contain alcohol, because it has a very drying effect.
- Try applying aromatherapy oils such as geranium, chamomile, rose and sandalwood. They can help soothe overly dry skin.

Cold-pressed apricot kernel oil is rich in vitamin E. Smooth it around your eyes to prevent dryness and wrinkling.

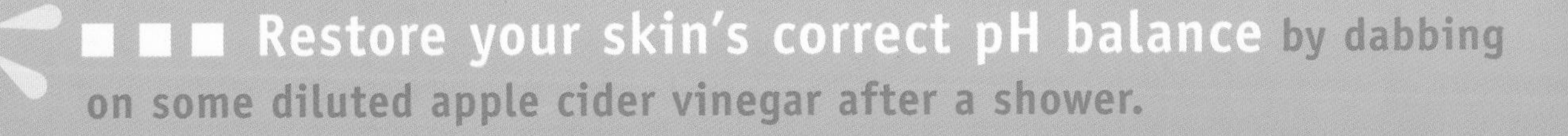

■ ■ ■ **Restore your skin's correct pH balance** by dabbing on some diluted apple cider vinegar after a shower.

PROS & CONS

IS SORBOLENE SAFE TO USE?

Sorbolenes are widely recommended by dermatologists for a variety of dry, irritated and itchy skin conditions. They have a high ratio of oil to water – the product sits on the skin's surface, acting as a barrier and slowing excess moisture loss, thus reducing symptoms such as flakiness and tautness. However, sorbolene is not for everyone, as it may lead to skin problems for some people. Also, be aware that some sorbolenes are made from petrochemical by-products, such as mineral oil. Vegetable sorbolenes, based on natural nut and seed oils, may be a more earth-wise choice. Before you buy sorbolene, always check the label to be sure.

TOP TIP

If you have dry, irritated skin, simply dip a clean cloth in a little chilled milk and dab on the affected area. Or pour a cupful into a warm bath for a skin-soothing soak.

OILY SKIN CARE

Oily skin may be the result of a high-fat diet, overstimulation of the sebaceous glands as a result of heat, or hormonal imbalances.

- Eat more raw vegetables and fruit and take B-group vitamins.
- Use mildly astringent and toning skincare products, with ingredients such as lavender and witch hazel.
- Use toners or fresheners that do not contain alcohol. Stripping the skin of its natural oil (sebum) will only cause it to produce more.
- If you also have pimples, use herbs with mildly antibacterial and antiseptic properties, such as calendula, in skin washes and masks.
- To help rebalance oily skin, use these ingredients in skin treatments: cucumber (soothing, toning; helps bleach freckles), lemon (mild bleach, disinfectant with antiseptic properties) and tomato (soothes inflamed skin, rebalances skin acidity).

FACE TREATMENTS

ANTI-AGE SPOTS MASK

Used regularly, this easy-to-make face mask is very effective and is a fraction of the price of similar commercial salon treatments and anti-ageing preparations.

2 egg whites
2 tbsp runny honey
1 tsp almond oil
juice of 1 lemon

- Whisk ingredients together in a bowl.
- Brush the mixture onto clean, damp skin, avoiding the eye area.
- Leave for 15 minutes and then rinse off.

CUCUMBER SKIN FRESHENER

Cucumber is a time-tested remedy for spots and blemishes, and benzoin is a mild preservative that is also good for skin problems.

1 large cucumber
hot water
½ tsp tincture of benzoin

- Slice a large, unpeeled cucumber and place it in a bowl with enough hot water to cover. Leave it to cool for 1 hour.
- Strain the mixture through a fine sieve or cloth, squeezing thoroughly.
- Stir through the benzoin and store the mixture in a glass bottle.
- Apply it to the skin with a cotton wool ball. Use it to refresh your skin, especially in summer. Store it in the fridge and discard it after a week.

For dry skin, take 1 tablespoon apricot kernel oil daily. It boosts the manufacture of sebum, the skin's natural oil.

Cleanse, tone and moisturise

Deciding whether to use natural products instead of synthetic ones comes down to two questions – your skin absorbs substances, so why put unnecessary chemicals on it? And why waste money on expensive packaging and ingredients when you can make something just as effective yourself? Here's how to give yourself a home spa treatment for a fraction of the cost you'd pay in a salon.

NATURAL INGREDIENTS

Many foods can double as cheap, handy beauty treatments. Try to be creative and experiment – adjust the quantities to suit your skin type, but you may need to make allowances for differences in raw materials.

- For a nourishing face mask, mash the flesh of 1 avocado with 1–2 teaspoons honey and enough fine oatmeal to make a workable paste. Massage into your face and throat, avoiding your eye area and lips, then leave on for 10 minutes before rinsing off with warm water.
- To make a mild astringent and refreshing skin toner, pour 200 ml boiling water over 2–3 teaspoons green tea leaves. Steep for about 5–10 minutes, then strain. Store the tea in the fridge in a plastic pump-spray bottle.
- Smooth about 1–2 tablespoons mayonnaise over clean, dry skin, avoiding the eye area and lips, and lie down for 10 minutes. Rinse off with warm water and pat dry. The vegetable oils and egg protein make this treatment particularly suitable for older skin types.
- To help slough off dull, dead skin cells and revitalise the skin, crush 5–6 ripe, hulled strawberries. Mix with enough fine oatmeal or cornflour to make a paste and then spread over clean, dry skin, avoiding the eye area and lips. Leave for about 15 minutes, then rinse off with warm water and pat dry.

WARNING!

▼ If you have sensitive skin, patch-test commercial facial scrubs, peels and masks on the inside of your arm before using them, as they can cause redness and irritation.

OPEN THE PORES

Facial steams improve your circulation, open your pores for deep cleansing and soften dead cells, making it easier to remove them.

- Bring 3 cups water to the boil and pour into a bowl. Add 4 drops of an essential oil: ylang-ylang for dry skin, calendula for normal or peppermint for oily.

- Lean over the bowl and tent your head with a towel, keeping your face at least 25 cm from the hot water. After 5 minutes, remove the towel and splash your face with cool water.

■ ■ ■ **For shine control** on hot summer days, dab your face with a 50:50 mix of strained lemon juice and witch hazel.

What you need

- Measuring cups and spoons
- Non-aluminium saucepans, including a double boiler
- Non-metallic strainers (try cheesecloth or muslin and coffee filter papers)
- Funnel
- Eye-dropper (optional)
- Wooden spoons
- Airtight glass jars and bottles that have non-metallic caps
- Food processor, blender or coffee grinder

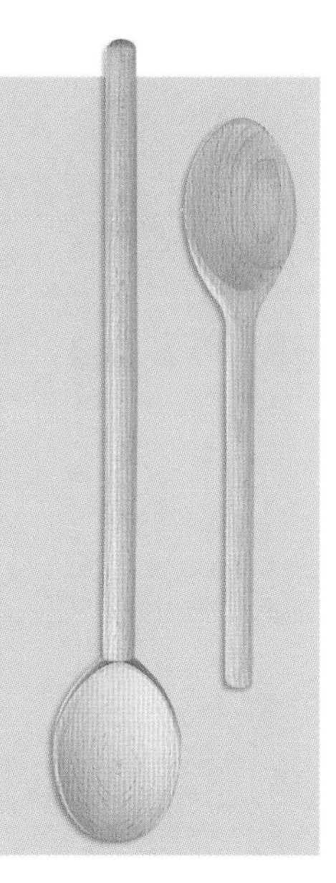

LAVENDER

Essential oils can be expensive, but if you only buy one, make sure it's lavender. Its aroma has a relaxing effect, and it can be used with all skin combinations and hair types.

- Lavender's antiseptic qualities make it particularly useful for blemished skin. To reduce the swelling and inflammation of a pimple, and to reduce the risk of an infection that could lead to scarring, add 5 drops lavender oil to 1 teaspoon warm water and stir. Dip a clean cotton bud into the mixture, and hold to the head of the pimple. Repeat as often as desired. (Do not allow the mixture to go into your eyes.)
- Make a refreshing skin toner by mixing 2 drops lavender oil with ½ cup witch hazel, 1 tablespoon apple cider vinegar and 1 tablespoon rosewater. Apply after cleansing.
- For a soothing and aromatic facial cleanser, add 5 drops lavender oil to 50 ml sweet almond oil and mix together thoroughly. Store in a dark-coloured, airtight glass bottle. Shake contents gently before use, and apply to face with a clean cotton wool ball.

SKINCARE PROGRAM

All the ingredients for making your own natural cleanser, toner and moisturiser can be purchased at most health food shops and chemists.

CLEANSING GRAINS

1 cup rolled oats
½ cup flaked almonds
1 tsp dried lavender
1 tsp dried rosemary
½ cup rice flour

- Finely grind the oats, almonds, lavender and rosemary. Stir through the rice flour and store the mixture in an airtight glass jar.
- To use, mix approximately 1 tbsp of the mixture with a little water. (If you have very dry skin, mix grains with 1 tbsp natural yoghurt and 2 tsp honey.)
- Massage into your skin, then rinse off.
- Discard any unused mixture immediately as it won't keep.

MINTY TONER

1 tbsp dried peppermint
½ cup witch hazel
½ cup rosewater
1 tsp vegetable glycerine

- Place peppermint in a jar, pour over witch hazel and cap.
- Let the mixture stand for 1 week, shaking daily. Strain through coffee filter paper and combine liquid with rosewater and glycerine.
- Shake contents gently before use, and apply to face with a clean cotton wool ball.

OIL MOISTURISER

1 tbsp each avocado oil, almond oil, sesame oil
2 x 500 IU (international units) vitamin E capsules

- Combine the three oils in a small, dark-coloured glass jar (this will help protect the oils from the light).
- Pierce the capsules and add their contents to the jar. Shake well.
- To use, place a few drops of the moisturiser on your palms and rub together. Pat gently over skin.

Looking your best

Your eyes are 'the windows to your soul', says the proverb. As well as showing your moods, they reflect your lifestyle and diet. Healthy teeth and gums also indicate peak nutrition and care. Combine a healthy diet with preventive dentistry and natural remedies to discourage tooth decay and gum disease.

EYE CARE

Simple, inexpensive lifestyle changes and dietary measures may arrest deterioration of and, in some cases, improve your eyesight. And easy exercises can 're-educate' and strengthen eye muscles, helping delay expensive and debilitating disorders.

- Wear sunglasses to reduce the risk of cataracts resulting from cumulative ultraviolet damage.
- Protect your eyes with safety goggles whenever you're doing hazardous jobs, such as using power tools or sanding.
- Nourish the blood vessels and nerves in your eyes with a diet that includes vitamins A, C and E – eat plenty of fresh fruit and dark green leafy vegetables, such as brussels sprouts.
- Limit your intake of saturated fats and avoid cigarette smoke to stop free radicals forming on the retina and causing macular degeneration.
- Each morning, refresh your eyes by splashing your eyelids 20 times with warm water, then 20 times with cold water.
- To rest your eyes, completely cover them with the palms of your hands for at least 1 minute. Repeat about four times a day.
- Try exercises to strengthen your eye muscles. Hold a forefinger 15–25 cm from your eyes. Move it from your left shoulder to your right, and back again, following it with your eyes. Repeat 10 times.
- Pick an object just out of your field of vision. Imagine your nose is a pointer, then move your head slowly as you trace around it. Repeat in the opposite direction.

WARNING!

▼ If an eye infection hasn't improved within 3 days, or if you experience an unusual amount of pain or loss of vision, see your doctor immediately.

BEAT BAD BREATH

Bad breath can be a sign of major gum disease. It's also a side effect of more than 100 drugs – from cold tablets to penicillin – which decrease the amount of saliva in the mouth, causing what's known as 'dry mouth'.

- Avoid highly spiced foods such as garlic, onions, chillies, salami, strong cheeses or smoked foods. They recirculate through essential oils left in your mouth.

~ STAR SAVER ~

There's no need to spend a fortune on clinical whitening treatments: just combine 1 tbsp bicarbonate of soda with 1 tsp fine sea salt. Dip a moistened toothbrush directly into the mixture and use to brush your teeth. Use no more than once a month. Be sure to rinse your mouth out thoroughly and do not 'scrub' your teeth.

Try bilberry extract for cataracts. It's an inexpensive herb with an ANTI-OXIDANT that helps slow cataract development.

ALMOND LIP BALM

Save money, and avoid the artificial additives found in many commercial lip balms, with this easy recipe.

1 ½ tbsp beeswax grains (available from some chemists)
1 tbsp almond oil
½ tbsp cocoa butter

- Combine grains, oil and butter in a small double boiler.
- Set over a low heat, and whisk thoroughly.
- Once combined, remove from heat and pour into a clean, airtight glass jar.
- Allow to cool and set.

PROS & CONS

SHOULD YOU USE EYE-DROPS?

Over-the-counter eye-drops are fine if you need them only occasionally. They work by shrinking the eye's blood vessels with decongestants, thus reducing mild irritation and redness. However, if you wear contact lenses or suffer from glaucoma, some eye drops may trigger an allergic reaction. If you regularly experience dry, itchy eyes, avoid using eye-drops as prolonged use can actually exacerbate the problem. A milder alternative is eyebright tea (from health food shops), which contains soothing and cooling anti-inflammatory glycosides.

- Drink plenty of water. Coffee, beer, wine and whisky leave residues that infiltrate the digestive system, so that for some time afterward each breath expels traces of them back into the air.
- Try natural breath fresheners. Chew up a few sprigs of parsley or garnish your sandwich with parsley – it's a great breath-saver.
- Cloves, fennel and anise seeds are also effective breath fresheners. Mix together a small amount of each and carry a small bag of them so you can chew a few after meals – that is, if you don't mind the rather strong taste.
- Gently brush the top of your tongue with your toothbrush when brushing your teeth, to get rid of the food particles and bacteria that can cause bad breath.
- Lavender is an effective mouth freshening herb. Mix a few drops of lavender essential oil into warm water and gargle.
- Try this cleansing mouthwash to ward off offensive breath: stir 1 teaspoon powdered cloves into 1 cup white vinegar. Shake before gargling the mixture.

ORAL HEALTH

- Brush your teeth regularly. The main cause of tooth decay is plaque, a film of bacteria that clings to the teeth and gums. Cleaning after meals will help to get rid of it and also reduce stains.
- Floss regularly. Using a gentle back-and-forth motion, pass the floss between two teeth. At the gumline, curve the floss in a C-shape against one tooth, then scrape downward on the upper teeth, upward on the lower teeth.
- Consider investing in an electric toothbrush. Although it costs more, over time it is more effective than a regular toothbrush in removing plaque from your teeth.
- Gargle regularly with cold black tea. The tannin in tea acts as an astringent, strengthening gums.
- Massage your gums. Using your fingertip or a patented rubber gum massager (available from chemists) gently massage your gums in small circular movements several times a week to improve circulation and boost oral health.
- Add 2 drops tea-tree oil to water to make a powerful antiseptic gargle (but make sure you don't swallow it). Or try gargling with salt, a general antiseptic. Salty water also soothes a sore throat.
- To help reduce inflammation and fight plaque, stir 1 teaspoon aloe vera gel into warm water and gargle.
- Treat a mouth ulcer by rinsing your mouth out with a solution of 1 teaspoon 3 per cent hydrogen peroxide in 50 ml water. This will disinfect your mouth, clean up bacteria and speed healing. Finally, to put a protective coating on the ulcer, dab it with vegetable glycerine.
- For bleeding gums, gargle with 1 teaspoon witch hazel in 50 ml water. Alternatively, use 1 cup warm water with ½ teaspoon salt and 6 drops goldenseal tincture.

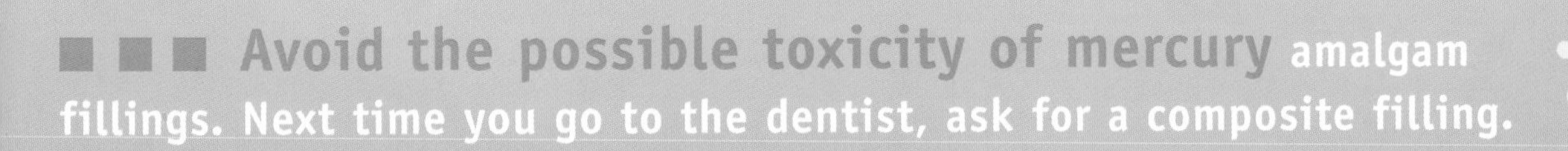

Avoid the possible toxicity of mercury amalgam fillings. Next time you go to the dentist, ask for a composite filling.

Healthy, shining hair

The type, thickness and curl of your hair depend on heredity – but its condition depends on your diet and how you care for it. For hair to be beautiful it needs to be fed from within. Your hair may also be damaged by conventional medicines and harsh commercial hair products, so choose wisely.

SIX TIPS FOR HEALTHY HAIR

1 Feed your hair by eating a healthy diet. The condition of your hair depends on the internal state of your body. A diet that is adequate in vitamins and minerals – especially silica, iron, sulphur, zinc, the B vitamins and vitamin C – is vital for good hair nutrition.

2 Avoid blow-dryers, curling wands and electric heated rollers, as they make hair brittle. Instead, allow your hair to dry naturally.

3 Protect your hair from the elements. Wear a sun hat in summer and a bathing cap when swimming because the sun, salt and chlorine all damage your hair. For extra hair protection, rub a little olive oil onto the ends of your hair before you go swimming.

WARNING!

▼ The contraceptive pill affects a woman's hormone balance, which in turn affects the skin's oil production. Discuss excessively oily hair with your gynaecologist.

4 Be wary of prescription medicines. The contraceptive Pill, diet pills, thyroid drugs, cortisone and antibiotics are just some that can cause brittleness, and even hair loss.

5 Massage your head to improve scalp health. Besides daily brushing, it's the best thing you can do for your circulation. Use your fingertips and palms and rotate them in small circles for 3–5 minutes every day.

6 For a rich conditioning treatment, warm ½ cup apricot kernel or sweet almond oil and massage it into your scalp and hair. Wrap a warm, damp towel around your head, then cover it with a plastic shower cap. After about 45 minutes, shampoo it out.

CLEANSING RINSE

Epsom salts – a cheap staple best known for easing muscle strain – also helps remove the build-up of commercial hair sprays and gels that leave your hair dry and dull.

1 litre water
1 cup lemon juice
1 cup Epsom salts

- Combine all the ingredients in a jug. Pour through dry hair.
- Leave for 15 minutes, then shampoo out.

DANDRUFF TREATMENTS

If you suffer from recurring dandruff, try some of these remedies.

- Try to avoid using commercial antidandruff preparations. Not only are they expensive, but their overuse can actually worsen the problem. They can trigger a condition known as reactive seborrhoea, where the scalp produces more oil and the skin flakes faster.
- Boil 4 tablespoons dried thyme, which has mild antiseptic properties, in 2 cups water for 10 minutes. Strain, then cool and pour over clean, damp hair. Do not rinse out.
- Massage the scalp with apple juice – its natural fruit acids will help get rid of dandruff. After massaging, shampoo your hair then rinse with apple cider vinegar, which acts as both an exfoliant and an astringent.

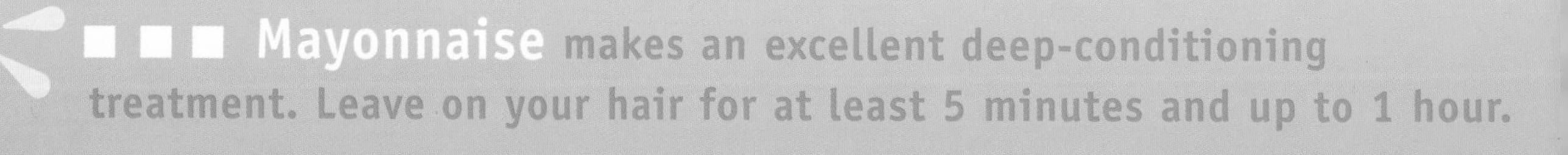

- Add 10 drops tea-tree oil to 1 cup strained black tea. Work the mixture into the scalp. If possible, leave it in your hair overnight before washing it out.
- Restore sheen to your hair and relieve an itchy or over-dry scalp with a vitamin E treatment. Simply prick 1–2 vitamin E capsules. Squeeze the oil onto your fingertips and rub the contents directly onto the roots, then massage it gently into the scalp.

STYLING TIPS

- Smooth very thick and unruly hair by rubbing 1–2 drops rosemary essential oil between your palms and then stroking it over dry hair. It will condition your hair, making it easier to control.
- Wrap an old silk scarf around your hairbrush and smooth it over your hair to add shine and get rid of static electricity.

- To control fly-away hair, try this simple hair spray. Simmer 2 sliced lemons in 2 cups water until reduced to about ½ cup of liquid. Pour into a pump-spray bottle and spray on your hair.

HAIR LOSS REMEDIES

Stress, dieting and prescription medicines are just some of the possible causes of hair loss. Any sudden hair loss may be a symptom of a serious health disorder. See your doctor.

- To disguise thinning hair, crack an egg over your hair, massage it in well, then rinse thoroughly. Since egg is basically protein, it coats your hair and will help give it more life and body.
- To help ward off thinning hair, drink stinging nettle tea and also use the tea as a final rinse on your hair. Used traditionally as a hair tonic, dried stinging nettles are available from most health food shops.
- If you are beginning to suffer from baldness, consider taking mineral silica tablets. Silica has a long history of helping hair and nails to grow. Make sure you follow the recommended dosage on the packet.

DIY NATURAL TINTS

Having your hair tinted professionally can cost a small fortune. Save time and money by making your own natural hair tint using dried herbs.

- For a blonde tint, use 2 tbsp dried chamomile flowers. For a darker colour, use 1 tbsp dried rosemary, 1 tbsp dried sage and 1 black tea bag. For red highlights, use 2 tbsp dried marigold flowers.
- Simmer the appropriate herb in ½ cup water for 15 minutes. Strain, cool, add to ½ cup mild shampoo, then work through your hair. Leave the mixture on for 5–10 minutes, or for longer if you want a stronger effect. Rinse.
- The longer you steep the herbs, the darker your hair colour. The intensity of the colour and how long it lasts depend on, for example, your hair's texture and the strength and age of the herbs.

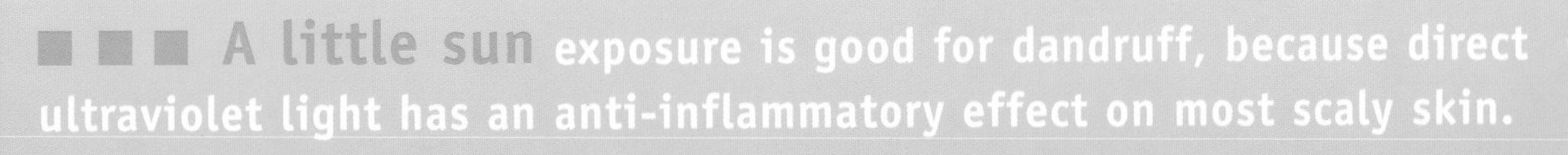

■ ■ ■ **A little sun** exposure is good for dandruff, because direct ultraviolet light has an anti-inflammatory effect on most scaly skin.

Caring for your body

Your body reveals many things about you – how you think and feel, how much (or little) exercise you take and how well you look after yourself. Caring for your hands and feet, and making scented powders and massage oils, aren't just extravagant indulgences – they are an important part of your self-esteem.

SILKY SKIN

- Remove dead skin cells and improve your circulation by brushing your body with a natural bristle body brush or an inexpensive loofah. Using gentle circular strokes, brush upwards from your feet, over your hips and stomach, moving lightly up your arms and across your chest, shoulders and back.
- Smooth almond oil all over your body and relax in a comfortably warm place for about 15 minutes. Afterwards, have a bath or shower and use a loofah or face washer to gently buff the oil away.
- Soften and naturally lighten any leathery, discoloured skin on your knees and elbows. Soak cotton squares in lemon juice and massage them into your knees. Then place your elbows in the pre-squeezed lemon halves for 5 minutes. Finish by rinsing with water and gently drying your skin.
- Treat rough, bumpy skin by spreading sour cream over the backs of your arms and legs. Leave it on for 10 minutes, then rinse it off. The lactic acid exfoliates the skin via a natural chemical action.
- For dry, cracked hands try this old-fashioned remedy – it really works! Combine 2 boiled, mashed potatoes with 1 tablespoon vegetable glycerine and enough milk to make a workable paste. Massage thoroughly into your hands, leave for about 5 minutes, then rinse.
- Relieve itchy skin by adding 2 tablespoons bicarbonate of soda to your bath water. If you are sensitive to highly scented bath preparations, it's an ideal alternative.
- For softer skin, put a handful of rice bran into a clean cut-off stocking, knotted at the top, and drop it into the bath to release vitamin-rich oils. In Japan, this is known as a *nuka* bath. Or sprinkle ½ cup powdered milk into the bath water and swish to disperse. Another one to try is ½ cup oatmeal in a muslin bag, added to the bath water.

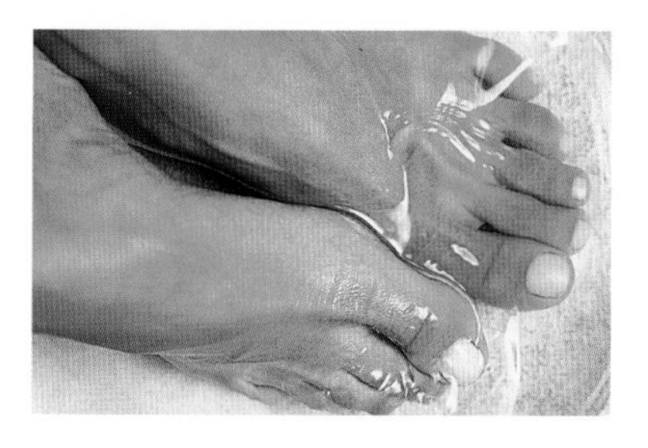

SMELLING SWEET

- Have a bath or shower every day and wash your body thoroughly to get rid of perspiration and bacteria, the two main causes of body odour.
- Wear clothes and nightwear made from natural fabrics. They absorb perspiration better than synthetic materials.
- Try a crystal stick as a deodorant (available from health food shops). It's a chunk of mineral salts that keeps bacteria under control without irritating the skin.
- Watch what you eat. Certain foods and spices – such as fish and curry – impart a strong odour.
- Make your own pleasant-smelling deodorant. Combine 10 drops lavender essential oil with ½ cup witch hazel. Use a pump bottle to spray it on.

THE TRUTH ABOUT...

ALUMINIUM SALTS

Used in most commercial deodorants, aluminium salts have powerful astringent properties that shrink the sweat glands and so reduce perspiration. Aluminium is sometimes added to baby powder to increase its water-repellent effect, and to eyeshadows, to create a silvery finish. Despite industry assurances that aluminium is not linked to health problems, natural health practitioners continue to recommend avoiding its ingestion and topical application.

■ ■ ■ **Give yourself a regular buff** with a textured face washer or a home-made scrub to help slough off dead skin cells.

DO-IT-YOURSELF PAMPERING

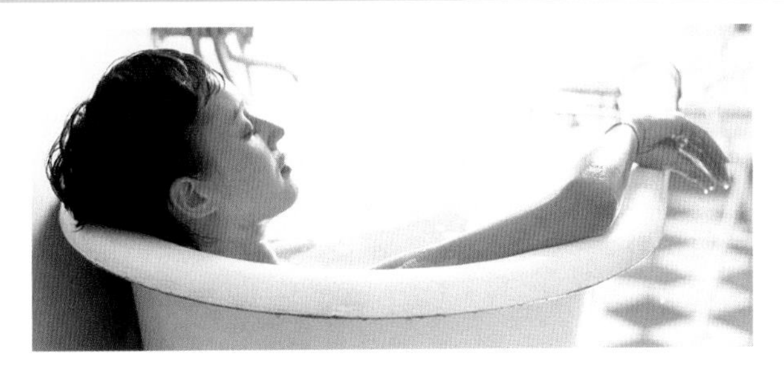

DETOX BATH SALTS

This detox eliminates toxins. The hot water encourages your body to sweat, while essential oils and salts stimulate elimination and circulation.

1 cup Epsom salts
4 drops rosemary essential oil
4 drops juniper essential oil
4 drops grapefruit essential oil

- Add to warm bath water and enjoy soaking for 20 minutes.

MUSCLE MASSAGE OIL

Vegetable oils such as almond and avocado restore the skin's natural elasticity and sheen. This blend helps to relax tight muscles.

2 tbsp apple cider vinegar
good pinch dry mustard powder
3 drops wintergreen essential oil
5 drops rosemary essential oil
2 drops juniper essential oil
200 ml olive oil

- Warm the vinegar and blend it with the mustard so that the powder dissolves.
- Add essential oils and mix well. Combine with olive oil in a plastic squeeze bottle. Store in a cool, dry place, and shake well before use.

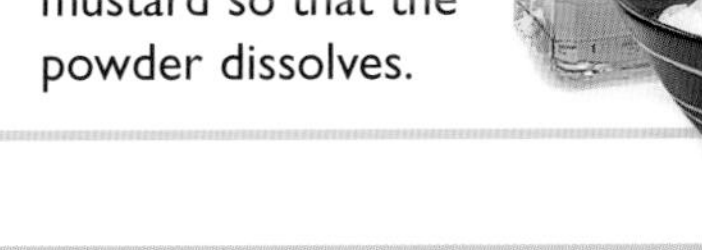

BODY SCRUB

This naturopathic treatment will rejuvenate your skin and improve circulation of the blood and lymph.

1 cup coarse sea salt
2 tbsp olive oil

- Mix the ingredients to form a paste.
- In the shower, massage small amounts into your legs, arms and stomach with circular movements, always moving up and in towards your heart but avoiding your breasts.
- Rinse off. End with a cold shower for a fresh and tingling sensation.

BODY FIZZ

After the body scrub, finish off by spritzing your skin with this all-over body fizz. This mixture will last about 6 weeks if kept in the fridge. Discard it as soon as the scent fades.

150 ml soda water
100 ml apple cider vinegar
1 tbsp vodka
2–3 drops grapefruit essential oil
2–3 drops lemon essential oil

- Combine all the ingredients and pour the mixture into a clean plastic pump-spray bottle that has a non-metallic cap.
- Store your body fizz in the fridge. Shake well before using it.

FRAGRANT POWDER

To avoid the potentially irritating artificial fragrances found in commercial talcum powders, make your own dusting powder.

1 cup rice flour
1 ½ cups cornflour
8 drops ylang-ylang essential oil
4 drops lemon essential oil
4 drops vanilla essence

- Mix the flours together, then sift them through a sieve to remove any lumps.
- Add the oils and the vanilla essence, then sift once more.
- Store in a moisture-proof container.

DEODORANT

This scented deodorant is an effective alternative to the aluminium salts used in most commercial deodorants.

20 drops lavender essential oil
12 drops tea tree essential oil
10 drops lemon essential oil
100 ml apple cider vinegar
50 ml witch hazel

- Mix all the ingredients together and pour into a pump-spray bottle.
- Shake before use and either spray onto the body or under the arms. (Do not spray the deodorant on or around the genital area.)

Soften hard skin and calluses by soaking your feet in weak, warm chamomile tea.

Plants and herbs for naturally glowing skin

Almond 	Used as an ingredient in many good-quality lotions and creams, almond oil is one of the oldest of all cosmetics. It's good for cleansing and nourishing dry and sensitive skin.
Angelica	A pretty, lush plant that will thrive in the smallest kitchen garden. Its stems and leaves can be used in home-made recipes for toilet waters and light fragrances.
Anise	The aromatic seeds have mildly antibacterial properties and can be used to freshen the breath. The essential oil can be used in massages – but don't use it if you have a rash.
Apricot 	The fine-textured oil, derived from apricot kernels, is a very good all-purpose body moisturiser, helping to erase stretch marks. It can also be used as a facial anti-wrinkle treatment.
Avocado	Contains lecithin, a protein which is good for dry or damaged hair. Use avocado in oil form as a moisturiser and hair conditioner. It's also good for softening nails and cuticles.
Banana 	Banana is rich in vitamin A and potassium. The mashed pulp is very gentle when used on the skin, making good refining and cleansing face masks.
Basil	Steep the dried leaves of this herb in hot water, then cool and strain before using the tea as a fresh-smelling bath fragrance.
Calendula	Strain and cool an infusion of calendula leaves to make an effective skin toner. It can also be used as a hair rinse, as it is particularly good in highlighting tints in brown and reddish hair.
Chamomile	A good highlighter for fair hair, it is also effective in soothing tired eyes and chapped or dry skin. It makes a gentle skin toner and can be incorporated into a variety of bath treatments and face masks.
Chervil	Use a cooled infusion to soothe blemishes or fresh juice from the plant to treat various skin conditions, including pimples.
Chives	Chives have a high sulphur and iron content, so the juice makes an excellent skin tonic and cleanser when dabbed on to the skin.
Cloves 	Clove oil's antiseptic qualities make it a valuable ingredient in toothpastes. Use it in mouthwashes and other oral hygiene preparations.
Coconut	Blended with other ingredients, coconut makes a nourishing pre-wash hair-conditioning treatment. It may also be used as an intensive skin moisturiser.
Coriander	The oil, made from the seeds, is a traditional ingredient in many famous perfume recipes. Try it in home-made toilet waters and bath fragrances.
Cornflower 	Use an infusion as an eyebath, a mildly refreshing mouthwash, a facial steam treatment or a bath additive, or apply as a dressing for itchy skin.
Cucumber	Slices placed on the eyelids can reduce puffiness. The pulp can be used in after-sun body splashes, cleansers and soothing masks for sensitive skin.
Evening primrose	Traditional Native American medicine uses the oil, made from the seeds, to treat skin disorders and dandruff. It contains gamma linolenic acid, which helps in treating acne and strengthening nails.
Eyebright	Contains anti-inflammatory plant glycosides. Use the strained tea in a compress or eyebath for sore eyes and dark under-eye circles.
Fennel 	Chew the seeds to neutralise the effects of bad breath. An infusion of seeds in water will soothe inflamed and swollen eyelids. A steam made from fennel seeds is good for deep-cleansing skin pores.
Grapeseed	A light, fine-textured colourless oil that is a good choice for massage oil blends and cosmetics, as it leaves a barely noticeable film on hair and skin.
Hazelnut	An expensive specialty oil with good penetrative powers that is very light and fine in texture. Use in skincare blends, as a base for essential massage oils and as an alternative to almond oil.
Jojoba	Jojoba oil is actually a wax that remains liquid at room temperature. It's expensive, but a little goes a long way in facial oil blends and hair conditioners.
Kelp 	Kelp is rich in vitamins and minerals, so it is a useful ingredient in face masks and bodycare treatments for skin problems. Use dried or powdered.

■ ■ ■ **Steep chamomile tea bags** in boiling water then, when they have cooled, apply them to swollen and puffy eyes.

Plants and herbs for naturally glowing skin

Lemon

The juice makes a useful gargle and, being a good source of vitamin C and bioflavonoids, helps maintain skin health. It also has toning and mild deodorising properties.

Lemon balm

The sweet scent of this herb makes it a relaxing tonic, helping to reduce feelings of nervousness and panic. Use the crushed leaves in bath sachets and cosmetic vinegars.

Lovage A strong tea made from the fresh leaves has mild bleaching and deodorant properties. Try it in skin tonics and perfumes.

Macadamia A thick-textured oil that can be used in small quantities in home-made cosmetics, it is a natural skin soother. Use on its own on dry or chapped skin or mix with a fragrant oil for hair gloss.

Melon Rich in vitamins B and C, melon flesh is useful in home-made recipes for cooling face masks and nourishing skin treatments.

Nasturtium The flowers, leaves and seedpods all contain large amounts of vitamin C and sulphur, making it useful for fighting skin infections. Make an infusion to soothe skin troubled by pimples.

Nettle An astringent herb that helps cleanse skin and speed healing. Use in home-made skin and hair tonics and bath soaks for its stimulating properties.

Olive Extra-virgin olive oil is a good choice for home-made beauty care products, though it has a distinctive smell. Choose pure olive oil (from chemists) if you prefer no fragrance.

Parsley Parsley tea makes an excellent mouthwash and anti-freckle lotion. Pulp it in a food processor to add to tonics, toners and skin cleansers.

Peppermint Drink as a tea with spearmint to freshen the breath. Once cooled, the tea can be used as a refreshing toner or blended with other ingredients to make a cleanser, hair rinse or footbath.

Potato

Mashed and cooled, it can be used as an intensive moisturising treatment and facial mask that is particularly suitable for dry complexions. It may also be used to soothe swollen eyelids and sunburn.

Rose

Use the perfumed oil in home-made perfumes and bath splashes, face masks, hand lotions and hair rinses. Rosewater is an excellent mouthwash and a soothing and softening remedy for dry skin.

Rosemary Has refreshing, stimulating qualities that are useful in facial steams, bath splashes and footbaths. The leaves can be made into a useful remedy for dandruff and a wonderful tonic for hair.

Sage Use a tea made from the leaves as an antiseptic gargle and to strengthen gums. It darkens hair naturally and has strong deodorant properties.

Savory The leaves are sometimes used by herbalists for their mildly astringent and antibacterial properties. The essential oil is useful in skin toners and fresheners, particularly for troubled skin.

Sesame In oil form, sesame can be used in a variety of nourishing skin treatments. As it is very fine-textured and light, it has excellent lubricating qualities and makes a good base oil for massage.

Sorrel Better known as a salad herb, sorrel also has strong antiseptic properties. Apply a cooled tea as a treatment for troubled skin or acne.

Southernwood Long cultivated as a medicinal and cosmetic herb, it makes a soothing bath additive and a stimulating hair tonic or after-shampoo rinse.

Strawberries

Being mildly astringent, strawberries are a refreshing natural cosmetic for cleansing and toning the skin. Fresh strawberries contain an acid that whitens teeth.

Tarragon The essential oil is thought to be helpful in combating a variety of skin conditions, acting as a tonic without being an irritant.

Thyme Strongly antiseptic, thyme is useful in gargles and mouthwashes. Cooled and strained, an infusion makes a refreshing skin tonic and mild astringent as well as a stimulating bath additive.

Witch hazel An alcohol-free toner good for dry complexions, it tightens the skin, has antiseptic properties and promotes blood circulation. It also contains tannins, which help soothe and heal pimples.

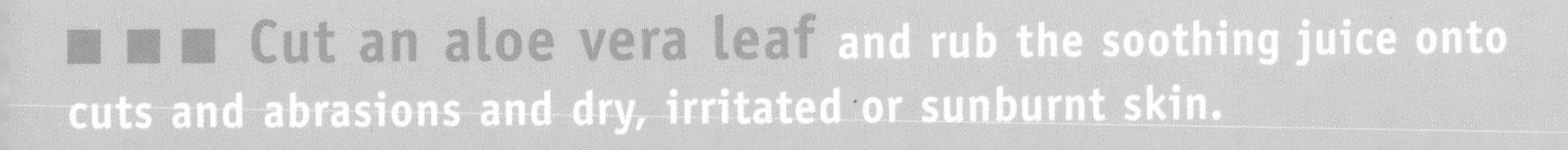

To stay well, we need to take account of the full range of factors that can influence our health.

Coping with modern life

The philosophy of holistic health recognises that the body and mind are interrelated and that if one is out of balance, it can affect the other. While it's not possible to avoid stress entirely, there are practical ways to restore our equilibrium that don't involve stimulants or medical intervention.

SIX HANDY STRESS BUSTERS

A demanding job, too many personal commitments and a polluted environment are just some of the factors that can put us at risk of stress and affect our health and wellbeing. Try these earth-wise remedies to counter the effects of stress.

1 Laugh more. It's a cliché, but laughter really is the best medicine. It disrupts negative thoughts, boosts the immune system, relaxes the muscles and stimulates the release of feel-good brain chemicals called endorphins. Laughter clubs have become popular in some areas.

2 Move vigorously. Aerobic activity helps metabolise the stress hormones created when we're angry or tense. If you can exercise out of doors, fresh air and sunshine can also improve your mood.

3 Practise breathing properly. When we're tense, we don't breathe deeply, and the shallow breaths we take contribute to our feeling of anxiety. Try taking one breath every 6 seconds or 10 breaths a minute. Do this twice a day, 10 minutes per session, and it will become a healthy habit.

4 Avoid the triggers that lead to stressful situations. If you find crowds difficult to cope with, for example, rearrange your timetable to avoid travelling during rush hour.

5 Rethink your medications. Often the very things you take to reduce stress may be having the opposite effect. Sleeping pills, for example, can produce a next-day 'hangover' effect, and some high blood pressure medicines and cough syrups can have unexpected side effects such as poor sleep.

6 Try to cut down on cigarettes, which contain nicotine, and coffee and chocolate, which contain caffeine. These stimulants provide a temporary lift, but can produce jittery feelings as a side effect.

STRESS ALERT

Sometimes life is so busy it's hard to notice when stress is affecting our health. If you have any or all of these symptoms, nature is telling you it's time to take action.

- ✗ Frequent colds and sore throats
- ✗ Insomnia or restless sleep
- ✗ Headaches or backache
- ✗ General feeling of fatigue
- ✗ Heart palpitations
- ✗ Skin problems
- ✗ Mood swings, sudden emotional outbursts, hostility
- ✗ Stomach and digestive upsets
- ✗ Increased reliance on alcohol or pills to help sleep

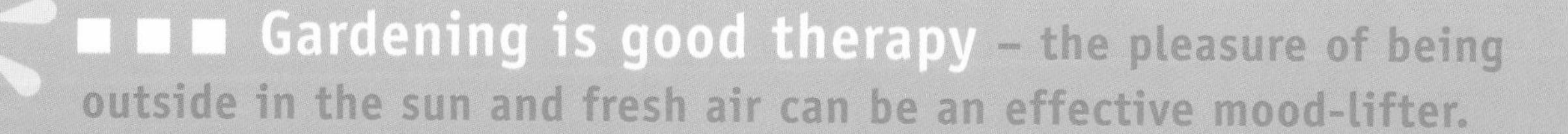

■ ■ ■ **Gardening is good therapy** – the pleasure of being outside in the sun and fresh air can be an effective mood-lifter.

COPING WITH POLLUTION

It's almost impossible to avoid pollution in all its forms in cities, but there are steps you can take to minimise your exposure.

- Stay indoors and keep the windows closed when pollution or pollen counts are high. Ask someone else to mow the lawn if grass pollen triggers your hay fever.
- Avoid places where smoking is allowed if you're concerned about the dangers of passive smoking.
- Stand back from the kerb at traffic lights or intersections to avoid breathing in the worst of petrol exhaust fumes from idling cars.
- Wear a proper cycling mask if you're susceptible to headaches or eye or throat irritation, especially on still days if you cycle daily in heavy traffic. The benefits to your heart of cycling vastly outweigh the health risks.
- Check the daily pollution report before going to the beach.
- Wear earplugs. They can be very effective against noise pollution. Or use your own noise – in the form of a personal stereo – to counter the effects of more unpleasant sounds.

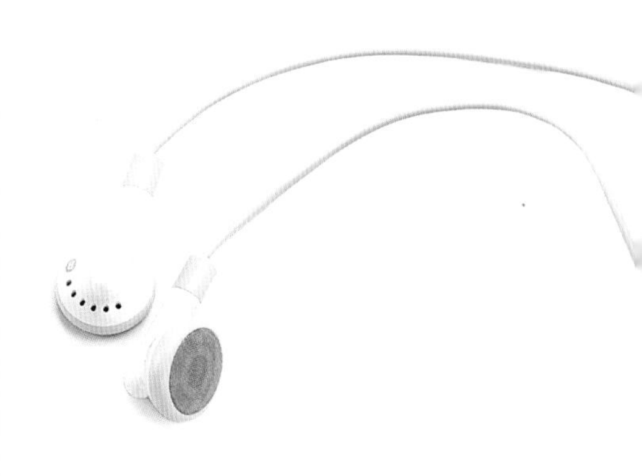

WARNING!

▼ If you have persistent feelings of pessimism, have difficulty concentrating and/or have lost interest in ordinary activities, including eating and sex, consult a mental health professional as soon as possible.

BE PREPARED

If waiting and delays are a major source of stress, take control by thinking ahead.

- Make appointments with people, such as doctors, who have many clients well in advance, and request the first slot of the day.
- If you have a later appointment, phone before leaving home to find out if the person you are seeing is on time or running late.
- Shop early in the week and early in the day to avoid long lines at the supermarket checkout – or better still, shop online.
- If you have a mobile phone, keep it with you so you can easily let people know if you are running late.
- Carry work or reading matter to use downtime productively. Play music CDs or audio books when you are caught in traffic.
- If you are on 'hold' waiting to speak to someone in a call centre, try to get on with some simple tasks. Alternatively, hang up and call again outside peak time.
- Use your computer to transact as much business as possible. You can now do your banking, pay many bills, order food, buy books and hire DVDs on line without leaving your home, and without any delays.

QUICK FIXES

Try these effective natural remedies for everyday ailments.

- For frazzled nerves, sip oat straw tea. It's inexpensive and soothing. Or try chamomile, valerian, lime flower or lemon balm.
- Drink grapefruit juice to cure a hangover. The juice is a liver tonic and also contains a sugar called fructose that helps the body burn alcohol faster.
- Use vitamins and natural extracts to ward off hay fever. Vitamin C has a mildly antihistamine effect. Vitamin A supports the health of the mucous membranes. Licorice and marshmallow teas ease irritation. Horseradish tablets contain a volatile oil that dilates the sinuses and reduces congestion.
- Take willow bark tablets to treat headaches. Willow bark contains a natural form of salicylate, the active ingredient in aspirin.
- If you suffer from indigestion, try some simple reflexology. Points of the left hand correspond to points for the stomach, so massage the base of your left palm to the base of the fingertips with creeping movements of your right hand.
- To quell nausea, nibble crystallised ginger. Ginger is one of the most effective natural remedies for feeling sick. Alternatively, sip peppermint tea.
- Try activated charcoal for an inexpensive, old-time remedy for the 'sour' stomach brought on by overindulgence or stress. Buy the tablets from the chemist, and keep them handy in your earth-wise medicine cabinet.

■ ■ ■ **Snack on dried organic apricots** when you crave a sweet treat – they're a healthy source of nerve-soothing minerals.

Achieving a balance

If you perceive your quality of life to be reasonably high, chances are that you've struck a happy medium between the things you have to do and the things you love to do, and between your role as an individual and as part of a wider community. If, on the other hand, you're stressed, here's how to get the balance back.

TAKE A BREAK

Everyone has different needs – some people thrive on the fast track, others need to operate at a slower pace – but we all need a breathing space now and then.

- If necessary, make time for yourself in the form of diary appointments and treat them as seriously as you treat business meetings. Make it clear to others that you expect them to treat these appointments equally seriously.
- Avoid over-commitment by learning to say no, both to yourself and to other people. Taking on too much, whether it be work or family commitments, can lead to a breakdown in health.
- If you work in an analytical occupation such as accounting or law, try to spend some of your leisure time engaging your creative side. It doesn't have to be painting or playing a musical instrument. Gardening, cooking and woodwork all involve the imagination.
- Plan regular treats for yourself if you're under pressure over which you have no control. A lunch with your funniest friend, an aromatherapy massage or a bottle of your favourite perfume can all help to alleviate stress.
- Give yourself a reward when you have achieved something. It's important to recognise your own milestones, however small, and be good to yourself now and again.
- Consider putting some time aside for meditation. It can take as little as 20 minutes, you can do it at home and it can be an oasis of calm to escape into if the rest of your life is on fast-forward.

TIME MANAGEMENT

Keep on top of things, rather than letting them get on top of you, and you'll avoid the stress of running to catch up with your life.

- Fix things as soon as they start to malfunction; don't wait until repairs become so expensive that it's cheaper to replace the item.
- Don't let clutter accumulate. Return things to their place as soon as you have finished with

Try to keep a sense of wonder in the natural world. It's a great antidote to stress.

RE-CHARGE YOUR BATTERIES

Qi kung (pronounced *chee gung*) is an ancient Chinese healing system that works with the same 'meridians', or channels of energy flow, that are used in acupuncture. Try this terrific energy-boosting stretch.

- Sit cross-legged on the floor, making sure you are comfortable. Cross your arms and place one hand over each knee. Breathe in steadily for a count of ten.
- Breathe out, bending forward and dropping your head down, for a count of ten.
- Breathe in, return to an upright position and repeat, this time re-crossing your legs and arms so that the arm and leg that were at the bottom are now on top.

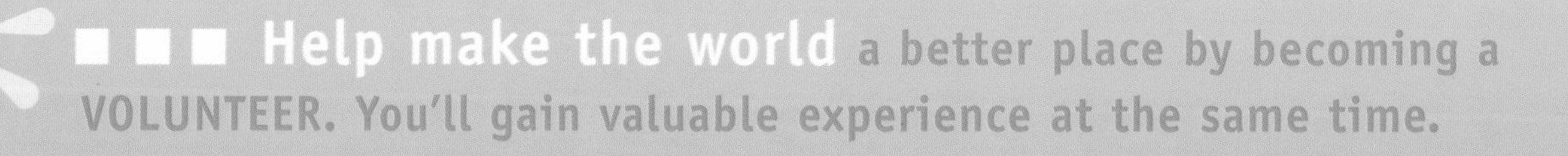

■ ■ ■ **Help make the world** a better place by becoming a VOLUNTEER. You'll gain valuable experience at the same time.

TOP TIP

Keep your brain active and lessen the risk of age-related memory decline by exercising your grey cells. Try doing newspaper crosswords or take up a pastime like bridge.

LOOKING OUTWARDS

Make a positive impact on the world by getting involved with your community. Participating in the wider world, away from your immediate circle of family and friends, can take your mind off your own troubles and be extremely rewarding.

- **VOLUNTARY WORK** There's a huge range of humanitarian and earth-wise opportunities to choose from – from community aid to environmental restoration projects. Pick a cause you're passionate about and try to match it with your skills, interests and schedule.
- **BUSH REGENERATION** Join a bush regeneration group to make a difference to your local area. Your local council should be able to put you in touch with one. As a bonus, if you're thinking about planting a native garden, the knowledge you'll gain about what grows well in your area will be invaluable.
- **SAVING WILDLIFE** Help rehabilitate injured wildlife by becoming a carer in an animal rescue organisation. Many animals and birds at risk from traffic, domestic pets and encroaching development have been saved in this way.
- **MONITORING THE ENVIRONMENT** Become involved in a wildlife monitoring project. There are many environmental and conservation projects that need volunteers to help identify and record native plants and animals or endangered species.

them. Give anything you haven't used in a long time to charity.

- Tidy your work or hobby area before you finish for the day. It's not only easier to find everything the next day, you'll feel much better coming back to a tidy set-up.
- Replenish supplies at home and at the office before they run out. That way you won't have to shop for supplies at an inconvenient time.
- Whenever you take something out of a folder at the office, take a couple of minutes to put the other papers in order before returning it to the drawer. It's a painless way of reorganising your filing system.
- Every time you walk around your garden, pull out a few weeds, dead-head some flowers and remove dead foliage. Small amounts of regular maintenance add up to a tidy-looking garden.

KEEP IT INTERESTING

Lethargy is bad for your mental health and it can also have an adverse impact on your physical health. Set yourself the challenge of learning something new on a regular basis. Nothing gives a greater mental charge than mastering an unfamiliar skill.

- Stretch yourself in some way every day. Try a new activity or visit somewhere you haven't been before. Even finding ways to improve and streamline everyday tasks can be a satisfying challenge.
- Go to evening classes. Learn a new language, learn to paint or take better photographs, join a choir or take dancing lessons.
- Don't be a couch potato. Television can be a fascinating adjunct to real life, but it shouldn't take its place. If you watch too much television, try to be more selective and cut back on viewing. Use the time you save to do something different and more stimulating.

hot links

Join Australia's largest wildlife rescue organisation: www.wires.org.au
Help care for Australia's natural environment: www.greeningaustralia.org.au
Volunteering in New Zealand: www.volunteernow.org.nz/home.html

Make someone's day – write a thankyou note, pay a genuine compliment or SMILE at a neighbour.

Mind over matter

It's now recognised in both mainstream and alternative medicine that mind and body each have an effect on the other. That's why meditation and positive thinking can enhance physical wellbeing and why relaxation and massage can calm the mind. The techniques below are all things you can do for yourself.

GOOD THINKING

- Focus on the good things in life. On bad days, this may be a challenge, but keep looking. Sources of joy may come from something as simple as your cat's antics, the first tomatoes of the season from your own vegetable garden or a wonderful book you've just read.
- If a plan goes wrong, don't get angry; instead, think of it as an opportunity to try something different. It could even be something that you've been wanting to do for a long time!
- Choose to remain calm. It's much kinder to your mind and body. Your reaction to annoying or traumatic events, people and circumstances outside your control determines whether they will be stressful or not.
- Learn to deflect 'worry' thoughts. It takes practice, but there are techniques to help (see *Think positive,* at right). By replacing gloomy beliefs with life-affirming ones, you'll break the cycle of stress that accompanies negativity.
- Let go of all or nothing thinking. No one is perfect.
- To help you relax, listen to meditation music and guided-meditation recordings, available from New Age bookshops. These are particularly useful at the end of the day, to help prepare you for a good night's sleep.

Take advantage of beautiful days and meditate in the open air.

- Keep a gratitude journal if it helps you identify and be reminded of the positive things in your life. Choose a beautiful book that's a pleasure to use, and try to write down three things every day for which you are grateful.
- Try listening to New Age or baroque music. These types of music have been found to induce alpha brainwaves, which in turn instil deep physical and mental relaxation.
- Make a point of focusing on the positive things you desire rather than the negative things you don't want. In time, you'll find that your thinking shifts effortlessly from negative to positive.

THINK POSITIVE

This technique is used by cognitive behavioural psychologists to help people think more positively. It's very effective if practised regularly.

- Bring to mind a situation that is generating negative thoughts. As the thought enters your mind, think or say a sharp 'Stop!' The thought will disappear, along with any accompanying emotions.
- Next, replace the negative thought with a positive or calming thought.
- To prepare, write down everything that's worrying you and come up with positive thoughts to replace these ones.
- Monitor your thoughts and whenever the black ones start forming, mentally call a sharp 'Stop!' and choose to think the corresponding positive thought.

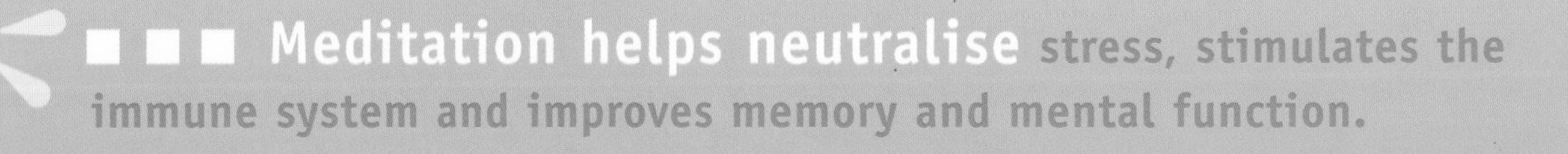

Meditation helps neutralise stress, stimulates the immune system and improves memory and mental function.

RELAXATION TECHNIQUES

SITTING MEDITATION

Meditation exerts a powerfully calming effect on the body as well as the mind, slowing the heart rate, lowering blood pressure, increasing blood flow to the brain and balancing brainwave patterns.

- Sit comfortably – cross-legged if you wish – in a quiet spot where you won't be disturbed. Close your eyes and breathe deeply and slowly.
- Now, calm your mind and clear it of all thoughts. To help you achieve this, focus your attention on an object such as the flame of a candle or a flower in a vase, on your breathing, or on a sound such as 'Om', which you quietly hum.
- Sit quietly for 2 or 3 minutes to start with. (As you become more comfortable with the practice, increase the time to 20 minutes.) Focus on the object you've chosen.
- When your mind wanders, simply return your attention to the object. This becomes easier with practice, so persevere!

MUSCLE RELEASE TECHNIQUE

With our nonstop lifestyles, many of us have forgotten what true relaxation actually feels like. Experience it again with this simple exercise.

- Lie on your back on the floor or your bed, with a pillow underneath your knees to support your lower back, and the flattest pillow you can tolerate under your head. Relax in this position for a couple of minutes.
- For the next 10 minutes, systematically tense and release every major muscle group three times. Start with your feet and work progressively towards your head in the following order: calves, thighs, buttocks, stomach, chest, back, hands, arms, shoulders, neck and face.
- Hold each muscle tense for 3 seconds, then very slowly release the tension. With each successive relaxation, you'll find you can relax the muscles a little more deeply.
- Rest for 5 minutes, enjoying the sensation of deep relaxation. When you get up, do so gradually to avoid dizziness, and then move very slowly at first.

DIY ACUPRESSURE

This technique can be used to relieve tension unobtrusively at an office desk or on a bus.

- With your fingertips, massage in circular movements from the centre of the face outwards.
- Whenever you encounter an indentation in the bone structure, hold your fingertips on the spot and work it for several seconds, applying gentle pressure.

SCALP MASSAGE

Try this if a headache threatens or if you feel tense. It sounds rough but is effective.

- Grab a handful of hair close to the scalp and clench and release your fist several times.
- Without letting go, move your fist back and forth, feeling your scalp moving over the skull.
- Repeat all over your head.

FOOT MASSAGE

In this treatment, the combination of heat and small pressure points from the pebbles gives new life to tired feet.

- Place smooth pebbles or marbles in the bottom of a large bowl, and cover with water as hot as you can bear. Add a couple of drops of lavender essential oil.
- Put your feet in the bowl and roll them back and forth over the pebbles, applying gentle pressure.

CHEST MASSAGE

Use this technique to relieve tightening of the chest muscles as a result of stress.

- Massage firmly across the top of your rib cage, putting pressure into the heels of your hands as you circle them outwards.

Natural therapies

Natural therapies aim to heal the whole person, not just the symptom. Many people believe that these therapies offer less intrusive ways to treat illness, are better at treating stress-related problems and have fewer side effects than conventional drugs. Consider whether such treatments are for you.

FINDING A THERAPIST

- Go through the relevant practitioner body. In Australia, contact the Australian Traditional Medicine Society or the Australian Natural Therapists Association for details of the appropriate professional organisation. In New Zealand, get in touch with the South Pacific Association of Natural Therapists.
- Ask your therapist to list his or her qualifications if you have any concerns. These credentials can normally be verified with the relevant practitioner body.
- Check the price up front. It can vary per session, depending on the therapy and the time involved. Again, the practitioner body can suggest a reasonable price range. The initial consultation is often longer and more expensive than the normal charge, as it involves taking a detailed case history.

Anything that reduces stress is not only good for you, it's good for the economy. Stress-related illness accounts for millions of days of annual sick leave.

- Avoid any therapist who suggests that you stop taking conventional medication, or who promises results that sound unrealistic.
- Don't stop taking any prescribed medication without consulting your doctor. If you have any worrying symptoms after seeing a natural therapist, talk to your doctor.

VITAL SIGNS

- Iridology is founded on the idea that the iris contains a 'map' of the body. For example, a dark rim around the iris may indicate inefficient elimination. Those who want early warning of a condition before it gets worse, or who simply want to monitor their health, may also benefit from it.
- Kinesiology is a system of diagnosis based on the testing of the muscles. Responses indicate how the body is functioning and whether there are any chemical or energy imbalances. It can help identify allergies and sensitivities, and benefit children with learning difficulties.
- Biofeedback uses a computer to analyse heart rate, pulse and brain waves. The results are used to design a program for controlling the symptoms of any existing condition. For example, if your condition is worsened by stress, you will be taught stress-reduction techniques, such as deep breathing.

EVERYDAY AROMATHERAPY

- Place a couple of drops of energising orange oil in the shower recess before turning on the water.
- In the car, dot a few drops of lavender oil on the dashboard to help you keep calm while driving.
- Burn geranium oil in a desk vaporiser to promote a peaceful atmosphere at work.
- Sniff invigorating rosemary if your blood sugar plummets after lunch.
- Light a vanilla-scented candle to soothe and relax yourself at the end of the day.

GENTLE ADJUSTMENT

Osteopathy and chiropractic have a common aim – to remove aches and pains by adjusting the spine – but different approaches. This is what to expect.

Natural therapies aim to achieve health and wellbeing through the connection of body, mind and spirit.

THE TRUTH ABOUT...

COMPLEMENTARY MEDICINE

Practitioners of mainstream medicine are increasingly recognising that complementary therapies, such as acupuncture and herbalism, have much to offer in treating specific ailments. Anecdotal evidence can also be strong, but how can you be sure that they really work? The answer is that we don't know because the industry is less regulated and researched than conventional medicine. In the end, it's up to you to give natural therapies a go and then decide whether they are working.

hot links

Find a therapist: www.naturaltherapypages.com.au
Australian Traditional Medicine Society: www.atms.com.au
Australian Natural Therapists Association: www.anta.com.au
South Pacific Association of Natural Therapists: www.spant.org.nz
Chiropractors' associations: www.chiropractors.asn.au; www.chiropractic.org.nz
Osteopathic associations: www.osteopathic.com.au; www.osteopathiccouncil.org.nz

- A chiropractor will endeavour to restore balance to the spine through gentle manipulation of joints and by making small adjustments that assist the spine's mechanical function. This in turn helps muscles, nerves, joints and ligaments to work better.
- An osteopath will try to bring the structure of the body into balance through massage and manipulation of the spine and may also apply similar techniques to the limbs and skull.
- A first visit can last up to 1 hour. A good chiropractor or osteopath will normally request X-rays of your spine and check your blood pressure.
- In most cases, you'll be examined sitting, standing and lying down. Your reflexes will also be tested.
- You won't just be asked about your skeletal or muscular problem – you will also be quizzed on your lifestyle, work and leisure activities.
- Both types of therapist will apply gentle manipulative techniques to your joints and may also massage your muscles. They may also try a technique known as the high-velocity thrust – a rapid, painless movement that makes the joint move and click and the muscles around the joint then quickly relax.
- You'll be given follow-up advice about exercises you can do to maintain the mobility of your joints.

KEEPING COSTS DOWN

- Check your health fund. Osteopathy and chiropractic, for example, are common inclusions.
- Rehabilitation patients and pensioners may find hospitals and hospices provide natural therapists' services at a reduced rate.
- If you're expecting to have long-term treatment, ask about discounts or a sliding scale for fees.
- Try a therapist who is starting a practice. They may charge less in order to build up the business.
- Try a training college. It will often be cheaper, provided you don't mind being treated by students. They may lack experience, but will work under a qualified practitioner.

WHICH THERAPY?

AROMATHERAPY Involves the use of essential oils from plants and herbs, and is often combined with massage. Frequently a component of beauty treatments, and regularly employed to treat gynaecological and skin problems and muscle injuries.

HERBALISM The use of plants and herbs with medicinal properties that stimulate the body's natural healing processes. Used to treat: pain, gynaecological problems, PMS, stress, sleep disturbance, digestive problems, headaches, acne and eczema.

HOMEOPATHY A system of healing that involves taking a detailed history of the patient and introducing small amounts of a remedy to exacerbate and then cure a problem. Used to treat: emotional issues, allergies, and menstrual and menopausal disorders.

NATUROPATHY Combines mainstream health science with a range of natural therapies to provide protection against common health problems. Used to treat: weight problems, addictions, allergies, eczema and digestive problems (such as irritable bowel syndrome).

REFLEXOLOGY Reflex points in the feet and hands are believed to correspond to various organs in the body. Used to treat: stress, anxiety, asthma, menstrual problems and also digestive problems (such as constipation).

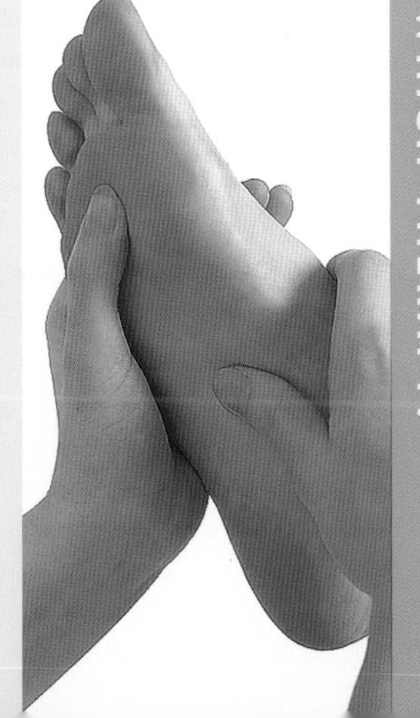

Hands-on healing

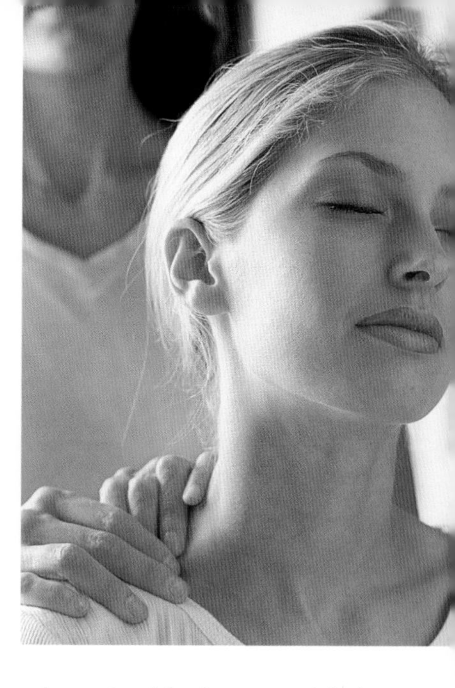

Massage has been used for thousands of years as a wonderfully effective way to relax, invigorate and heal. Whether you invest in a professional massage or learn a few basic strokes yourself, it will enhance your life by helping to prevent illness, by boosting circulation, lowering blood pressure and expelling toxins.

THE POWER OF TOUCH

Massage can be used on a daily basis or to alleviate unexpected aches and pains. These are just some of the reasons to use it.

- It's especially good for people in sedentary occupations. If you work at a desk all day long, it's worth asking your human resources department if the company would be willing to subsidise a massage therapist. Some organisations recognise the benefits to their workers and help to cover the cost.
- It will help your muscles recover quickly after exercise and reduce spasms, tension and cramping.
- Massage can help lower blood pressure and reduce your pulse rate, in turn helping to relieve tension and stress.
- It can help reduce emotional stress, which often manifests as a dramatic tightening of the chest muscles and shortness of breath.
- Massage can accelerate the process of healing tissue by stimulating the circulation of blood. This in turn can help minimise swelling and contusions.
- It works as an aid for digestive problems by reducing cramping and spasms in the digestive tract and facilitating elimination through the large intestines.
- It can instil both a general feeling of relaxation and wellbeing and a strong sense of invigoration.
- Note that massage is not advised if you are in the first trimester of pregnancy, suffer from cancer, have a broken bone, have a serious back injury, suffer from severe skin problems such as psoriasis or eczema, or have tissue damage – in particular, direct pressure should never be applied to varicose veins.

DIFFERENT STROKES

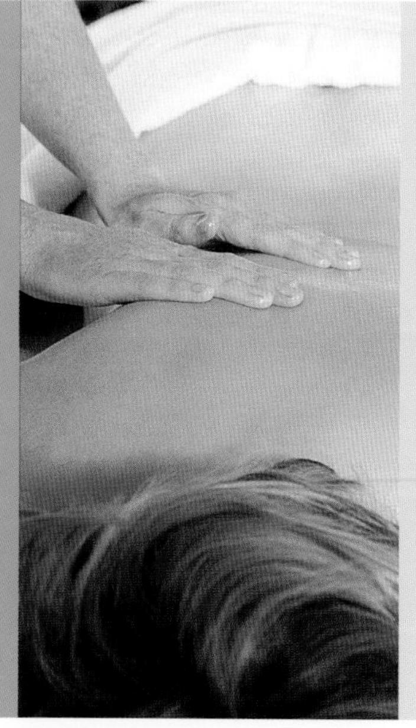

Therapeutic or remedial massage draws on a number of techniques taken from different healing traditions. Here are just a few examples.

- **KA HUNA** This wonderfully relaxing technique was once practised only by the mysterious *kahunas*, or Hawaiian native priests. It involves placing warmed rocks on the spine, applying scented oils and using long, fluid massage strokes. It's especially good for stress-related neck and upper back tension.
- **SHIATSU** The therapist applies firm pressure to particular points on the body – known as *tsubos* – and stretches muscles. Shiatsu works especially well for back pain, headaches and digestive problems.
- **SWEDISH** This typically involves light fingertip stroking with kneading and friction. It's effective at relieving tension and promoting relaxation.
- **THAI** Nicknamed 'the lazy person's yoga' because it flexes you into positions you might never have thought you could reach. This type is great for improving flexibility and circulation.
- **TUINA** Originating in China, the words *tui* and *na* literally mean 'push' and 'grasp', referring to the deep pressure the therapist uses. It's excellent for frozen shoulder, sciatica and tension-related conditions.

■ ■ ■ **Massage increases** levels of dopamine – a 'feel-good' neurotransmitter – benefiting both the body and the mind.

ACUPRESSURE

This self-help technique is nicknamed 'acupuncture without needles' because it uses finger massage to stimulate 'acupoints' that restore the flow of energy – or *qi* – through the body.

- The next time you feel your neck and shoulders becoming stiff and sore, place your fingers at the base of your neck, where it meets your shoulders, on either side of your spine. Press for 15 seconds, take a deep breath in, and breathe out.
- Move your fingers 2 cm outwards, then repeat. Move your fingers another 2 cm outwards and repeat.
- Give yourself a big hug to stretch your back; swap your hands over and hug yourself again.

LYMPHATIC DRAINAGE

Manual lymphatic drainage is a gentle technique based on circular, 'pumping' movements. These are its benefits.

- It is highly effective at countering oedema (fluid retention) after surgery and after radiotherapy and chemotherapy.
- It's a way of easing the painful pressure that can build up with chronic catarrhal and sinus infections.
- Regular lymphatic drainage massage can save you money in the long run by improving your general immune system.

DIY MASSAGE

You can adapt a range of techniques for use on yourself or a partner.

- Try friction. It's particularly useful on stiff joints. Place palms side by side on the body and, using even pressure, briskly rub or 'scissor' them backwards and forwards.
- Use kneading for fleshy areas such as thighs. Squeeze the muscles rhythmically between the thumb and fingers.
- Knuckling is especially good for shoulder tension. Curl hands into loose fists, placing the middle section of the fingers on the skin, then rotate.

hot links

Australian Association of Massage Therapists: www.aamt.com.au
Australian Acupuncture and Chinese Medicine Association: www.acupuncture.org.au
Therapeutic Massage Association New Zealand: www.tmanz.org.nz

MASSAGE FOR BABIES

Massage has a bonding effect on baby and parents. It also helps to settle premature babies, and is particularly recommended for adoptive parents wanting to establish a connection with their baby.

- Before you start, make sure the room is warm – a good time to massage a baby is after a bath.
- Lie the baby down on a towel or bunny-rug at waist level so you aren't bending over uncomfortably. Prop some pillows around the baby to ensure he or she doesn't roll off.
- Place a small amount of massage oil in the palm of your hand. Wait a few seconds to let it warm up and gently massage over the baby.
- Be careful to avoid baby's eyes, and be careful around the umbilical cord when massaging a young baby. Never extend the arms and legs too firmly.
- Soothe a colicky baby by stroking the tummy, putting one hand on each side, and sliding the baby back and forth in a gentle crisscross motion. Then stroke clockwise around the belly button, with one hand following the other.
- To calm a teething baby, massage from the base of the ears out to the base of the neck and in towards the centre of the chin.
- Make your own delicately scented baby massage oil by mixing 75 ml sweet almond oil, 1 tsp jojoba oil and 2 drops chamomile essential oil. The mixture can also be used as a cleansing oil on a cotton wool ball to wipe the nappy area clean. Presented in an attractive bottle, it makes a thoughtful and useful gift for a new parent.

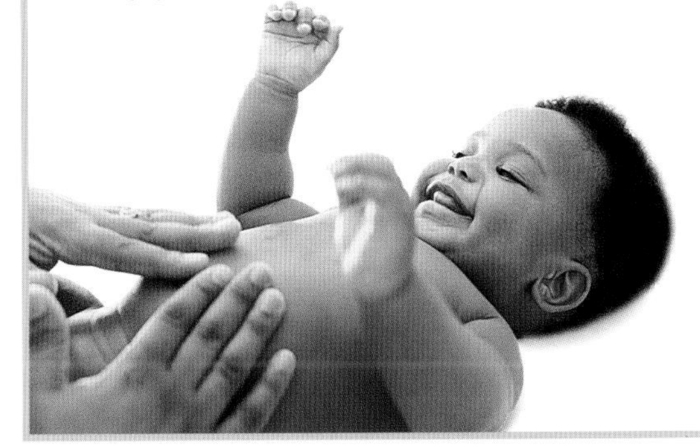

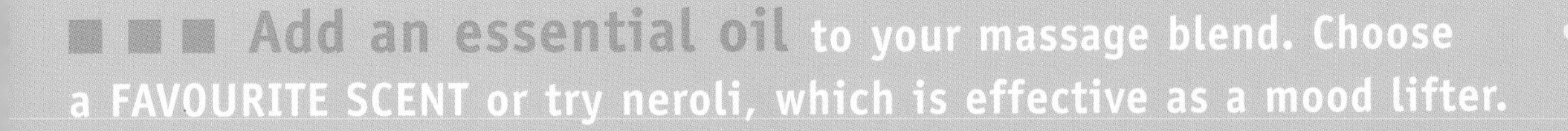

NATURAL REMEDIES

Earth-wise medicines and a healthy lifestyle will help you to deal with many ailments, safely and naturally.

Feeling good on the inside

Constipation, indigestion and heartburn are no fun, but it's a sure bet that at least one of them will bother you at some time. There is usually no serious underlying problem, but it helps to learn some gentle ways to remedy the situation or to simply prevent it from occurring in the first place.

TEN TIPS FOR BETTER DIGESTION

1 Make the milk connection. Lactose intolerance could be the culprit behind your digestive upsets. Calcium-fortified rice or soy milk are great substitutes.

2 Check your medications. A wide variety of drugs, including antihistamines and antidepressants, can upset your stomach. Ease acid reflux and indigestion by taking 1–2 teaspoons slippery elm powder in a glass of warm water.

3 Antibiotics not only attack harmful bacteria, they also kill off the 'friendly' bacteria (probiotics) that help digest food in the gut. To replace the good bacteria, take a probiotic supplement. Fermented milk drinks and some yoghurts are a good source, or take in capsule, tablet or powder form (available from health food shops).

4 Are you drinking enough water? Every adult needs a minimum of about 2 litres of fluid daily to ensure efficient digestion and elimination.

5 Focus on fibre. It's not difficult to get the recommended daily 30 grams of fibre if you choose foods carefully. Try fresh or dried fruit, vegetables, nuts, cooked dried beans and whole grains. (Increase your intake slowly to avoid gas attacks.)

6 Get moving. Inactivity can result in a sluggish digestion. Regular exercise moves food through the bowel faster.

7 Go to the toilet as soon as you feel the need. Ignoring the urge to go can cause a variety of digestive problems.

8 Have a good laugh! Laughing has a 'massaging' effect on the intestines, and counters stress, which can make the bowel sluggish.

9 Eat pineapple or kiwi fruit after meals. These foods contain enzymes that assist digestion. Or try chewing cardamom or caraway seeds. Flavour food with rosemary and mint, and eat watercress or artichokes occasionally. All these foods make the digestive juices flow.

10 Go easy on your intake of caffeine (found in coffee and chocolate), and avoid soft drinks and greasy foods, all of which can exacerbate digestive problems.

TOP TIP

For constipation, take a dose of psyllium seed, a natural bulking agent sold in supermarkets and health food shops. It's tasteless, inexpensive and very safe, even if taken over long periods. Grind together 2 parts psyllium seed with 1 part flaxseed and 1 part chopped dried figs or prunes. Take 1 tbsp mixed with yoghurt every night before bed.

■ ■ ■ **If you have coeliac disease,** eat some sunflower seeds each day to protect against inflammation of the intestinal lining.

QUICK FIXES FOR HICCUPS

More of a nuisance than a medical problem, hiccups are caused by a spasm in the diaphragm. The triggers range from a nervous reaction to swallowing too much air and eating too quickly.

✔ Swallow 1 tsp sugar.
✔ Bend over forwards, and drink a full glass of water upside-down.
✔ Suck on a lemon wedge.
✔ Blow in and out of a brown paper bag 10 times, very quickly.
✔ Hold your breath and swallow the moment you feel the hiccup coming.

Chew coriander seeds or drink coriander tea to help reduce flatulence, nausea and indigestion.

DIARRHOEA

Try these gentle remedies to soothe diarrhoea, but seek prompt medical attention if the problem does not subside in 2 days, if it's accompanied by a fever and severe abdominal pain or if blood or mucus is present in the stool.

- Increase your intake of soluble fibre. This may help to absorb excess fluid. Try apples, porridge or red kidney beans.
- Steep 2 teaspoons dried fennel seeds in 200 ml boiling water for 5–10 minutes, strain and drink. Fennel is mildly antiseptic and helps to relieve the cramping pains that often accompany diarrhoea.
- Steep 1 tablespoon barley in 200 ml boiling water for 20 minutes, strain and drink. It's a gentle traditional remedy for an upset stomach and diarrhoea.
- Vomiting and diarrhoea can flush out important nutrients, such as potassium, sodium and glucose. Side-step expensive, commercially prepared electrolyte products with this handy home-made rehydration recipe: just mix diluted fruit juice (to replace lost potassium) with ½ teaspoon honey (to replace glucose) and a pinch of table salt (for sodium chloride).

HEARTBURN

When digestive acids back up out of your stomach for any reason, it gives you an unpleasant burning sensation in your oesophagus, the tube connecting your mouth with your stomach. To help put out the fire, keep these herbal remedies in your earth-wise medicine cabinet.

- Take ginger tablets or capsules. Ginger works by absorbing the acid, and it also calms the nerves.
- Slippery elm produces mucilage, a thick, sticky substance that coats your digestive tract, creating a protective barrier. Take 1 teaspoon slippery elm, mashed with a little banana, before each meal.
- Try apple cider vinegar, an inexpensive old-fashioned remedy that really works. Take 1 teaspoon in ½ glass water during a meal.

IRRITABLE BOWEL SYNDROME (IBS)

The symptoms of IBS – a condition in which parts of the bowel contract too quickly – include constipation, diarrhoea, cramps and bloating.

- Stress can make IBS worse, so if you're under pressure, regularly practise a relaxation technique, such as yoga. Or breathe slowly and deeply through your diaphragm.
- Moderate physical exercise can help to control the condition.
- Try to avoid coffee, spicy meals and acidic foods such as oranges, tomatoes and vinegary salad dressings, all of which contribute to IBS.
- Try psyllium seed, which is a very safe natural laxative.
- Fat is a major stimulus to bowel contractions, so avoid fatty foods.
- Keep a diary to help you identify the triggers – for example, certain foods, stress or hormonal changes.
- Check food labels before you buy. Lollies that are artificially sweetened with sorbitol can upset the digestion, and may even aggravate IBS.

Wintering wisely

With foresight and practical intervention, make this the year you didn't succumb to winter ailments as soon as the weather turned chilly. The beauty of earth-wise remedies is that they naturally enhance your body's ability to fight infection and build up resistance.

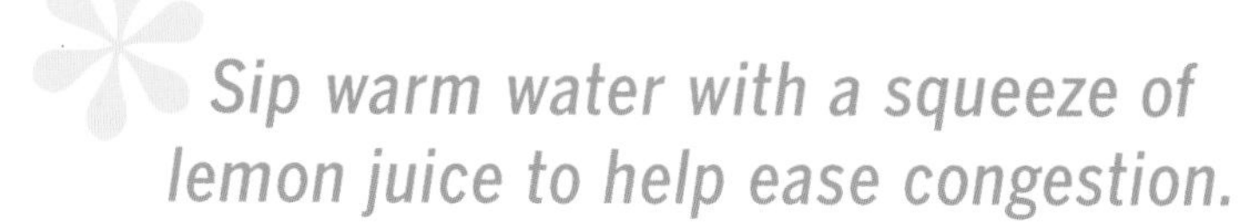

KEEPING WARM

- Aerobic exercise is an excellent way of providing internal central heating, because you'll feel warm long after you've stopped moving. Make sure you wrap up well afterwards to conserve the benefit.
- You lose most of your body heat through your head, so choose a hat that you can pull over your ears, preferably one made from a natural fabric, such as lambswool.
- Wear an earth-wise polar fleece. It's made from recycled plastic soft-drink bottles and, unlike most synthetics, it will keep you dry. This is important because damp skin leads directly to chills.
- Raise your body's metabolism by eating small meals throughout the day, rather than 2–3 large ones.
- Rub your arms and legs with a loofah when you're showering and cover up well afterwards. This should warm you for several hours.
- Massage cold feet with a warming mix of 1 tablespoon olive oil and 3 drops each rosemary and black pepper essential oils. Firmly sweep your hand up towards your ankle and then lightly sweep down towards your toes.

COUGHS AND COLDS

Don't overuse decongestants, nose drops and sprays – they can damage the delicate lining of your nose. Instead, try these gentler remedies.

- At the first sign of a dry tickle in the back of your throat, sip warm blackcurrant cordial. It soothes a sore throat and provides extra vitamin C, which helps your body fight infection.
- If you suddenly develop a sore throat, but experience no other symptoms of a cold or flu, check your prescription drugs with your doctor. Some drugs, including blood pressure and thyroid medications, can cause sore throats because they have dehydrating properties.
- Take vitamin C. It may shorten a cold's duration because of its ability to boost the immune system by producing antibodies to fight infections.
- Get some rest so you don't compromise your immune system and become even sicker.
- Treat yourself to some chicken soup. This long-time folk remedy helps to unclog sinuses. Another trick is to tent your head over a bowl of hot water to which 3 drops peppermint oil have been added, then inhale.
- Drink lots of fluids, especially if you have a fever. Try diluted carrot or apple juice but avoid milk. Natural therapists believe dairy products stimulate the production of excess mucus.
- Clear your stuffed-up nose and help yourself to a good night's sleep with this blend: add 1 tablespoon whisky, the juice of ½ lemon and a little honey to hot chamomile tea. (Warning: don't drink any more alcohol than this, as it will stress your system.)
- Prepare an old-fashioned mustard footbath. Add 2 teaspoons mustard powder to 1 litre hot water, and soak your feet. This is said to draw blood down to your feet, thereby relieving congestion in your head and lungs.
- Gargle with tea-tree oil to soothe a sore throat. Add 5 drops tea-tree oil to a glass of water. (Warning: do not swallow the gargle as tea-tree oil is toxic.)

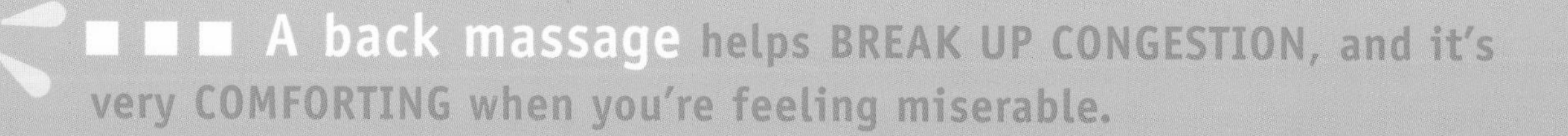

CHILBLAINS

- Don't toast your feet in front of a fire or add a direct source of heat to sore toes. It will make chilblains worse. Wear warm socks and move around to get your circulation going.
- Drink a ginger and cinnamon tea to stimulate your circulation and possibly help prevent chilblains. Add 3 teaspoons grated fresh ginger and 2 cinnamon sticks to 500 ml water in a saucepan. Bring to the boil, then simmer for 15 minutes. Strain. Drink a cup of this tea 3 times a day.
- Give yourself a warming hand- or footbath with the same mixture. This time, however, make four times the amount and add 225 grams Epsom salts.

DRYNESS

- Drink about 2 litres of water a day. The ability of your body's cells to retain moisture decreases as you get older, worsening any dry skin problem.
- Try not to spend too long in hot showers and baths. Although it's tempting to do so in winter, hot water can dehydrate your skin. If you feel cold before you bathe, do some stretching or some other gentle exercise. The exertion will warm you up.
- If you have central heating in your home, turn it down. Your skin tends to feel itchier when you're hot, so save both energy and your complexion by turning down the the thermostat a few degrees.
- Use oatmeal as a soap substitute to soothe flaky, irritated skin characterised by 'winter itch'. Oatmeal is recommended by dermatologists and is safe, effective and inexpensive. Tie some oatmeal in a handkerchief, dunk it in water, then squeeze out the excess and use it as you would a normal face washer.
- If you have an electric blanket on your bed, turn it off as soon as you go to bed. Leaving it on overnight will overheat you and you'll wake up feeling dehydrated.
- To avoid dry or splitting nails, massage some nourishing oil into them. Mix together 2 teaspoons wheat germ oil, the contents of 2 vitamin E capsules and 10 drops lavender oil. Store the mixture in a small, dark-coloured glass bottle. Massage the oil into your nails and cuticles daily.

RESISTING THE FLU

- ✔ Take a daily garlic supplement
- ✔ Stay warm
- ✔ Get enough sleep
- ✘ Cut down on smoking and alcohol
- ✘ Avoid crowds

HELP FROM HERBS

EUCALYPTUS OIL Suck eucalyptus lozenges to clear your nasal passages and suppress coughing.

GARLIC Take a garlic supplement daily. It is said to reduce your risk of catching a cold by more than half.

LICORICE This relaxes bronchial spasms and loosens phlegm. Combined with other expectorants such as thyme and garlic, it is available in teas and tinctures. (Warning: too much licorice tea can raise your blood pressure.)

MARSHMALLOW Steep the herb marshmallow (*Althea officinalis*, not the confectionery) in hot water to release a gel-like substance that will soothe your throat.

THYME This herb has antiviral properties and may help to alleviate throat infections. Other useful herbs are elderflower (anti-catarrhal), plantain (soothes mucous membranes) and sage (mildly antibacterial). (Warning: avoid thyme and sage if you are pregnant.)

A good diet of brightly coloured vegetables and fruits contains every vitamin you need to COMBAT the common cold.

Treating minor ailments

Bumps, bruises, swellings, bites and stings are part of everyday life, especially if you have small children. For minor ailments there's often no need to visit the chemist. Stock your medicine cabinet with safe, natural solutions – you'll avoid potential side effects from synthetic ingredients, and save money too.

BITES AND STINGS

Wearing perfume and brightly coloured clothes and eating sweet, sticky food increase your chances of being stung or bitten by insects. Cover your skin and hair and wear pale clothing.

- Consider taking bromelain (available from health food shops). An enzyme derived from pineapple, it may help to reduce swelling.
- Try taking vitamin B_1 to repel mosquitoes. It's thought to produce a skin odour they dislike.
- Use an ice pack or calamine lotion to calm red, irritated or itchy skin. Use a paste of bicarbonate of soda and water to ease pain and itchiness.
- Apply calendula ointment to relieve the inflammation.

BOILS

Don't squeeze a boil. Doing so will be painful and you'll risk spreading the infection. Always bring a boil to a head by using gentle heat.

- Mix 250 grams slippery elm powder (from health food shops) with enough hot water to make a paste. Carefully spread the poultice over the boil, and then cover with sterile gauze. Leave it in place until it is cool. Repeat twice a day until the boil discharges.
- If you're prone to boils, drink immune-boosting teas, such as red clover, goldenseal and echinacea.

COLD SORES

If you're prone to cold sores, avoid eating nuts, seeds and chocolate. They contain the amino acid arginine, which may trigger the problem.

- Take natural supplements. You can take the amino acid lysine orally, or apply it in cream form. Vitamin C and the flavonoids may help boost your immunity; the herbs echinacea and goldenseal have natural antiviral and antibiotic properties.
- When you first feel the tingling, hold an ice cube against the spot or, to numb the irritation, apply neat spirits, such as gin or vodka.
- Use witch hazel to help dry up a cold sore. Or combine 10 drops geranium or eucalyptus essential oil with 25 ml water, shake and apply with a cotton bud several times a day. Both remedies are astringent

EARTH-WISE REMEDIES

ALOE VERA The sap of *Aloe barbadensis* soothes bites and stings and eases minor burns and scalds. It's also an effective reliever of sunburn.

CABBAGE LEAVES Poultices made from cabbage leaves are an inexpensive and effective treatment for abscesses: dip the leaves in boiling water until they are just wilted. Cool, wrap in gauze and place over an abscess every 2 hours to relieve pain.

TEA Soak your feet in black tea to make the skin tougher and less blister-prone, a trick athletes use to build themselves up for long distances. Cooled, wet tea bags can alleviate the tingling of a cold sore and reduce stinging and redness.

TEA-TREE OIL This oil has powerful antimicrobial and disinfectant properties. Add 6–10 drops to 1 cup warm water and use it to bathe cuts and grazes. Insects dislike the scent of tea-tree – try burning a few drops in a vaporiser to repel biting pests.

To speed healing, pierce a vitamin E capsule and massage the oil into a burn once a skin has formed over it.

~ STAR SAVER ~

There's a range of gels and creams containing aloe vera, one of nature's most useful remedies. As a general rule, the more aloe concentrate they contain, the more expensive they are. Save money by keeping a pot plant handy and simply snap off a leaf tip to access your own free supply.

WARNING!

▼ Never try to burst an abscess or a boil. Large painful boils and abscesses require medical assistance. See your doctor.

and antiseptic. Thuja ointment (from health food shops) speeds healing.

- Apply sunscreen to block out sun and wind, both triggers of cold sores for some people, and to prevent recurrences.

HAEMORRHOIDS

Haemorrhoids, swellings of the veins in and around the anus, affect 7 out of 10 people.

- Increase your intake of dietary fibre and fluid, and avoid salt, spices and carbonated drinks.
- Avoid lifting heavy objects. The action has the same effect on haemorrhoids as straining on the toilet and can exacerbate the problem.
- To help reduce swelling and irritation, add a strong brew of strained marigold tea to a shallow bath. Or add 4 drops cypress essential oil, which is soothing and cooling.
- To shrink haemorrhoids and reduce the pain, dab them with chilled witch hazel.

HIVES

Hives are itchy lumps that can be caused by stress, emotional upset or a reaction to allergies. Try to relieve the itch and swelling without taking antihistamines.

- Rub ice cubes over the lumps to shrink the blood vessels and reduce the swelling caused by the cells' release of histamine.
- Use calamine lotion, an old-fashioned astringent famous for its ability to soothe rashes. Witch hazel and milk of magnesia may also help, especially when chilled.
- If you suspect emotional upsets bring on your hives, try some nerve-calming teas, such as passionflower, chamomile and catnip.

SUNBURN

- Before spending a day at the beach, take anti-oxidant supplements such as vitamins A, C and E. Although vitamins won't protect you from becoming sunburnt, research has found that they may slow the sun's ageing effects.
- If you are badly sunburnt, you may also be dehydrated. Until the symptoms of sunburn ease, drink 2 litres of water a day, and avoid alcohol.
- Add 10 drops each of chamomile and lavender essential oil to a cool bath and soak in it for 15 minutes.
- Alternatively, try 1 cup of either dissolved bicarbonate of soda or apple cider vinegar, or fill a sock or cut-off stocking with oatmeal, and swish that through the bathwater.
- Use a lip balm to soothe burnt lips. Remember to re-apply it after eating or drinking.

TREATING AND AVOIDING BRUISES

✔ Eat more citrus fruits, red and green capsicums, kiwi fruit, spinach and broccoli for their vitamin C content. It's thought that people with low levels of vitamin C bruise more easily.

✔ Apply an ice pack quickly – cooling numbs the area and also constricts blood vessels, so that less blood spills into the surrounding tissues to cause discolouration.

✔ Use a menthol-based ointment to increase circulation, which speeds healing and reduces discolouration.

✔ Avoid taking aspirin or antihypertensive drugs if you can. These two medications may increase bruising. Ask your doctor for advice if you bruise easily.

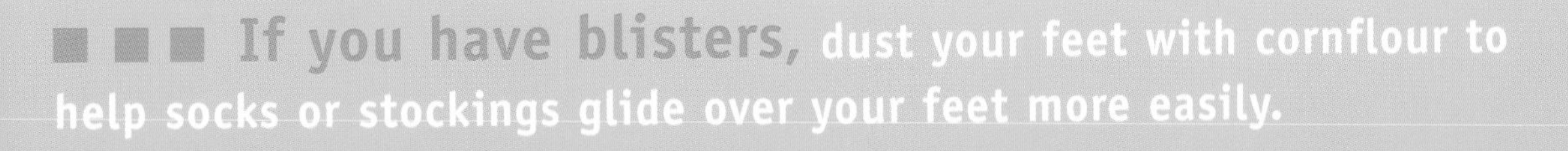

If you have blisters, dust your feet with cornflour to help socks or stockings glide over your feet more easily.

Aches and pains

No matter where it hurts – your head, your feet or anywhere in between – aches and pains can wear you out. Fortunately, you don't have to rely on strong and often expensive painkillers. Instead, use natural therapies and remedies to help ease your discomfort.

EARACHE

- Try this garlic oil treatment. Rub a garlic oil capsule between your hands to warm the oil, then pierce the capsule and place 1–2 drops in the affected ear. (Warning: if you think your eardrum is ruptured, never drip fluids into your ear.)
- If your ears become painfully blocked whenever you travel by plane, take horseradish tablets, a herbal decongestant.
- Try the herbal form of chamomile for a mild earache and the homoeopathic form for a more painful one.

EYE STRAIN

Soothe tired, aching eyes with these easy treatments you can do at home.

- Lie down and place either cucumber slices or cold used tea bags over both eyes. Relax for 10–15 minutes, then remove the cucumber or bags.
- If you suffer from dry eyes, boil 2 cups water with a pinch of bicarbonate of soda. Leave the solution to cool, then bathe your eyes.
- Add 1 teaspoon dried eyebright (available from health food shops) to 1 teacup boiling water. Cover, cool and strain through coffee filter paper before using the solution to bathe your eyes.

HEADACHES

If you are unfortunate enough to suffer regularly from headaches, consider possible environmental causes as well as other common triggers, such as food sensitivities and eating habits.

- If you're prone to headaches, make sure you snack little and often. Eating too little or infrequently results in fluctuating blood sugar levels, which can kick-start a headache.
- Try white willow tablets or capsules (available from health food shops). This natural herbal anti-inflammatory is very similar to aspirin but doesn't cause stomach bleeding, which is one of aspirin's potentially serious side effects. (Warning: people who are allergic to aspirin or who suffer from ulcers should avoid this herb.)
- Be aware that food sensitivities can be the cause of headaches. The four 'Cs' – cheese, chocolate, citrus and caffeine – are known culprits, as are red wine and port. If you notice that you suffer a headache every time you eat a certain food, eliminate that food from your diet.
- Boost your fibre intake with brown rice, oats and bran because constipation, surprisingly, can be a cause of headaches.

~ *FLYING START* ~

Avoiding aged cheese, pickles, cured meats, red wine, beer, nuts, oranges and caffeinated drinks can make an immediate difference to migraine sufferers. These foods contain compounds known as amines that are notorious migraine triggers. Chocolate is also a culprit.

■ ■ ■ **To relieve a painful tooth,** dab a few drops of CLOVE OIL on a cotton wool ball and place it on or near the tooth.

MIGRAINE

The good news for migraine sufferers is that natural remedies and therapies are not only an earth-wise choice – for some people they can be as effective as conventional drugs.

- Take magnesium and calcium to help maintain blood vessels and nerve health. When taken over several months, the herb feverfew can reduce the frequency of migraines.
- If you know that stress brings on a migraine, try biofeedback or relaxation training.
- Eating fish rich in omega-3 fatty acids – for example, salmon and tuna – reduces the likelihood of clotting, and so may help to prevent your migraines.

STOMACH ACHE

- Have a cup of tea. Chamomile is especially good for pain from tension or sluggish digestion. Parsley-seed tea reduces wind and relaxes the intestinal muscles. Peppermint tea is excellent for cramping.
- Depending on your symptoms, try these homoeopathic remedies: *Nux vomica*, if you've eaten or drunk too much and feel queasy, or *Arsenicum album* if you have heartburn and you also feel chilled.
- Try stress-relieving strategies, such as regular exercise and relaxation. When you're stressed, blood levels of stimulating hormones increase and make the muscles in your stomach tense, leading to the sensation of 'butterflies' in the stomach, or actual pain.

TIRED FEET

- Take off your shoes and sit down. Stretch your legs out and rotate both ankles clockwise and then anticlockwise. Wiggle your toes.
- Massage your feet. Use your thumbs to rub up and down the arch of each foot with firm circular movements. Roll each foot over a rolling pin or empty bottle while seated for a quick mini-massage.
- Soak your feet for 10 minutes in a basin of warm water containing 2 tablespoons Epsom salts. Pat dry, then wrap a few ice cubes in a wet face washer and rub it over your feet and ankles for a 'zingy' effect.

HOME-MADE TREATMENTS

MUSCLE AND JOINT SORENESS

Whether you're a weekend gardener or a serious athlete, these make-it-yourself oil treatments can help alleviate muscle and joint soreness.

- Blend 15 ml of a neutral-scented oil, such as almond, with 3–5 drops eucalyptus, lavender, peppermint or wintergreen essential oil. Gently rub the mixture into sore muscles. Store in a cool, dry place in a dark-coloured glass bottle.
- Infuse 1 tsp dried chilli flakes in 2 tbsp sunflower oil overnight. Strain through a coffee filter before use. Test for sensitivity on a small area first, and keep away from the eyes.
- Spread castor oil all over the afflicted joint. Put cotton wool or a piece of flannel over the oil, then apply a heating pad or hot-water bottle.

SINUSITIS

If you're prone to bouts of sinusitis, get off the antihistamine merry-go-round and do what the traditional yogis of India do: flush your nasal passages daily with a neti pot (from health food shops).

- Fill the pot (pictured above) with warm, salty water.
- Tip your head back and put the spout in one nostril. The fluid will run down the nostril and out through the other nostril.

The brush-off

When you feel a headache coming on, don't reach for pain-killers – try 'brushing' it away by relieving muscle tension. Use either your fingertips or a moderately stiff hairbrush.

- Starting above an eyebrow, draw your fingertips or the brush over your head, back over your ear and down the back of your neck.
- Go back to the top of the eyebrow and do it again, starting a little to the right of the previous stroke.
- Do the same above the other eyebrow until you've covered your head.
- To make sure the headache really has gone, repeat the whole procedure about half an hour later.

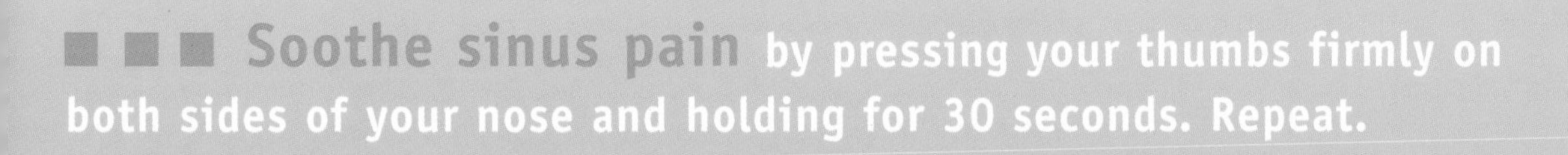

Health for women

Adopt a 'prevention-is-better-than-cure' perspective and use relaxation techniques and easy lifestyle tips, rather than reaching for antidepressants or pain-killers to treat problems such as breast pain, menstrual cramps and thrush. Here is a small sample of time-honoured tips and inexpensive drug-free treatments from the world of alternative medicine.

PMS AND MENSTRUATION

- Gentle exercise, such as walking, will ease the emotional as well as the physical symptoms of PMS. However, if you suffer from aches and pains in the days before and during the menstrual cycle, listen to your body and rest instead.
- Practise relaxation techniques such as yoga. Calming the mind can also have a calming effect on the body.
- Try this yoga stretch: kneel on your heels, drop your forehead to the floor and place your arms against your body. Close your eyes. Hold for 5 minutes.
- Use acupressure. Points in the foot are said to be connected to the pelvic area. These spots are in the depressions above either side of your heel. Gently press in with your thumb and fingertips.
- Avoid, or limit your intake of, alcohol and caffeine-containing drinks: though they may make you feel better in the short term, they worsen tension.
- Allow yourself to snack at this time of the month. Frequent small meals help to stabilise your blood sugar, reducing cravings and irritability.
- Use 3–5 drops essential oil of geranium in an oil burner, or add it to warm bathwater. It is said to balance the emotions – useful for coping with moodiness.
- Gently massage your abdomen, lower back and thighs with a blend of 4 drops clary sage essential oil in 1 tablespoon vegetable oil.

BREAST PAIN

Try to relieve the tenderness triggered by hormonal changes without resorting to pain-killers.

- Try self-massage. Use plain vegetable oil and rotate your fingertips along the skin in coin-size circles. Finish by gently pressing the breasts in, then up, with your palms.
- Stay as calm as possible. Adrenalin, produced during periods of stress, can aggravate breast tenderness.

WARNING!

▼ If you're over the age of 40, regularly discuss your symptoms with your doctor – you're at an age when you're more likely to suffer from diabetes and blood pressure conditions.

COPING WITH THRUSH

Anything that disturbs the normal vaginal environment can trigger an attack of thrush, a common infection caused by an excess of the yeast *Candida albicans*. The symptoms include a discharge and itching.

✔ To restore healthy bacteria to the digestive system, eat yoghurt that contains *acidophilus* cultures.

✔ Choose low-glycaemic index carbohydrates to slow the release of sugars into your bloodstream.

✔ Eliminate the possibility that you have a food allergy as this has been shown to worsen the symptoms.

✘ Try to avoid stress, which can contribute to the condition.

✘ When washing after intercourse, use plain water, not soap.

✘ Don't wear tight trousers, shorts or underwear and avoid synthetic materials. Loose cotton underpants are best.

■ ■ ■ **If you take evening primrose oil** for several months, it may help alleviate MENSTRUAL PROBLEMS, such as breast tenderness.

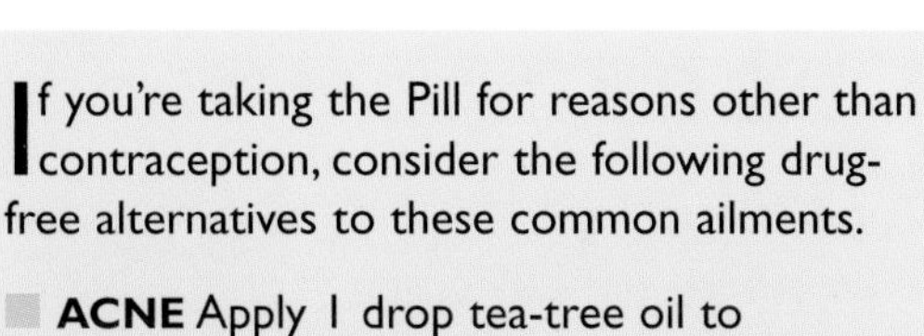

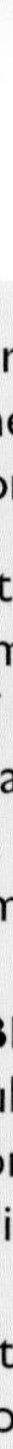

ALTERNATIVES TO THE PILL

If you're taking the Pill for reasons other than contraception, consider the following drug-free alternatives to these common ailments.

- **ACNE** Apply 1 drop tea-tree oil to blemishes. Try a herbal steam to deep-cleanse your skin: boil 2 tsp each of dried red clover and chamomile in 500 ml water. Take it off the stove and pour it into a bowl. Tent your head with a towel and steam your face for 10 minutes.
- **CRAMPS and HEAVY BLEEDING** Chaste tree is a herb that is particularly effective when taken in tablet or capsule form or as a tea. If you suffer from heavy bleeding, ask your doctor to check your iron levels.
- **HEADACHES** Feverfew tablets may reduce the frequency and severity of migraines.

- Cutting out caffeine and highly salted foods may decrease bloating.
- Use castor oil to soothe the pain. First saturate an old towel with the oil and wring it out. Then lie down somewhere comfortable, place the folded towel over your breasts, cover with a piece of plastic wrap, and apply a warm hot-water bottle. Leave in place for 15 minutes.

MENOPAUSE

Hormone replacement therapy (HRT) is often used to balance the lack of oestrogen after menopause. If you prefer not to interfere with natural processes or suffer from side effects, here are some earth-wise alternatives to consider.

- Eat more soy foods for the phyto-oestrogens they contain. These are plant substances that behave like natural oestrogen in the body and help reduce symptoms. Also try drinking licorice root tea for its oestrogenic properties.
- Stock your medicine cabinet with black cohosh for hot flushes.
- Try powdered maca (from health food shops), a root vegetable used as food and medicine by Peruvians. Anecdotal evidence suggests it may help menopausal symptoms. Because it seems to affect hormones, ask your doctor before using it.
- Ease night sweats by sponging your face and chest with a face washer dipped in lavender water. Simply add 2–5 drops lavender essential oil to 250 ml water.

URINARY TRACT INFECTIONS (UTIs)

Ten times more women than men suffer from recurring UTIs. If you're one of them, consider these natural alternatives to prescription drugs.

- Try drinking cranberry juice. Once a traditional remedy, it's now also regarded as an effective preventive by orthodox medicine. Cranberries contain chemicals that prevent *E. coli* bacteria (that cause urinary infections) from sticking to the wall of the urinary tract.
- Sandalwood oil has anti-inflammatory properties, and is used as a urinary antiseptic in traditional Ayurvedic medicine. Fill the bathtub with warm water and add 2 cups Epsom salts, 1 cup bicarbonate of soda and 5 drops sandalwood oil. Soak in the bath for 15 minutes.

CYSTITIS

To combat cystitis, make up this infection-fighting blend of herbs from your health food shop, to sip when you feel an attack coming on.

- Take 1 tsp each of these dried herbs – uva-ursi, goldenseal and echinacea.
- Pour 2 cups boiling water over the dried herbs.
- Steep and strain.
- Drink up to 4 cups a day.

The older body

As you age, your susceptibility to both minor ailments and more serious diseases increases. However, there's a lot you can do to reduce their impact – and perhaps even to avoid them altogether – by staying active, eating a nutritious earth-wise diet and also harnessing the power of preventive medicine.

ARTHRITIS

Arthritis generally occurs when bones and joints suffer natural deterioration with ageing. Instead of depending entirely on medication to relieve the symptoms, such as pain and stiffness, try these earth-wise remedies.

- If you take sleeping pills and pain-killers to ease the discomfort and pain of arthritis, talk to your doctor about natural alternatives. For many people, prescription drugs end up creating more problems than they solve.
- If you're overweight, try to shed a few kilograms. Even a reduction of 2 kg can significantly diminish the impact of the stress suffered by the knees, and may also help in slowing the progress of the arthritis.
- Choose a form of exercise that improves joint mobility and may reduce pain while being gentle on the body – check with your doctor or physiotherapist.
- Eat more fish. Studies show that omega-3 fatty acids, the active ingredient in oily fish such as salmon and mackerel, may help to alleviate joint tenderness.
- Take glucosamine, a cartilage-building sugar compound. While not absolutely proven as an effective treatment, it appears to slow damage over time, and has fewer serious side effects than prescription drugs. Look for a glucosamine supplement that's combined with chondroitin, also a cartilage-building compound.
- Use a little heat. Mix together ½ teaspoon eucalyptus oil and 50 g calendula ointment or capsaicin cream over a gentle heat. Cool, then rub on the sore area. Wrap in plastic film and a warm, moist towel and leave for 10–15 minutes.

PROSTATE SOLUTIONS

Benign prostate hyperplasia (BPH), or prostate enlargement, is becoming increasingly prevalent in men over the age of 50. These natural remedies may help reduce the risk of BPH.

- **NETTLE ROOT** (*Urticae radix*) Taken over a number of weeks, this may reduce the frequency of urination that accompanies an enlarged prostate. It's often used in combination with other herbs, such as saw palmetto.
- **SAW PALMETTO** (*Serenoa repens*) (*top right*) Available from chemists or herbalists, it's a herb long used by Native Americans. Research suggests it may be beneficial for prostate health.
- **TOMATOES** Eat these cooked, rather than raw, to access lycopene, a flavonoid (anti-oxidant) that helps prevent prostate cancer.

VARICOSE VEINS

Avoid surgery by exercising, eating a high-fibre diet and trying these helpful vitamins, herbs and foods.

- Vitamin C and bioflavonoids: strengthen capillaries.
- Gotu kola (a herb): supports connective tissue health and keeps veins supple.
- Horse chestnut (a herb): helps control the inflammation and swelling of varicose veins.
- Chillies, garlic, onion and ginger: improve circulation.

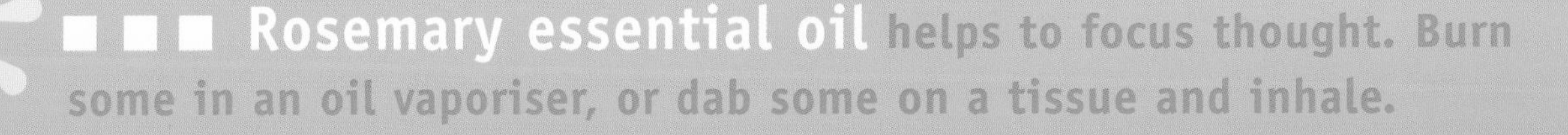

■ ■ ■ **Rosemary essential oil** helps to focus thought. Burn some in an oil vaporiser, or dab some on a tissue and inhale.

INCONTINENCE ADVICE

- ✔ Help prevent infection in the kidneys, bladder and urinary tract by drinking cranberry juice. It stops bacteria from adhering to the linings of these organs. The high vitamin C content of cranberry juice also helps to reduce or prevent infection.
- ✔ Practise Kegel exercises at least three times a day: imagine you are trying to stop the flow of urine and tighten your pelvic muscles. With each contraction, count to three slowly and then release.
- ✘ Don't drink too much alcohol and avoid caffeine and nicotine if possible. They are all powerful diuretics.
- ✘ Don't be tempted to drink less fluid. The best policy is to drink enough to ensure that you urinate at regular intervals. This helps to retrain the bladder and keeps urine dilute so you won't be susceptible to kidney problems.

EYESIGHT

Deterioration of vision often occurs in old age. However, if it is treated early, it can be improved or even reversed.

- Eat lots of yellow and orange vegetables. They are rich in carotenoids, the types of nutrients that prevent damage to the area of the retina responsible for vision.
- Eat foods rich in anti-oxidants daily. Include in your diet fruit and vegetables – especially green leafy varieties such as spinach – and make sure you eat fish and nuts regularly. These foods have been found to significantly cut the risk of macular degeneration.
- If you suffer from macular degeneration, a loss of vision in the central part of the retina, consider taking lutein and zeaxanthin, anti-oxidant supplements. Vitamins A, C and E are believed to help prevent macular degeneration, cataracts and glaucoma.

MENTAL HEALTH

Stay as mentally active as you can, and also give your brain cells some internal help. Consider these suggestions.

- Oily fish – such as salmon, mackerel and tuna – are high in omega-3 fatty acids, which are essential for normal, healthy brain function.

~ STAR SAVER ~

If you wear dentures, an inexpensive alternative to overpriced, sometimes harsh-tasting mouthwashes is to rinse your mouth daily with a glass of warm water mixed with 1 tsp salt and a few drops myrrh tincture (from chemists).

- Lecithin – which is found in soy beans, eggs and wheat germ – can be broken down in the body to produce choline, which is then used to make acetylcholine, the most abundant neurotransmitter in the brain.
- Ginkgo, a herb, may boost oxygen flow to the brain by improving peripheral circulation.

OSTEOPOROSIS

After the age of 30, the loss of calcium from your bones can result in osteoporosis (brittle bone disease) and fractures.

- Include in your diet low-fat dairy products, red salmon (with the bones) and soy foods, all good sources of calcium.

- Watch your consumption of soft drinks. The calcium to phosphate ratio in them discourages the retention of calcium in the bones, and can therefore affect your bone density.
- To help increase your bone density, add some powdered, non-fat, dry milk to soups, casseroles and drinks. Each teaspoon of dry milk provides about 50 mg of calcium. To work out how much you need, check the manufacturer's instructions.
- If you prefer to take a calcium supplement, try calcium carbonate. It's usually the cheapest type.
- Perform some regular weight-bearing exercise to increase bone density. Walking is the most convenient form, but strength training is also excellent (for exercise routines, see *Strength training*, p. 166).
- Make sure you get enough exposure to daylight. It produces vitamin D, which helps with calcium absorption.

■ ■ ■ If you have gout, a form of arthritis, eat cherries. They contain ANTHOCYANINS, which help lower levels of uric acid.

Serious health conditions

There are many effective results to be gained from modern drugs and surgical treatments. However, simple earth-wise lifestyle choices – including preventive screening procedures, natural supplements, herbs and 'super foods' – can all dramatically lower your risk of developing certain diseases in the first place.

ANAEMIA

Being anaemic means having too little haemoglobin, the iron-containing blood pigment that conveys oxygen around your body. Only take iron supplements if your doctor has tested you and confirmed that you have low iron levels.

- Boost your iron intake by eating lean red meat, whole grains (such as fortified breakfast cereals), legumes (including kidney beans, baked beans and lentils) and leafy green vegetables, such as spinach and brussels sprouts.
- Foods rich in vitamin C improve iron absorption, so eat iron-rich foods with vegetables such as red capsicum and broccoli, or drink orange juice with meals.
- Try spirulina tablets (from health food shops). They are rich in iron, minerals and trace elements.
- Avoid drinking tea or coffee with meals as they reduce your body's ability to absorb iron.

ASTHMA

Take these remedies along with conventional treatment, but never stop taking asthma medication without consulting your doctor.

- Take vitamin C, a powerful anti-oxidant. It may help to reduce the severity of an attack by slowing the cells' release of histamine. It also helps if you are on cortisone medication, which may deplete vitamin C from the adrenal glands.
- Drink licorice tea, traditionally used to loosen congestion. (Warning: high doses of licorice can raise blood pressure in some people.)

CANCER

Gentle natural remedies taken in conjunction with conventional medical treatment for cancer can help alleviate unpleasant side effects and boost the immune system. However, never take supplements without consulting your doctor first.

- Take anti-oxidants. Evidence suggests that cancer may be related to damaging, destructive molecules called free radicals. Certain nutrients – including beta-carotene, vitamins A, C and E and the minerals zinc and selenium – appear to help counter free radical activity and may therefore reduce the risk of some cancers.
- To help counter nausea caused by chemotherapy, have some acupuncture treatment.

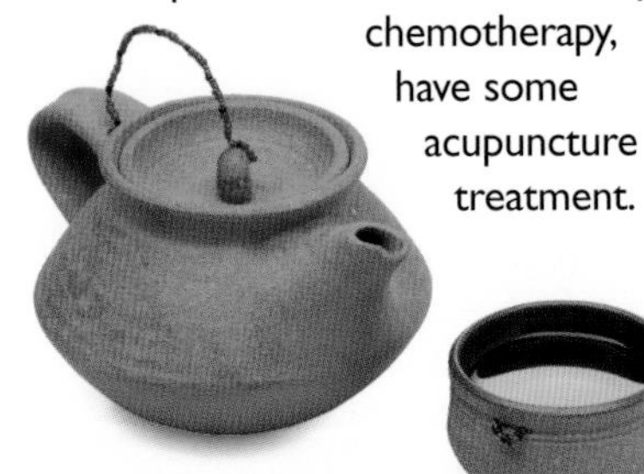

HEALTH CHECKS

Regular health checks can detect signs of serious diseases before you notice any symptoms. Ask your doctor for advice.

- **BLOOD PRESSURE CHECK** High blood pressure can make you susceptible to heart attack, stroke and kidney failure.
- **BONE DENSITY SCAN** A test for osteoporosis (brittle bone disease).
- **CHOLESTEROL TEST** A blood test to determine whether the blood levels of low-density lipoprotein (LDL), which can increase the risk of heart disease, are too high.
- **EYE TEST** This can reveal high blood pressure, glaucoma and diabetes.
- **FAECAL OCCULT BLOOD TEST** A screen for bowel or colon cancer.
- **MAMMOGRAM** An X-ray for detecting breast abnormalities and early-stage breast cancer.
- **PAP SMEAR** A cervical swab shows cell changes that could develop into cancer.
- **PROSTATE-SPECIFIC ANTIGEN SCREENING** Early PSA screening may reduce the risk of metastatic prostate cancer by up to 35 per cent.
- **SKIN CANCER CHECK** Malignant melanomas are curable if identified and treated at an early stage.

THE TRUTH ABOUT...

ANTIBIOTICS
Antibiotics are lifesavers for serious bacterial infections such as pneumonia. However, excessive use of antibiotics can breed antibiotic-resistant bacteria and also destroy large numbers of the protective 'good' bacteria that reside in the intestine, making you more vulnerable to other infections. If you're prescribed antibiotics, take a probiotic supplement such as *acidophilus* during and following the course to replace the beneficial bacteria and help keep your immune function strong.

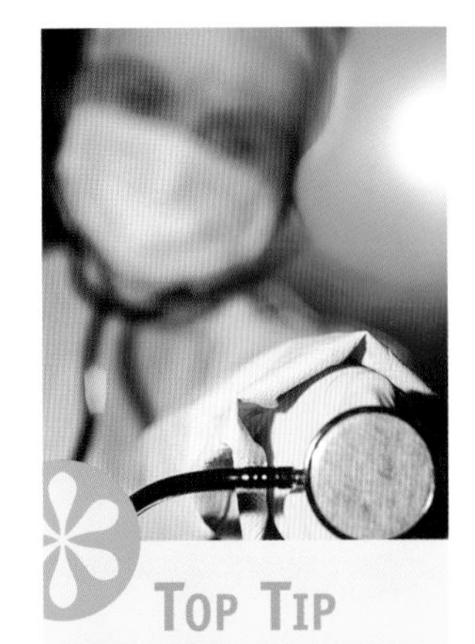

TOP TIP

If you have to go to hospital, listening to a relaxation tape could shorten your stay. Research has shown that visualisation and guided imagery can reduce pre- and post-operative anxiety. Ask at a bookshop or a New Age store for suggestions.

Ginseng helps to increase energy and stamina and may therefore be a useful adjunct to stressful cancer treatments, such as chemotherapy and radiotherapy.

- A daily glass of diluted aloe vera juice helps protect the gut and guard against digestive upsets, such as the nausea related to chemotherapy treatment.
- Mix a good-quality vitamin E cream with a little aloe vera gel and apply it to areas of the skin that have been exposed to radiotherapy. Use before and after each treatment, subject to medical advice.
- To help digestive problems and reduce reflux, sip a mixture of 1 teaspoon each of slippery elm powder and *acidophilus* powder in a glass of warm water.
- Ensuring your diet is low in fat will reduce the severity of diarrhoea, a possible side effect of conventional treatment. Temporarily reducing your intake of vegetable fibre – such as skins and seeds – may also help to counter diarrhoea.
- To improve appetite and digestion, take ½ teaspoon Swedish bitters, a mixture of bitter herbs, in a little warm water before eating.

DIABETES

Those who do not produce enough insulin, or who have bodies that become less sensitive to insulin, have Type 2 diabetes. Insulin is a hormone produced in the body to regulate blood sugar levels. These tips will help in most cases.

- Eat a variety of nutritious low-glycaemic index foods. These include oats, untoasted muesli, pasta and brown rice, lentils, beans, yoghurt and apples. These foods will slowly increase your blood sugar levels, not just supply you with a quick burst.
- Use exercise to help control your blood sugar levels: physical activity increases the sensitivity of your body cells to insulin.
- Keep your weight in check. Ensuring your weight is within your healthy weight range for your age and height will make your insulin more effective.

HEART DISEASE

Evidence shows that making significant changes to exercise and diet can not only stop heart disease from advancing, it can also undo some of the damage.

- Protect your heart by eating more dark green, leafy vegetables, lean meat, wholegrain cereals and breads, all good sources of folic acid. This helps to reduce levels of homocystine, linked to an increased risk of heart disease. Or take a folic acid supplement.
- Factor more fish into your diet. The beneficial fatty acids found in oily fish, such as salmon and mackerel, support heart health by reducing the risk of blood clotting. They can also help to reduce high blood cholesterol levels.

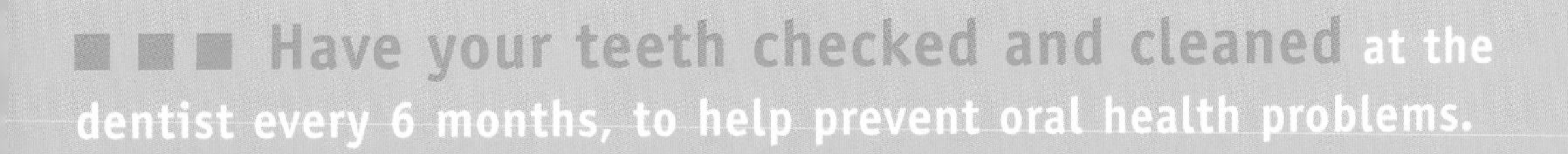

Go for a brisk half-hour walk every day. Exercise is one of the best ways to prevent heart disease.

- Reduce the risk of angina (severe chest pain, which can be an early warning sign of a heart attack) by avoiding stress. Do relaxation exercises or meditate.
- Take hawthorn (*Crataegus oxyacantha*) supplements to improve blood and oxygen supply to the heart.
- Drink cranberry juice. It has antioxidants that help protect against plaque build-up in the arteries.

HIGH BLOOD PRESSURE

Some non-drug therapies can help reduce high blood pressure, also known as hypertension. Try these earth-wise remedies to avoid the possible unpleasant side effects of prescription drugs.

- Discuss with your doctor the possibility of making lifestyle changes – such as exercising more, drinking less alcohol and giving up cigarettes – to reduce or eliminate your dependence on medication for high blood pressure.
- Consider becoming a vegetarian. Generally speaking, vegetarians tend to have lower blood pressure and a lower risk of cardiovascular disease. This is due to their higher intake of fibre, complex carbohydrates and the vitamins and nutrients in fruit and vegetables that help to keep blood pressure at a normal level.
- Being overweight is a prime cause of high blood pressure. Just losing the extra kilograms can help reduce your blood pressure. Focus on exercise and healthy eating rather than go on a diet.
- Take a two-pronged approach: cut down on salt and boost potassium because a combination of high salt and low potassium produces high blood pressure in some people. Bananas, wholegrain cereals, broad beans, potatoes, avocados and orange juice are all good natural sources of potassium.

WARNING!

▼ A dangerous interaction between a drug and a vitamin or herb is rare, but it can happen. Always tell your doctor exactly what you are taking.

Supplement alert

Drug type	Examples	Don't take with	Risk
Anti-anxiety	Alprazolam	Sedative herbs (e.g., kava, St John's wort)	Extreme lethargy
	Diazepam		Possible disorientation
Anticoagulants	Aspirin, Warfarin	Feverfew, garlic, ginkgo or vitamin E	The herbs and vitamin E act like blood thinners in the body
Laxatives	Magnesium hydroxide	Aloe	Could bring on severe diarrhoea
	Senna	Cascara	Could bring on severe diarrhoea

■ ■ ■ **Ginger, fennel and chamomile teas** are calming and soothing, and may help counter the nausea caused by chemotherapy.

hot links

Information about specific types of cancer, treatment information and advice, and support groups: www.cancer.org.au; www.cancersoc.org.nz
Complementary and Alternative Medicine website with practical information and self-help resources: www.wholehealthmd.com
Understanding Complementary and Alternative Medicine: http://nccam.nih.gov/health

HIGH CHOLESTEROL

Changing your diet and doing more exercise can help you to avoid the build-up of cholesterol, a fatty deposit linked to an increased risk of heart attacks and stroke. (See also, *Cholesterol busters*, p. 159.)

- Always eat breakfast, and include whole grains in the form of cereals (for example, whole-wheat flakes or rolled oats) or multigrain bread. It's been found that cholesterol levels are highest in adults who don't eat breakfast and lowest in those who eat a wholegrain cereal.
- Increase your intake of fresh fruit and vegetables. For example, apples are rich in pectin, which helps to reduce your cholesterol level.
- Eat fish such as mackerel and salmon for their beneficial omega-3 fatty oils, which help to lower cholesterol. Choose lean meats and trim off any visible fat; remove the skin from chicken before cooking.
- Take the herb gugulipid (*Commiphora mukul*), which can lower cholesterol by increasing the liver's metabolism of LDL cholesterol. But if you suffer from liver disease, inflammatory bowel disease or diarrhoea, consult your doctor before taking this herb.

KIDNEY STONES

Kidney stones, crystallised minerals that become lodged in kidney tissue, can be excruciatingly painful. If you're prone to developing kidney stones, try these gentle preventive measures.

- If you're taking a supplement, check with your doctor to make sure it's appropriate. It may include calcium, a substance most kidney stones contain, so you don't want to add to the load you already have. Some antacid formulas, for example, are very high in calcium. The ingredient panel on the packet will provide you with the relevant information.
- Limit oxalate-containing foods such as chocolate, chocolate drinks and cocoa and carob powder.

SHINGLES

Shingles are painful blisters caused by the same virus that leads to chickenpox. It mainly affects people over the age of fifty.

- Try capsaicin cream (from chemists). Based on the ingredient that makes cayenne chillies hot, it blocks the action of neurotransmitters in the skin's nerve endings that help send pain signals to the brain. The cream can irritate sensitive skin, so always check with your doctor, and patch-test first.
- Your immune system and nerves will benefit from extra doses of vitamin C and B-complex vitamins.
- Use an aromatherapy compress. Add 6 drops lavender essential oil and 2 drops each of lemon and geranium essential oils to 500 ml cold water. Dip a soft, clean cloth in the solution, squeeze it out and apply it to the affected area.
- For a soothing effect, throw a handful of cornflour or finely ground oatmeal into your bathwater and have a soak.
- Consider using homoeopathy. For itching, burning skin, take *Mezereum*; for sharp nerve pain that is worse at night take *Arsenicum album*.
- If the blisters have healed, but you still feel pain, gently stroke your skin with ice cubes wrapped in plastic.

Increase the fibre in your diet and help **REDUCE CHOLESTEROL** levels by adding wheat bran to breakfast cereals.

Earth-wise medicines

Vitamin and mineral supplements and herbal remedies can often do the job of drugs, but more safely and cheaply. If you find yourself regularly reaching for over-the-counter and prescription medicines, empty your medicine chest and refill it with these top 30 all-natural alternative treatments for common problems.

ALOE VERA GEL

- This gel soothes irritated skin and increases the rate at which burns, wounds and other skin problems heal.
- Use for acne, burns, sunburn, cuts, itchiness, bites and stings. Soak cotton wool in the gel and dab it directly onto the affected area.

APPLE CIDER VINEGAR

- Suitable for a variety of hair and scalp problems, including dandruff. Also counters indigestion.

ARNICA OINTMENT

- Use for back pain, bruises, muscular aches and sprains and chilblains to reduce pain and swelling. (Warning: do not use on open wounds or broken skin.)

BICARBONATE OF SODA

- Suitable for cuts and grazes, bites and stings, allergic skin reactions and gum disease.

BLACK COHOSH

- This herb is said to reduce the number and intensity of menopausal hot flushes. It has also had a long history of use as a folk medicine for treating menstrual cramps.
- Take it in either tablet or capsule form, according to the manufacturer's instructions.

CALENDULA

- This herb has healing and anti-inflammatory properties. Use it for red, sore or irritated skin.
- Apply the tincture to cuts and grazes, and use the ointment for athlete's foot and itchy skin.

CHAMOMILE

- Drink as a tea for anxiety, wind, colic, indigestion, mild diarrhoea and sleep problems; especially helpful for babies and children.

CHARCOAL TABLETS

- Take tablets or capsules after meals for wind, bloating and indigestion. (Warning: charcoal can turn your stools black.)

CLOVE OIL

- Mildly analgesic, and very useful for toothache. Suck on a clove peg, or apply a drop of clove oil to the tooth, until you are able to see a dentist.

COD LIVER OIL

- An inexpensive source of the omega-3 fatty acids. Also, a powerful anti-inflammatory that eases the pain of rheumatoid arthritis.

COLLOIDAL SILVER

- This is a weak antimicrobial preparation that can be either taken internally or squirted into cuts or grazes. Ask your naturopath or health food shop to recommend a reputable brand.

COMFREY-BASED OINTMENT

- For sprains and strains, where the skin is not broken. May also help alleviate the pain of arthritis.

ECHINACEA

- Good for all infections, including colds, flu, thrush, sinusitis and catarrh. Helps to increase the body's natural resistance and immunity, thus speeding recovery. May also help counter some allergic reactions and inflammation.
- Take echinacea as a tincture, or in tablet or capsule form to boost your resistance to infections.

EUCALYPTUS OIL

- Use as a steam inhalation for coughs and colds.
- Add several drops to a vaporiser in a sick room to help deodorise and disinfect.

EVENING PRIMROSE OIL

- A good source of omega-6 fatty acids. Recommended if you suffer from premenstrual syndrome.

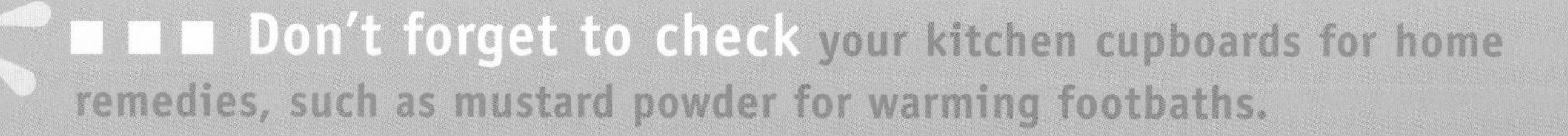

Don't forget to check your kitchen cupboards for home remedies, such as mustard powder for warming footbaths.

FEVERFEW
- Long-term use helps reduce the frequency and severity of migraines. Rich in flavonoids, it may also help relieve some allergic reactions.

GARLIC
- Well known for its antibacterial properties, garlic is a natural antibiotic. Take capsules or tablets for all kinds of infections, particularly those of the nose, throat and chest.

GINGER
- Take either tablets or capsules for nausea, travel sickness and morning sickness. Ginger may also help some circulatory disorders.

LAVENDER
- Drink lavender tea to help relieve headaches and counter stress.
- Use the essential oil for minor burns, insect bites, stings and cold sores. Add 5 drops to a bedtime bath to encourage sound sleep.

LICORICE ROOT
- Research has identified a key component of this herb (deglycyrrhizinated licorice) as promoting the healing of ulcers.
- Also a soothing treatment for gastrointestinal inflammation and various disorders, including indigestion. (Warning: don't take high doses because it can cause high blood pressure in some people.)

PROBIOTICS
- Probiotics, such as *Lactobacillus acidophilus*, are the 'friendly' bacteria that inhabit the gastrointestinal tract. To restore those destroyed by antibiotics, take tablets or capsules.

RED CLOVER
- A 'blood cleanser', traditionally used to treat blemished skin.
- Also a source of plant chemicals with mild oestrogen-like properties; may assist menopausal women. Take in capsule or tea form.

RESCUE REMEDY
- A gentle blend of flower essences that rebalances emotions. Also said to relieve the emotional component of accidents, injuries and shock.

SLIPPERY ELM
- Effective in treating acid indigestion, heartburn, gastritis, diarrhoea, constipation, bronchitis and coughs.
- Take tablets, or mix powder in liquid, or mash with a little banana.

SWEDISH BITTERS
- These bitter herbs stimulate the digestion and relieve intestinal wind.

TEA-TREE OIL
- For bacterial and fungal skin infections. For vaginal yeast infections, use it diluted in a shallow bath.
- Apply tea-tree oil neat to small problem areas, such as pimples or around an inflamed hangnail. For larger areas, dilute it by adding 10 drops to 5 ml almond oil or witch hazel.

VITAMIN C
- Helps boost the immune system, builds protective collagen around blood vessels in the skin, and may also have an antihistamine-like effect on rashes and hay fever.
- Take tablets or powder at the first sign of a viral or bacterial infection. To reduce stomach acidity, choose a brand that is 'buffered' with mineral ascorbates.

VITAMIN E
- Helps protect against heart disease; especially good if you have circulatory disorders.
- Use liquid from the capsules to dress minor cuts and scrapes, and also to help heal scars.

WITCH HAZEL
- Dab liquid on cuts, scrapes, bruises and also insect bites or stings.
- Makes a soothing, astringent treatment for haemorrhoids and varicose veins. Chill before applying.

ZINC LOZENGES
- If you feel a cold coming on, suck on a lozenge to greatly relieve the symptoms; it may even reduce the duration of a cold.

Honey works well for coughs and colds, hay fever and for sweetening herbal teas. Apply a thin layer to minor burns.

Earth-wise Gardening

Look after your soil, choose plants that suit your climate and situation, use water wisely and try organic methods before resorting to chemicals, and your earth-wise garden will reward you with healthy plants and produce all year round.

EARTH-WISE GARDENING...

WORKING WITH NATURE

■ Which trees provide summer shade and winter warmth in your climate? See page 223. ■ Go organic and try our home-made sprays and repellents on page 224. ■ Follow our guide to building a 'no-dig' garden on page 231. ■ Mimic nature and make your garden wildlife-friendly with these planting suggestions. See page 232. See our pond feature on page 234.

GARDEN BASICS

■ What type of soil do you have and how can you improve it? See page 236. ■ Make your own compost heap, page 240. ■ Follow our step-by-step guide to building a worm farm, page 243. ■ What's the best watering system for your garden? See page 245. ■ Learn about water-wise gardens on page 248.

PLANTING GUIDE

■ Whatever the size of your garden, you can grow vegetables all year round. See our seasonal guide on page 252. ■ Grow your own fruit without using chemicals. Check out our tips on natural pest control on page 257.

■ Which are the right trees for you to plant in your garden? See page 258. ■ It's possible to have a green lawn all year round without wasting water. See our advice on lawn care and alternatives to grass on page 264.

DEALING WITH PROBLEMS

■ Keep weeds in check without using chemicals by following our top tips on weed control, page 266. ■ There are lots of natural ways to control pests in your garden. See page 270. ■ Sometimes you have no alternative but to use chemicals. Here's a guide to using them sparingly and safely, page 272.

■ Pets and wildlife can damage your plants. Find out how to deal with these unwelcome visitors without harming them. See page 276.

WORKING WITH NATURE

An earth-wise garden makes the most of an existing site and is easier and cheaper to maintain.

Getting started

The best way to be earth-wise in your garden is to work with nature, not against it. Think laterally when it comes to garden design. Understanding and accommodating the limitations of your particular site will save time, money, effort and the possibility of disappointment over the long term.

KEEP IT SIMPLE

- Develop what's already in your garden, rather than try to change it. If your land is badly drained, for example, instead of installing an expensive drainage system, think about planting a bog garden.
- Grow plants suited to the climate in which you live. Plants can become stressed and pest- or disease-prone when they are out of their comfort zone. Frangipanis, for example, aren't robust in areas that experience winter frost, and spring-flowering magnolias don't do well in the subtropics.
- Observe and record the names of plants that thrive in your area – and the ones that don't. Rather than visit show gardens, seek out overgrown areas and gardens with mature plants to identify the plants that will survive on neglect.
- Get rid of plants that continually struggle to survive. If you don't have a sunny aspect, stop hankering for agapanthus and learn to love shade-loving acanthus. If your lawn isn't getting enough light or there's too much root competition under trees, replace the grass with a groundcover that tolerates shade.
- Before buying a plant, find out about its growth habit, including its mature height and width, and plant accordingly, otherwise it will need a lot of maintenance.
- Mimic nature by covering the soil with organic mulch. As well as providing regular nourishment to the soil and suppressing weeds, mulch keeps the soil cool and cuts down on moisture loss.
- Don't persevere with poor soil. If your soil is clay-based, and you've been struggling unsuccessfully for years to improve it, build your garden beds on top of it.

PROS & CONS

TREES NEAR HOUSES

Trees are a natural and inexpensive solution to the long-term problem of heating and cooling your home. A deciduous tree on the sunny north or west side of your house will filter hot winds and provide shade in summer. In cooler months, when the leaves drop, it will let in warmth and reduce frost. But big trees can pose a threat in storms and bushfires, and roots can undermine foundations and drains. To enjoy the benefits of trees without the risks, always plant them at least 3–5 metres from your house and drains.

■ ■ ■ **Trees are nature's airconditioners.** If positioned well, they can reduce summer temperatures by up to 10°C.

Trees for summer shade and winter warmth

Tree	Size	Best climate	Comments
Bauhinia (*Bauhinia* species)	4–12 m	Subtropical to temperate	Fully deciduous in cool areas.
Birch (*Betula* species)	6–12 m	Cool to temperate	Grow tropical birch (*Betula nigra*) in warm climates.
Callery pear (*Pyrus calleryana*)	10–18 m	Cool to temperate	'Glen's Form' is a narrow variety for smaller spaces.
Cercis (*Cercis canadensis* 'Forest Pansy')	3–5 m	Cool to temperate	New leaves are colourful in spring.
Chinese tallow (*Sapium sebiferum*)	5–6 m	Cool to tropical	Will colour in autumn even in mild coastal climates.
Claret ash (*Fraxinus* 'Raywood')	8 m	Cool to subtropical	Ash trees tolerate coastal and urban conditions.
Crab-apple (*Malus floribunda*)	4 m	Cool to temperate	Produces fruit that can be made into jam or jelly.
Crepe myrtle (*Lagerstroemia indica*)	3–8 m	Cool to subtropical	The Indian Summer series is mildew-resistant.
Ginkgo (*Ginkgo biloba*)	7 m	Cool to temperate	Turns golden in autumn.
Japanese apricot (*Prunus mume*)	3–4 m	Cool to temperate	Flowers in winter on bare stems.

THE FUNDAMENTALS

No matter what type of garden you have or choose – be it cottage or native or balcony – there are three basic requirements.

- Sun and shade: north-facing means sunny and south-facing means shady. Choose the best place for your garden beds, lawns and outdoor living areas according to their aspect.
- Shelter from harsh winds is essential for plant growth and for your own comfort. Create a multi-layered windbreak with tall plants facing the prevailing winds and layers of lower plants facing the area you wish to shelter.
- Healthy soil: the composition of the earth in your garden – whether it is sand, clay or loam – and its depth, drainage patterns, pH and nutrient levels will determine what you can grow, although applying nutrient-rich mulches and organic matter can improve many unpromising sites.

BALCONY GARDENS

- Choose shade-tolerant plants if your balcony has an overhang. Go for varieties normally sold as indoor plants, such as peace lilies (*Spathiphyllum*) or potted *Ficus*. For a sun-drenched balcony, choose tough but not prickly succulents, such as *Kalanchoe*, or a potted citrus, such as a cumquat.

- Protect yourself from prevailing winds with a screen of plants in heavy pots or troughs. Hardy varieties include bamboo and coprosma.
- Buy a good potting mix to suit the types of plants you're growing.

hot links

Sustainable Gardening Australia: www.SGAonline.org.au/aboutsga.html
Garden design ideas: www.baag.com.au/designideas.html; www.garden-nz.co.nz/article/archive/17
Native flora information: www.anbg.gov.au; www.nzpcn.org.nz
Bush regeneration: www.nsw.nationaltrust.org.au/bush.html

■ ■ ■ **Solid windbreaks** create turbulence so use hedging plants such as bottlebrushes, conifers, grevilleas, photinia and viburnum.

Going organic

Many home gardeners are turning to organic gardening, an approach that doesn't use harmful chemicals and restores the natural relationship between plants and the environment. Going organic takes commitment, but it's well worth the effort if you want to be sure that your garden is 100 per cent earth-wise.

SIX GUIDELINES FOR ORGANIC GARDENING

Going organic is as much an attitude as a practice. The idea is to respect life in all its forms, instead of trying to dominate it. In the long run, your plants will actually become stronger.

1 Create healthy soil: add lots of mulch and dig in organic matter. If you need help to start with, buy certified organic soil treatments and manures from your local nursery.

2 Encourage biodiversity: plant many different species and intermingle them.

3 Rotate crops: in order not to deplete soil fertility and to reduce the build-up of diseases, don't grow the same annuals, plants and vegetables in the same place year after year.

4 Understand the terrain: choose plants suitable for the soil, climate and aspect of your area.

5 Use organic controls so that natural pest predators can find their place in the garden. Don't use chemicals at the first sign of insect infestation, and learn to tolerate some damage to your plants. In time, your garden will evolve into a balanced ecosystem.

6 Accept that in nature nothing is perfect, that some untidiness is natural and that mistakes and losses are an inevitable part of achieving a natural balance in your garden.

Home-made sprays and repellents

Problem	Solution	Recipe
Ants and caterpillars	Chillies and soap	■ Chop up a handful of fresh red chillies. Place in a spray bottle with some grated pure soap and water. ■ Shake the bottle well and use the solution as a spray.
Aphids	Detergent and a yellow container	■ Fill a bright yellow container with water, then add 1 tbsp colourless detergent. Place the container near the affected plants. ■ The yellow container will attract aphids and they'll drown in the water.
Aphids, mites and other sap-suckers	Pyrethrum and soap	■ Pour 1 litre hot soapy water over 2 tbsp pyrethrum flowers. ■ Allow to stand for 1 hour. Strain before spraying.
Black spot and powdery mildew on roses	Bicarbonate of soda and fish emulsion	■ To 4.5 litres water add 3 tsp bicarbonate of soda and 3 tsp fish emulsion. ■ Pour the solution into a spray bottle and use it 3 times over 2 weeks, then weekly.
Fungus and bacterial disease	Seaweed	■ Put some seaweed into a bucket and cover with water. ■ After a few weeks, dilute it with water. It should be the colour of weak tea. Pour the solution into a spray bottle and use it as needed.

■ ■ ■ **Visit a permaculture garden and discover how to create a healthy garden out of infertile, worn-out land.**

ORGANIC STRATEGIES

As an organic gardener, you don't have to sit back and do nothing when your plants are attacked by animals, birds and insects. If you have been using pesticides in your garden, expect some losses at first. However, in time the following organic strategies will work if you implement them early enough.

- Choose plant varieties that are resistant to disease – they will survive problems that less robust plants may succumb to.
- Walk around the garden every day to check for problems. Tackling pests and diseases at the first sign of trouble will give you a head start.
- Remove the pests you can see by hand. In the first stages of infestation, this method works well for leaf-munching caterpillars, snails and slugs.

~ STAR SAVER ~

A garden that's free of pesticides is kinder to all living organisms and costs much less to maintain. In addition, organic produce is expensive to buy, so growing your own will save you money.

BUY WISELY

- Fertilisers and manures may be labelled organic, but often this doesn't mean 'certified' organic. For example, fertilisers that contain more than 5.5 per cent nitrogen are rarely organic. Check on the package for the symbol of a nationally certified body or ask the nursery attendant.

- Drape lightweight netting over plants to protect them from birds and other small animals. Check the netting daily to make sure nothing is trapped in it.
- While they are becoming established, protect young trees and shrubs from larger animals by circling them with wire netting or sturdy plastic.
- Surround plants at risk from slugs and snails with wood ash, sawdust, blood and bone, lime or diatomaceous earth (garden grade, not swimming-pool grade).
- Prevent damage to ripening fruit by covering it with a cloth or waxed paper bag. This is a great way to stop fruit fly ruining tomatoes, peaches or nectarines.
- Use Dipel (*Bacillus thuringiensis*), a naturally occurring bacterium that controls caterpillars without harming other insects or mammals. It is safe to spray on vegetables or other plants under attack.
- If you don't have enough beneficial insects to begin with, buy some. Some commercially available species include *Cryptolaemus montrouzieri* ladybirds to control mealy bugs, *Chilocorus* species beetles for scale insects, lacewings to control aphids and *Phytoseiulus persimilis* mite for two-spotted mite.
- A natural way to attract birds and beneficial insects to your garden is to grow plants such as Queen Anne's lace and elderberry. (For some more planting suggestions, see *Natives for every situation*, p. 229.)
- Save seeds to help you achieve a self-perpetuating garden. Heirloom varieties ('open-pollinated' forms, more than 50 years old, which produce seed that is true to form) may be resistant to pests and diseases. Available from many nurseries.

hot links

Non-profit organisation promoting permaculture: www.permacultureinternational.org
Organic vegetable gardening: www.organicdownunder.com
Predatory insects for gardens: www.bugsforbugs.com.au; www.goodbugs.org.au; www.zonda.net.nz
Great garden tips: www.organicgardentips.com; www.rnzih.org.nz/pages/Garden-tips.htm

The first step in an organic garden is to SAFELY dispose of any chemicals. Your local council can advise you.

Natural partners

Companion planting is a way of employing the tactics used by plants themselves to survive. Take advantage of the strategies some species use to defend and disguise themselves, and plant them among your precious garden specimens and vegetables. There they will act as allies to entice, deter or confuse pests, or to provide protection from the sun, wind, frost and weeds.

Plant a fast-growing crop such as lettuce or radish to provide shade for slower growing tomatoes or cabbages.

SOME COMPANION PLANTING STRATEGIES

- Plant French marigolds (*Tagetes* sp.) to get rid of nematodes – (soil-borne pests that infest the root systems of plants). They don't like the chemicals that the marigolds exude from their roots. If one of your garden beds is infested with nematodes, mass-plant the area with marigolds, to the exclusion of any other plants, and you'll starve the nematodes out.
- Confuse the enemy by mixing a variety of plants together, one of the methods of permaculture gardening. A plethora of different aromas can put insects off the scent of their favourite foods.
- Use strong-smelling herbs, such as lavender and tansy, as a mask for the more delicate scents of other crops and herbs. This strategy will keep them free of sap-sucking pests, such as aphids.
- Protect slow-growing, delicate plants from sun, wind or frost by providing them with a nurse plant until they can stand on their own. Use a tough, fast-growing wattle or tall, robust species such as sunflowers as a sheltering canopy for newly planted seedlings.
- Disguise your vegetables and herbs by introducing differently shaped plants into your vegetable patch. This will fool some insect pests that seem to recognise their food sources by shape. It's believed that cabbage white butterflies, for example, are drawn to the round shape of cabbages.
- Allow some of your vegetables to mature to the flowering stage. The flowers of broccoli, cabbages, cauliflowers and other brassicas are favourite foods for aphids and cabbage white butterflies. The theory is that they will feed among the flowers and ignore the plants.

Traditional combinations

Plant	Companion	Benefits
Apples	Nasturtiums	Repel aphids
Carrots	Leeks	Repel carrot fly
Corn	Sweet potatoes	Attract parasitic wasps
Peaches	Strawberries	Control oriental fruit moth
Raspberries	Rue	Deter harlequin beetles
Roses	Chives	Keep black spot at bay

■ ■ ■ **Give companion plant species a HELPING HAND by planting them 2–4 weeks before pest-prone plants.**

HERB REPELLENTS

The following herbs exude volatile oils that repel the insects listed. Grow these herbs to keep away pests and as barrier plants to protect other plants.

- Basil – flies, mosquitoes
- Bay leaves – cockroaches
- Chamomile – flies
- Dill – cabbage moth
- Fennel – fleas
- Marigold – nematodes, aphids
- Mint – cabbage moth
- Nasturtium – ants, aphids
- Pennyroyal – ants
- Rue – flies, mosquitoes
- Sage – cabbage moth
- Tansy – ants

- Some plants, such as peas and beans, are nitrogen-fixers – they convert nitrogen from the atmosphere into soil-enriching nitrogen compounds. Plant them with a crop that thrives on extra nitrogen, such as corn.
- Don't leave areas of uncovered soil in your garden. Bare earth is sure to be colonised by weeds, so introduce ground-hugging plants. They'll leave no room for weeds to set seed and grow.
- Include plants that provide a safe haven for beneficial insects when times are tough. Many of these insects need a source of nectar and pollen to survive while they're waiting for the pests to arrive. Good choices are alyssum, coriander, gypsophila, nasturtium and Queen Anne's lace (*Anthriscus sylvestris*).

TOP TIP

Grow colourful self-seeding annuals and perennials around the edges of garden beds or fence lines where they can go wild. They're a great first line of defence against the pests that would otherwise make a beeline for your prized specimens, and they look good too.

GOOD AND BAD COMPANIONS

Some plants emit chemicals to prevent other plants growing nearby – a process known as allelopathy. If you know how it works, you'll be able to take advantage of the process or avoid potential problems.

- The black walnut tree (*Juglans nigra*) emits juglone, a substance that suppresses the growth of other plants, particularly tomatoes, potatoes, blueberries and blackberries. Rhododendrons and azaleas planted near a black walnut will die.
- Don't encourage camphor laurels as they also suppress competing growth, a factor that has contributed to this tree's success as an invasive environmental weed in temperate and subtropical climates.
- When brassicas, such as cabbages and brussels sprouts, are past harvesting and forming seed, they inhibit the germination of other seeds nearby. If you want to sow seeds for a new crop near an old crop of brassicas, pull them up first.
- Use the growth-inhibiting properties of pine needles as a mulch to prevent weeds. They break down slowly and are highly acidic, so work well around acid-loving plants such as azaleas and strawberries.
- The toxins in fallen rhododendron leaves break down into the soil, preventing grassy weed seeds from germinating nearby.
- Practise crop rotation. This strategy works not only for vegetables, but also for other plants. Rose sickness, for example, may be caused by growing a new rose where an old one previously grew.

Trees and lawns

Trees and grasses tend to make poor companions. Sometimes this is due to allelopathy, but more often it is due to root competition and shading. The easiest and best earth-wise solution to poor grass growth under or near trees is to cover the area immediately beneath a tree with an organic mulch. This way, grass can only grow beyond the canopy. In doing this, you're mimicking what happens naturally in a forested area.

Grow tall, fast-growing plants such as borage to SHELTER STRAWBERRIES, and corn to shade sprawling pumpkin vines.

Planting with natives

Growing native plants from your area will give you a head start in your garden. Because they are already ideally adapted to local conditions, you'll make fewer planting mistakes. Your council may provide a list of native plants suitable for the locality or you could join a bush regeneration group to learn what grows well in your area.

BUSH GARDEN BASICS

Though a well-mulched bush garden will look after itself once it's established, it does require care and attention initially.

- If you select plants that are indigenous to your area or from a similar climatic and soil situation, they will be more likely to thrive.
- Most native plants grow best in well-drained soils, so if you have heavy clay soils, you will need to improve the drainage or build your beds on top of them by adding good-quality topsoil and lots of organic mulch.
- Look for the grafted forms and named varieties of native plants that have been selected and cultivated for better performance in gardens. This will increase the range of native plants you can grow and enjoy.
- After planting, water new plants to establish them. Once they've settled in, some native plants will survive on little more than natural rainfall. If they need more, you can adjust the watering to suit their needs later.
- To keep native plants tidy, prune and train them regularly, just as you would exotic plants. That way you'll be shaping a native garden rather than just recreating a patch of bushland. Always trim back native plants after flowering.

GROWING FROM SEEDS

- When clearing a bush site for building, save the topsoil and take cuttings or collect seed from any native plants. Once the building has been completed, replace the topsoil and use the seeds and cuttings to revegetate the garden.
- Recycle milk cartons – they make great growing containers for gum tree seeds.
- Plant seedlings in the individual compartments of egg cartons, then place them directly into the ground, cardboard and all. This minimises root disturbance at transplanting time. The cardboard, an organic material, will quickly break down.
- Check the growing conditions for native plants. Some seeds need to be treated or they won't germinate. There are various pre-treatments including the use of hot water, smoke and heat. Ask your local native plant society for advice.
- If you want to collect seeds outside your own block, seek permission from the landholder. If you're collecting from bushland, check with your local council first. Only collect seed from healthy plants.

THE TRUTH ABOUT...

NATIVE PLANTS

The term 'native' refers to all the plants in a particular country. Indigenous plants are natives that have evolved to grow in the soil and climatic conditions in a specific area. Planting indigenous species helps to maintain local plant populations and may also provide food for the local native animals, birds and insects, whereas not all native plants are suitable for every area.

~ STAR SAVER ~

Buy small plants in tubes when establishing your garden. Tubestock is cheap, establishes quickly and grows vigorously when planted out. This way, if your plant choices don't thrive, you've only wasted a few dollars and can afford to start again.

Indigenous plants are well adapted to local soils and climatic conditions such as rainfall, temperature and salt exposure.

Native plants for every situation

Australia	New Zealand
For coastal areas	
Beach she-oak (*Casuarina equisetifolia*) Coastal rosemary (*Westringia fruticosa*) Coast banksia (*Banksia integrifolia*) Coast wattle (*Acacia longifolia* subsp. *sophorae*) Pandanus (*Pandanus tectorius* var. *australianus*)	Brachyglottis (*Brachyglottis greyi*) Coprosmas (*Coprosma* species) Karo (*Pittosporum crassifolium*) Pohutukawa (*Metrosideros excelsa*) Purple hebe, napuka (*Hebe speciosa*)
For shady places	
Common maidenhair fern (*Adiantum aethiopicum*) Dog rose (*Bauera* 'Ruby Glow') Elkhorn fern (*Platycerium bifurcatum*) Necklace fern (*Asplenium flabellifolium*) Soft tree fern (*Dicksonia antarctica*)	Chatham Island forget-me-not (*Myosotidium hortensia*) Five finger, whauwhaupaku (*Pseudopanax arboreus*) Pepepe (*Machaerina sinclairii*) Rosy maidenhair fern (*Adiantum hispidulum*) Rough tree fern, wheki (*Dicksonia squarrosa*)
For colour	
Banksias (*Banksia* species) Grevilleas (*Grevillea* species) Native daisy (*Brachyscome multifida*) Red flowering gum (*Eucalyptus* 'Summer Red') Wattles (*Acacia* species)	Coprosma (*Coprosma* 'Karo Red') Creeping fuchsia (*Fuchsia procumbens*) Hebe (*Hebe* 'Blue Gem') Kaka beak (*Clianthus puniceus*) Tea-trees (*Leptospermum* species)
For screening and privacy	
Bottlebrushes (*Callistemon* species) Grevillea (*Grevillea* 'Orange Marmalade') Lilly pilly (*Acmena smithii*) Paperbarks (*Melaleuca* species)	Kohukohu (*Pittosporum tenuifolium*) Manuka, tea-tree (*Leptospermum scoparium*) Ngaio (*Myoporum laetum*) Pohutukawa (*Metrosideros excelsa*)
Climbers	
Bower of beauty (*Pandorea jasminoides*) Climbing flame pea (*Chorizema diversifolium*) Native sarsaparilla (*Hardenbergia violacea*) Old man's beard (*Clematis aristata*) Wonga vine (*Pandorea pandorana*)	Crimson rata, akakura (*Metrosideros carminea*) Kaihua, New Zealand jasmine (*Parsonsia heterophylla*) Kaka beak (*Clianthus puniceus*) Native clematis (*Clematis* species) Three kings climber (*Tecomanthe speciosa*)
For boggy areas	
Broad-leaved paperbark (*Melaleuca quinquenervia*) Christmas bells (*Blandfordia cunninghamii*) Crimson bottlebrush (*Callistemon citrinus*) Knotted club rush (*Isolepis nodosa*) Native frangipani (*Hymenosporum flavum*)	Bartlett's rata (*Metrosideros bartlettii*) Carexes (*Carex* species) Giant rush, wiwi (*Juncus pallidus*) Giant umbrella sedge (*Cyperus ustulatus*) Swamp musk (*Mazus radicans*)
To attract birds	
Banksias (*Banksia* species) Grevilleas (*Grevillea* species) Hakeas (*Hakea* species) Illawarra flame tree (*Brachychiton acerifolius*) Wattles (*Acacia* species)	Cabbage tree, ti kouka (*Cordyline australis*) Kaka beak (*Clianthus puniceus*) Kowhais (*Sophora* species) New Zealand flaxes (*Phormium* species) Tree fuchsia, kotukutuku (*Fuchsia excorticata*)
For architectural form	
Burrawang (*Macrozamia communis*) Gymea lily (*Doryanthes excelsa*) Kangaroo paws (*Anigozanthos* species) Tree ferns (*Cyathea* species and *Dicksonia* species)	Harakeke, New Zealand flax (*Phormium tenax*) Puka (*Meryta sinclairii*) Rengarenga, renga lily (*Arthropodium cirratum*) Spaniards (*Aciphylla* species) Tree ferns (*Dicksonia* species)

■ ■ ■ **Help restore the native habitat** by joining a bush regeneration group. Your local council will put you in touch with one.

Low-maintenance strategies

When you buy a plant or design a garden, think about what it is going to take in terms of natural resources and effort to maintain that plant or to keep the effect you want. If you plan carefully from the outset, and choose plants that do well in your climate and situation, you'll have a garden that, once established, needs only routine care.

TEN EASY GARDENING TIPS

1 Start with a small garden area that you can easily maintain. It's easy to expand later if you wish.

2 Make paths or lay stepping stones to provide quick, easy access to all your garden beds and to utility areas such as the tool shed, compost and garbage bins, garden tap and clothes line.

3 Choose plant varieties that are resistant to pests and diseases. Also select varieties grafted onto hardy understocks, as these usually perform better than species growing on their own roots.

4 Consider how much work you're willing to do. Immaculate lawns, topiarised hedges and swimming pools are not only expensive but also require a great deal of time and energy to look after. Try to minimise the number of areas with high maintenance needs, such as annual beds, vegetable gardens or potted plants.

5 Group plants with the same needs together – for example, low water users such as succulents and ornamental grasses, shade-loving plants like ferns and sedges, and so on. Mulch all plants well in order to reduce their need for water.

6 Fill your garden beds with plants, leaving no room for weeds to grow. Grow prostrate shrubs and spreading groundcovers between larger shrubs. Use organic mulch or pebbles to cover any bare soil.

7 Plant informal hedges and screens that don't need clipping. Abelia, grevillea, Indian hawthorn, murraya, nandina, oleander and plumbago are all good choices.

8 Use a mulching mower on your lawn. It doesn't have a grasscatcher, so you won't have to keep emptying the clippings. The cut grass is scattered onto the lawn as you go, returning nutrients to the soil.

9 If you are fortunate enough to live in an area without water restrictions, use an irrigation system. A carefully monitored one with an automatic timer is more efficient than hand watering and wastes less water.

10 Save time and money by using a slow-release fertiliser. It will last for months and won't burn the root system. It is also kinder on the environment as nutrients are made available at a rate at which they can be taken up. Finally, less fertiliser is lost in run-off.

High-maintenance	Low-maintenance
Lawns	Shrub borders
Formal hedges and topiary	Native gardens
Vigorous growers	Trees with mulch
Annual and perennial beds	Paved areas
Vegetables and fruit trees	Succulent gardens
Pot plants	Dwarf ornamental grasses
Swimming pools and water features	Groundcovers

TOP TIP

Keep cutting tools – such as secateurs, shears and spades – sharp. Blunt tools are hard to use and take longer to do the job. More importantly, they may also damage your plants. Sharpen them with a sharpening stone or sharpening tool.

Save time by marking the handles of your tools with fluorescent tape so they can be easily located if dropped.

BUILDING A 'NO-DIG' GARDEN

A no-dig garden can be built on soil, over existing lawn or even on hard, barren ground. It's a great way to recycle waste materials, and, once established, a no-dig garden is virtually maintenance free. No matter where you live or how fit you are, it's an easy, cheap and practical way to grow plants. Here are the basic materials you'll need:

edging material
newspaper
1–2 bales straw or lucerne
organic fertiliser
well-rotted manure
compost
seedlings

- Choose a sunny position with good drainage. If you are starting the garden on lawn and can't remove the grass, keep it at bay by laying down some old carpet as a base for the other materials. With no oxygen or sunlight, the grass will eventually die off.
- Decide what size your garden bed will be. The idea is to start with a small area, which you can expand later if you wish. Edge the bed with bricks, logs, rocks or railway sleepers – in fact, any material that will allow you to contain the soil.
- To suppress weeds, cover the ground with a thick layer of wet newspaper, about 1 cm thick. Use plain rather than glossy sheets, and overlap the edges.
- Cover the newspaper with pads of straw or lucerne. Next, add a layer of organic fertiliser, such as pellets of chicken manure or blood and bone.
- Cover the fertiliser with a 20 cm layer of straw or lucerne. Add a generous amount of manure with further layers of straw or lucerne, then cover with a layer of compost.
- Water the garden and allow it to settle for a few days.
- Plant seedlings into the compost. Start with shallow-rooted vegetables, such as lettuce. As your garden begins to make its own compost, and the layers turn into rich, brown soil, plant deep-rooted crops such as carrot.

To reduce your lawn's watering needs, cut only the top third of the grass and keep mower blades sharp.

PROS & CONS

KEEPING YOUR SWIMMING POOL

Backyard swimming pools are a great way of cooling off in summer. However, as any pool owner knows, they are a high-maintenance item and incur expensive water bills. They also lose a lot of water through evaporation, and the chemicals used to keep them clean are hazardous to wildlife. If you don't get as much use out of your pool as you once did, consider filling it in or turning part of it into a fish or frog pond. Make sure you advise your local council of your plans.

Avoid planting fast-growing climbers, as they need a lot of pruning and training to keep them in check.

A wildlife garden

The presence – or absence – of wildlife in the garden is an important indicator of its health. Frogs are especially sensitive to changes in the ecosystem, so if you have a thriving frog pond, you'll know you're on the right track environmentally. Even dedicating just a corner of the garden as a small wildlife sanctuary will yield results, and you'll also find it incredibly satisfying.

LIVING WITH WILDLIFE

- Keep your wildlife-friendly garden from invading your neighbours' properties by pruning and mowing along boundaries and fence lines.
- Mow areas next to the house so that animals and insects don't live in too close proximity to humans. Both species will be happier!
- Take simple precautions. For instance, when lifting an object that could shelter an animal, lift it towards you so any hidden creature can make a break away from you.
- If you keep your lawn long, mow an access path and be careful when walking through long grass. In Australia, a lizard-friendly garden may also attract snakes.
- Protect native animals from your pets. If you have a cat, attach a bell to its collar to warn birds and other creatures of its approach. Also, both cats and dogs should be kept inside at night.

BIRDS

Attract native birds to your garden by growing a variety of native plants, especially those from your region. Many birds, particularly when they are feeding their young, will also eat a wide range of insect pests, so you'll benefit from their visits.

- In Australia, plant grevilleas, banksias and bottlebrushes to attract nectar-feeding birds, such as honeyeaters, lorikeets and spinebills. In New Zealand, include flax in your garden – its tall flowers are a magnet to tuis, a black honeyeater.
- To cater for birds of all sizes, include some groundcovers, low to medium-sized shrubs and small trees. Larger trees, such as gum trees and casuarinas, will attract seed-eaters, such as cockatoos, galahs and finches.
- Construct a bird bath. Simply place a layer of rinsed river pebbles in a shallow dish and add clean water to a depth of about 30 mm. Then hang the dish from a branch or place it on a pedestal – any spot that is safe from cats.
- If you enjoy the company of birds, learn to share the fruit from your trees with them. Otherwise, near harvest time, cover your fruit trees with bird-proof netting.

INSECTS

- Learn to identify the insect visitors to your garden and the role they play in keeping it healthy. Not all of them eat plants. Some insects, such as ladybirds and their larvae,

~ FLYING START ~

Attract wildlife to your garden by planting native grasses, leaving the lawn to grow long and including a water feature.

TOP TIP

Wildlife corridors – created by linking wildlife-friendly gardens through bush regeneration and planting – act as transport routes for native animals, birds and insects. Contact your national park ranger, local council or wildlife protection society to find out more about wildlife corridors in your area.

■ ■ ■ **Kangaroo paw flowers act as handy perches that birds can use to access their nectar reserves.**

eat other insects. These are known as beneficial insects.

- Avoid using pesticides, as they will kill not only destructive insects but also beneficial bugs, such as hover-flies, parasitic wasps and spiders.
- Attract butterflies to your garden by planting achillea, buddleias, cosmos and zinnias.
- Encourage native bees to visit your garden by planting abelia, bottlebrush, buddleia, eucalypt, grevillea, lavender, melaleuca, tea-tree and westringia. Bees are pollinators, so if you have a productive garden, the more bees you have, the better.

LIZARDS AND SKINKS

Lizards and skinks will help to keep your garden free of snails and grasshoppers.

- Create a safe haven for skinks and lizards by keeping cats and dogs under control.
- Provide some flat rocks where lizards can sit and bask on sunny days, and also hollow logs, pipes and low spiky shrubs where they can hide from predators.
- Don't use snail bait – lizards will eat the poisoned snails and die. With any luck your resident blue-tongue lizard will eat all the snails anyway.

Garden allies	What they eat
Assassin beetles	Many garden pests
Centipedes	Slugs (adults and eggs), other soil-dwelling insects
Damselflies (nymphs and adults)	Small insects, including mosquitoes and their larvae
Dragonflies (nymphs and adults)	Mosquitoes and their larvae
Hoverflies (larvae)	Aphids and other small insects
Lacewings (larvae)	Aphids and other small insects
Ladybirds (adults and larvae)	Aphids, scale insects, mealy bugs, mites, leaf-hoppers and other insects
Millipedes	Decaying plant matter
Praying mantis	Many pests
Spiders	Many insects, especially night-flying species
Wasps (mud-daubing, paper, parasitic, etc.)	Caterpillars, spiders and other insects

hot links

How to make bird- and wildlife-friendly gardens:
www.floraforfauna.com.au;
www.zoo.org.au/education/factsheets.htm
www.bestgardening.com/bgc/hub/ecobirds01.htm
How to build nest boxes for native birds and mammals:
www.gould.edu.au/wildlifecams/habitats.asp;
www.wwf.org.nz/earthsaver/es_16.cfm

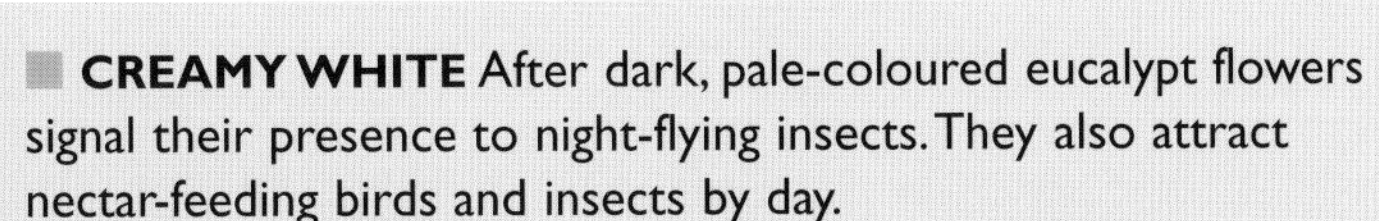

COLOUR-CODED BLOOMS

CREAMY WHITE After dark, pale-coloured eucalypt flowers signal their presence to night-flying insects. They also attract nectar-feeding birds and insects by day.

PINK and ORANGE These colours advertise nectar to birds. Choose sasanqua and japonica camellias in pink. There are many banksias with orange-coloured blooms, while the orange flowers of the silky oak literally drip with nectar.

RED Nectar-feeding birds are attracted to red, though bees and most butterflies can't see this colour. Top red flowers for attracting birds include bottlebrushes, grevilleas, kangaroo paw and New Zealand flax.

YELLOW and PURPLE These colours indicate pollen-rich flowers, which are attractive to insects. Top yellow flowers include daisies, eucalypts and wattles. For purple blooms, choose from buddleia, foxgloves, mint bush and penstemons.

PLANNING A POND

- Before you start excavating your pond, locate the service lines so that you don't cut them by accident. If you want to light the pond or run a fountain or pump, you'll need to dig a trench from the power supply to the pond to accommodate a power line.
- When running electrical cables outdoors, always use an isolating transformer to protect yourself from shocks. Keep power tools well away from electrical cables so that there is no danger of cutting them.
- While you're still at the planning stage, check with your local council on the safety regulations for backyard pools. Generally, pools accessible to children should not exceed a depth of 5 cm. However, in some areas, ponds that are over 2 cm deep may need fencing.
- To make a pond child-safe, place a layer of pebbles or river gravel to 5 cm below the water level. The pebbles or gravel can also be used to conceal the pump.

FROGS AND FISH

- If you're patient, animals and insects will eventually colonise your pond, but you may have to wait up to two years before frogs arrive. If you don't want to wait that long, ask a friend or neighbour who has a frog pond for some frogspawn.
- Don't introduce frogs from more than 20 km away, as this may spread a type of fungal disease. Check with your local wildlife authority in case a permit is required.
- Include some means of exit for little frogs – a piece of wood or a stone placed at an angle to the rim of a pot or the edge of a pond will help them to hop out.
- Buy only frog-friendly native fish if you want to have both frogs and fish in your pond. Your local aquarium shop should be able to advise you which species to choose.

AVOIDING ALGAE

There are several forms of algae. Particularly damaging is angel's hair, a green, hair-like weed that feeds on excess nutrients and wraps itself around other water plants, killing them and reducing light levels in the pond.

- Don't use chemicals to get rid of algae. They may be harmful to fish, animals and insects and may also damage other plants. Instead, remove it by hand or fish it out with a stick or scoop. Algae can be added to the compost heap.
- Reduce nutrient run-off to the pond by restricting the use of fertilisers (particularly lawn fertilisers) in the area.
- Install a submersible pump to aerate the water in a fountain: algae thrives in still, stagnant conditions, not in agitated water.
- Add barley straw (available at some hardware and produce stores) to the water. As it decays in oxygenated water, it releases chemicals that inhibit the growth of algae.

PLANTS FOR PONDS

- ✔ Nardoo (*Marsilea drummondii*): An Australian fern species with fan-shaped leaflets that float on the water.
- ✔ Sacred lotus (*Nelumbo nucifera*): Perfumed flowers and decorative seed pods that resemble a bathroom shower rose.
- ✔ Sweet flag (*Acorus species*): Has attractive, sword-like foliage that is aromatic when crushed. Some variegated varieties are also available.
- ✔ Water lilies (*Nymphaea species*): Heart-shaped, floating leaves and beautiful (sometimes fragrant) flowers of a number of different colours.
- ✘ Alligator weed (*Alternanthera philoxeroides*)
- ✘ Duckweed (*Wolffia species*)
- ✘ Elodea (*Elodea canadensis*)
- ✘ Fanwort (*Cabomba caroliniana*)
- ✘ Floating water chestnut (*Trapa species*)
- ✘ Hornwort (*Ceratophyllum demersum*)
- ✘ Hydrilla (*Hydrilla verticillata*)
- ✘ Lagarosiphon (*Lagarosiphon major*)
- ✘ Parrot's feather (*Myriophyllum aquaticum*)
- ✘ Salvinia (*Salvinia molesta*)
- ✘ Water hyacinth (*Eichhornia crassipes*)

■ ■ ■ **For a natural look, site a pond at the lowest point of your garden where water might naturally accumulate.**

MAKING A BUSH POND

A pond in your garden will attract a variety of wildlife, including frogs, insects and birds. Here's an easy way to make a pond. You'll need:

sand
butyl rubber liner
some large rocks
aquatic plants

- Before starting work, check the regulations for backyard pools with your local council. You may need to install a fence.
- Choose a level, partly shaded position. Don't put the pond under large trees, which may drop leaves, flowers and fruit.
- Use a garden hose to mark out the shape of your pond. Once you're happy with the layout, sprinkle flour to mark the outline.
- Excavate to the required depth, removing anything sharp that could puncture the liner.
- Line the hole with a layer of sand. Cut the liner so that there is plenty of overlap around the pond edges. Place the liner in the hole, and half-fill it with water to allow it to settle into place.
- Hide the edge of the liner with some large rocks and some aquatic plants. Ask at your local nursery for advice on some suitable plants for your climate and situation. Avoid weedy aquatics.
- Place water plants (in their pots) in the pond. Water lilies should be planted so that the water barely covers the crowns. As the plants grow, increase the water depth to around 30 cm. If necessary, put the pots on bricks or pebbles to raise them to the correct level.
- Before introducing fish, add a water conditioner containing hydrosulphite salts to neutralise chlorine and other impurities.
- Use a swimming-pool kit to check the pH of the water. It should be neutral. If not, add either bicarbonate of soda to make it more alkaline or sodium phosphate to make it more acidic.

Mosquito control

Most tadpoles are vegetarians and don't eat mosquito larvae. If you have a mosquito problem, add some native fish such as these to your pond.
- Marjorie's hardyhead (*Craterocephalus marjoriae*).
- Olive perchlet (*Ambassis agassizii*).
- Pacific blue-eye (*Pseudomugil signifer*).

Note that crimson-spotted rainbowfish (*Melanotaenia duboulayi*) eat tadpoles, so make sure you don't introduce this species to your frog pond.

The world's worst aquatic weed, water hyacinth, looks pretty but is very invasive and can double its size in a few weeks.

Plants for boggy patches near the pond

- Arrow arum (*Peltandra virginica*)
- Arum lily (*Zantedeschia* 'Childsiana')
- Canna lily (*Canna* species), at right
- Dwarf papyrus (*Cyperus papyrus* 'Nana')
- Louisiana iris (*Iris* Louisiana hybrids)
- Maidenhair fern (*Adiantum* species)
- Stream lily (*Helmholtzia glaberrima*)
- Yellow flag iris (*Iris pseudacorus*)

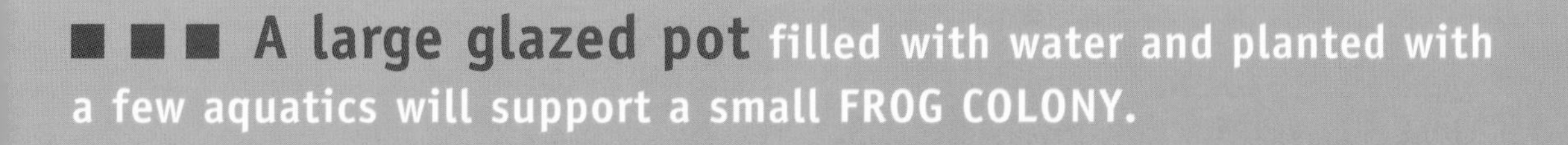

GARDEN BASICS

To have an earth-wise garden, you need to know your soil and understand how to improve it.

Down to earth

The biggest factor in your garden's success is what goes on underground. For best results, most roots need a soil or potting medium with a ready supply of nutrients that's moist, but not waterlogged, and easy to grow in. The better the drainage, structure and chemical balance of the soil, the better your plants will grow and flower.

SOIL SENSE

- Work with the soil you have rather than replace it with new material. Not only is new earth expensive and hard work to import, it may also contain weed seeds.

Identify your soil

To find out whether your soil is sand, loam, clay or a mixture, follow these steps.

• Take a handful of soil from your garden and mix it with a little water.
• Try to form the soil into a sausage shape. If the soil crumbles and falls apart, you have sandy soil. If it just holds together, it is loam. If you can mould it into a firm sausage shape, then you have clay soil.

Methodically repeat this test throughout your garden, as different areas may have different kinds of soil.

- Grow plants that are native to your area. They will be perfectly suited to the chemical composition of the soil, so you won't have to worry about changing it.
- The easiest way to improve just about any soil is to add compost and organic matter, but there are also lots of other products that will benefit your soil, including gypsum and humic acids (that is, acids that are derived from humus). These are naturally occurring materials that improve soil structure and the way the soil absorbs water. You can purchase these products from your local nursery.
- Avoid adding lots of fertilisers to soils that are poorly drained or too dry. Work on the drainage and soil structure first.

SAND

Although sandy soils drain very efficiently, their small particles don't hold onto nutrients well and can dry out rapidly.

- Dig in lots of compost and well-rotted manure before you start planting. Add more manure and organic mulch on a regular basis in order to replenish the nutrients in the soil. This will also improve the soil's water-holding capacity.
- Line the base of the planting hole with a few sheets of newspaper. This slows down water loss and allows the plant to gather more moisture. Eventually the newspaper will break down, but by the time it does, the root system should be well established.
- Add a layer of either loam or sandy loam to improve the soil structure. Mix it in with a rotary hoe, fork or shovel.
- Add some lime to correct the level of acidity in your soil. This will also improve the soil structure because lime helps to bind sand particles together.

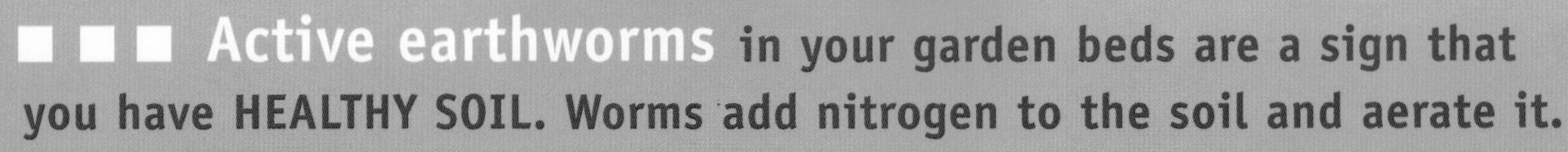

■ ■ ■ **Active earthworms** in your garden beds are a sign that you have HEALTHY SOIL. Worms add nitrogen to the soil and aerate it.

Azaleas, camellias and rhododendrons only grow well in an acid soil. Lavenders, sweet peas and carnations prefer an alkaline soil.

LOAM

This is the best type of soil you can have in your garden. Usually rich in nutrients and easy to dig, it drains well yet holds moisture.

- Keep loam in good shape with regular additions of compost.

CLAY

Clay can be hard to dig. It can also crack when dry and become a mud bath when wet. But don't despair, you can transform clay into a workable soil.

- Add gypsum, a naturally occurring mineral composed of calcium sulphate. If the spade bounces off the surface, hire a rotary hoe to turn the gypsum into the soil.
- Add well-rotted organic matter, such as compost and animal manures, to improve the drainage and aeration of the soil.
- Add some sand. As sand doesn't mix easily with heavy clay, combine it with some organic matter first.
- If all else fails, build raised beds of good-quality soil on top of the clay.

IMPROVING DRAINAGE

To check how well your soil drains, dig a 30 cm hole, then fill it with water. If the water drains away in minutes, the soil is water-repellent. If it takes more than 8 hours, it is waterlogged.

- To fix water-repellent soil, dig in plenty of well-rotted animal manure or compost. Apply a wetting agent, or, for new plantings, add a few water-storing crystals to the planting hole. Mulch the garden beds to help preserve soil moisture.
- To fix waterlogged soil, add sub-surface drainage to remove excess water. Build raised garden beds so that plants are not growing in wet conditions. If neither works, create a bog or water garden and grow water-loving plants.

WARNING!

▼ Don't go overboard with water-storing crystals – too many will actually push plants out of the soil as they swell up!

- Most plants prefer neutral soil. Very acidic or very alkaline soils will 'lock up' some nutrients (such as iron), causing growth problems.
- Use a pH kit (available from nurseries or hardware stores) to test if the soil is likely to cause nutrient deficiencies. The pH (potential Hydrogen) of the soil measures the soil acidity on a scale of 1–14.
- If your soil has a pH over 7, it is alkaline. Add sulphur or iron sulphate and organic matter to grow acid-loving plants. If your soil has a pH below 7, it is acidic. Add some lime to grow plants that like a more alkaline soil.

• *Check out the hydrangeas in your area – pink or red blooms show the soil is alkaline, mauve and blue flowers indicate it is acidic.*

■ ■ ■ **If your garden beds** are hard to dig, let the plants do the work. As they grow, their roots will break up the soil.

The magic of mulch

Bare earth is rare in nature. In a eucalypt forest or rainforest most of the ground is covered with mulch – fallen leaves, flowers, twigs and fruit. In the garden, all organic material can be used as mulch. If you can, use what's native to your area so that you are recycling local materials.

WHY MULCH?

- Organic mulches break down, releasing nutrients into the soil. Inorganic mulches, such as pebbles, stabilise soil temperature in the root zone and help to prevent erosion.
- Applying mulch is a cheap, easy and effective way to reduce surface evaporation caused by wind and hot sun.
- A layer of mulch works well as a natural weed mat, reducing the need for chemicals and time-consuming weeding.
- Mulch provides food and shelter for insects and increases the activity of worms and micro-organisms in the soil, which is good for plants.

MULCH FROM GARDEN WASTE

- If there's enough waste material in your garden to recycle regularly, buy a shredder and use disease-free garden prunings.
- If you don't have a shredder but you do have a lot of pruning to do, hire one for a day. Aim to produce a load that is big enough to last for months in your garden. Share the cost of hire with a neighbour if you can.
- Run over leaves and small prunings with the lawnmower to make an instant mulch. Collect and put it on garden beds.
- Collect fallen leaves in autumn and put them straight onto garden beds. Extra leaves can be stored in heaps to break down into leaf mould.
- Start a compost heap. Having a place to put plant waste will help to keep the garden tidy, and well-rotted compost makes an excellent mulch.

HOW TO MULCH

- The best time to apply mulch is in spring, but keep it topped up throughout the year. The key is to avoid leaving any soil bare, so always mulch around new plantings straight away.
- Prepare the ground. Dig out all traces of perennial weeds, and water garden beds before and after applying mulch.
- Spread mulch over the soil and around the base of plants. Don't mound it around stems and trunks as it can cause rot. Aim for a depth of about 7.5–10 cm.
- If you use organic mulch, add an organic fertiliser, such as chicken manure, because the mulch tends to rob the soil of nitrogen as it breaks down.
- Mulch around fruit and vegetables, such as strawberries and tomatoes, to keep the produce clean and help prevent soil-borne disease from attacking crops.
- Prevent mulch such as gravel from spilling out onto the lawn by installing a solid edge around all your garden beds.

THE TRUTH ABOUT...

MULCH MYTHS

- Mulch does not attract frost. It actually protects plant roots and bulbs underground from cold damage.
- Mulch made from the needles of pine or she-oak trees is not poisonous to plants. It may break down slowly.
- Fallen camphor laurel leaves are not harmful to plants. They can be used as mulch.
- Thicker is not necessarily better: if mulch is too thick it may stop moisture from reaching the soil.

TOP TIP

Apply mulch to the garden after rain or a thorough watering in order to retain moisture in the soil.

Mulches can prevent up to 75 per cent water loss from evaporation and run-off from garden beds.

Types of mulch

Organic mulch	Comments
Compost	If using your own, make sure it's well rotted. Or, buy in bags or in bulk.
Garden prunings	Shred before using. Avoid diseased material or plants that have recently been sprayed with herbicides.
Grass clippings	Mix well with other materials or compost before use, as they can pack down into a water-shedding layer.
Leaf litter	Don't use in bushfire areas, as it burns easily.
Lucerne	Use spoiled hay that's unsuitable for stock feed.
Manure	Age the manure, or compost it first.
Mushroom compost	May be alkaline, so check its pH before applying.
Native plants (eucalypt, bottlebrush, tea-tree)	Break down very slowly, but this is an advantage.
Pea straw	Sold in bales or bags. Ideal for fast-growing plants such as annuals and perennials.
Sugarcane	Good to use around roses and vegetables.
Weeds	Fresh, seed-free green weeds break down well in garden beds.

Organic mulch	Comments
Pine needles	Suitable around acid-loving plants like azaleas. Slow to decompose.
Rice hulls	Good on its own or can be mixed with other mulches. Has good resistance to compaction. It is not a fire hazard. Slow to decompose.
Shredded pine bark	Attractive in a bush garden, but can be flammable. Slow to decompose.
Wood chips	Burns easily, so don't use it in bushfire areas. Slow to decompose.

Living mulch	Comments
Groundcover plants	Suppress weeds; keep roots of other plants cool.

Inert mulch	Comments
Crushed bricks or roof tiles	Use for paths or around low water-using plants.
Gravel	Easy to spread. Many forms are inexpensive.
Pebbles	Good for pot plants and around succulents and cacti.
Recycled glass	Attractive as a feature in courtyards or in pots.
Rocks	Decorative; excellent for keeping soils cool.

Use inert or inorganic mulches in bushfire areas as they are **LESS FLAMMABLE** than organic ones.

Building a compost heap

Plants get most of their nutrients from compost, which is decomposed organic matter in the soil. By adding extra compost into the soil, you not only boost the health of your garden, but by recycling organic matter, you can also reduce the amount of waste going to landfill by as much as 30 per cent.

SETTING UP

- Work out the most convenient spot in your garden for a compost heap. If possible, locate it near the kitchen, so that it is handy for the disposal of food scraps.
- Use recycled materials such as brick, stone, timber or plastic to make your compost heap. For example, an old plastic garbage bin is an easy and economical option. Just cut the bottom out, press the bin into the soil and keep the lid to cover it.
- To aid drainage and provide access to soil organisms, position the bin on a level, well-drained area so it is in contact with the earth.
- If you're making your own, build a four-sided structure that's at least 1 metre high and open at the top. Make sure that one side is easy to remove so you can turn the heap and remove finished compost.
- If you decide to buy a compost bin, consider a plastic tumbler. It's a drum that aerates the compost very effectively when it is spun round. A full tumbler produces good-quality compost quickly. If you regularly dispose of large amounts of material, buy a large one.
- Make sure your compost heap, tumbler or bin is in the shade during the day because it shouldn't dry out too rapidly, nor should temperatures become so high that soil organisms can't survive.

Troubleshooting problems

Symptom	Problem	Solution
Ammonia smell	Excess nitrogen.	Add more carbon in the form of straw, newspaper or hay.
Rats and mice	Wrong items added.	Don't compost meat, fish and fatty scraps. Build a rodent-proof bin.
Rotten egg smell	Pile too wet or compacted.	Aerate the heap. Add more dry material. Mix small particles with larger particles. Add lime.
Slow decomposition	Material may be too dry, or heap may be too small. Could be due to lack of nitrogen or oxygen.	Add water. Build a larger pile. Add nitrogen-rich materials such as green prunings and vegetable scraps. Aerate regularly.
Steam	Excess nitrogen. Or the heap may be too big to turn properly, leaving the centre too hot.	Add more carbon-rich material (straw, newspaper or hay). Limit the size of the heap.

COMPOST TEA

Use this rich liquid fertiliser to water your plants, or (diluted to about half strength) as a leaf spray.

compost
1 bucket water

- Put the compost into a porous bag.
- Immerse it in a bucket of water for about 2 weeks.
- Remove the bag and use the liquid as required.

Making compost yourself costs you nothing and saves you buying expensive fertilisers.

Top Tip

Contract mowers are often looking for places to drop off lawn clippings from the gardens they mow on a regular basis. If you notice a contractor working nearby, try offering your compost bin. You could gain plenty of local, weed-free grass to add to the compost for your garden.

Life in the compost

Hundreds of species of micro-organisms, such as bacteria and fungi, are present in a compost heap, and they do the work of breaking down organic materials. It is also quite normal for compost heaps to attract small 'vinegar' or 'compost' flies that swarm around the surface. These do no harm and are just part of the natural process of composting. However, if there are blowflies and vermin in your compost you could be adding the wrong kind of scraps.

Compost improves the quality of clay or sandy soil, improving water-holding capacity and reducing run-off.

MAKING YOUR OWN

- Alternate layers of carbon-rich 'brown' materials – straw, hay, dried leaves, sawdust and shredded newspaper and shredded cardboard – with layers of nitrogen-rich 'green' materials – animal manures, grass clippings, fresh leaves, prunings, tea bags, coffee grounds, and vegetable and fruit peelings.
- Don't compost meat, grease, cooking oil, dairy products, dead animals, pet faeces, diseased plants or plant material that has been treated with herbicides or other chemicals (see also *Compost checklist*, p. 43).
- Don't compost invasive weeds that are going to seed. Although a hot compost heap will kill most seeds, it's best to be on the safe side and throw them out.
- Use a shredder to chop up leaves and thick prunings before adding them to the compost heap. Shredding helps to increase the surface area of the materials, making them more accessible to decomposing agents.
- Don't use packaged compost 'accelerators' or 'activators' – they usually give a quick fix of nitrogen that won't last long and is of little benefit. Instead use organic sources of nitrogen such as grass clippings or manure.
- Add manures such as horse, cow, goat, pig, sheep and chicken, but avoid dog and cat droppings, as they may contain pathogens or wormicides. Age manure before adding it.
- Boost your compost by adding a few shovelfuls of finished compost from the previous heap. Manure and comfrey leaves are also good boosters. Or add an infusion made from 1 kilogram chopped nettles and 10 litres water, turning the heap with a spade or fork to add air.

FIVE TIPS FOR TOP COMPOST

1. Turn the heap regularly – at least once a month, but more often to accelerate the process.
2. Don't let it get too wet or too dry – it should be about as damp as a wrung-out sponge.
3. Don't add too much of any one material, or decomposition will slow down or stop.
4. Keep a balanced mix of brown and green material.
5. A good-sized heap generates enough heat for decomposition to occur. However, if it is too big, you won't be able to turn it properly to aerate it. The ideal size is about 1 x 1 metre.

■ ■ ■ **If you don't have a garden** but do have balcony space, get a worm farm instead of a bin for compost.

Feeding your garden

To germinate, grow, flower and set seed, plants need 16 essential elements. Some come from the air and water, but most are found in the soil. By adding organic fertilisers, it's possible to remedy nutrient deficiencies. Animal manures, vermicompost (from worms), chicken manure and seaweed are all good earth-wise fertilisers and they are all either cheap or free.

Chickens provide manure, consume insects and weeds, and cut down on garden and kitchen waste by eating it.

HOW TO USE FERTILISERS

- Always thoroughly water garden beds before and after fertilising, otherwise the fertiliser may damage plant roots. Conserve water and save money by fertilising your garden during periods of heavy rain.
- Fertilise plants in the warmer months of the year, when they are actively growing. In the cooler months they are dormant and don't need much food, so save money by not using fertiliser in winter. Fertilise lawns twice a year, during spring and autumn.
- Follow the directions on the fertiliser container – some plants, such as ferns, only require half-strength applications. Feed any Australian native plants with a fertiliser that is low in phosphorus.
- Learn which plants need a large quantity of fertiliser. These plants are known as 'gross' feeders and include citrus, roses, hibiscus, bougainvilleas, gardenias, lawns and most vegetables.
- Add slow-release fertilisers – they're safe to use and won't burn plant roots. For a quick boost, consider using a leaf fertiliser.

NATURAL FERTILISERS

The essential fertilisers are nitrogen (promotes green growth), phosphorus (for general health) and potassium (for fruit and flower development).

ANIMAL MANURES These contain all the basic plant nutrients and add bulk fibre to the soil. They also encourage beneficial organisms such as earthworms. Apply them as mulch or dig in to improve the soil.

CHICKEN MANURE This provides all the basic plant nutrients and makes a good mulch around plants that require lots of fertiliser. Free-range chickens add the manure directly to the garden.

SEAWEED This contains naturally occurring hormones that stimulate root growth. Seaweed helps to minimise transplant stress and provides better tolerance to cold and heat. Some kelps are low in nitrogen. Before collecting seaweed, check with the local council to find out if it is legal to do so.

VERMICOMPOST As well as being an excellent fertiliser, vermicompost (worm castings) is great for other jobs in the garden. Use it as a soil conditioner, garden mulch, top dressing for lawns and in seed-raising and potting mixes. Dilute it in water (until it becomes the colour of weak tea) and use it on potted plants.

WHAT TO FEED WORMS

✔ Do feed the worms with vegetable and fruit scraps, coffee grounds, tea bags, crushed egg shells, aged grass clippings and manure.

✔ Do bury the scraps in the bedding. Exposed scraps will attract flies and other pests.

✔ Do keep the bedding moist, but not too wet, and at an even temperature.

✘ Don't feed the worms meat, dairy products, fat, onions, garlic, banana skins, or too much citrus or spicy food.

✘ Don't add too much food material at once, or the worms won't be able to keep up!

✘ Don't use spray insecticides in the vicinity of the worm farm.

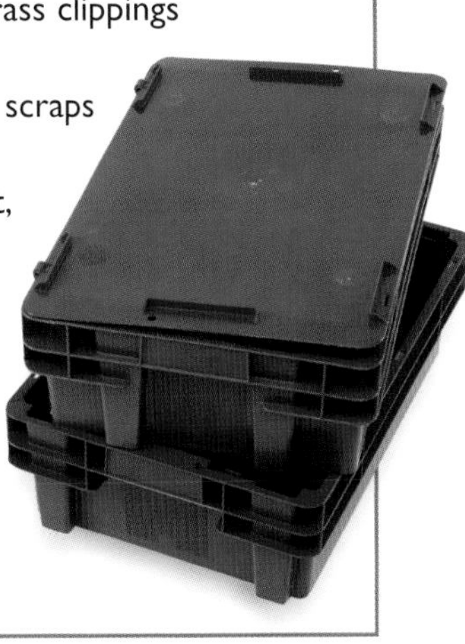

TOP TIP

If you travel to the city fringes or visit local stables you may be able to find manure for free. At most, you'll pay a couple of dollars for a feed bag full.

BUILD YOUR OWN WORM FARM

A worm farm is small enough to be kept on a balcony, so if you have a limited amount of space, it's ideal for producing your own fertiliser. Here's how to build your own.

1 You'll need a moisture-proof container that is 30 centimetres deep with drainage holes in the base, bedding (in the form of straw or shredded newspaper), water and some kitchen scraps.

2 Place some bricks in a tray and sit the container on the bricks. Excess liquid from the worm farm will fall into the tray.

3 Fill the container to about three-quarters full with bedding, moistened to the consistency of a damp sponge. Add a little soil or sand to help the worms digest the waste. Leave it to settle for a couple of days.

4 Introduce tiger worms (*Eisenia fetida*), available from worm farms or the Internet. Or ask at your local hardware store or nursery. Don't use worms from the garden as that type prefers ordinary garden soil and won't thrive.

5 Loosely cover the box with a sheet of plastic or sacking. If you keep your worm farm outdoors, a container with a lid is best.

hot links

How to build a worm farm: www.cleanup.com.au; www.earthworms.co.nz/Worms/worms.html; www.wwf.org.nz/earthsaver/es_23.cfm
How to make fish or seaweed fertiliser: www.organicpathways.co.nz/garden/story/356_html

ANIMAL MANURES

- Check the horse manure you obtain from stables. If it contains lots of wood shavings, it will take longer to decompose. If you find grain seeds, just think of them as green manure – when they sprout, simply pull the seedlings out and throw them on the compost heap.
- Allow cow manure to rot down before you use it on the garden. Milled cow manure is available by the bag from nurseries.
- Chicken manure is very strong, so age it for at least six weeks before you use it. If you don't keep chickens, you can buy the manure from garden centres. Make sure it's from a free-range poultry farm if you disapprove of battery or deep-litter poultry farms (the litter is not changed for weeks).

■ ■ ■ **Slow-release fertilisers** save time and money because one application often lasts for six months or more.

Irrigation systems

Using some form of watering system in your garden will save you time. If it's well designed, it will irrigate your plants more effectively and more efficiently than hand-watering with a hose. Knowing what time of day to water will also avoid loss through evaporation, thus saving you money.

TOP TIPS FOR WATERING

There's more to watering a garden than splashing the hose around. The trick is to provide enough water so that the soil not only looks damp, but also feels wet below the surface.

Don't forget to check and fix dripping taps – a slowly dripping tap wastes about 90 litres of water a week.

- Check whether your watering system is penetrating the ground at root level. Run the system for about 20 minutes (longer for weeping, drip or micro-irrigation systems), then probe the soil to see if it's moist. If it is, turn the water off. If it's still dry, leave the system to run longer.
- To avoid evaporation, water only in the early morning or late in the afternoon when it's cool. However, if it's especially hot in the middle of the day, break this rule and give your plants some extra relief. Water stress can lead to other problems, such as pest and disease attack.
- If watering by hand, water the soil, not the foliage, so the water reaches the roots. On hot days, be very careful not to splash the leaves – the magnifying power of water droplets can concentrate the sun-light and burn them.
- Allow the soil to dry out between waterings, but don't leave it for so long that plants become water stressed. Remember to adjust your watering patterns to reflect changes in season and local weather conditions and also check to see if any water restrictions apply.
- Give plants extra help during periods of drought and heat. In addition, water more often in windy weather and when plants are actively growing or blooming.

BUY WISELY

- A DIY irrigation system will save you money and allow you to develop a system that suits your garden layout, soil and plants. You may need to combine several different methods, such as those in the table opposite.
- Draw a diagram of your garden and take it to an irrigation specialist for advice. Over-the-counter advice is usually free and you won't waste money buying the wrong fittings.
- Install a double-tap fitting at taps so you can operate a fixed watering system and still have a tap available for filling a bucket or attaching a hose.
- Keep on hand some 'goof plugs' – devices that block unwanted holes if you make a mistake when installing your irrigation system.

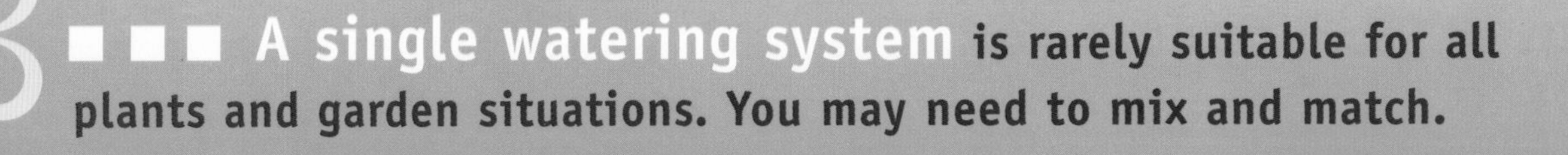

- If you have an automatic system, run it during the night, when the water pressure is stronger due to lower demands on the water supply.
- Don't leave a hose in the sun. The water that collects in it heats up and can burn foliage. Store hoses in the shade, cover irrigation pipes with mulch or set them just below ground level, or allow water to run cold before hosing plants.
- Regularly check and clean all irrigation heads and filters to ensure the water is flowing correctly. A tap filter will catch dirt before it enters the system. To flush out the system, remove the end cap and let the water run for several minutes.
- In cold winter areas, the water in hoses and irrigation systems can freeze overnight. This is a problem if water systems are set to automatically come on early in the morning. On cold nights, adjust the watering times to avoid early mornings.
- Where water is being used to avoid frost damage on plants, set the timer so the system comes on several times during the night.

THE TRUTH ABOUT...

WATER-GUZZLING PLANTS

Are ornamental garden plants water guzzlers? And would we be better off without them in times of drought and water restrictions? No, and no. Not much is known about how much water garden plants actually need. What we do know is that all plants need water to get established, but after this stage, if they're well mulched, most survive with little extra irrigation, especially where there is regular rainfall.

hot links

Water-saving tips: **www.waitakere.govt.nz/CnlSer/wtr/wtrsavetips.asp; www.watersmart.co.nz/tips.html; www.sydneywater.com.au/SavingWater**

Which watering system?

Type	Advantages	Disadvantages
Watering cans	Useful for watering individual plants (especially hanging baskets, balcony and indoor plants), applying liquid fertiliser or tonics and for watering in new plantings.	When full of water, large metal watering cans are very heavy to lift. If you have a lot of ground to cover, a plastic can may be a better choice.
Hand-held hoses	Ideal for watering potted and individual plants. Can be adjusted to a hard squirt setting for washing off aphids or to a gentle shower for watering newly planted seedlings.	In times of water shortages, their use is restricted. Also, most of us don't have enough time or patience to water a garden thoroughly with a hand-held hose.
Weeping hoses	Often made from recycled materials, such as old tyres. Cheap to buy and easy to install. Place beneath mulch in order to direct water to root level, where it's needed.	Several hoses may be needed to deliver sufficient water to plants in a large garden bed. Slow rate of delivery means the water may need to run for a long time.
Sprinklers	One of the best ways of thoroughly watering lawns or large garden areas. Cheap and easy to install, sprinklers mimic natural rainfall and distribute water evenly.	Not available to everyone. In some areas of Australia council regulations now prohibit the use of sprinklers during times of water shortage. Can waste water.
Micro-irrigation	An efficient irrigation method. The small spray heads give a good range of coverage, from 90 to 360 degrees, and can be tailored to the needs of individual areas.	Spray heads can get blocked with dirt or insect nests. If you don't remember where the concealed supply hose is, it's easy to put a garden fork through it.
Drip systems	Water isn't wasted because it can be directed to the roots of individual plants and there is little loss through evaporation. Effective where water pressure is low.	Difficult to fit into established gardens with many different types of plants. Can be expensive and labour-intensive to install. May need to run for many hours.

■ ■ ■ **Stick a finger** in the soil to see if your garden is getting enough water – it's the most accurate gauge.

Water for the garden

In many areas water is a limited resource. Plants don't need drinking-quality water, so make the most of what's available naturally by collecting rain and diverting run-off, or by recycling household waste water. While it may not be possible to become completely self-sufficient, you can reduce your water consumption as well as the costs to you and the environment.

TANK TIPS

Install a rainwater tank to collect water for the garden. Consider what type will best suit your needs (see *Collecting water*, p. 36). Correctly siting your tank is also important for maximising efficiency.

- Never install a rainwater tank without first checking the local council regulations, including details on required distances from boundaries and drains.
- Look at where your downpipes are and consider siting your tank close by. It will save on extra pipes and you can easily redirect any overflow into the stormwater.
- Choose to site your tank in a naturally cool spot – on the south or east side of the house is ideal. Unwanted algae is likely to multiply in tanks where the water is warm.
- If you can, try to site your tank at a high point in the garden. This way you can use gravity, rather than a pump, to move the water around.
- If you do need a pump – to increase pressure for sprayers or to push water uphill – make sure you have a weatherproof power outlet nearby. Your external electricity box can be useful for this.
- For units and small houses where space is limited, consider a water wall, a vertical storage system available from hardware stores, which can double as a fence.
- Use some form of meshing, such as shadecloth, to prevent your tank becoming a breeding ground for mosquitoes.

Rainwater should provide between 30 and 40 per cent of the water you use on your garden.

SCREENS FOR TANKS

Although water tanks provide environmental and economic benefits, they are not particularly attractive and can be an eyesore in a small area. Here are some ideas for concealing a tank.

- You may be able to install a tank underground. It will depend on the type of soil or rock in your garden, whether there's enough access for excavation equipment and the amount of money you want to spend.
- Paint the tank the same colour as the wall so it will blend in better with its surroundings.
- Put tubs of bamboo in front of the tank for an instant screen.
- Another idea for a ready-made screen is to erect panels of reed, bamboo or tea-tree (from hardware stores and landscape suppliers).

WHY USE RAINWATER?

Installing a rainwater tank will save you money on water bills and provide a backup supply during droughts and periods of restrictions. You'll also be doing your bit to help the environment by:

- ✔ Reducing pressure on water supplies
- ✔ Conserving valuable drinking water
- ✔ Protecting river catchments
- ✔ Limiting stormwater run-off
- ✔ Creating a ready resource for firefighting

■ ■ ■ **Plastic rainwater tanks known as water walls can double as garden fences or patio dividers.**

- For a fast, seasonal cover, grow tall annuals, such as sunflowers and sweet peas.
- Place a trellis around the tank and cover it with a fast-growing evergreen climbing plant, such as orange trumpet creeper (*Pyrostegia venusta*).
- Plant a row of evergreen shrubs in front of the tank and train them as a narrow living screen. Some suitable choices include bottlebrushes, dwarf conifers, pohutukawa (New Zealand Christmas tree), photinia or viburnum.
- Stretch wires between two posts in front of the tank and train a plant, such as a citrus, as an espalier. Tie the branches to the wires and prune them in order to achieve a horizontal effect.

THE TRUTH ABOUT...

MAINS WATER

Some people believe that because of its chlorine content, mains water is bad for their plants. In fact, the low levels of chlorine in mains water and its fast rate of dispersal when it is exposed to light mean that chlorine has no effect on garden plants. In some areas where the mains water is alkaline, however, the neutral to slightly acid pH of rainwater is better for acid-loving plants such as camellias, azaleas, rhododendrons and citrus. This is another benefit of using rainwater on your garden.

USING GREY WATER

The water from the laundry and bathroom is a great additional resource for gardens where rainwater is scarce. The average household produces between 200 and 800 litres of grey water a week. If your system is set up efficiently, it will need little effort to use this regularly. Take these precautions to make grey water safe (see also *Recycling water*, p. 38).

- Check the legal requirements with your local council. Most authorities insist that water must be kept within the boundary of where it was produced. Therefore it mustn't go onto a neighbour's land, or into stormwater drains.
- It's best to apply grey water to your garden using a subsurface irrigation system. If you pour it directly onto the surface of your garden, it can become a health hazard for humans and animals.
- Use only the rinsing water from a load of washing, so that you're not introducing concentrated detergents into the garden.

- Don't use any water from a washing-machine load of nappies as it may contain faecal matter that carries pathogens.
- Use grey water only when it has cooled, as hot water can damage plant roots.
- Where grey water is continually applied, treat the soil with gypsum to help break down salts such as sodium (present in some detergents and washing powders), which could eventually kill plant life. Diluting with rain or mains water will also help.

• *Recycle rinsing water from your washing machine onto your garden.*

- The fats from the soap in grey water can make the soil water-repellent. If this occurs, treat the soil with a wetting agent every 6 months or so.
- When it's raining, don't use grey water – let it run down the drain.
- Don't use grey water to water vegetables or children's play areas.
- Check the pH of your soil. Grey water tends to increase its alkalinity, which can lead to iron deficiencies in plants. (Symptoms include new yellow leaves and green veins.) If necessary, remedy the problem by adding sulphate or iron to the soil.
- Don't use grey water on the garden if it is likely to contain phosphorus (present in some detergents). Native plants and proteas struggle with excess phosphorus, as it is toxic to them. Too much phosphorus in other plants can cause iron deficiencies.
- Use less fertiliser.

■ ■ ■ **Add a few drops of vegetable oil** to the water in tanks and barrels to PREVENT MOSQUITOES from breeding.

Water-wise design

The key to creating a water-wise garden lies in good soil preparation before you plant and appropriate care immediately after planting. The main ingredients are lots of organic matter and mulch. If you want to cut down on garden maintenance and conserve water, these are good principles for all gardens, not just those in dry areas.

GETTING STARTED

- Dig over the soil to break up large clods and remove any stones. This will help moisture to permeate the earth particles.
- Check how well your soil drains by using the *Draining check*, at right. Good drainage is essential for a water-wise garden.
- Add lots of organic matter – compost, mushroom compost and manure – to the soil, digging it in to at least a spade's depth.
- Group plants according to their water needs. That way, you can water all the thirsty plants together and leave the tougher ones to survive on rainfall.
- Make a saucer-shaped depression around the base of each plant so that any rainfall will be directed towards the root system.
- Even the most drought-tolerant plant will need watering when it is first planted, so drench the area with a watering can full of water, adding it gradually and making sure that it soaks in.
- Cover the root area with mulch, taking care not to allow it to build up around the stem or trunk of the plant. Otherwise, the plant could develop collar rot.
- Allow the roots to become established and gradually reduce watering until the plants are surviving on natural rainfall.

DRAINAGE CHECK

To find out how well water is held in your soil, dig a hole and fill it with water. Time how long it takes for the soil to absorb the water.

- ✗ 0–60 minutes: You need to improve the soil before you start planting.
- ✗ 1–4 hours: Add plenty of organic matter.
- ✓ 4–8 hours: The soil is great, start planting.
- ✗ More than 8 hours: The soil is badly drained, dig in some gypsum and try again.

WATER-WISE CHOICES

Conserve water and save money by choosing your plants carefully. Research their moisture requirements before you buy.

- Native Australian trees, shrubs and grasses from low rainfall areas all cope well with prolonged dry periods.
- Eucalypts and wattles (*Acacia* species) are good choices for a water-wise garden, because their leaves hang vertically, reducing exposure to the sun and cutting down on the amount of water loss.
- Choose plants with silver or grey leaves, such as lamb's ear (*Stachys byzantina*). These are covered with a downy hair that reduces water loss.
- Most air plants, such as Spanish moss (*Tillandsia usneoides*), need no watering at all, managing to survive on the moisture they draw from the atmosphere.

Many exotic plants are drought-tolerant too. Do some research to find out which plants are suited to your area.

Ten 'plant and forget' choices

Plant	Plant type	Conditions
Blue chalk sticks (*Senecio serpens*)	Groundcover	Full sun, well-drained soil
Bromeliads (many genera)	Groundcover or clumps	Full sun to shade
Coastal rosemary (*Westringia fruticosa*)	Shrub	Full sun, well-drained soil
Creeping boobialla (*Myoporum parvifolium*)	Groundcover	Full sun to part shade
Dianella (*Dianella* species)	Grass-like clump	Shade
Lomandra (*Lomandra longifolia*)	Grass	Full sun
New Zealand flaxes (*Phormium* species)	Stiff clump/perennial	Full sun
Succulents (many genera)	Groundcover to shrubs	Full sun
Tussock grasses (*Poa* species)	Grass	Full sun
Yuccas (*Yucca* species)	Clump-forming shrub	Full sun

WHAT IS XERISCAPING?

Xeriscaping, or dry landscaping, is a garden design technique that aims to conserve water.

- Use contouring, in the form of low mounds and shallow channels, to direct the flow of any available water towards larger plants.
- Replace the lawn with paving and hard surfaces.
- Select plants that grow naturally in arid regions and will survive without additional water once they are established.
- To retain moisture, cover soil with mulch. Gravel or pebbles provide a decorative effect in low-water gardens.

SMART SOLUTIONS

Gardens that use little water don't have to look like deserts. Here are some alternatives.

- It may seem illogical, but once established, rainforest gardens need little extra water. Many rainforest plants, such as palms and tree ferns, can survive long dry periods outside the wet season. They need a good layer of organic mulch and the occasional deep watering when rainfall is scarce.
- Without their leaves, deciduous plants need little water during winter, and many survive with little extra moisture in summer. They need water most in spring, when they're forming new leaves and flowers. Fortunately, in many areas, this coincides with the period of highest rainfall.
- Water gardens don't use a lot of water after they've been set up. Just top them up occasionally with small quantities of water to balance what is lost through evaporation.

DRY SPECIALISTS

Cacti enjoy dry, humidity-free conditions, particularly in winter, and need very little water.

- Grow cacti in pots or in the ground depending on your climate. They need very well-drained soils or potting mixes. To flourish, cacti also need good light, warmth and ventilation.
- Give them some additional water in early spring as this is the time when they are flowering and forming fruit and seeds.
- To reduce overwatering in poorly drained or damp areas, grow cacti in raised beds or under eaves.
- Use a mulch of gravel around cacti. As well as conserving soil moisture and reducing evaporation, the gravel keeps humidity in check.

hot links

Plant lists and tips for water-efficient gardens:
www.conservewater.melbournewater.com.au;
www.plantsinternational.com.au/info/waterw.php;
www.nreta.nt.gov.au/whatwedo/waterwise/gardening.html
Xeriscape site: www.xeriscape.org

In prolonged dry times, all plants – even the most water-wise – will benefit from extra moisture.

PLANTING GUIDE

Save money and look after the environment by growing your own chemical-free produce and flowers.

Creating a vegetable patch

There's nothing like the taste of fresh vegetables, just pulled from the earth or picked from the vine. A vegetable patch gives you the convenience of having instant produce to hand, and, by growing your own, you can minimise or avoid the use of pesticides or manufactured fertilisers. That's good for your health and good for the environment. And if you plan carefully, it's possible to have fresh vegetables all year.

VEGIE PATCH KNOW-HOW

1 Don't make your first vegetable patch too big. Start on a small scale, and if you find you need more space, you can extend the area later.

2 Choose disease-resistant varieties that will grow well in your climate or situation.

3 For a continuous supply of vegetables, make small, successive sowings. Use seeds or advanced seedlings rather than buy entire punnets that may have more plants than you need.

4 Use a mulch between the rows and between individual plants to suppress weed growth. If any weeds do appear, pull them up straight away.

5 Provide shade for plantings made in summer with a temporary shadecloth screen, which you can then remove as the plants become established.

6 Give the growing crops a quick check every day. All you need is 5 minutes for watering, harvesting any crops and keeping an eye out for pests and diseases.

7 Accept some damage to leaves and other parts of the plant that you won't eat rather than use chemicals to control pests. Try companion planting (see *Natural partners*, p. 226) as your first line of defence. If you need extra help, consider using biological controls or introduce some beneficial insects.

8 Water your vegetable garden in the early morning or evening, never in the heat of the day as the moisture will be lost through evaporation.

9 To maximise the use of nutrients and to prevent the build-up of pests and diseases, avoid growing members of the same vegetable family in the same part of your garden in successive seasons. For instance, don't grow broccoli after a crop of cabbage – they are both members of the brassica family.

10 Plant flowering ornamentals such as lavender among vegetables to attract pollinating insects. Planting sweet peas next to runner beans will encourage early pollination of beans.

■ ■ ■ **Coordinate your plantings** with neighbours or family, so that you don't all grow the same crop and can share the harvest.

Dwarf vegetable varieties

Vegetable	Variety	Harvest time
Bean	'Pioneer'	Summer
Beetroot	'Baby'	Spring to summer
Carrot	'Baby'	Year round
Chilli	'Thai Chilli'	Spring to autumn
Lettuce	'Salad Bowl'	Year round
Peas	'Earlicrop Massey'	Autumn to spring
Radish	'Salad Crunch'	Year round
Tomato	'Tiny Tim'	Spring to autumn

PROS & CONS

DO HOME-GROWN VEGIES SAVE MONEY?

In the first year, savings will be hard to make with set-up costs – for fencing, edging, fertilisers and plants. Ongoing costs can outweigh savings too, if you continue to buy seedlings and fertilisers. For maximum savings, grow your plants from seed, make your own compost and mulch, look for free manure from farms and minimise your use of chemicals. In addition, choose to grow plants that can be costly at the greengrocers such as tomatoes, Asian greens, runner beans, sugar snap peas, snow peas and silver beet.

~ FLYING START ~

Try planting old-fashioned vegetable varieties, called heirloom vegetables. Many of these have superior flavour, crop abundantly and have good disease resistance. They're perfect for home gardens where they can be picked and used straight away.

SELECTING THE RIGHT SITE

- Check the drainage. Dig a hole about 30 cm deep and fill it with water. If the water sits in the hole for hours, you will need to either install agricultural pipe, to carry excess water away, or grow your vegetables in raised beds.
- Choose an area that receives at least 6 hours of sun every day, preferably from the morning onwards. If your backyard isn't sunny enough, think about locating your plot in the front yard.
- If the lawn is in the sunniest spot in your garden, consider replacing it. Dig up the turf and use it elsewhere, kill the grass by covering it with newspaper and plastic, or build a raised garden (see *Building a 'no-dig' garden*, p. 231).
- Don't plant your vegetable patch too close to large, established trees. The trees will shade the vegetables and compete with them for water and nutrients.

MAKING A MINI VEGETABLE GARDEN

- If space is tight, grow a salad in a large container. Surround a small-growing tomato with soft-hearted lettuce and clumps of chives.
- Look for non-running forms of vegetables such as bush zucchini and bush pumpkin.
- Try the dwarf form of these varieties, which are also suitable for growing in containers: beetroot (you'll need a soil depth of at least 20 cm so the roots have room to form), capsicum, chillies, eggplant, beans, lettuce, rhubarb, shallots, silver beet and tomato.
- Don't forget that you can garden vertically as well as horizontally! Make a tripod for climbing peas and beans by tying three hardwood stakes or bamboo poles together at the top, and then wrapping some wire netting around the stakes.

hot links

Groups dedicated to conserving heirloom vegetable varieties: www.seedsavers.net; www.seedsavers.org.nz; www.diggers.com.au; www.koanga.co.nz/pages/buy_seeds.html
Starting a vegetable garden: www.thevegetablepatch.com; www.bestgardening.com/bgc/howto/vege.htm

■ ■ ■ Vegetables can be grown very successfully in flower beds, in pots, on a patio or balcony, or on a sunny windowsill.

Vegetables for all seasons

Crop	Harvest time	Harvesting tips	Storage and cooking tips
Asparagus	Spring	Leave uncut in the first year. In the second year, cut the spear just below the soil, using a sharp knife.	Cut ends off then stand in a small container of water in the fridge. Cover with plastic.
Beetroot	10 weeks from sowing	Young beetroot has the best flavour, but the crop can be stored in the ground and harvested over many months.	The leaves can also be picked for salads.
Cabbage	Summer to autumn or 8–16 weeks from sowing	Harvest the entire plant when heads are firm and plump.	Can be sliced, blanched for 3–4 minutes and stored in the freezer.
Carrots	Year round	Pick continuously to spread the harvest.	Small young carrots have the best flavour.
Parsnips	18–20 weeks after planting	Pick continuously to spread the harvest. Pull baby parsnips at 2–3 months or leave in the ground for up to 6 months.	Store out of the light for 1–2 weeks, or in the vegetable crisper for several weeks.
Potatoes	Spring	Pick after flowering, when the leaves start to turn yellow.	Store out of the light to prevent greening (the formation of alkaloids).
Pumpkin	Autumn	Harvest when the stems begin to wither and when the vine starts to die off.	Cure (harden the skin) in a warm spot, but store in a cool, dry space on a wire rack.
Sweet corn	Spring to autumn or 10 weeks after sowing	When the silks turn brown, the corn is ready to pick.	To maximise flavour, cook as soon as possible after picking.
Sweet potatoes	Autumn or 20 weeks after planting	Tubers are mature when the plants turn yellow.	Leave tubers in the sun to cure for a few days after digging up.
Tomatoes	Early summer to autumn (year round in warm climates)	For the best flavour, allow fruits to ripen on the vine.	In fruit fly zones, pick full-sized green tomatoes and ripen them inside the home to reduce pest damage.

TOMATOES

If you plan well, you can have home-grown tomatoes on the table at Christmas, a time of year when they're expensive to buy.

- Plant seedlings in late spring. In cool areas, keep plants in pots and in a warm, sheltered spot until all threat of frost has passed. In all areas, if frost or cold nights are forecast, cover seedlings at night because low temperatures inhibit fruit from forming.
- Select early-maturing varieties such as the 'Marmande' forms. These take less time to form fruit than other varieties and have greater cold tolerance, so they are more likely to be cropping by mid-summer. 'Rouge de Marmande' matures 77 days after planting.
- Choose the sunniest part of the garden for a tomato bed, and dig in lots of organic matter such as compost and well-rotted manure that will improve the moisture-holding capacity of your soil.
- Keep your tomato plants well watered. Begin liquid feeding with an organic fertiliser once the first flowers appear.

■ ■ ■ **Early-maturing tomatoes** are less likely to be affected by fruit fly than later-maturing varieties, making them easy to grow.

CARROTS

Carrots are fun to grow because they are easy. They can be grown from seed, take about three months to mature and can be eaten raw or cooked.

- In warm areas, sow carrot seed at any time. In temperate areas, sow from July to March. In cold climates, sow from August to February.
- Prepare the soil carefully. Carrots need deep, sandy or loam soils with good drainage. If you have clay soil, sow carrots in a raised bed and try stump-rooted varieties, such as 'Early Chantenay'.
- Remove all rocks, stones and lumps, as these will cause the roots to become forked and misshapen.
- Carrot seeds are tiny and difficult to handle, so mix them with fine sand before sowing (or buy seeds on paper tape). Then simply pour the sand and seed mixture along the prepared row.
- Thin out excess carrots to 2–3 cm apart when they're around 5 cm high. Thin them again to about 5 cm apart when the plants are around 15 cm high.

Easy vegetables for beginners include Asian greens, carrots, cherry tomatoes, green beans, pumpkin, radishes, repeat harvest lettuce, silver beet and zucchini.

LETTUCE

- Ask your local nursery for advice about the best varieties of lettuce to sow. There are several different varieties available for sowing at different times of the year.
- Avoid sowing in hot weather. If the temperature is 30°C or above, moisten the seeds, place them on a paper towel and place in the fridge for about a day before sowing.
- Plant out in the garden or, if space is limited, use a large bowl-shaped container with a good-quality potting mix. This is ideal for a balcony or small patio. Some varieties make an attractive display.
- Keep the soil moist until the seedlings appear. Water every day in summer, but avoid overhead watering in the heat of the day.
- Although mature plants need full sun, use shadecloth, cardboard or taller plants such as beans to shade new plantings from afternoon sun until they're established. In hot inland climates, lettuce need light shade in summer.

GROWING POTATOES IN OLD TYRES

Here's how to recycle tyres and grow a delicious crop at the same time. You'll need:

2 old car tyres
hay, compost or potting mix
seed potatoes (potato tuber)

- Place an old car tyre flat on the ground.
- Add a layer of hay, compost or potting mix, and then place a couple of seed potatoes on top.
- Bury the potatoes by placing more hay, compost or potting mix on top of them.
- Water well.
- As the potatoes grow, put another tyre on top of the first and add more hay, compost or potting mix. If necessary, repeat the process as the plants grow.
- Begin to harvest the first small potatoes after a few months.
- Harvest the full crop after the tops have started to die down.

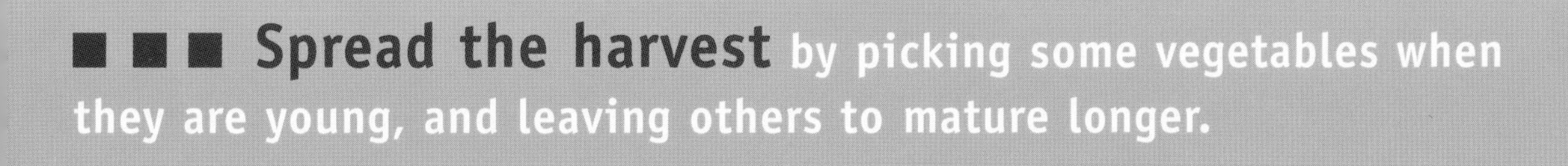

Spread the harvest by picking some vegetables when they are young, and leaving others to mature longer.

Growing a herb garden

The scent of herbs wafting through the garden on a warm, sunny day is the essence of summer. Even if you don't have room for a full-sized vegetable garden, you can always squeeze in a few herbs to add freshness and flavour to your food. Some herbs also function as earth-wise insect controllers and many have medicinal properties.

CHOOSING THE RIGHT SPOT

If you're planning to use herbs for cooking, select an area that is convenient to the kitchen door. If you just want to enjoy their beauty and aroma, or to attract bees, consider these options.

~ *FLYING START* ~

Try growing basil, chives, dill, garlic, mint, oregano, parsley, rocket and thyme if you're new to herb cultivation – they're easy to cultivate, and ideal for beginners.

- Plant herbs at random in the garden, wherever there's a sunny spot, or create a dedicated area for them. You could grow them in beds of their own, arranged in rows with brick or stone paths in between the beds, or in a geometric pattern.
- Consider planting herbs in rockeries where heat-loving varieties such as thyme will thrive. They can also be grown as borders along the edges of garden beds or paths, or in pots. Parsley, for example, looks great used in this way.
- To attract bees and other beneficial insects, grow herbs such as rosemary, lavender, coriander and dill in the vegetable garden.

GROWING HERBS IN POTS

- If space is limited, plant herbs in pots. You could also use troughs, tubs and window boxes. Use hanging baskets for herbs with a cascading or trailing habit, such as thyme, mint and oregano.
- Use a strawberry pot for growing herbs. This has planting pockets in the sides, which make good spots for herbs. Put low-growing varieties, such as thyme, in the sides of the pot and taller ones, such as chives, in the top.
- Use containers for growing mints and other invasive herbs. Large troughs or recycled laundry tubs are ideal.

TIPS FOR HEALTHY HERBS

- Protect annual herbs from extreme summer heat by covering them with shadecloth or by misting the leaves.
- Avoid the problem of bolting – when a plant sends up flower stalks and goes to seed prematurely, making the herb lose its flavour and become bitter – by selecting 'bolt-resistant' or 'slow-bolting' varieties.
- Grow herbs at the correct time of year because temperature extremes may encourage bolting. Coriander, for example, is best grown in the cooler months, when it will develop more slowly.
- Sow dill seed directly into the soil. Thin the seedlings and harvest regularly, as crowded plants are more likely to bolt.
- Remove insect pests by hand and always wash herbs thoroughly before use in case any pests remain.
- As a last resort, use a spray oil or soap spray to get rid of pests. Or try Dipel (*Bacillus thuringiensis*), a bacterium that will control caterpillars but is harmless to other insects.
- Trim back damaged growth, and apply a liquid fertiliser and water to encourage new, undamaged growth.

■ ■ ■ The key to growing herbs SUCCESSFULLY is planting them in a sunny, well-drained spot.

HARVESTING AND STORING HERBS

- Pick herbs just as they begin to flower. This is the time when the oil content in the leaves is greatest so the taste is at its peak.
- So the herbs will dry without attracting mould or mildew, tie the stems and hang them upside down in a warm, airy place. When they are dry, pick off the leaves and store them in an airtight container.
- To dry herbs in the microwave, place leaves between two sheets of paper towel and cook them on 'high' until the leaves become brittle (about 1 or 2 minutes, depending on your microwave).
- To dry herbs in the oven, place leaves on an oven tray and dry on the lowest temperature setting. Herbs can also be dried in home food dehydrators.
- Some herbs – including basil, parsley and tarragon – keep well if frozen. Pick the herbs, give them a quick wash and then chop the leaves. Put the chopped leaves into ice-cube trays filled with water. When frozen, store the herb cubes in a plastic bag in the freezer, ready to add to any bubbling pot for both flavour and fragrance.

MEDICINAL HERBS

- Aloe vera has both antibacterial and antifungal properties, and helps cuts and burns to heal. To use, just break open a leaf to access the gel.
- Calendula (*Calendula officinalis*) is widely used to heal wounds, burns, insect bites, eczema, skin ulcers and rashes. It is often used in commercial ointments.
- Chamomile (*Chamaemelum nobile*) flowers can be dried and used to make a tea that soothes nausea.
- Feverfew (*Chrysanthemum parthenium* syn. *Tanacetum parthenium*) is believed to alleviate headaches. It is often included in herbal medicines.
- Garlic (*Allium sativum*) is said to lower cholesterol levels, reduce blood pressure, prevent cancer, treat infection and enhance the body's immunity to infection.
- Ginger (*Zingiber officinale*) helps to alleviate digestive ailments, motion sickness and nausea. It can be used to make a refreshing tea.
- Valerian (*Valeriana officinalis*) has traditionally been used to treat anxiety, stress and insomnia. For a relaxing soak, add it to a warm bath.

Culinary herbs

Style	Herbs
French	Chives, lemon verbena, marjoram, tarragon, thyme
Greek	Chives, Greek basil, marjoram, oregano, sweet basil
Italian	Chives, garlic, oregano, parsley, rosemary, sage, sweet basil
Mexican	Chillies, chives, coriander, nasturtiums
Thai	Coriander, ginger, lemon basil, lemon grass, Thai mint, Vietnamese mint

hot links

General information on herbs and their uses:
www.global-garden.com.au/gardenherbs.htm;
www.organicdownunder.com/Herbs.htm;
www.botanical.com; www.livingherbs.co.nz

BAY TREE Native to the Mediterranean region, bay trees grow to around 10 metres tall but can be kept clipped as small shrubs. They can also be grown in large tubs as ornamental topiary plants. Use the leaves in bouquet garni, soups, stocks and stews but remove them before serving.

LAVENDER (*Right*) Grown for its attractive flower spikes and fragrant leaves, lavender can be used as an informal hedge or a cottage garden plant. Oil from this hardy perennial is used in perfumes and soaps and as a disinfectant. It is also used to treat insomnia, anxiety and depression.

ROSEMARY This is an attractive shrub that grows to around 1.5 metres tall, making it ideal for hedges. Add sprigs of rosemary to a lamb roast or use rosemary stalks instead of skewers.

Creating a backyard orchard

While the idea of an orchard may sound ambitious for a suburban backyard, there are some clever ways to cram fruit-bearing plants into small spaces. Wherever possible, plant a productive tree, shrub or climber – grow a nut tree for shade, train a passionfruit, grapevine or kiwi fruit over an arbour, or plant a hedge of fruit-bearing plants for a privacy screen.

✓ BUY WISELY

- Purchase bare-rooted fruit trees in winter. They're cost-effective because you don't pay for the transporting and handling of heavy pots and soil.
- Choose dwarf varieties of fruit trees. You'll save money because smaller trees cost less to fertilise, water and maintain.
- Plant a 'fruit salad' tree. Multi-grafted trees are cheaper because there are several fruit varieties on the one plant.

PLANTING FRUIT TREES

- Always plant grafted, named varieties, rather than grow your fruit trees from pips. Seedlings can be unreliable and they may take many years to bear fruit.
- Choose varieties that are suitable for your climate and situation. When you bring the trees home from the nursery, plant them as soon as possible – it's important not to let the roots dry out.
- Mound the soil in the bottom of the hole, and then spread the roots over the mound. Position the strongest root in the direction of the prevailing wind. Make sure that the bud or graft union is above the soil level.
- Apply a slow-release fertiliser at planting time, or a complete fertiliser in spring when growth begins. Fertilisers rich in potash encourage flowering and fruit.
- Is your tree self-fertile or does it need cross-pollination from another variety? Many fruit trees will not set fruit unless their pollination requirements are met. Some are self-pollinating (only one plant is required), while others require pollen from a tree of a different variety but of the same species.
- When planting for pollination, plant the pollinator no more than 30 metres away so the bees don't have too far to travel!
- Try planting these easy-to-grow citrus varieties – 'Emperor' mandarin, 'Valencia' orange, 'Eureka' lemon (in cool areas, plant 'Meyer' lemon), 'Tahitian' lime and 'Marsh' grapefruit.

MAKING A MINI ORCHARD

- Plant dwarf varieties. They produce the same-sized fruit, but take up less space. There are dwarf cultivars of apples, citrus, nectarines, peaches and plums that can be grown in small spaces or even in containers – perfect for a balcony.
- Save space by planting multi-grafted trees. Different varieties are available, including citrus, apple, pear and stone fruit. You can select combinations for your climate, and include compatible varieties for cross-pollination on the one tree.
- Espalier fruit trees against a fence or trellis to save space and to create a feature (pictured at left).

■ ■ ■ **Prune deciduous fruit trees** to an open, vase shape, to let in light and encourage flowers and fruit.

MAKING A FRUIT FLY TRAP

In many areas, fruit fly is the fruit grower's number one enemy. A fruit fly trap will not only reduce the fruit fly population but it will also allow you to monitor their presence so you'll know when to begin preventive treatments.

- Punch several 6 mm holes in the neck of a 1 litre plastic bottle. To attract the fruit fly, put a bait in the bottle, along with a few drops of methylated spirits. Suitable baits include yeast spread, port wine, vanilla essence and sugar.
- Hang the bottle in the tree, just above the lower leaves. Replace the bait at least twice a week. Start using the traps about 6 weeks before harvest time, as the fruit begins to ripen, and continue until the fruit has been picked.

ORCHARDS FOR LARGER GARDENS

- If you have enough room, dedicate an area of the garden to the orchard. A well-drained position in full sun is best. A north-facing slope is ideal.
- When you're planning your orchard, bear in mind that most fruit trees take two years to begin cropping, and that trees grown from seed may take seven years or longer.
- Fence off the orchard to keep animals out. Before planting, establish windbreaks on the south, west and east sides of the area.
- Don't plant your fruit trees too close together or they will compete for sunlight and nutrients. They will also be stressed, susceptible to insect and fungal attack and will not crop well. To work out how much space to leave between them, check the mature size and height of all the varieties you've chosen.
- If you decide to have grassy paths between the trees, make sure there's enough access for a lawn mower. Plant in straight lines to make mowing easier.
- Think about grouping fruit trees with similar pest and disease management needs. For example, treating citrus trees suffering from citrus leaf miner will be easier if all the trees are together.

NATURAL PEST CONTROL

- Hang bird scarers such as fake snakes, unwanted CDs, the empty and inflated bladders of wine casks, wind chimes or small mirrors in your trees.
- Grow a line of 'sacrificial' trees along the orchard boundary. Leave these for the possums, birds and bats who may leave the fruit on the other trees for you!
- Drape bird netting over your trees. It's the most effective way of stopping birds from eating your fruit, but make sure you check the nets regularly and release any trapped birds.
- Let your chickens forage in the orchard. They'll help control pests and fertilise the trees at the same time.
- To avoid attracting flies, remove rotten or infested fruit. Don't compost it, but wrap it in newspaper and put it in the garbage bin.

Nectarines, peaches and plums are ideal for bottling. Alternatively, turn your excess crop into jam.

hot links

Fruit fly and tropical fruit information: www.dpi.qld.gov.au/horticulture
Fruit production information: www.agric.nsw.gov.au/reader/hort
Netting of garden fruit trees: www.nationalparks.nsw.gov.au/npws.nsf/Content/Netting+of+garden+fruit+trees+-+guidelines+to+protect+wildlife

Find out if your neighbour has fruit trees – they might serve as POLLINATORS for your trees.

Nature's powerhouses

Every garden needs at least one tree. Trees offer a wealth of earth-wise benefits, such as water conservation, to your immediate surroundings and add to the natural beauty of your local area. And if you plant a tree, you're providing shade, shelter, perches, roosts and food for birds, animals and insects.

PLANT FOR THE FUTURE

The lifespan of a tree depends on its species, growing conditions and climate. Trees can live for centuries or they can reach decline in seven to ten years, so it's worth considering the future.

- To find out which trees are likely to grow well in your area, look at mature trees in nearby gardens, parks or street plantings.
- If you live in a bushfire area, don't plant trees that may add to the danger. Eucalypts, for example, harbour leaf and bark debris and contain high levels of volatile oils.
- Research the maximum height and habit of the tree you want to plant. Check books, read plant labels and ask the local nursery to point out a mature tree of the sort you're thinking of planting.
- Avoid potential disputes with your neighbours by avoiding trees with invasive root systems. These can block drains and cause severe structural damage to your own house as well as your neighbour's.
- Don't plant trees that can become environmental weeds. Ask your local council for a list.
- Keep paths, paved areas, gutters and drains clear of leaves and debris from your tree.
- Replace old or damaged drainage pipes with plastic pipes that will not be damaged by tree roots.
- Seek local council permission before removing or heavily pruning a tree. Most trees are protected by tree preservation orders.
- Each winter, check deciduous trees while they are leafless for signs of borer, invading climbing plants or broken limbs.
- Watch for signs of weakness such as dieback. Dead twigs at the tips of branches indicate problems with the tree's root system.

Trees that need room		Trees for small spaces	
Evergreen	Deciduous	Evergreen	Deciduous
Conifers (large species, including *Cupressus torulosa*)	Coral trees (*Erythrina* species)	Blueberry ash (*Elaeocarpus reticulatus*)	Chinese tallow tree (*Sapium sebiferum*)
Evergreen alder (*Alnus acuminata*)	Elm (*Ulmus* species)	Citrus (*Citrus* species)	Crab-apple (*Malus* species)
Evergreen figs (*Ficus* species)	Fiddlewood (*Citharexylum spinosum*)	Dwarf flowering gum (*Eucalyptus* 'Summer Beauty' and 'Summer Red')	Crepe myrtle (*Lagerstroemia indica*)
Gum trees (*Eucalyptus* species)	Jacaranda (*Jacaranda mimosifolia*)	Gordonia (*Gordonia axillaris*)	Japanese maple (*Acer palmatum*)
Norfolk Island pine (*Araucaria heterophylla*)	Liquidambar (*Liquidambar styraciflua*)	Ivory curl (*Buckinghamia celsissima*)	Pistachio (*Pistacia chinensis*)
Plum pine (*Podocarpus elatus*)	Poplars (*Populus* species)	*Magnolia grandiflora* 'Little Gem'	*Prunus cerasifera* 'Nigra'
	Robinia (*Robinia pseudoacacia*)		Silk tree (*Albizia julibrissin*)

■ ■ ■ **Free mulch** from fallen leaves and bark is a bonus of growing a tree in your garden.

HOW TO PLANT A TREE

Deciduous trees are sold bare-rooted in winter (and are cheaper and easier to manage at this time). Container-grown trees, from tiny tube stock to mature specimens, are available all year.

• *Bare-rooted trees are wrapped in hessian for sale.*

1 Dig a hole wider and deeper than the root ball. Remove the tree from its container, or unwrap a bare-rooted tree. If the roots are congested, cut them or gently tease them out.

2 Place the tree in the hole so the top of the root ball is level with the soil surface. Backfill, adding organic matter, and gently firm the soil around the root ball. Water in and mulch.

Houses in tree-lined streets sell faster and usually demand a higher price than similar houses in streets with no trees.

WHY PLANT TREES?

✔ They help to prevent erosion.
✔ They take up carbon dioxide from the atmosphere and release oxygen.
✔ They act as filters of undesirable nutrients and pesticides, improving water quality.

LIVING WITH A MATURE TREE

A mature tree is a valuable commodity, both in dollar terms and in its beneficial effect on the environment. So, if you have one in your garden, cherish it.

- Think again if you're considering replacing an old tree with a new, young tree. It will be many years before the young tree can give the same value to the environment that its predecessor provided.
- Water mature trees in times of drought. And don't forget the ones out on the footpath.
- Regularly inspect mature trees for signs of damage and remove encroaching growth from climbing plants, weeds and groundcovers. If you notice problems, call a qualified tree surgeon for advice.
- Seek professional advice before pruning an older tree – it is less likely to tolerate pruning errors, and removing large branches can endanger both tree and pruner. It may be better to thin the canopy.

hot links

Non-profit organisation dedicated to planting trees to improve the environment: www.menofthetrees.org.au
Tree regulations from the International Society of Arboriculture Association: www.isaac.org.au
New Zealand Arboricultural Association: www.nzarbor.org.nz
Planting tips: www.forestfloor.co.nz/ff/plantingtips.htm
The Tree Doctor: www.treedoc.com.au

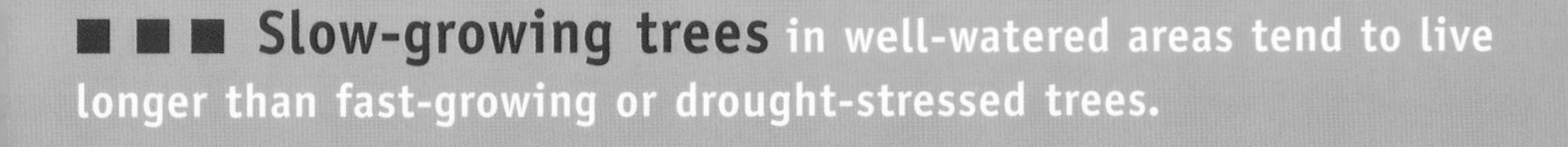

■ ■ ■ **Slow-growing trees** in well-watered areas tend to live longer than fast-growing or drought-stressed trees.

Foliage and fragrance

The workhorses of the plant world, shrubs provide the structure around which the rest of your garden can be designed. They're easy to establish, and cuttings provide a quick and economical way to establish a new garden. They are mostly long-lived and, once established, can survive on minimum care.

CHOOSING A SHRUB

The key to a long-lasting, healthy shrub is buying a good-quality plant in the first place.

- Avoid plants that are pot-bound, with roots spiralling around inside the container, as these will fail to establish when planted.
- Watch out for signs that a plant has been in the pot for too long – faded labels, cracked pots, and roots growing through the drainage holes.
- Check for weeds growing in the pot. They are potential problems.
- Avoid plants with leaves that are discoloured, wilting or damaged. Make sure the branches are strong and not broken.
- Buy extra shrubs as tube stock and grow them in pots so you'll always have spare plants on hand.

~ STAR SAVER ~

For great home-grown presents, try striking these popular plants from cuttings in late summer or autumn: fuchsias, gardenias, hebes, hydrangeas, lavenders and marguerite daisies.

WARNING!

▼ When opening bags of potting mix, take care not to inhale any dust. This is to avoid contact with *Legionella* bacteria. It's best to wear protective clothing such as a dust mask and gloves.

TOP TIP

Roses have a reputation for needing lots of care and attention but in fact, they are drought- and heat-hardy, making them a water-wise choice for your garden, especially in dry inland areas.

POTTED SHRUBS

Shrubs make good, long-lived container plants. They can be used as a screen, as a backdrop for seasonal colour or to accent an entrance.

- Transfer a shrub from its nursery pot to a larger container and then, as it grows, regularly repot it into an increasingly larger container.
- If a shrub is growing in a windy or exposed situation, make sure the pot is large enough to support it.
- Use pot feet or bricks under the pot to improve drainage, but make sure the plant doesn't send roots down to the earth.
- If there is only one drainage hole in the bottom of the pot, use a drill bit to add more.
- Choose a good-quality potting mix with the Australian Standards 'ticks' on the bag. In New Zealand, select a mix from a reliable supplier. Premium mixes need no added fertiliser for 6–8 weeks after planting.
- If the potting mix doesn't contain water-saving crystals, add some. Make sure you carefully follow the instructions on the packet.
- At planting time, sprinkle a few slow-release fertiliser pellets around the plant.
- Lastly, mulch the top of the pot with either an organic mulch, such as compost, or an inert mulch, such as gravel.

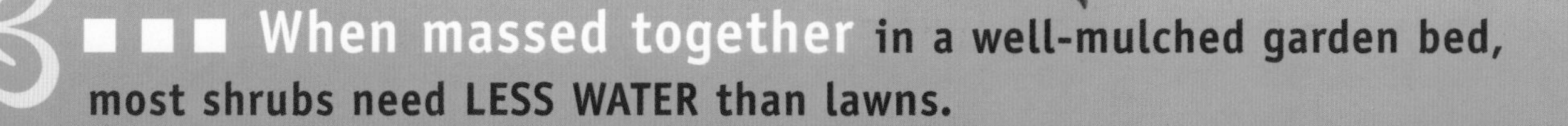

■ ■ ■ **When massed together in a well-mulched garden bed, most shrubs need LESS WATER than lawns.**

HEDGES AND SCREENS

The following shrubs grow to about 3–5 metres but can be pruned for a hedge.

- For an evergreen hedge, try lemonwood (*Pittosporum eugenioides* 'Variegatum'), lilly pilly (*Acmena* and *Syzygium* species) and photinia (*Photinia* species).
- For seasonal flowers and lush green foliage all year round, choose murraya and sasanqua camellias.

HOW TO ESPALIER

An espalier is an ornamental shrub or small tree that is trained to grow flat against a support. Camellias are ideal espaliers.

- Choose to espalier a plant when you want to save space or to hide an ugly wall or fence.
- Select a young plant with open, sprawling growth and several horizontal branches.
- Decide on a type of support. It could be a trellis, a framework made of galvanised wire or just nails or screws.
- Plant the shrub about 5–10 cm out from the wall.
- Attach the branches to the support in either a formal or an informal pattern. Adjust your ties as the plant grows.
- Prune regularly to achieve the desired effect.

SHRUB CARE

You don't need expensive or dangerous chemicals to protect your shrubs from pests or diseases.

- Use lime sulphur straight after winter-pruning dormant shrubs to control scale and fungal diseases.
- Spray aphids with a mild soap solution. Use either pure soap or a soap-based commercial spray.
- For more recipes, see *Going organic*, p. 224, and *Keeping plants healthy*, p. 274.

hot links

National Rose Society of Australia with links to state groups: www.rose.org.au
Help for New Zealand rose enthusiasts: www.nzroseinfo.co.nz

Shrubs for year-round interest

Shrub	Features	Best season	Size
Banksias	Evergreen; bird-attracting flowers	Winter to spring	Groundcover to tall shrub (3–5 m)
Camellias	Glossy evergreen foliage; long-flowering; bird-attracting	Late summer to early spring	Groundcover to tall shrub (3–5 m)
Gardenias	Glossy evergreen foliage; highly fragrant cream flowers	Late spring to autumn	Groundcover to medium-sized shrub (1–3 m)
Grevilleas	Evergreen; colourful, nectar-rich flowers; bird-attracting	Year round, peak flowering autumn to spring	Groundcover to tall shrub (3–5 m)
Hebes	Naturally compact; evergreen; attractive spires of purple, pink or white flowers	Year round, peak flowering spring and autumn	Rounded shrub (1–1.5 m)
Hibiscus	Evergreen; glossy foliage; highly coloured and varied flowers	Spring to autumn	Low to medium-sized shrub (1–3 m)
Osmanthus	Evergreen; highly fragrant, apricot-scented flowers	Autumn to winter	Low to medium-sized shrub (1–2 m)

■ ■ ■ **For a uniform hedge,** look for a named variety and check how high it will GROW and SPREAD. Always plant only one variety.

Flowers for beds and borders

If trees are the roof of the garden and shrubs the walls, then annuals, perennials and bulbs are the colourful cushions. They are also among the best plants for budget-conscious gardeners. And, as an added benefit, the flowers from these plants encourage beneficial insects, including bees and hoverflies, to visit your garden.

ANNUALS

Annuals are plants that grow, flower, set seed and die in one year, or part of a year. Grown from seed or seedlings, annuals are among the cheapest of plants to grow. Here's how to use them.

- As spectacular floral displays, in the form of mass- and drift-plantings, borders, edgings and groundcovers, and in meadow gardens.
- As colourful container plants, in window boxes, pots, tubs and hanging baskets.
- For their scent. Many annuals have beautiful perfumes – sweet pea and stock, for example – and can be included in fragrant and sensory gardens.
- As rapid-growing 'fill-in' plants, to keep down weeds and provide colour, while slower-growing, permanent plantings are establishing.
- To vary your colour scheme from year to year and season to season.
- As cut flowers for indoors. Or buy annuals already in flower. Known as 'potted colour', they are a great alternative to cut flowers.
- To attract beneficial insects. Simple, open flowers, such as *Linaria maroccana,* will do the trick.

PERENNIALS

A perennial is a plant that lives for three or more growing seasons. Very easy to propagate, perennials are a cheap and effective method of stocking a new garden. Once established, they tend to be low maintenance.

- Choose plants to suit your soil, climate and situation. Consider colour, reliability, length of flowering, longevity and form as well as light and shade requirements.
- Before planting, dig over the ground and remove any weeds. Dig in manure and compost, and mulch well to reduce water stress.
- Allow room for plants to expand through their growing season. This will reduce the need for pruning.
- To obtain more plants at no cost, divide an existing clump. Do this

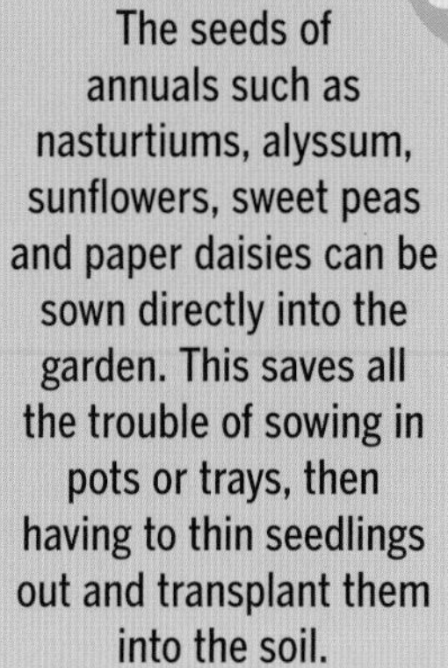

EASY-GOING ANNUALS

Try these undemanding warm-season annuals:

- ✔ Amaranthus
- ✔ Begonia
- ✔ Impatiens
- ✔ Marigold (African and French)
- ✔ Nasturtium
- ✔ Nicotiana
- ✔ Petunia
- ✔ Phlox
- ✔ Salvia
- ✔ Torenia
- ✔ Zinnia

Plant these easy cool-season annuals:

- ✔ Calendula
- ✔ Gomphrena
- ✔ Lobelia
- ✔ Mignonette
- ✔ Nemesia
- ✔ Pansy
- ✔ Poppy
- ✔ Salvia
- ✔ Sweet pea
- ✔ Sweet William
- ✔ Viola
- ✔ Wallflower

TOP TIP

The seeds of annuals such as nasturtiums, alyssum, sunflowers, sweet peas and paper daisies can be sown directly into the garden. This saves all the trouble of sowing in pots or trays, then having to thin seedlings out and transplant them into the soil.

■ ■ ■ **After planting** spring-flowering bulbs, plant pansy seedlings on top as a colourful groundcover until the bulbs shoot.

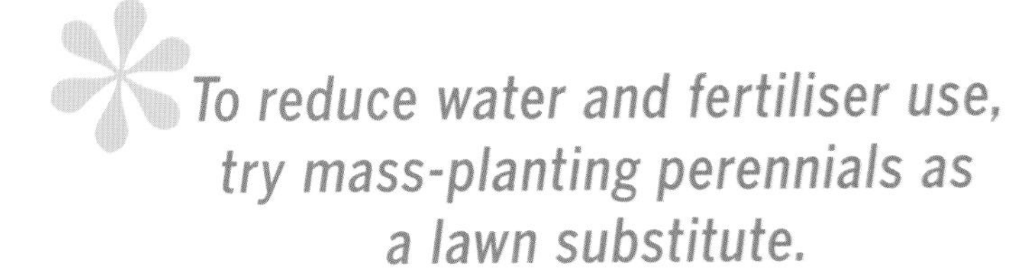

in autumn, when most plants are dormant – just one clump can yield dozens of new plants. Simply dig up the clump and pull it apart, or cut it into sections with a sharp knife.

- Save money by buying perennials in winter, while they are dormant, from mail-order specialists.

BULBS

Grouped together, bulbs require little maintenance. Plant them under trees and leave them to naturalise as a groundcover. Many bulbs, such as bluebells, do well in shady situations, especially under deciduous trees.

- Choose bulbs that are firm and healthy. Avoid smelly, brown and soft ones, as they won't grow, and also bulbs that have started to shoot (unless you plant them straight away).
- Prepare the soil. Bulbs require a well-drained, slightly acidic soil, enriched with organic material and covered with a thick layer of mulch.
- Plant spring-flowering bulbs twice as deep as their diameter – if the bulbs are 2 cm wide, plant them 4 cm deep, pointy end up.
- If mass-planting, use a bulb planter to dig the holes. Or excavate the entire area to the required depth, then simply place bulbs in position and cover them.
- Water well after planting and when bulbs are actively growing. After flowering, continue watering until the leaves start to yellow.

Foolproof perennials

Plant	Aspect	Flowering	Growing notes
Agapanthus	Full sun; drought-tolerant	Summer	Dead-head after flowering to prevent unwanted seeding. Divide in late winter for more plants.
Bearded iris	Full sun; drought-tolerant	Spring to summer; some varieties re-flower in autumn	Great choice for hot, sunbaked spots. Plants are very long-lived and can be divided in late spring or autumn.
Canna	Full sun; moist soil (good for boggy spots)	Spring to autumn	Cut back in late autumn or early spring to make way for new growth. Divide in winter or early spring for more plants.
Clivia	Shade; tolerates poor soil	Winter to spring	Good for mass-planting under trees. Divide clumps or grow from seed for more plants.
Daylily	Full sun	Spring to autumn	In frost-prone areas, choose forms that are dormant over winter. Mass-plant for a long-flowering, trouble-free display.
Geraniums and pelargoniums	Full sun; well-drained soil; tolerate dry conditions	Spring to autumn	Prune in autumn. Pelargoniums grow very easily from cuttings and are great beginner's plants.
Oyster plant	Shade to part shade; tolerates dry soil	Spring to summer	Plants benefit from extra water in dry periods. Divide in winter or sow seed in spring.
Shasta daisy	Full sun; well-drained soil; drought-hardy	Spring to late summer	Pick flowers to encourage more blooms. Easy to divide in late winter: just use a sharp spade.

■ ■ ■ **Order bulbs in bulk** when they are dormant – spring-flowering bulbs in autumn and summer-flowering bulbs in spring.

Lawns and grasses

If you decide to grow a lawn, you can save water by learning which grasses do best in your area and climate and how to look after them. On the other hand, if you want the aesthetic appeal of a green space without the trouble of mowing, there are attractive and earth-wise alternatives to grass.

MAINTAINING AN EARTH-WISE LAWN

- If you live in a warm climate, choose grasses that form runners, such as couch, buffalo and kikuyu. These grasses die back in cold or dry periods, but reshoot from runners with warm weather or rain.
- In a cold climate, plant grasses that form deep-rooted clumps, such as tall fescue, as they can withstand periods with low rainfall.
- Before laying new lawn or sowing seed, mix some water-saving crystals into the turf underlay. This will help the soil to retain moisture.
- When establishing a lawn, water well to ensure the grass puts down a strong root system. Once it is growing well, it can be left to survive on minimal water.
- Cutting the grass too short weakens it, slows the growth, makes it less drought-tolerant and more susceptible to attack by various pests and diseases. Try to keep your grass about 3 cm high.
- Don't mow during very hot or very wet weather.
- Take the catcher off the mower, or use a mulching mower, in order to leave the grass clippings on the lawn. The clippings break down, returning nutrients to the grass.
- Hold off fertilising lawns until good rains fall. Lawns that are fertilised regularly require more water to support lush growth.
- For an economical lawn food, use chicken manure pellets. Apply in spring or autumn when the lawn is growing, after rain. Water in well.
- To even up the surface of your lawn, use river sand as an economical top dressing. Spread the sand with a lawn leveller so the grass is still visible. Water well.
- Aerate the grass to reduce weeds, help prevent compaction and improve drainage and water penetration. Use a garden fork or hire a power aerator from an equipment hire company.
- To discourage lawn weeds that prefer acidic soils, spread garden lime, which is alkaline, over the grass. Water in well. The optimum pH for lawns is 5.5–7.5.

Warm-season grasses	Cool-season grasses
Creeping; grow from runners – for example, buffalo, couch, kikuyu.	Upright – for example, bent, fescue, Kentucky bluegrass, rye.
Grow actively during the warmer months.	Lush and green all year round.
Readily self-repair damaged areas.	Usually don't self-repair, so patch damaged areas from seed.
Slow down over winter, becoming almost dormant and sometimes losing their colour.	Not as robust as warm-season types, particularly over summer, requiring more water than warm-season grasses during summer.
If well-grown, kikuyu and the new varieties of soft buffalo such as 'Palmetto' and 'Sir Walter' have excellent drought-tolerance.	Grows well, with a deep root system; tall fescue varieties have excellent ability to withstand dry times.
When your lawn is 4–5 cm long, set the blades of the lawnmower to cut about 2.5 cm above the ground.	When your lawn is 5–6 cm long, set the blades of the lawnmower to mow about 4 cm above the ground.

■ ■ ■ **Tolerate clover** because it ADDS NITROGEN to the soil. If it looks unruly, just run over it with the mower.

PROS & CONS

HAVING A LAWN

To look lush and green, lawns require regular maintenance, in the form of mowing, edging, fertilising, aerating and weeding. They soak up a lot of water, though there are some drought-hardy varieties, such as buffalo grass, which are suitable for a warm climate. On the other hand, lawns provide a play area for children and pets, and reduce reflected heat near buildings, keeping indoor temperatures down. Grass is also a useful design element, creating visual unity by forming a green link between various planting areas.

GRASS ALL YEAR ROUND

To keep using the lawn during winter in temperate zones, plant both warm-season and cool-season grasses.

- Oversow warm-season lawns with cool-season grass seed in autumn. Just water, scuff up the soil and scatter a cool-season grass seed mix.
- As the warm-season grasses naturally stop growing, the cool-season grass sprouts up, giving a green lawn during the winter. Then, as the weather begins to warm up, the fine cool-season grasses will die down to make way for the warm-season grass as it resumes growing.
- There are various grass seed mixtures available – for instance, some mixtures are suitable for sun and shade, while others suit the climate of a particular region. Ask your local nursery for advice on which mixes are most suitable for your area.
- Try growing a native grass, such as kangaroo grass (*Themeda triandra* syn. *T. australis*). It is drought-hardy and stays green for long periods, especially if you cut back the leaves in spring.

More than three-quarters of the water used in our gardens goes on lawns.

ALTERNATIVES TO GRASS

If you find lawn maintenance too demanding, yet like the look of a large green area, consider these alternatives. Although they won't tolerate heavy traffic (such as children playing), they won't need as much water or maintenance as a grassy lawn, and will never need mowing.

- **AUSTRALIAN NATIVE VIOLET** (*Viola hederacea; left, top*) Blue, violet-like flowers. Likes moist shade.
- **CHAMOMILE** Look for non-flowering forms. Best in cool to mild areas; not for warm to tropical areas.
- **CORSICAN MINT** Low, dense and fragrant when crushed underfoot.
- **DIANELLA** 'Little Rev' forms a dwarf plant to around 30 cm.
- **DICHONDRA** (*Left, bottom*) Tolerates light traffic. Never needs mowing.
- **LIPPIA** Considered weedy in some areas but has a good mat-like cover and is tolerant of shade.
- **MINGO GRASS** A low-spreading, blue form of native kangaroo grass for sun or part shade.
- **MONDO GRASS** The dwarf form will mimic the look of green lawn. Expensive and slow-growing, but ideal for small spaces.
- **MYOPORUM PARVIFOLIUM** A taller growing groundcover to 50 cm that spreads a metre or more. Suitable for a bushland garden.
- **PRATIA PEDUNCULATA** White flowers, with dense mat-like growth. Sun to part shade.
- **THYME** Needs excellent drainage and full sun but is a great aromatic groundcover for small, sunny spaces.

DEALING WITH PROBLEMS

To control weeds, pests and diseases in your garden, try to avoid chemicals. Use natural methods instead.

Keeping weeds in check

Not all weeds are a nuisance – some can actually be useful by covering soil which would otherwise be exposed, while others provide food and shelter for wildlife. However, environmental weeds that compete with native vegetation and noxious weeds that pose a threat to humans and pets should be removed. There are several effective control methods that don't involve chemicals.

TEN TIPS ON WEED CONTROL

1 Try not to bring weeds into your garden in the first place. Avoid importing soil, including top-soil, that may contain weed seeds or pieces. Check for weeds in the pots of new plants.

2 Avoid leaving areas of soil bare or weeds will soon colonise them. Replant these cleared areas as soon as possible with native or non-invasive groundcovers.

3 Cover weeded areas with plenty of mulch to prevent weed seeds from germinating. Remove any new weeds as they appear.

4 Remove weeds before they mature. Mow annual weeds to remove flower heads and seeds.

5 Smother weeds with a thick layer of newspaper or card-board and cover with mulch, then plant through the mulch and paper, keeping the soil covered.

6 Cover larger areas of weedy ground with clear plastic and let it bake in the hot sun for several days. Heat will build up in the soil beneath the plastic and kill both weed seeds and soil pathogens. Or try a weed mat, made from woven mesh (pictured below left).

7 Put hard-to-kill weeds into a plastic bag and leave it in the hot sun for a few weeks. Then put it in the garbage to avoid spreading weeds to other areas.

8 With persistent weeds, make sure you remove the whole root and all underground parts. Some weeds can grow from a tiny piece.

9 Pour boiling water on weeds. This will kill many species. Or use steam via a steamer unit (sold in nurseries), a device developed for non-chemical weed control.

10 Kill weeds that need plenty of sunshine, such as paspalum and cudweed, by covering them with bricks or sheets of roofing iron for a few days.

■ ■ ■ **Learn which weeds** spread from cuttings and dispose of them by sealing them in a bag before throwing in the garbage bin.

Dandelions have very long tap roots, so make sure you remove the whole root when you weed.

ANNUALS

Annual weeds complete their life cycle in one season and spread by seeding. These include bindii, cobbler's pegs, green amaranth, milk thistles and petty spurge.

- Pull annuals out by hand as soon as they emerge and before they get a chance to seed.
- Use a hoe to weed flower beds or vegetable plots.
- In awkward places, you may need to use a chemical control. To kill broad-leaved weeds such as dandelions in paths, try this recipe. Dissolve 2 tablespoons iron sulphate (from nurseries or hardware stores) in 4.5 litres water, then sprinkle the solution over the weeds.

PERENNIALS

These include onion weed, oxalis and turkey rhubarb. Perennial weeds take longer to mature than annuals, setting seed and also forming bulbs, corms, rhizomes, suckers or some other underground growth system that allows regrowth and spread even if the top growth is removed.

- Prevent seeding by removing the top growth and the underground bulb or tuber. If hand weeding is unsuccessful, use carefully targeted applications of herbicide.
- To kill creeping oxalis, a weed of lawns and garden beds, try a solution of brown vinegar diluted with an equal amount of water.
- Keep lawn weeds under control by looking after your lawn – lush turf that is regularly fertilised and mowed won't have any bare spots for weeds to colonise.

TOP TIP

For weeding an established area, try the Bradley Method, named after two sisters who pioneered this technique in Sydney in the 1960s. Start hand-weeding where there is good native plant cover, working towards the weed-infested area. Work carefully and slowly (because soil disturbance encourages weeds to regenerate) and replace the earth afterwards.

MAKE WEEDING EASIER

✔ When weeding, work in the cool part of the day and kneel on something comfortable, such as an old cushion or a thick piece of foam, cut to size.

✔ Use the right tools. A blunt, broad-bladed knife is great for digging out deep-rooted weeds from lawns or from between pavers.

✔ Divide the area to be weeded into manageable sections. It is unrealistic to tackle a huge area all at once.

✔ Weed after a good soaking rain or after you have thoroughly watered the target area. Dry earth is much harder to weed.

✔ Always wear gloves when weeding – many common weeds, such as wandering jew (*Tradescantia alba*), can cause itchiness on contact with the skin.

■ ■ ■ **Drown leafy green weeds** in a bucket of water and leave them for a few weeks to produce a rich liquid garden fertiliser.

Winter grass is a favourite food of small, seed-eating birds such as finches.

FIRST THINGS FIRST

Not all weeds are pests. If you learn which ones are invasive, you can leave the plants that are harmless. This will save you a lot of time and work. Some weeds can even be put to good use in the garden.

- Some gardeners consider winter grass (*Poa annua*) a weed. But don't be too quick to remove its bright green tufts if they appear in your lawn during the cooler months. The seeds may be a valuable food source for small seed-eating birds. When the warm weather returns, the winter grass will disappear – naturally.
- Established weeds such as lantana and cotoneaster provide a habitat and food for native animals, birds and insects. If you remove them and don't replace them with substitute plantings, the survival of these animals may be at risk. However, both these plants are spreading into bushland and are regarded as environmental weeds so keep them under control.
- Just like other plants, weeds hold the soil together. It may be preferable to have weeds than exposed topsoil, which will result in erosion. Wait until you're ready to plant before removing weeds. (However, don't allow weeds to set seed, or you'll have much more work to do.)

LAWN WEEDS

Keeping a lawn completely weed-free is time-consuming; and can be an unrealistic goal. A more relaxed attitude towards lawn weeds will save you work. It can also be good for the health of the lawn. Consider these facts:

- Non-chemical controls include mowing and hand-weeding, along with a fertilising and watering regimen, to keep the grass growing vigorously so it can compete successfully with weeds.
- Clover adds nitrogen to the soil (but it also attracts bees, so make sure you're wearing shoes when you walk on it).
- Turf weeds usually have a low-growing habit, which helps them avoid mower blades.
- The quickest method of stopping lawn weeds from spreading is to mow the grass before it sets seed. Most weeds set seed in summer.
- Infrequent but deep watering will encourage the grass to send its roots deeper. This will result in a tougher lawn.
- Repeated applications of herbicide will result in a weed-free lawn, but may also reduce the lawn's vigour in the long term. Make sure you carefully follow the manufacturer's instructions when applying herbicide to lawn weeds.

EDIBLE WEEDS

Some weeds are delicious to eat, and many have medicinal value. Check a plant guide or enrol in a course on wild foods. Don't eat any plant or feed it to an animal unless you can identify it and are sure it hasn't been treated with any herbicide or insecticide.

- **DANDELIONS** (*Taraxacum officinale*) have roots that can be made into a coffee substitute and leaves that add an interesting flavour to salads. Another edible weed is pigweed (*Portulaca oleracea*).
- **MILK THISTLES** (*Silybum marianum, Sonchus oleraceus*) and chickweed (*Stellaria media*) (*right*) are favourite treats for birds, including chickens and caged birds. You might like to give these weeds a try too.
- **WILD BLACKBERRIES** (*Far right*) may be a blot on the landscape, but they can't be beaten for flavour when the fruit is ripe in late summer.

THE TRUTH ABOUT...

CLOVER

Many gardeners don't like clover because it can colonise lawns and attract stinging bees. However, it's worth tolerating because it gives lawns a lush green look in winter and improves the soil for other grasses, adding nitrogen via nodules on its roots. As it grows mainly in the cool months, clover will die back in spring and summer as the weather warms up.

WARNING!

▼ In Australia, purple-flowered *Echium plantagineum* covers many hectares of land, from pastures to road verges. It's poisonous to livestock, and many graziers and farmers call it Paterson's curse.

ENVIRONMENTAL WEEDS

An environmental weed is a plant that is capable of invading, outcompeting and preventing the regeneration of native vegetation. These once well-loved plants are now on the 'not wanted' list in our gardens (note that this list may vary from state to state).

- Bitou bush (*Chrysanthemoides monilifera*), a yellow-flowering shrub with a spreading habit, is out of control in some coastal sand dunes.

- Cotoneaster is an evergreen, thornless, pest- and disease-free screening shrub with the bonus of red autumn to winter berries. However, this shrub is now spreading to bushland.
- Crocosmia (*Crocosmia* x *crocosmiiflora*), above, also called montbretia, is an easy-growing corm that naturalises in gardens. Loved for its carefree orange, yellow and red flowers that bloom in summer, it is now an invasive weed.
- Another weed is Dutchman's pipe (*Aristolochia macrophylla*), a flowering climber related to native species. It attracts an endangered butterfly, the Richmond birdwing, but fails to provide food for the caterpillars.
- Gloriosa lily (*Gloriosa superba*), a herbaceous climber, has red and green trumpet flowers. It has invaded coastal areas in the tropics and subtropics. However, large-flowered named varieties, such as 'Rothschildiana', are not considered a problem.
- Gorse bush (*Ulex europaeus*) is a major weed in New Zealand. A yellow-flowering shrub with spiny leaves, it provides cover for rabbits and prevents stock from grazing.
- Ivy (*Hedera helix*) was once hailed as an ornamental solution to difficult, dry-shade areas but it can cause structural damage to buildings. It supports itself by means of aerial roots and once it gets into a tree, it can kill it. Ivy can also cause allergies.
- Lantana used to be popular as a drought-hardy shrub, but it is now regarded as invasive and is known to be poisonous to stock.
- Pampas grass (*Cortaderia* species) was a used as a garden accessory to the Spanish-mission style of architecture, which was popular in the 20th century, but it spread into bushland and coastal areas and is now considered a weed.
- Privet (*Ligustrum* species) was once popular as a tough, evergreen hedge for city gardens. Its berries are attractive to birds, which spread them into bushland. The perfume from its flowers can cause allergies.
- Trident maple (*Acer negundo*) is an easy-to-grow shade tree. Its seeds spread so easily it is now growing in areas where it's not wanted.
- Willow (*Salix* species) was once considered a useful tree for damp spots. However, many species grow readily from broken branches and supplant native vegetation along water courses.

hot links

Weed lists and links to related sites: www.weeds.crc.org.au
Australia's national weed site: www.weeds.org.au
Environmental weeds and links to bush care groups: www.weedsbluemountains.org.au
New Zealand weed information: www.doc.govt.nz
Weed awareness programs: www.weedbusterweek.info.au; www.weedbusters.org.nz

■ ■ ■ **Pour boiling water** over weeds – it's a good NON-CHEMICAL METHOD of killing hard-to-get-at plants embedded between pavers.

Common garden pests

Choose the right plants for your climate and situation and you'll have fewer problems with plant-damaging pests. But sometimes, despite all your precautions, you'll need to give your plants a helping hand. Wherever possible, use non-chemical methods. There are plenty of earth-wise methods that won't harm the beneficial insects in your garden.

NATURAL PEST CONTROL

Remove pests manually and either squash them, or drop them into a bucket containing water and a little detergent.

- Use diversity as a strategy against plant pests. Avoid monocultures – instead, mix plants together to avoid providing pests with a banquet of their one favourite food.
- Find out about companion planting. Combinations of certain plant varieties can help keep certain pests away from food plants. French marigolds (*Tagetes* species), for example, repel the nematodes (eel worms) that attack tomatoes. For more information, see *Natural partners*, p. 226.
- Plant vegetables when pest numbers in your area are low – for example, in autumn or winter.
- Encourage beneficial insects such as hoverflies, predatory mites and spiders to your garden by avoiding the use of pesticides.
- Attract insect-eating birds to your garden by planting native species such as tea trees, eucalypts and melaleucas. Exotics such as camellias, roses and citrus also attract insect-eating birds.
- Collect and dispose of infested, rotten and mummified fruit as it may harbour pest eggs.

LEAF-EATERS

- Deter grasshoppers from your vegetable garden by planting a barrier crop such as coriander, or nitrogen-fixing crops such as peas or beans, both of which they dislike. Grasshoppers lay their eggs in neglected, untilled ground so regularly digging the soil and a big autumn clean-up will help control numbers.
- In New Zealand, to reduce the impact of porina caterpillars on lawns in autumn, flood the grass to flush the caterpillars from their burrows. Mowing the lawn to remove the thatch in summer and fertilising and watering it well in autumn will also help.
- To kill other caterpillars, try a spray of vinegar and water.
- If you spot leaf-eating ladybirds, pick them off by hand, or sprinkle garden-grade diatomaceous earth or lime around the infested plants. And encourage birds, their natural predators, to visit your garden.

HELPERS, NOT PESTS

These creatures all fulfil the useful function of eating decaying organic matter and do no harm to plants.

- ✔ Centipedes prey on many garden pests.
- ✔ Leopard slugs feed on carrion and pet faeces, and also hunt other slugs.
- ✔ Millipedes eat organic matter, such as plant mulch.
- ✔ Slaters feed on decaying vegetable and animal matter and their associated fungi.

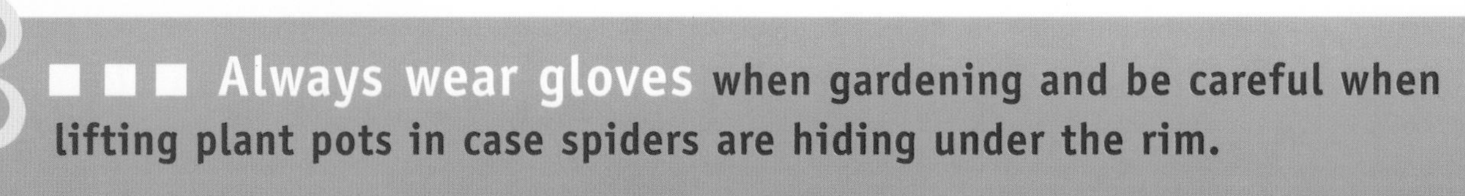

Always wear gloves when gardening and be careful when lifting plant pots in case spiders are hiding under the rim.

Save money and reduce harm to the environment by choosing manual methods of insect control.

TOP TIP

For large infestations of clustering insects, such as paperbark sawfly larvae on tea-trees and melaleucas, prune off the branch on which the larvae are feeding or resting and destroy them. This removes the pest and keeps the plant bushy.

SAP-SUCKERS

These pests can excrete a sugary waste that encourages the growth of sooty mould.

- Aphids infest the new shoots of plants, causing distorted leaves. Hose them off or squash them with your fingers.
- Whitefly nymphs also suck sap, resulting in mottled and papery leaves. Use yellow sticky traps to attract and trap them.
- Scale can be kept under control by its natural predators, which include native birds (for example, honeyeaters), lacewing larvae and introduced and native wasps.

SNAILS AND SLUGS

- One of the best ways to deal with snails and slugs is to walk around the garden with a torch at night, particularly after it has been raining, and squash any you see.
- Eliminate rough, weedy areas, piles of rocks and rubbish. These are the places where snails and slugs shelter and breed.
- Fill a shallow container with stale beer. The snails and slugs will be attracted to the beer and drown. Mixing a little flour with the beer makes it even more attractive.
- Make traps out of grapefruit and oranges. For example, cut an orange in half, squeeze out all the juice and cut a little door large enough for a snail to go through. Or make a trap from a can filled with bran.
- Snails and slugs dislike crossing rough surfaces. Put physical barriers – such as sawdust, garden-grade diatomaceous earth and eggshells – around plants.
- Surround plants with copper strips. Copper reacts with the mucus secreted by slugs and snails, creating an electrical charge.

ANTS

Most species of ant are harmless. However, smaller ants can infest pot plants, making air-filled chambers around the roots, which may affect plant growth.

- To get rid of ants in pots, flood the container or place it in a tub of water. Take out the plant and remove the ant nest at the base. Repot the plant in fresh potting mix, and use clay feet or bricks to keep the pot off the ground.
- Slowly pour boiling water into the nest. Or try sprinkling a mixture of equal parts of borax and icing sugar. (Store any leftovers in a child- and pet-proof container in a secure place.)
- Smear grease or calendula jelly onto a metal strip padded with cloth and use it to encircle tree trunks or plant stems. This will stop ants farming honeydew excreted by insects, such as scale and aphids.
- Squirt ants with water and disturb places where ants are nesting. The workers will be less likely to return to the colony with food, and, in time, the colony will decrease.

hot links

Integrated Pest Management: www.tec.nccnsw.org.au/ipm/online
Natural alternatives in the garden: www.marlborough.govt.nz/enviromonitoring/enviroeducation.cfm
Good or bad?: www.landcareresearch.co.nz/research/biodiversity/invertebratesprog/invertid/good_bad.asp

■ ■ ■ **Disrupt ant trails** with pennyroyal or eucalyptus oil, or sprinkle them with garden-grade diatomaceous earth.

Chemicals in the garden

Chemical control should be the last resort of the earth-wise gardener. Some pesticides are not safe to use near waterways because of their toxicity to plants, fish and amphibians, whereas others can persist in the soil, affecting regrowth. So use an environmentally preferred alternative where possible, but if you do choose to use chemicals, always do so in accordance with the instructions on the label.

SAFE USE OF HERBICIDES

Herbicides are chemicals used to kill weeds. Some are selective, specially formulated to kill a particular weed, whereas others are broad-spectrum, designed to kill a wide range of plants.

- Resist using herbicides anywhere near food plants.
- Choose the most appropriate herbicide for the job you need to do: contact herbicides kill plants on contact; systemic herbicides get into the vascular system of plants, eventually killing the roots; and residual herbicides act on the soil, not the foliage, and may remain in the soil for about a year.
- When applying herbicides, carefully follow the instructions. Always wear gloves and only spray on wind-free days as these chemicals can cause skin and eye irritation and may spread to other plants.
- If using broad-spectrum weedkillers such as glyphosate, which will kill most plants, target weeds carefully and use in dry weather. The safest approach is to use a weed wand, or soaked sponge or cloth, to 'paint' the weeds with the chemical rather than spray. This ensures that the substance hits its target and nothing else.
- Use a plant-specific weedkiller strictly in accordance with the instructions on the label, applying it carefully to only the target plants, and taking particular care

How insecticides work

Type	How they work	Environmental impact
Contact	Must touch the pest to kill it, much like a fly spray.	Fast and effective, and usually breaks down quickly in the environment. However, can harm beneficial insects.
Penetrant	Moves a short distance into the plant and is eaten by the pest as it eats the plant.	In general, penetrants are safer than contact insecticides as they are less likely to come into contact with beneficial insects. However, they do target insects that feed on plants.
Systemic	Moves through the vascular system of the plant protecting the whole plant from pests.	Some systemics last for weeks while others can remain in the system for as long as a year. Little is known about what else they may be doing to the environment.
Broad-spectrum	Kills a wide range of insects, including beneficial predatory insects.	Marketed as environmentally friendly, but as they kill a wide range of beneficial insects, including bees and wasps, use them with care.
Selective	Targets a particular pest.	Leaves other insects unharmed. Very useful for spot-treating outbreaks of a pest that may get quickly out of hand.

■ ■ ■ **Always make sure you are using an insecticide that is registered to control the insect pest you want to eradicate.**

PROS & CONS

USING GLYPHOSATE

Glyphosate has been widely used to control weeds for many decades and is the main weed control chemical available to home gardeners. It is a non-selective, systemic herbicide with an added surfactant (a soapy additive) to make it stick to plants. But is it safe? Authorities argue that it is not toxic to mammals, birds and bees; however, there are concerns about the long-term effects on waterways and amphibians of both glyphosate and some of the surfactants used in glyphosate products. As a result, new formulations that are considered safer near waterways have been developed. For home gardens, choose formulations without POEA (polyoxyethyleneamine, a group of surfactants) and 'paint' it on the weeds rather than spray it on.

near trees. There are plant-specific weedkillers that target only bindii and clover, broad-leaved weeds or winter grass without harming other plants.

GETTING RID OF IVY

Ivy is now generally regarded as a weed as it is so invasive. It is also linked to allergies such as asthma and severe lung conditions. Follow these steps to remove ivy from walls without leaving unsightly marks.

- Wear gloves and long sleeves to prevent the sap or dust from irritating your skin, and a dust mask so that you won't inhale dust and ivy mites. Water the foliage before you start, to reduce dust and allergen problems.
- Cut the stems at the base and poison with a glyphosate-based product. Repeat applications may be necessary.
- Wait for the top growth to die before trying to remove the foliage and stems from the wall. Remove the aerial roots using a stiff brush or paint scraper.

USING INSECTICIDES RESPONSIBLY

Insecticides are chemicals that kill insects either by contact or as the insect eats the chemical after it has been sprayed on target plants. A little understanding about how insecticides work will help you to select the most effective, safe and efficient product.

- Read the label to make sure you are using an insecticide that is registered to control the insect pest you want to remove, and follow the directions carefully.
- Observe the withholding period – that is, the time lapse between spraying the plant and being able to eat it.
- Wear protective clothing. Insecticides can be breathed in or absorbed via the skin, so cover your arms and legs; wear gloves, boots, hat, goggles and a suitable respirator.
- Be careful when mixing the concentrate. Avoid breathing the fumes or inhaling toxic dust. To avoid any accidental ingestion, wash your hands after use.

Is pyrethrum safe?

The botanical insecticide pyrethrum comes from the pyrethrum daisy (*Tanacetum cinerariifolium*). Commercial pyrethrum sprays may be natural, but often they are synthetic and contain additives. These are known as pyrethroids.

- Generally, synthetic pyrethroids are of high toxicity to insects (at low concentrations) but of low toxicity to mammals. Both natural and synthetic pyrethrum are toxic to aquatic life, so take extreme care to avoid run-off into waterways.
- Commercial sprays often contain the 'carrier' piperonyl butoxide, which makes the spray more effective and long-lasting, but it is moderately toxic to fish and highly toxic to other aquatic organisms.

WARNING!

▼ If using insecticides, strictly observe the withholding period specified on the container. This is the length of time that must pass between applying an insecticide and harvesting or eating any part of the plant you are treating.

- Don't spray on windy days, if rain is predicted, in very hot weather or in frosty conditions. If you use insecticides to control aphids or thrips, spray late in the day when bees have returned to their hives.
- Store insecticides in their original containers, in a locked cupboard or shed out of reach of children.

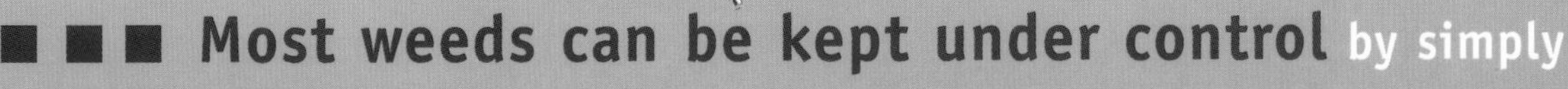

Keeping plants healthy

Plant diseases are a natural, if unwanted, part of the growing process. While it's difficult to isolate your garden from attack, employing good hygiene, dealing promptly with disease outbreaks and growing resistant varieties are all earth-wise practices that will help to keep plants strong and reduce the need for chemicals.

AVOIDING DISEASES

- Deal with disease outbreaks quickly. Check your garden regularly and remove infected leaves, flowers, fruit or entire plants. Always pick up and dispose of infected windfalls or mummified fruit hanging on the branches.
- Never take cuttings from plants that are diseased – use only healthy material. As an added precaution, disinfect secateurs and other pruning tools after each cut, or before starting to cut another plant.
- Keep pruning tools sharp – jagged, rough cuts made by blunt tools may become infected.
- To effectively control overwintering spores, spray fruit trees with a lime- or a copper-based fungicide in winter.
- Don't compost weeds and diseased or virus-infected plant leaves and prunings. Your compost heap may not be hot enough to kill them. Instead, place them in a bag and put it straight in the rubbish bin.
- To improve air circulation, prune out the centre of plants subject to leaf diseases.
- To reduce the chance of soil-borne disease, viruses and pests, avoid growing members of the same vegetable family in the same part of your garden in successive seasons. For instance, alternate potatoes with turnips.
- Keep insects that spread viral diseases, such as aphids, under control. Squash them, hose them off with a jet of water, spray them with soapy water or try another home-made remedy, such as garlic spray.
- Check tree trunks in autumn, when fungal growths flourish. Bracket fungi on the tree trunk indicates that the tree is probably rotten inside and may need to be removed. Consult a tree surgeon.
- Take care of the root systems of trees because damaged roots are susceptible to root rot. Don't park the car over them, don't cut them and don't use lawn weedkillers near them.

ROOT PROBLEMS

Although root problems are hidden underground, symptoms of their diseases – such as phytophthora, a type of rot that makes roots die back – show in the plant above ground.

- Check for signs of root rot. These include wilting when the plant doesn't need water, the tips of twigs or branches dying, and splitting or oozing from low down on the trunk. The plant may also

Causes of plant disease

Non-infectious diseases are caused by environmental factors, such as nutrient deficiencies and lack of water. Infectious diseases are usually caused by fungi, bacteria and viruses and can be spread in a number of ways.

- Humans: via hands, shoes, pruning tools and machinery.
- Insects: via bodies and mouthparts.
- Water: from groundwater, rainwater and water from overhead irrigation.
- Wind: carries fungal spores and other pathogens long distances.

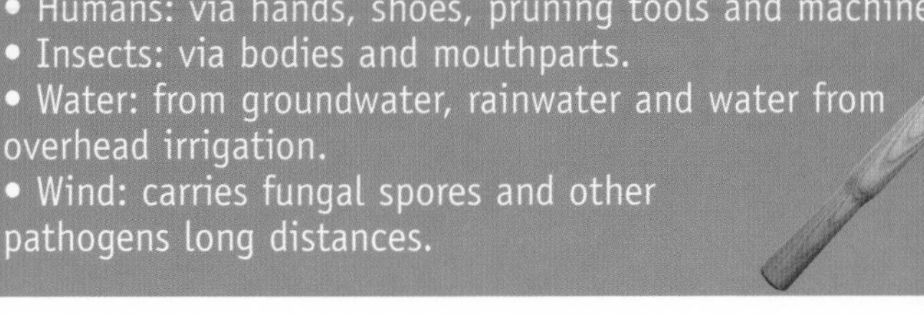

■ ■ ■ **To avoid spreading disease, wipe your pruning tools with a cloth dipped in tea-tree oil after pruning each plant.**

be unsteady in the ground if its root system is dying.

- Monitor avocados, azaleas, citrus, daphne and pieris for symptoms. These plants, as well as many Australian native plants, are susceptible to root diseases.
- Don't keep the soil constantly wet. To reduce the likelihood of root rot, allow the soil to dry out slightly between watering.
- Use phosphorus acid, a registered food additive that is now being used to combat plant diseases. It's an effective fungicide and prevents root rot in sensitive plants. Follow the instructions on the container and water it over the foliage and soil.

BLACK SPOT ON ROSES

A fungal disease, black spot (pictured at right) disfigures roses and will lead to excessive leaf drop if it is not controlled.

- Plant roses in full sun, not too close to trees and shrubs, leaving enough room between the plants to provide adequate air movement.
- Cover the ground over the root area with 5–7 cm organic mulch, such as chopped sugarcane, pea straw or lucerne.
- Regularly check for any diseased leaves around the base of the plant. Pick them up and dispose of them.
- Also, avoid overhead watering, particularly late in the day.
- When roses are dormant in winter, spray with a clean-up fungicide such as lime sulphur. Spray immediately after pruning, before new growth occurs.

Yellow leaf problem solver

Symptom	Cause	Solution
A few older leaves yellowing	Normal ageing	Do nothing
New leaves pale yellow	Iron deficiency	Iron chelates
All leaves pale yellow	Nitrogen deficiency	Complete fertiliser
Yellow 'V' on leaves	Magnesium deficiency	Magnesium sulphate
Yellow mottling/marbling	Virus infection	Do nothing, or remove badly affected plants
Yellowing and excessive leaf drop	Too dry or too wet	Water properly

FUNGUS REMEDIES

These earth-wise sprays will help keep various fungal diseases under control. For each one, decant the solution into a spray bottle and shake well before using.

- Cover 90 g chopped garlic with vegetable oil and add 1 litre soapy water. Let stand for a day or so and then strain. Use 1 part solution to 50 parts water to treat fungal disease.
- Pour boiling water over fresh or dried chamomile flowers (or use a chamomile tea bag). Allow to steep, then cool. Use this herbal tea to treat fungal disease.
- Dilute 1 cup full cream milk (or milk powder) with 9 cups water and use it as a spray for downy or powdery mildew.
- During the growing season, make your own powdery mildew spray by adding 1 tsp bicarb soda to 1 litre water. Apply every 3–4 days until the problem is brought under control. Then spray on roses every few weeks while the weather is hot and humid.
- Use Condy's crystals (available from chemists) to make an excellent remedy for azalea petal blight and other fungal diseases. To a bucket of water add just enough crystals to colour the water pale pink.

Regularly fertilising and mulching plants increases their strength and makes them less susceptible to common diseases.

Unwelcome garden visitors

The animals and birds that eat plants present a dilemma for the earth-wise gardener. On the one hand, you may want to create a garden that is a haven for wildlife; on the other, you don't want the same creatures to destroy your garden. Luckily, there are a number of things you can do to discourage animals and birds from eating your plants without harming them.

BANDICOOTS

If you see funnel-shaped holes in your lawn, then you'll know bandicoots have been around. Don't be alarmed – they can do you a service by eating lawn pests, so try to put up with the holes.

- To protect bandicoots, keep your pets inside the house at night.
- Or, if you can't tolerate the holes in your lawn, use fine, galvanised wire mesh to build a fence. Make it a minimum of 50 cm above the ground, and bury the foot at least 15 cm deep.

BIRDS

To keep birds away from your fruit trees, see the ideas in *Natural pest control* on p. 257 as well as the one below.

- Attach a bird-scarer to a branch – fake birds of prey are available from hardware stores, gift shops, some nurseries and by mail order.

CANE TOADS

Cane toads were introduced to Queensland in the 1930s to control sugarcane pests. They cause great damage to native flora and fauna.

- To kill a cane toad humanely, pick it up in a plastic bag and put it in the fridge for 4 hours. Then place it in the freezer for 24 hours.
- Contact Frogwatch, which is researching trapping methods.

FLYING FOXES

These fruit- and nectar-feeders roost in large groups, or camps.

Animals may invade your garden during a drought or after a fire. Providing some food and water may help protect your plants.

- Net any fruit trees or blossoming natives, but check them regularly to make sure there are no trapped animals or birds.
- Encourage flying foxes to move by removing branches from their roosting trees and clearing the understorey.

SAYING 'NO' TO VISITORS

If you can't tolerate the wildlife visitors in your garden, here are some harmless deterrents.

- Sprinkle blood and bone around plants to discourage rabbits. (However, you may find that your dog or cat finds the smell attractive.)
- Buy a repellent containing Bitrex, a bitter-tasting ingredient available from nurseries that will protect new shoots from browsing birds and animals, such as foxes, dogs, possums and cats.
- To deter possums and kangaroos from foraging in your garden, apply a sticky camphor product on the upper surface of leaves.
- Squirt birds and cats with a pump-action water pistol — it won't harm them, but it will keep them away from plants.
- Provide a dedicated pile of mulch or compost for digging animals. Bandicoots or brush turkeys may prefer this alternative food source to your plants.

To scare away cockatoos and other persistent visitors, hang old CDs, bells, wine cask bladders and plastic snakes in trees.

POSSUMS

Possums can damage plants by eating fruit, new shoots, flowers and buds. They can also damage bark as they climb up and down.

- Try to block access to your garden from fences or railings, and place movement-sensitive lights at strategic points.
- Plant lavender around the shrubs and trees for which possums have shown a preference. The smell of the flowers is said to deter them. If it doesn't, cover particularly vulnerable plants with shadecloth at night.
- Band the trunks of trees with a slippery material, such as metal, so possums can't scale them. Banding should only be a temporary method as anything that encircles a tree trunk long-term can harm the tree.

HOP OFF

To discourage kangaroos and wallabies from eating your plants, mix these ingredients in a spray bottle. Shake before spraying it on leaves.

5 eggs
600 ml water
150 ml acrylic paint

POSSUMS AND THE LAW

If you have a possum nesting in your roof space, check where it is getting in while it's out foraging at night, then repair the hole. Or call a licensed possum remover.

IN AUSTRALIA, there are several species of possums and all are protected. They are territorial and will not survive if you move them to another possum's territory. It is illegal to trap a possum without a licence (from your local National Parks and Wildlife centre) and to release it more than 50 metres away from where it was caught.

IN NEW ZEALAND, brushtail possums are an introduced animal, and are considered a pest. There are programs in place to eradicate them. Contact your local Department of Conservation or regional council.

CATS

Cats will often damage plants by lying on them or by digging around them when they bury their droppings.

- Minimise areas of soft earth where cats like to dig by planting lots of groundcovers, including pungent-smelling plants, such as rue.
- Place a forest of small twigs around any young plants, either in the garden or in pots. If cats are an ongoing problem, try covering plants with a layer of chickenwire.
- If you have only a few plants on a balcony or in a courtyard, drape them with shadecloth – pots and all – each evening. Remove the cover in the morning. This method also deters possums.

DOGS

Some dogs dig holes because they're bored. Exercise will help, so will a large bone to chew. Here's how to deal with a hole-digger.

- Provide your dog with a place of its own to dig and encourage it to use the area by burying treats there, such as a bone. Cordon off the areas you want to protect.
- Every time the dog digs, put some of its droppings into the hole and cover them with soil. The dog is very unlikely to dig in the same spot again.

hot links

Living with wildlife:
www.nationalparks.nsw.gov.au/npws.nsf/Content/Living+with+wildlife
Animal pests in NZ: www.doc.govt.nz/Conservation/002~Animal-Pests
Cane toads: www.amonline.net.au/factsheets/canetoad.htm

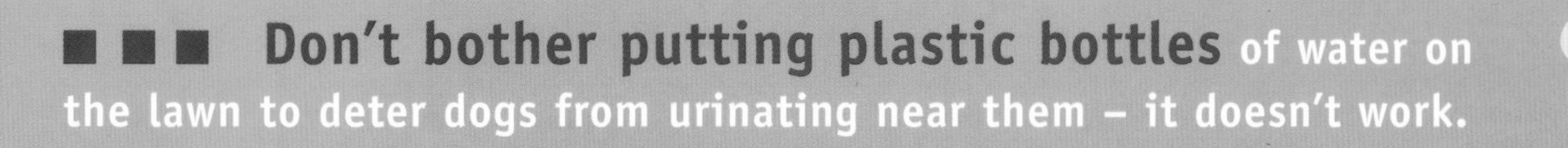

Don't bother putting plastic bottles of water on the lawn to deter dogs from urinating near them – it doesn't work.

Out and About

It's surprisingly easy to make earth-wise changes to your buying and commuting habits, and even to the way you travel. The benefits range from increased fitness to knowing that you're minimising your impact on the environment.

OUT AND ABOUT...

BUYING POWER

■ Follow our easy tips and greatly reduce your consumption of plastic products, page 283. ■ Our A–Z guide will help you to make earth-wise choices next time you shop, page 284. ■ You'll be surprised by some of the ingredients in cosmetics and toiletries. Find out what to avoid on page 291. ■ Learn about investing in socially responsible companies on page 296.

ON THE ROAD

■ Check out our 10 tips on how to save fuel, and money, on page 298. ■ Choose the right car for your situation and needs, and find out about the latest innovations in car manufacture, page 300. ■ Learn how to keep your car in top working order, page 304. ■ Get fit and save money by riding a bike, page 308.

TRAVELLING LIGHT

■ Whether you prefer wilderness areas or large cities, try walking next time you go on holiday – you'll leave a much lighter ecological footprint as you go. See page 310. ■ Check out our inspiring ideas for eco-friendly holidays as well as our advice on how to feel good when you get there, page 312.

BUYING POWER

How you shop and spend can make an important contribution to protecting your health and resources.

The choice is yours

Today's consumers are faced with a wider range of choices than ever before, and a steady stream of sophisticated sales campaigns. To buy economically, as well as to reduce waste, safeguard health and protect the environment, you need to follow some basic principles, learn to interpret the claims of salespeople, and have a clear idea of what you want.

EIGHT WAYS TO SHOP ECO-SMART

1 Before making any major purchase, do your research. Avoid buying in a hurry and don't be persuaded by overzealous salespeople. Sleep on it, if necessary.

2 Consider the running costs as well as the initial price of any item you buy. Many environmentally preferred products, such as compact fluorescent lamps (CFLs), cost more to buy but will save you money in the long run.

3 Select products made from renewable resources, such as plantation timber, wool and silk.

4 Choose items that are built to last. For example, choose a sofa that has a hardwood or steel frame rather than one made of softwood or chipboard, which may warp or break easily. You may pay more up front, but a well-made piece will last longer.

5 Buy reusable products rather than disposable ones. For example, buy washable cloth towels, handkerchiefs, serviettes and cleaning cloths rather than paper, single-use varieties. Avoid disposable cups, glasses and cutlery, too.

6 Buy local produce that is in season. It is usually cheaper and fresher and has less impact on the environment. Markets and roadside stalls are good sources, but some supermarkets also buy from local producers. Support your local food co-op if you have one.

7 Look for all-natural, fully biodegradable, non-toxic products that break down without leaving harmful residues in the environment. (Most materials will biodegrade eventually, but some leave toxic residues.)

8 Avoid products that have excessive and/or non-biodegradable packaging. It is estimated that approximately 10 per cent of every shopping bill goes towards paying for packaging – which you normally just throw away! Moreover, significant amounts of energy are used in the manufacture of packaging. Purchasing refillable containers can help cut this kind of waste.

BREAKING THE PLASTIC HABIT

Plastics have a highly detrimental effect on the environment, but are so much a part of life today that it would be very difficult to do without them. However, you can at least reduce how often you use these materials. Think about the plastics you use each week: include plastic bags used for shopping and storing food, plastic containers in the refrigerator and pantry, and plastic wrap used to cover food. Then set a goal to reduce your consumption by, say, half. The following tips will help you achieve this.

■ ■ ■ **If the styrofoam cups used in Australia each year were placed end to end, they would circle the world ten times.**

Don't be swayed by special reductions and two-for-one offers. If you don't need it, don't buy it.

THE TRUTH ABOUT...

PLASTICS

Plastics represent a massive environmental problem. Not only is their manufacture energy-intensive and highly polluting, but, in addition, only a few plastics can be recycled – and then only once. Plastics never decay and even if they are incinerated (a process that produces dioxins), 90 per cent of the material remains as toxic waste. Some plastics are also suspected of causing health problems. Soft plastics leach harmful volatile organic compounds (VOCs) into the air and into food. VOCs have been linked to headaches, irritation, depression, respiratory-system damage and nausea. Chemicals known as phthalates are used to give plastic its flexibility. Possibly carcinogenic, phthalates have also been implicated in reproductive defects, endometriosis, fibrocystic breast disease and birth defects.

WHAT TO AVOID

- ✗ Products containing aerosol propellants (such as propane, pentane and halons) and solvents (such as methyl chloroform and methyl bromide), which damage the ozone layer or increase global warming.
- ✗ Products whose production is highly polluting. Examples include chlorine-bleached paper, cleaning products that contain phosphates, or cosmetics made with petroleum derivatives.
- ✗ Products made from finite resources. For example, avoid buying furniture made with the wood from old-growth forests.

- Choose glass, ceramic or stainless steel containers for storing food.
- To wrap food, opt for waxed or greaseproof paper or cellophane (made from plant fibre).
- Substitute paper bags for plastic bags as often as you can.
- Avoid prepacked foods. Buy in bulk whenever possible, taking along your own containers.
- Try to cut down your use of foods packed in plastic-lined cans.
- Look for cellulose freezer bags, which should soon be available in Australia and New Zealand. These are made from natural materials and are biodegradable.
- Take your own reusable bags when you go shopping. Bags made from polypropylene can be purchased cheaply from most major supermarkets. Although they are manufactured using non-renewable fossil fuels, they last much longer than plastic shopping bags and can be reused many times over.
- If you have to use plastic bags at the supermarket, make sure at least eight items go into each one – assuming they are not too heavy.
- Aim to reuse plastic bags at least once or twice.
- Buy plastics that your local council will recycle. To identify recyclable plastics, manufacturers stamp an identification code on all products (see *Getting started*, p. 13). Councils usually publish lists of the plastics they collect and recycle.

SAFER USE OF PLASTIC

Taking a few simple precautions will help you to avoid the harmful health effects of plastics.

- Transfer food from takeaway containers to glass or ceramic dishes before reheating them in a microwave. Microwaving some plastic containers and plastic bags speeds up the migration of chemicals into the food. Leaching is most likely to occur with hot, fatty foods, so always choose glass containers for reheating these foods.
- Try to buy cheese off the block instead of prepacked. If you can't avoid buying plastic-wrapped cheese, remove the plastic as soon as you get home.
- Throw out plastic containers that are cracked, discoloured or show other signs of wear: they may be leaching harmful chemicals into your food.
- Harsh dishwashing detergents and the high temperature of water used in dishwashers can cause plastics to break down. Wash all plastic containers, including those labelled as dishwasher-safe, by hand in warm water, using a mild, plant-based, detergent.

■ ■ ■ **Recycling plastic into** new material requires just 30 per cent of the energy needed to make plastics from fossil fuels.

Shopping off the shelf

Before reaching automatically for the product you always buy, look through this A–Z list of commonly purchased items for information about problem ingredients and healthy alternatives. You may be surprised to learn that earth-wise choices are often the most cost-effective.

AIR FRESHENERS

- Whether aerosol or wick-based, many air fresheners contain toxic chemicals, such as formaldehyde and dichlorobenzene, which are both possibly carcinogenic and also tend to persist in the environment for a long time. Most air fresheners also contain synthetic fragrances, which may cause adverse reactions in some people.
- As alternatives, try bicarbonate of soda or vinegar. Both will absorb odours at a fraction of the cost of commercial fresheners. Or, if you like a scent, use products made with herbs or essential oils – the main thing is to avoid synthetic fragrances. Also don't forget that fresh air works wonders too.

ALUMINIUM FOIL

- The production of aluminium requires large amounts of energy and aluminium never breaks down.
- Try to use aluminium foil sheets and containers sparingly, reusing and recycling whenever possible. Recycling aluminium uses just 5 per cent of the energy used in producing new aluminium.

BABY BOTTLES

- Clear plastic baby bottles are usually made of polycarbonate, a plastic that has been shown to leach out minute amounts of the hormone disruptor Bisphenol A, especially when heated.
- Polycarbonate is one of several plastics grouped and identified by a number 7 inside the recycling triangle symbol. As an alternative, look for glass bottles or safer kinds of plastics, such as polyethylene (recycling symbol 1, 2, 4) or polypropylene (symbol 5). Contact the manufacturer if you are unsure.

BABYCARE PRODUCTS

- Baby oil often contains mineral oil, a petroleum derivative. Gentler, more earth-wise choices include cold-pressed vegetable and nut oils such as grapeseed, jojoba, almond and apricot kernel.

THE TRUTH ABOUT...

ALUMINIUM

Aluminium is the third most abundant element in the earth's crust, and is found in air, water, soil, plants and animals. In recent decades, several studies have suggested a link between increased levels of aluminium in the brain and Alzheimer's disease. Sources suspected of raising aluminium levels include drinking water and saucepans. Makers of aluminium cookware acknowledge that cooking acid foods such as tomatoes in aluminium pans can increase the amount of the metal entering food. But, as the Alzheimer's Association has acknowledged, there is as yet 'no proof that aluminium causes Alzheimer's disease'.

Australians spend about $400 million a year at supermarkets on cleaning products.

■ ■ ■ **Buy pump sprays and trigger packs instead of aerosol cans that use hydrocarbon propellants such as propane and pentane.**

- To protect your baby's skin from the detergents, preservatives and fragrances found in many commercial soaps, shampoos and creams, choose plant-based alternatives.

BARBECUES

- Look for clean fuel such as untreated wood, or buy a gas barbecue that doesn't produce smoke. Avoid compressed charcoal briquettes and fire starters.
- An LPG cylinder produces fewer emissions than solid fuel, but if you barbecue a lot and have natural gas in the house, consider installing a permanent gas outlet as it is considerably cheaper and produces even fewer emissions than LPG.

BOTTLED WATER

- Plastic bottles for water contribute to environmental pollution both in their manufacture and their eventual disposal. It is much more cost-effective and more earth-wise to drink filtered tap water.
- Before installing an under-sink water filter, research the pros and cons of each type carefully. Jug systems using activated carbon filter cartridges should filter out chlorine and pesticides but the cartridges need replacing regularly (about every 150 litres).
- Avoid buying mineral water with a high sodium content – above 30 mg sodium per 100 ml.

CAT LITTER

- Two of the most popular types of cat litter are a clay-based product and a clumping litter. Clay for litter is obtained by potentially environmentally destructive strip-mining and may also contain crystalline silica, a lung irritant. Clumping litters often contain sodium bentonite, which can cause respiratory distress in cats, and harm to kittens, who ingest it after licking their fur.
- Look for 100 per cent biodegradable, non-clay organic products such as 100 per cent recycled paper, organic wheat or pelletised lucerne. If odour is a problem, sprinkle the litter with bicarbonate of soda.

COFFEE

- Choose to drink natural ground coffee, as huge amounts of energy are consumed in the dehydration of instant and decaffeinated varieties.
- If you like decaffeinated coffee, choose one that has been decaffeinated using the water extraction or carbon dioxide methods. Some methods involve the use of chemical solvents such as methylene chloride, which has been linked to cancer in humans.
- Coffee is a heavily sprayed crop. Consider buying certified organic brands, or buy locally grown beans. Subtropical Australian plantations don't use the fungicides needed for high-altitude plantings in other countries, and the coffee is naturally lower in caffeine.

COFFEE FILTER PAPERS

- Look for reusable unbleached cotton filters or disposable unbleached or oxygen-bleached paper filters. Chlorine-based bleaching leaves dioxin residues in the filters and also releases dioxins into the environment. Dioxins have been identified as carcinogens by the World Health Organisation.
- Consider buying a reusable gold mesh filter or change to plunger or espresso coffee-making methods.

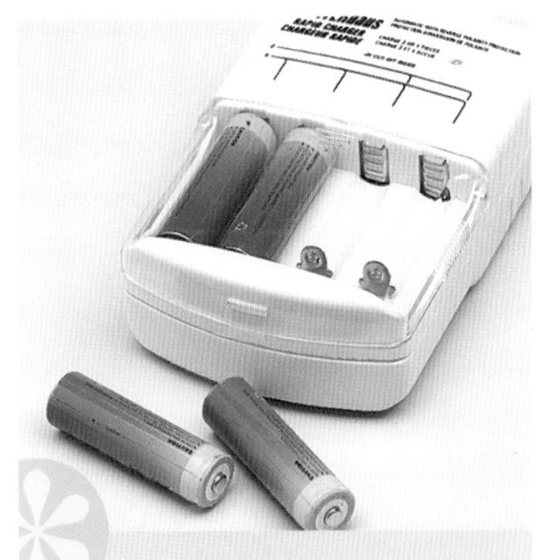

TOP TIP

Next time you need to replace batteries, consider rechargeable nickel metal hydride (NIMH) models. These require a charger unit and cost about three times as much as standard alkaline batteries, but can be recharged more than 500 times, making them much more economical in the long run. And with some models, recharging takes only 15 minutes, which is usually quicker than going to the shops! What's more, you'll help to reduce the amount of waste going to landfill.

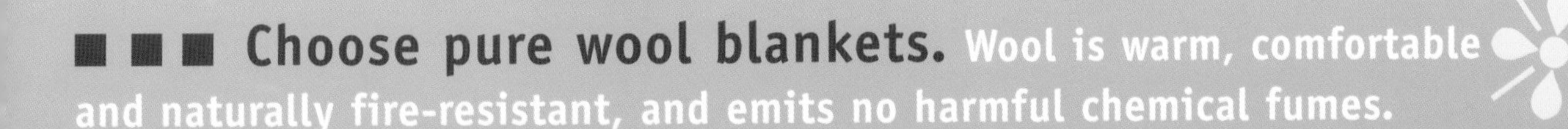

CLEANING PRODUCTS

Household cleaning and laundry products contain a huge array of synthetic chemicals, some of which are harmful to both humans and the environment. (See also *Choose carefully*, p. 74.)

■ **ALL-PURPOSE CLEANERS** Try to buy fewer cleaning products. One simple earth-wise, all-purpose cleaner, whether home-made or a commercial product, is really all you need to do the vast majority of household cleaning jobs.

■ **PHOSPHATE-FREE DETERGENTS** Choose unperfumed, phosphate-free or low-phosphate laundry powders and liquids.

■ **BIODEGRADABLE PRODUCTS** Try to use only products that are 80–100 per cent biodegradable and free from phosphates, petrochemicals, optical brighteners (or fluorescers), enzymes, chlorine and caustic soda.

■ **PRODUCTS WITH WARNINGS** Many products do not carry a full ingredients list, but they are required by law to carry warnings if they are hazardous or poisonous. Avoid products that carry such warnings. If they're toxic enough to poison or burn you, they're best left on the shelf. (The exception is borax: though poisonous if ingested in large amounts, it still has a valuable place in an earth-wise cleaning kit.)

■ **ECO-FRIENDLY LABELS** Look for labels that indicate that a product is eco-friendly, but read such labels critically – 'natural', 'organic' and 'biodegradable' are often used in very loose ways and may not mean much. For example, almost everything will break down (biodegrade) eventually: you need to know that it will do so in a matter of weeks rather than decades!

■ **PACKAGING** Think about how the cleaning products you buy are packaged: can you get them in a larger size or in bulk? In a concentrated form? In a recycled container?

FABRIC SOFTENERS

- Fabric softeners are designed to stay in your clothes for considerable periods of time and can slowly release a range of chemicals that have been linked with a variety of ailments. Given that if you use these products on all clothes and sheets you will be in contact with them almost around the clock, it's worth considering whether they are really necessary.
- Use bicarbonate of soda or vinegar to soften your wash – and add an essential oil if you like fragrance.

GARBAGE BAGS

- Instead of reaching for standard plastic garbage bags, read the labels carefully and choose biodegradable bags instead. Slightly more expensive plastic bags, made primarily from starches derived from plants such as corn and potato, will biodegrade in about 3 months.

GLUE

- The most dangerous ingredient in many glues is the solvent – rapid-drying solvent-based glues give off toxic fumes. Try to select a water-based product rather than a solvent-based one.
- It is difficult to find alternatives for some special-purpose adhesives such as epoxy glues, contact adhesives, rubber cements, instant glues and hobby glues. But most contain toxic ingredients, such as hexane, xylene, trichloroethane, acetone and toluene, so use them with caution and always in well-ventilated areas.
- The least toxic glues are white glue (PVA), and paste-based glue sticks. For children, the best glue is a combination of flour and water.

INSECT REPELLENT (PERSONAL)

- Many personal insect repellents contain DEET (N, N-diethyl-m-toluamide), which is a mosquito repellent but also a skin irritant as well as a neurotoxin. If you have to use a repellent

■ ■ ■ **Seek out biodegradable plastic bags, which will break down safely in landfills, without leaving any chemical residue.**

containing DEET, choose one with minimal levels of the chemical, preferably less than 10 per cent, and use it only when you really need to, for example where mosquito-borne diseases, such as malaria, are prevalent. Avoid repeated use and applying the repellent to broken skin. Be particularly cautious with children.

- Look for DEET-free repellents containing herbal essential oils, such as citronella, lavender, lemon grass, pennyroyal and peppermint. You will need to apply these more often and they may not be as effective as DEET-based types, but they are safer for long-term use.

IRONING AIDS

- An ironing aid is likely to contain: corn starch to give the fabric body silicone to stop the iron sticking to the fabric, borax to stabilise the starch, and fabric softener, preservatives and fragrance. Some may contain acetic acid, a mild irritant to the respiratory system. Ironing aids in aerosol packs contain propellants such as hydrocarbons.
- A cheap and safe alternative is to use a steam iron or iron over a damp cotton cloth placed on the fabric. For a badly creased cotton or linen item, sprinkle the garment with warm water, roll it up and put it aside for an hour or so before you iron it.

LIGHT BULBS

- Both incandescent and halogen lights are inefficient, wasting most of their energy as heat.
- Try to replace as many incandescent globes and halogen lamps as you can with compact fluorescent lamps. These cost more initially, but last up to 15 times longer and use up to 80 per cent less energy. They come in various shapes and sizes.

MOSQUITO COILS AND MATS

- Many mosquito repellents contain allethrin, a synthetic pyrethroid that is a central nervous system stimulant. Prolonged use should be avoided, especially by children.
- Use allethrin-based products only outdoors. Safer alternatives are to burn a citronella candle outdoors and use screens and nets indoors.

NAPPIES

- Even allowing for their manufacture and the necessarily high level of washing required, cloth nappies are generally a more earth-wise choice than disposable nappies. If you can't abide the idea of fiddling with pins and pilchers, seek out the nappy systems that consist of a fitted non-plastic, waterproof cover with elasticised legs and waist and velcro tabs, into which you insert the cloth nappy.
- Disposable nappies might seem convenient, but they have many drawbacks, so they should be used sparingly, if possible. They are more expensive,

MOBILE PHONES

An estimated 17 million Australians own a mobile phone and most of these people upgrade their phone every couple of years or so. If discarded phones are sent to landfill, the batteries and circuit boards break down, releasing nickel and other metals into the soil and groundwater.

- **When disposing of a mobile phone, make sure you have it recycled. Numerous recycling programs now operate in Australia and New Zealand. Check the Internet for local initiatives and participating outlets. A good starting point is www.recyclingnearyou.com.au**

Ironing aids often contain an array of toxic chemicals. Use a steam iron or apply a fine spray of water just before ironing.

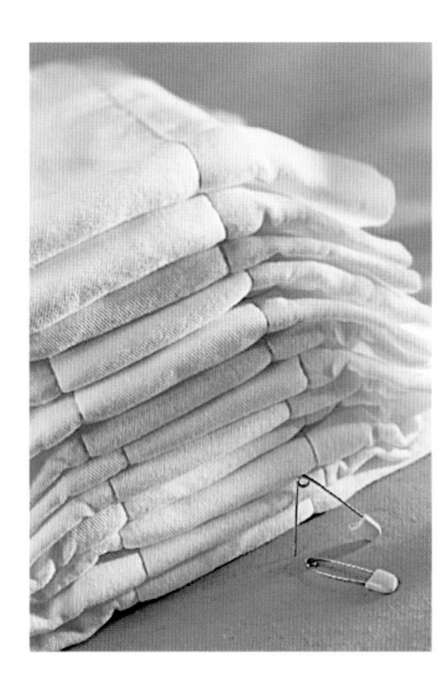

OFFICE SUPPLIES

- ✔ Choose copy/printing paper made from recycled paper.
- ✔ Look for 'chlorine-free' or 'oxygen-bleached' labels.
- ✔ If you need to use envelopes with windows, don't use the ones with plastic windows. Look for envelopes with windows made from a material called 'glassine', which is recyclable.
- ✔ Buy folders, binders and dividers made from recyclable materials.
- ✔ All printer cartridges can be recycled. In Australia, many post offices and retailers participate in the Cartridges 4 Planet Ark scheme, so look for recycling bins in these locations.

both financially and environmentally, than cloth nappies. Most are bleached, a process that yields, as a by-product, , which are highly toxic and have been linked to cancer. Most contain fragrances and polyacrylate crystals or gel (used to increase absorbency), which are possible irritants to infants. Finally, their disposal presents major environmental problems because they are often made of non-biodegradable plastics, and also because of the sheer number of nappies that are thrown away.

- If you feel you can't do without disposable nappies, try to find non-bleached, non-gel, natural cotton or wood-pulp ones. You might also consider a nappy system of disposable pads held inside washable pants – these are non-bleached, non-perfumed, non-plastic and fully compostable, although they do contain super-absorbent gel. Look also for the newly emerging disposable nappy recycling services – the paper and plastic in disposables can be separated and reused.
- See www.rwh.org.au/wellwomens/whic.cfm?doc_id=7691 for more information.

PENS AND PENCILS

- Many felt-tipped permanent marker pens are solvent based, and some contain xylene and/or toluene, which have been linked to damage to the nervous system, kidneys and liver. A strong odour usually indicates a chemical solvent.

Safer models of permanent markers use alcohol as a solvent.

- If you need a permanent pen, choose a fine-point rather than a broad point, as less solvent is released onto the paper.
- As a better alternative, choose a non-permanent pen, marked 'water-based' or 'non-toxic'.

PLASTIC WRAP

- Most plastic wraps are made from polyethylene, but chemicals called plasticisers are added to some types of commercial wrapping to make them pliable. Many of these chemicals, including phthalates and adipates, are toxic and have been shown to leach into food.
- To protect against this, try to minimise your use of plastic wrap, especially for storing food.
- If you buy food sold in plastic wrapping, particularly cheese or other fatty foods, remove the plastic when you get home and rewrap the food in waxed or greaseproof paper or cellophane (which is plant-based).

■ ■ ■ Tea crops are often treated with chemicals. Choose teas made without pesticides, preferably brands that are certified organic.

An infant's skin is thinner and significantly more permeable than an adult's – invest in natural soaps, shampoos and creams for your child.

SMOKE DETECTORS

- Although smoke detectors contain tiny amounts of radioactive material, the benefits of having an alarm far outweigh the almost negligible risk of direct radiation.
- A more important factor is the safe disposal of a disused smoke alarm, since the radioactive material has a very long half-life and could conceivably leach into landfill. Consider buying a photo-electronic alarm. These contain no radioactive material, but are more expensive.

TEA BAGS

- Buy loose-leaf tea and use a teapot or a stainless steel infuser, or look for unbleached natural-fibre bags. If possible, buy tea bags without staples so that they are completely biodegradable.
- If your tea of choice has been grown overseas, it may have been exposed to chemical pesticides and fertilisers. One of these could be DDT, which has been banned in most parts of the developed world. Look in health food shops for certified organic or Australian-grown teas that have been produced without fungicides or pesticides.
- Herbal teas aren't necessarily a healthy alternative, as the herbs are often grown in soil-free conditions in glasshouses, and doused with chemicals before and after harvest. If you can, choose a certified organic herbal tea.

TINNED FOOD

- Opinion is divided over whether the material used to line food cans (an epoxy resin that contains a hormone disruptor called Bisphenol A) leaches into the canned food in dangerous amounts.
- Do try to avoid canned baby foods, as babies are more susceptible to minute amounts of any chemical. Look for baby food in glass containers instead.
- Use your canned food sensibly: avoid overlong storage periods and rotate the cans in your pantry so that the oldest items are used first. Never heat food directly in the can.

WINE

- In conventional viticulture, fungicides, insecticides and herbicides are applied to grape vines. After harvesting, winemakers use preservatives (usually sulphur dioxide or sulfites), which can cause allergic reactions. In Australia, all additives must be named on the label; in New Zealand, only sulphur dioxide must be listed.
- If you are concerned about additives, seek out certified organic wines (which contain a minimum level of preservatives) or wines that are labelled preservative-free. Bear in mind that the latter may be difficult to cellar for the long term.

PERFLUOROCHEMICALS

Perfluorochemicals, or PFCs, are found in a wide range of consumer goods. They can biodegrade to form perfluoro-octane sulfonate (PFOS), which persists in the environment and our bodies, and has been linked to an increased risk of cancer in humans, as well as developmental defects in animals. You can't avoid PFCs entirely as they are present in the atmosphere, but you can minimise exposure by limiting use of the following.

■ **NON-STICK COOKWARE** Non-stick coatings often contain PFCs. When heated to high temperatures they emit harmful fumes (which have been shown to kill pet birds). Buy stainless steel, glass or cast-iron cookware.

■ **WATER AND STAIN REPELLENTS** When buying furniture and all-weather clothing, avoid products that have been treated for water or stain resistance, and reject any additional treatments of this kind that you are offered, as they often contain PFCs.

■ **FAST-FOOD PACKAGING** PFCs are frequently added to pizza, French fry and popcorn boxes to prevent grease soaking through the cardboard.

■ ■ ■ **Look for solar-powered** or wind-up models of small electrical items, such as torches, calculators and radios.

Cosmetics and toiletries

Many personal care products are designed to penetrate the skin, but few have been evaluated for safety. So it pays to take a little time to check what's in those lotions and potions you use every day. With a little knowledge and a bit of patience, your grooming needn't cost the earth – nor affect your health.

COSMETIC CAUTION

Many cosmetics and personal care products contain petroleum derivatives, preservatives, synthetic fragrances and genetically modified ingredients, and other potentially harmful chemicals.

- Shop for toiletries in health food shops rather than supermarkets.
- Consider using beeswax-based cosmetics, such as skin creams, lip salves, eyebrow pencils, lipsticks and stick eyeshadows.
- Long chemical names in ingredients lists aren't necessarily an indication of something toxic. Use information on these pages and on the Internet to check such lists.
- Buy pump spray, roll-on or stick products, rather than aerosols, which contain greenhouse gases.
- Look for 'cruelty-free', organic and plant-based products.
- Many items labelled 'cruelty-free' or 'not tested on animals' may still contain ingredients that have been tested on animals. Examples include collagen, glycerine, keratin and lanolin. For a list of companies that adhere to a strict cruelty-free ethic, see www.choosecrueltyfree.org.au/list.html

INGREDIENTS TO LOOK FOR

- ✔ **Aloe vera** Gentle, healing, anti-inflammatory.
- ✔ **Ginseng** Has regenerative and stimulating properties.
- ✔ **Glycerine (vegetable)** Thick plant-derived liquid that is a rich moisturiser.
- ✔ **Horsetail** Astringent herb, used to strengthen hair and stimulate healthy growth.
- ✔ **Lavender** Soothing and anti-inflammatory; widely used to treat burns.
- ✔ **Lecithin** Soya bean extract that nourishes and hydrates skin.
- ✔ **Lemon grass** Toning and mildly astringent herb; used in preparations for acne.
- ✔ **Neem** Leaves from tree can be used to treat dermatitis and eczema.
- ✔ **Oats** Used to soften water, reduce redness, and relieve itching and inflammation.
- ✔ **Vitamins E and C** Both are anti-oxidants, which help skin counter damage from the sun and other environmental hazards. Vitamin C also stimulates collagen and elastin production, and has some mild bleaching properties.

SHOPPING GUIDE

These tips will help you make earth-wise choices when shopping for cosmetics and toiletries.

DEODORANTS

- Most antiperspirants and deodorants contain aluminium salts to shrink sweat glands. A link between aluminium and illness has not been proven, but experts recommend avoiding its use. Choose aluminium-free deodorant, or make your own (see *Caring for your body*, p. 187).

DEPILATORIES

- Most depilatory creams and lotions contain an array of chemicals, including irritants and allergens, as well as alkaline, corrosive substances such as sodium thioglycolate.
- Consider natural methods of hair removal – such as shaving or sugar waxing (sometimes called 'sugaring'). This involves removing unwanted hair with a mixture of sugar, lemon juice, water and citric acid, so look for those ingredients when buying a sugar-waxing product. If you prefer traditional waxing, look for beeswax as an ingredient.

■ ■ ■ **Opt for packaging made of hard plastics and glass. It's less likely to leach chemicals, especially into oil-based products.**

Ingredients to avoid

Ingredient	Comments
Alpha-hydroxy acids (AHAs)	Found in facial scrubs, peels and masks. Usually derived from citric or lactic acid, they work by having an exfoliating effect on the skin. Can cause redness and irritation; regular use may increase risk of skin cancer.
Artificial colours	FDC Red 4, FDC Red 1 (or Food Red 1) are banned in food, but may still be used in some cosmetics.
Coal tar	A petroleum derivative, usually described on labels as FD&C or D&C colours. Its antibacterial properties mean it is widely used in medicated soaps and shampoos; it is also used in some hair dyes. It contains aromatic amines that are potentially carcinogenic.
Diethanolamine (DEA)	A toxic nitrosamine believed to cause tumours in laboratory animals. Can cause allergic reactions in susceptible individuals and can form carcinogenic compounds on the skin or in the body after absorption.
Formaldehyde-releasing preservatives	Usually listed as imidazolidinyl urea, diazolidinyl urea, 2-bromo-2-nitropane-1, 3-dio, DMDM hydantoin, or quaternium 15. Formaldehyde can cause skin reactions such as dermatitis, and is a probable carcinogen.
Isopropyl alcohol	Has antibacterial, antiseptic and astringent properties, so is often included in toners and aftershaves. It is a neurotoxin and can be toxic if inhaled in large quantities.
Methylisothiazolinone	A preservative that may trigger allergic skin reactions. If inhaled, it may sensitise the lungs, resulting in asthma attacks and other respiratory problems.
Parabens	These common preservatives can affect the endocrine system and trigger allergic reactions. Derivatives have the prefixes butyl-, ethyl-, methyl- and propyl-.
Paraffin	Included in a wide variety of products, from hair removers to eye shadows and eye pencils. Prolonged contact may cause irritation, particularly of the skin.
Perfluorochemicals	Used in lotions, pressed powders, nail polish and shaving cream. Linked to cancer and reproductive damage.
Phthalates	Usually covered by the word 'fragrance'. Have been linked to reproductive and developmental problems. The most commonly used phthalate, diethylhexylphthalate (DEHP), is a probable carcinogen.
Propylene glycol (PEG)	Widely used as a hydrating ingredient, it is a skin sensitiser and causes other chemicals to penetrate skin.
Sodium lauryl sulphate	A detergent and emulsifier used in shampoos, bath additives and cleansers. Can have an irritant and drying effect on skin.
Synthetic fragrances	May be petroleum-derived. Can trigger adverse reactions, including headaches, dizziness and skin pigmentation. Almost all synthetic fragrances contain phthalates (see above). Choose natural, essential oil-based fragrances.
Tallow	Used in soaps, lipsticks, shampoos and shaving cream. Derived from the organs and tissues of sheep and cattle.
Triclosan	An antibacterial ingredient, often used in soaps and lotions marked 'antibacterial'. Its overuse may be promoting the resistance of the so-called antibiotic-resistant superbugs (MRSA).
Triethanolamine (TEA)	Used as an emulsifier. Can form carcinogenic compounds on the skin or in the body after absorption. Can cause itching, burning and blistering of skin.

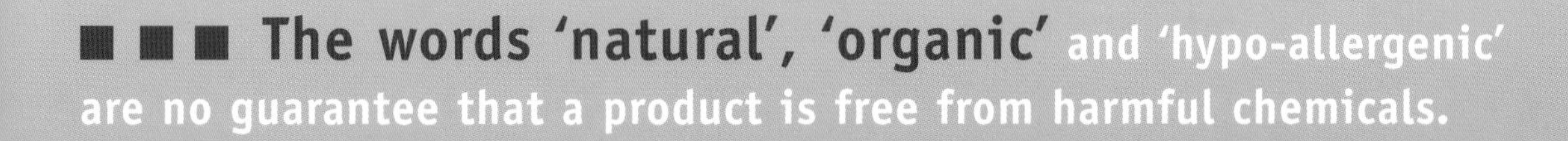

TOP TIP

If you only make one change to your usual cosmetic purchases, make it your lipstick. It's been estimated that lipstick wearers eat up to four whole tubes of lipstick in a lifetime, so make sure you're not swallowing undesirable synthetic preservatives and chemicals.

WARNING!

▼ Avoid cosmetics and toiletries whose ingredients include the terms 'fluoro-' or 'perfluoro-' as these indicate the presence of PFCs or perfluorochemicals. PFCs persist in the environment and have been linked to cancer and reproductive damage.

HAIRCARE PRODUCTS

- Look for organic shampoos and conditioners, available from some health food shops and suppliers of organic goods. Choose fragrance-free items, or those scented with botanical essential oils. The safest preservatives are grapefruit seed extract and vitamins A, C and E.
- Many mousses, hair sprays and hair gels contain phthalates – often listed as 'fragrance'.
- Permanent and semi-permanent hair dyes may contain potentially carcinogenic aromatic amines. Their use has been linked with an increased risk of some cancers, though the link is still disputed.
- Rinses and temporary dyes are safer and therefore a wiser choice. Alternatively, ask your hairdresser about less toxic dyes that have recently become available.
- Highlights or 'foils' added to your natural colour are an even safer option, since the hair dye doesn't saturate the scalp.

MAKE-UP

- It is difficult to find any eye make-up, foundation, lipstick or blusher that does not contain some chemical products. All invariably contain preservatives of some kind, because unpreserved cosmetics are prone to bacterial growth.
- Cosmetics may also contain penetration enhancers such as PEG and TEA, which sensitise the skin and allow chemicals to enter the body. TEA (triethanolamine) can form carcinogenic compounds.
- Look for the most natural, least fragranced options, preferably preserved with vitamins A, C or E. Use the Internet to check your favourite brand, or to find a better one.

NAIL CARE

- Nail polish and nail polish remover are both solvent-based products, likely to contain formaldehyde, toluene and phthalates, as well as acetone, which, if breathed in large quantities, can cause eye and respiratory-system irritation, nausea and headaches.

- It is safer to buff your nails to a natural shine. If you want to use polish, search for products that contain as few of these toxic chemicals as possible. Choose acetone-free polish remover.

PERFUME

- Discovering the ingredients of perfumes can be difficult because manufacturers are not required to list every ingredient – often the word 'fragrance' is all that is required, and it may simply be a byword for synthetic perfume. Many fragrance ingredients can be irritants, but the most worrying ingredients are the group of chemicals called phthalates, which appear in almost all perfumes and scented products, from soaps and shaving creams to air fresheners.
- A number of large international cosmetics companies are voluntarily removing two of the most dangerous phthalates – dibutyl phthalate and diethylhexyl phthalate – from their products. However, it is difficult for consumers to tell whether these components are present, as manufacturers are not required to stipulate this.
- If you are allergic to synthetic fragrances, choose fragrance-free or organic products scented with essential oils.

■ ■ ■ **Chemical residues from cotton wool balls or make-up removal pads can penetrate your skin over time.**

SANITARY PROTECTION

- Look for 100 per cent organic cotton tampons or pads. It's also possible to find cotton pads that are unbleached, or bleached with hydrogen peroxide or oxygen bleach, rather than chlorine.
- The most earth-wise solution is to opt for reusable pads. These are made from 100 per cent soft cotton fabric, come in a variety of thicknesses, and can be used for menstruation or incontinence. Check the Internet for suppliers.
- There is an alternative to tampons – a small, soft rubber cup called a menstrual cup, which collects the menstrual flow instead of absorbing it. Check the Internet for specialist suppliers.

SHAVING PRODUCTS

- Look for non-aerosol, fragrance-free, soap-based shaving creams.
- The petroleum derivative isopropyl alcohol is often included in aftershaves and toners. As alternatives, look for plant-based products containing witch hazel, rosewater, lemon grass, chamomile or cucumber. Peppermint is effective for oily skin and is also anti-inflammatory and mildly antiseptic.

SKINCARE PRODUCTS

- Look for moisturisers, body lotions and hand creams that are fragrance-free (or scented with essential oils) and contain no artificial colours. In particular, try to avoid the commonly included paraben preservatives – look for safer products that use vitamins A, C and E as preservatives.
- Seek out skincare products that are based on vegetable oil. Better still, consider making your own creams (see *Looking good*, p. 176).

SOAPS

- Choose a vegetable-based pure soap that is either fragrance-free or has an essential oil fragrance.
- Try to avoid 'antibacterial' or 'deodorant' soaps as they are likely to contain triclosan. Implicated in the growth of antibiotic-resistant 'superbugs', it can also react with chlorine in water to create chloroform, which may be inhaled, and is not readily biodegradable.

SUNSCREEN

- A sunscreen should protect you against both types of ultraviolet light – UVA and UVB. It should be labelled 'broad spectrum'.
- Although the toxic PABAs have now been eliminated from most sunscreens, almost all sunscreens still contain potentially harmful chemicals, including diethanolamine, triethanolamine and the parabens, and benzophenone, which can interfere with reproductive cycles and is thought to increase the risk of certain cancers.
- The safest alternatives are the physical UV-blockers zinc oxide and titanium dioxide, and, of course, a hat and protective clothing. (Note that the majority of the newer zinc oxide-based sunscreens don't sit on top of the skin in a thick layer like the old ones did.)

TALCUM POWDER

- Talcum powder is made from talc, a magnesium trisilicate mineral, which in its natural form may contain asbestos, a known carcinogen. As a result of this link with asbestos, all personal talcum products are now required to be certified asbestos-free. If you are still concerned but like to use a body powder, try cornflour in a fine shaker. Scent it with dried lavender – the lavender heads won't pass through the holes of the shaker. Commercial preparations are also available.

TISSUES AND TOILET PAPER

- It's hard to believe that something as simple as toilet paper could contain formaldehyde, artificial fragrance and dye, but it often does. Look for undyed, unbleached, fragrance-free tissues and toilet paper made from recycled paper.

TOOTHCARE PRODUCTS

- Some toothpastes and over-the-counter mouthwashes may contain triclosan. It reacts with chlorine in water to form chloroform and is not readily biodegradable.
- Look in your health food shop for toothpaste that is made from natural ingredients, or simply use bicarbonate of soda on a soft toothbrush. For a mouth wash, try rinsing with water and a few drops of clove or peppermint essential oil.

■ ■ ■ **To reduce waste,** avoid one-piece disposable razors. Choose a quality razor with a disposable blade instead.

Fabric matters

Making an earth-wise choice about what to wear is not as straightforward as it sounds. Just because something comes from a natural source doesn't mean it's earth-friendly. And just because it's manufactured from synthetic fibres doesn't make it all bad. These are the options to consider when shopping for fabrics.

CHOOSING FABRICS

There are two main issues to consider when choosing materials: whether the fabric is healthy and comfortable to wear and use, and whether it has been produced without damaging the environment.

- Cotton fabrics have many virtues, but conventional cotton production uses large amounts of water as well as pesticides, fertilisers and bleaches; large doses of chemicals are also required to fix dyes. Consider buying organic cotton.
- Try to avoid cotton products labelled 'easy care' or 'non-iron'. These terms indicate that the fabric has been coated with chemical resins or formaldehyde to improve wrinkle resistance. As well as exposing the wearer to potential off-gassing of these chemicals, this coating decreases the absorbency and 'breathability' of the fabric, making it less comfortable to wear. Cotton products that are 'unbleached' are less likely to be treated with formaldehyde.
- For a durable, breathable fabric that grows softer with wear, choose linen. It's made from the fibres of flax, a sustainable crop. It is sometimes combined with other natural fabrics such as hemp.
- If you suffer from allergies or asthma, hemp is a good choice as it has natural antibacterial and antiviral properties and is cool in summer and warm in winter. It's also the ultimate eco-friendly crop!

Synthetic fibres

Fibre	Production and use	Advantages	Disadvantages
Acrylic	Produced from a petrochemical called acrylontrile. Widely used, notably in sportswear.	Good elasticity, shape retention and moisture control – acrylic fabrics draw moisture away from the skin, making the wearer more comfortable.	Sensitive to heat; has static cling.
Nylon	Developed in the 1930s as an alternative to silk, nylon is made from adipic acid and hexamethylene diamine. Used in clothing, ropes, carpets, etc.	Strong, elastic, light.	Prone to static build-up; absorbs oil.
Polyester	Made from chemicals found mainly in petroleum. Used in everything from sheets to shirts and stockings.	Resists wrinkling, stretching and shrinking; easy to launder, dries quickly. Polyethylene terephthalate (PET), the most common polyester, can be recycled.	Not absorbent, doesn't breathe, so retains body odours and can make wearer hot.
Rayon	The oldest artificial fibre, dating from the late 19th century, rayon is made from cellulose obtained from wood pulp. Used mainly in clothing.	Relatively inexpensive and derived from a renewable resource. Soft and absorbent.	Processing requires high water and energy use. May be treated with formaldehyde for crease-resistance.

Hemp is prolific and requires little water and no pesticides. Clothes made from its fibres are durable but comfortable.

HEMP, THE WONDER PLANT

Hardy and prolific, hemp can be grown just about anywhere and, unlike cotton, requires little water and no chemical fertilisers. It also outgrows most weeds, resists pests and reinvigorates the soil. It's a great earth-wise choice for clothing and much more.

■ Hemp fibres are long and strong, and absorb dyes without the use of chemical fixatives. Hemp fabrics are durable, comfortable and breathable.
■ Hemp seeds can be ground into flour and yield a nutritious edible oil that is also a suitable foundation for beauty products. The oil can even be used to make ethanol fuel and as an ingredient in paints and plastics.
■ Hemp can be made into naturally acid-free paper. Production requires less energy and fewer chemicals than the production of conventional paper.
■ The strength of hemp fibres makes them ideal for use in fibreboard. Combined with lime, hemp can also provide a building material that is light, flexible, waterproof, rot- and pest-resistant and a good insulator.
■ Use of hemp has been hampered by its link with marijuana. But although it belongs to the *Cannabis* genus, it contains virtually no intoxicants.

● Sheep's wool is a versatile and resilient fibre that is absorbent and naturally dust- and flame-resistant and has good insulating properties. Compared with cotton production, wool production involves far fewer chemicals, though some treatments are used and wool can contain pesticide residues. To avoid chemicals altogether, seek out organic wool.
● Silk comes from cocoons spun by silkworms that feed on mulberry leaves. It has the highest tensile strength of any fabric and silk production has a low environmental impact. Formaldehyde is sometimes applied to silk to increase wrinkle-resistance but should not be used on products labelled '100 per cent silk'.
● Tencel is a wrinkle-free fabric made from renewable wood pulp, using non-toxic methods. It's highly absorbent, so it requires less dye than cotton, and is breathable, durable and biodegradable.
● Look for recycled polyester fleeces. Available from a number of specialist trekking shops, these garments have been made from recycled PET plastic bottles and are normally free of formaldehyde and chlorine bleaches. Remember, however, that these garments will not biodegrade.
● Other eco-friendly choices include clothing made from bamboo, which has natural antibacterial properties; ramie, made from the bark of China grass stalks (*Boehmeria nivea*), which looks and feels like linen; and soy silk, made from the by-products of the tofu-making process. Look on the Internet to find suppliers.

DYES

Wool, silk and many synthetics may be coloured with petro-chemical based dyes. Many of these leach heavy metals into groundwater and waterways during the production process.

● Where possible, choose naturally coloured cotton, which is whitened using non-polluting active oxygen, rather than chlorine bleaching.
● If you choose dyed cotton, favour lighter colours, because the darker the colour, the more chemicals are required to fix the dye.
● Consider using fabrics that have been coloured with natural dyes, which are derived from plants and minerals. Use of natural dyes is usually indicated on labels.
● Alternatively, choose undyed materials. Look for wool in its natural shades of black, grey, brown, fawn or ecru. Alpaca fibre comes in a large range of colours, from white to reddish brown and black.

■ ■ ■ **Look for eco-friendly** 'wild rubber', a faux-leather used for making hats and bags, which is becoming popular with designers.

Making your money work positively

Another way to make your money work for the benefit of the environment is to put it into socially responsible investments, or SRIs. Encompassing savings accounts, superannuation and shares, SRIs direct funds only to companies that adhere to widely accepted ethical standards. That normally means the companies follow sound environmental and employment practices, and do not produce harmful products such as arms or tobacco.

THE ETHICS OF INVESTING

Evaluation of companies for their appropriateness for socially responsible investing may cover a broad range of issues, and different funds – and individuals – have different priorities. But the following are normally assessed.

- Environmental practices: for example, pollution reduction, recycling and energy-saving measures.
- Community relations: community service projects, scholarships, philanthropic investments.
- Employee relations: wages relative to the industry, employee empowerment.
- Equal opportunities: percentage of minority groups and women in the workforce.
- Customer relations: stringent quality control, monitoring of feedback from customers.

TEN TIPS FOR ETHICAL INVESTING

1. Decide which issues are most important to you. Environmental issues may be top of the list, but you might also feel strongly about employment conditions or fair trade.

2. Research the grey areas. You may be determined to avoid the timber industry, but if you find out a company replants disused farmland, you might reconsider.

3. Take your time. Shop around for investment opportunities that are not only compatible with your personal values but also give you a good return on your money.

4. Ask questions. Request written information about where the financial organisation invests its money and how it makes its selections. Ask for rationales and any documents that support its claims. Just because a company claims to be ethical, it doesn't mean it is.

5. Make sure that the investment mix is acceptable. Often, the pros and cons are not clear-cut. Even a bank or superannuation fund that claims to be ethical may invest in what you may judge to be unethical businesses. It may exclude armaments, gambling and tobacco stocks, for instance, but still invest in petrochemical industries.

6. Check out the top 10 to 20 holdings in an investment company's portfolio. This information is available from the fund manager's web site or call centre.

7. Ask about fees. SRI management fees may be higher than mainstream ones because of the level of checking and screening. However, you may consider any extra costs worthwhile to ensure that your money is being invested responsibly.

8. Look for regularly updated rankings of socially responsible companies on the Internet.

9. Learn the language. Portfolios can include investments such as equities, property, offshore investments and venture capital, all of which may be confusing for the uninitiated. Seek out specialist advice, attend seminars and courses, and read as much as you can.

10. Make your voice heard. Shareholders have the right to raise questions about corporate governance and to table resolutions on social and environmental issues.

■ ■ ■ **When making investment choices, weigh up the environmental advantages of a scheme against any additional cost.**

Ethical investments

Favoured	Avoided
Conservation	Logging of old-growth forests
Environmental stewardship programs	Petroleum-based mining and manufacturing activities
Organic agriculture	The tobacco industry
Renewable energy	Weapons manufacturing
Human rights	Nuclear power
Fair trade	Gambling
Domestic violence counselling services	The alcohol industry
Housing cooperatives	Industries that exploit child labour
Sustainable housing	Industries that exploit the underprivileged
Community kindergartens	Factory farming
Animal welfare	Cattle feedlots
	Animal testing

SCREENING METHODS

SRI fund managers use two main methods of screening to assess businesses and industries for investment.

- **Negative screening** is the more common method. It is used to weed out enterprises involved with environmentally and ethically unacceptable practices such as deforestation, weapons manufacturing, nuclear power, animal testing, gambling and the tobacco industry.
- **Positive screening** is a much more stringent approach. Fund managers seek out enterprises that not only avoid unethical practices but also yield social and environmental benefits.

GETTING A GOOD RETURN

As banks and finance companies respond to public demand, the indicators for a growth in SRIs are encouraging. As with any investment, however, there is never a guarantee that you will make money. Points to bear in mind include the following.

- Although the percentage rise in ethical investing in recent years has outstripped mainstream investing, it starts from a much smaller base, making comparisons difficult.
- Returns on SRI can lag behind the mainstream, but that may not always be the case.
- It is up to you to assess whether your choice of investment is likely to make sufficient profit and pay an acceptable dividend. A deliberately conservative strategy will suit some investors and not others.

Socially responsible investments include ethical banking, ethical superannuation funds and ethical share portfolios.

hot links

Articles on ethical investment opportunities and developments: www.ethicalinvestor.com.au
General information about SRIs: www.csri.org.nz
Directory of SRI financial advisers and fund managers: www.eia.org.au
Social and environmental information about the companies behind the brand names: www.ethicalconsumer.org
Information about multinational companies profiting from environmental and human rights abuse: www.corpwatch.org
Rating of Australian companies and SRI funds according to environmental, social and corporate governance performance: www.corporatemonitor.com.au
Indexes tracking the performance of international and Australian companies that lead their industry in terms of corporate sustainability: www.sustainability-indexes.com/htmle/sustainability/sustinvestment.html; www.aussi.net.au/htmle/sustainability/sustinvestment.html

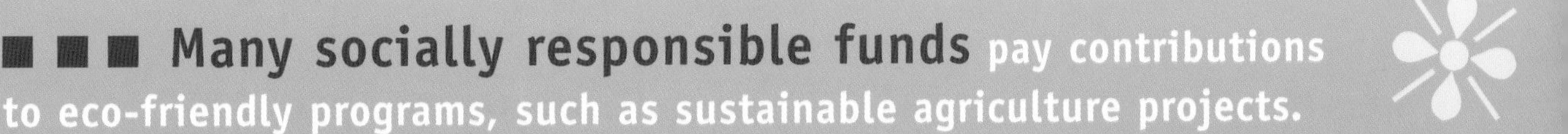

Many socially responsible funds pay contributions to eco-friendly programs, such as sustainable agriculture projects.

ON THE ROAD

If you choose the right car, drive your car less and use other forms of transport, you'll cut fuel emissions.

Using your car

For many of us, cars are indispensable, even though they are not the most earth-wise form of transport. If you can't do without one, you can easily modify your driving habits to cut your fuel consumption. In the process, you will significantly lessen your car's impact on the environment. You'll also be surprised at the savings you can make.

TEN TIPS FOR LOW-ENERGY DRIVING

1 Always try to drive smoothly. Avoid accelerating and braking unnecessarily and use your gears to help you slow down. Speeding up and slowing down (between traffic lights, for instance) wastes fuel. To drive smoothly, you need to become more alert to road conditions and anticipate traffic flow. If you can work out what's about to happen on the road ahead, you won't be caught by surprise.

2 Leave a reasonable distance between your car and the vehicle in front. If the other car changes its speed, you should have enough space and time to take your foot off the accelerator and slow down without breaking, or to accelerate gently and smoothly to keep up with traffic flow.

3 To avoid either braking or accelerating sharply, which wastes fuel, pretend there's an egg between your foot and the pedals – doing so will help you to press on them more gently.

4 If your car is a manual, shift up through the gears as soon as possible to avoid the coughing or chugging sound that indicates the engine is strained. Driving in top gear is much more economical than driving in a lower gear.

5 On a long stretch of road, use overdrive if you have it. This top gear (usually the fifth) enables the drive shaft to turn faster than the engine crankshaft, thus allowing the engine to run more slowly. This will in turn save fuel and reduce engine wear and noise.

6 Cut down your driving speed to save fuel. At 110 km/h, your car uses up to 25 per cent more fuel than it would cruising along at 90 km/h.

7 Consider turning off your car's airconditioner and opening the window. If you run your car's cooling system on a hot day in city driving conditions, you'll increase your fuel consumption by about 15 per cent. At faster cruising speeds, airconditioning is more efficient – but you'll still use about 11 per cent more fuel than if you switched it off.

8 Clean out your car every now and then so you're not carrying any unnecessary extra weight. It's easy to forget about items you may have left in the boot.

9 You can cut your fuel consumption by as much as 20 per cent simply by removing unnecessary extras such as roof-racks and spoilers. They increase wind resistance, making the trip harder work for your car.

10 Whenever you're stuck in a traffic jam or idling for longer than a few minutes, turn off your engine. You'll save more fuel than you'll use in restarting the engine.

■ ■ ■ **If you use a roof-rack for a one-off purpose such as a camping trip, reduce wind resistance by taking it off afterwards.**

CAR-SHARING SCHEMES

Car-sharing schemes are popular in Europe and the United States. It's a new concept in Australia and New Zealand, but it has been predicted that such schemes will bring about a revolution in private car ownership. Essentially, the concept is similar to a short-term rental. You pay a periodic membership fee to the company running the scheme and then an hourly rate whenever you use a vehicle, plus a certain amount per kilometre. These are the advantages.

- It's convenient. You have access to a car whenever you need it. The scheme is ideal for people who use public transport to travel to work, but need a car for short periods on weekends or for holidays.
- It's economical. You don't have to incur the considerable expense of buying a vehicle or paying for ongoing costs, such as registration, insurance and regular parking fees.
- It's earth-wise. If the scheme takes off, it will reduce the number of cars on the road, cutting the environmental impact of fuel emissions.

Making a number of short trips can use twice as much fuel as one multi-purpose trip covering the same distance when the engine is warmed up and efficient.

PLANNING AHEAD

Here are some ideas on how to reduce the number of times you use the car on a regular basis. Once again, you'll save money.

- Combine shopping with as many other errands as possible. Even in a small, modern, fuel-efficient car, a 6-km round-trip can use half a litre of fuel – that's close to 80 litres per year if you make the trip three times a week.
- Avoid peak-hour traffic whenever possible. In terms of fuel use, peak hour is the most expensive time to drive. If you're driving in start–stop driving conditions in heavy traffic, your car will typically use 20–30 per cent more fuel than if you're driving on free-flowing highways.
- Use Park 'n' Ride. With this scheme, commuters park their cars in a designated and secure place on the city outskirts and transfer to public transport (usually a train) to complete their journeys. Find out if the Park 'n' Ride scheme is available in your city.
- Car pool. Share the drive and split the fuel costs. Check with friends or neighbours who travel to similar destinations at similar times. If there are three or more passengers, you may be able to use a transit lane, which will make your journey much faster.

hot links

How a car-share scheme works: www.portphillip.vic.gov.au/car_share.html
Car-pooling information: www.travelsmart.gov.au/employers/carpool.html; www.carshare.co.nz
Not-for-profit organisations that plant trees to absorb the greenhouse gases emitted by your car: www.greenfleet.com.au; www.carbonneutral.com.au

Driving at 60 km per hour in third gear uses about 25 PER CENT MORE fuel than driving at the same speed in fifth gear.

Choosing a car

Before you choose your next car, ask yourself whether you really need one, or whether you'd be better off using taxis or renting a car occasionally when necessary. Most motorists don't realise how much it costs just to keep a car on the road. If you must have a car, consider buying a smaller model that is more economical to run.

ASSESSING YOUR NEEDS

After a house, a car is likely to be the second biggest purchase you'll ever make. Before you buy one, realistically assess your needs. Ask yourself the following questions and answer them honestly.

Australia has the world's second-highest car ownership rate after the United States, with New Zealand ranking third.

- Can you afford to run a car? Apart from fuel, the less obvious on-road costs include depreciation, regular servicing and repairs, registration and insurance – plus the time you spend on cleaning, servicing and fuelling your vehicle.
- Can you afford to buy a new car? Big savings can be made if you find a good second-hand car, but remember that more recent models are less polluting than older cars, making them more environmentally friendly. Also, the use of lighter materials and better technology in newer models mean you'll spend less on fuel.
- If most of your journeys are city-based, do you really need an off-road vehicle such as a four-wheel-drive? The operating cost for large 4WDs can be three times that of the smallest cars.
- How many passengers do you usually carry? Larger, heavier vehicles use more fuel than smaller, lighter alternatives. Big cars can cost two and a half times as much to run as their petite counterparts. If you need a large car occasionally, it's more economical to buy a smaller one for everyday use and hire a larger model when necessary.
- Could you manage with a smaller car? A vehicle's fuel economy improves by 7 per cent for each 10 per cent of weight removed from its body. A smaller car also helps reduce greenhouse car emissions.

TOP TIP

If you decide to buy a new vehicle in Australia, check the fuel consumption label on the windscreen. It will tell you how many litres of petrol the car uses to travel a standard 100 km. A difference of 2 litres of fuel every 100 km will save about 1500 litres of fuel over 5 years of average driving.

PROS & CONS

FOUR-WHEEL-DRIVES

Four-wheel-drive (4WD) vehicles are popular for their towing power and their off-road performance. However, they can use more than twice the amount of fuel of smaller vehicles and cost more to run in tyres and servicing. They don't fare well in terms of safety either – large models, which may weigh more than 2 tonnes, take longer to stop, and are more likely to roll over. Also, in the event of an accident, vehicles fitted with bull-bars are more likely to kill pedestrians. Off the road, the power of 4WD vehicles to churn up unstable soil causes environmental damage.

Eco plastic, made from renewable sources such as sugar-cane, is now being used to make car accessories, such as floor mats.

- Is an automatic vehicle better than a manual one? A mid-size, modern, petrol-driven car with five-speed automatic gearing might do 8.9 km per litre in city conditions and 12.7 km per litre on highways. The same car with five-speed manual gearing is about 14 per cent more fuel-efficient.
- Is a diesel engine better than a petrol one? Although diesel contains more energy per litre than petrol, and diesel engines are more efficient to run, it is a more polluting fuel than petrol.
- Should you buy or rent a hybrid car? A hybrid car uses both electric and petrol engines in combination and cuts fuel consumption significantly. Although the saving in fuel costs doesn't yet cover the cost of the technology, this may change as the cost of fuel rises. A few models are available.
- Would it be cheaper to take a taxi than drive when you need to go somewhere? If you only use one occasionally, taxis are cheaper than owning and running a car.

OVERSEAS TRENDS

In Europe both individual governments and the European Union (EU) have been supporting the push for greener cars.

- The European Union is encouraging the development of low emissions from conventional fuels as well as lower emissions from alternative fuels.
- The French goverment is introducing a higher car registration tax, based on a car's pollution levels, and is also funding research to design a family car that will consume less than 3.5 litres of fuel every 100 km.

hot links

Estimate your annual carbon dioxide emissions:
www.greenhouse.gov.au/fuellabel/environment.html
Compare car-operating expenses:
www.mynrma.com.au/operating_costs.asp
The Australian Government's Green Vehicle Guide:
www.greenvehicleguide.gov.au

FUTURE GLIMPSES

Car manufacturers are constantly trying to come up with alternatives to fuel-guzzling petrol engines. Watch out for these innovations.

■ **BUILT-IN FUEL SAVERS** These range from simple devices, such as one that switches the engine off when idling and back on again when you accelerate, to complex technologies, such as 'lean burn' engines that combine less fuel per volume of air than conventional engines.

■ **HYDROGEN FUEL CELL CAR** In theory, this car, invented by the Swiss, can drive around the globe using only 8 litres of fuel. Hydrogen is pollution-free – its only waste product is water. However, production, provision and storage issues remain unresolved, and the vehicle is still too expensive to be commercially viable.

■ **LIGHTWEIGHT MATERIALS** Researchers constantly try to reduce aerodynamic drag, partly caused by the type of materials cars are made from. Traditionally, steel has been used, but these days manufacturers are using more plastic, aluminium and carbon fibre.

■ **ZERO-POLLUTION CAR** French-designed, this vehicle runs on compressed air technology (CAT). About to go into production, it can run for 10 hours around the city and is able to reach 110 km/h on less congested roads. This car can be refuelled quickly with just an air pump at a petrol station.

■ ■ ■ **A car with a 5-speed** manual transmission is about 14 per cent more fuel-efficient than an equivalent automatic car.

Reducing emissions

Although petrol-driven cars are bad news for the environment, today's cars are ten to twenty times cleaner – in terms of emissions – than cars in the 1970s, and cleaner, greener fuels are now being developed. In the meantime, driving carefully and looking after your car will minimise its environmental impact.

REDUCING EMISSIONS

- Buy a new or late-model car and think small! Since 1986, new cars sold in Australia and New Zealand have been fitted with catalytic converters to reduce the level of harmful exhaust emissions. On average, the smaller and newer your car, the less polluting it will be.
- If you're purchasing a new car in Australia, check the fuel information label before you buy. The fuel consumption is shown in a red box and carbon dioxide emission in a green box. A low CO_2 figure indicates that the car is a relatively environmentally friendly vehicle.
- Have your car serviced regularly. Expert maintenance will ensure the engine is tuned so that it runs at an optimum level, delivering power without burning excessive fuel. The service should include checking components such as spark plugs and air filters, which are crucial to an engine's efficiency.

PROS & CONS

ETHANOL

A type of alcohol made from agricultural crops, ethanol has been proposed as an eco-friendly alternative fuel, and a 10 per cent blend, E10, has been approved for use in new cars by most car manufacturers. Ethanol does have some green credentials: when burned as a fuel, its only by-products are water and carbon dioxide, and the latter is offset by carbon dioxide emitted by the crops. However, growing and transporting the crops and manufacturing the ethanol require significant amounts of fossil fuel energy. Indeed, studies have shown that the use of E10 is likely to reduce vehicle greenhouse emissions by just 1–5 per cent – at most, only 0.4 per cent of Australia's total emissions. Moreover, the different chemical properties of E10 relative to conventional fuel result in higher levels of groundwater pollution by benzene, a known carcinogen.

- Make sure your tyres have the recommended air pressure. Underinflated tyres offer more resistance, so your engine has to work harder, using more fuel and emitting more carbon dioxide. Check the tyre pressure about once a month. For an accurate reading, check your tyres when they are cold (when you drive your car, the tyres heat up and the pressure increases).
- Avoid petrol spills at the pump – don't overfill your tank. Spilled petrol is especially polluting because it evaporates straight into the atmosphere. On average, to emit the same amount of hydrocarbons in your exhaust as you would release by spilling 1 litre of petrol, you'd have to drive 12,000 km.

AVOIDING POLLUTION

- Before entering a long tunnel and in a traffic jam, close your windows and either turn off the air-conditioner or set it to recirculate the air already inside. Otherwise, the pollution levels inside the car can build up to more than ten times the levels outside.
- Turn off the car engine in a lengthy traffic jam or when waiting for someone.
- Don't run your car engine in enclosed spaces, where poisonous fumes can build up. The deadliest exhaust gas is carbon monoxide, which is colourless, odourless and poisonous. It is slightly lighter than air, so it floats away rather than builds up from the ground.

■ ■ ■ **Governments are legislating** to progressively reduce sulphur levels in diesel fuel in order to reduce air pollution.

Alternative fuels

Type	Advantages	Disadvantages
Biodiesel	Made from any fat or oil and runs in conventional diesel engines without modification. Reduces carbon monoxide (a greenhouse gas) by 33% and black smoke by 26%.	Biodiesel dates back to the early 20th century, but it's still virtually unobtainable commercially in Australia and New Zealand. This may change as world demand for oil continues to grow, making biodiesel more price competitive.
Compressed natural gas (CNG)	Efficient, compared with commercial diesel engines, CNG-burning engines can reduce carbon monoxide emissions by 90% and particulate matter by 50%. Already used by some urban buses. Made up of 95% methane, CNG reduces greenhouse emissions by about 30–40% for cars.	Having your car converted to CNG is expensive, and only a small number of refuelling stations stock it.
Electricity	New batteries are lighter, longer lasting and less toxic than conventional batteries – and can be charged either by being refilled or plugged into a charger. Electricity is generally better for the environment than petrol, as it can be produced en masse by turbines at a power station more efficiently than petrol can be turned into energy in thousands of separate car engines.	Conventional batteries tend to be bulky and slow to recharge. Electric cars generally have lower top speeds because they are smaller vehicles, designed for urban, rather than highway, use.
Ethanol	Derived from agricultural crops, and added to petrol. The carbon dioxide released by burning the ethanol is offset by the carbon dioxide absorbed from the atmosphere by the crops before harvesting.	Has less energy than petrol, so motorists must buy 3.5% more E10 fuel to travel the same distance. Releases higher levels of benzene into groundwater than conventional fuel. Using ethanol/petrol blends may cause starting difficulties, engine knock and other problems.
Liquified petroleum gas (LPG)	A mixture of propane and butane (the same mix that fuels suburban barbecues). Has been used in transport for more than 60 years and is popular with taxi firms. Compared with petrol or diesel, cuts greenhouse gas emissions by about 10%.	LPG consumption on the open road can be up to 30% higher than that for petrol, although in the city it is only 10–20% higher. Not all service stations stock LPG. Also, an LPG tank can take up a lot of boot space. Taxi drivers report LPG doesn't always give the same acceleration as petrol.

- If you can, use trains more often. A Sydney study showed that car commuters were exposed to the highest levels of several pollutants. Bus commuters were exposed to the highest levels of nitrogen dioxide. Train commuters breathed the cleanest air.
- Walkers and cyclists have significantly lower levels of exposure to benzene compared with car commuters and significantly lower levels of exposure to nitrogen dioxide than bus commuters.

FUEL CHOICES

- Diesel contains more energy per litre than petrol. Unfortunately, diesel engines pollute the air more than comparable petrol or liquified petroleum gas (LPG) vehicles and they emit particulate matter and nitrogen oxides that can cause health problems. Diesel with minimal sulphur will soon become mandatory.
- Lead-replacement petrol is required by some cars with older engines (mainly those built before 1986) but few vehicles now use it. If you run an old car and can't find lead-replacement petrol, use premium unleaded and a lead-replacement additive.
- Depending on the make and model of car, high-octane petrol may or may not improve engine performance and fuel economy.
- Lobby groups want no more than 10 per cent of ethanol in petrol until research shows it won't damage either fuel systems or engines.

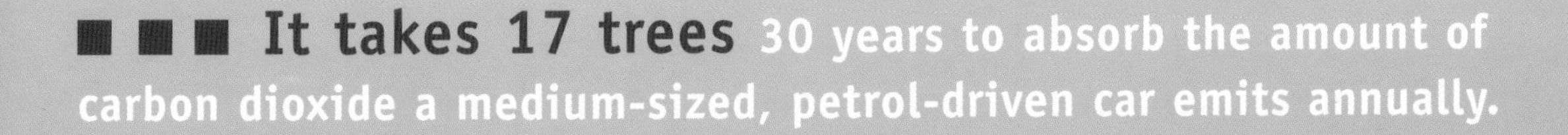

Earth-wise maintenance

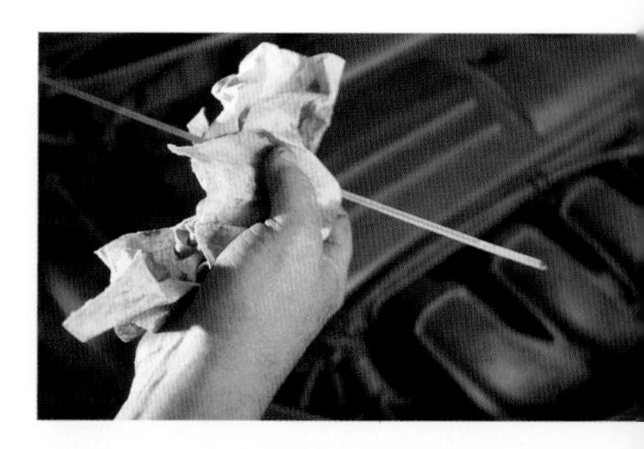

Maintaining your car in top working order will have the engine working at maximum efficiency while burning minimum fuel. For instance, not only does the oil lubricate metal engine parts, it also helps to keep the engine free of the dirty by-products of fuel combustion.

Just 1 litre of oil can contaminate 1 million litres of water.

REGULAR CAR CARE

- When filling your petrol tank, stop when you hear the first click of the petrol pump switching off. That click indicates the tank's optimum level. If you keep filling, it's likely to overflow.
- Measure your tyre pressure regularly. Driving on under-inflated tyres can add 15 per cent to your petrol bill and take 15 per cent off the life of your tyres.
- You should change your oil every 5000–7000 km if you frequently make short runs of under 10 km, if you drive in city traffic with many stops and starts, if you tow a caravan, trailer or heavy load regularly, or if you drive in dusty, sandy or salty conditions.
- Check your vehicle's fluid levels every 500 km in order to top them up or replace them. These fluids may include: coolant, anti-freeze, brake/clutch, battery electrolyte, windscreen wiper and headlamp cleaner.
- If you often drive your car on rough roads, or on surfaces covered with anti-freeze or salt, inspect the chassis – including the axle shafts and steering box – to prevent or remedy corrosion and rust. Joints, hinges and door catches may all need lubrication.

- Check and replace windscreen wipers when the rubber in them has worn out; if you don't, not only will they be ineffective, but they may also scratch the windscreen.

SAVING WATER

Before washing your car, find out if there are any water restrictions in force. During a drought, car washing is one of the first activities to be restricted.

- Avoid washing your car on the driveway with a hose as it wastes water and allows dirt, grease and detergents to run down drains. Place it on a grassy area instead, to minimise run-off.
- Try to use vegetable oil based soaps to wash your car, but if you do use car shampoos, always wash your car on the lawn. Car shampoos contain phosphates similar to those found in fertilisers.
- Use a sponge and bucket or watering can. It takes a little more time than using a hose but saves water. Washing your car with a hose typically uses four or five times as much water as the sponge-and-bucket option.
- Consider reusing your laundry rinse water to wash the car. Using grey water, as it's known, is a good way of getting twice as much use out of a precious resource.
- Wash your car in the shade – slower evaporation helps conserve water and avoids streaks on the paint as the car dries.
- Don't bother buying expensive finishing treatments. A chamois and vigorous rubbing is the best way to achieve a streak-free finish.
- Try using a commercial spray to clean your car. It cleans and polishes without using any water or chemicals and is biodegradable. All you need to do is rub with a towel or microfibre cleaning cloth.

■ ■ ■ **You can wash your car thoroughly with a sponge, bucket and just 54 litres, or 6 buckets, of water.**

- If you don't want to clean your car yourself, take it to a car wash. It will probably use less water than a hose, and the oil from your car will be diverted into the sewer, not into the stormwater drain. Many car wash companies are now recycling their water.

How much water?

- Hose wash: 220 litres
- Automatic car wash: 100 litres
- Self-serve car wash: 60 litres
- Hand wash, 6 buckets of water: 54 litres

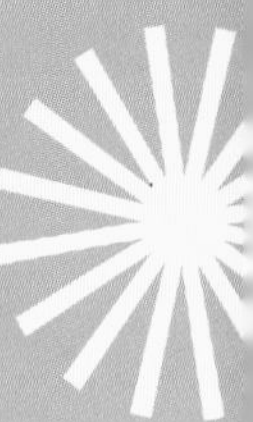

RECYCLING OIL

Even if you don't use your car very often, you should change the oil in your car at least every 10,000–12,000 km or every year. Here's what to do with the used oil, which is toxic, carcinogenic and a potential fire hazard.

- When you top up your car's oil levels, place a container under the engine to catch drips. Clean any spills immediately with a damp cloth.
- If you change the oil yourself, dispose of it responsibly. Place the used oil in a secure container. Don't pour it into a drum in the corner of your garage and forget about it, or dump it with the garbage, as it may eventually leach out to pollute the environment. And never pour it down a drain.
- If you have the oil changed at a licensed service station, the mechanic will store the used oil (sump oil) for recycling. This involves de-watering, filtering and de-mineralising the oil before it can be used in industrial burners.
- In Australia, check the Department of the Environment and Heritage's oil recycling web site for the location of your nearest used-oil recycler or drop-off depot. If you live in New Zealand, ask your local garage if it accepts used oil for recycling. If it doesn't, check with your local council to find out where you should take it.

HOME-MADE CAR CLEANERS

CAR WAX

Wax forms a protective layer between your car's paint and the corrosive emissions from other cars and road dirt.

1 cup linseed oil
4 tbsp carnauba wax (from hardware stores)
2 tbsp beeswax (from hardware stores and large supermarkets)
½ cup vinegar

- Place the ingredients in a saucepan or the top half of a double boiler and heat slowly, stirring gently until the wax melts.
- Pour the mixture into a heat-resistant container.

- Once the wax is solid, rub it onto your car with a lint-free cloth, using a brisk side-to-side motion without undue pressure.
- To finish off, soak the corner of a clean cotton rag in a little extra vinegar and polish the wax to a rich shine.

WINDSCREEN CLEANER

This cleaning mixture will keep your windscreen free of ice and frost in cold weather.

vinegar
water

- In a pump spray bottle mix 3 parts vinegar with 1 part water.
- Wet a clean cloth with the mixture and coat the car windows with it.
- Allow to dry.

Use vegetable oil based liquid soap to wash your car. It's better for the environment than detergents.

Green wheels

If you live in the city but don't want to use a car, you can choose an earth-wise alternative, such as riding a bicycle or catching public transport. There are several benefits for you, including improved fitness and cost savings, and there are benefits for the environment too. Fewer cars on the road mean a cleaner, healthier environment for all.

USING THE SYSTEM

Public transport helps reduce greenhouse gas emissions, improves local air quality and reduces traffic congestion.

If the number of people using public transport increased by 45 per cent, there would be a 28 per cent decrease in air pollution.

- Travel by train or bus whenever you can. It takes another car off the road and it uses less fuel per passenger, provided most of the seats on your bus or train are full.
- If your area isn't well served by public transport, consider driving part of the way and switching to train, bus, light rail or tram on the city outskirts.

- Check whether your local transit authority provides an Internet link or phone service listing timetables. The Internet is an especially useful tool for accessing integrated transport information, allowing you to work out the most efficient way of getting around.
- Travel in off-peak periods when you can. If you avoid the peak hour you'll find a seat more easily. Also rail networks typically offer off-peak tickets for at least a third of the price of a regular return ticket – that's a significant saving over a year.

THE SAVVY COMMUTER

Travel to and from work accounts for a quarter of all car travel. Here are some suggestions for changing the way you use commuter transport.

- Find out if your employer has a strategy for encouraging staff to use their cars less. Options include allowing staff to work from home if possible, interest-free loans to purchase public transport season tickets and salary package alternatives to a company car.
- Ask your employer if working flexible hours is a possibility. If so, you will be able to avoid peak commuting times, at least on some days.
- If public transport in your area is inadequate, set the ball rolling by joining a lobby group to improve it. Talk to other commuters in your area, then work out what sort of changes are needed. Finally, write letters to your local political representative, council or newspaper.

SHORT COMMUTES

If you only have a short distance to travel, you have several transport options – from your own two feet to motorbikes or scooters that use fuel economically.

■ ■ ■ Trains are responsible for LESS POLLUTION than any other commonly used form of transport.

Public transport

Type	Earth-wise rating
Eco buses	Some buses use compressed natural gas, hybrid combustion engines or battery or fuel cells. One type uses biodiesel, made from renewable sources such as sunflower oil. All these alternative power sources create less carbon monoxide than conventional engines.
Ferries	Most ferries are powered by diesel or diesel-electric engines, which generate air pollution. Environmentally friendly anti-fouling paint (which also reduces fuel consumption) and catamaran hulls designed to minimise wash are innovations that are helping to minimise the vessels' effect on the environment.
Light rail	A newer and lighter version of trams, light rail is enjoying a renaissance as its speedy, efficient and non-polluting advantages are recognised. In the past 25 years, more than 35 cities – including Sydney, Paris, Buenos Aires and Houston – have introduced new light rail systems.
Trains	Trains are responsible for less air pollution than any other commonly used form of transport. Compared with individual petrol engines, trains use a relatively clean form of power – electricity.
Trams	Trams run on electricity, so they don't release any fumes into city streets. But unless they run on dedicated routes, trams contribute to pollution by slowing other traffic and causing congestion.
Trolleybuses	Trolleybuses use an electrical charge transmitted through overhead wires, so they don't contribute to city fumes. However, if their transmission poles come off the overhead wires, they can cause traffic congestion. Some are fitted with emergency battery power.

Future ferries

Future ferries are likely to use hybrid marine power (HMP), which combines electric drives with hydrocarbon or alternative fuels – and sometimes uses sail power, too. HMP is optimised by computer, like a hybrid car. The system powers a 100-passenger charter cruise catamaran called *Sydney Solar Sailor*, now plying Sydney Harbour. Solar panels mounted on the deck and on special, wing-like 'sails' provide electricity to drive the propellers. An Australian invention, HMP suits a wide range of marine applications, from ferries and private yachts to large tankers.

- If you're fit and agile, and traffic conditions are safe in your area, consider buying a scooter, a skateboard, rollerskates or rollerblades. They're relatively cheap to buy and faster than walking. But check the council by-laws in your local area first. And be sure to wear the appropriate safety gear for each mode of transport.
- For a little extra power, consider an electric bike. Both earth-wise and convenient, it's powered by a rechargeable nickel-hydride battery, weighs only 18 kilograms and can travel about 25 km without being recharged. The whole bike folds neatly into a car boot. With a 200-watt motor, the bike has a top speed of 20–25 km/h. You'll need to ride it on bike paths and in other safe areas. For safety, do not ride on the road with fast-moving traffic.
- If you need to go further than a bike could take you, consider the benefits of a small motorcycle. On average it uses less fuel than a car – a smaller model may average about 40 km per litre – and is more manoeuvrable. Choose a lightweight model with an engine of 125 cc or less for maximum fuel economy.
- If you want a powered bike but don't want anything as big as a motorbike – or something you must straddle – consider a motor scooter (pictured, opposite top). It's more economical than a motorcycle, with engine capacities as small as 50 cc. Some scooters can travel 50 km or further on a litre of petrol. And you don't necessarily need a licence to drive one.

■ ■ ■ **One of the advantages** of using PUBLIC TRANSPORT is that you can work on a laptop, read or meditate while you travel.

On two wheels

Not only is cycling fun, it will also save you money in transport costs. It's easy on the environment and, if you ride a bicycle regularly, it will keep you fit. While today's bikes look much the same as they did 50 years ago, technological advances and new materials have made them lighter, stronger and faster.

GETTING STARTED

- Buy a second-hand bike to begin with, or wait until your nearest cycle shop has its next sale. There's no point in buying an expensive model, with all the bells and whistles, if you don't take to cycling.
- Ask for advice. Critical aspects – such as seat height, the position of handlebars and gear adjustment – can make all the difference between a comfortable ride and an unnecessarily arduous one. So be honest with the bike shop about your fitness level and your needs.
- If you enjoy the social aspect of cycling and want to become involved with a group, look out for a Bicycle Users Group (BUG) in your area. BUGs regularly organise rides as well as lobby the government for better facilities for cyclists.
- Check the Internet for foreign cycling tours that combine exercise with cultural tourism. There's a huge variety from which to choose – from exploring medieval villages in Spain by bicycle to pedalling around the Andes – and it's a great way to meet people.

CHOOSING A BIKE

Bicycles are designed for different purposes. You'll save a lot of energy if you choose the right one for your needs.

- **RACING BIKES** These suit dedicated cyclists who ride on well-surfaced roads. Built for speed rather than strength, their wheels and tyres are narrow and their frames are lightweight. However, racing bike tyres tend to get punctures very easily.
- **TOURING BIKES** More robust than racing bikes, touring bikes are less speedy but better equipped to deal with standard road conditions. This makes them a good choice for commuting or recreational rides, where reliability rather than speed is the issue.
- **MOUNTAIN BIKES** Robust, with fatter wheels than racing or touring bikes, these have very low 'granny gears' for riding up hills. Sometimes they have suspension. You need a mountain bike for handling off-road tracks without getting a puncture. However, it does have more drag, so you need more energy to ride one.
- **HYBRID BIKES** These bikes combine elements of touring and mountain bikes. Like the latter, they have fatter wheels than touring bikes. Often they feature more gears (for easier hill-climbing) and have straight handlebars. They're good for commuting and weekend riding with the family.

COMMUTING

If you live within 10 km of work or school (or more if you're fit), bicycle commuting is an excellent option.

- If it's safe, get children to ride their bikes to school.
- Plan your route before setting out. Use cycle paths when they're available and roads when you have to. You may need maps and information provided by local cycling groups to find the best route.
- Check out the parking facilities where you work. You'll need somewhere convenient and dry to store your bike. Car parks often have corner spaces that aren't large enough for cars.
- Ask your employer to consider providing bike racks where you can lock your bike while at work.
- Contact your local cycling organisation or council. They may be able to offer helpful suggestions. Many cities support bicycle commuting as part of a strategy to cut the number of cars on the roads.
- Check with your travel agent if you want to take your bicycle overseas. Many airlines take bikes free of charge, provided it's within your baggage allowance.

■ ■ ■ **If you find you enjoy cycling,** consider getting fit for a long-distance bike ride – it's a great goal to aim for.

BIKE SMART

Urban cycle paths are often shared with other traffic, even when they are marked with bicycle symbols, so take care at all times.

✔ Look for a safe route if you're commuting to work or school. In many cities busy streets are often complemented by quieter back roads.

✔ Always wear a helmet. In a serious accident, it can be the difference between life and death. In Australia and New Zealand, helmets are compulsory for cyclists, although there are specific limited exemptions that vary according to the jurisdiction.

✔ Wear reflective clothing if you're going to be out after dark. Fix a light to the front and rear of your bicycle and make sure both lights are switched on from dusk onwards.

✔ Watch out for people in parked cars opening doors. Often they don't check for cyclists before they get out.

✔ Buy a sturdy lock so you can park your bike, confident that it will be there when you return. If it has a removable front wheel, make sure the lock secures both wheels.

✘ Don't be tempted to run traffic lights or use footpaths. Obey the rules of the road, just like other road users.

✘ Don't lean your bike against shop windows or park it in the way of pedestrians.

✘ If you're taking your bicycle on the train, make sure your bicycle doesn't block doorways or aisles, making it difficult for other passengers.

A study in Denmark involving 30,000 people, followed over 14 years, found that cycling to work decreased the risk of early death by 40 per cent.

hot links

Australia's top cycling portal with links to Australian cycling organisations: www.bicycles.net.au
Cycling and Loving it: www.womenscycling.com.au
The Cycling Promoting Fund: www.cyclingpromotion.com
Rail Trails in Australia: www.railtrails.org.au
Bicycle Industry Association of New Zealand: www.bianz.org.nz

- To boost the range of your bicycle, consider taking it on a train for part of the journey. The rules and charges vary from place to place, so check beforehand. In some cities, you can convey your bike for free on weekends and in off-peak periods. Otherwise, you must buy a child ticket for the bicycle as well as a ticket for yourself.

SHOPPING BY BIKE

- Bikes are great for shopping if it's practical for you to shop frequently for small amounts. Consider home delivery only for bulky or heavy items, or use the car for these when necessary.
- If your local shopping centre doesn't provide bike racks, ask shopkeepers, the shopping centre management or your local council to install some. Your local cycling organisation can advise you on the best way to go about it.
- Buy sturdy, capacious and waterproof pannier bags. You can fit a surprising amount into them.
- Keep your tyres pumped up – it reduces drag, which is greater when you have a heavier load.

■ ■ ■ **Cycling reduces the risk** of heart disease, high blood pressure, obesity and the most common form of diabetes.

TRAVELLING LIGHT

Wherever you travel, tread lightly on the earth by taking eco holidays and exploring on foot.

Your own two feet

No matter where you're holidaying, walking is often the best way to experience a different place. Instead of rushing past scenery at high speed in a car or train, you'll be able to hear birdsong, spot animals and see wildflowers, as well as take the time to simply stop and reconnect with the natural world.

WHY WALK?

- It's a slower way of getting around that lets you really wind down. If you've been working hard and sitting at a desk all year, a walking holiday is the perfect antidote.
- It's cheap. Many long-distance walks are well signposted with inexpensive or free accommodation along the way, so you don't have to book an expensive organised tour.
- You don't have to be super-fit to enjoy a walking holiday. If you're not up to marathon walks, base yourself somewhere beautiful and walk just a little each day.
- Walking is an unobtrusive way of being in the landscape. If you move quietly, you'll see wildlife that you wouldn't normally see from a car.
- If you're out in the country, walking gives you a break from the built environment and pollution, and lets you breathe fresh air.
- You'll be able to reach out-of-the-way places. Mountain terrain is often inaccessible to cars, but a network of tracks may be open to walkers. Being away from traffic and noise enjoying spectacular scenery can be an exhilarating experience.
- It's satisfying being self-sufficient.

FIVE WALKS FOR BEGINNERS

Walking has become a distinct sector of the travel industry, with specialist walking tour operators around the world. If you do your research, it's easy to arrange shorter walks yourself. Here are five good walks around Australia and New Zealand for reasonably fit beginners.

- Tasmania's Cradle Mountain–Lake St Clair National Park offers excellent bushwalks. Beginners can try a circuit of Dove Lake, about 90 minutes on prepared paths, which is mostly flat.
- In Sydney, the renowned coastal walk between Bondi and Bronte is invigorating, spectacular and just 3.5 km in length, proving that scenic walks don't have to be in the wilderness.
- In Queensland, you can walk shorter stretches of the 30-km Whitsunday Great Walk near Proserpine, which offers paths through majestic tropical rainforest as well as views of the Whitsunday Islands. These shorter walks are linked to the main track so you can join or leave it as you wish.
- Auckland's 16-km Coast to Coast Walkway has panoramic views of sea, gardens and ancient Maori fortification sites.
- A walk around sleepy Akaroa – an historic town on the South Island's Banks Peninsula, about 85 km from Christchurch – takes about 2 hours.

BE PREPARED

- If you're interested in joining an organised tour, find out how much walking is involved. Tours range from a kilometre or two of city sightseeing to walks covering substantial distances – perhaps as much as 10–18 km most days.
- Check what sort of terrain and distances you'll be facing. Trekking tours frequently involve arduous walking as well as some climbing.
- Buy footwear at least 6 weeks in advance so you can break it in gradually and avoid blisters on your walking holiday.

■ ■ ■ **In Europe,** some walking tours are designed around GOURMET CUISINE, and stop at inns serving regional specialties.

WHAT TO TAKE

- ✔ A broad-brimmed hat
- ✔ Sunscreen
- ✔ Insect repellent
- ✔ Sunglasses
- ✔ Clothes suitable for varied weather
- ✔ Wet weather gear
- ✔ A map and compass (if necessary)
- ✔ Plenty of water, especially in hot countries

TOP TIP

After a hard day's walking or sightseeing, soak your tired feet in a warm bath of lavender tea. If you've developed a blister, apply a compress of soothing lavender oil to the area – it will help the blister go down and its antibacterial properties should prevent infection.

- Don't assume that willpower and enthusiasm alone will sustain you. When did you last walk 18 km in one day? Before you commit yourself to a booking, take a test walk on similar terrain.
- Choose sturdy, comfortable, lightweight walking shoes or boots with good ankle support. Your footwear should provide stability for your entire foot, ankle and leg, cushioning the heel and supporting it.
- Find out how much you'll need to carry. Many organised walks will transport your luggage from one night's lodging to the next, so that you only need to carry a light daypack, camera and perhaps a packed lunch. If you plan a more independent approach, be prepared to carry more supplies.

RULES OF THE ROAD

- If you're walking alone, always tell someone where you're going and when you expect to be back. Some walks have a registration scheme – make sure you use it.
- Respect other people's property: don't trespass, and remember to leave gates as you find them.
- Be cautious before entering fields containing livestock. Goats and bulls, and sometimes cows, can be aggressive.
- Watch out for dogs. Carry a stick with you, or pick up a large stone if you see a dog approaching you in a threatening manner.

SIGHTSEEING

Travel almost always involves more walking than you would normally do at home. Even traversing airport terminals can involve long distances, so plan ahead to avoid exhaustion.

- Buy a good pair of comfortable shoes with rubber soles. They're essential for city sightseeing. It's easy to forget how tiring walking on hard surfaces can be when you're exploring a city.
- Check out city walking tours. They can be a good way of familiarising yourself with a place and are often run by local people with specialised knowledge.
- When planning your day, don't forget to allow for the distances involved in seeing interior attractions, such as art galleries. The kilometres can add up very quickly.
- Try to be selective when seeing the sights, or both cultural overload and foot fatigue could overwhelm you. The Louvre Museum in Paris, for instance, contains more than a million works of art displayed in 13 km of galleries. If you have time, it may be better to make several short visits rather than try to tackle it all in one day.
- Read guidebooks or surf the Internet if you're concerned about your personal security. Some cities have districts that are not safe to walk through, particularly at night. Research your destination so you don't end up walking through unsafe areas.

The earth-wise traveller

Regular travellers know that doing your homework before you leave home is the best way to make your trip an enjoyable experience – and one that is respectful of the local people and environment. Just reaching the destination can be exhausting, so it's well worth equipping yourself with a little natural know-how before you take off.

BEATING JET LAG

- Try taking Siberian ginseng a week before flying and for several days afterwards. It may help your body adapt more quickly to jet lag.
- Consider taking a melatonin supplement (available only on prescription in Australia). Melatonin is the hormone that helps to regulate the sleep–wake cycle.
- On board, drink plenty of water because the recycled air in planes is very dehydrating. Avoid carbonated drinks because they can cause wind when the plane changes altitude.
- Move around to avoid the risk of deep vein thrombosis, a condition caused by sitting in cramped conditions for hours at a time. At regular intervals, walk around and do some simple stretching exercises.
- Try to sleep during the hours that correspond to night-time at your destination.
- If you find noise stressful, wear earplugs. The noise of jet engines for a long journey may exhaust you.
- Use rehydrating salts once or twice during the flight and again after you arrive, to avoid cramping, another symptom of dehydration.
- Try to avoid drinking alcohol as it also contributes to dehydration.

WHERE TO STAY?

- To find eco-friendly hotels, use the Internet. Some of the larger hotels will have web sites listing the practices they have in place.
- Some big hotels may not promote themselves as eco-friendly, but do give you the opportunity to conserve power and water – for example, by asking you to use your towels and bedding for more than one night. Also, turn off lights and heaters or airconditioning when you're not actually in the room.

ECO HOLIDAYS

Increasingly popular, eco holidays allow you to explore the beauty of the natural environment or gain a greater understanding of local cultures without contributing to their decline.

- Check the credentials of the tour organisation by contacting the company itself, talking to travel agents and surfing the Internet.
- Ask whether the organisation hires local people and uses local services in the communities it visits.
- Find out if the accommodation is appropriate to local conditions. Will you be staying in mid-range, locally owned hotels or guesthouses or in an international-brand hotel?
- Feedback from other travellers can be invaluable, so log onto Internet chat rooms – travel guides list some of the best ones.

SOUVENIRS TO AVOID

Knowing what to buy and how much to pay for it can be a complicated issue in some countries. If you want to avoid exploiting the local people or environment, do some research before you go. To make sure you're not unwittingly encouraging trade in endangered animals, don't buy:

- ✗ Ivory
- ✗ Tortoiseshell
- ✗ Reptile skins
- ✗ Furs/skins
- ✗ Some corals and seashells

■ ■ ■ **Take Vitamin C** (about 1500 milligrams) a few hours before flying to protect against the airborne germs in the cabin.

MAKE A DIFFERENCE

A holiday spent volunteering is a great way to get to know local people and the environment, as well as make a real difference.

■ Assist scientists in their work with the Earthwatch Institute. This international non-profit organisation puts people in the field to help scientists working on rainforest conservation and similar projects. You can choose from more than 130 expeditions in 47 countries.
■ Support charitable work by undertaking an overseas challenge – such as cycling through Vietnam, Cambodia or Sri Lanka – as part of the Oxfam Challenge or CARE Australia programs. Participants must qualify by meeting a fundraising target first, whereby the proceeds are split between the costs of the trip and supporting overseas charitable work.
■ Work with communities in Africa, Asia and the Pacific with Volunteer Service Abroad. Since 1962, this non-religious, non-government, non-profit organisation, based in Wellington, New Zealand, has recruited skilled New Zealanders for overseas voluntary work in developing countries.
■ Help educate children in the Peruvian Andes, raising their living standard and general health, by volunteering with Peru's Challenge. Volunteers book their own trips and devote some of their travel time to the project. So far, the youngest volunteer has been 13 and the oldest 72.
■ Clean up some of the world's beauty spots by booking a tour that allows you to devote a day to tidying Mt Sinai in Egypt or Mt Kilimanjaro in Tanzania, just to name a few. These tours sometimes coincide with the Clean Up the World initiative every September.

TREADING LIGHTLY

Wherever you go, leave a light footprint on the earth. Respect native flora and fauna, and follow National Parks rules.

- Resist the temptation to stray from designated tracks or board-walks in rainforests. Otherwise you may step on and damage delicate plant life, or contribute to erosion in fragile environments.
- Don't feed animals in the wild. Some become addicted to human food, to the detriment of their natural diet. It also causes animals to become less wary of people, so they're more likely to be run over.
- Remember to dispose of rubbish properly, especially at cooler, higher altitudes, where it takes much longer to biodegrade. This usually means carrying out rubbish with you, so if you're camping in alpine regions, compress your garbage and carry it out. Alternatively, book with a tour operator who organises responsible garbage removal.

- If you're camping or staying in a hut in a wilderness area, scatter waste water at least 50 m from any watercourse so that you don't contaminate it.
- When reef diving or snorkelling, ensure your equipment is well secured so it won't drag on coral. In some areas, divers are discouraged from wearing gloves so they aren't tempted to grab onto coral.
- Photograph marine life but don't handle or feed it unless an expert is guiding you. Never chase or ride marine animals.

YOUR OWN BACKYARD

Australia and New Zealand both provide high-quality eco-tour experiences that conserve the natural environment.

- Many of Australia's natural wonders are World Heritage-listed and protected by legislation. The Wet Tropics Management Authority manages almost a million hectares of rainforest, regulating visits and providing signage and infrastructure.
- Take part in bush regeneration schemes while on holiday. You'll enjoy beautiful scenery and contribute to protecting the natural environment. For example, every winter volunteers visit World Heritage-listed Lord Howe Island, off the coast of New South Wales, to help eradicate introduced weeds.
- In New Zealand, consider becoming a conservation volunteer. You might find yourself helping to plant native trees in parks and reserves, or maintaining tracks in offshore wildlife refuges.

■ ■ ■ **Health food shops** sell inexpensive acupressure wristbands, a must-have for anyone who suffers from motion sickness.

RESOURCES

BUILDING

BASIX
www.basix.nsw.gov.au/information/about.jsp
Find out how to ensure that new homes are designed and built to use less water and energy, and produce fewer greenhouse gas emissions.

Building Biology and Ecology Institute
www.ecoprojects.co.nz/Electrobiology.asp
Discover what electro-stress is and how to protect yourself from electro-pollution in your home.

Designing an Energy Efficient Home
www.sustainable.energy.sa.gov.au/pages/advisory/residential/residential.htm
This South Australian Government site covers all the elements of design for a house to be energy efficient, from orientation and siting to landscaping and thermal mass.
Tel: 08 8204 1888 (Australia)

Easy Guide to Eco-Building
www.branz.co.nz/main.php?page=Eco-Building
Discover how to carry out construction projects with consideration for the environment, and what to take into account from the early stages of design right through to the end of a building's lifetime.
Tel: 04 237 1170 (New Zealand)

5 Star Houses
www.5starhouse.vic.gov.au
A Victorian Government web site explaining how to achieve a 5 Star standard house.

Home Energy Efficiency
http://energysavers.gov/homeowners.html
Links to sites that provide practical information on how to improve the energy efficiency of properties.

Home Help
www.state.co.nz/Homehelp/Environment
Advice on good home design, choosing materials to build an environmentally friendly home and saving energy and water.

Ortech Industries
www.ortech.com.au
Find out about durras straw building panels, which offer innovative acoustical solutions for sound transmission and noise reduction.
Tel: 03 9580 7766 (Australia)

Renewable Energy Businesses by Country
http://energy.sourceguides.com/businesses/byGeo/byGeo.shtml
A comprehensive online buyer's guide and business directory to over 9000 renewable energy businesses and organisations worldwide.

Warm Homes Project
www.mfe.govt.nz/issues/energy/warm-homes/index.html
This New Zealand Government site explains the initiatives based on the findings of the Warm Homes Project, which aims to improve air quality by encouraging the use of energy-efficient heating in homes.

CLEANING

Eco Store
www.ecostore.co.nz
A site offering safe, natural, plant-based ingredients from sustainable resources. Products include household cleaners, organic gardening goods and skin and body care. Search the directory for NZ and Australian stockists.
Tel: 09 360 8477 (New Zealand)

Green Cleaning
www.penrithcity.nsw.gov.au/index.asp?id=2867
Information on how to reduce the chemicals used in domestic cleaning, as well as 17 steps to 'detoxing' your home.

Healthier Alternatives to Household Chemicals
www.arc.govt.nz/arc/big-clean-up/healthier-alternatives-to-household-chemicals
Information on safe storage, use and disposal of chemicals and safe alternatives for the entire household.

Healthy Habitat
www.healthyhabitat.com.au
An extensive range of healthy home products for sale, for cleaning, personal care, skin care, baby care, pet care and painting, along with advice on which ingredients to avoid in general and other useful information.
Tel: 02 9437 0829 (Australia)

Pesticide Action Network
www.pesticideinfo.org/Index.html
Find out about current toxicity and regulatory information for pesticides on the international database.

Planet Ark Direct
www.planetarkdirect.com
Find products free from harmful chemicals, that are not tested on animals and do not contain animal ingredients.
Tel: 02 9557 9658 (Australia)

EDUCATION

Eco'tude

www.powerhousemuseum.com/ecotude

Learn how to understand the environmental impact of schools in order to take action and change ecological attitudes. The site includes an Eco'tude calculator to estimate your school's ecological footprint.

EcoWater Education

www.waitakere.govt.nz/AbtCit/ei/EcoWtr/index.asp

Useful information from the New Zealand Government for teachers, students and anyone else interested in learning more about water.

5+ A Day

www.5aday.co.nz

A site that aims to encourage and educate parents and children on the benefits of healthy eating.

5 Fun Ways to Kids' Health & Fitness

www.kidshealthandfitness.org.au/default.asp

This site provides a set of guidelines that aims to give children a holistic and fun approach to balancing nutrition and physical activity, in order to achieve health and fitness.

Kiwi Conservation Club

www.kcc.org.nz

A site encouraging children to enjoy, understand and love the natural environment around them.

Millennium Kids

www.millenniumkids.com.au

Discover how to develop local, regional and international partnerships that will empower young people to explore, identify and address environmental issues through information exchange and membership networks.

Waterwatch

www.waterwatch.org.au/contacts.html

Find out about this water quality monitoring and catchment education program. It includes planning water monitoring activities with individuals, schools and community groups with aid of program facilitators.

WSN Environmental Solutions

www.wasteservice.nsw.gov.au/dir138/publish.nsf/Content/education

Educational resources for those who are interested in learning about waste avoidance, resource recovery and environmentally responsible waste-disposal options.

ENERGY

Cent-A-Meter

www.centameter.com.au; www.centameter.co.nz

Online buyers can purchase the award-winning Cent-A-Meter to measure overall power use, energy cost per hour and greenhouse-gas emissions, and to monitor how individual appliances affect overall energy consumption. It can also be purchased in Australia through AGL retail outlets.

Energy Efficiency and Conservation Authority

www.eeca.govt.nz

This site is dedicated to helping businesses get more from their energy dollar; promoting warmer, drier homes; helping people make better personal transport choices; and protecting the environment through energy efficiency and renewable energy supply.

Energy ratings

www.energyrating.gov.au/productmenu.html

Australia's leading guide to choosing an energy-efficient appliance.

EnergyWise

www.energywise.org.nz

This site provides practical guides on improving energy efficiency. Search the Energy Services Database for companies and organisations that provide energy-efficient products and services.

Energy Savings Calculators

www.countryenergy.com.au/internet/cewebpub.nsf/Content/h_eff_cover
www.originenergy.com.au/efficiency
www.actewagl.com.au/default.aspx?loc=/energysavingscalculator.htm
www.meridianenergy.co.nz/Energysavingscalculator

These web sites offer information on improving the energy efficiency of your home, and incorporate energy calculators that allow you to tally the approximate cost of operating individual household appliances.

Household Self Energy Auditing

www.sustainable.energy.sa.gov.au/pages/advisory/residential/residential.htm

This site helps you identify practical ways in which you can be more energy efficient at home by observing and assessing the types of energy-using appliances you have and the way you use them.

ENVIRONMENT

Australian Conservation Foundation

www.acfonline.org.au

Australia's leading non-profit environment organisation. Find out what your environmental impact is using the Eco-calculator.
02 8270 9900 (Australia)

Australian Environment Directory

www.environmentdirectory.com.au

A comprehensive guide to environmental technologies, products and services available from companies operating in Australia.

Australian Greenhouse Office
www.greenhouse.gov.au
Learn how you can make a difference through commonsense actions for reducing greenhouse gas emissions at home, work, school and in your local community.

Carbon Neutral
www.carbonneutral.com.au
Find out how to offset the carbon dioxide produced by your vehicle and daily activities. You can calculate your CO_2 emissions online.

David Suzuki Foundation
www.davidsuzuki.org
This foundation is dedicated to protecting the future in terms of diversity of nature and quality of life. Discover ten simple things that you can do to protect nature.

Earth Garden
www.earthgarden.com.au
Discover practical ways to lead a simpler, healthier, less stressful lifestyle, while also using the earth's resources more wisely.

Ecology Discovery Foundation New Zealand
www.ecoglobe.org/nz/index.htm
Information about the local and global ecology, and the balance between human activities and nature.

Eco-village
www.converge.org.nz/evcnz/index.html
This site explains the benefits of cohousing with a view to building sustainable human settlements.

Eco Voice
www.ecovoice.com.au
An overview of environmental information from renewable energy to natural living and organic agriculture. Includes a directory of eco-friendly products and services.

Enviro-Friendly Products
www.enviro-friendly.com/environmentally-friendly-products-resources.shtml
A listing of environmentally friendly products and resources to help you save water, save energy, save money and save the environment.
Tel: 02 6231 9235 (Australia)

Environment ACT
www.environment.act.gov.au/yourenvironmenthwp/yourenvironmenthwp.html
Find out how to make a contribution to the wellbeing of the environment in the home, the garden, the bush, out shopping, at work and while travelling out and about.

Environment Canterbury
www.ecan.govt.nz/Our+Environment/
A Christchurch-based organisation addressing the problems of pollution and poor waste management. Find the answers to some troublesome questions regarding the environment. Includes educational resources.

Friends of the Earth
A broadly based activist environmental organisation with groups in more than 60 countries, this group has some 5000 local branches. It is the largest environmental federation in the world, and is active on many of the main global environmental and social issues.
Adelaide: www.adelaide.foe.org.au
Tel: 03 8212 0182
Brisbane: www.brisbane.foe.org.au
Tel: 07 3846 5793.
Melbourne:
www.melbourne.foe.org.au
Tel: 03 9419 8700
Perth: Tel: 0411 220 704
Sydney: www.sydney.foe.org.au
Tel: 02 9567 6222
Tasmania: Tel: 03 6363 5171
New Zealand: Tel: 09 3034319
e-mail: foenz@kcbbs.gen.nz

Global Warming: Early Warning Signs
http://climatehotmap.org
Check the impact of global warming: heat waves and periods of unusually warm weather; downpours, heavy snowfalls and flooding; droughts and fires; ocean warming, sea-level rise and coastal flooding.

Go Smarter
www.gosmarter.org.nz
Find out how to reduce the time and money spent travelling. Includes tips on planning ahead.

Green Innovations
www.green-innovations.asn.au
This non-profit environmental services organisation pursues sustainability projects, both locally and globally, for the benefit of future generations and the environment.

Greenpeace Australia Pacific
www.greenpeace.org.au
Find out how Greenpeace Australia aims to create a peaceful future; prevent climate change; save the forests; eliminate toxics; ensure a GE-free future; save the oceans and end the nuclear threat.
Tel: 1800 815 151 (Australia)

Greenpeace New Zealand
www.greenpeace.org.nz
This is the New Zealand arm of the global, non-profit organisation that is dedicated to protecting the enviroment for everyone and future generations. Become a cyberactivitst!
Tel: 0800 22 33 44 (New Zealand)

GreenTick
www.greentick.com
Find out what the standards are that make a product eligible to bear the GreenTick brand, certifying that it meets international standards for sustainability.
Tel: 09 430 8612 (New Zealand)

Green Vehicle Guide
www.greenvehicleguide.gov.au
This site provides ratings on the environmental performance of new vehicles sold in Australia. Find out how different vehicles compare on greenhouse and air-pollution emissions.

Men of the Trees
www.menofthetrees.com.au
An international, non-profit organisation dedicated to the planting and protection of trees, to reduce greenhouse gases and combat salinity.
Tel: 08 9250 1888 (WA);
02 4572 8556 or 9743 1487 (NSW);
07 3262 1096 (Qld)

Mineral Policy Institute
www.mpi.org.au
Find out more about this Australian-based, non-government organisation that specialises in advocacy, campaigning and research to prevent environmentally and socially destructive mining and energy projects in Australia, Asia and the Pacific region.
Tel: 02 9557 9019 (Australia)

Rainforest Information Centre
www.rainforestinfo.org.au
A non-profit organisation dedicated to the protection of the last remaining rainforests and the indigenous people who depend on them.

Sustainable Wellington Net
www.sustainable.wellington.net.nz/Resources
Information about sustainable development, divided up according to the type of resource you are looking for.

The Timber Shop
www.timbershop.org
A comprehensive guide to forest-friendly and recycled timbers. This site has a searchable database of recycled timber stocks and has regularly updated national information about preferable timbers.

TravelSmart Australia
www.travelsmart.gov.au
Find out how you can reduce your reliance on cars and make sensible and informed choices about other types of transport.

Trees For Life
www.treesforlife.org.au
The world's largest local native plant growing organisation of its kind.
Tel: 08 8372 0150 (Australia)

The Wilderness Society
www.wilderness.org.au
A national, community-based, environmental advocacy organisation whose purpose is to protect, promote and restore wilderness and natural processes across Australia.
Tel: 03 6270 1701 (Australia)

Worldwatch Institute
www.worldwatch.org
This site provides an accessible and fact-based analysis of critical global environmental issues.

FOOD

Clean Food Organic
www.cleanfood.com.au
The web site of the publication, which is available from newsagents or you can subscribe online. A complete guide to organics.
Tel: 02 9664 6670 (Australia)

GeneEthics Network
www.geneethics.org
An organisation promoting community education, discussion and debate on the economic, market, environmental, social and ethical impacts of the technologies behind genetic engineering.
Tel: 1300 133868 (Australia)

Healthy Eating Club
www.healthyeating.org
This site provides nutrition fact sheets, a food database with nutritional information and recipes. Monthly newsletters give the latest in nutrition research. Find out how what you eat can help the environment.

Nutrition Australia
www.nutritionaustralia.org
An organisation that aims to provide scientifically based nutrition information to encourage everyone to achieve optimal health through food variety and physical activity.
Tel: 02 4257 9011 (NSW);
07 3257 4393 (Qld); 03 9650 5165 (Vic); 08 6304 5096 (WA)

Organic Certifiers
Australian Certified Organic (ACO)
www.australianorganic.com.au
Tel: 07 3350 5716
Australian Quarantine & Inspection Service (AQIS)
www.aqis.gov.au/organic
Tel: 02 6271 6638
Bio-Dynamic Research Institute (BDRI)
www.demeter.org.au
Tel: 03 5966 7333 (Australia)
National Association For Sustainable Agriculture Australia Ltd (NASAA)
www.nasaa.com.au
Tel: 08 8370 8455
Organic Food Chain (OFC)
www.organicfoodchain.com.au
Tel: 07 4637 2600 (Australia)
Organic Growers Of Australia – OGA Certified
www.organicgrowers.org.au
Tel: 02 6622 0100
Safe Food Queensland (SFQ)
www.safefood.qld.gov.au
Tel: 07 3253 9800; 1800 300 815 (Qld only)
Tasmanian Organic-Dynamic Producers Inc. (T.O.P)
Tel: 03 6363 5162

AgriQuality New Zealand
www.agriquality.co.nz
Tel: 09 237 1807

The Bio Dynamic Farming and Gardening Association (Demeter)
www.biodynamic.org.nz
Tel: 04 589 5366 (New Zealand)

Bio-Gro New Zealand
www.bio-gro.co.nz
Tel: 04 801-9741

International Federation of Organic Agriculture Movements (IFOAM)
www.ifoam.org

Organic Choice
www.organicchoice.com.au
This site contains extensive product information with links to retail outlets throughout Australia that supply certified organic and biodynamic products.
Tel: 08 8370 2563 (Australia)

The Organic Center for Education & Promotion
www.organic-center.org
This organisation provides consumers, health care professionals, educators, public officials and government agencies with scientific information about the benefits of organics. It is dedicated to increasing the awareness of and demand for organic produce.

The Organic Consumers Association (OCA)
www.organicconsumers.org
This web site will help you discover more about issues concerning food safety, industrial agriculture, genetic engineering, corporate accountability and environmental sustainability.

Organic Federation of Australia
www.ofa.org.au
The free electronic monthly newsletter provides updates on organic food; pesticides, chemicals and health; GMO news and events around the world.

The Organics Directory
www.theorganicsdirectory.com.au/
Learn about organics and wholefoods through seminars and campaigns. Search the directory online or download a copy. To receive a free copy of the directory of the region that you live in, send a 50c stamp (not a self-addressed envelope) to:
PO Box 3335 Tamarama
NSW 2026

Safe Food Campaign
www.safefood.org.nz
A nationwide New Zealand organisation campaigning for safer, healthier food. It provides consumers with the necessary information so that they can make up their own minds about what is safe to eat.

Soil & Health Association of New Zealand
www.soil-health.org.nz
This site includes a list of 10 good reasons to go organic, and it also has an organic goods and services directory

True Food Guide
www.greenpeace.org.au/truefood/index2.html
With this site you can make your own GM-free shopping list using the True Food Guide. Then edit, print and save your list for future use.

GARDENING

Brisbane Organic Growers (BOG)
www.bog.powerup.com.au/default.htm
This site will show you how to grow your own fruit and vegetables without using harmful chemicals, hormones, artificial herbicides and pesticides. Includes a month-by-month guide to planting and caring for your garden.
PO Box 236 Lutwyche
Queensland 4030

Canberra Organic Growers Society (COGS)
www.cogs.asn.au
Find out about community gardens in the Canberra area, and how members can get a plot at one of these gardens to grow organic produce. Includes a seasonal planting guide and a directory of organic products.

Centre for Plant Biodiversity Research
www.cpbr.gov.au/gnp/index.html
Comprehensive information on growing Australian native plants.

Down to Earth Manual
www.epa.nsw.gov.au/publications/html/downtoearth/index.htm
Learn about composting, worm farming and how to create a no-dig garden.

New Zealand Plant Conservation Network
www.nzpcn.org.nz
Information about native plants. Search for a plant-specific fact sheet.

Organic Gardening from Down Under
www.organicdownunder.com
Find out how easy organic vegetable growing is for beginners. Fresh vegetables, which are chemical-free, can be grown in your own garden. Includes a 'how-to' table on growing.

Organic Garden Tips
www.organicgardentips.com
Over 250 great tips for organic gardening at home.

Organic Pathways
www.organicpathways.co.nz/garden/index.html
Information on gardening by the Moon, easy-care gardening, how to build a raised garden bed, recipes for fish or seaweed fertiliser, how to create a 'wildgarden' and more.

Plants for Mediterranean Climates
www.mediterraneangardensociety.org/plants
Plant selection for gardening and horticulture in the world's mediterranean climates.

Royal New Zealand Institute of Horticulture
www.rnzih.org.nz/pages/Garden-tips.htm
A site with a combination of great garden tips and 'did you knows?'.

HEALTH & BEAUTY

Biome Living
www.biome.com.au
Buy environmentally friendly alternatives for the items you use every day. Organic, natural and eco-friendly shopping for all purposes.
Tel: 1300 301 767 (Australia)

Body Burden Community Monitoring Handbook
www.oztoxics.org/cmwg/index.html
Information on the body burdens of chemicals and community monitoring initiatives. Downloadable chemical fact sheets are available.

Chemical Body Burden
www.chemicalbodyburden.org
Information on the chemical body burden, including fact sheets on commonly used pesticides and dioxin. Includes a link to the Coming Clean Home Page.

The LEAD Group
www.lead.org.au
This group is working towards eliminating childhood and foetal lead poisoning, and protecting the environment from lead, through community education and assisting government policy development for lead risk reduction.
Tel: 02 9716 0014 (Australia)

National Center for Complementary and Alternative Medicine
http://nccam.nih.gov
Explore complementary and alternative healing practices within the context of science, training and research. Includes FAQs and links to other related resources.

Nga Tipu Whakaoranga/People Plants Database
http://peopleplants.landcareresearch.co.nz
Information on traditional uses of plants that are native to New Zealand.

Ozganics
www.ozganics.net.au
Find out about natural and organic alternatives to everyday household items, from body and hair care to soap and cleaning products.

Planet Ark Direct
www.planetarkdirect.com
Buy products free from harmful chemicals, making them kinder to you and the environment. Products listed are not tested on animals and do not contain animal ingredients.
Tel: 02 9557 9658 (Australia)

Silicon Valley Toxics Coalition
www.svtc.org/hu_health/index.html
A comprehensive site covering high-tech impacts on communities, workers and environmental health in general.

Skin Deep
www.ewg.org/reports/skindeep
This online, brand-by-brand personal care product safety guide has in-depth information on 14,228 products – 988 brands of lotion, lip balm, deodorant, sunscreen and other popular products. Includes safety ratings and brand-by-brand comparisons.

Soap Kitchen
www.soapkitchen.com.au/catalog
Natural body- and face-care products including soaps, cosmetics, cleansers, toners and shampoos. Products are carefully selected and do not contain harmful petrochemicals, mineral oils or chemical preservatives.
Tel: 02 9516 0018 (Australia)

Washington Toxic Coalition
www.watoxics.org/redirect/TIH_MAIN.aspx?fromMenu=0&pos=5&name=TIH_MAIN
A US site outlining the Home Safe Home Program, which includes a series of fact sheets that identify hazards associated with various products for use in and around the home, and suggest alternatives.

RECYCLING

ACT NOWaste
www.nowaste.act.gov.au
Information about recycling and the waste-collection service operating in ACT, including where recycling and waste goes. Useful information for people living outside the Canberra community, too.

The Bower
http://home.pacific.net.au/~thebower
A cooperative that operates a repair and re-use centre that collects, repairs and resells goods diverted from the municipal waste stream. They also aim to educate the community about waste reduction.
Tel: 02 9568 6280 (Australia)

Cartridges 4 Planet Ark
www.planetark.org/index.cfm
Find out what you can do with used toner cartridges, inkjet cartridges, photocopier toner bottles and drums, to avoid adding to the already massive landfill of more than 5000 tonnes a year.

Clean Up Australia
www.cleanup.com.au
An organisation dedicated to litter reduction and environmental conservation in Australia and around the world. Includes information on plastic bags, electronic waste, glass and paper recycling, and more.
Tel: 02 9552 6177 (Australia)

Computer Take Back Campaign
www.computertakeback.com
Discover what it means to protect the health and wellbeing of workers who use electronics, as well as the communities where electronics are produced and discarded.

EcoRecycle Victoria
www.ecorecycle.sustainability.vic.gov.au
This site provides advice and assistance for individuals, businesses, governments and communities so that they can make informed decisions in a more environmentally sustainable way. Includes information on managing and minimising waste, and the sustainable use of resources.

Green Office Guide
www.greenoffice.org.nz/greenpages.php
Find out about green purchasing. Includes links to preferred suppliers; check the lists of addresses for recycling.

Green PC
www.greenpc.com.au
Find out how to reduce technological waste by buying a recycled personal computer that has been refurbished and repackaged into a usable, Internet-ready computer. The computers are made available to low-income communities, individuals and community organisations.
Tel: 03 9418 7400 (Vic); 07 3255 8300 (Qld); 08 9434 0530 (WA); 02 6251 5617 (ACT)

Greenworld
www.greenworld.com.au
Supplier of remanufactured laser toner cartridges and other environmentally friendly products.
Tel: 03 9545 0700 (Australia)

Mobile Phone Recycling
www.phonerecycling.com.au
Find out how your old mobile phones and their batteries can be recycled.
Tel: 1300 730 070 (Australia)

Recycling Near You
www.RecyclingNearYou.com.au
This site tells you how and where to recycle mobile phones, printer cartridges and even cars within Australia. Check the collection dates and where drop-off centres are for old or leftover chemicals.

Resources NSW
www.resource.nsw.gov.au/index-RNSW.htm
A site explaining how to achieve a reduction in waste generation and how to turn waste into recoverable resources.

Resource Work Co-operative Society Limited
http://resourcetipshop.com
The aim of this Tasmanian society is to reduce waste, educate and create employment. The Tip Shop (not for online buyers) is stocked with items salvaged from the tip face.
Tel: 03 6234 3772 (Australia)

Reverse Garbage
www.reversegarbage.com.au
This Brisbane group have a warehouse full of recyclable materials that would otherwise become landfill. All materials in the warehouse are clean, safe and non-toxic. Includes information on practical and creative ways to promote sustainability.
Tel: 07 3844 9744 (Australia)

The Steel Can Recycling Council
www.cansmart.org
This site has the latest news on steel can recycling, information and resources for students, and a 'Kids' Corner'. Find out what recycling services Australian local councils offer, and how to recycle steel cans, including empty paint cans and aerosol cans.

Sustainable Households
www.sustainablehouseholds.org.nz/issues1.htm
Discover how you can do your bit at home to help care for the planet, save resources and enjoy a healthier lifestyle. Includes downloadable practical guides for taking action at home.

Tasmanian Dept. of Primary Industries, Water & Environment
www.dpiwe.tas.gov.au/inter.nsf/WebPages/BHAN-53LUW4?open
A Tasmania-specific site providing information on waste disposal and collection facilities. Check with your local council or recycler, reprocesser or reuser regarding the availability of a particular service.
Tel: 03 6233 6599 (Australia)

Unwanted Medicines
www.returnmed.com.au
Find out how to return your old and unwanted medicines to any pharmacy, for free within Australia, and ensure their safe disposal.
Tel: 1300 650 835 (Australia)

Waste Wise WA
www.wastewise.wa.gov.au
Information about waste, including handy hints on how to reduce, reuse and recycle to minimise the environmental impact. Check the WA local council database to find out how to dispose of specific waste items in that state.
Tel: 08 9278 0300 (Australia)

Zero Waste New Zealand Trust
www.zerowaste.co.nz
The aim of this group is to promote recycling; minimise residual waste; reduce consumption; and also ensure that products are made to be reused, repaired, recycled or composted.
Tel: 09 486 0734 or 09 486 0738 (New Zealand)

Zero Waste SA
www.zerowaste.sa.gov.au/
This web site provides information to help businesses, governments and communities become involved in waste avoidance. Includes information on what can be recycled in local council areas throughout South Australia.
Tel: 08 8204 2051 (Australia)

WATER

GreenPlumbers
www.greenplumbers.com.au
This site includes a directory of licensed GreenPlumbers. GreenPlumbers can assist you in making informed choices that will help you save water and energy, from water recycling to water harvesting . They also offer advice about government rebate schemes.

Grey Water
www.greywater.com
Find out what you have to do to treat grey water before it can be used safely in and around the home.

NZ Ministry for the Environment
www.mfe.govt.nz/issues/water/prog-action/index.html
Find out what the New Zealand Government is doing about water as a resource: for drinking, the environment, irrigation, energy, cultural values and tourism. The site explains the Sustainable Water Programme of Action in detail, with background information and reports.

Savewater!
www.savewater.com.au
This group is dedicated to water conservation. The site includes water-saver tips and tricks and a comprehensive guide to water-saving products, including rainwater tanks, dishwashers, shower heads, tapware and irrigation systems.

Sydney Water
www.sydneywater.com.au/SavingWater/GreyWater
Find out about grey water and how much wastewater Australian households produce. Includes information on uses for grey water, such as diverting it to your garden via a grey water diversion device or a domestic grey water treatment system (DGTS).

Waterforever
www.waterforever.com.au
This site has the answers to most FAQs regarding residential water restrictions and also has links to regional councils in Australia.
Tel: 1300 789 906 (Australia)

Water Conservation
www.wellington.govt.nz/services/watersupply/tips/tips.html
This Wellington City Council web site has a collection of tips for saving water in the home, along with information about testing water quality and emergency water supplies.

Water for Life Plan
www.waterforlife.nsw.gov.au/households/index.shtml
This site has simple and easy water-saving tips to make a difference in helping to conserve this resource.

Water Magazine
www.watermagazine.com
This online magazine examines issues to do with urban water systems in New Zealand and internationally.

Water Services Association of Australia
www.wsaa.asn.au
Find out how to check the A-water efficiency rate of your household appliances.

Yarra Valley Water
www.yvw.com.au/yvw/Home/HelpingOurEnvironment
This site has tips for saving water in the home, the garden and at work, using grey water.

INDEX

Page numbers in **bold** print refer to main entries

A

B

C

T

U

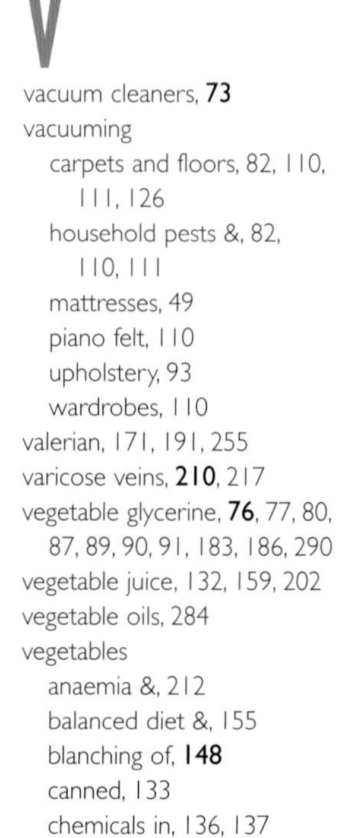

V

Y

Z

ACKNOWLEDGMENTS

The position of photographs on each page is indicated by letters after the page number: *t* = top; *c* = centre; *b* = bottom; *l* = left; *r* = right

Front cover *b* from left to right: Getty Images, Getty Images, Fotomorgana/Corbis/Australian Picture Library, Getty Images, RD; background Getty Images. **Back cover** *l* Royalty-Free/Corbis; *c* Digital Vision; *r* Ivy Hansen. **Endpapers** PhotoDisc.
2 *tl* PhotoDisc; *tr* RD/GID; *bl* Linda Burgess/Garden Picture Library; *br* Royalty-Free/Corbis. **5** *t* RD; *b* Royalty-Free/Corbis. **6** *t* RD; *b* PhotoDisc. **7** Ivy Hansen. **8** PhotoDisc. **9** *tl* Digital Vision; *tr* Royalty-Free/Corbis; *bl* PhotoDisc; *br* Juliette Wade/Garden Picture Library. **10** *t* RD/GID; *bl* Digital Vision. **11** PhotoAlto. **12** Lorna Rose. **13** All logos reproduced with permission from relevant organisations. **14–15** Brand X Pictures. **16** *t* Royalty-Free/Corbis; *c* & *b* PhotoDisc. **17** *tl* Royalty-Free/Corbis; *tr* Stockbyte; *bl* Brand X Pictures; *br* PhotoDisc. **18** *bl* Reproduced with permission from Energy Rating, Australian Greenhouse Office. **18–19** Stockbyte. **19** *b* RD. **20** *both* PhotoDisc. **22** RD. **23** *c* RD; *bl* RD/GID. **24** *t* Royalty-Free/Corbis; *c* RD. **25** PhotoDisc. **26** *The Family Handyman*. **27** *t* PhotoDisc; *b* Courtesy Masport www.masport.com. **28** Stockbyte. **29** *tr* Courtesy Solahart Australia www.solahart.com.au; *bl* Reproduced with permission from The Australian Gas Association. **30** *t* PhotoDisc; *b* Royalty-Free/Corbis. **31** PhotoDisc. **32** *tr* Royalty-Free/Corbis; *c* Courtesy Skydome Skylight Systems www.skydome.com.au. **33** *t* RD; *br* David Boehm. **34** *t* Royalty-Free/Corbis; *b* Image Source. **35** *tl* Image Source; *tr* Brand X Pictures; *bl* Reproduced with permission from the Water Services Association of Australia; *br* Reproduced with permission from the Department of the Environment and Heritage. **36–37** Lorna Rose. **37** *tr* Courtesy Waterwall Solutions www.waterwall.com.au; *b* PhotoDisc. **38** *tr* Courtesy Sydney Water Corporation; *br* PhotoDisc. **39** *t* RD; *b* Lorna Rose/Dora Scott Garden, Sydney. **40–41** Brand X Pictures. **41** *b* RD. **42** *tl* PhotoDisc; *br* Royalty-Free/Corbis. **43** *t* RD/GID; *b* Royalty-Free/Corbis. **44** Imagestate. **45** *t* ImageDJ; *b* Courtesy Nature Loo www.nature-loo.com.au. **46** Royalty-Free/Corbis. **47** PhotoDisc. **48** *b* PhotoDisc. **48–49** PhotoDisc. **49** *br all* RD. **50** *t* Digital Vision; *c* Royalty-Free/Corbis. **51** *t* PhotoDisc; *b* Reproduced with permission from Energy Rating, Australian Greenhouse Office. **52** *t* Digital Vision; *b* Royalty-Free/Corbis. **54–55** Brand X Pictures. **56** *both* PhotoDisc. **57** Courtesy Designer Blinds. **58** Image 100. **59** John Benfer/Gloria Lee Environmental Centre. **60–61** RD. **62** *both The Family Handyman*. **63** PhotoDisc. **64** *tr The Family Handyman*; *br* RD. **65** *rt* Courtesy Style Plantation www.styleplantation.com; *rc The Family Handyman*; *rb* PhotoDisc. **66** Stockbyte. **67** *bl* RD/GID; *br* RD. **68–69** PhotoDisc. **70** *tl* Digital Vision; *tr* & *br* Royalty-Free/Corbis. **71** *t* Janet Seaton/Garden Picture Library; *bl* Jean-Michel Labat/Auscape; *br* PhotoDisc. **72** *t* RD; *b* Digital Vision. **73** RD. **74** *both* RD. **75** *tl* Digital Vision; *tc* & *br* RD. **76** *both* RD. **77** *t* & *cr* RD; *cl* PhotoDisc. **78** *tr* RD; *cl* Digital Vision; *b* PhotoDisc. **79** *t* Digital Vision; *bl* RD. **80** *t* Digital Vision; *b* Royalty-Free/Corbis. **81** *tl* Royalty-Free/Corbis; *tr* Digital Vision; *c* RD; *br* Brand X Pictures. **82** *t* Royalty-Free/Corbis; *c* & *b* RD. **83** *both* RD. **84** *b* RD. **84–85** PhotoDisc. **85** *b* PhotoDisc. **86** *t* PhotoDisc; *b both* RD. **87** PhotoDisc. **88** *tl* Digital Vision; *c* Brand X Pictures. **89** *cr* PhotoDisc; *br* RD. **90** Royalty-Free/Corbis. **92** Brand X Pictures. **93** *c* PhotoDisc; *br* RD. **94** *both* RD. **95** *both* RD. **96** PhotoDisc. **97** *tl* PhotoDisc; *tr* RD. **98** *t* Comstock Images; *b* Digital Vision. **100** *t* Bilderlounge; *b* RD. **101** RD. **102** *t* Brand X Pictures; *c* RD; *b* Janet Seaton/Garden Picture Library. **103** *both* RD. **104** *t* PhotoDisc; *b* RD. **105** Digital Vision. **106** *b* AbleStock.com. **106–07** PhotoDisc. **107** *c* PhotoDisc. **108** *t* PhotoDisc; *b* RD. **109** *tl* RD; *cr* PhotoDisc; *b* Denis Crawford/Graphic Science. **110** *both* RD. **111** *all* RD/GID. **112** *tr* Michael Maconachie/Auscape; *c* NHPA/ANTPhoto.com; *bl* RD; *br* Denis Crawford/Graphic Science. **113** *all* RD. **114** *tr* & *c* Denis Crawford/Graphic Science; *br* RD/GID. **116** *tr* PhotoDisc; *cl* Brand X Pictures; *br* Royalty-Free/Corbis. **117** Greg Harold/Auscape. **118** *tr* RD; *cl* Jean-Michel Labat/Auscape. **119** *both* RD. **120** *tl* Pixtal; *c* PhotoDisc. **121** *tr* Comstock Images; *cl* PhotoDisc; *cr* Royalty-Free/Corbis. **122** *tr* PhotoDisc; *bl* RD. **123** *tr* & *br* Comstock Images; *cl* RD. **124** *tl* Jean-Michel Labat/Auscape; *b* PhotoDisc. **125** Comstock Images. **126** *tr* Image 100; *bl* Jean-Michel Labat/Auscape; *br* RD. **127** Photick. **128–29** Chassenet/BSIP/Auscape. **130** *all* RD/GID. **131** *tl* Digital Vision; *cr* & *bl* PhotoDisc. **132** *t* RD/GID; *b* RD. **133** *tr* RD; *c* RD/GID. **134–35** RD/GID. **135** *c* RD/GID. **136** *tl* Digital Vision; *cr* Brand X Pictures. **137** Brand X Pictures. **138** *t* Image 100; *c* PhotoDisc; *b* RD/GID. **139** RD. **140** *t* PhotoDisc; *b* Image 100. **141** Reproduced with permission from the Heart Foundation. **142** *t* Image 100; *b* RD. **143** RD/GID. **144** *t* RD/GID; *c* FoodCollection. **145** *both* RD/GID. **146** *both* RD/GID. **147** RD/GID. **148** *tr* & *cl* RD/GID; *cr* PhotoDisc. **149** *t* RD; *bl* RD/GID. **150** *bl* RD/GID. **150–51** RD/GID. **151** *both* RD/GID. **152** *both* RD/GID. **153** PhotoDisc. **154** *all* RD/GID. **155** *both* RD/GID. **156** *t* RD; *b* RD/GID. **157** *tr* RD/GID; *cr* PhotoDisc; *b* RD. **158** *both* RD/GID. **160** *t* PhotoDisc; *b* RD. **161** *all* RD/GID. **162** *t* Digital Vision; *b* RD. **163** PhotoDisc. **164** *t* PhotoDisc; *b* RD. **165** *t* PhotoDisc; *b* RD. **166** *t* PhotoDisc; *b* RD.
167 *tl* RD; *tr* Pixtal; *bl* Stockbyte. **168** *t* Imagestate; *bl* PhotoDisc; *br* Stockbyte. **169** PhotoDisc. **170** *t* PhotoAlto; *b* PhotoDisc. **171** *t* Andrew Lord/Garden Picture Library; *b* RD/GID. **172–73** Peter Hendrie/Lonely Planet Images. **174** *t* PhotoAlto; *cr* RD; *bl* PhotoDisc. **175** *t* PhotoDisc; *cr* Thinkstock Images; *bl* RD/GID. **176** *t* PhotoDisc; *b* RD. **177** *t* RD/GID; *c* RD. **178** *t* Stockbyte; *bl* RD/GID. **179** *tr* & *br* RD; *bl* RD/GID. **180** *t* Stockbyte; *bl* RD; *br* RubberBall Productions. **181** *t* RD; *bl* PhotoDisc; *br* RD/GID. **182** *t* ImageDJ; *b* PhotoDisc. **183** *both* RD. **184** *tr* PhotoAlto; *bl* RD. **185** *tr* PhotoDisc; *cl* & *br* RD. **186** *tl* RD; *cr* Goodshoot. **187** *t* PhotoAlto; *b* RD. **188** Almonds, apricot, chervil, cornflower & fennel RD/GID; bananas, cloves & kelp RD. **189** Lemon & potato RD; lemon balm, melon, parsley, sage & thyme RD/GID; rose & strawberries PhotoDisc. **190** *tr* PhotoDisc; *bl* Thinkstock Images. **191** RD. **192** *t* Creatas Images; *b* Eoin Clarke/Lonely Planet Images. **193** *tl* Digital Vision; *cr* RD. **194** *t* PhotoDisc; *b* Pixland. **195** *tr* RD/GID; *cl* PhotoDisc; *b* RD. **196** *t* Image Source; *b* RD. **197** RD/GID. **198** *t* PhotoDisc; *b* Image 100. **199** Bananastock. **200** *t* PhotoDisc; *c* RD. **201** *both* RD. **202** *t* Brand X Pictures; *b* RD. **203** *both* RD/GID. **204** *t* RD/GID; *c* & *b* RD. **205** Stockbyte. **206** *t* PhotoDisc; *bl* Stockbyte; *br* RD/GID. **207** *both* RD. **208** *tr* RD/GID; *cl* PhotoDisc. **209** *tl* Pixland; *tr* RD. **210** *t* PhotoDisc; *b both* RD. **211** PhotoDisc. **212** *tl* RD/GID; *br* RD. **213** PhotoDisc. **214** PhotoDisc. **215** *t* PhotoDisc; *c* RD. **216** *both* RD. **217** RD. **218–19** David Cavagnaro/Garden Picture Library. **220** *t* Ivy Hansen; *c* Lorna Rose; *b* Jean-Paul Ferrero/Auscape. **221** *tl* C. Andrew Henley/Auscape; *tr* RD; *b* Brand X Pictures. **222** *t* Wayne Lawler/Auscape; *b* Ivy Hansen. **223** RD. **224** Lorna Rose. **225** *cl* C. Andrew Henley/Auscape; *cr* PhotoDisc. **226** Mayer-Le Scanff/Garden Picture Library. **227** *t* Ivy Hansen; *cl* RD/GID. **228** *tl* Ivy Hansen; *tr* RD. **230** *t* Lorna Rose; *b* RD/GID. **231** Lorna Rose. **232** *t* Jean-Paul Ferrero/Auscape; *b* Lorna Rose. **233** *bl* Jean-Paul Ferrero/Auscape; *br* Lorna Rose. **234** Ivy Hansen. **235** *t* Ken Griffiths/ANTPhoto.com; *cr* Lorna Rose; *b* Ivy Hansen. **236** *b* Linda Burgess/Garden Picture Library. **236–37** Lorna Rose/Jill Morrow Garden, Wagga Wagga, NSW. **237** *both* Lorna Rose. **238** *t* Jerry Pavia/Garden Picture Library; *b* Brand X Pictures. **239** *all* RD. **240** *t* PhotoDisc; *b* RD. **241** *tl* Brigitte Dufour/Garden Picture Library; *b* RD. **242** *tr* PhotoDisc; *cl* Lorna Rose; *b* Grant Dixon/ANTPhoto.com. **243** *tl* RD; *tr* Brand X Pictures. **244** *tr* Georgia Glynn-Smith/Garden Picture Library; *bl* RD. **245** RD/GID. **246** *t* Royalty-Free/Corbis; *bl* Lorna Rose. **247** Digital Vision. **248** *both* RD. **249** RD. **250** *tr* Ivy Hansen; *bl* Suzie Gibons/Garden Picture Library. **251** Brand X Pictures. **252** RD. **253** *all* Brand X Pictures. **254** *t* Lorna Rose; *b* RD/GID. **255** *t* & *cl* RD; *br* Ivy Hansen. **256** *tr* Lorna Rose; *cl* Eric Crichton/Garden Picture Library; *br* RD/GID. **257** RD. **258** Lorna Rose. **259** *tl* PhotoDisc; *tc* & *tr* Marie O'Hara/Garden Picture Library. **260** *tr* Mark Bolton/Garden Picture Library; *bl* PhotoDisc; *br* Lorna Rose. **262** *t* Lorna Rose; *bl* Ivy Hansen; *bc* PhotoDisc. **263** PhotoDisc. **264** Brand X Pictures. **265** *t* PhotoDisc; *b both* Lorna Rose. **266** *t* Brand X Pictures; *b* Lorna Rose. **267** *tl* RD/GID; *tr* Lorna Rose/Hodge Garden, Logan View, Qld. **268** *t* RD/GID; *bl* François De Heel/Garden Picture Library; *br* Mayer-Le Scanff/Garden Picture Library. **269** RD/GID. **270** *t* Roger Brown/Auscape; *b* Lorna Rose. **271** *tr* Lorna Rose; *c* PhotoDisc. **272** Jacqui Hurst/Garden Picture Library. **273** RD. **274** *tr* Howard Rice/Garden Picture Library; *cl* RD/GID; *br* PhotoDisc. **275** *cl* RD/GID; *br* RD. **276** *tl* Lena Lowe; *b* Jean-Paul Ferrero/Auscape. **277** *tc* Jean-Paul Ferrero/Auscape; *cr* Jean-Michel Labat/Auscape. **278–79** Image Source. **280** *t* PhotoDisc; *c* Stockbyte; *b* Royalty-Free/Corbis. **281** *t* Richard Nebesky/Lonely Planet Images; *cr* RD; *b* Nick Groves/Focus New Zealand. **282** *t* PhotoDisc; *b* Digital Vision. **284** *b* RD. **284–85** Imagestate. **285** *tr* RD; *b* Stockbyte. **286** *both* RD. **287** *tl* & *cr* RD; *b* PhotoAlto. **288** *tl* Brand X Pictures; *tr* RD; *b* RD/GID. **289** RD. **290** *t* Stockbyte; *c* RD/GID; *b* RD. **292** *both* Stockbyte. **293** RD. **294** Image 100. **295** *t* Gordon Claridge/ANTPhoto.com; *b* Juliet Coombe/Lonely Planet Images. **296** *t* MedioImages; *b* RD. **298** *b* Courtesy Toyota. **298–99** Brian Moorhead/Focus New Zealand. **299** *cl* Image 100. **300** *tr* Image 100; *bl* Creatas Images. **301** *t* PhotoDisc; *b* Courtesy Toyota. **302** *t* Powerstock ZEFA Limited/Focus New Zealand; *b* Digital Vision. **304** *t* Thinkstock Images; *b* Stockbyte. **305** *t* PhotoDisc; *b both* RD. **306** *t* Royalty-Free/Corbis; *bl* PhotoDisc; *br* Digital Vision. **307** Stockbyte. **308** Pixtal. **309** Stockbyte. **310–11** Nick Groves/Focus New Zealand. **311** *tr* RD/GID; *tc* RD; *cl* Anders Blomqvist/Lonely Planet Images; **312** *t* Richard Nebesky/Lonely Planet Images; *b* Scott Darsney/Lonely Planet Images. **313** David Else/Lonely Planet Images.

The publisher would also like to thank the following people and organisations for their assistance: Bunnings Warehouse, Mascot, NSW; Nature's Energy, Glebe, NSW; Rebel Sport, Broadway, NSW; Filomena Pezzimenti.

Concept code AU0542/IC; Product code 041.3070